Remarriage in Early Christianity

Remarriage in Early Christianity

―

A. Andrew Das

WILLIAM B. EERDMANS PUBLISHING COMPANY
GRAND RAPIDS, MICHIGAN

Wm. B. Eerdmans Publishing Co.
4035 Park East Court SE, Grand Rapids, Michigan 49546
www.eerdmans.com

© 2024 A. Andrew Das
All rights reserved
Published 2024

Book design by Lydia Hall

Printed in the United States of America

30 29 28 27 26 25 24   1 2 3 4 5 6 7

ISBN 978-0-8028-8374-2

Library of Congress Cataloging-in-Publication Data

A catalog record for this book is available from the Library of Congress.

Scripture quotations are from the New Revised Standard Version unless otherwise indicated.

χάριτι θεοῦ

μιᾶς γυναικὸς ἄνδρα

for Susan, my beloved wife

ἑνὸς ἀνδρὸς γυνή

χάριτι θεοῦ

Contents

	Acknowledgments	ix
	List of Abbreviations	x
	Introduction	1
1.	The Widespread Acceptance of Remarriage in Antiquity	15
2.	Jesus "behind" the Gospels, or Jesus Remembered	56
3.	The Meaning of Words in the Matthean Exceptions	105
4.	The Matthean Divorce-Remarriage Texts in Context	145
5.	"Not Bound" and "Free" in the Apostle Paul?	193
6.	The Witness of the Early Church	232
	Conclusion	282
	Bibliography	293
	Index of Authors	327
	Index of Subjects	336
	Index of Scripture	340
	Index of Other Ancient Sources	349

Acknowledgments

Several conversations over the years led to this project, and some of the conversation partners engaged with the manuscript at various points, including the Revs. Neal R. Blanke, Dean H. Duncan, Randy Emmons, Nathan Cordes, Edward L. Bryant, David Lau, and Mark Drevlow. For technical assistance with the research, I am grateful to the Rev. Jason Foreman. Each of them will likely attest that the topic is not merely academic but intensely personal and of great ecclesiastical relevance. I am also thankful for the careful editorial work of Dr. Blake A. Jurgens.

Abbreviations

Nonbiblical Ancient Sources

Old Testament Apocrypha and Pseudepigrapha

1 En.	1 Enoch
Jub.	Jubilees
2 Macc.	2 Maccabees
Ps.-Phoc.	Pseudo-Phocylides
Pss. Sol.	Psalms of Solomon
Sus.	Susanna
T. Benj.	Testament of Benjamin
T. Isaac	Testament of Isaac
T. Iss.	Testament of Issachar
T. Jos.	Testament of Joseph
T. Jud.	Testament of Judah
T. Levi	Testament of Levi
T. Naph.	Testament of Naphtali
T. Reu.	Testament of Reuben
T. Sim.	Testament of Simeon
T. Zeb.	Testament of Zebulun
Tob.	Tobit

Dead Sea Scrolls

CD	Damascus Document
1QapGen	Genesis Apocryphon

Abbreviations

4Q76	Minor Prophets[a]
4QD[a]	4QDamascus Document[a]
4QD[e]	4QDamascus Document[e]
4QD[f]	4QDamascus Document[f]
11QT[a]	Temple Scroll[a]

Rabbinic Sources

ʿArak.	ʿArakin
b.	Babylonian Talmud
Ber.	Berakot
B. Meṣ.	Baba Meṣiʿa
Giṭ.	Giṭṭin
Ketub.	Ketubbot
m.	Mishnah
Ned.	Nedarim
Num. Rab.	Numbers Rabbah
Qidd.	Qiddušin
Sanh.	Sanhedrin
Šeb.	Šebiʿit
t.	Tosefta
Yebam.	Yebamot

Greco-Roman Sources

Ab urbe cond.	Livy, *Ab urbe condita libri*
Adelph.	Philemon, *Adelphoi*
Adol. poet. aud.	Plutarch, *Quomodo adolescens poetas audire debeat*
Aen.	Vergil, *Aeneid*
Ag. Ap.	Josephus, *Against Apion*
Am. prol.	Plutarch, *De amore prolis*
Andr.	Euripides, *Andromache*
Ann.	Tacitus, *Annals*
Ant.	Josephus, *Antiquities*
Anth. Gr.	Aeschines, *Anthologia Graeca*
Ant. rom.	Dionysius of Halicarnassus, *Antiquitates romanae*
Aug.	Suetonius, *Divus Augustus*
Ben.	Seneca, *De beneficiis*
Bib. hist.	Diodorus Siculus, *Bibliotheca historica*
Cato Min.	Plutarch, *Cato Minor*

ABBREVIATIONS

Chaer.	Chariton, *De Chaerea et Callirhoe*
Cher.	Philo of Alexandria, *De cherubim*
Chron.	Malalas, *Chronographia*
CJ	Justinian, *Codex Justinianus*
Decal.	Philo of Alexandria, *De decalogo*
Deipn.	Athenaeus, *Deipnosophistae*
De or.	Cicero, *De oratore*
Descr.	Pausanias, *Graeciae descriptio*
Det.	Philo of Alexandria, *Quod deterius potiori insidari soleat*
Dial. mar.	Lucian, *Dialogi marini*
Diatr.	Epictetus, *Diatribai*
Dig.	Justinian, *Digesta*
Eleg.	Propertius, *Elegiae*; Tibullus, *Elegiae*
Ep.	Apollodorus, *Epitome*; Ovid, *Epistulae*; Pliny the Younger, *Epistulae*
Epigr.	Martial, *Epigrammata*
Fact.	Valerius Maximus, *Factorum ac dictorum memorabilium libri IX*
Fals leg.	Aeschines, *De falsa legatione*; Demosthenes, *De falsa legatione*
Frag.	Theopompus, *Fragments*
Germ.	Tacitus, *Germania*
Gyn.	Soranus, *Gynaeceia*
Hel.	Euripides, *Helena*
Hist.	Herodotus, *Historiae*; Polybius, *Historiae*; Tacitus, *Historiae*
Hist. an.	Aristotle, *Historia animalium*
Hist. rom.	Dio Cassius, *Historia romana*
Hypoth.	Philo of Alexandria, *Hypothetica*
Ios.	Philo of Alexandria, *De Iosepho*
Iph. taur.	Euripides, *Iphigenia taurica*
Is. Os.	Plutarch, *De Iside et Osiride*
J.W.	Josephus, *Jewish War*
Leg.	Plato, *Leges*
Leoch.	Demosthenes, *Contra Leocharem*
Leuc. Clit.	Tatius, *Leucippe et Clitophon*
Life	Josephus, *Life*
Mag. mor.	Aristotle, *Magna moralia*
Mem.	Xenophon, *Memorabilia*
Merc.	Plautus, *Mercator*
Metam.	Apuleius, *Metamorphoses*
Mor.	Plutarch, *Moralia*
Mos.	Philo of Alexandria, *De vita Mosis*

Abbreviations

Most.	Plautus, *Mostellaria*
Neaer.	Demosthenes, *In Neaeram*
Noct. att.	Gellius, *Noctes atticae*
Od.	Homer, *Odyssea*
Onir.	Artemidorus, *Onirocritica*
Or.	Lysias, *Orations*
Quaest. rom.	Plutarch, *Quaestiones romanae et graecae*
Rom.	Plutarch, *Romulus*
Sacr.	Lucian, *De sacrificiis*; Philo of Alexandria, *De sacrificiis Abelis et Caini*
Sat.	Horace, *Satirae*; Juvenal, *Satirae*; Petronius, *Satyrica*
Silv.	Statius, *Silvae*
Spec.	Philo of Alexandria, *De specialibus legibus*
Tim.	Aeschines, *In Timarchum*; Lucian, *Timon*
Tr.	Ovid, *Tristia*
Virt. vit.	Plutarch, *De virtute et vitio*

Early Christian Sources

1 Apol.	Justin Martyr, *Apologia I*
2 Apol.	Justin Martyr, *Apologia II*
Comm. Matt.	Origen, *Commentarium in evangelium Matthaei*
Dial.	Justin Martyr, *Dialogus cum Tryphone*
Did.	Didache
Did. apost.	*Didascalia apostolorum*
Disc.	Musonius Rufus, *Discourses*
Ep. virg.	Athanasius, *Epistula ad virgines*
Exh. cast.	Tertullian, *De exhortatione castitatis*
Gub.	Salvian, *De gubernatione Dei*
Haer.	Hippolytus, *Refutatio omnium haeresium*; Irenaeus, *Adversus haereses*
Herm. Mand.	Shepherd of Hermas, Mandate(s)
Herm. Vis.	Shepherd of Hermas, Visions
Hist. eccl.	Eusebius, *Historia ecclesiastica*
Hom. 1 Cor.	John Chrysostom, *Homily on 1 Corinthians*
Hom. Matt.	John Chrysostom, *Homily on Matthew*
Iter. conj.	John Chrysostom, *De non iterando conjugio*
Marc.	Tertullian, *Adversus Marcionem*
Mon.	Tertullian, *De monogamia*
Oct.	Minucius Felix, *Octavius*
Ord.	Augustine, *De ordine*

ABBREVIATIONS

Pan.   Epiphanius, *Panarion*
Praescr.   Tertullian, *De praescriptione haereticorum*
Pud.   Tertullian, *De pudicitia*
Strom.   Clement of Alexandria, *Stromateis*
Symp.   Methodius, *Symposium*
Ux.   Tertullian, *Ad uxorem*
Virg.   Tertullian, *De virginibus velandis*
Virginit.   John Chrysostom, *De virginitate*

Ancient Inscriptions and Papyri

BGU   *Aegyptische Urkunden aus den Königlichen Staatlichen Museen zu Berlin, Griechische Urkunden*. 9 vols. Berlin: Weidmann, 1892–1937

Carm. Epigr.   *Carmina Latina Epigraphica*. Edited by Franz Bücheler. Leipzig: Teubner, 1895

Chr.M.   L. Mitteis and U. Wilcken. *Grundzüge und Chrestomathie der Papyruskunde*. Vol. 2, *Juristischer Teil*. Part 2, *Chrestomathie*. Leipzig: Teubner, 1912

CIJ   *Corpus Inscriptionum Judaicarum*. Edited by Jean-Baptiste Frey. Rome: Pontifical Biblical Institute, 1936–1952

CIL   *Corpus Inscriptionum Latinarum*. Berlin, 1862–

CPJ   *Corpus Papyrorum Judaicarum*. Edited by Victor A. Tcherikover and Alexander Fuks. Cambridge: Harvard University Press, 1957–1964

IG   *Inscriptiones Graecae. Editio Minor*. Berlin: de Gruyter, 1924–

ILCV   *Inscriptiones Latinae Christianae Veteres*. Edited by Ernst Diehl. 2nd ed. Berlin: Druckerei Hildebrand, 1961

P.Brookl.   *Greek and Latin Papyri, Ostraca, and Wooden Tablets in the Collection of the Brooklyn Museum*. Edited by John C. Shelton. Papyrologica Florentina 22. Florence: Edizioni Gonnelli, 1992

P.Dura.   *The Excavations at Dura-Europos Conducted by Yale University and the French Academy of Inscriptions and Letters*. Final Report 5, Part 1, *The Parchments and Papyri*. Edited by C. Bradford Welles, Robert O. Fink, and J. Frank Gilliam. New Haven: Yale University Press, 1959

P.Eleph.   *Aegyptische Urkunden aus den Königlichen Staatlichen Museen zu Berlin, Griechische Urkunden: Elephantine-Papyri*. Edited by Otto Rubensohn. Berlin: Weidmann, 1907

P.Fam.Tebt.   *A Family Archive from Tebtunis*. Edited by B. A. van Groningen. Papyrologica Lugduno-Batava 6. Leiden: Brill, 1950

Abbreviations

P.Fay.	*Fayum Towns and Their Papyri.* Edited by Bernard P. Grenfell, Arthur S. Hunt, and David G. Hogarth. Graeco-Roman Memoirs 3. London: Egypt Exploration Fund, 1900
P.Freib.	*Juristische Urkunden der Ptolemäerzeit.* Edited by Josef Partsch. Vol. 3 of *Mitteilungen aus der Freiburger Papyrussammlung.* Heidelberg: Winter, 1927
P.Gen.	*Les papyrus de Genève.* Edited by Paul Schubert and Isabelle Jornot. 2nd ed. Geneva: Bibliothèque Publique et Universitaire, 2002
P.Giss.	*Griechische Papyri im Museum des oberhessischen Geschichtsvereins zu Giessen.* Edited by O. Eger, E. Kornemann, and P. M. Meyer. Leipzig: Teubner, 1910–1912
P.Grenf.	*New Classical Fragments and Other Greek and Latin Papyri.* Edited by Bernard P. Grenfell and Arthur S. Hunt. Oxford: Oxford University Press, 1897
P.Lips.	*Griechische Urkunden der Papyrussammlung zu Leipzig.* Edited by Ludwig Mitteis. Leipzig: Teubner, 1906
P.Mil.Vogl.	*Papiri della Università degli Studi di Milano.* Edited by A. Vogliano et al. Milan: Istitution Editorale Cisaplino, 1937–1981
P.Münch.	*Die Papyri der Bayerischen Staatsbibliothek München.* Edited by Dieter Hagedorn, Ursula Hagedorn, Robert Hübner, and John C. Shelton. Berlin: de Gruyter, 1986
P. Mur.	*Les grottes de Murabba'ât.* Edited by P. Benoit, J. T. Milik, and R. de Vaux. DJD 2. Oxford: Oxford University Press, 1961
P.Oxy.	*The Oxyrhynchus Papyri.* Edited by Bernard P. Grenfell et al. London: Egypt Exploration Fund, 1898–
P.Oxy.Hels.	*Fifty Oxyrhynchus Papyri.* Edited by Henrik Zilliacus et al. Commentationes Humanarum Litterarum 63. Helsinki: Societas Scientiarum Fennica, 1979
P.Ryl.	*Catalogue of the Greek and Latin Papyri in the John Rylands Library, Manchester.* Edited by Arthur S. Hunt et al. Manchester: Manchester University Press, 1911–1952
PSI	*Papiri greci e latini.* Edited by G. Vitelli and M. Norsa et al. Florence: le Monnier, 1912–1979
P.Tebt.	*The Tebtunis Papyri.* Edited by Bernard P. Grenfell et al. Cambridge: Cambridge University Press, 1902
SB	*Sammelbuch griechischer Urkunden aus Ägypten.* Edited by Friedrich Preisigke et al. Wiesbaden: Harrassowitz, 1915–2002

Secondary Sources

AB	Anchor Bible
ABRL	Anchor Bible Reference Library
ACW	Ancient Christian Writers
AnBib	Analecta Biblica
ANE	Ancient Near East
ANF	*Ante-Nicene Fathers*
AnSt	*Anatolian Studies*
ANTC	Abingdon New Testament Commentaries
ASNU	Acta Seminarii Neotestamentici Upsaliensis
ATANT	Abhandlungen zur Theologie des Alten und Neuen Testaments
AThR	*Anglican Theological Review*
Aug	*Augustinianum*
AYBRL	Anchor Yale Bible Reference Library
BA	*Biblical Archaeologist*
BASP	*Bulletin of the American Society of Papyrologists*
BBR	*Bulletin for Biblical Research*
BDAG	Danker, Frederick W., Walter Bauer, William F. Arndt, and F. Wilbur Gingrich. *Greek-English Lexicon of the New Testament and Other Early Christian Literature*. 3rd ed. Chicago: University of Chicago Press, 2000
BECNT	Baker Exegetical Commentary on the New Testament
BETL	Bibliotheca Ephemeridum Theologicarum Lovaniensium
Bib	*Biblica*
BibInt	*Biblical Interpretation*
BJRL	*Bulletin of the John Rylands University Library of Manchester*
BJS	Brown Judaic Studies
BSac	*Bibliotheca Sacra*
BTB	*Biblical Theology Bulletin*
BZNW	Beihefte zur Zeitschrift für die Neutestamentliche Wissenschaft
CBQ	*Catholic Biblical Quarterly*
CC	Continental Commentaries
CRINT	Compendia Rerum Iudaicarum ad Novum Testamentum
CSCO	Corpus Scriptorum Christianorum Orientalium. Edited by Jean Baptiste Chabot et al. Paris, 1903–
CTM	*Concordia Theological Monthly*
CTR	*Criswell Theological Review*
CurTM	*Currents in Theology and Mission*

DJD	Discoveries in the Judaean Desert
EBib	Études biblique
EKKNT	Evangelisch-Katholischer Kommentar zum Neuen Testament
ERE	*Encyclopedia of Religion and Ethics.* Edited by James Hastings. 13 vols. New York: Scribner's Sons, 1908–1927
EvJ	*Evangelical Journal*
EvT	*Evangelische Theologie*
ExpTim	*Expository Times*
FC	Fathers of the Church
FRLANT	Forschungen zur Religion und Literatur des Alten und Neuen Testaments
GCS	Die griechische christliche Schriftsteller der ersten [drei] Jahrhunderte
GNS	Good News Studies
HNTC	Harper's New Testament Commentaries
HTR	Harvard Theological Review
HR	*History of Religions*
HS	*Hebrew Studies*
HvTSt	*Hervormde Teologiese Studies*
ICC	International Critical Commentary
IEJ	*Israel Exploration Journal*
ITQ	*Irish Theological Quarterly*
JAC	*Jahrbuch für Antike und Christentum*
JANESCU	*Journal of the Ancient Near Eastern Society of Columbia University*
JB	Jerusalem Bible
JBL	*Journal of Biblical Literature*
JEH	*Journal of Ecclesiastical History*
JES	*Journal of Ecumenical Studies*
JESOT	*Journal for the Evangelical Study of the Old Testament*
JETS	*Journal of the Evangelical Theological Society*
JJS	*Journal of Jewish Studies*
JLA	*Jewish Law Annual*
JNES	*Journal of Near Eastern Studies*
JSHJ	*Journal for the Study of the Historical Jesus*
JSNT	*Journal for the Study of the New Testament*
JSNTSup	Journal for the Study of the New Testament: Supplement Series
JSOT	*Journal for the Study of the Old Testament*
JSOTSup	Journal for the Study of the Old Testament: Supplement Series
JTS	*Journal of Theological Studies*
LCC	Library of Christian Classics

ABBREVIATIONS

LCL	Loeb Classical Library
LNTS	Library of New Testament Studies
LSJ	Liddell, Henry George, Robert Scott, Henry Stuart Jones. *A Greek-English Lexicon*. 9th ed. with revised supplement. Oxford: Clarendon, 1996
LXX	Septuagint
MT	Masoretic Text
NCB	New Century Bible
Neot	*Neotestamentica*
NETS	*A New English Translation of the Septuagint*. Edited by Albert Pietersma and Benjamn G. Wright. New York: Oxford University Press, 2007
NICNT	New International Commentary on the New Testament
NIDB	*New Interpreter's Dictionary of the Bible*. Edited by Katharine Doob Sakenfeld. Nashville: Abingdon, 2006–2009
NIDNTT	*New International Dictionary of New Testament Theology*. Edited by C. Brown. Grand Rapids: Eerdmans, 1975–1985
NIGTC	New International Greek Testament Commentary
NJB	New Jerusalem Bible
NovT	*Novum Testamentum*
NovTSup	Novum Testamentum Supplements
NTD	Das Neue Testament Deutsch
NPNF1	*Nicene and Post-Nicene Fathers*, Series 1
NPNF2	*Nicene and Post-Nicene Fathers*, Series 2
NTAbh	Neutestamentliche Abhandlungen
NTL	New Testament Library
NTS	*New Testament Studies*
OTP	*Old Testament Pseudepigrapha*. Edited by James H. Charlesworth. 2 vols. New York: Doubleday, 1983, 1985
PAAJR	*Proceedings of the American Academy of Jewish Research*
Presb	*Presbyterion*
PRSt	*Perspectives in Religious Studies*
PTSDSSP	Princeton Theological Seminary Dead Sea Scrolls Project
RAC	*Reallexikon für Antike und Christentum*. Edited by Theodor Klauser et al. Stuttgart: Hiersemann, 1950–
RB	*Revue Biblique*
RevQ	*Revue de Qumran*
RHE	*Revue d'histoire ecclésiastique*
RSR	*Recherches de Science Religieuse*
SBJT	*Southern Baptist Journal of Theology*
SBLSP	Society of Biblical Literature Seminar Papers

Abbreviations

SBLSymS	Society of Biblical Literature Symposium Series
ScEs	*Science et Esprit*
SemeiaSt	Semeia Studies
SHBC	Smyth & Helwys Bible Commentary
SNTMS	Society for New Testament Studies Monograph Series
SNTW	Studies of the New Testament and Its World
SP	Sacra Pagina
StBibLit	Studies in Biblical Literature (Lang)
STDJ	Studies on the Texts of the Desert of Judah
SVTG	Septuaginta: Vetus Testamentum Graecum
TDNT	*Theological Dictionary of the New Testament*. Edited by Gerhard Kittel and Gerhard Friedrich. Translated by Geoffrey W. Bromiley. Grand Rapids: Eerdmans, 1964–1976
TDOT	*Theological Dictionary of the Old Testament*. Edited by G. Johannes Botterweck and Helmer Ringgren. Translated by John T. Willis et al. Grand Rapids: Eerdmans, 1974–2006
ThH	Théologie Historique
THKNT	Theologischer Handkommentar zum Neuen Testament
TJ	*Trinity Journal*
TJT	*Toronto Journal of Theology*
TNTC	Tyndale New Testament Commentaries
TQ	*Theologische Quartalschrift*
TS	*Theological Studies*
TynBul	*Tyndale Bulletin*
TZ	*Theologische Zeitschrift*
VT	*Vetus Testamentum*
WBC	Word Biblical Commentary
WMANT	Wissenschaftliche Monographien zue Alten und Neuen Testament
WTJ	*Westminster Theological Journal*
ZAC	*Zeitschrift für Antikes Christentum/Journal of Ancient Christianity*
ZAW	*Zeitschrift für die alttestamentliche Wissenschaft*
ZBK	Zürcher Bibelkommentare
ZNW	*Zeitschrift für die neutestamentliche Wissenschaft*

Introduction

Reconstructions of the ancient world are often controversial, and remarriage in early Christianity is no exception. A paucity of key information, debate over how to incorporate new artifacts and materials, unverified scholarly assumptions, and potentially disqualifying problems hinder efforts to understand remarriage in its ancient Christian context. A modern synthesis of remarriage in early Christianity must plunge into disputed waters. At least one firm anchor in that discussion is the ancient divorce certificate. Whether in the ancient Near East or in the Greco-Roman world, these certificates frequently proclaim a wife's freedom to remarry after a divorce. The certificates confirm that a first-century person would have assumed upon leaving a marriage that the woman was no longer obligated to her former husband and enjoyed the right to marry again. The question remains, however, to what extent early Christians shared this cultural assumption. A paradigm shift is in order.

Remarriage has always been a hotly debated topic, but never more so than in 1984 when William A. Heth and Gordon J. Wenham rocked the evangelical world with the publication of *Jesus and Divorce: The Problem with the Evangelical Consensus*.[1] Many seminary students, pastors, and priests gave serious thought to what an appropriate pastoral practice should be. Heth and Wenham followed up their book with a series of journal articles further refining their case.[2] Challenging what

1. William A. Heth and Gordon J. Wenham, *Jesus and Divorce: The Problem with the Evangelical Consensus* (Nashville: Nelson, 1984).
2. E.g., William A. Heth, "The Changing Basis for Permitting Remarriage after Divorce for Adultery: The Influence of R. H. Charles," *TJ* 11 (1990): 143–59; Heth, "Divorce and Remarriage: The Search for an Evangelical Hermeneutic," *TJ* 16 (1995): 63–100; Heth, "Divorce and Remarriage," in *Applying the Scriptures: Papers from ICBI Summit III*, ed. Kenneth S. Kantzer (Grand

they labeled an "evangelical consensus," their work advocated for a minority view: the impermissibility of remarriage while the former spouse remained alive.[3] Prior to Heth and Wenham's work, Roman Catholics had historically taken this position, although the instrument of annulment allowed some flexibility in particular instances where an original marriage could be declared not a marriage after all.

Inevitably, Heth and Wenham's book drew sharp and vigorous scholarly response. David Instone-Brewer in 2002 published *Divorce and Remarriage in the Bible: The Social and Literary Context*.[4] Instone-Brewer's work surveys how widespread the assumption that divorce entailed a corresponding freedom to remarry was among the ancients. He comprehensively documents the divorce certificates from the ancient Near East and Greco-Roman world with their legal expressions of freedom or the permission to remarry.[5] He comments: "The right to remarriage was embedded so deeply in Graeco-Roman marriage law that there was no need to mention it.... The right to remarry after divorce was the fundamental right that was communicated by the Jewish divorce certificate. It was also seen as an undeniable right in Graeco-Roman marriage and divorce law."[6] Instone-Brewer also surveys and identifies several New Testament passages that reflect that right (e.g., 1 Cor 7:29; Rom 7:3), arguing that early Christians would have assumed the freedom inherent in any ancient divorce certificate.

Paving the way for Instone-Brewer's study was Craig Keener's 1991 book *And Marries Another: Divorce and Remarriage in the Teaching of the New Testament*. Attending to the first-century social setting with great care, Keener meticulously reconstructs just how common and unobjectionable divorce and remarriage were in the ancient world while also stressing an additional element: "This book particularly addresses those who would judge or penalize the innocent party."[7] The concept of an innocent party was popularized by Desiderius Erasmus in the early sixteenth century and adopted by the Reformers, who maintained that the innocent victim of a divorce should be permitted to remarry. The rationale behind this

---

Rapids: Zondervan, 1987), 219–39; Gordon J. Wenham, "The Syntax of Matthew 19:9," *JSNT* 28 (1986): 17–23; Wenham, "Matthew and Divorce: An Old Crux Revisited," *JSNT* 22 (1984): 95–107.

3. Heth and Wenham, *Jesus and Divorce*.

4. David Instone-Brewer, *Divorce and Remarriage in the Bible: The Social and Literary Context* (Grand Rapids: Eerdmans, 2001).

5. The argument that divorce *assumed* the right to remarry has been persuasive to many; e.g., Craig L. Blomberg, "Marriage, Divorce, Remarriage, and Celibacy: An Exegesis of Matthew 19:3–12," *TJ* 11 (1990): 196.

6. Instone-Brewer, *Divorce and Remarriage*, 211.

7. Craig S. Keener, *And Marries Another: Divorce and Remarriage in the Teachings of the New Testament* (Peabody, MA: Hendrickson, 1991), xii.

concept derived from the requirement in the Jewish Scriptures that an adulterer suffer the penalty of death (Lev 20:10; Deut 22:22; cf. Deut 22:23–27). Although the death penalty for adultery was no longer enforced in the first century, the guilty party in a divorce would be considered as if he or she were dead to the innocent victim. Later Protestant interpreters agreed with this practice and added that the freedom of the gospel surely placed no further constraint on the innocent.[8] For some Protestants, *even the guilty* who had repented could enjoy absolution and a chance to begin again.[9] Nevertheless, Keener's study explains why the first Christians did not divorce and remarry as frequently as others within their larger world. Jesus's teaching in Mark 10:2–12 and Matt 19:3–9 on one man and one woman in a lifelong marriage had a constraining effect.

Another potential limiting factor for the innocent party of an ancient divorce was the notion that some divorces were legitimate or valid while others were not. Matthew 5:32 and 19:9 both forbid a husband from divorcing his wife except in instances in which she has sinned sexually. For a Christ-believing man to divorce a nonadulterous, believing wife would be an illegitimate divorce in view of Jesus's teaching; neither party should subsequently remarry. Despite the divorce (and even the divorce certificate) and the presence of an innocent party, the original marriage would somehow endure. First Corinthians 7:12–16 permits a believing spouse to suffer divorce by a non-Christ-believing spouse. Such divorces are therefore legitimate. In *these* instances, remarriage would be freely permitted to the innocent party. The partners in an illegitimate divorce, however, should remain single rather than remarry (e.g., 1 Cor 7:10–11).[10]

This bewildering array of perspectives on early Christian remarriage clearly overlaps with questions regarding how early Christians approached divorce. Why not a more ambitious study of *both* divorce and remarriage? A comprehensive study of both is becoming increasingly difficult, if not impossible. In 2002 David

---

8. Keener (*And Marries Another*, 5) censures a "rigid" application of "Christian" doctrines to prohibit the innocent's remarriage, and with potent rhetoric he compares "the oppression of innocent divorced people in some of our churches" to "the oppression the slaves experienced" in an even more severe form.

9. With Instone-Brewer, *Divorce and Remarriage*, 312; Keener, *And Marries Another*, xii.

10. The classic articulation of this perspective is John Murray, *Divorce* (Philadelphia: Committee on Christian Education, 1953). This work is a reprint of a single essay published in parts: See Murray, "Divorce," *WTJ* 9.1 (1946): 31–46; "Divorce: Second Article," *WTJ* 9.2 (1947): 181–97; "Divorce: Third Article," *WTJ* 10.1 (1947): 1–22; "Divorce: Fourth Article," *WTJ* 10.2 (1948): 168–91; "Divorce: Fifth Article," *WTJ* 11.2 (1949): 105–22. For a recent exponent of this position, see Blomberg, "Marriage," 161–96. For a representative commentator articulating this approach in his exposition, see Craig A. Evans, *Matthew*, New Cambridge Bible Commentary (Cambridge: Cambridge University Press, 2012), 126.

INTRODUCTION

Instone-Brewer complained: "A recent search on the American Theological Library Association bibliographic database of academic publications in the area of Religion found more than one thousand articles and book reviews since 1970 that contained the word 'divorce' or 'remarriage' in the title."[11] Instone-Brewer's tome, much like Craig Keener's earlier one, is especially thorough in its treatment of divorce in antiquity and remains a valuable resource. The coverage of remarriage is significantly briefer and heavily reliant on the freedom proclaimed in ancient divorce certificates.[12] What follows, then, is a dedicated study of early Christian perspectives on remarriage that engages debates over divorce only where they are directly relevant to the question of remarriage. Several thorny issues that may be bypassed, at least in large measure, include betrothal customs, dowries, marital customs across ancient cultures, and the legitimate grounds for divorce.[13] Yet another thorny issue is whether marriage as a covenant may be dissolved.[14] Even with these limitations, the task remains challenging and not simply because of the array of scholarly perspectives.

Rocking the evangelical world perhaps as much as Heth and Wenham's original 1984 book was Heth's 2002 recantation of his position. In large measure that turnabout reflected a reevaluation of the cultural "given" in the Greco-Roman world that a divorce assumed the freedom to remarry.[15] Even in Jewish circles,

---

11. Instone-Brewer, *Divorce and Remarriage*, 269. In view of the quantity of literature on the topic, this study will not attempt to document each claim comprehensively but will document claims *strategically* with key, representative sources.

12. Instone-Brewer, *Divorce and Remarriage*, 28–32, 125–32, 203–12, 282–89.

13. Many of these questions are already well covered by Instone-Brewer, *Divorce and Remarriage*, although his attempt at a comprehensive treatment had its inevitable gaps and would have been more accurately titled *Marriage and Divorce in the Bible*. His treatment of remarriage is largely limited to pages 118–25 and, not surprisingly, is grounded in the documented divorce certificates. This begs the question whether Jesus or Paul would agree with the freedom to remarry expressed in these divorce certificates.

14. Hebrew Bible specialists have debated whether and how a particular covenant instrument may be set aside or annulled, even when one party violated the covenant stipulations. In favor of covenantal permanency is David W. Jones and John K. Tarwater, "Are Biblical Covenants Dissoluble? Toward a Theology of Marriage," *Reformed Perspectives Magazine* 7.38 (2005): 1–13. On dissolving a covenant instrument, see Gordon P. Hugenberger, *Marriage as a Covenant: Biblical Law and Ethics as Developed from Malachi*, VTSup 52 (Leiden: Brill, 1994). See also the discussions in Jeffrey J. Niehaus, "God's Covenant with Abraham," *JETS* 56.2 (2013): 249–71; in response to Niehaus, see David Andrew Dean, "Covenant, Conditionality, and Consequence: New Terminology and a Case Study in the Abrahamic Covenant," *JETS* 57.2 (2014): 281–308. This trend sees a bilateral covenant as capable of dissolution.

15. William A. Heth repeatedly mentions how he had felt the pressure of representing a minority position on the topic; see Heth, "Jesus on Divorce: How My Mind Has Changed," *SBJT* 6.1

"almost never was a divorcée or the one who initiated divorce prohibited from remarrying."[16] One senses in his revised thinking not a clear resolution of the debate but rather a thickening plot. The ranks of those advocating Heth's former position have certainly thinned.[17]

Any study of early Christian attitudes toward remarriage is inevitably going to evoke strong emotions since the topic is intensely *personal* and since many modern adherents of a Christian faith take their cues from the biblical text. While reconstructing the ancient world and ancient belief systems, many will recognize familiar situations with which the modern may empathize, including the divorced enjoying remarriage or even *wishing* to enjoy remarriage. Modern researchers have increasingly recognized that a fully neutral perspective is impossible. A person's situation and experiences influence the contours of the study and maybe even the results. This is certainly the case in modern Western societies.

(2002): 4–29, esp. 13–14. Of particular interest is how Heth's argumentation for his newfound acceptance of remarriage compares to his earlier critique of that position. He ignores much of his earlier argumentation. Readers of Heth's recantation should also consult in the same publication Gordon Wenham, "Does the New Testament Approve Remarriage after Divorce?" *SBJT* 6.1 (2002): 30–45. Trumpeting Heth's recantation, for instance, is Andrew David Naselli, "What the New Testament Teaches about Divorce and Remarriage," *Detroit Baptist Seminary Journal* 24 (2019): 4, 4–5 n. 3, 14–15.

What, in part, motivated Heth's shift on the topic was his change of position on marriage as a permanent, unbreakable covenant thanks to the work of Hugenberger, *Marriage as a Covenant*; Heth, "Jesus and Divorce," 5, 17–20. Jesus and the gospel authors do not appeal to a marital covenant instrument. Paul distances himself from covenantal categories; see A. Andrew Das, "Rethinking the Covenantal Paul," in *Paul and the Stories of Israel: Grand Thematic Narratives in Galatians* (Minneapolis: Fortress, 2016), 65–92. Jesus affirms that God's *will* in creation is for the one man to be married to one woman. Divorce involves a violation of God's will for marriage, but this does not mean that people cannot separate what God had joined.

16. See the section titled "'Divorce' in the First Century Was Synonymous with the Right to Remarry," in William A. Heth, "Remarriage for Adultery or Desertion," in *Remarriage after Divorce in Today's Church: Three Views*, ed. Mark L. Strauss, Counterpoints (Grand Rapids: Zondervan, 2006), 68.

17. Naselli ("What the New Testament Teaches," 4) does not include Roman Catholic scholars in his estimates, but among evangelicals he could point only to Gordon J. Wenham—Heth's former coauthor—and John Piper, who has not authored a full study of this topic. Wenham recently published *Jesus, Divorce, and Remarriage in Their Historical Setting* (Bellingham, WA: Lexham, 2019). Unfortunately, this is a rather brief, popular treatment of the topic and does not advance the position beyond his former work. Even Gordon D. Fee, who writes against remarriage in his exegesis of 1 Corinthians 7, has subsequently endorsed Craig Keener's 1991 book *And Marries Another*. See Gordon D. Fee, *The First Epistle to the Corinthians*, rev. ed., NICNT (Grand Rapids: Eerdmans, 2014), 777–78. Among Roman Catholic biblical scholars, the historic position of the church does not currently have a strong champion engaged in these debates.

INTRODUCTION

The Western Context

In 2006 Rose Kreider of the US Census Bureau gave a poster presentation at the American Sociological Association on remarriage in the United States.[18] She based her study on the results of the 1996, 2000, and 2004 Census Bureau surveys of income and program participation. These surveys had collated data on marital histories and identified 33,891 (unweighted) people who had been married two or more times among those age fifteen or older. For all three census years, the percentage of marriages in the United States including at least one formerly married partner remained steadily between 29 and 30 percent. Of the formerly married partners, 91 percent had remarried after divorce and the other 9 percent after being widowed. Kreider discovered that most of those who remarried did so within five years of a divorce. Almost half of these households had biological children under the age of eighteen. Kreider then teamed with Jamie Lewis in issuing an updated report in March 2015 on the basis of Census Bureau data collected in 2014.[19] Almost 42 percent of recent marriages in 2014 involved at least one formerly married spouse, and 21 percent represented remarriages for both spouses. Just over 32 percent of all US marriages included at least one partner who had remarried.

The Pew Research Center issued a report on November 14, 2014 with more recent data entitled "Four-in-Ten Couples Are Saying 'I Do,' Again."[20] The senior researcher for the report was Gretchen Livingston. The study documented a rise in remarriage from 1960 to 2013. In 2013, 40 percent of marriages included at least one partner who had been married before. In 20 percent of all marriages, one spouse had been previously married, and in another 20 percent both spouses were previously married. Forty-two million married adults in the United States in 2013 had been previously married as compared to twenty-two million in 1980 and fourteen million in 1960. This increase may be partially attributed to an aging (and growing) population with increased lifespans allowing for more opportunities for remarriage. Overall, almost one-fourth of all married adults in the United

---

18. Rose M. Kreider, "Remarriage in the United States," *United States Census Bureau*, August 2006, https://www.census.gov/library/working-papers/2006/demo/kreider-02.html.

19. Jamie M. Lewis and Rose M. Kreider, "Remarriage in the United States: American Community Survey Reports," *American Community Survey Reports* 30, March 2015, https://www.census.gov/content/dam/Census/library/publications/2015/acs/acs-30.pdf.

20. Gretchen Livingston, "Four-in-Ten Couples Are Saying 'I Do,' Again: Growing Number of Adults Have Remarried," *Pew Research Center*, November 14, 2014, http://www.pewsocialtrends.org/2014/11/14/chapter-1-trends-in-remarriage-in-the-u-s/#.

States had been previously married. Another study concluded that 75 percent of North Americans who divorce will later remarry.[21] According to a 2008 Barna Group study, 78 percent of the total American population in 2007 had previously been or was currently married, and one-third of those currently married had been divorced at least once.[22]

The rising percentage of those remarrying can be attributed to several additional factors. To start, marriage as a whole has been on the decline. In the 1950s, 95 percent of young adults were married.[23] By 1970 only 68 percent of all adults over the age of eighteen were married, and that percentage decreased again in 1990 to 59 percent.[24] In 1950 there were 90.2 marriages for every 1,000 unmarried women, but in 2019 that number fell to 43.4.[25] Westerners are also choosing to marry for the first time at a later age. In 1950 the average age at marriage was twenty for women and twenty-two for men; by 2019 those numbers rose to twenty-eight for women and thirty for men.[26] The number of people opting for a single lifestyle has also increased. In Western societies in 1950, an average of 10 percent of households consisted of a single person. By 2000 that percentage increased to 25 percent in the United States and 20 percent across Europe.[27] As the proportion of adults choosing not to marry has increased, so also the rate of cohabitation has increased eightfold since the 1960s from less than 500,000 in the United States to more than four million in 1998. (The population increased in that time period from 200 to 275 million.) More than 50 percent of cohabiting adults in the United States in 1994 have never been married. According to a 2007 study, while 33 percent of women by the age of twenty-four have married, 60 percent were cohabiting in 2007.[28] American adults are shifting away from marital relationships,

---

21. David H. Olson and John DeFrain, *Marriage and the Family: Diversity and Strengths*, 3rd ed. (Mountain View, CA: Mayfield, 2000), 15.

22. The Barna Group, "New Marriage and Divorce Statistics Released," March 31, 2008, https://www.barna.com/research/new-marriage-and-divorce-statistics-released/.

23. Andrew J. Cherlin, "The Deinstitutionalization of American Marriage," *Journal of Marriage and Family* 66.4 (2004): 852.

24. Olson and DeFrain, *Marriage and the Family*, 11.

25. National Center for Family & Marriage Research, "Fast Facts on American Marriages," Bowling Green State University, n.d., https://www.bgsu.edu/ncfmr/resources/data/fast-facts.html.

26. National Center for Family & Marriage Research, "Fast Facts on American Marriages."

27. Stephanie Coontz, "The World Historical Transformation of Marriage," *Journal of Marriage and Family* 66.4 (2004): 975.

28. Jeremy E. Uecker and Charles E. Stokes, "Early Marriage in the United States," *Journal of Marriage and Family* 70.4 (2008): 837; The Barna Group, "New Marriage and Divorce Statistics

INTRODUCTION

affecting marriage and remarriage rates.[29] Even so, one-third of all marriages in 2010 were remarriages.[30]

The United States is not unique among Western countries. Four out of every ten marriages in the United Kingdom in 2009 included a partner who was remarrying.[31] C. Simó, J. J. A. Spijker, and M. Solsona have noted the proportion of marriages that consist of previously divorced partners across the countries of the European Union.[32] Over 20 percent of remarriages during this period consisted of divorced men and another 20 percent of divorced women not only in the United Kingdom, but also in Estonia, Belgium, Latvia, Luxembourg, Austria, the Czech Republic, Germany, Switzerland, Denmark, Lithuania, Finland, Hungary, Norway, and Sweden. The number of divorced persons remarrying has been steadily on the rise in Europe since 1980. The US statistics are representative, then, of a widespread acceptance of divorce and remarriage in Western countries.[33] Personal experience and cultural acceptance of divorce and remarriage are factors that must be considered in the interpretation of ancient texts.

Released"; Judith A. Seltzer, "Families Formed outside of Marriage," *Journal of Marriage and Family* 62.4 (2000): 1249–50.

29. Olson and DeFrain, *Marriage and the Family*, 13. On the falling rate of remarriages, see Sharon Jayson, "Remarriage Rate Declining as More Opt for Cohabitation," *USA Today*, September 12, 2013, https://www.usatoday.com/story/news/nation/2013/09/12/remarriage-rates-divorce/2783187/; see also Sharon Jayson, "Interest in Remarriage Is on the Wane," *Christianity Today*, October 16, 2013, 16–17. Jayson notes a 40 percent drop in marriage rates over twenty years, during which the rate of cohabitation exploded.

30. Jayson, "Interest in Remarriage," 16.

31. Sally Williams, "'I Do, I Do, I Do . . .': The Remarriage Game," *The Guardian*, January 20, 2009, https://www.theguardian.com/lifeandstyle/2009/jan/31/remarriage-family. In England and Wales, there has been a departure from this trend with some decline in the proportion of marriages that involve a remarrying partner (42 percent of marriages in 2000 versus 33 percent in 2013). See Elizabeth McLaren, "Marriages in England and Wales, 2013," *Office for National Statistics*, April 27, 2016, https://www.ons.gov.uk/peoplepopulationandcommunity/birthsdeathsandmarriages/marriagecohabitationandcivilpartnerships/bulletins/marriagesinenglandandwalesprovisional/2013.

32. C. Simó, "Atlas of Divorce and Post-Divorce Indicators," (paper presented at the XXVI IUSSP Conference, Marrakech, Morocco, 27 September–2 October, 2009); Jeroen Spijker and Montserrat Solsona, "Atlas of Divorce and Post-Divorce Indicators," *Papers de Demografia* 412 (2012): 1–110.

33. On international divorce statistics, see DivorceScience, "World Divorce Statistics—Comparisons among Countries," n.d., https://divorcescience.org/for-students/world-divorce-statistics-comparisons-among-countries/. Of course, complicating the analysis is a rapidly changing context since marriages may now be between people of the same gender.

The Personal Context of the Researcher

John Meier, a Roman Catholic historical Jesus researcher, recalled a telling incident: "I remember with a smile how, after discussing the possible celibacy of Jesus during a lecture at the University of California, San Diego, the wife of my professor-host told me that the best proof that Jesus was celibate was that he totally forbade divorce—something no married man would ever have done." Reflecting on her comment, Meier remarked on how celibate Catholic bishops and priests tend to teach that divorce and remarriage are not permitted while Protestant clergy, although frowning on the divorce rate, generally allow divorce and remarriage in their churches.[34] Personal contexts impact the conclusions of the researcher. If historical Jesus specialists regularly lament the images of themselves that they find at the bottom of the well of their research staring back up at them, the same danger faces those who investigate remarriage. Those active in church leadership minister to many who are divorced and remarried and are often themselves divorced and remarried. Modern cultural assumptions, personal predilections, denominational divisions, and life experiences are all too easily read back upon the ancient world. The social location of the researcher is always a factor. Personal biography provides necessary context for evaluating the results of a researcher's labors.[35]

Even modern contexts resist casual generalizations. In the fall of 2015 Roman Catholic bishops gathered in Rome to discuss the church's teaching on divorce and remarriage in the wake of the pronouncements of Vatican II on the subject and the 1981 *Familiaris Consortio* of Pope John Paul II. A progressive party advocated for a wider application of annulments that would permit remarriage, which traditionalists resisted.[36] Following the October 2015 publication of their *Final Report*, Pope Francis issued a call urging more sensitive pastoral care for the remarried.[37]

---

34. John P. Meier, *Law and Love*, vol. 4 of *A Marginal Jew: Rethinking the Historical Jesus*, AYBRL (New Haven: Yale University Press, 2009), 118.

35. This author is the "husband of one wife" (1 Tim 3:2)—in whatever sense one wishes to understand that phrase—and comes from a Protestant tradition that permits the remarriage of the innocent party of a divorce. For that matter, a reconstruction in defense of the historic Protestant approach would be personally preferable (and ecclesiastically more convenient), especially in view of the criticism that the conclusions of this study will inevitably evoke.

36. On the dramatic expansion of annulments in the United States, see Pierre Hegy and Joseph Martos, eds., *Catholic Divorce: The Deception of Annulments* (New York: Continuum, 2000); Robert H. Vasoli, *What God Has Joined Together: The Annulment Crisis in American Catholicism* (New York: Oxford University Press, 1998), 4–6, 14–28, 200–201.

37. Pope Francis had been calling for greater sensitivity in the pastoral care of the remarried

INTRODUCTION

His March 2016 *Amoris Laetitia* (The Joy of Love) seemed to some observers to sanction communion for those who had divorced and remarried without an annulment. Whereas the *Familiaris Consortio* reaffirmed a ban on the communion of those civilly remarried after divorce, the *Final Report* did not affirm an unqualified ban.[38] Although historic Roman Catholic doctrine has prohibited remarriage, the winds of change were in the air.[39]

---

well before this; see Bernd Jochen Hilberath, "Die prinzipielle Unauflösichkeit der Ehe und die prinzipielle Bedeutung einer evangeliumsgemäβen Barmherzigkeit," *TQ* 194 (2014): 399–401.

38. Gerald O'Collins, "The Joy of Love (*Amoris Laetitia*): The Papal Exhortation in Its Context," *TS* 77 (2016): 912. On Pope Francis's urging of pastoral sensitivity toward the remarried, see 918–20. The position that a remarried Roman Catholic may not receive the Eucharist is by no means popular among American Catholics (cf. African Catholics); see Michael G. Lawler and Todd A. Salzman, "Catholic Doctrine on Divorce and Remarriage: A Practical Theological Examination," *TS* 78 (2017): 338–39. Many remarried Roman Catholics leave the church. See also Eberhard Schockenhoff, "Traditionsbruch oder notwendige Weiterbildung? Zwei Lesarten des Nachsynodalen Schreibens 'Amoris Laititia,'" *Stimmen der Zeit* 235 (2017): 147–58.

39. For Roman Catholic teaching on remarriage and the widening extent of its practice, see Timothy J. Buckley, *What Binds Marriage? Roman Catholic Theology in Practice*, rev. ed. (London: Continuum, 2002), 3–16, 28–73; Denise Lardner Carmody, "Marriage in Roman Catholicism," *JES* 22.1 (1985): 28–40; Gerald D. Coleman, *Divorce and Remarriage in the Catholic Church* (New York: Paulist, 1988), 5–12; Michael G. Lawler, *Marriage and the Catholic Church: Disputed Questions* (Collegeville, MN: Liturgical, 2002), 92–117; Theodore Mackin, "The International Theological Commission and Indissolubility," in *Divorce and Remarriage: Religious and Psychological Perspectives*, ed. William P. Roberts (Kansas City, MO: Sheed and Ward, 1990), 27–69. As Dale B. Martin observes: "These days it is difficult to pick up a study of divorce among Roman Catholics that does not begin with lamentation about how common divorce and remarriage are among even faithful Catholics, including the admission that Catholics are divorcing and remarrying at about the same rate as Protestants, even though the Roman Catholic official position has been, and still is, that marriage is indissoluble"; *Sex and the Single Savior: Gender and Sexuality in Biblical Interpretation* (Louisville: Westminster John Knox, 2006), 141. Martin adds from the perspective of a non–Roman Catholic: "The doctrine and practice of annulment have always looked like sophistry and casuistry run amok at best, and downright hypocrisy and dishonesty at worst. And today, even many loyal Roman Catholics are beginning to say the same" (141). As Michael Lawler writes: "The actual number of marriages the Church holds to be canonically indissoluble is, in reality, very limited" (*Marriage and the Catholic Church*, 98).

The Council of Trent in Canon 7 of Session 24 responded to the Reformers' insistence on the freedom of the innocent party to remarry: "If anyone says that the Church errs in that she taught and teaches that in accordance with evangelical and apostolic doctrine the bond of matrimony cannot be dissolved by reason of adultery on the part of one of the parties, and that both, or even the innocent party who gave no occasion for adultery, cannot contract another marriage during the lifetime of the other, and that he is guilty of adultery who, having put away the adulteress, shall marry another, and she also who, having put away the adulterer, shall marry another, let him be anathema." See H. J. Schroeder, *Canons and Decrees of the Council of Trent* (St. Louis, MO: Herder, 1941), 181–82.

Introduction

In agreement with the recent Roman Catholic trends, Eastern Orthodox teaching has generally sanctioned remarriage, especially in situations where divorce has been caused by adultery.[40] As for Protestant interpretation, due in no small part to the influence of Erasmus, Martin Luther defended the remarriage of innocent parties. Divorce and remarriage remain widely accepted and practiced in modern Western societies and in much of the rest of the world. Contemporary biblical scholars are not immune to the cultural influences of their day; such influences (and emotions) may (literally) hit quite close to home. A discussion of remarriage in early Christianity, again, must recognize the relevant social contexts, both ancient and modern.

A Scholarly Rorschach Test

Reconstructing *the* early Christian perspective on remarriage presents its share of riddles and controversy with a dizzying array of intersecting disciplines and methods. The biblical gospels are documents of faith often reflecting the interests of their authors and the needs of the communities to which they were addressed. The gospels were composed several decades after the events they describe. Many specialists therefore endeavor to reconstruct what the Jesus *behind* these gospels taught during his life and ministry, with due recognition that this methodology of reconstruction is imperfect and incomplete. Some researchers are convinced that the critically reconstructed Jesus denied any possibility of remarriage for his followers. Perhaps not surprisingly, many scholars advocating for this position have also served in Catholic institutions or as Catholic priests. Others are not certain whether the Jesus behind the gospels had anything to say about remarriage at all. Still others question the methodology itself and the value of such reconstructions. Many scholars stress a version of Jesus as he was *remembered* in the pages of the gospels and in the communities of his followers.

As for the gospel narratives, Jesus forbids divorce and remarriage in the Gospels of Mark and Luke in apparently absolute terms. Matthew's Jesus, on the

---

40. On Orthodox attitudes historically tolerating remarriage, see Demetris J. Constantelos, "Marriage in the Greek Orthodox Church," *JES* 22.1 (1985): 21–27; Kevin Schembri, "The Orthodox Tradition on Divorced and Remarried Faithful: What Can the Catholic Church Learn," *Melita Theologica* 65.1 (2015): 121–41, esp. 125–33; John H. Erickson, "Eastern Orthodox Perspectives on Divorce and Remarriage," in Roberts, *Divorce and Remarriage*, 15–26; Lorenzo Lorusso and George Gallaro, "Divorced and Remarried in the Eastern Orthodox Churches," *Studia Canonica* 50 (2016): 485–502; Peter L'Huillier, "The Indissolubility of Marriage in Orthodox Law and Practice," in Hegy and Martos, *Catholic Divorce*, 108–26.

other hand, includes an exception clause that most think allows for divorce and remarriage in instances where the other partner had been guilty of sexual infidelity (depending on how one defines the Greek word πορνεία). Contrarians have contended that Matthew's Jesus, while allowing for divorce, denies the possibility of remarriage. While Roman Catholics begin with Mark and Luke, Protestants instead stress the Matthean exception clauses.

With respect to the apostle Paul, most have surmised from 1 Cor 7:10–16 that Paul permitted divorce and remarriage in instances where an unbelieving spouse initiated the divorce. Perhaps there are *other* places in 1 Cor 7 that suggest the acceptability of remarriage. Once again, a minority of scholars claims that Paul made no provision for remarriage. Still other passages—1 Cor 7:39 and Rom 7:1–3—seem to claim that a woman is married to a man for the duration of his life, although many think those passages should be taken metaphorically.

As for ecclesiastical authors from the end of the New Testament era through the early fourth century, many modern church historians believe early Christians generally denied any possibility of remarriage while the divorced partner was still alive and that this remained the predominant Christian position through the Council of Nicaea. Others have highlighted significant exceptions to that trend. Once again, the results of such scholarly labor are conflicting.

As a rough generalization, historical Jesus researchers and early Christian specialists working in the ante-Nicene (and even post-Nicene) period are more likely to affirm that early ecclesiastical authors denied the possibility of remarriage after divorce while the former spouse still lived. Matthean and Pauline specialists tend to conclude that remarriage after divorce in certain instances was acceptable. Clearly, minority positions abound. Any synthesis of early Christian thought on remarriage must address these differences within individual disciplines.

An Early Christian Consensus?

This study goes against the headwinds of an emerging consensus that remarriage was permitted by the first Christians, a consensus that has often overlooked the variety of perspectives within individual disciplines. Indeed, one might contend that if modern scholars are on all sides of the remarriage issue, early Christians likely held multiple positions as well. Along these lines, a reasonable conclusion would be that the historical Jesus, the gospels authors, the apostle Paul, and subsequent Christian generations held varying points of view on remarriage. Nevertheless, the thesis of this work is that early Christianity manifests a greater consistency regarding remarriage. From a critically reconstructed Jesus to the third- and early

Introduction

fourth-century Christian authors, the first Christ-believers tended to reject remarriage apart from cases where a spouse had died.

The first chapter documents the widespread acceptance of divorce and remarriage in the ancient world, whether among the ancient Israelites, Second Temple Jews, or the gentile inhabitants of the Roman Empire. This broad social consent raises the question whether any ancient Jew, Greek, or Roman would have questioned remarriage. Some have therefore claimed that early Christian resistance to remarriage would have been culturally unprecedented and unwarranted. Nevertheless, perhaps surprisingly, in some quarters of the ancient world were groups valuing single marriage.

The second chapter tackles how Jesus was remembered by reconstructing a "minimal" or "historic" Jesus behind the gospels as documents of faith for individual communities. Such methods of reconstruction have come under increased critical scrutiny of late, especially among those working in memory studies. However one might methodologically tackle Jesus and memories of him, one of the most certain results of such work is that Jesus taught against divorce and remarriage, save for one important witness (the Gospel of Matthew) that recalls Jesus making an exception to that teaching.

The third chapter analyzes the language used in Matthew's recollection of the exception made by Jesus to his divorce and remarriage teaching. The precise meaning of key words in these passages can dramatically shift how these Matthean statements are understood, even to the point that they may not offer an exception after all. For example, if the Greek verbs usually rendered as "to commit adultery" (μοιχεύω and μοιχάω) are best translated as "to be stigmatized as an adulterer" or "to be victimized by adultery," then Matthew's Jesus was teaching that the innocent may marry again without themselves committing adultery: They would enjoy a clear freedom to remarry. This potential exception to Jesus's prohibition against divorce and remarriage also depends on how one defines and understands the key word πορνεία in these Matthean verses—a word whose meaning has its own story across different times and cultures.

The fourth chapter explores the context behind the exception to Jesus's strict divorce and remarriage teaching in Matt 5:31–32 and 19:3–12. Matthew 5:32 casts light on whether Jesus would have endorsed the freedom of divorce certificates or the notion of an innocent party. Scholars have debated whether the exception clause in both Matthean texts extended also to remarriage. Finally, the chapter assesses the perplexing relationship between the eunuch saying in Matt 19:12 and the divorce and remarriage teaching of 19:9. If the eunuch saying relates to Jesus's teaching on divorce and remarriage, then Jesus would be explaining that celibacy is necessary for his followers in the wake of divorce. Most, however, think that 19:12

INTRODUCTION

is a freestanding logion and not further commentary on Jesus's teaching on divorce and remarriage.

The fifth chapter shifts from the gospels to the apostle Paul, who in 1 Cor 7 tackles at some length divorce and remarriage by taking Jesus's teaching as his starting point (1 Cor 7:10–11). Paul also treats remarriage briefly in Rom 7:1–3. At least five distinct elements in 1 Cor 7 suggest the possibility of remarriage for the divorced. This chapter also tests claims that Paul appears to be drawing on the language of freedom in ancient divorce certificates.

The sixth and final chapter surveys how the earliest Christian writers and confessions up to the time of the Council of Nicaea (325 CE) interpret the permissibility in Scripture to remarry. The question here is whether early Christian viewpoints are more indebted to scriptural teaching or to the growing asceticism of their age. Early Christians may have varied in their approach to divorce, but the first Christians from Jesus to Nicaea remained relatively consistent in opposing remarriage in cases where a former spouse remained living. Their thinking remained anchored in the interpretation of biblical texts, which may even manifest ascetic elements themselves.

Too many important questions and issues regarding remarriage among early Christians have been brushed aside, such as whether the New Testament authors endorsed divorce certificates or the notion of an innocent party. Sometimes an overeager conclusion—such as rushing to translate a passage in a convenient way—prematurely concludes a discussion. Such claims require more rigorous testing. Even the discussion of Greco-Roman and Second Temple Jewish sources may be influenced by one's personal perspective. Reengaging these matters afresh will hopefully reopen a question that, in the minds of many interpreters of antiquity, had been closed long ago.

1

The Widespread Acceptance of Remarriage in Antiquity

At least in its acceptance of divorce and remarriage, the ancient world resembles the modern, but there were different social contexts intersecting in the early Christian movement. The Jewish Scriptures reflect their ancient Near Eastern context, but the Jews would find themselves enveloped first by an emerging Hellenistic world and the subsequent realities of the Roman Empire. Throughout this, the Jews would continue to seek guidance in their ancient scriptural texts, and those texts speak at various points about divorce and occasionally remarriage as well. These texts were received and interpreted in the centuries prior to and contemporaneous with Jesus in what is called the Second Temple Period—an age that began after the return from Babylonian exile in the sixth century BCE and would last until the latter half of the first century CE when the second Jewish temple was destroyed by the Romans after the First Jewish Revolt. By the time of Jesus, most of his fellow Jews would take divorce and remarriage for granted. Greeks and Romans likewise permitted divorce and remarriage.

The divorce certificates issued by Jewish spouses (usually husbands) parallel closely the certificates issued by their Greco-Roman peers. The divorced enjoyed a legal "freedom" or permission to remarry. Most ancients would assume that freedom, as do most moderns. Some current researchers would have their readers believe that the ancient acceptance of remarriage was unanimous. This chapter will test that thesis while keeping in mind the two different cultural streams at play here: the ancient Near Eastern and Jewish trajectory, and Greco-Roman perspectives. Not everyone in the ancient world would have agreed with what was expressed on the divorce certificates. There were dissenting voices, whether Roman or Jewish.

CHAPTER 1

The Ancient Jewish Context

The Scriptures

The Jewish Scriptures do not offer a comprehensive body of divorce law. Only four passages in the Pentateuch mention it. Since these passages are more relevant to discussions of divorce than remarriage, the examination in what follows will be brief. According to Lev 21:7, 13–14: "They [the priests] shall not marry a prostitute or a woman who has been defiled; neither shall they marry a woman divorced from her husband. . . . He [the priest] shall marry only a woman who is a virgin. A widow, or a divorced woman, or a woman who has been defiled, a prostitute, these he shall not marry. He shall marry a virgin of his own kin." The law here assumes that there will be divorced women in the land of Israel and does not censure divorce. The priests, for purposes of cultic holiness, are to marry only virgins. Thus the widow, like the divorced woman, is not a marital option for a priest. That this was required of priests and not more generally suggests that divorce and remarriage were commonplace in the Israelite population.

In Deut 22:13–19:

> Suppose a man marries a woman, but after going in to her, he dislikes her and makes up charges against her, slandering her by saying, "I married this woman; but when I lay with her, I did not find evidence of her virginity." The father of the young woman and her mother shall then submit the evidence of the young woman's virginity to the elders of the city at the gate. The father of the young woman shall say to the elders: "I gave my daughter in marriage to this man but he dislikes her; now he has made up charges against her, saying, 'I did not find evidence of your daughter's virginity.' But here is the evidence of my daughter's virginity." Then they shall spread out the cloth before the elders of the town. The elders of that town shall take the man and punish him; they shall fine him one hundred shekels of silver (which they shall give to the young woman's father) because he has slandered a virgin of Israel. She shall remain his wife; he shall not be permitted to divorce her as long as he lives.

A man is not allowed to divorce his wife if he has falsely accused her of not being a virgin at the time of their marriage. He loses what appears to be a general right to divorce. Nothing indicates that divorce or remarriage is otherwise impermissible.

In Deut 22:28–29: "If a man meets a virgin who is not engaged, and seizes her and lies with her, and they are caught in the act, the man who lay with her shall give fifty shekels of silver to the young woman's father, and she shall become his wife. Because he violated her he shall not be permitted to divorce her as long as he lives." In this passage a man who rapes a virgin must marry her and is not permitted to divorce her.[1] The restriction in this particular instance again assumes that divorces were commonly taking place.

Last, in Deut 24:1–4:

> Suppose a man enters into marriage with a woman, but she does not please him because he finds something objectionable about her, and so he writes her a certificate of divorce, puts it in her hand, and sends her out of his house; she then leaves his house and goes off to become another man's wife. Then suppose the second man dislikes her, writes her a bill of divorce, puts it in her hand, and sends her out of his house (or the second man who married her dies); her first husband, who sent her away, is not permitted to take her again to be his wife after she has been defiled; for that would be abhorrent to the Lord, and you shall not bring guilt on the land the Lord your God is giving you as a possession.

Rabbinic authors took great interest in applying v. 1 more widely, but this passage does not legislate divorce. A husband may give his wife a divorce certificate and send her away without any involvement of the governing authorities.[2] The passage censures remarriage in a particular situation. Deuteronomy 24:1–4 is a single sentence in the Hebrew. Most scholars consider v. 4—"[then] her first husband, who sent her, is not permitted to take her again to be his wife"—to be the apodosis after a lengthy protasis in the first three verses.[3] If a husband dislikes his wife and divorces her, she may not return to him in marriage after she has married a second man. Obviously, the original marriage bond is no longer in effect.[4] The phrase "something objectionable" in v. 1 is more literally translated "the shame/nakedness of a thing" (*'erwat dābār*).[5] Rabbinic authors claimed that Second Temple (pre-

---

1. Note that sexual relations with a woman does not of itself constitute a marriage.
2. The certificate would likely have been the standard one permitting remarriage for the divorced wife. Alternatively, it could have been a legal document that the dowry had been returned.
3. E.g., Martin Rose, *5. Mose 12–25: Einführung und Gesetze*, vol. 1 of *5. Mose*, ZBK 5.1 (Zurich: Theologischer Verlag, 1994), 173; Jeffrey H. Tigay, *Deuteronomy: The JPS Torah Commentary* (Philadelphia: Jewish Publication Society, 1996), 220–21.
4. Joe M. Sprinkle, "Old Testament Perspectives on Divorce and Remarriage," *JETS* 40.4 (1997): 532: "Marriages can become irreconcilably dissolved."
5. The only other instance of the phrase in the Masoretic Text is Deut 23:14 (MT 23:15). The Israelites must dig a hole and then cover over their excrement since Yahweh is in the camp and must not see "the shame/nakedness of a thing" (*'erwat dābār*). Apparently, this would be indecent. This instance of the phrase indicates that its use should not be limited to instances

CHAPTER 1

rabbinic) teachers had debated what this phrase meant and the extent to which it justified divorce. The Pentateuch itself, however, clearly assumes divorce and remarriage were taking place in the nonpriestly majority of the populace. Apart from a few restrictions, those practices seem largely unchallenged.

Deuteronomy 24:1–4 addresses the relatively uncommon situation of a man seeking to take back a former wife after she has married and been divorced from another man. Although the Torah recognizes that divorces and remarriages were taking place, the legal code rarely *commands* divorce (Exod 21:10–11, assuming a slave *wife*; Deut 21:10–14) and typically *restricts* divorce and remarriage.[6] The Deut 24:1–4 text is very difficult, and no consensus has emerged regarding its interpretation. One recent reviewer of the literature has even concluded that it was not just remarriage to the original spouse (the third marriage) that defiled but also the second marriage to a different partner.[7]

---

of sexual misconduct. Thus the Septuagint translates it as ἄσχημον πρᾶγμα "a shameful thing," in Deut 24:1 and similarly in Deut 23:15.

The phrase does not likely refer to adultery since adultery's penalty is death in the Pentateuch (Lev 20:10; Deut 22:22; cf. Deut 22:23–27). Numbers 5:11–31 provides instructions for instances in which a wife is suspected of adultery. The charge of uncleanness against a *newly* wedded wife is treated in Deut 22:13–21. The uncleanness of a betrothed virgin is addressed in Deut 22:23–24, and a betrothed virgin forced into uncleanness is addressed in Deut 22:25–27, with the man sleeping with an unbetrothed virgin in Deut 22:28–29. John Murray concludes on the basis of these texts that the stricter interpretation of the school of Shammai that Deut 24:1–4 dealt *only* with adultery is likely wrong; see *Divorce*, 9–12. The school of Hillel's liberal approach to the Deut 24:1 phrase is unlikely as well since the only other use of the phrase in Deut 23:14 (MT 23:15) is for a failure to cover human excrement. The word ʿerwat is used for the shameful exposure of the human body (e.g., Gen 9:22–23; Exod 20:26; Lam 1:8; Ezek 16:36–37). Murray (*Divorce*, 12–13) therefore advocates for a position *between* Hillel and Shammai.

6. On the pentateuchal verses commending divorce in certain situations, see the discussion of Sprinkle, "Divorce and Remarriage," 533–36.

7. Todd Scacewater reasons that the first or second divorces could not have been defiling since defilement in the instance of the first divorce would have been flagged. Remarriage to the original husband would not have been defiling either since the defilement took place *prior* to the original couple's reuniting (note the preposition ʾaḥar): "The only option left is that the defilement takes place through the second marriage." Going back to her former spouse would be *doubly* defiling, hence an abomination; see "Divorce and Remarriage in Deuteronomy 24:1–4," *JESOT* 1.1 (2012): 71, but see the full discussion in 71–73. If Scacewater is correct, then John Murray (*Divorce*, 14) would be in error in claiming, "The remarriage on the part of the divorced woman is not expressly stated to be defilement irrespective of return to the first husband." The return to the first husband would be a step further to an "abomination" that pollutes the land. Murray cautiously adds: "[I]t is not at all so certain that the remarriage is not regarded as involving defilement" (15). It is difficult to understand why such defilement, if present, would not also be adulterous. At the same time, despite the defilement involved, the Torah does not expressly

The remainder of the Jewish Scriptures offers a handful of additional relevant passages.[8] In Isa 50:1: "Thus says the Lord: Where is your mother's bill of divorce with which I put her away? ... for your transgressions your mother was put away." The verse recognizes the practice of giving a woman a bill of divorce and does not censure the practice. In Jer 3:1–2, 8:

> If a man divorces his wife and she goes from him and becomes another man's wife, will he return to her? Would not such a land be greatly polluted? You have played the whore with many lovers; and would you return to me? says the Lord. Look up to the bare heights and see! Where have you not been lain with? By the waysides you have sat waiting for lovers, like a nomad in the wilderness. You have polluted the land with your whoring and wickedness. . . . She saw that for all the adulteries of that faithless one, Israel, I had sent her away with a decree of divorce; yet her false sister Judah did not fear, but she too went and played the whore.

For Jeremiah God is like a husband who issues his unfaithful wife a decree or certificate of divorce. The passage again assumes the practice. (The apocryphal Tob 7:13 is the first text explicitly mentioning a marriage contract.) At the same time, while God has divorced his spouse in these prophetic texts, the book of Hosea describes God as willing to be reconciled to the erring partner (e.g., Hos 2:14–15; 3:4–5; 5:14–6:3; 14:1–2).

Ezra 9–10, written after the return from the Babylonian exile, *requires* Israelite men to divorce their foreign wives. This does not appear to have been a rule in the postexilic period and was not the practice after Ezra. Ezra 9–10 appears to be the basis for the comments of Mal 2:10–16:

> Have we not all one father? Has not one God created us? Why then are we faithless to one another, profaning the covenant of our ancestors? Judah has

---

prohibit remarriage. Also, the defilement may have been adultery in the woman's marriage to another (second) man after her divorce from her first husband; see Moshe Weinfeld, *Deuteronomy and the Deuteronomic School* (Winona Lake, IN: Eisenbrauns, 1992), 269–70 n. 4: "committed by the woman with the man whom she afterwards married" (cf. Lev 18:20; Num 5:13, 14, 20), thus placing her first husband in a situation that prevents him from remarrying her; so also Jacob J. Rabinowitz, "The 'Great Sin' in Ancient Egyptian Marriage Contracts," *JNES* 18.1 (1959): 73.

8. The book of Hosea is not of value for this question since it is not clear if Hosea formally divorced his wife or if the same woman is involved in Hos 1–3. For a concise summary of the problems that Hosea presents, along with pertinent bibliography, see Meier, *Law and Love*, 145 n. 24.

CHAPTER 1

been faithless, and abomination has been committed in Israel and in Jerusalem; for Judah has profaned the sanctuary of the Lord, which he loves, and has married the daughter of a foreign god. May the Lord cut off from the tents of Jacob anyone who does this—any to witness or answer, or to bring an offering to the Lord of hosts.

And this you do as well: You cover the Lord's altar with tears, with weeping and groaning because he no longer regards the offering or accepts it with favor at your hand. You ask, "Why does he not?" Because the Lord was a witness between you and the wife of your youth, to whom you have been faithless, though she is your companion and your wife by covenant. Did not one God make her? Both flesh and spirit are his. And what does the one God desire? Godly offspring. So look to yourselves, and do not let anyone be faithless to the wife of his youth. For I hate divorce, says the Lord, the God of Israel, and covering one's garment with violence, says the Lord of hosts. So take heed to yourselves and do not be faithless.

The Malachi text is a difficult passage to interpret since it is not entirely clear to what Malachi was objecting. Clearly God is disappointed with the faithlessness of the people. The pertinent statement is in v. 16. Several interpreters have insisted that "I hate divorce" is not a viable translation of the verse.[9] The Masoretic Text appears corrupted at this point. To render the text intelligible, for a skeptical Meier, requires "changing vowel points, adding consonants, assigning words unusual meanings, or understanding words not expressed in the verse."[10]

John Nolland, on the other hand, stresses that the unpointed Masoretic Text reading best accounts for all the other readings.[11] The Masoretic Text may be repointed in a way that makes good sense as "one who hates divorce," a reading that enjoys Septuagintal support.[12] If Nolland is correct "that Mal 2:16 is to be read

---

9. Meier (*Law and Love*, 81–82) provides as literal a translation as possible of the MT: "For/if/when/indeed he hated, send away!" Each word in the Hebrew text has more than one possible meaning, and no combination makes sense in the larger context (e.g., "for he hated to send away"). Thus, as Meier comments: "A fortiori, it takes no little imagination to twist the three Hebrew words into a declaration of Yahweh stating 'For I hate divorce'" (147 n. 29). In other words, only with some interpretive license does the received MT text read "I hate divorce."

10. Meier, *Law and Love*, 82.

11. John Nolland, *The Gospel of Matthew*, NIGTC (Grand Rapids: Eerdmans, 2005), 770: "Most likely a 'correction' in Hebrew to the second person in the first clause—perhaps on the basis of the unintelligibility of the Hebrew as construed in the MT pointing—opened the way for the range of variants now represented, as well as for an understanding of the text as more hospitable to divorce."

12. Nolland (*Gospel of Matthew*, 769) repoints the MT from the usual *śānē šallaḥ* as *śōnē* (par-

as profoundly hostile to divorce," the prophetic acceptance of divorce would be softened or changed altogether.[13]

Some Old Greek manuscripts of Mal 2:16 read: "if, hating her, you send her away" (ἐὰν μισήσας ἐξαποστείλης; B Q V). This Greek textual tradition censures a man's divorcing a wife on the grounds of hatred and conveys no sentiment with respect to divorce on the part of God. Two other Old Greek manuscripts read: "But if you hate [her], send [her] away!" (ἐὰν μισήσας ἐξαποστείλας ἐξαποστείλον; L and the mixed reading of W).[14] This reading agrees with a copy of the Book of the Twelve (4Q76) from Qumran, in which the verb is rendered as an imperative: "Send her away if you hate her" (II, 4–7). This would be a command to divorce. Thus a Qumran scroll and the Old Greek translation tradition of Malachi affirm, or even command, divorce. The Targum, the Vulgate, and the Greek manuscripts W and L, all have "divorce" in the imperative.[15]

In response to 4Q76 II, 4–7, Nolland proposes the text could be read instead as, "If you hate divorce... they [the wives] will cover your garment with violence," in which case "divorce must be retained as the ultimate sanction for the behaviour of wives" (cf. Sir 25:13–26).[16] Adela Yarbro Collins concurs that the Old Greek manuscripts of Malachi and 4Q76 attest a later tradition that relaxed the originally strict prohibition against divorce in the Hebrew text of Malachi and thus resolved the perceived conflict with a man's freedom to divorce in Deut 24:1.[17] The Jewish Scriptures lack any discussion of the details of divorce procedures and simply assume that divorces are taking place. There is no general prohibition of divorce, with the possible exception of Malachi. However, the New Testament authors did not appeal to the Malachi text in their teachings on divorce and remarriage, and recently specialists have increasingly translated Mal 2:16 *not* as "I hate divorce" but along the lines of "one who divorces because of hate covers his garment with

---

ticiple) *šallēaḥ*: "one who hates divorce." The Septuagintal participle "one who hates" (μισήσας in ℵ B A Q) supports the repointing. Phillip Sigal spiritedly writes: "It is not what modern scholars ingeniously determine the original meaning of verses to have been that counts in this connection, but how this meaning was understood in ancient Judaism"; see *The Halakah of Jesus of Nazareth according to the Gospel of Matthew* (Lanham, MD: University Press of America, 1986), 93.

13. Nolland, *Gospel of Matthew*, 770.

14. Joseph Ziegler, ed., *Duodecim Prophetae*, SVTG 13 (Göttingen: Vandenhoeck & Ruprecht, 1943), 334.

15. The syntax of W and L is broken, however, with no clear sense; see Nolland, *Gospel of Matthew*, 769–70.

16. Nolland, *Gospel of Matthew*, 769.

17. Adela Yarbro Collins, *Mark*, Hermeneia (Minneapolis: Fortress, 2007), 460: "[Malachi] most likely... originally expressed an unqualified rejection of divorce."

CHAPTER 1

violence."[18] Thus, the Jewish Scriptures provide no clear prohibition of remarriage, except that the priests are not to marry divorced women.

Second Temple Jewish Literature

The earliest extant Jewish marriage and divorce documents (*ketubōth*) are contracts from the Egyptian city of Elephantine dated from the fifth century BCE.[19] These documents state that divorced women were to enjoy a return of their dowry unless certain conditions excused the husband from payment. Nothing in these documents prohibits divorce or remarriage. In fact, *either* spouse could make a public declaration to divorce the other partner.[20] The Jewish Scriptures only envision husbands divorcing wives.[21] The openness expressed in the Elephantine documents to wives divorcing husbands may reflect a syncretistic form of Judaism at a location in which Yahweh had a goddess consort.[22]

Both Philo and Josephus are of the opinion that divorce may be for any reason. Philo comments on Deut 24:1-4 in *Spec.* 3.30–31. There he reviews the content of the verses and identifies the apodosis in Deut 24:4. He interprets a "shameful thing" in Deut 24:1 broadly: A divorce may be initiated for any reason, but the wife must not go back to her first husband. Philo adds a rationale: If a wife were to return to her first husband, then both parties would be guilty of immorality. The wife would be crossing boundary lines, the man would be an adulterer, and both should be punished with death for their immorality.[23] Josephus agrees with Philo

---

18. Those supporting this reading include David Clyde Jones, "A Note on the LXX of Malachi 2:16," *JBL* 109.4 (1990): 683–85; Russell Fuller, "Text-Critical Problems in Malachi 2:10–16," *JBL* 100.1 (1991): 54–57; C. John Collins, "The (Intelligible) Masoretic Text of Malachi 2:16, or, How Does God Feel about Divorce," *Presb* 20.1 (1994): 36–40; Martin A. Shields, "Syncretism and Divorce in Malachi 2,10–16," *ZAW* 111 (1999): 81–85; Markus Zehnder, "A Fresh Look at Malachi II 13–16," *VT* 53.2 (2003): 251–58. Favoring "I hate divorce," see Walter C. Kaiser Jr., "Divorce in Malachi 2:10–16," *CTR* 2.1 (1987): 76–78.

19. A. E. Cowley, *Aramaic Papyri of the Fifth Century BC* (Oxford: Oxford University Press, 1923), esp. nos. 9 and 15; Emil G. Kraeling, ed., *The Brooklyn Museum Aramaic Papyri: New Documents of the Fifth Century B.C. from the Jewish Colony at Elephantine* (New Haven: Yale University Press, 1953).

20. E. Lipiński, "The Wife's Right to Divorce Her Husband in the Light of an Ancient Near Eastern Tradition," *JLA* 4 (1981): 9–27, esp. 21, 26; Alfredo Mordechai Rabello, "Divorce of Jews in the Roman Empire," *JLA* 4 (1981): 79–102, esp. 91.

21. On wives not divorcing their husbands (generally) in Second Temple Judaism and beyond, see especially the review of the literature and arguments in Meier, *Law and Love*, 149–52 n. 38. There were (rare) exceptions.

22. T. W. Manson, *The Sayings of Jesus* (Grand Rapids: Eerdmans, 1957), 137.

23. Meier, *Law and Love*, 154 n. 45. Perhaps Philo views the initial divorce as a sham, and thus both partners are implicated in adultery.

that a divorce may occur for any reason (*Ant.* 4.8.23 §253). Whereas Philo discusses Deut 24:1-4 in relation to the wife, Josephus closely paraphrases Deut 24:1-4 with his focus on the husband. He identifies in Deut 24:1 a *separate* command for a divorce certificate.[24] Remarriage appears to be assumed.

Jewish Divorce Certificates

The late second-century CE mishnaic tractate Giṭṭin 9:3 reads: "The essential formula in the bill of divorce [*gēt*] is, 'Lo, thou art free to marry any man'. R. Judah says: 'Let this be from me thy writ of divorce and letter of dismissal and deed of liberation, that thou mayest marry whatsoever man thou wilt'. The essential emancipation formula in a writ of emancipation is, 'Lo, thou art a freedwoman; lo, thou belongest to thyself.'"[25] Synonymous with the "freedom" language is the explicitly stated "permission" to remarry (e.g., m. Yebam. 1:2). The Mishnah (ca. 200 CE) describes divorce certificate wording that dates back at least to the first century BCE. Toward the end of the first century CE, with no indication of any sense of impropriety, Josephus matter-of-factly describes how he divorced his wife and married another woman whom he judged to be far better (*Life* 76 §§426-427). He credits Moses with the procedures for a proper divorce: the husband may divorce his wife for any cause but must place in writing that he will have no further intercourse with her. As Josephus writes, "For thus will the woman obtain the right to consort with another" (λάβοι γὰρ ἂν οὕτως ἐξουσίαν συνοικεῖν ἑτέρῳ; *Ant.* 4.8.23 §253 [Thackeray, LCL]). This divorce certificate would allow the former wife to marry another man without any concern that the rights of the original husband were being violated. A divorce document from Masada plausibly dated to 72 CE reads in part: "You are free on your part to go and become the wife of any Jewish man that you wish" (DJD 2.19 = P.Mur. 19 [AD72]).[26] Another papyrus dating to 13 BCE documents the divorce of a Jewish couple and reads: "It shall be lawful [ἐξεῖναι]

---

24. Meier, *Law and Love*, 86-87.

25. Unless otherwise noted, translation of the Mishnah by Herbert Danby, *The Mishnah* (Oxford: Oxford University Press, 1987).

26. AD72 refers to an Aramaic divorce document (AD) dating to 72 CE in the collection of ancient marriage and divorce documents assembled by David Instone-Brewer, "Marriage & Divorce Papyri of the Ancient Greek, Roman and Jewish World," 2000, http://www.tyndalearchive.com/Brewer/MarriagePapyri/Index.html. The original text is in P. Benoit, J. T. Milik, and R. de Vaux, *Les grottes de Murabba'ât*, DJD 2 (Oxford: Oxford University Press, 1961), 104-9; translation by Tal Ilan, "Notes and Observations on a Newly Published Divorce Bill from the Judaean Desert," *HTR* 89.2 (1996): 199-200, based on Léone J. Archer, *Her Price Is beyond Rubies: The Jewish Woman in Graeco-Roman Palestine*, JSOTSup 60 (Sheffield: Sheffield Academic Press, 1990), 297-99. Note the emendation of the original text by Yigael Yadin, Jonas C. Greenfield, and Ada Yardeni,

CHAPTER 1

for Apollonia to marry another man and Hermogenes to marry another woman without penalty [ἀνυπευθύνοις]" (*BGU* 4.1102 = *CPJ* 2.144 [JD13]).[27] The documented witnesses to the legality and freedom of a wife to remarry thus span from 13 BCE to roughly 200 CE. Josephus reports the scandal of Salome divorcing her husband without receiving the requisite certificate from him allowing for remarriage (*Ant.* 15.7.10 §§259–260). The only limitation on a woman's remarrying would be if the divorce occurred because she had adulterated or had improperly divorced her former husband (m. Giṭ. 8:5; m. Yebam. 10:1; b. Giṭ. 90b).[28]

These Jewish documents, with their explicit statements of the freedom to remarry, correspond to ancient precursors. Again, Deut 24:1 posits a husband giving his wife a divorce certificate prior to a subsequent remarriage. The divorce certificate, even in earlier antiquity, facilitated subsequent remarriage. Two ancient Near Eastern divorce certificates are extant. In a Middle Assyrian document from Kirkuk, dating to approximately 1400 BCE, the husband declares that his wife "has received her freedom [*zi-iz-z*] and in the future I will make no demand on [her]."[29] Another ancient certificate reads: "[Husband] expelled [wife]. She has obtained her freedom and she has received her divorce money."[30] Two of the three surviving marriage documents from the fifth century BCE Jewish community at Elephantine include the language "She may go wherever she wishes" ("going" here is synonymous with "marry").[31] Finally, seven Babylonian marriage documents use the similar phrase "she may go wherever she wishes" with two slightly different

---

"Babatha's '*Ketubba*,'" *IEJ* 44.1–2 (1994): 86 n. 36, and Y. Yadin, "Expedition D—The Cave of the Letters," *IEJ* 12.3–4 (1962): 249.

27. JD-13 refers to a Jewish and Samaritan Greek Aramaic divorce document (JD) from 13 BCE in Instone-Brewer, "Marriage & Divorce Papyri."

28. On limitations in remarriage, especially after adultery or an invalid divorce, see the helpful review of the primary sources in Instone-Brewer, *Divorce and Remarriage*, 121–32.

29. See document 33 in C. J. Gadd, "Tablets from Kirkuk," *Revue d'Assyriologie et d'Archéologie Orientale* 23 (1926): 111–12.

30. Translation from David Instone-Brewer, "Deuteronomy 24:1–4 and the Origin of the Jewish Divorce Certificate," *JJS* 49.2 (1998): 237. This document was originally published in Bruno Meissner, *Beiträge zum Altbabylonischen Privatrecht* (Leipzig: Hinrichs, 1893), 72 (document 99). According to Instone-Brewer, such certificates facilitated the wife's ability to marry another man (237).

31. The first is published as papyrus no. 15 in Cowley, *Aramaic Papyri*, 44–50 and reads on line 25: "she shall go away whither she will." The second, labeled papyrus 7, appears in Kraeling, *Brooklyn Museum Aramaic Papyri*, 201–22, esp. 206–7: "she shall go [where]ver [she will]." Both documents are respectively translated in Bezalel Porten and Ada Yardeni, *Textbook of Aramaic Documents from Ancient Egypt*, 3 vols. (Jerusalem: Hebrew University, 1986–1996), 2:30–33 (= Cowley 15): "she shall go away wherever she desires"; 2:78–83 (= Kraeling 7): "she shall go [*away from him*] wher[ever] she desires."

wordings.[32] Jewish divorce certificates were therefore based on ancient precedents in granting the wife explicit permission to remarry.

Although Jewish society assumed a freedom to remarry in instances where the wife had received a divorce certificate from her former husband, thus avoiding a charge of adultery, what typically goes unnoticed is that Deut 24:1–4 does not assume a blanket freedom to remarry. The woman who has married another man is *not* free, despite the certificate, to marry her former husband—even if she should become "free" again after a second marriage.[33] The "freedom" featured in the divorce certificates is here qualified.

The Ancient Greco-Roman Legal Context

The Greco-Roman world widely sanctioned divorce and remarriage as well. The main source for Roman law is the much later sixth-century compilation of the Roman jurists by Justinian. Gaius, the second-century CE jurist, reportedly defines divorce as a difference of minds or as a case in which the two parties of a marriage end up going in different ways (*Dig.* 24.2.2).[34] Legally, divorce was freely available and without penalty (*Dig.* 45.1.19; *CJ* 5.4.14; 5.10.1; 6.46.2). A quotation of the third-century emperor Alexander in the *Code of Justinian* states: "The freedom of marriage has been established from ancient times, and therefore agreements providing that it shall not be lawful for the parties to be separate are void, and it has been decided

---

32. See Martha T. Roth, *Babylonian Marriage Agreements: 7th–3rd Centuries. B.C.*, Alter Orient und Altes Testament 222 (Neukirchen-Vluyn: Neukirchener, 1989), 39–40, 42–44, 47–49, 64–68, 73–76. The phrase *asar sebat* appears in nos. 2 (625–623 BCE), 6 (564 BCE), 19 (535–534 BCE), and 20 (523 BCE); *asar mahri* appears in nos. 4 (592 BCE), 15 (543 BCE). The version in no. 16 (543–542 BCE) is corrupt; see also Instone-Brewer, "Deuteronomy 24:1–4," 240. On the other hand, Raymond Westbrook stresses that Old Babylonian divorce documents more typically pronounce a divorce (e.g., "You are not my wife"); 69–70, 76, 83, 112 (ARN 37), 114–15 (BE 6/2 40), 115 (BE 6/2 48), 116 (BIN 7 173), 116–17 (CT 2 44), 119 (CT 8 7b), 122–24 (CT 48 50; 48 51; 48 52; 48 56; 48 61), 127 (BAP 89, 90), 128 (PBS 8/2 107), 129 (PRAK 1 B17). In other words, expressions of freedom or permission to marry were relatively unusual; see *Old Babylonian Marriage Law*, Archiv für Orientforschung 23 (Horn: Berger & Söhne, 1988). See also the Old Babylonian documents cited concerning the same point (i.e., "You are not my wife/husband") in Lipiński, "Wife's Right to Divorce," 14–19.

33. Raymond F. Collins, *Divorce in the New Testament*, GNS 38 (Collegeville, MN: Liturgical, 1992), 84. Again, there are some who conclude that even the second marriage had already been defiling; see Scacewater, "Divorce and Remarriage," 71–73.

34. For a translation, see Theodor Mommsen and Paul Krueger, eds., *The Digest of Justinian*, trans. Alan Watson, 4 vols. (Philadelphia: University of Pennsylvania Press, 1985).

that stipulations by whose terms penalties are imposed upon those who obtain divorces are not to be considered valid" (*CJ* 8.39.2).[35] Ulpian, the late second- and early third-century jurist, claims remarriage is the right of a divorced wife: if the husband becomes betrothed or married to another woman, the former wife—in this instance a freedwoman—enjoys the right to marry another man (*Dig.* 24.2.11). The legal corpus treats remarriage after divorce as commonplace (e.g., *Dig.* 24.3.66).

Unfortunately, Justinian's legal compilations date centuries after the figures they quote and may not reflect first-century social realities. Justinian ordered these ancient legal texts to be altered, where necessary, to resolve potential contradictions that might stand in the way of a prescriptive synthesis for his own day. The compilers were more concerned with general rules rather than with the actual daily application of the law. Of greater value are the extant legal papyri.

Almost all the extant papyri on marriage and divorce—dating from the fourth century BCE to the fourth century CE—have been collated on a website established by David Instone-Brewer prior to the publication of his book on divorce and remarriage in the New Testament.[36] He also published a series of articles explaining the implications of his research.[37] Thirty-seven of the legal papyri are divorce certificates.[38] Most of these papyri are from Egypt, but consistent patterns become clear when this group is compared with the few extant papyri from outside of Egypt. Although the wording of the divorce papyri is not fixed, certain

---

35. The Latin text is in Part 2 of *Corpus Juris Civilis*, ed. Albert Kriegel and Moritz Kriegel (Leipzig: Baumgartner, 1987). The English translation is from S. P. Scott, trans., *The Civil Law Including The Twelve Tables, the Institutes of Gaius, the Rules of Ulpian, the Opinions of Paulus, the Enactments of Justinian, and the Constitutions of Leo*, 17 vols. (Cincinnati: Central Trust Company, 1932), 14:294–95; cf. 13:148, 171–72, 14:58.

36. http://www.tyndalearchive.com/Brewer/MarriagePapyri/Index.html; Instone-Brewer's classification is included for each papyrus. GD-13 is a Graeco-Roman divorce deed from 13 BCE (hence the "-" before the number, not present in documents from the Common Era); Instone-Brewer, *Divorce and Remarriage*.

37. David Instone-Brewer, "1 Corinthians 7 in the Light of the Graeco-Roman Marriage and Divorce Papyri," *TynBul* 51 (2001): 101–15; Instone-Brewer, "1 Corinthians 7 in the Light of the Jewish Greek and Aramaic Marriage and Divorce Papyri," *TynBul* 52 (2001): 225–43.

38. Only one papyrus is extant that witnesses to Greek law. The papyrus stipulates the return of the dowry and the need to support the wife should she be pregnant when divorced (*Chr.M.* 291 = P.Fay. 22 [GR50b]). Only one side of the two-sided papyrus is accessible and provides only the general thrust of the document; see the comments of Bernard P. Grenfell, Arthur S. Hunt, and David G. Hogarth, *Fayum Towns and Their Papyri*, Graeco-Roman Memoirs 3 (London: Egypt Exploration Fund, 1900), 126; L. Mitteis and U. Wilcken, *Grundzüge und Chrestomathie der Papyruskunde*, vol. 2: *Juristischer Teil*; Second Half: *Chrestomathie* (Leipzig: Teubner, 1912), 329–30; Instone-Brewer, "Graeco-Roman Marriage," 102. The remainder of the papyri attest to Roman legal practice.

features regularly recur. Divorce documents typically include the date and place of the agreement, the names of the parties involved and their hometowns, a certification that the dowry had been returned, a certification that neither party had grounds to litigate against the other, and, finally, the signature of the witnesses. Several other secondary features are present in some cases. For instance, several of the papyri include an affirmation that the parties are legally permitted after the divorce to remarry anyone they wish.[39] That permission is usually worded as follows: it is lawful or permitted (ἐξεῖναι) for each of the partners to cohabit (οἰκονομεῖν) or marry another (e.g., συναρμόζεσθαι), if desired. Despite the differing Greek terms, cohabitation and marriage were the same. The oldest example of a divorce document that mentions the legality of remarriage is from 13 BCE. The relevant text reads: "And hereafter it shall be lawful [ἐξεῖναι] both for Zois [the wife] to marry another man and for Antipater [the husband] to marry another woman without either of them being answerable [ἀνυπευθύνοις]" (*BGU* 4.1103 [GD13]).[40] Ten more papyri include this language:

> *BGU* 4.1104 (10 BCE): "She is permitted [ἐξεῖναι] . . . to join herself in marriage [συναρμόζεσθαι] to another husband."[41]
>
> P.Mil.Vogl. 3.184 (GD47 lines 19–21) (41–54 CE): ἐξεῖναι
>
> P.Fam.Tebt. 13 (GD113 lines 13–16) (113–114 CE): ἐξεῖναι: "Kronous shall be free [ἐξεῖναι] to conclude a new marriage with the man whom she prefers."[42]
>
> P.Lips. 27 (= *Chr.M.* 293; GD123 lines 23–26) (123 CE): ἐξῖναι [ἐξεῖναι]
>
> P.Mil.Vogl. 3.185 (= *SB* 6.9381; GD139 lines 18–19) (139 CE): ἐξεῖναι
>
> *PSI* 8.921.25–31 (GD143 line 29) (143–144 CE): ἐξεῖναι
>
> P.Oxy.Hels. 35 (GD151 lines 42–45) (151 CE): ἐξεῖναι: "Henceforth it shall be lawful [ἐξεῖναι] for the same Chaeremon and Tnephersois, either of them, to marry [ἁρμόζεσθαι], as they choose without incurring liability [ἀνυπευθύνῳ]."[43]
>
> P.Brookl. 8 (= *SB* 8.9740; GD177 lines 15–19) (177 CE): ἐξεῖναι
>
> P.Oxy.906 (GD200) (200 CE): ἐξεῖναι
>
> P.Grenf. 2.76 (= *Chr.M.* 295; GD305) (305–306 CE): ἐξεῖναι

---

39. Instone-Brewer, "Graeco-Roman Marriage," 103.

40. Text and translation are available in A. S. Hunt and C. C. Edgar, trans., *Select Papyri, Volume I: Private Documents*, LCL (Cambridge: Harvard University Press, 1959), 22–25.

41. Translation by Mary R. Lefkowitz in Lefkowitz and Maureen B. Fant, *Women's Life in Greece and Rome* (Baltimore: Johns Hopkins University Press, 1982), 60.

42. Text and translation in B. A. van Groningen, ed., *A Family Archive from Tebtunis*, Papyrologica Lugduno-Batava 6 (Leiden: Brill, 1950), 40–44.

43. Henrik Zilliacus et al., *Fifty Oxyrhynchus Papyri*, Commentationes Humanarum Litterarum 63 (Helsinki: Societas Scientiarum Fennica, 1979), 131–32.

CHAPTER 1

Other papyri formulate the legality of remarriage slightly differently. The partners give each other permission and authority (διδόναι ἀλλήλοις ἔφεσιν καὶ ἐξουσίαν) to cohabit or marry someone else (P.Dura. 31 [GD204]; P.Oxy. 2770 [GD304]).[44] Another papyrus (P.Dura. 32 [GD254]) follows the same formula, but the verb indicating the permission is not clear in the text.[45] Still another text is an application for remarriage from 201 CE that includes reference to the discharge (λύω) from a previous marriage contract (P.Oxy. 1473 [GM201]).

The Roman divorce documents in Greek were likely influenced by still older language such as, for instance, in the ancient Egyptian Demotic papyri (dated as early as 548 BCE), which include language such as: "I am the one who has said to you: 'take yourself a husband'; I shall not be able to stand in your way in any place where you will go in order to take yourself a husband there."[46] As P. W. Pestman points out concerning these deeds: "In respect of legal effects pertaining to family law it is stated that the husband has no rights any more as regards the wife and that she is free to marry again."[47]

A significant proportion of the extant divorce papyri (at least a third) render the permission to marry another explicit. As Instone-Brewer concludes: "The legal permission to remarry was a traditional element of the divorce deed. It was not strictly necessary, because divorce by itself gave an individual the legal right to remarry."[48] The permission to remarry was often assumed even when it was

44. For P.Dura. 31, see C. Bradford Welles, Robert O. Fink, and J. Frank Gilliam, eds., *The Excavations at Dura-Europos Conducted by Yale University and the French Academy of Inscriptions and Letters*, Final Report V, Part 1, *The Parchments and Papyri* (New Haven: Yale University Press, 1959), 160–66; upper text and lower text: the former marital partners "give each other permission and power [/authority]" (διδόναι ἀλλήλοις ἔφεσιν καὶ ἐξουσίαν) to cohabit or marry anyone he or she chooses. For P.Oxy. 2770, see volume 36 of *The Oxyrhynchus Papyri*, ed. and trans. by R. A. Coles et al. Graeco-Roman Memoirs 51 (London: Egypt Exploration Society, 1970). In this fragmented portion of the papyrus, the partners grant each other the power/authority (ἐξουσίαν) to marry someone else.

45. Welles, Fink, and Gilliam, *Excavations at Dura-Europos*, 166–69; the text indicates a permission for the wife "to marry another man," but the verb indicating the permission is not clear.

46. P. W. Pestman, *Marriage and Matrimonial Property in Ancient Egypt: A Contribution to Establishing the Legal Position of the Woman*, Papyrologica Lugduno-Batava 9 (Leiden: Brill, 1961), 72.

47. Pestman, *Marriage and Matrimonial Property*, 181. With Erich Lüddeckens, *Ägyptische Eheverträge*, Ägyptische Abhandlugen 1 (Wiesbaden: Harrassowitz, 1960), 276: "Der Grund dafür ist, daß die Frau durch die Scheidungsklausel in der Eheurkunde für eine zukünftige Scheidung gesichert, durch den Scheidebrief aber zu einer zukünftigen Wiederheirat berechtigt werden soll. Das allein ist der Zweck des Scheidebriefes."

48. Instone-Brewer, "Graeco-Roman Marriage," 112. David Atkinson applies this reasoning to the New Testament divorce passages: "In Jesus' day divorce was practically automatically

not explicitly stated. The later Justinianic right to remarry is thus amply confirmed by the divorce papyri in Greek from the first century BCE to the early fourth century CE.

The Ancient Greco-Roman Political and Social Context

The first-century BCE Roman statesman Cicero narrates how a Roman citizen left his pregnant wife in Spain to go to Rome (*De or.* 1.40.183). There this citizen married another woman without the first wife's knowledge of any intent to divorce. After he died, both women gave birth to sons. Cicero wonders whether the son of the second woman was illegitimate because the first marriage had not been dissolved by means of a divorce document with its specific formula. The second woman might be considered merely a concubine. Or perhaps, on the other hand, the second woman should be considered his wife. After all, would not cohabitation with another be sufficient indication that the first marriage had ended in divorce? Legal experts of the day were divided on a situation of this type (*De or.* 1.56.238).[49] Prior to the advent of Augustus's marriage laws, a divorce document was not required.[50] The freedom to marry, divorce, and remarry without any formality could create problems, as Cicero's instance shows.

In the Greco-Roman world, a man and a woman's living together constituted a marriage. One Greco-Roman marriage contract from 66 CE refers to a couple as *already* having been parties to a marriage prior to the contract itself (P.Ryl. 2.154 [GM66]).[51] The agreement to live together constituted an "unwritten marriage" (γάμος ἄγραφος) and could be supplemented, if need be, by a "written marriage" (γάμος ἔγγραφος), usually for when children were born or a significant dowry was involved.[52] The end of the marriage would consist simply of one party

---

followed by remarriage.... If right of remarriage after divorce was assumed, however, then divorce-and-remarriage belong together in Jesus' thinking." See *To Have and to Hold: The Marriage Covenant and the Discipline of Divorce* (London: Collins, 1979), 113. He adds: "The assumption that remarriage normally followed divorce underlies all the Synoptic references to divorce," although possibly "certain covenant obligations remain" after the divorce (121–22).

49. See the discussion of these two texts from Cicero in Rabello, "Divorce," 80–81.

50. Alan Watson, *The Law of Persons in the Later Roman Republic* (Oxford: Oxford University Press, 1967), 53–54.

51. Instone-Brewer, "Graeco-Roman Marriage," 103–4. The text and translation are also in Hunt and Edgar, *Select Papyri, Volume I*, 12–17.

52. Instone-Brewer, "Graeco-Roman Marriage," 104–5; Hans Julius Wolff, *Written and Unwritten Marriages in Hellenistic and Postclassical Roman Law*, Monograph of American Philological Association 9 (Haverford, PA: American Philological Association, 1939), esp. 1–6.

CHAPTER 1

leaving the other, provided the dowry and the wife's personal belongings had been returned.[53]

Divorce was freely permitted in the late Roman Republic, whether on the basis of a husband's lack of affection for his wife or even for the trivial objection of her having gone out in public without his knowledge (Plautus, *Merc.* 817–829). A man might divorce his wife for her failure to give birth to a child. Plutarch recounts the orator Quintus Hortensius (114–50 BCE) requesting that Cato the Younger dissolve his own daughter's marriage so that Hortensius might marry her, thus bringing their two houses together. Cato refused. Hortensius then persuaded Cato and Cato's father-in-law that Cato divorce his *own* wife, whom Hortensius then married (Plutarch, *Cato Min.* 25.2–5).

Such freedom was not limited to husbands. Upper-class Roman women could very easily obtain divorces as well. The first-century CE Stoic philosopher Seneca complains that some women do not number the years by consuls but by their husbands as they divorce to marry and marry to divorce (*Ben.* 3.16.2). The first-century CE poet Martial points to a woman who over the course of thirty days had married and divorced ten men; he considered this adulterous (*Epigr.* 6.7). One study of Roman consuls estimates that at least 47 percent of consular-married couples would involve a remarriage on the part of one or both parties.[54] Most women, of course, did not enjoy the means of the wealthy and elite to dissolve marriage so easily, and estimates concerning nonelite marriage are more difficult to make. If any indication, the remarriage rate for Roman consular couples (the upper crust) was significantly higher than the modern Western average.

At the beginning of the imperial period, between 29 and 22 BCE, Emperor Augustus was engaged in the reorganization of the provinces and with other external affairs. The landscape was dramatically changing with the rapid growth of provinces and the skyrocketing influx of slaves and foreigners into Rome. As a consequence, the older social and political structures were becoming obsolete,

53. Suzanne Dixon, *The Roman Family* (Baltimore: The Johns Hopkins University Press, 1992), 81; Jane F. Gardner, *Women in Roman Law and Society* (Bloomington, IN: Indiana University Press, 1986), 81.

54. K. R. Bradley, "Remarriage and the Structure of the Upper-Class Roman Family," in *Marriage, Divorce, and Children in Ancient Rome*, ed. Beryl Rawson (Oxford: Oxford University Press, 1991), 83; cf. the modern US rate in the 40th percentile. One would not expect the same rate among the general population as among the elite consular families. See especially also Michel Humbert, *Le remariage à Rome: Étude d'historie juridique et sociale*, Università di Roma 44 (Milan: Giuffrè, 1972), 76–112. Humbert traces literary witnesses and inscriptions, especially for the better-attested elite families, and notes the rarity of long single marriages. High divorce and remarriage rates at the end of the Republic and the beginning of the Empire had created a crisis for the institution of marriage.

provoking a conservative backlash. Augustus returned to Rome in 19 BCE only to have the office of *cura mora et legum* bestowed on him. He took very seriously the newfound responsibility to oversee public morality, which he judged as having become particularly lax (Dio Cassius, *Hist. rom.* 54.10.5–7).[55] He issued legislation to respond to the weakening of the traditional power of the paterfamilias, the disintegration of the family, growing urbanization, and rank moral depravity. Roman men were opting for fewer or, preferably, a *single* heir to their large estates.[56] Infanticide was not uncommon. Many in Roman society were remaining celibate and childless. Women were becoming increasingly libertine among the upper classes. In response, Augustus hoped to encourage both marriage and children with his legislation. With his edicts of 18–16 BCE (*Lex Iulia de maritandis ordinibus* and *Lex Iulia de adulteriis coercendis*), Augustus sought to formalize marriage and discourage divorce. Divorce would require a letter and seven adult Roman witnesses.[57]

Out of concern for their estates, some men were encouraged by these laws to marry and have children (Plutarch, *Am. prol.* 2 [*Mor.* 493e]). On the whole, however, Augustus's reforms faced heavy resistance. According to Suetonius, he was forced to revise and mitigate some of their requirements "because of an open revolt against its provisions" by rescinding or mitigating the legislation's penalties while increasing rewards and allowing a three-year exception from marriage after the death of a spouse (Suetonius, *Aug.* 34.1 [Rolfe, LCL]). The equestrian order continued to call publicly for the reforms to be repealed. Augustus concluded that "the spirit of the law was being evaded" (*Aug.* 34.2 [Rolfe, LCL]). As Csillag writes, "Because of the strong opposition of his contemporaries, Augustus was able to enforce the provisions of the *Lex Iulia de maritandis ordinibus* only by consenting to their continual amendment, mitigation and even the suspension of their operation."[58]

In 9 CE, five years before his death, Augustus decreed his *Lex Papia Poppaea nuptialis*; he had to weaken some of the provisions of his earlier laws. The 18 BCE edicts and this new edict were later merged into a single law (*Lex Iulia et Papia*). In general, the results of these laws were unimpressive. Seneca and Tacitus both complain of the continuing moral depravity (Seneca, *Ben.* 3.16; Tacitus, *Hist.* 1.2). According to the latter, Augustus's laws "failed ... to make marriage and the family popular—childlessness remained the vogue" (Tacitus, *Ann.* 3.25 [Jackson, LCL]). Dio Cassius reports that Augustus had realized startlingly on one occasion in the

---

55. Pál Csillag, *The Augustan Laws on Family Relations* (Budapest: Akadémiai Kiadó, 1976), 30.
56. Csillag, *Augustan Laws*, 43–44; Humbert, *Remariage*, 138–78.
57. On the need for witnesses, see Justinian, *Dig.* 24.2.9.
58. Csillag, *Augustan Laws*, 33.

CHAPTER 1

wake of the *Lex Iulia et Papia* in 9 CE that a majority of the assembled members of the equestrian order remained unmarried (*Hist. rom.* 56.1.2–1.4.3). The ruling classes were indignant at Augustus's legislation.

One motivating factor for Augustus's moral legislation was the freewheeling lifestyle of his daughter Julia, and she was hardly an isolated instance (Seneca, *Ben.* 3.16.2; Martial, *Epigr.* 6.7). Julia became an exemplar for many upper-class women in her lifestyle, even as husbands and fathers longed for the days when women tended to be more like Augustus's wife, the faithful and proper Livia. The laws aimed to encourage marriage, to allow for adultery to be punished, and to restrict divorce in order to increase the number of children born to citizens. Widows were to be remarried within two to three years, and divorcées within eighteen months.

Although Augustus's financial incentives for bearing children would be more successful, overall Augustus's laws failed to have any real effect in reducing adultery or divorce, since the measures relied on private citizens bringing formal charges against offenders.[59] Such rewards and penalties required significant wealth. That such laws targeted the behavior of elite women in divorce and remarriage and required the financial means to make use of the court systems leaves it doubtful whether these laws filtered down to the masses and the provinces. Augustus's laws also required the return of a woman's dowry before they could marry again and aimed to protect the children of an earlier marriage from a stepfather.[60] The laws did not accomplish much more and certainly did little to stem divorce or encourage remarriage. Remarriages took place freely quite apart from Augustus's legislation.

Pre-Christian Roman marriage remained largely a private matter. Divorce by mutual consent without documentation remained common even with Justinian's later legislation. If both parties did not anticipate a challenge and mutually consented, a formal divorce document would be unnecessary. Without that mutual consent, one partner could not easily initiate a divorce.[61] Augustus required a divorce certificate witnessed by seven Roman citizens in instances where a divorce had been initiated unilaterally. This protected a party against a charge of adultery or would establish an accusation against a wife.[62] Having a letter of divorce was insisted on in instances where someone might challenge the legality of the di-

---

59. Instone-Brewer, *Divorce and Remarriage*, 73.
60. Dixon, *Roman Family*, 89.
61. Dixon, *Roman Family*, 81.
62. Percy Ellwood Corbett, *The Roman Law of Marriage* (Oxford: Oxford University Press, 1930), 228–34, 238–39.

vorce.[63] The limitation to these particular situations explains why many ancient texts bear witness to a lack of formality in divorce.[64]

Of greater consequence is whether remarriage would have been assumed in any case where a divorce had taken place. Was remarriage universally accepted in the Greco-Roman world? Were there other points of view? Just as ancient Near Eastern and Jewish divorce certificates regularly express a "freedom" or "permission" to marry again, Instone-Brewer stresses that the Greco-Roman freedom to remarry was universal. Many follow Instone-Brewer's lead in claiming a blanket freedom to remarry in view of ancient divorce certificates. Andrew David Naselli, for instance, notes how both Hillel and Shammai permitted remarriage, "as did all known Jewish and Graeco-Roman views at that time.... [E]veryone—Jew or Gentile—assumed that remarriage is legitimate when the divorce is legitimate."[65] R. T. France's judgment (citing Instone-Brewer) is commonplace among gospel commentators: "The standard wording [of the divorce certificate], according to *m. Giṭ.* 9:3, was, 'You are free to marry any man.' Without that permission it was not divorce. Divorce and the right to remarry are thus inseparable, and the Jewish world knew nothing of a legal separation which did not allow remarriage."[66] Instone-Brewer's survey of the universal acceptability of remarriage has clearly been influential. He convinced William Heth to drop his well-known earlier position against remarriage, since apparently everyone in the first-century world would have assumed it. Heth titled a section of a later essay: "'Divorce' in the First Century Was Synonymous with the Right to Remarry."[67] The time has come to test that assertion.

The Roman Ideal of the Woman Married Only Once

Augustus's *Lex Iulia et Papia* aimed to correct the decline in morals that had been taking place for some time and that was also impacting the institution of marriage. Roman customs in the prior centuries had been more conservative, and earlier practices continued to exert a countervailing influence. A prime example is the lingering ideal of the *univira* (literally "a one-husband [woman]") still heralded in some quarters of Roman society, an ideal that Augustus with his legislation had sought to counteract by mandating remarriage for the sake of more children.

---

63. Dixon, *Roman Family*, 79, 81.
64. Corbett, *Roman Law*, 229.
65. Naselli, "What the New Testament Teaches," 12.
66. R. T. France, *The Gospel of Matthew*, NICNT (Grand Rapids: Eerdmans, 2007), 212.
67. Heth, "Remarriage for Adultery or Desertion," 67–68.

CHAPTER 1

Originally, *univira* described a woman who was eligible to participate in particular Roman religious cults and rituals. No explanation has survived from antiquity why only single-married women were permitted to take part in these rituals when other matronal cults allowed remarried women to participate. The cults that preferred the *univira* did not just exclude the divorced and remarried but also the widowed. In the *flaminica dialis* cult of Jupiter, a perpetual and unique union of a woman and a man was a favorable omen.[68] Even as touching the dead would render a male *flamen* or a female *flaminica* impure, so also would a divorce or remarriage. If a *flaminica* died, her *dialis* was obliged to resign his office.[69] Cultic purity required an ideal union of one husband and one wife, just like Jupiter and Juno, unsullied by death. In the cults of Fortuna (Muliebris and Virgo) and the Mater Matuta, only a once-wedded woman could hang the wreath.[70] Tacitus narrates how a decision was rendered in the appointment to the office of the Vestal Virgins: "Pollio's child was preferred, for no reason save that her mother was still living with the same husband, while Agrippa's divorce had impaired the credit of his household" (*Ann.* 2.86 [Jackson, LCL]).[71] Similar qualifications were required for the cults of the Achaian Juno, the Scythian Diana, and the Pythian Apollo.[72] The Roman historian Livy relates how the sacrifice at the shrine of Pudititia could be performed only by a once-married woman, and only such women could serve as *pronubae* at weddings, a practice that encouraged the bride to remain faithful to and have only one husband.[73]

In the early Roman Republic, divorce was uncommon and a *matrona* was often eligible to serve as a *univira*. The husband had the right to divorce his wife only if the wife was gravely at fault (Dionysius of Halicarnassus, *Ant. rom.* 2.25; Aulus Gellius, *Noct. att.* 10.23.3–5). With the increasing divorce rate in the late first century BCE, *matrona* was no longer necessarily assumed a single marriage; the term *univira* was extended from those eligible for the archaic cults to *any* woman married to only one man in her lifetime.[74] The *univira* would ultimately refer to

68. Humbert, *Remariage*, 36.
69. Humbert, *Remariage*, 41; Plutarch, *Quaest. rom.* 50 (*Mor.* 276d).
70. Tertullian, *Mon.* 17; *Exh. cast.* 13.
71. Csillag, *Augustan Laws*, 30, 232 n. 235.
72. Tertullian, *Mon.* 17; *Exh. cast.* 13.
73. *Uni nuptam ad quem virgo deducta sit*; *uni virae nupti*; "wedded to the one man she had been given as a maiden; wedded to one man alone" (Livy, *Ab urbe cond.* 10.23.5, 10 [Foster, LCL]). "Women in the married state" would implore the gods (Tacitus, *Ann.* 15.64 [Jackson, LCL]); so also Susan Treggiari, *Roman Marriage: Iusti Coniuges from the Time of Cicero to the Time of Ulpian* (Oxford: Oxford University Press, 1991), 233.
74. Majorie Lightman and William Zeisel, "Univira: An Example of Continuity and Change in Roman Society," *CH* 46 (1977): 25; see also Hermann Funke, "Univira: Ein Beispiel heidnischer Geschichtsapologetik," *JAC* 8/9 (1965–1966): 183–88.

a widow who had been married as a virgin at a young age and transferred from her father's power to the husband's *manus*. In the era of the late Republic, many widows were still choosing to remain single out of loyalty to their dead husbands. Often the decision was for the benefit of the children.

Few women in the imperial period boasted *univira* status.[75] As a vestige of earlier sensibilities, Roman authors occasionally criticized remarriages, especially while the first spouse was still alive. Tacitus condemned the adulterous Messalina's behavior prior to her third marriage to the previously unwed Silius: "Yet, for the sake of that transcendent infamy which constitutes the last delight of the profligate, she coveted the name of wife; and waiting only till Claudius left for Ostia to hold a sacrifice, she celebrated the full solemnities of marriage" (*Ann*. 11.26 [Jackson, LCL]). Despite the frequency and widespread acceptance of remarriage in their society, many Romans continued to praise the ideal practiced by those women who had remained married to a single spouse, the *univira*.

Imperial-era Latin authors decried the decline in marital faithfulness. Tacitus casts a sideways glance at Germanic society and morals: "Adulteries are very few for the number of the people" and the punishment by the husband very severe (*Germ*. 19.2 [Hutton, LCL]). He adds: "Better still are those tribes where only maids marry, and where a woman makes a pact, once for all, in the hopes and vows of a wife; so they take one husband only, just as one body and one life" (*Germ*. 19.4). The comments say as much about Tacitus's attitude as the Germans.

Despite the increasing frequency of divorce and remarriage in Roman society, especially among the upper classes with greater financial means, many tombstones are extant that celebrate the woman of one husband with the varied language for the *univira*:

nulli dedita—CIL 6.6976

uniuira/uniuiria/unicuba—CIL 3.3572 (*unicuba*, adding *coniugi incomparabili*); 5.7763 (*univiriae*; admittedly "a woman most rare" [*femin rarissimae*]); 6.2308 (*univiriae*); 6.2318 (*univiriae*); 6.12405 (*unibyria*); 6.13299 (*univiriae*); 6.13303 (*univiriae*); 6.14771 (*univiriae*); 6.25392 (*incomparabili univiriae*); 6.26268 (*univiriae*); 6.31711 (*univira*); 9.5142 (*univiria*); 10.3058 (*univirae*); 10.3351 (*unovirae*); 11.4593 (*univiriae*); 14.418 (*unibyriae*); 14.839; 14.963 (*univiriae*); *Carm. Epigr*. 1306 (*Celsino nupta univira unanimis*); CIL 6.3604 (*incomparabili univiriae*); 8.7384; 8.11294 (note the virtues listed, including *fides*; adding *inconparabilis coniux*); 8.19470 (all three with *univira*); 11.1800 (*univirie*); with some variation in *Carm. Epigr*. 558.4 (*unicuba uniiuga*)

---

75. Humbert, *Remariage*, 68 in reference to five imperial-era epitaphs.

CHAPTER 1

> *uno contenta marito*—*CIL* 3.2667
> *solo contento marito*—*CIL* 13.5383
> *virginia/verginiae*—*CIL* 3.1992; 3.2741; 3.14292; 6.12829 (= 6.10867, [*virgo*]); 11.216 (*virginiae*); 14.1641 (*virgo*); the words *virginius, virginia,* and *virginalis* also referred to the once-married (e.g., *CIL* 6.19253; 6.37207; 10.3058; 11.216; 13.2000)[76]
> *cum quo uixit a virginitate*—*CIL* 6.9810; 10.3720
> *unum ab virginitate*—*CIL* 6.7732
> *unimaritae*—*CIL* 6.30428
> *solus coniunx/unicus maritus*—*CIL* 3.1537; 3.8178; 8.1542 (*post maritum, quem solum norat*); 9.2272 (*unum sortita maritum*); 13.2216 (*uniusq maritae*).

Other epitaphs identify the woman as married to a single man (*solus*).[77] Even more frequent are those that describe the woman's relationship to only *one* (*unus*) husband.[78] *CIL* 6.13303 reads: "For Aurelia Domitia, freedwoman of Augustus, *univira*, a spouse most blessed, most devoted, most proper and respectful to her family. Pompeianus, her husband, with whom she lived twenty years. She was thirty-six years old." After translating this epitaph, Lightman and Zeisel conclude: "The inscriptions indicate that *univira* had lost its specifically religious and cultic associations as well as its elite social status, to become one of the many pagan epithets for the good wife."[79] Some epitaphs would simply state that the woman had remained content with a single husband, another expression of the *univira* language.[80] Other epitaphs praise those who remained widows. For example, *CIL* 9.5517 eulogizes a widow, who died at the age of eighty-five after living thirty years beyond the death of her husband. Elsewhere another widow is celebrated for dying at seventy-eight years of age as a *univira* (*CIL* 11.6281). Likewise, *CIL*

---

76. Richmond Lattimore, *Themes in Greek and Latin Epitaphs* (Urbana, IL: University of Illinois Press, 1942), 278 n. 98.

77. E.g., *Carm. Epigr.* 455 (*solo contenta marito*); 548.5 (*dedita coniugi soli suo*); 597.3 (*que mihi solus coniunx Aelius*); 652.7 (*soli seruasses marito*); cf. 1142.15–17: *quod solum licuit coniunx fidissima fecit*.

78. E.g., *Carm. Epigr.* 643.5 (*uno contenta marito*); 693.4 (*unius viri consortio . . . coniuncta*); 736.3 (*uni devota marito*); 968.3 (*coniuge namque uno vixit contenta probato*); 1523.7 (*unum sortita maritum/servavi casta pudorem*); 1693.1 (*u[no cont]enta marito*). See also Gordon Williams, "Some Aspects of Roman Marriage Ceremonies and Ideals," *Journal of Roman Studies* 48.1–2 (1958): 23.

79. Lightman and Zeisel, "Univira," 24.

80. Treggiari, *Roman Marriage*, 234. Jean-Baptiste Frey, "Signification des termes ΜΟΝΑΝΔΡΟΣ et Univira," *RSR* 20 (1930): 57, comments on the twelve *univira* inscriptions he had located: Nine were left behind by the surviving husband, and the remaining three offered no indication that the deceased wife was remarried.

13.2056 describes a mother and grandmother who died at fifty-four years of age after having remained unmarried for eighteen years (similarly *CIL* 6.19838).[81] Such widows were the exception since most women remarried, usually of necessity.

As a legacy of the pre-Augustan era, the Roman poets likewise celebrated the memory of *uxores univires*. Statius in the first century CE applauds how a woman "knew marriage by a single torch; yours was a single love" (*Silv.* 5.3.240 [Bailey and Parrott, LCL]; so also 5.1.43–74). In an early Augustan poem, Propertius relays a mother, Cornelia, speaking to her daughter: "Follow mine example and wed one and only one," although Cornelia grants that her husband, Lucius Aemilius Paullus, may marry again (*Eleg.* 4.11.68 [Butler, LCL]).[82] Earlier Cornelia dictates: "Behold the legend on this stone: 'To one and one alone was she espoused'" (4.11.36 [Butler, LCL]). She was a woman of a single marriage. Even at a lower social level, one inscription describes a woman "to Celsinus married, an harmonious *univira*" (*CIL* 6.31711).[83] Catullus in his poem 111 writes: "To live content with one her husband and no other husband is a glory for brides one of the most excellent" (Cornish, LCL). To live content with one man" appears in inscriptions from a less affluent social milieu than Catullus's literary reference (e.g., *viro contentam . . . solo* or *uno contenta viro* as in *CIL* 6.5162).[84] Such descriptions are widely attested at different social levels.

Valerius Maximus similarly describes this single-marriage ideal:

> Women who had been content with a single marriage used to be honoured with a crown of chastity. For they thought that the mind of a married woman was particularly loyal and uncorrupted if it knew not how to leave the bed on which she had surrendered her virginity, believing that trial of many marriages was as it were the sign of a legalized incontinence (*Fact.* 2.1.3 [Shackleton Bailey, LCL]).

He offers as an example Antonia, who "balanced her husband's love with outstanding loyalty." She shared a bed with her mother-in-law in lieu of a husband as "the vigour of youth was quenched for the old and the experience of widowhood turned to old age for the other" (*Fact.* 4.3.3 [Shackleton Bailey, LCL]). Even Josephus, despite his own multiple marriages, esteems Antonia: "For despite her youth she remained steadfast in her widowhood and refused to marry again although

---

81. In several instances these women remained unmarried for the sake of their children; see Humbert, *Remariage*, 67–68.

82. See Lightman and Zeisel, "Univira," 21–22.

83. Translation from Lightman and Ziesel, "Univira." *Domo orta* in the inscription may indicate a *verna*, a houseborn slave (see 23).

84. Lightman and Zeisel, "Univira," 22.

CHAPTER 1

the emperor urged her to do so. She thus kept her life free from reproach" (*Ant.* 18.6.6 §180 [Feldman, LCL]). Widows were praised for mourning until the end of life (*CIL* 3.3241; 6.7243; 6.15806; 6.15546).

Plutarch expresses a similar sentiment:

> For what reason is it not the custom for maidens to marry on public holidays, but widows do not marry at this time? . . . Is it rather because it is seemly that not a few should be present when maidens marry, but disgraceful when widows marry? Now the first marriage is enviable; but the second is to be deprecated, for women are ashamed [αἰσχύνονται] if they take a second husband while the first husband is still living, and they feel sad if they do so when he is dead (*Quaest. rom.* 105 [289a–b] [Babbitt, LCL]).

The ideal is therefore for the widow to remain unmarried (*univira*). A widow's wedding should be quiet with only a few witnesses. It is particularly shameful if a woman marries while the first husband remains alive. Because of this ideal, Horace describes Livia, despite her previous marriage and the inaccuracy of the description, as "rejoicing in her peerless husband [Augustus]" (*Odes* 3.14.5: *unico gaudens mulier marito* [Bennett, LCL]). She had not remarried after Augustus. Some epitaphs would award the title for the ideal to the unworthy.

Although remarriage was possible, poets echoed the sentiment that spouses would be reunited with their partners in the afterlife. Statius remarks on Polla's devotion and faithfulness to her dead husband (*Silv.* 2.7.126–129). Pliny recalls one wife who enabled a mutual death for herself and her gravely ill husband so that they would remain together (Pliny, *Ep.* 6.24). Several other Roman authors recall women following their husband's examples in death.[85] When Porcia M. Cato's daughter learned of her husband Brutus's death, she took burning coals into her mouth to suffer an even braver death than her father (Valerius Maximus, *Fact.* 4.6.5; Martial, *Epigr.* 1.42). Some wives would even throw themselves on their husband's funeral pyre (Ovid, *Tr.* 5.14.7, 38; Propertius, *Eleg.* 3.13.23).

For many ancient Romans the marital union remained permanent, even in the face of the death of a spouse.[86] The eternal union would survive death (e.g., *CIL* 10.1310: *Iulius cum Trebia bene uixit multosque per annos, coniugio aeterno hic quoque nunc remanet*). Some inscriptions express the couple's desire not to be sep-

---

85. E.g., Tacitus, *Ann.* 6.29 [Paxaea]; 16.34 [Arria almost]; Martial, *Epigr.* 1.13; Dio Cassius, *Hist rom.* 60.16.6

86. E.g., *CIL* 6.11082; 6.30111a (*aeternum foedus*, if reconstructed correctly); 6.434 (*dum u[i]ta manet, toto est in corde maritus*); 8.648 (*semper vivit sibi*).

arated into different tombs (e.g., *CIL* 8.27380: *crudelis quae sola potest disiu[n]gere amantes*) or their wish to remain together even after death (e.g., *CIL* 2.3596; 6.9693; 6.30115). Some vow in inscriptions never to marry again (*CIL* 6.14404; 8.16737) or to remain chaste after the death of the spouse (e.g., *CIL* 6.25427). A wife might even promise to wait for her reunion with her husband (*CIL* 12.5193: *virum expecto meum*). One Spanish inscription states the ashes within the chamber and tomb were to be respected in the same manner as the nuptial bed (*CIL* 2.301). Death was just a cruel, temporary separation (e.g., *CIL* 6.7579; 6.12652; 6.18817). The surviving spouse would mourn to the very end (e.g., *CIL* 6.7243; 6.15546; 6.15806: *flet amissam aeterno tempore coniunx*). Some epitaphs describe death as a chance to be reunited with a predeceased spouse for a perpetual union or for the predeceased spouse to receive the partner for a renewed, perpetual union.[87]

Vergil celebrates the *univira* through the character of Dido in his *Aeneid*. At the heart of her tragedy is her one, eternal marriage to Sychaeus.[88] She was given to him as a virgin, and she adored (*amore*) him (*Aen.* 1.343–346). After he was murdered, she desired not to break honor's laws or falter (*culpa*); she wanted to stay faithful to her dead husband (4.18–19, 27–29).[89] She calls her passion "marriage . . . to conceal her shame" (4.171–172; cf. 4.307, 316).[90] Despite the gods' orchestrating another union (4.45, 123–128, 165–168, 575), ultimately, she sorrowfully confesses: "I broke my promise to the dead Sychaeus" (4.551–552). As a result, Aeneas eventually leaves her, and Dido joins Sychaeus in the afterlife after committing suicide in repentance for her lack of fidelity to her dead husband (6.473–474). There in the afterlife she refuses to recognize Aeneas and returns to Sychaeus (6.450–475).[91] Earlier versions of the story call her Elissa, and in those accounts she remains fully faithful to her dead husband.[92] Vergil describes the marriage of one man and one woman that, despite Dido's love for Aeneas, lasts eternally, even into the afterlife. Similarly, Chariton's Callirhoe (*Chaer.* 3.6.6)—if not also the Jewish heroine Ju-

---

87. E.g., *CIL* 6.1779 (*sed tamen felix, tua quia sum fuique postque mortem mox ero*); 6.11252 (*quod praecessi sustineo in aeterno toro adventum tuum*); 6.13528 (*parato hospitium; cara iungant corpora haec rursum nostrae sed perpetuae nuptiae*); 6.19008 (*coniugi perpetuae . . . nunc mortis iuncti iacent*). See also the hopes among Greeks to meet again after death in Lattimore, *Themes in Greek and Latin Epitaphs*, 58 (e.g., *IG* 12.8.449.12–14: "Theodorus, my husband, I pray that, late though it be, you will come and I shall meet you and we shall share our bed, so that we shall forget our misfortunes").

88. Williams, "Some Aspects," 23.

89. Ovid (*Ep.* 7.123–124) celebrates Dido's refusal of countless potential suitors after his death.

90. Translation, unless otherwise noted, from Vergil, *The Aeneid*, trans. Sarah Ruden (New Haven: Yale University Press, 2008).

91. Williams, "Some Aspects," 23–24.

92. Reportedly in the lost writings of Timaeus of Sicily (c. 356–260 BCE).

dith (Jud. 16:22)—exhibits faithfulness to a dead spouse by not remarrying. The romance genre's ideal wife, mourning and starving at the grave of the husband, would even be satirized (Petronius, *Sat.* 111).

The ancients often celebrated the single, eternal union. One wife's tombstone inscription conveys that the marriage is *coniugi perpetuae*, a perpetual or unceasing marital union (*Carm. Epigr.* 1571.3).[93] The Roman grammarian Festus (second century CE) writes of the once-married who enjoyed a perpetual union.[94] Propertius frequently refers to the eternal bond of marriage while idealizing his relationship with his Cynthia: "As for me, no wife nor mistress shall ever steal me from thee; for me thou shalt at once be mistress and wife" (*Eleg.* 2.6.41–42 [Butler, LCL]). He adds: "He errs that seeks to set a term to the frenzy of love; true love hath no bound. . . . hers will I be in life and hers in death" (2.15.29, 36). Propertius continues: "I will abide true to thee, my life, until darkness close my day; one selfsame love, one selfsame hour, shall sweep us both away" (2.20.17–18). As Scapha says in Plautus's *Mostellaria*: "This giving yourself up to one lover is all right for married women, but not for mistresses" (*Most.* 187–189 [Nixon, LCL]). Scapha then laments: "I was loved no less than you are now; I devoted myself to just one man—and he, oh well, when age came on and changed the colour of this head of mine, he left me, deserted me" (199–202). The ideal is that "he'll be food for you eternally and be your own fond lover all your life" and that "you . . . put yourself at his sole disposal" (223–226). The bond of marriage is for a lifetime with eternal implications.[95] Occasionally, Jewish inscriptions similarly attest to the *monandros* or *univira* ideal.[96]

Such descriptions are sometimes applied to the husband as well. As Propertius's fidelity to his wife suggests, the *univira* tradition was apparently not limited to women. For instance, *CIL* 10.3720 is an epitaph that praises two parties who have married only once: *cum quo vixit ab virginitate sua ad finem vitae suae*.[97] Although

---

93. Bücheler, *Carmina Latina Epigraphica*, 758–59.

94. Sextus Pompeius Festus, *De verborum significatu quae supersunt cum Pauli Epitome*, ed. Wallace M. Lindsey (Leipzig: Teubner, 1913), 282.16–18: *pronubae adhibentur nuptis, quae semel nupserunt, ut matrimonii perpetuitatem auspicantes*. Festus's manuscript had *paupertatem* instead of *perpetuitatem*, but Augustine suggests the reading *perpetuitatem* instead, and a Paulus excerpt reads: *ut singulare perseveret matrimonium*; Williams, "Some Aspects," 25 n. 42.

95. See the detailed analysis of this text as exhibiting the Roman belief in the eternal marriage bond in Williams, "Some Aspects," 25–27.

96. E.g., *CIJ* 1.81, 158, 392, 541. See also Harry J. Leon, *The Jews of Ancient Rome*, rev. ed. (Peabody, MA: Hendrickson, 1995), 129–30, cf. Leon's statement that it was precisely because Jewish widows generally remarried that "it was apparently regarded as a noteworthy mark of devotion to her dead husband if a widow did not take another husband" (232). Note also Frey, "Signification," 48–60.

97. See the discussion in Lattimore, *Themes in Greek and Latin Epitaphs*, 278; cf. *CIL* 12.2244 (*virginitate*); 14.5210.

women are praised in four times as many inscriptions for this, men are occasionally lauded for remaining *virginii*.[98] Valerius Maximus praises the senator C. Plautius Numida, who, after his wife's death, stabbed himself and died of the wound in mourning: "By so violent a death he testified how mighty a conjugal flame was hidden in that breast of his" (*Fact.* 4.6.2 [Shackleton Bailey, LCL]). Likewise, Plautius fell on his drawn sword following his wife Orestilla's sickness and death. Valerius Maximus concludes from the couple: "Surely where love is both at its greatest and most honourable, it is far better to be joined by death than separated by life" (4.6.3). Carphyllides, who may be dated either prior to 90 BCE or in the second century CE, boasted of being a "one wife" man: "I enjoyed the company of one wife (μιῆς ἀπέλαυσα γυναικός) who grew old together with me" (*Anth. Gr.* 7.260 [Paton, LCL]).

Such conservative ideals with respect to marriage did not subside in the Julio-Claudian period, even in the face of the excesses of the emperors. Pliny and Suetonius's respective commentaries on married life are evidence of a Flavian reaction to the excesses of the Julio-Claudian period.[99] As Keith Bradley concludes: "Thus ideal perception of Roman marriage still retained vitality and validity, and made evaluation of imperial performance possible and meaningful to an author interested in the 'abstinentia et moderatio insequentium principum' as well as the *virtutes* and *vita* of their predecessors."[100] Despite the fact that actual marriages rarely emulated this ideal, during the reigns of Trajan and Hadrian historians and commentators still held concerning the ideal Roman marriage that the wife should be married only once during her lifetime and praised as a *univira*, that the wife should obey her husband, and that the marriage would last a lifetime and be brought to an end by spousal death alone, if even then.[101]

Such traditions may well be attested elsewhere in the Greco-Roman world. One ancient marriage certificate reads: "It shall not be lawful for Philiscus [the husband] to bring in another wife besides Apollonia [the wife], nor to keep a concubine or boy, nor to have children by another woman while Apollonia lives, nor

---

98. E.g., *CIL* 3.2739; 3.2868; 3.7507 (*virginio*); 3.7553 (*virginio*); 3.7694 (*virginio*); 3.10577 (*virginio*); 3.14910 (*virginius*); 6.37207; 13.2189 (*virginio*); 14.2841 (*virginio*).

99. Keith R. Bradley, "Ideals of Marriage in Suetonius' *Caesares*," *Rivista storica dell'antichità* 15 (1985): 91–93. On the continuing influence of the *univira* traditions into earliest Christianity and the resultant debate over whether widows may remarry, see Jens-Uwe Krause, *Witwen und Waisen im Römischen Reich I: Verwitwung und Wiederverheiratung*, Heidelberger Althistorische Beiträge und Epigraphische Studien 16 (Stuttgart: Franz Steiner, 1994), 102–7, 153–91.

100. Bradley, "Ideals of Marriage," 93, who earlier had emphasized: "[T]he ideals of the past had not lost vogue but were still being cultivated in the era of Suetonius" (91).

101. Bradley, "Ideals of Marriage," 86–87.

CHAPTER 1

to inhabit another house over which Apollonia is not mistress."[102] This language is identical to that found in several other papyri.[103] David Instone-Brewer summarily dismisses that these papyri forbid remarriage:

> The contract might appear, at first glance, to forbid remarriage during the lifetime of the wife. . . . This reading would be totally contrary to everything we know about Greek and Egyptian marriages. All the marriage, divorce and related legal papyri suggest that remarriage was not only normal but expected. The sentence presumably means '. . . while Apollonia lives (and continues to be his wife)'. There was no need to state this only applied while she was his wife because this was implied.[104]

For Instone-Brewer, societal attitudes *uniformly* sanctioned remarriage. Any departure from that norm would be unprecedented. Humbert, on the other hand, recognizes that these Egyptian Greek marriage contracts did indeed introduce the duty of a husband to have neither a concubine nor children with another spouse. The contracts maintained that the husband could neither break the conjugal union by a divorce nor enter into a second marriage.[105] These marriage contracts *are* different from others in antiquity, and the differences must be taken seriously and not dismissed. The older Roman traditions of the *univira*—which Instone-Brewer largely ignores—place these second- and early first-century BCE papyri in a different light and render his generalized claims doubtful. These papyri reflect a minority position in the East that parallels the older Roman traditions in the West. Some of these papyri are intended to protect the wife and to make provisions for her if the union does not last her entire lifetime. The intent appears to be for the spouses to remain faithful exclusively to each other for life.

Language associated with the *univira* tradition parallels the apostle Paul's in Rom 7:1–3 and 1 Cor 7:39. Livy attributes to Lucius Valerius in 195 BCE these words: "Never while their males survive is feminine slavery [*servitus*] shaken off; and even they abhor the freedom [*libertatem*] which the loss of husbands and fathers gives" (*Ab urbe cond.* 34.7.12 [Sage, LCL]). The wife is subject to the husband while he lives, and only his death brings about freedom. In the tradition of the *univira*, the wife does not avail herself of that freedom. Many women in the midst of their

---

102. P.Tebt. 1.104 (= *Chr.M.* 285; GM92). Text and translation are available in Hunt and Edgar, *Select Papyri, Volume I*, 6–7.

103. P.Freib. 3.30 (GM179g), esp. lines 29–30; P.Giss. 2 (GM173), lines 16–24; P.Gen. 1.21 (= *Chr.M.* 284; P.Münch. 3.62; GM150), lines 4–6; P.Eleph. 1.2.1–18 (= *Chr.M.* 283; GM311).

104. Instone-Brewer, "Graeco-Roman Marriage," 109–10.

105. Humbert, *Remariage*, 67.

newfound freedom keenly felt the tension between faithfulness to a deceased husband and the prospect of a new marriage (e.g., Apuleius, *Metam.* 8.8.7).[106]

Christian authors as early as Tertullian openly promoted the tradition of the *univira* and the idea that widows must remain single and not remarry. He exhorted his own wife to remain *ad univiratum* as a widow.[107] A number of Christian epitaphs likewise celebrate the *univira* in their ranks (*CIL* 10.7196; *ICLV* 1581). The Roman ideal was thus reprised in Latin Christianity in the West, with figures like Tertullian relying on the *univira* tradition to deny the possibility of widows marrying second husbands. This raises the question whether the author of 1 Timothy, one of Tertullian's source texts, had been influenced by the *univira* ideals already within the first century, at least for church office holders. First Timothy states the bishop is to be the husband of one wife (3:2) even as the woman within the parallel office of widow is to have been the wife of one husband (5:9). It may be that the phrases "husband of one wife" (1 Tim 3:2; Titus 1:6) and "the wife of one husband" (1 Tim 5:9) in the Pastoral Epistles reflect the tradition of the *univira*. The stipulations are reminiscent of the *univira* ideal among leaders in some of the ancient Roman cults, but the evidence for the influence of the *univira* tradition may be stronger for Tertullian than the author of 1 Timothy in view of another popular explanation (see the appendix to this chapter: The Pastoral Epistles and the *Univira* Tradition).

The idealization of a wife's devotion to a single man, and occasionally also the husband's devotion to a single wife, is largely limited to the Romans although there are some parallels among the Egyptians and Greeks. Many have concluded that the Greek parallels may be "the product of direct Roman influence."[108] There is certainly no clear evidence to demonstrate the influence of the older Roman ideals on Jesus or the New Testament authors with the exception of the Pastoral Epistles. The Roman ideals demonstrate that resistance to remarriage was present in some sectors of the first-century Greco-Roman world, and these ideals would be reclaimed by early Christian authors after the time of the New Testament. Such attitudes may, nevertheless, have enjoyed wider currency.

---

106. Ben Witherington III objects to an application of *univira* traditions to the New Testament witness: "It is furthermore often overlooked that the *univira* inscription is about a woman who did not remarry after the mentioned spouse died." See *A Socio-Rhetorical Commentary on Titus, 1–2 Timothy, and 1–3 John*, vol. 1 of *Letters and Homilies for Hellenized Christians* (Downers Grove, IL: InterVarsity, 2006), 110. The problem with Witherington's reasoning is that these women were likewise being praised for having been married and faithful to a single man, even after his death!

107. E.g., *Virg.* 9; *Mon.* 8; *Exh. cast.* 11, 13; *Ux.* 1.7–8; 2.1; cf. *Mon.* 13, 17; *Pud.* 16; *Exh. cast.* 4–7.

108. Williams, "Some Aspects," 24; followed by Sarah B. Pomeroy, *Goddesses, Whores, Wives, and Slaves: Women in Classical Antiquity* (New York: Schocken, 1975), 161.

CHAPTER 1

The Dead Sea Scrolls as a Second Temple Jewish Witness against Remarriage

Even as the Roman world had its *univira* traditions, the diversity of Second Temple Judaism included those who had adopted a more restrictive stance on remarriage. The Qumran scrolls include two substantive texts on the topic, one in the Damascus Document (CD) and the other in the Temple Scroll (11QT^a). The Damascus Document offers rules for sectarian communities located throughout Palestine. The Temple Scroll offers a vision of a future temple and temple city. In other words, one document deals with real lives and the other with an imaginary, future ideal. Also, while the Damascus Document is associated with the Essenes, the Temple Scroll may or may not be Essene literature.[109] These differences must be kept in mind while interpreting their statements on divorce and remarriage. "Nonetheless, one could argue that these regulations reflect the ideal values of the [Qumran] group."[110]

11QT^a LVII, 15–19 legislates the marital life of the future king: "He shall take no other wife apart from her because only she will be with him all the days of her life. If she dies, he shall take for himself another."[111] Thus the king is permitted only one wife while she lives, and he is apparently not to divorce her.[112] Joseph Fitzmyer maintains that the limitations on the king would apply to his people as well.[113] While possible, that conclusion ignores the two-tier approach in a number of Dead Sea Scrolls.[114] The king is to maintain a level of holiness greater

---

109. Meier, *Law and Love*, 87.

110. Yarbro Collins, *Mark*, 462; Yarbro Collins thinks the document "may" predate the settlement of the Qumran site (mid-second century BCE) and thus may "not necessarily" express the values held at the Qumran site or the related towns.

111. The earliest textual witnesses for the Temple Scroll date to the mid-second century BCE. This may therefore be the earliest Qumran witness on the subject; C. D. Elledge, "'From the Beginning It Was Not So . . .': Jesus, Divorce, and Remarriage in Light of the Dead Sea Scrolls," *PRSt* 37 (2010): 379. All translations of the Dead Sea Scrolls, unless otherwise noted, from Florentino García Martínez, *The Dead Sea Scrolls Translated: The Qumran Texts in English* (Grand Rapids: Eerdmans, 1992).

112. Ben Zion Wacholder, *The New Damascus Document: The Midrash on the Eschatological Torah of the Dead Sea Scrolls: Reconstruction, Translation, and Commentary*, STDJ 56 (Leiden: Brill, 2007), 191; cf. the full discussion on 188–200.

113. Joseph A. Fitzmyer, "The Matthean Divorce Texts and Some New Palestinian Evidence," *TS* 37 (1976): 216.

114. Fitzmyer ("Matthean Divorce Texts," 216) does, however, point to the extension of application of Deut 17:17 from the king to the prince of the congregation; cf. Elledge, "From the Beginning," 380–81, who notes elsewhere that 11QT^a LXVI, 8–11 presupposes divorce, and the imposition of lifelong marriage on a man who seduces a virgin suggests that divorce was common. On the other hand, C. D. Elledge maintains that "the Statutes of the King" applied Scriptures

than the people, at the level of the high priest.[115] The wife of the king functions along with other special types of guardians in 11QT[a] LVII (12,000 soldiers, twelve princes, twelve Levites, and twelve priests) to protect the king from the danger of a harem.[116] Some have reasoned that since the Temple Scroll may not be of Essene origin, the forbidding of another wife while the first still lives in this document should not influence the interpretation of CD IV, 19–V, 9.[117] Peter Tomson and others disagree and instead hold that the prohibition of the king remarrying while the wife lives *does* influence how CD IV, 19–V, 3, should be interpreted.[118] Whether remarriage or polygyny is at issue, the Temple Scroll demonstrates a concern regarding *remarriage* in at least one text.

The second text, CD IV, 19–V, 9 accuses the "builders of the wall" of having been snared by zənût, a word that can refer to prostitution as well as other types of sexual infidelity.[119] These opponents were snared by zənût because they had taken "two wives/women in their lifetimes" (IV, 21). The third-person masculine plural suffix

---

pertaining to nonroyals to the king; *The Statutes of the King: The Temple Scroll's Legislation on Kingship (11Q19 LVI 12-LIX 21)*, Cahiers de la Revue biblique 56 (Paris: Gabalda, 2004), 147–56. Thus Elledge writes: "Such compositional methods may imply that in the eschatological future all Israelites will keep the same laws prohibiting foreign wives, polygamy, and divorce" ("From the Beginning," 381).

115. Lawrence H. Schiffman, "Laws Pertaining to Women in the Temple Scroll," in *The Dead Sea Scrolls: Forty Years of Research*, ed. Devorah Dimant and Uriel Rappaport, STDJ 10 (Leiden: Brill, 1992), 213. See also David Instone-Brewer, "Nomological Exegesis in Qumran 'Divorce' Texts," *RevQ* 72 (1998): 567–68, although he concedes that it may apply more generally than to just the king. Schiffman and Instone-Brewer are followed by Meier, *Law and Love*, 92, 161.

116. Other Temple Scroll passages take divorce for granted (11QT[a] LIII and LIV; see esp. the use of Num 30:10 in LIV, 4–5, assuming a divorced woman). The prohibition against divorce in LXVI, 8–11 (Deut 22:18–19) is only applicable to those who have seduced a virgin.

117. Tom Holmén, "Divorce in *CD* 4:20–5:2 and *11QT* 57:17–18: Some Remarks on the Pertinence of the Question," *RevQ* 18 (1998): 397–408; Meier, *Law and Love*, 91–93. Meier later comments on Murphy-O'Connor's work: "We have no right to presuppose that all the documents found at Qumran espouse one homogeneous doctrinal position on a given point and that (even if one grants that both of these documents come from Qumran) there was no evolution in the doctrines professed by the sect. Then, too, there is the question of the tradition and redaction of various sources that may have gone into the final composition of the two works" (155 n. 48). He adds that the relative dates of the two works, their provenances, and tradition histories are unknown, all of which "cautions us against a naïve use of one document to interpret the other" (158 n. 57).

118. Peter J. Tomson, *Paul and the Jewish Law: Halakha in the Letters of the Apostle to the Gentiles*, CRINT 3.1 (Minneapolis: Fortress, 1990), 111. Wacholder (*New Damascus Document*, 190–91) goes so far as to contend that the author of CD V, 1b–2a was quoting this Temple Scroll passage.

119. This text is likewise dated from the second century BCE and likely circulated beyond Qumran; see Elledge, "From the Beginning," 381.

CHAPTER 1

"their" here is ambiguous. The suffix could very naturally refer to the lifetimes of the individual *men*. This could include that these men married two women at the same time (polygamy), remarried after a divorce, or remarried after being widowed. The husband would be forbidden from a second marriage during his lifetime, regardless of the status of the first marriages.[120] He would be permitted only one wife.[121] Divorce would be permissible, provided a second marriage did not follow.[122]

The Hebrew suffix could also refer to the lifetime of the two wives. In this case, the masculine plural form of the noun "women/wives" (*nāšîm*) would be attracting the masculine plural suffix.[123] This would indicate that the male opponents took two wives during the lifetimes of the *women* involved (i.e., while both women were alive).[124] Thus the Damascus Document would not be censuring divorce; a man might divorce his wife and simply not marry another woman. The prohibition during "their lifetimes" would then refer to having two wives at the same time

---

120. E.g., Philip R. Davies, *Behind the Essenes: History and Ideology in the Dead Sea Scrolls*, BJS 94 (Atlanta: Scholars, 1987), 73–85; Jerome Murphy-O'Connor, "An Essene Missionary Document? CD II, 14–VI, 1," *RB* 77.2 (1970): 220; A. Dupont-Sommer, *The Essene Writings from Qumran*, trans. Geza Vermes (Cleveland: World, 1961), 129 n. 1.

Some have taken the Hebrew suffix *-hem* to refer to *both* the husband and the wife; e.g., Fitzmyer, "Matthean Divorce Texts," 220; Lawrence H. Schiffman, *Reclaiming the Dead Sea Scrolls: The History of Judaism, the Background of Christianity, and the Lost Library of Qumran* (Philadelphia: Jewish Publication Society, 1994), 130; and Schiffman, "Laws Pertaining to Women," 217, who (tentatively) holds that neither party may remarry. Meier (*Law and Love*, 157 n. 56) responds that this results in a convoluted reading. For the man, "in their lifetimes" would refer to both polygyny and divorce with remarriage while the first spouse still lived. For the woman, it would prohibit only divorce with remarriage since polyandry was not a factor in Second Temple Jewish society. The man would not be able to execute a divorce. Even in this reading, the man is not allowed polygyny or divorce followed by remarriage.

121. On the other hand, according to Holmén ("Divorce," 400, 408), marriage ends when a spouse dies; see also Meier, *Law and Love*, 89.

122. Richard B. Hays, *The Moral Vision of the New Testament: A Contemporary Introduction to New Testament Ethics* (New York: HarperCollins, 1996), 351–52: "Particularly interesting is the Damascus Document's citation of Gen 1:27 as the scriptural basis for condemning remarriage (cf. Mark 10:6); this demonstrates that the position ascribed to Jesus in Mark 10 has clear points of contact with one stream of rigoristic pre-Christian Judaism."

123. Some have wrongly presupposed that a reference to wives would require presupposing a scribal error that had to be emended; thus Instone-Brewer, "Nomological Exegesis," 571. The suffix in the Cairo Geniza text (CD) is clearly the masculine form *-hem*, and it can bear a feminine sense in late biblical and Qumran Hebrew, in this particular instance as a result of attraction; see Meier, *Law and Love*, 88, 156 n. 52.

124. Some Second Temple Jews, most notably Herod the Great and his relatives, practiced polygyny (Josephus, *J.W.* 1.24.2 §477; *Ant.* 17.1.2 §14). Polyandry—a woman's having two husbands at the same time—was not practiced.

(polygyny), marrying a second woman while the divorced spouse was still living, or both.[125] This would suggest a similar reading for the Damascus Document as in 11QT[a] LVII, 15–19, which identifies the *wife's lifetime* as the period in which the king may not have a second wife (whether through bigamy or remarriage).[126] This second possibility raises the question whether bigamy or remarriage (or both) is in view in the CD IV text.

The phrase "in their lives" could also refer collectively to both the husband and the wife, in which case a single marriage is in view. The Damascus Document would thus be prohibiting *both* polygamy and remarriage after divorce.[127] Fitzmyer takes CD IV, 21 and 11QTa LVII, 15–19 as parallel prohibitions of remarriage during the lifetime of the spouse, if not also of divorce.

Perhaps the target of the Damascus Document author's ire is strictly polygyny and not remarriage after divorce. Some specialists have sought leverage in how CD IV, 21 then quotes Gen 1:27: "Male and female he [God] created them." They conclude that CD IV, 21 only prohibits having multiple wives *at the same time* (polygyny) and not a taking a second wife after divorcing a first wife who is still alive. This passage, however, may not necessarily be limited to prohibiting polygamy but may just as well be ruling out taking a second wife after divorce. Jesus, for his part, uses the same Genesis text to argue against *divorce* in the gospels, thus maintaining a marriage between one man and one woman (Mark 10:6; Matt 19:4). CD V, 1 next observes how in Gen. 7:9 the animals went into Noah's ark two by two, male and female, perhaps serving as proof that the male must have only one female partner. On the other hand, the key word in Gen. 7:9 is "two" (i.e., a single pair for the purpose of procreation). CD V, 2 then quotes Deut 17:17 on the king and his potential harem: "He must not acquire many wives for himself."[128] Even this text, however, could apply also to a second wife after a divorce.[129] The immediate context of CD IV, 21 is not decisive, then, whether multiple wives at the same time are at issue or a second wife while the first was still alive.

---

125. Meier, *Law and Love*, 89; Collins, *Divorce*, 81–85; Hays, *Moral Vision*, 351. See also Murphy-O'Connor, "Essene Missionary Document," 220: "The suffix should be taken at its face value, unless there are strongs reason to the contrary. This is not the case here; the masculine suffix yields [sic] perfect sense."

126. R. Collins, *Divorce*, 84.

127. Fitzmyer, "Matthean Divorce Texts, 216–21; Joseph A. Fitzmyer, "Divorce among First-Century Palestinian Jews," *Eretz-Israel* 14 (1978): 103–10; Joseph A. Fitzmyer, "Marriage and Divorce," in *Encyclopedia of the Dead Sea Scrolls*, ed. Lawrence H. Schiffman and James C. VanderKam (Oxford: Oxford University Press, 2000), 1:511–14.

128. CD XIII, 17 *might* use the verb *grš* "drive out," to refer to a permission for divorce; see Meier, *Law and Love*, 90–91.

129. Davies, *Behind the Essenes*, 82–83.

CHAPTER 1

Louis Ginzburg over fifty years ago firmly declared that CD IV, 19–V, 9 addresses polygyny with no implications for divorce or subsequent remarriage. The expectations for Israelite men thus matched the requirement expressed in Deut 17:17 of a single wife for Israel's king.[130] Others followed in that judgment. David Instone-Brewer draws attention to three Qumran texts that refer to divorce (11QT^a LIV, 4–5; LXVI, 11; CD XIII, 15–18, esp. 17). He notes that none of the three passages offers any regulations or strictures against divorce or subsequent remarriage.[131] In view of these texts, for Instone-Brewer, one would not expect any censure of divorce or remarriage in CD IV, 19–V, 9.[132] Brin notes how 4Q76 II, 4–7's version of Mal 2:16 appears to have altered the reading attested in the Masoretic Text "for I hate divorce" (*ky śn' šlḥ*) with "but if you hate her, divorce her" (*ky 'm śnth šlḥ*), betraying Qumran acceptance of divorce.[133] In its collection of ordinances 4Q159 2–4 9–10 reads: "[He may not] divorce her for his entire lifetime," a prohibition of divorce in a special instance that presumes a freedom otherwise to divorce.[134] Adiel Schremer concludes his analysis of CD IV, 19–V, 9: "Divorce was not forbidden by the Qumran community."[135] The

---

130. Louis Ginzburg, *An Unknown Jewish Sect*, Moreshet Series 1 (New York: Jewish Theological Seminary of America, 1970), 19–20.

131. Instone-Brewer, "Nomological Exegesis," 572–73; Adiel Schremer, "Qumran Polemic on Marital Law: CD 4:20–5:11 and Its Social Background," in *The Damascus Document: A Centennial of Discovery. Proceedings of the Third International Symposium of the Orion Center for the Study of the Dead Sea Scrolls and Related Literature, 4–8 February, 1998*, ed. Joseph M. Baumgarten, Esther G. Chazon, and Avital Pinnick, STDJ 34 (Leiden: Brill, 2000), 158–59; Gershon Brin, "Divorce at Qumran," in *Legal Texts and Legal Issues: Proceedings of the Second Meeting of the International Organization for Qumran Studies Cambridge 1995*, ed. Moshe Bernstein, Florentino García Martínez, and John Kampen, STDJ 23 (Leiden: Brill, 1997), 232–38. Meier (*Law and Love*, 90–91) and Davies (*Behind the Essenes*, 80–81) both dispute whether CD XIII, 17 is referring to divorce and point to the variety of interpretations of this problematic text.

132. Meier (*Law and Love*, 157 n. 56), however, faults Instone-Brewer for "convoluted hermeneutical principles and scriptural allusions supposedly underlying CD IV.20–21" that one could hardly expect the ancient reader to understand.

133. Brin, "Divorce at Qumran," 234–36, who remains convinced that "I hate divorce" is the original reading and was adapted in practice at Qumran, since the covenanters seem to be encouraging divorce.

134. Lawrence H. Schiffman, "Ordinances and Rules," in *Rule of the Community and Related Documents*, vol. 1 of *The Dead Sea Scrolls: Hebrew, Aramaic, and Greek Texts with English Translations*, ed. James H. Charlesworth et al., PTSDSSP 1 (Tübingen: Mohr Siebeck, 1994), 145–75; Jeffrey H. Tigay, "Examination of the Accused Bride in 4Q159 Forensic Medicine at Qumran, *JANESCU* 22 (1993): 129–34; Vered Noam, "Divorce in Qumran in Light of Early Halakhah," *JJS* 56.2 (2005): 209–10.

135. Schremer, "Qumran Polemic," 159–60, adding that had the text been prohibiting remarriage after the divorce of a living first wife, Lev 18:18 would have been cited.

acceptance of divorce would presumably entail a corresponding acceptance of remarriage. Geza Vermes further points out that ancient Hebrew scribes would have connected Gen 1:27 and 7:9 on the basis of the common phrase "male and female," a hermeneutical practice labeled by the later rabbis *gĕzērâ šāwâ*. In this case, only polygyny would be the target of the critique, since any of the four men who entered the ark might have remarried after a divorce or spousal death and thus still entered the ark "two by two."[136]

Some scholars go further to express *great confidence* that only polygyny is in view. Cecilia Wassen, for instance, identifies two possible interpretations of CD IV, 20–21: (1) the community recognized divorce but not remarriage after divorce; or (2) divorce and subsequent remarriage were permitted, since the text only refers to polygyny. She offers three lines of evidence to support her decision: (1) in 4QD^f 3 10–15 a widow is permitted to remarry after the death of her husband; (2) other Qumran texts allow for divorce (4QD^a III, 5 // CD XIII, 7) and Jewish certificates found at Elephantine and the Wadi Murabba'at permit the divorced woman to remarry; and (3) 11QT^a accepts divorce among the general population.[137] From this, she concludes that only polygyny must be in view.[138] Strikingly, none of Wassen's evidence from Qumran demonstrates a permission to remarry after divorce: (1) that a Qumran text relays a *widow's* permission to remarry does not demonstrate the same for a *divorced* woman; (2) Wassen's citation of permission for the divorced to remarry does not come from the Qumran community but rather from Elephantine and the Wadi Murabba'at; and (3) a permission to divorce does not demonstrate that the community was tolerant of remarriage, especially in instances in which the first spouse was still living.[139] The three lines of evidence substantiating her confidence are simply irrelevant to the discussion.

---

136. Geza Vermes, "Sectarian Matrimonial Halakhah in the Damascus Rule," *JJS* 25.1 (1974): 200. Fitzmyer faults Vermes for overlooking that texts addressing polygamy may be reappropriated to prohibit divorce and remarriage; "Divorce among First-Century Palestinian Jews," 109.

137. 11QT^a LIV, 4–5 paraphrases Num 30 regarding the law on oaths of women; also 11QT^a LXVI, 8–11 requires the seducer to marry the seduced with no opportunity for divorce (Deut 22:28–29), which assumes divorce was ordinarily allowed. So also Mal 2:16 in 4Q76: "If you hate her, send her away." See Brin, "Divorce at Qumran," 231–44. One might contend, in view of the live issue of divorce at Qumran, that remarriage after divorce would be far more pertinent than polygyny.

138. Cecilia Wassen, *Women in the Damascus Document* (Leiden: Brill, 2005), 114–18.

139. Note how Wassen's problematic argumentation is uncritically considered conclusive by Tal Ilan, "Women in Qumran and the Dead Sea Scrolls," in *The Oxford Handbook of the Dead Sea Scrolls*, ed. Timothy H. Lim and John J. Collins (Oxford: Oxford University Press, 2010), 135.

Several indications point toward CD IV, 20–21 prohibiting remarriage. A man marrying another woman after a divorce would have taken place far more frequently than having multiple wives at the same time. The latter practice took place typically among only the wealthy or royalty (e.g., the Herodians).[140] Further, as Jerome Murphy-O'Connor stresses, the text does not say "simultaneously" as one would expect were only polygyny in view.[141] "In their lifetimes" indicates that *more* is at issue.[142] Had only polygyny been in view, Paul Winter points out that the phrase "during their lives" would have been unnecessary.[143]

Many scholars now consider the Damascus Document fragment 4QD^f 3 10–15 decisive evidence that CD IV, 20–21 should indeed be interpreted in terms of a prohibition of remarriage while the first wife was still alive (and not strictly polygyny):

> Let no man bring [a woman into the ho]ly [covenant?] who has had sexual experience, (whether) she had such [experience in the home] of her father or as a widow [*'almānâ*] who had intercourse after she was widowed. And any [woman upon whom there is a] bad [na]me in her maidenhood in her father's house, let no man take her, except [upon examination] by trustworthy [women] of

---

140. Josephus refers to the permission for polygyny: "For it is an ancestral custom of ours to have several wives at the same time" (*Ant.* 17.1.2 §14 [Marcus, LCL]; cf. *J.W.* 1.24.2 §477). Justin Martyr charges the Jews with the practice (*Dial.* 134). The Mishnah allows the ordinary Jewish man multiple wives if he can afford them and the king as many as eighteen (m. Sanh. 2:4).

In a document from Naḥal Ḥever from a remote, rural area of moderate means, an illiterate woman named Babatha was married twice and, after her second husband died, she inherited property from him. In a dispute with the late man's family about the property, she summoned a woman named Miriam to appear before the governor with her and referred to "my and your [Miriam's] husband" in the absence of any divorce as having ever taken place: "From Babatha's second marriage it is evident, therefore, that polygamy, or at least bigamy, was not in her time restricted to men of power and distinction, but was indulged in as a matter of course considerably farther down the social scale than has hitherto been recognized." See *The Documents from the Bar Kokhba Region in the Cave of Letters: Greek Papyri*, ed. Naphtali Lewis (Jerusalem: Israel Exploration Society, 1989), 22–26. John Collins qualifies that one cannot generalize about the frequency of the practice. Nevertheless, Collins continues, bigamy was not limited to the Herodians, thus challenging the usual view among specialists that, despite the legal permission, monogamy was the norm in this period; see John J. Collins, "Marriage, Divorce, and Family in Second Temple Judaism," in *Families in Ancient Israel*, ed. Leo G. Perdue, Joseph Blenkinsopp, John J. Collins, and Carol Meyers (Louisville: Westminster John Knox, 1997), 122.

141. Murphy-O'Connor, "Essene Missionary Document?," 220 (even after the death of the spouse); Jerome Murphy-O'Connor, "Remarques sur l'exposé du Professeur Y. Yadin," *RB* 79.1 (1972): 99–100; followed by Davies, *Behind the Essenes*, 76.

142. Paul Winter, "Ṣadokite Fragments IV, 20, 21 and the Exegesis of Genesis 1, 27 in Late Judaism," *ZAW* 68 (1956): 71–84.

143. Winter, "Ṣadokite Fragments," 77–78.

repute selected by command of the supervisor over [the many. After]ward he may take her, and when he takes her he shall act in accordance with the l[a]w [and he shall not t]ell about [her.] (4QD^f 3 10–15)[144]

The permission here is for a male member of the community to marry an unmarried virgin or a widow if she has not had sexual relations with anyone since her husband died. The *widow* is thus permitted to be remarried (cf. 1 Cor 7:39; Rom 7:3). The fragment does not even consider as a possibility that the man might marry a divorcée.[145] Later rabbinic Hebrew uses the same noun employed in 4QD^f 3 5–10 for widows (*'almānâ*) but uses a *different* word for the divorced party (*gərûšâ*), and the two categories are regularly distinguished (e.g., m. Ketub. 1:2; 5:1).[146] This fragment renders it likely that CD IV, 19–V, 2 also condemns second marriages while the first wife is still alive. With Adela Yarbro Collins: "The reason for forbidding polygamy and remarriage during the lifetime of the first spouse is probably a concern about purity."[147] The Qumran community was emulating priestly holiness (Lev 21:7, 13–14).

Both John J. Collins and Lawrence Schiffman agree that CD IV, 9–V, 2 (esp. IV, 21) applies primarily to polygyny but also to remarriage after divorce while the former spouse still lives.[148] The parallel with 11QT^a LVII, 15–19 demonstrates that not just polygyny is in view there either as the king remains limited to one wife in his lifetime, unless she should die.[149] Again, the most natural use of the pronoun in CD IV, 20–21 would be for a prohibition of a subsequent marriage while the man's first wife is still alive. Remarriage is categorically censured as a matter of priestly

---

144. Joseph M. Baumgarten, *Qumran Cave 4: XIII The Damascus Document (4Q266–273)*, DJD 18 (Oxford: Oxford University Press, 1996), 175–76.

145. Aharon Shemesh, "4Q271.3: A Key to Sectarian Matrimonial Law," *JJS* 49.2 (1998): 246: "[T]he halakhah's omission of the divorcee attests that sectarian halakhah outlawed remarriage subsequent to divorce as long as the former spouse was still living." See also Noam, "Divorce in Qumran," 219–20.

146. Yarbro Collins, *Mark*, 463 n. 41.

147. Yarbro Collins, *Mark*, 463.

148. J. Collins, "Marriage, Divorce, and Family," 129, 158; Schiffman, "Relationship," 138.

Fitzmyer thinks a prohibition of remarriage could have been a result of the influence of Mal 2:14–16; see "Marriage and Divorce," 1:512. See, however—against Fitzmyer's understanding of Mal 2:14–16—the existence of divorce in CD XIII, 14–18; 11QT^a LIV, 4–5; LXVI, 8–11. In spite of this, John Kampen has taken 11QT^a LVII, 18 as revising the feminine singular of Lev 18:18 "her sister's lifetime," to the masculine plural in 11QT^a LVII to prohibit divorce. Kampen stresses that recognition that divorce is taking place does not mean agreement with the practice. See "A Fresh Look at the Masculine Plural Suffix in CD IV, 21," *RevQ* 16.1 (1993): 91–97.

149. Fitzmyer, "Matthean Divorce Texts," 220.

CHAPTER 1

holiness in one sector of Second Temple Judaism.[150] While divorce was permitted, the Qumran scrolls *in multiple places* warn against illicit remarriage: the king of 11QT[a] LVII having to wait until his spouse dies before remarrying, the equation of second marriages with fornication in CD IV, and the permission to marry only unmarried virgins or chaste widows in 4QD[f] 3 10–15.[151] As Elledge concludes from his review: "[The Qumran scrolls] exhibit a clear and strong trajectory of the utmost concern for the endangerments posed by remarriage."[152]

Conclusion

Whatever the grounds for divorce, once a marriage had been terminated the (former) partners were free under Augustan law to remarry.[153] While the older ideal was for the woman to remain single after her husband's death, Augustus legally required remarriage for fertile widows. Divorced women between the ages of twenty and fifty were to remarry after eighteen months, and widows after two years.[154] Some scholars have stressed these laws as potential background for the New Testament: Paul's readers might have assumed the right, or even legal requirement, to remarry after a valid divorce. Such assumptions must be tempered by reality. Augustus's marital legislation was not enforced and depended on the action of private citizens. Although the imperial era attests to widespread acceptance of divorce and remarriage, many in Roman society continued to praise the ideal of the *univira*. Jesus taught in a social context—whether Jewish, Greek, or Roman—in which divorce and remarriage were widely accepted, but attitudes toward remarriage were by no means monolithic. The most likely interpretation of the Damascus Document manifests a similarly conservative position of priestly

---

150. Meier, *Law and Love*, 93.

151. Elledge, "From the Beginning," 386, while hunting for a diversity of Qumran perspectives with which to compare various New Testament perspectives.
Even here, William Loader, *The Dead Sea Scrolls on Sexuality: Attitudes toward Sexuality in Sectarian and Related Literature at Qumran* (Grand Rapids: Eerdmans, 2009), 115, appeals, as decisive, to the wider Jewish context's permission for the divorced to remarry, citing m. Giṭ. 9:3; the Babatha archive; Josephus, *Ant.* 4.8.23 §253 [*sic*]; and Elephantine.

152. Elledge, "From the Beginning," 386. He adds: "Remarriage is the most frequently attested concern among the Qumran writings that pertain to this question. Moreover, Jesus himself forbids divorce through a retrojective logic in which the dangers of remarriage are so great that divorce itself must be forbidden altogether" (388). Elledge assumes the Matthean exception clauses are redactional.

153. Csillag, *Augustan Laws*, 135.

154. Csillag, *Augustan Laws*, 87–89. Gardner, *Women*, 50–56.

holiness in avoiding remarriage. In short, some Jews and Romans held to the ideal of faithful lifelong marriage to a single spouse. Were the first Christians to adopt a stance against remarriage, such a view would not be unprecedented.

Appendix: The Pastoral Epistles and the *Univira* Tradition

On the Pastoral Letters reflecting the *univira* ideal, see Andreas J. Köstenberger, *Commentary on 1–2 Timothy and Titus*, Biblical Theology for Christian Proclamation (Nashville: B&H, 2017), 127. A prohibition of the remarried in leadership is possible here.

Polygamy is an unlikely target of the qualification, since monogamy was the norm in both Greco-Roman and Jewish society, and polyandry (cf. 1 Tim 5:9) was unknown, even among Jews more open to polygamy; note also Justinian, *CJ* 9.18; Lefkowitz and Fant, *Women's Life*, 183; Gardner, *Women*, 92–93. Jewish practice outside Palestine likewise avoided polygamy. Inscriptional evidence indicates monogamy among the Jews (*CIJ* 1:cxii).

A prohibition of the leadership of the unmarried is unlikely in the Pauline churches in view of Paul's advocacy of the single life and service in 1 Cor 7:32–40. The emphasis on "one" in the phrasing militates against a requirement to be married rather than single, and it leads to a tautology for the widow in 1 Tim 5:9 since, had she remarried, she would no longer be a widow eligible for the office; see I. Howard Marshall, *A Critical and Exegetical Commentary on the Pastoral Epistles*, ICC (Edinburgh: T&T Clark, 1999), 155. Philip H. Towner, *The Letters to Timothy and Titus*, NICNT (Grand Rapids: Eerdmans, 2006), 250–51 n. 42, disagrees with reading the Pastoral Epistles in light of the *univira* traditions since the inscriptions praise *women* who had remained single after the death of their husbands but, as clear above, there is also attestation for men claiming the same toward their one wife. See, however, the argumentation otherwise in Sydney Page, "Marital Expectations of Church Leaders in the Pastoral Epistles," *JSNT* 50 (1993): 105–20. Page disagrees with the consensus of English translations that have the unusual expression "husband of one wife" or "married only once." Page contends that "faithful to his one wife" is more accurate, since it is the marital relationship and not the marital status per se that is in view; note the parallel issues in 1 Tim 5:9: "wife of one husband" or "faithful to one husband." Even if the first Christian authors understood the Pastoral Epistles in terms of the *univira* tradition (e.g., Tertullian), that does not make it the most likely interpretation. On the other hand, Page does not adequately address the possibility that 1 Tim 3:2 and 5:9 are excluding the *remarried* from church offices. Page rightly recognizes that the New Testament

CHAPTER 1

permits divorce in certain situations but simply *assumes* that divorce included the right to remarry (109–10); so also Towner, *Letters to Timothy and Titus*, 251 n. 42. Page also recognizes that it is "not certain" whether exclusion of the remarried is to be ruled out as the likeliest option (110). Page confuses matters to label an aversion to second marriages a matter of asceticism (see 111–12). Extreme asceticism would have been averse to any marriage *at all*. The earliest Christians *defended* marriage against such positions, even as they allowed for only one marriage. These matters, of course, will need to be discussed further in what follows.

In a case that Page does not adequately address, "husband of one wife" and "wife of one husband" could be targeting primarily the *divorced* and not the widows (or widowers) in view of 1 Tim 5:9's provision for the remarriage of younger widows. This approach is *not exclusive* of marital behavior and fidelity, with Page, "Marital Expectations," 113–19. It is not an either-or: *Both* marital status (one spouse) *and* faithfulness (behavior) are in view in 1 Tim 3 and 5 offices. Even if the office qualifications represent how *all* Christians should be, likewise the New Testament *may* teach against remarriage for all Christians with the exception of widows and widowers. In short, the Pastorals do not of themselves *demonstrate* that remarriage after divorce was proscribed, but they would neatly conform to that position were it taught elsewhere in the New Testament, which would agree with how the first Christians were interpreting the texts prior to and during the Council of Nicaea. Were the *univira* traditions casting a shadow *earlier* on the Christian movement than Tertullian?

The most difficult problem for the influence of the *univira* traditions on the Pastorals is the contradictory advice in 1 Tim 5:14 for the younger widows to remarry, which would disqualify them from the office of widow at an older age since they would have been married to more than one man (5:9); see Witherington, *Titus, 1–2 Timothy, and 1–3 John*, 110. Nevertheless, 1 Tim 5:11–12 addresses the matter of younger widows who are making the pledging to remain single. They incur condemnation if they renounce their pledge. J. N. D. Kelly comments on these verses: "Christ is thought of as a spiritual bridegroom (cf. 2 Cor. xi. 2). Hence the desire to marry again, natural enough in young women who have lost their husbands, is in effect an act of unfaithfulness to him." See *A Commentary on the Pastoral Epistles* (Grand Rapids: Baker, 1981), 117 and his earlier statement, "In pagan, Jewish and Christian inscriptions of the first centuries the noun *monandria* (lit. 'having one husband') is always applied, usually as a term of obvious eulogy, to widows who have been content with one marriage" (116). Note also the remarks of (preconversion) in William A. Heth, "Unmarried 'For the Sake of the Kingdom' (Matthew 19:12) in the Early Church," *Grace Theological Journal* 8.1 (1987): 67–68: Since younger widows might become gossips and busybodies, giving the adversary a reason to accuse, marrying again is the lesser of these two evils. The 1 Tim 5 passage is simply acknowledging an understandable impediment to the *preferred* outcome of remaining single in widowhood in the service of the Lord. The Roman *univira* traditions were upheld especially for cultic functionaries, unlike the general population, and such may be the case here as well since not all widows are in view, only those who have made the pledge. The *univira* tradition's influence on the Pastoral Epistles deserves further examination.

2

Jesus "behind" the Gospels, or Jesus Remembered

Early Christianity began with the teaching of Jesus. The first generations of Christ-believing authors conveyed that teaching in the hope that others too would come to believe in Jesus as the Christ. In a relative abundance of riches, *five* New Testament passages relay Jesus's teaching about divorce and remarriage:

Matt 5:32: But I say to you that anyone who divorces his wife, except on the ground of unchastity, causes her to commit adultery; and whoever marries a divorced woman commits adultery.

Matt 19:9: And I say to you, whoever divorces his wife, except for unchastity, and marries another commits adultery.

Mark 10:11–12: Whoever divorces his wife and marries another commits adultery against her; and if she divorces her husband and marries another, she commits adultery.

Luke 16:18: Anyone who divorces his wife and marries another commits adultery, and whoever marries a woman divorced from her husband commits adultery.

1 Cor 7:10–11 (Paul): To the married I give this command—not I but the Lord—that the wife should not separate from her husband (but if she does separate, let her remain unmarried or else be reconciled to her husband), and that the husband should not divorce his wife.

With their similarities but also significant differences, these five texts are the basis for reconstructing what Jesus taught about divorce and remarriage.

The differences have led many to attempt to reconstruct what the Jesus *behind* the gospel accounts taught—the "historical" Jesus. This more traditional scholarly reconstruction has, of late, been heavily criticized for problematic criteria and for not accounting for how Jesus was *remembered*. One must take seriously the gospel narratives themselves as preserving the memories of Jesus. That critique will therefore lead to a discussion of how Jesus was remembered in two of those gospels, the narratives of Mark and Luke.

The "Historical" Jesus Reconstructed on Divorce and Remarriage

In the earliest of the five texts, 1 Cor 7:10–11, Paul reports a saying of the Lord. The saying addresses the *wife* and employs *imperatival* constructions. The Lord does not completely forbid divorce for her, but she must not marry another. As for Matt 5:32 and Luke 16:18, most gospel specialists consider these verses to be relaying a teaching independently derived from a hypothetical source labeled Q.[1] Luke 16:18 identifies as adultery a *man* marrying another woman in the wake of his own divorce; for any man to marry a divorced woman is also an act of adultery. Matthew 5:32 claims that a man who divorces his wife makes her an adulteress.[2] The second half of Matt 5:32 parallels the second half of Luke 16:18: for a man to marry a divorced woman is adultery. The teaching of Jesus in Luke 16:18 and Matt 5:32, unlike 1 Cor 7:10–11, is worded in the form of *indicative* statements. Matthew 5:32 also includes an exception clause that is not in Luke 16:18.

Most scholars believe that Matthew drew upon Mark, which would connect Jesus's teaching in Matt 19:9 to Mark 10:11–12. There are differences here as well. Mark mentions a woman divorcing her husband (as does Paul) whereas Matt 19:9 does not. Matthew 19:9, like 5:32, includes another exception clause that is not in Mark 10:11–12 (or Luke 16:18; cf. Matt 5:32). Mark 10:10–12 concludes privately "in the house" a conversation that had begun outside with the Pharisees, whereas Matt 19:3–12 does not indicate any change of setting. The comment that Moses allowed divorce is placed earlier in the Markan narrative (10:4) than in Matthew 19, where

---

1. From the German word *Quelle*, "source." The teaching of Jesus will also be considered from the point of view of those who dispense with this hypothesis.

2. Matthew's Jesus does not explicitly say that divorcing the wife also makes the man an adulterer.

CHAPTER 2

it is placed *immediately* before Jesus's censure of divorce and remarriage. Despite the wealth of witnesses to Jesus's teaching on divorce and remarriage, those witnesses obviously do not present that teaching in quite the same way or in the same narratival contexts. These differences require explanation. Can an original version of Jesus's teaching be reconstructed when no two versions of that teaching in the gospels are exactly the same? Or is there a single version of that teaching that might be traced to the Jesus who stands *behind* the gospel reports?

Posing such questions is unavoidable. Hyperskepticism about Jesus as a figure in history falters with the Jewish historian Josephus's account of Jesus—albeit in what may be an edited passage (*Ant.* 18.3.3 §§63–64). Possible later Christian additions in Josephus may be peeled away. In the most likely reconstruction of the original text of Josephus, Jesus was a wise man and a miracle worker, hardly unusual in the first-century world. He was also a teacher with quite a following. When accused by the Jewish leadership, Pilate had him crucified, but the Christian movement continued.[3] More recent work, however, has defended the authenticity of the entire passage.[4] Tacitus in the early second century, a generation after Josephus, describes the "Christ" as an individual who had been executed by the procurator Pontius Pilate during the reign of Tiberius (*Ann.* 15.44). Multiple, later non-Christian historical sources mention Jesus Christ, but nothing more of relevance is said outside the bare descriptions of his ministry and crucifixion in Josephus and Tacitus. Other ancient sources appear dependent on the New Testament documents.

For a fuller picture of Jesus's life and ministry, the New Testament Gospels are indispensable. The critical historian treats the gospels as hostile witnesses to reconstruct what the "historical" Jesus taught, a Jesus *behind* these overt documents of faith. The methodology is imperfect and cannot capture all that Jesus said and did. Much accurate information about Jesus in the gospels will simply not be identified as such because of the imperfections of the method. Despite those imperfections, employing a critical method allows the historian to reconstruct a minimal, more assured picture of Jesus's teaching in the face of the gospels' own expressions of belief.

---

3. See the thorough exercise in peeling back the later additions in John P. Meier, *The Roots of the Problem and the Person*, vol. 1 of *A Marginal Jew: Rethinking the Historical Jesus* (New York: Doubleday, 1991), 56–88.

4. See, e.g., Alice Whealey, *Josephus on Jesus: The Testimonium Flavianum Controversy from Late Antiquity to Modern Times*, StBibLit 36 (New York: Lang, 2003), esp. 1–52; Whealey, "Josephus, Eusebius of Caesarea, and the *Testimonium Flavianum*," in *Josephus und das Neue Testament: Wechselseitige Wahrnehmungen*, ed. Christfried Böttrich and Jens Herzer, WUNT 209 (Tübingen: Mohr Siebeck, 2007), 73–116; Gary J. Goldberg, "Josephus's Paraphrase Style and the *Testimonium Flavianum*," *JSHJ* 20.1 (2021): 1–32; John Curran, "'To Be or to Be Thought to Be': The *Testimonium Flavianum* Again," *NovT* 59.1 (2017): 71–94.

Jesus "behind" the Gospels, or Jesus Remembered

Many conservative Christians have expressed concerns over this sort of enterprise, and remarriage has been a topic of interest in those circles, especially since two evangelicals raised the matter of divorce and remarriage in an acute way in the 1980s.[5] As Craig Evans explains for the sake of a conservative audience, "If the story of Jesus is to be commended to skeptics as worthy of acceptance, then critical, historically sound reasons must be given."[6] A critical historian can affirm much about Jesus in the face of radical skepticism. Again, the methodology is imperfect and cannot lead to a complete picture of Jesus. Some have even argued that the gospels, from the standpoint of critical reconstruction, are far more reliable as witnesses.[7]

Again, historical Jesus reconstruction is not a scientific enterprise, and the results are rather modest at best. Scholars dispute which criteria to use, how to apply those criteria and, especially, which criteria to prioritize. A scholar who prioritizes dissimilarity—where Jesus says or does something that differs from other Jews of his day or the first Christians—will yield different results than the scholar who starts with multiple, independent attestation.

John Meier has published an unusually detailed reconstruction of Jesus's teaching on divorce and remarriage, and what follows is unavoidably indebted to his exhaustive analysis.[8] Meier relies in his labors on the existence of Q even though other gospel specialists, albeit a minority, are skeptical of the existence of such a document, if "document" is even the best word for it. Matthew and Luke independently appear to rely on a collection of Jesus's sayings. Sometimes that reliance appears to be word for word, but in other places they could be drawing on shared oral traditions. Meier also relies on the traditional criteria of historical Jesus scholarship but does not resolve how to *prioritize* those criteria. Again, this sort of reconstruction will not yield *the* historical Jesus, only *a* historical Jesus. Even the criteria themselves have sustained increased scrutiny and criticism in recent years. Despite that, in a volume seriously questioning the various criteria for reconstruction, several of the authors continue to affirm the importance of the historical Jesus venture itself.[9] The criteria, properly qualified and nuanced,

---

5. Heth and Wenham, *Jesus and Divorce*.

6. Craig A. Evans, "Authenticity Criteria in Life of Jesus Research," *Christian Scholar's Review* 19.1 (1989): 7.

7. Craig L. Blomberg, *The Historical Reliability of the Gospels*, 2nd ed. (Downers Grove, IL: InterVarsity, 2007); Craig S. Keener, *The Historical Jesus of the Gospels* (Grand Rapids: Eerdmans, 2009). See esp. Lydia McGrew, *The Mirror and the Mask: Liberating the Gospels from Literary Devices* (Tampa, FL: DeWard, 2019); McGrew, *The Eye of the Beholder: The Gospel of John as Historical Reportage* (Tampa, FL: DeWard, 2021).

8. Meier, *Law and Love*, 74–181.

9. Anthony Le Donne, Dagmar Winter, and Mark Goodacre over against the greater skepti-

CHAPTER 2

can identify certain traditions that are more likely original than others. This venture cannot yield assured results, only more probable ones—and divorce and remarriage texts appear, relatively speaking, to abound. Several early Christian communities, including those of Mark and Luke, were engaging such teaching.

First Corinthians 7:10–11 as the Earliest Witness to a Dominical Saying

Witness to the Earthly Jesus's Teaching or to Early Christian Prophetic Teaching

The earliest potential source for Jesus's teaching on divorce and remarriage is not a gospel narration but rather the apostle Paul in 1 Corinthians, which was written to the Corinthians in 54–55 CE. Some have questioned whether 1 Cor 7:10–11 relays a saying from Jesus during his earthly ministry or a later, post-Easter Christian proclamation uttered in Jesus's name in the 40s or early 50s. As E. P. Sanders, a leading historical Jesus researcher, poses the question: "Did early Christians, besides altering and reapplying stories about and sayings of Jesus, also simply make up material and attribute it to him? The answer is 'Yes,' though 'simply make up' mis-states their perception."[10] Sanders then adds: "People who 'discovered' a new saying or a new meaning were presumably sincere. They believed in revelation—that the Spirit of God spoke through inspired humans or that the Lord spoke directly to them—and thus could honestly attribute to Jesus things that came to them from some source other than his pre-crucifixion teaching."[11] Christians were receiving the gift of prophecy (e.g., 1 Cor 12:28–29; 14:3, 5). It is quite possible that prophetic utterances were received as teachings of Jesus and confused with his actual earthly teaching. According to Paul in 2 Cor 12:9, the postcrucifixion Lord spoke to him and said, "My grace is sufficient for you, for power is made perfect in weakness." Sanders wonders how long it would have been before someone confused what the Lord said to Paul and what the Lord said during his earthly ministry.[12]

---

cism of Chris Keith, Dale Allison, and Rafael Rodríguez in Chris Keith and Anthony Le Donne, eds., *Jesus, Criteria, and the Demise of Authenticity* (London: T&T Clark, 2012).

10. E. P. Sanders and Margaret Davies, *Studying the Synoptic Gospels* (Harrisburg, PA: Trinity Press International, 1989), 138. Sanders authored the chapters on form criticism.

11. Sanders and Davies, *Studying*, 139.

12. Sanders and Davies, *Studying*, 139. Sanders was by no means the first to suggest that early Christian prophecy had been confused with earthly Jesus teaching; see especially the work of Eugene M. Boring in the early 1970s: "How May We Identify Oracles of Christian Prophets in the Synoptic Traditions? Mark 3:28–29 as a Test Case," *JBL* 91.4 (1972): 501–21.

Mary Rose D'Angelo, in Sanders-like fashion, concludes that the saying of "the Lord" in 1 Cor 7:10–11 on divorce and remarriage is a later prophetic saying attributed to the Lord that should not be confused with Jesus's earthly ministry and teaching.[13] As precedent, she points to 1 Cor 14:26–33 with its liturgical regulations. Paul concludes that these (later) regulations are "a command of the Lord" (1 Cor 14:27). The same phenomenon is likely at work in 1 Cor 7:10–11. Later words and teachings are being attributed to Jesus, argues D'Angelo.

D'Angelo concedes that Paul distinguishes his own teaching from the Lord's in 1 Cor 7:12. Sanders also recognizes that Paul modeled the opposite approach as he carefully distinguished between his own teaching and the Lord's in 1 Cor 7:10, 12.[14] The apostle is clear in 1 Cor 7:25 when he did *not* have a command of the Lord.[15] Instead of Paul's distinguishing between his own prophetic spirit and the sayings of the historical Jesus—as most readers of 1 Cor 7:12 have concluded—D'Angelo proposes that Paul here distinguishes between his own teachings that are *with* prophetic authority from those that are not and that come from other Christian prophets.[16] In 1 Cor 7:40, in giving his own teaching, Paul reminds the community of his own possession of the Spirit and appears to treat his Spirit-inspired teaching as fully authoritative. Perhaps other Christian prophetic teachings were not as authoritative as Paul's. D'Angelo notes how in 1 Cor 14:26–33, 37–38 Paul gives his instructions on the Corinthians' worship setting and then claims that his (later) instructions are "the command of the Lord." The instructions of the "Lord" in 1 Cor 7:10–11 could likewise be later and from a Christian prophet, whether in the Corinthian community or some other community.[17]

The New Testament witness poses problems for this approach. Luke in Acts 11:28 narrates a prophet predicting "by the Spirit" and *not* in the name of the earthly Jesus. Likewise the prophet Agabus proclaims in Acts 21:11: "Thus says the Holy Spirit." In 2 Cor 12:9 Paul is clear that this was *his* exchange with the Lord regarding the thorn in the flesh that he had experienced. The words in Rev 3:20, "I am standing at the door knocking," are "what the Spirit is saying to the churches" (3:22). These passages offer no evidence of an attempt to read later revelations back into the

---

13. Mary Rose D'Angelo, "Remarriage and the Divorce Sayings Attributed to Jesus," in *Divorce and Remarriage: Religious and Psychological Perspectives*, ed. William P. Roberts (Kansas City, MO: Sheed and Ward, 1990), 88.

14. Sanders and Davies, *Studying*, 139.

15. D'Angelo, "Remarriage," 87.

16. Such a distinction is unlikely; see Kenneth L. Gentry Jr., *The Charismatic Gift of Prophecy: A Reformed Response to Wayne Grudem* (Memphis: Footstool, 1989).

17. Assuming a distinction between Paul's own teaching and prophetic utterances is D'Angelo, "Remarriage," 88.

CHAPTER 2

earthly Jesus. The New Testament authors frequently stress eyewitness testimony.[18] Jesus in John 14:26 promises that the Spirit would "remind" the disciples of what he had said during his earthly ministry and indeed, as attested in John 2:13–22, the disciples would later reflect on what Jesus had said and done while on earth. The New Testament authors esteem and value what Jesus had said during his earthly ministry and distinguish those memories from later sayings and events.

D'Angelo relies on the work of Eugene Boring, but Boring considers Paul to be relying on *authentic* Jesus traditions in 1 Cor 7:10–11, 9:14, and 11:23–26. Rather than conclude that 1 Cor 7:10 and 14:37 are both later creations, Jerome Murphy-O'Connor, in a critique of D'Angelo, points out that the unique wording of 1 Cor 14:37 "is clearly different from the language of 1 Cor 7:10."[19] The saying in 1 Cor 7:10 thus represents an authentic Jesus tradition in contrast to the subsequent teaching of 1 Cor 14:37.

D'Angelo's thesis is unlikely. First, although Paul *may* be appealing to the revelation of the Lord mediated through a prophet, Paul still makes a firm, even emphatic, distinction between "*not* I but the Lord" who "*commands*" and "I and *not* the Lord" who "*says*" in 1 Cor 7:10 (compared to 7:8, 12). The Lord commands (παραγγέλλω) but Paul says (λέγω). Paul only uses "command" in two other places (1 Cor 11:17 and 1 Thess 4:11), but here it is the Lord's own command. In the prior verses, Paul had been directing the Corinthians consistently on the basis of his *own* authority ("I say," v. 6; "I wish," v. 7; "I say," v. 8) before making an emphatic distinction in 7:8–12 by appealing to the Lord's own authority, a distinction that is unique within the Pauline corpus.[20] Second, Paul considered his own teaching on the same level as Peter's (Gal 1:11–2:14; 1 Cor 9:1–18). His apostolic office was of a *higher* rank than the prophets (1 Cor 12:28). As John Meier notes, for an apostle who boasts the mind of Christ and heavenly revelations (1 Cor 2:16; 7:40; 2 Cor 12:1–4), it is unlikely that he would appeal *away from* his own authority to an unnamed Christian prophet speaking in Christ's name.[21] Third, the Synoptic parallels to 1 Cor 7:10–11 reinforce that Paul is appealing to Jesus's earthly teach-

---

18. E.g., Luke 1:2; John 19:35; 21:24; Acts 1:21–22; 10:39, 41; 1 Cor 15:6; 1 Pet 5:1; 2 Pet 1:16; 1 John 1:1–3.

19. Jerome Murphy-O'Connor, *Divorce in the New Testament*, GNS 38 (Collegeville, MN: Liturgical, 1992), 31.

20. Meier, *Law and Love*, 98–99; Joseph A. Fitzmyer, "The Matthean Divorce Texts and Some New Palestinian Evidence," in *To Advance the Gospel: New Testament Studies*, 2nd ed., Biblical Resource Series (Grand Rapids: Eerdmans, 1981), 103 n. 13. This chapter is a republished version of Fitzmyer's 1976 *Theological Studies* article of the same title with an additional footnote at the end.

21. Meier, *Law and Love*, 99; Fee, *First Epistle to the Corinthians*, 777–78.

ing rather than to later prophetic revelations. As Meier states, "Granted this rare coincidence of Paul appealing to a specific teaching of Jesus for which we have multiple attestation in two primitive Gospel sources [Mark and Q], the most natural reading of Paul is that he intends to appeal to what Jesus commanded during his public ministry."[22] Fourth, 1 Cor 7:10–11 is only one of several quotations of the earthly Jesus's teachings or actions within this letter.[23] D'Angelo did not apply her analysis to 1 Cor 9:14 or 11:23–25, two of the other verses that most consider to be conveying authentic Jesus traditions from his earthly ministry.[24] Paul's wording in 1 Cor 11:23–25 closely parallels the Synoptics.[25] Most likely he is appealing to the Jesus tradition in 1 Cor 7:10–11 as well.[26]

Paul's Rephrasing of Jesus's Teaching for His Own Context

The vocabulary for divorce in 1 Cor 7:10–11 parallels Paul's own teaching in vv. 12–16 rather than the Synoptic parallels (vv. 10–11 use ἀφίημι and χωρίζω while the Synoptic traditions employ ἀπολύω). Paul's own teaching in 1 Cor 7:12–16 states that Christians are not to divorce their non-Christian spouses (ἀφίημι, vv. 12, 13) but may let the non-Christian spouse separate (χωρίζω, v. 15), if that spouse is determined to do so. The apostle also adapts Jesus's words to the Hellenistic setting of the Corinthian community, in which women were more frequently divorcing their husbands than in Jewish communities.[27] Unlike the verbatim quotation of the words of institution in 1 Cor 11:23–25, the differences in vocabulary in 1 Cor 7:10–11 betray that Paul is rephrasing in his own words Jesus's prohibition against divorce.[28]

Despite the paraphrase, Paul's version of Jesus's teaching retains the two-part structure of the Synoptic versions.[29] The fact that Paul is comfortable paraphras-

---

22. Meier, *Law and Love*, 99.
23. See also 1 Cor 9:14 (Luke 10:7); 11:23–25; 15:3–5; Meier, *Law and Love*, 99–100.
24. R. Collins, *Divorce*, 243 n. 114.
25. Sanders and Davies, *Studying*, 329.
26. Paul draws on the Jesus tradition elsewhere as well in 1 Corinthians: Jesus's brothers (9:5), including James (15:7); the Twelve (15:5); Cephas's prominence (15:4).
27. R. Collins, *Divorce*, 34; Meier, *Law and Love*, 100.
28. There is no available evidence to suggest that Paul knew more than the oral traditions of what Jesus had taught. Paul's variation in wording does not indicate any sort of quotation of gospel sources; with Dale B. Martin, *Sex and the Single Savior: Gender and Sexuality in Biblical Interpretation* (Louisville: Westminster John Knox, 2006), 230 n. 14; contra Robert G. Olender, "Paul's Source for 1 Corinthians 6:10—7:11," *Faith and Mission* 18.3 (2001): 60–73.
29. David Wenham, "Paul's Use of the Jesus Tradition: Three Samples," in *The Jesus Tradition outside the Gospels*, vol. 5 of *Gospel Perspectives*, ed. David Wenham (Sheffield: JSOT Press,

CHAPTER 2

ing the Lord's teaching demonstrates that the teaching itself is uncontroverted. "The allusive character of Paul's reference shows that Paul and the Corinthians were well aware of this teaching and that its authority can be taken for granted."[30] The value of Paul's witness should not be underestimated. Whereas some gospel scholars have questioned the criterion of multiple attestation in Jesus research because of the difficulty of knowing which sources are independent (i.e., did Q exist?), "the paucity of verbal agreement between Paul and the Gospels [in shared traditions about Jesus] is itself a likely indicator of their independence," concludes Mark Goodacre, who adds, "Here, then, there is the possibility of some genuinely independent tradition about Jesus."[31]

The Husband's Divorcing Activity and the Wife's Being Separated

The NRSV translates 1 Cor 7:10–11: "The wife should not separate [χωρίζω] from her husband ... and ... the husband should not divorce [ἀφίημι] his wife." The varied vocabulary with two distinct Greek verbs, rendered by different English verbs in the NRSV, might suggest a distinction between divorce and separation. Fee is representative of those scholars who conclude that there is a difference between these two verbs, although he is tentative: "Either the man sent his wife away (= 'divorce' in the sense of v. 12), or else either of them 'left' the other (= 'to separate')."[32] Spouses may separate but not divorce, or so Fee and others have thought.

The ancient world—whether Jewish, Greek, or Roman—did not distinguish separation and divorce. Most divorces were without any documentation by a divorce certificate.[33] For spouses to separate was considered a divorce. That the two

---

1984), 8 (1 Cor 7:10a parallels Mark 10:9 // Matt 19:6; 1 Cor 7:10b parallels Mark 10:11 // Matt 19:9); Meier, *Law and Love*, 100. Wenham ("Paul's Use," 9) contends for Pauline knowledge of the tradition behind the Synoptics since the "one-flesh" of 1 Cor 6:12–20, the emphasis on the gift of celibacy, and even the holiness of children in 1 Cor 7:15 could reflect the "M" tradition (cf. Matt 19). Compare also 1 Cor 7:15 and Mark 9:50. See "Paul's Use," 10–15 for Wenham's attempt to relate 1 Cor 7:10 to the two strands of Synoptic tradition.

30. Roy E. Ciampa and Brian S. Rosner, *The First Letter to the Corinthians*, Pillar New Testament Commentary (Grand Rapids: Eerdmans, 2010), 292; following James D. G. Dunn, *1 Corinthians*, New Testament Guides (Sheffield: Sheffield Academic, 1995), 101: "He [Paul] only cites it [a word from the Lord] because he is qualifying it, whereas the allusion implies an accepted authority."

31. Mark Goodacre, "Criticizing the Criterion of Multiple Attestation: The Historical Jesus and the Question of Sources," in *Jesus, Criteria, and the Demise of Authenticity*, ed. Chris Keith and Anthony Le Donne (London: T&T Clark, 2012), 168.

32. Fee, *First Epistle to the Corinthians*, 324–25.

33. See the discussion of this point in chapter 1. As David Field rightly explains: "The modern

Jesus "behind" the Gospels, or Jesus Remembered

Greek words Paul employs (χωρίζω and ἀφίημι) are synonymous is clear from the parallelism of vv. 10–11: "a *wife* should not separate from (her) *husband* . . . and . . . a *husband* should not divorce (his) *wife*." The actions are parallel.[34] Indeed, the extant divorce documents from the Greco-Roman world employ a variety of terms for "divorce."[35] The gospels use the verb ἀπολύω.[36] This verb also refers to divorce in Greek legal documents (Dionysius of Halicarnassus, *Ant. rom.* 2.25.7; Diodorus Siculus, *Bib. hist.* 12.18.1–2).[37] There was no technical word for divorce in the Greek language, and the variety of words for divorce could be used interchangeably (cf. Latin *divortium* and *divorto*). Although ἀφίημι is not employed in extant Greco-Roman divorce certificates, in Euripides: "I prayed to set thee free [ἀφεῖναι] (from a marriage)" (*Andr.* 973 [Way, LCL]).[38] Josephus distinguishes divorce by mere separation (διαχωρίζω) from divorce with a certificate (ἀφίημι) in the context of Salome sending her husband a divorce certificate: "Not even a divorced woman [διαχωρισθείσῃ] may marry again of her own initiative unless her former husband consents [ἐφιέντος]" (*Ant.* 15.7.10 §259 [Marcus and Wikgren, LCL]). Both verbs in 1 Cor 7:10–11 (χωρίζω and ἀφίημι) should be understood, then, as synonyms. In the same vein, the wife in 7:13 is not to divorce (ἀφίημι) her husband, even as in v. 12 the husband is not to divorce (ἀφίημι) his wife. Moreover, Paul states in v. 15 that if the unbeliever decides to separate or divorce (χωρίζω; cf. Mark 10:9), let them "divorce."[39] The word χωρίζω, like ἀφίημι, "has almost become a technical term in connexion [*sic*] with divorce."[40]

---

distinction between divorce proper (*a vinculo*) and legal separation (*a mensa et thoro*) was not something a Jew would have easily grasped"; see "Talking Points: The Divorce Debate—Where Are We Now?" *Themelios* 8.3 (1983): 29; Murray, *Divorce*, 35–43; David Atkinson, "A Response," *The Churchman* 95 (1981): 163; Bruce Vawter, "The Divorce Clauses in Mt 5,32 and 19,9," *CBQ* 16 (1954): 158: "It is unthinkable that our Lord's hearers would have grasped this second meaning ["separation" for *apoluo*] for *separatio a mensa et toro* was unknown among the Jews."

34. Meier, *Law and Love*, 100.

35. These include χωρίζω, "separate"; ἀποπέμπω, "send away" or "dismiss"; ἀπολάσσω, "set free"; ἀποπομπή, "sending away"; ἀπαλλαγή, "deliverance"; and ἀποπλοκή, "separation." See David Instone-Brewer, "Graeco-Roman Marriage," 105–6.

36. E.g., Matt 5:31–32; 19:3, 7, 9; Mark 10:2, 4, 11–12; Luke 16:18.

37. Papyri 19 and 115 in P. Benoit, J. T. Milik, and R. de Vaux, *Les grottes de Murabba'ât*, DJD 2 (Oxford: Oxford University Press, 1961): 104–9 (Aramaic), 243–54 (Greek: ἀπολύω); Fitzmyer, "Matthean Divorce Texts," 212.

38. Herodotus, *Hist.* 5.39, sometimes cited in this connection, uses a different word: "Therefore send away [ἔξεο] the wife that you have, seeing that she bears you no children, and wed another" (Godley, LCL).

39. Meier, *Law and Love*, 101.

40. J. H. Moulton and G. Milligan, *Vocabulary of the Greek Testament* (Peabody, MA: Hendrickson, 1930), 696 no. 5563; note the papyri instances.

CHAPTER 2

Yet a further potential distinction in 1 Cor 7:10–11 lies in the use of an active infinitive for the husband's divorcing but a passive verb for the woman's being separated or divorced (which English translations sometimes obscure with an active translation; e.g., NRSV). Perhaps the aorist passive infinitive χωρισθῆναι reflects Paul's Jewish background in which men were more commonly the initiators of divorce.[41] The wife does not separate herself (middle or reflexive), but separation is forced upon her.[42] The passive sometimes bears the sense of "allow oneself to be"; thus, "the wife should not allow herself to be separated from her husband."[43] Many manuscripts of 1 Cor 7:10 attest the aorist passive infinitive χωρισθῆναι (א, B, C Ψ 33), and even the variant present infinitive is passive (χωρίζεσθαι; p[46] A D F G 614 1505 1881). First Corinthians 7:10–11 would thus reflect the Jewish perspective on divorce, while vv. 12–13 turn to the Greco-Roman milieu with the wife potentially initiating divorce. This line of reasoning, however, has become problematic in view of *BGU* 4.1101 (GM-13).[44] In this papyrus, the spouses "separate from *each other*" (ἐχωρίσθημεν ἀπ' ἀλλή[λων]). The aorist passive verb form functions reflexively: "It is not possible they could both *be* separated from each other."[45] The distinction in tense between the aorist and the present should therefore not be pressed.[46] The reflexive sense of the verb is consistent throughout vv. 10–15. The active translation in the English rephrasing of the Greek reflexive usage is therefore justifiable. Spouses are not to divorce each other.

Paul's Jesus forbids divorce and yet, when divorce does take place, the wife is to remain single or be reconciled to her husband. The saying of Jesus that Paul relays in 1 Cor 7:10–11 is countercultural. David Instone-Brewer comments on the countercultural element of Jesus's saying in 7:10–11: "Graeco-Roman marriage certificates were worded as though they expected the marriage to end in divorce, not death."[47] According to a first-century BCE funeral inscription cited by Instone-Brewer: "Uncommon are marriages which last so long, brought to an end by death,

---

41. There has been debate on the extent to which wives divorce their husbands in Jewish society.

42. Thus Hays, *Moral Vision*, 358; Fitzmyer ("Matthean Divorce Texts," 199) poses a Palestinian Jewish context as a possibility, in which the husband initiates the divorce.

43. Jerome Murphy-O'Connor, "The Divorced Woman in 1 Cor 7:10–11," *JBL* 100.4 (1981): 602.

44. *Griechische Urkunden*, vol. 4 of *Aegyptische Urkunden aus den Koeniglichen Museen zu Berlin* (Berlin: Weidmann, 1912), 170.

45. Instone-Brewer, "Graeco-Roman Marriage," 105 n. 10.

46. Joseph Fitzmyer ("Matthean Divorce Texts," 199–200) notes that the middle (reflexive) mood is only with the present tense verb form, whereas the best manuscripts of 1 Cor 7:10 are aorist. Fitzmyer therefore believes it to be a viable translation that the woman is not separating herself but is *being* separated by her husband's divorce. The value of this papyrus is that it demonstrates the same reflexive usage with the aorist as with the present.

47. Instone-Brewer, *Divorce and Remarriage*, 191.

not broken apart by divorce; for it was our happy lot that it should be prolonged to the 41st year without estrangement."[48] Remarriage was then taken for granted in the wake of a divorce. "Paul makes it clear that whatever her motivation she is not to use her divorce as a way of marrying someone else."[49] In a world of widespread divorce and remarriage, Paul's Jesus taught that the marital bond had long-term implications. If divorced, remarriage was not an option.

Jesus "behind" the Gospels

Matthew 5:32 and Luke 16:18

Matthew 5:32 and Luke 16:18 each offer a version of Jesus's saying on divorce and remarriage that share some striking, word-for-word similarities, although they are placed in different literary settings. Matthew 5:32 is located within the Sermon on the Mount, and Luke 16:18 appears within a cluster of legal and moral sayings. The story of the dishonest steward, unique to Luke, precedes Jesus's teaching on divorce and remarriage, and the Lukan story of the rich man and Lazarus follows it. The similarities are more obvious when the sayings are placed side by side:

	Matt 5:32	Luke 16:18
1a	Anyone who divorces his wife	Anyone who divorces his wife
	Πᾶς ὁ ἀπολύων τὴν γυναῖκα αὐτοῦ	Πᾶς ὁ ἀπολύων τὴν γυναῖκα αὐτοῦ
	except on the ground of "unchastity"	
	παρεκτὸς λόγου πορνείας	
		and marries another
		καὶ γαμῶν ἑτέραν
1b	causes her to commit adultery	commits adultery
	ποιεῖ αὐτὴν μοιχευθῆναι,	μοιχεύει
2a	and whoever marries a divorced woman	and the one who marries a woman divorced from (her) husband
	καὶ ὃς ἐὰν ἀπολελυμένην γαμήσῃ,	καὶ ὁ ἀπολελυμένην ἀπὸ ἀνδρὸς γαμῶν
2b	commits adultery	commits adultery
	μοιχᾶται.	μοιχεύει.

48. Inscription from G. H. R. Horsley, *New Documents Illustrating Early Christianity: A Review of the Greek Inscriptions and Papyri Published in 1978* (Sydney: Macquarie University Press, 1983), 3: 35.

49. Ciampa and Rosner, *First Letter to the Corinthians*, 293.

CHAPTER 2

Both verses consist of a single sentence with two main parts (1 and 2), and each of those two main parts is subdivided into two subportions (a and b). Both gospels focus on the man as the responsible agent and as the subject of the finite verbs and active participles. While the two verses are similar to each other, they both differ from the version of Jesus's saying that is in Mark 10:11, which consists of two sentences, the first about the husband and the second about the wife. As a further difference, the two Markan statements, unlike Matt 5:32 // Luke 16:18, do not begin with participial phrases (nominative, masculine, singular participles modified by πᾶς "every"). Both of the Markan statements employ an indefinite relative clause and a conditional clause. Mark 10:11 further diverges from Matt 5:32 and Luke 16:18 in having the husband commit adultery "against [ἐπί] her (i.e., the first wife)."[50] Moreover, whereas Matt 5:32 and Luke 16:18 are both embedded within the larger context of Jesus's sayings, Mark 10:11–12 is part of what form critics have labeled a controversy story.[51] The saying in Mark 10:12 about the woman's divorcing her husband finds no parallel in Matt 5:32 // Luke 16:18. In other words, Matt 5:32 // Luke 16:18 and Mark 10:11 appear to represent two *separate* streams of tradition.[52] The Matt 5:32 // Luke 16:18 saying also diverges from Paul's version. Historical Jesus specialists thus stress the criterion of multiple attestation. Paul represents one stream of tradition attesting to a saying of Jesus on divorce and remarriage, Matt 5:32 // Luke 16:18 a second stream, and Mark 10:11 (and Matt 19:9) yet a third.

The majority of gospel scholars subscribe to the Two Source Hypothesis and thus would not be surprised by the Matt 5:32 // Luke 16:18 parallels since this version of Jesus's saying would be from Q, the hypothetical source drawn upon independently by Matthew and Luke. Some gospel specialists have lodged vigorous objections to the Q hypothesis.[53] James D. G. Dunn, an advocate of Q, has further complicated the hypothesis by distinguishing those portions of the Q material that may reflect a written document (greater verbal agreement, up to 100 percent)

50. Robert H. Gundry, *Mark: A Commentary on His Apology for the Cross* (Grand Rapids: Eerdmans, 1993), 541–42: Mark's Jesus does not use the preposition in the sense of "with her." The preposition, as elsewhere in Mark (3:24, 25, 26; 13:8, 12; 14:48), should be translated "against her" and in reference to the first wife.

51. Meier, *Law and Love*, 102–4.

52. Matthew draws on the Markan tradition later in Matt. 19:9; see W. D. Davies and Dale C. Allison Jr., *A Critical and Exegetical Commentary on the Gospel according to Matthew*, ICC (Edinburgh: T&T Clark, 1988–1997), 1:91–92.

53. E.g., Mark Goodacre, *The Case against Q: Studies in Markan Priority and the Synoptic Problem* (Harrisburg, PA: Trinity Press International, 2002); Mark Goodacre and Nicholas Perrin, eds., *Questioning Q: A Multidimensional Critique* (Downers Grove, IL: InterVarsity, 2004). For a valuable older critique, see Sanders and Davies, *Studying*, 51–119.

from those portions that may reflect shared oral traditions, which he labels with the lowercase "q" (less verbal agreement, as low as 8 percent).[54] Putting aside for a moment the potential Synoptic relationships, the Matt 5:32 // Luke 16:18 version of Jesus's saying differs significantly in structure and wording from Paul's version and from Mark 10:11 // Matt 19:9. Doubts about Q do not diminish the likelihood of independent streams of tradition.

Both Matt 5:32 and Luke 16:18 begin with the same participial phrase, which is therefore likely original (Πᾶς ὁ ἀπολύων τὴν γυναῖκα αὐτοῦ ["Anyone who divorces his wife"]). Matthew includes an exception clause, which is considered secondary since only Matthew includes it. Similarly, Matt 19:9 includes an exception clause for the material that parallels Mark 10:9, another apparent Matthean addition. As John Meier observes: "In both Matt 5:32 and 19:9, the phrase expressing the exception overloads the clause in which it occurs, making ... the prohibition unwieldy, overlong, and not a little obscure (at least to an endless line of Christian interpreters from the patristic period onward)."[55] Had the Matthean exception clause been original to Jesus's wording of the divorce saying, it is difficult to understand why Paul would state Jesus's teaching in an absolute form, only to maintain an exception based on the apostle's *own* authority.[56]

Some have maintained that the exception in Matt 5:32 appears to be a Semitic construction (παρεκτὸς λόγου πορνείας) unlike the exception in Matt 19:9 (μὴ ἐπὶ πορνείᾳ, "except for unchastity"). The two exception clauses differ from *each other* even within the same gospel. For John Nolland, Matthew in 5:32 had access to a different form of the shared material than Luke. The setting for the Matt 5:32 exception clause may well have been the strict Jewish view of adultery, a capital crime that brought the marriage to an end (Lev 20:10; Deut 22:22). Intertestamental and rabbinic sources also grapple with how to apply these Old Testament laws.[57] Adultery could be viewed as having *already* destroyed the marriage.[58] Nolland therefore contends that Matt 5:32's exception clause is a pre-Matthean addition to Jesus's teaching that originated from a Jewish-Christian community.[59]

---

54. James D. G. Dunn, "Q¹ as Oral Tradition," in *The Written Gospel*, ed. Markus Bockmuehl and Donald A. Hagner (Cambridge: Cambridge University Press, 2005), 45–69; Dunn, *Jesus Remembered*, vol. 1 of *Christianity in the Making* (Grand Rapids: Eerdmans, 2003), 147–49.

55. Meier, *Law and Love*, 104.

56. Meier, *Law and Love*, 104–5—that is, from the point of view of historical Jesus reconstruction. Jesus's teaching could have been remembered differently or have taken place on several occasions, to anticipate the discussion later in the chapter.

57. E.g., Jub. 30:8–9; 33:9; m. Soṭah 3:6; 4:2 [in relation to Deut 24:4]; 5:1.

58. John Nolland, *Luke 9:21–18:34*, WBC 35B (Nashville: Nelson, 1993), 817–18.

59. Nolland, *Luke 9:21–18:34*, 816.

CHAPTER 2

Whether one judges Matt 5:32's exception clause to be Semitic (with Nolland) or not, it would still be deemed a later addition.[60]

Luke 16:18 includes an added clause not in Matt 5:32: καὶ γαμῶν ἑτέραν ("and marries another"). Fifty of the ninety-eight New Testament occurrences of "another" (ἑτέραν) are in Luke-Acts. "Another" is thus a Lukan adjective. Luke would have been rendering explicit what most in antiquity would have assumed, mainly, that the husband is divorcing his wife with the intention of marrying another. Divorce in the ancient world would typically lead to remarriage. John Meier nevertheless contends that this clause is original since it is multiply attested: Mark 10:11 includes the same clause, and Paul in 1 Cor 7:11 implies it in requiring the divorced parties to remain unmarried or be reconciled to their spouse. "Thus, directly or indirectly, the prohibition of a second marriage is present in the Pauline, Lucan, and Marcan versions." The phrase "and marries another" therefore represents "the primitive Q form behind Luke 16:18."[61] Furthermore, the Synoptic versions of Jesus's teaching all reject divorce because it involves adultery, a conclusion that only makes sense if a second union is assumed.[62] Had the spouses divorced and remained celibate, no adultery would be involved. "Without the mention of a second marriage, the image, metaphor, or stigma of adultery does not make rhetorical sense."[63] "And marries another" therefore appears to be original.

Matthew 5:32 describes divorce as causing the *wife* to be adulterated, since she would need to enter a second marriage (for her social security), and the first husband is complicit in the adultery by placing her in this situation. Luke 16:18 describes the adultery of a *husband* marrying another woman. As a common denominator, both verses blame the husband, as does Mark 10:11. As for which version is original, Luke 16:18, Mark 10:11–12, and Matt 19:9 multiply attest the *same* person who divorces and marries another as the adulterer.[64] John Meier contends that Matt 5:32's focus on the husband causing the wife to be adulterated reflects the Jewish milieu of Matthew's church in which husbands were usually the initiators of

---

60. It is not multiply attested and is not dissimilar from the views of the first Jewish Christians.

61. Meier, *Law and Love*, 105; with Fitzmyer, "Matthean Divorce Texts," 82–83. Why then is "and marries another" not in the Matt 5:32 parallel? Meier explains this as a result of the emphasis in Matt 5:31 on the bill of divorce from Deut 24:1: the focus remains on the husband's initiation of divorce and not remarriage.

62. Gundry, *Mark*, 543; Meier, *Law and Love*, 169–70 n. 106. The second marriage is adulterous because the original marriage bond continues. On the other hand, one need not interpret this as a continuation of the marital bond, but rather simply that God's intent in creation is for one man to be married to one woman, and thus the remarriage is contrary to his will for only one marriage to take place during the lifetime of the partners.

63. Meier, *Law and Love*, 105.

64. Meier, *Law and Love*, 105–7.

divorce.[65] The circumstances were the same in the time of Jesus. The first part of the saying is therefore likely, "Everyone who divorces his wife and marries another commits adultery," with the words "and marries another" somewhat less certain.[66]

In the second part of the saying, both Matt 5:32 and Luke 16:18 are in agreement that whoever marries a divorced woman commits adultery.[67] Luke's phrasing ἀπὸ ἀνδρός, "by/from (her) husband," includes one of his favorite nouns ἀνήρ ("man").[68] The Matthean wording here is more likely original.

A reconstructed, more "original" form of the saying behind Matt 5:32 and Luke 16:18 would thus read:

> Anyone who divorces his wife and marries another
>   commits adultery;
> And the one who/whoever marries a divorced woman
>   commits adultery

The two parts are balanced with the husband as the actor and the wife as the object of his action. The verb μοιχεύει ("commit adultery") is also used in both parts.[69]

Mark 10:11–12 and Matthew 19:9

Similar to Matt 5:32 // Luke 16:18, Mark 10:11–12 has a two-part saying consisting of two separate sentences, with each sentence consisting of two parts. Unlike Matt 5:32 // Luke 16:18, which remains riveted on the husband, here the first sentence is focused on the husband but the second on the wife:

(1) Whoever divorces his wife and marries another (woman),
ὃς ἂν ἀπολύσῃ τὴν γυναῖκα αὐτοῦ καὶ γαμήσῃ ἄλλην
commits adultery against her.
μοιχᾶται ἐπ' αὐτήν.

---

65. Meier, *Law and Love*, 107. Just because this traditional practice might be Jewish does not mean that it is necessarily original; with Corrodo Marucci, *Parole di Gesù sul divorzio: Ricerche scritturistiche previe ad un ripensamento teologico, canonistico e pastorale della dottrina cattolica dell'indissolubilità del matrimonio* (Naples: Morcelliana, 1982), 308–9.

66. With Meier, *Law and Love*, 107.

67. The divorce does not appear to have completely severed the marital union, perhaps in the sense that God's original plan is for the marriage to be lifelong and thus the second marriage sins against God's will for the first marriage. The divorce has had no real effect *before God*.

68. 127 of 216 New Testament occurrences of ἀνήρ are in Luke-Acts.

69. With Meier, *Law and Love*, 107–8; Matthew's phrase "makes her an adulteress" (ποιεῖ αὐτὴν μοιχευθῆναι) is a result of focusing on the divorced wife; see Nolland, *Luke 9:21–18:34*, 818.

(2) And if she, divorcing her husband, marries another (man),
καὶ ἐὰν αὐτὴ ἀπολύσασα τὸν ἄνδρα αὐτῆς γαμήσῃ ἄλλον
she commits adultery.
μοιχᾶται.

The woman divorcing her husband assumes a situation more common in Greco-Roman society. Meier asks: "If ordinary Jewish women in Palestine did not have the power to divorce their husbands, what would be the point of Jesus going out of his way to prohibit it?"[70] Many scholars have therefore denied the authenticity of Mark 10:12. Certainly a woman divorcing her husband would be far more infrequent in Jewish society than among the Greeks or Romans.[71] Many Palestinians were also gentiles and not Jews, and the possibility of a woman initiating divorce in their circles could be a factor in the articulation of Jesus's teaching. "What is important is to note that it is conceivable and quite probable that Jesus could have said things that reflect a non-Palestinian environment, if we assume that Palestinian means non-Gentile or non-Greek."[72] Others point out that the woman *could* divorce her husband in Jewish society.[73]

A viable backdrop for Jesus's prohibition of the wife divorcing her husband, some contend, is John the Baptist's censure of Herod Antipas and the woman who had divorced her husband to marry him.[74] Appeal to John the Baptist's criticism, however, is not helpful in this particular instance. Mark 6:18 narrates the Baptist's complaint that Herod Antipas married *his brother's wife* and *not* that he married a divorced

---

70. Meier, *Law and Love*, 110.

71. Striking the right balance on the point, see Tigay, *Deuteronomy*, 221.

72. Robert H. Stein, "The 'Criteria' for Authenticity," in *Studies of History and Tradition in the Four Gospels*, vol. 1 of *Gospel Perspectives*, ed. R. T. France and David Wenham (Sheffield: JSOT Press, 1980), 237.

73. On women divorcing their husbands in Jewish society, see Bernadette J. Brooten, "Könnten Frauen im alten Judentum die Scheidung betreiben?," *EvT* 42.1 (1982): 65–80; Eduard Schweizer, "Scheidungsrecht der jüdischen Frau? Weibliche Jünger Jesu?," *EvT* 42.3 (1982): 294–300; Hans Weder, "Perspektive der Frauen?," *EvT* 43.2 (1983): 175–79; Brooten, "Zur Debatte über das Scheidungsrecht der jüdischen Frau," *EvT* 43.5 (1983): 466–78; Brooten, "Early Christian Women and Their Cultural Contexts: Issues of Method in Historical Reconstruction," in *Feminist Perspectives on Biblical Scholarship*, ed. Adela Yarbro Collins (Chico, CA: Scholars, 1985): 73–74; Brooten, "Jewish Women's History in the Roman Period: A Task for Christian Theology," *HTR* 79.1 (1986): 23. For biblical evidence in favor of a woman's divorcing her husband, see Yair Zakovitch, "The Woman's Rights in the Biblical Law of Divorce," *JLA* 4 (1981): 35–40; Exod 21:7–11; Judg 19:1–2 (cf. *qere* vs. *ketiv*); Jer 3:1 LXX.

74. Stein, "'Criteria' for Authenticity," 237. See also the materials discovered from the Bar Kokhba revolt referenced in J. Duncan M. Derrett, *Law in the New Testament* (London: Dartman, Longman, and Todd, 1970), 382.

woman. The charge in this case is of incest (with Lev 18:16; 20:21). This portion of Jesus's saying may be authentic if in reference to the Greeks and other non-Jews in Palestine rather than to Herod Antipas's family. Ultimately, as Luz writes, "It does not really matter how much upper-class Jewish women in the time of Jesus claimed this right; under normal circumstances Jewish women did not have it."[75]

On the other hand, Mark 10:12 lacks any Synoptic parallel and also differs from 10:11 in grammar and content. In terms of grammar, the protasis of v. 12 is a conditional sentence, whereas v. 11 begins with an indefinite relative clause. Also, the protasis in v. 12 has a participle, whereas v. 11's opening dependent clause consists of two finite verbs. Mark 10:11 would have been a sufficient answer to the Pharisees' question articulated earlier in Mark 10. Verse 12 therefore appears to be a secondary Markan rewording.[76]

Additionally, "against her" (ἐπ' αὐτήν) in Mark 10:11 is likely secondary as well since the words are unique to this version of Jesus's saying. Once removed, the original version of the pre-Markan tradition would read: "Whoever divorces his wife and marries another commits adultery."[77] With minor differences in grammar and wording, the reconstructed original behind Mark 10:11 is similar to the statement behind Matt 5:32 // Luke 16:18: "Everyone who divorces his wife and marries another commits adultery." The three independent streams of tradition in 1 Cor 7:10–11, Mark 10:11, and Matt 5:32 // Luke 16:18 thus serve as multiple attestation to Jesus's teaching on divorce and remarriage.

Again, multiple attestation does not *prove* that Jesus uttered the divorce and remarriage logion.[78] What it *does* demonstrate is that the teaching on divorce and remarriage *predates* the various sources. An earlier member of the Christ movement may have manufactured this teaching, but at least the New Testament sources did not themselves do so. Multiple attestation increases the probability that a particular teaching goes back to Jesus himself.

Criteria Not Dependent on a Particular Source-Critical Solution

Some high-profile researchers have been skeptical of such source critical investigation and results. Recent criticism of the Q source has led some investigators to a more eclectic method.[79] E. P. Sanders, a fan of neither Q nor the Two Source

---

75. Ulrich Luz, *Matthew 8–20*, Hermeneia (Minneapolis: Fortress, 2001), 487 n. 6.
76. For some, again, due to the narratival role of Herod's wife in Mark 6; see Meier, *Law and Love*, 110–11.
77. Meier, *Law and Love*, 111.
78. See Eric Eve, "Meier, Miracle, and Multiple Attestation," *JSHJ* 3.1 (2005): 44–45.
79. E.g., Goodacre, *Case against Q*; Goodacre and Perrin, *Questioning Q*.

CHAPTER 2

Hypothesis, prefers instead to highlight what is *common* in the various strands of tradition.[80] Clearly, the traditions on divorce and remarriage are multiply attested in Paul and—apart from any particular solution to the Synoptic problem—appear in a longer form (Matt 19:3–12 // Mark 10:2–12) and in a shorter form (Matt 5:31–32 // Luke 16:18). Throughout the New Testament, Jesus's teaching on divorce and remarriage always consists of two parts and, in each instance, it is the prohibition of remarriage that forms the common denominator in Jesus's teaching:

> Matt 5:32: But I say to you that anyone who divorces his wife, except on the ground of unchastity, *causes her to commit adultery*; and *whoever marries a divorced woman commits adultery*.

> Matt 19:9: And I say to you, whoever divorces his wife, except for unchastity, and *marries another commits adultery*.

> Mark 10:11–12: Whoever divorces his wife and *marries another commits adultery against her*; and if she divorces her husband *and marries another, she commits adultery*.

> Luke 16:18: Anyone who divorces his wife *and marries another commits adultery*, and *whoever marries a woman divorced from her husband commits adultery*.

> 1 Cor 7:10–11 (Paul): To the married I give this command—not I but the Lord—that the wife should not separate from her husband (but *if she does separate, let her remain unmarried or else be reconciled to her husband*), and that the husband should not divorce his wife.

Each of the above gospel sayings censures remarriage. As for 1 Cor 7:10–11, Paul's two-part saying targets divorce, but the qualification is raised that, if divorce takes place, the wife must remain unmarried or be reconciled to the husband. Remarriage is not a possibility. As the common denominator in these sayings of Jesus, Sanders judges the prohibition against remarriage to be authentic Jesus tradition.

Another possible criterion that would avoid requiring a source-critical solution to the relationships between the gospels is to stress that these comments are made in passing and are not as well integrated into their respective contexts. A comment

---

80. Sanders and Davies, *Studying*, 324–28 (Sanders authored the chapters on the historical Jesus quest); cf. E. P. Sanders, *The Historical Figure of Jesus* (London: Penguin, 1993), 198–201.

made in passing is less encumbered with the author's own agenda than are those statements that receive greater attention and theological development. Many have noted that Jesus's teaching against remarriage in Luke 16:18 is within a context absorbed with the question of possessions and not marriage. The parable of the dishonest steward precedes the saying (vv. 1–15) and the rich man and Lazarus follows (vv. 19–31). Luke 16:18 represents a comment made by Jesus in passing not developed elsewhere in its surrounding context. As such, this saying of Jesus is likely pre-Lukan.[81]

Embarrassment

Another criterion employed in historical Jesus reconstruction is embarrassment. Actions or sayings of Jesus that would have embarrassed or caused difficulties for the first Christians are deemed more likely original. The early church would not generally have tried to manufacture traditions that would embarrass the Christian movement and detract from its kerygmatic or polemical concerns. Such creations would only serve the opponents of the movement. Embarrassing material would presumably be softened or deleted as gospel traditions evolved. Potentially embarrassing material is likely an indicator of reliable Jesus traditions.[82] Embarrassment is Meier's first criterion and Bruce Malina's second (after discontinuity).[83] Dale Allison ranks it third after coherence and dissimilarity.[84] Several scholars consider embarrassment to be a subset of the criterion of dissimilarity, since the researcher is identifying where a tradition departs from the interests of the first Christians, as takes place in the application of the dissimilarity criterion (more on that criterion shortly).[85]

---

81. The Lukan context of 16:18 will be assessed later in this chapter.

82. Meier, *Roots of the Problem*, 168–77; John P. Meier, *Mentor, Message, and Miracles*, vol. 2 of *A Marginal Jew: Rethinking the Historical Jesus*, ABRL (New York: Doubleday, 1994), 5–6, 100–5; John P. Meier, *Companions and Competitors*, vol. 3 of *A Marginal Jew: Rethinking the Historical Jesus*, ABRL (New York: Doubleday: 2001), 9–12; Meier, *Law and Love*, 13–15.

83. Bruce J. Malina, "Criteria for Assessing the Authentic Words of Jesus: Some Specifications," in *Authenticating the Words of Jesus*, ed. Bruce Chilton and Craig A. Evans (Leiden: Brill, 1999), 28.

84. Dale C. Allison Jr., *Jesus of Nazareth: Millenarian Prophet* (Minneapolis: Fortress, 1998), 5–6. Allison later abandoned the criterion as well as the historical Jesus criteria in general; see Dale C. Allison Jr., *The Historical Christ and the Theological Jesus* (Grand Rapids: Eerdmans, 2009), 53–60. James H. Charlesworth, *The Historical Jesus*, An Essential Guide (Nashville: Abingdon, 2008), 20–22 lists it first, and Anthony Le Donne, *The Historiographical Jesus: Memory, Typology, and the Son of David* (Waco, TX: Baylor University Press, 2009), 89, places it second.

85. Tom Holmén, "Authenticity Criteria," in *Encyclopedia of the Historical Jesus*, ed. Craig A.

CHAPTER 2

Embarrassment as a criterion is not free of cause for concern. To illustrate the point, one may consider the showcase example of Jesus's baptism. The early Christians considered Jesus to be sinless, and yet he received John's baptism of repentance for the forgiveness of sins.[86] Jesus thereby gave the appearance of being subordinate to John and in need of forgiveness. Matthew is therefore forced to explain the baptism by John as necessary "to fulfill all righteousness" (3:15; cf. Matt 28:19 and the command to baptize). Matthew also has John saying that he is not worthy to baptize Jesus (3:14).[87] Luke, for his part, includes John's denial that he is the Messiah in 3:15–16. Luke also reduces John's role by reporting his imprisonment *prior* to Jesus's baptism, which is then very briefly narrated. John's Gospel (in embarrassment?) does not report Jesus's baptism by John the Baptist and has the Baptist subordinating his ministry to the coming one (e.g., 1:15, 27, 30). Even Mark 1:7–8 presents John's preaching of the coming "stronger one" before Jesus's baptism. Despite the cognitive dissonance, the very first Christians obviously conveyed the story of Jesus's baptism by John.[88] The gospel writers' embarrassment did not prevent them from maintaining the tradition.

On the other hand, the cognitive dissonance that early Christians experienced with Jesus's baptism may have emerged at a later point in time than that of the very first followers of Jesus. In the earliest years of the Jesus movement, his association with John's baptism may well have *enhanced* Jesus's reputation.[89] What was embarrassing at one stage of the Jesus movement may not have been embarrassing at another stage. The criterion does not guarantee that a tradition, preserved despite the embarrassment of later Christians, had not been manufactured and

---

Evans (New York: Routledge, 2008), 44; Dennis Polkow, "Method and Criteria for Historical Jesus Research," *Society of Biblical Literature 1987 Seminar Papers*, SBLSP 26 (Atlanta: Scholars, 1987), 341; see also Stanley E. Porter, *The Criteria for Authenticity in Historical-Jesus Research: Previous Discussion and New Proposals*, JSNTSup 191 (Sheffield: Sheffield Academic Press, 2000), 106–10.

86. Meier, *Roots of the Problem*, 168–69; Paula Fredriksen, *From Jesus to Christ: The Origins of New Testament Images of Jesus* (New Haven: Yale University Press, 1988), 41; Dunn, *Jesus Remembered*, 350–51.

87. On the evolution of baptismal traditions, see, e.g., Meier, *Roots of the Problem*, 168–69; Meier, *Mentor, Message, and Miracles*, 100–105; Dunn, *Jesus Remembered*, 372–73; Fredriksen, *From Jesus to Christ*, 97–98.

88. As Allison (*Jesus of Nazareth*, 6) points out: embarrassing traditions obviously "were not sufficiently disconcerting to be expurgated."

89. William Arnal, "Major Episodes in the Biography of Jesus: An Assessment of the Historicity of the Narrative Tradition," *TJT* 13 (1997): 204; Rafael Rodríguez, "The Embarrassing Truth about Jesus: The Criterion of Embarrassment and the Failure of Historical Authenticity," in *Jesus, Criteria, and the Demise of Authenticity*, ed. Chris Keith and Anthony Le Donne (London: T&T Clark, 2012), 142–43.

of value earlier in the Christian movement. The criterion only increases the likelihood that the tradition predates the "embarrassed" stage.[90] The criterion increases the likelihood that a tradition comes from an earlier stage of the community's interpretation, and perhaps even from Jesus's ministry itself.[91]

With these important qualifiers and caveats in mind while employing this criterion, the New Testament teaching on remarriage may reflect a level of discomfort with what appears to be a difficult saying. Matthew 5:32 and 19:9 include an exception clause that is not in the other gospels. Jesus's otherwise absolute teaching against divorce and remarriage is thereby mitigated in instances of unchastity or sexual sin, however one defines πορνεία there. As Richard Hays states: "Mark's radical vision of marriage as an indissoluble one-flesh union is accommodated in the interest of creating a workable rule for the community's life."[92] Similarly, Meier observes all the "weaving and bobbing" in the search for "wiggle room" on the part of the apostle Paul to allow an exception to Jesus's teaching in instances where a partner is not a Christ-believer.[93] Matthew and Paul offer differing exceptions to what appears to be Jesus's originally absolute teaching. Such conclusions do not rely on any particular source-critical solution.

Dissimilarity

Practitioners of the dissimilarity criterion hunt for instances where the Jesus traditions differ from what other Second Temple Jews or early Christians thought and did. Thus no one's interests would be served to make such a tradition up.[94] Whereas embarrassment assesses Jesus traditions in relation to the first Christian authors, dissimilarity is broader in analyzing these traditions in relation to the fullness of early Christianity as well as Second Temple Judaism. The criterion involves both a forward and a backward dimension.

Dissimilarity emphasizes what is unique about Jesus but without any assurance that these unique aspects are necessarily *characteristic* of him. The criterion,

---

90. Arnal ("Major Episodes," 204) contends that the earliest Christian movement did not yet possess the exalted Christology of the Synoptic Gospels, and at that point John was more popular than Jesus (as indicated by Josephus, *Ant.* 18.5.2 §§116–119). These early followers of Christ may have wished to associate Jesus with the greater figure, John. Later Christians, with their higher Christology, became embarrassed by the connection with John and his baptism.

91. Rodríguez, "Embarrassing Truth," 146.

92. Hays, *Moral Vision*, 356.

93. Meier, *Law and Love*, 117.

94. Polkow therefore subsumes embarrassment under dissimilarity, "Method and Criteria," 341.

if followed rigorously and consistently, would result in a non-Jewish Jesus without any followers, which was obviously not the case. The rigorous application of this criterion thus results in a skewed, idiosyncratic picture of Jesus. Rather, Jesus was a Palestinian Jew, and the first Christ-believers certainly based their teachings and beliefs on what he did and taught. Again, the rigorous application of the dissimilarity criterion would result in a distorted picture that would remove from consideration much of what was characteristic of Jesus.[95]

In an attempt to mitigate these weaknesses in the criterion, N. T. Wright proposes that double dissimilarity be used in conjunction with double similarity in order to account for the fact that Jesus was a Jew with followers.[96] As Stein comments: "Again we must be careful, however, not to assume that a valid criticism of the misuse of this tool is in reality a valid criticism of the tool itself. The tool does not claim to be able to arrive at what is 'characteristic' of Jesus' teaching, even if some scholars have falsely assumed that what was distinct was in fact the essence of his teaching."[97] Multiple attestation would offer a supplementary approach that would be immune to this criticism in cases where traditions are multiply attested. Fortunately, in the divorce and remarriage traditions that is the case. The criterion of dissimilarity may be applied to these traditions, but so also may multiple attestation. What is dissimilar in these instances may indeed be characteristic.

Some scholars in their application of this criterion assume rather radically that anything the church would consider relevant must have originated with the church and not with Jesus.[98] Others have responded that dissimilarity should be applied to *increase* the probability of authentic traditions and *not* in order to disqualify traditions. Dissimilarity, applied in this way, would thus *affirm* traditions as more likely originating in Jesus's teaching and would not rule out traditions as inauthentic.[99] The criterion would simply not apply where there is no indication of dissimilarity.

The criterion also assumes that the modern researcher, despite the temporal distance, possesses a truly comprehensive knowledge of Second Temple Judaism and early Christianity. Jesus may appear dissimilar to some *known* forms of Second

---

95. Morna D. Hooker, "On Using the Wrong Tool," *Theology* 75 (1972): 574.
96. N. T. Wright, *Jesus and the Victory of God*, vol. 2 of *Christian Origins and the Question of God* (Minneapolis: Fortress, 1996), 131–33, 226, 450, 489.
97. Stein, "'Criteria' for Authenticity," 244.
98. Evans, "Authenticity Criteria," 15, which is a form-critical assumption.
99. Tom Holmén, "Doubts about Double Dissimilarity: Restructuring the Main Criterion of Jesus-of-History Research," in *Authenticating the Words of Jesus*, ed. Bruce Chilton and Craig A. Evans (Leiden: Brill, 1999), 49: "It has been acknowledged—correctly, I think—that the criterion must not be used negatively, to single out what is inauthentic." With Morna D. Hooker, "Christology and Methodology," *NTS* 17.4 (1971): 486; D. G. A. Calvert, "An Examination of the Criteria for Distinguishing the Authentic Words of Jesus," *NTS* 18.2 (1971–1972): 209–19, esp. 211–13.

Jesus "behind" the Gospels, or Jesus Remembered

Temple Judaism or early Christianity and yet be similar to other, yet *unknown* forms.[100] At the same time, even after recognizing the limits of current knowledge, the modern researcher does enjoy a wealth of material illumining Second Temple Judaism, and that body of knowledge permits a useful application of the criterion, pending new discoveries in the future.

Finally, still others place greater emphasis on discontinuity from the first Christians rather than from Judaism since Jesus's teaching originates within the context of first-century Palestine.[101] These scholars do not deny any value to assessing discontinuity from Judaism, but it is not a concern in their application of the criterion. Most specialists, however, prefer the two-sided application of dissimilarity since the first Christians were also Jewish.

Again, identifying Jesus traditions on the basis of this criterion does not disqualify other non-discontinuous traditions in which Jesus parallels his Palestinian Second Temple Jewish milieu. One would expect such parallels. Similarly, just because a particular tradition does not differ from the beliefs or practices of the first Christians does not, on that account, render it inauthentic. The criterion should be employed to increase the likelihood of a tradition rather than to exclude traditions, and what results from the dissimilarity is what is unique about Jesus but not necessarily what is characteristic. The results of this criterion must not become a grid by which to judge the remainder of the Jesus materials.[102]

With an awareness of the weaknesses of the criterion, Jesus's teaching on divorce and remarriage as adulterous is dissimilar to the Jewish Scriptures and Second Temple Judaism, with the likely exception of the Damascus Document. The teaching was dissimilar to that of the earliest Christians since they would qualify the prohibition against divorce (e.g., Matt 5:32; 1 Cor 7:12–16). This criterion would affirm a Jesus who had made an absolute statement against divorce and remarriage.

The Supposed Hillel-Shammai Debate

The previous chapter examined how the Jewish Scriptures and the broader Second Temple Jewish milieu understood divorce and remarriage—a background essential to the application of the criterion of discontinuity, but what of the later rab-

---

100. An objection raised already by Calvert, "Examination," 211; Hooker, "Christology and Methodology," 482; Hooker, "On Using the Wrong Tool," 575.

101. Thus Ben F. Meyer, *The Aims of Jesus* (London: SCM Press, 1979), 86; Holmén, "Doubts about Double Dissimilarity," 52–53; Holmén cites in support Hooker, "Christology and Methodology," 482, but Hooker explains that the same problems with reconstructing a full picture of Judaism to serve the dissimilarity criterion would also apply to reconstructing a full picture of early Christianity.

102. Thus Evans, "Authenticity Criteria," 26.

CHAPTER 2

binic materials and their potential for this criterion? The late second-century CE mishnaic tractate Giṭṭin discusses divorce documents and closes in 9:10 by discussing the grounds for divorce. Deuteronomy 24:1 posits "the shame of a thing" (*'erwat dābār*). The Mishnah claims that the house of Shammai had inverted the phrase to place emphasis on the word "shame" (*'erwat*). The wife who is to be divorced must have done something shameful. As Meier puts it: "Hence, contrary to what is claimed in many treatments of the subject, the House of Shammai does not limit the grounds of divorce to adultery. Any action that would bring shame upon her husband qualifies as grounds for divorce."[103] This would, of course, include adultery.[104] In contrast, the house of Hillel emphasized the word "thing" (*dābār*) of the phrase. In other words, *any* thing could be grounds for divorce. Rabbi Akiva therefore thought that finding a more beautiful woman could be grounds to divorce a wife. He justified his position with another phrase in Deut 24:1: "if she (the first wife) does not find favor [*ḥēn*]." The Hebrew word *ḥēn* used in Deut 24:1 can also be translated as "grace" or "beauty." Reading it as such, the house of Hillel, much like Philo and Josephus, considered virtually anything a ground for divorce.

The gospels do not identify differences in the Pharisaic position; they question Jesus on his divorce teaching, and he responds to them as a group. Josephus adheres to a generous Hillel-like position on divorce with no suggestion that there were other views. Further, for the Pharisees to have convinced Jesus to agree with one or the other subgroup would not have demonstrated their point that he was taking a position opposed to Moses, as they attempt in their other confrontations with him. Finally, the Jewish divorce rate in Judea is thought to have been around 4 percent.[105] In view of this low divorce rate, it would have been counterproductive for Hillelites arguing for a more generous divorce policy to get Jesus to agree with the more conservative Shammaites in order to discredit him.[106] That Jesus was being pressed by the Hillel position to side with the Shammai position does not seem obvious.

John Meier faults New Testament interpreters for not realizing that m. Giṭṭin is the first attestation in Jewish literature of a dispute over the proper grounds for divorce. "As far as datable documents are concerned, this is something startlingly new in Judaism."[107] Josephus, Philo, and Deuteronomy all presume the near abso-

---

103. Meier, *Law and Love*, 94.
104. For other Shammaite grounds for divorce, see their interpretation of Exod 21:10–11 in m. Ketub. 5:6; Instone-Brewer, "Jewish Greek and Aramaic Marriage," 235.
105. Joachim Jeremias, *Jerusalem in the Time of Jesus: An Investigation into Economic and Social Conditions during the New Testament Period* (Philadelphia: Fortress, 1969), 371.
106. William F. Luck, Sr., *Divorce and Re-Marriage: Recovering the Biblical View*, 2nd ed. (Richardson, TX: Biblical Studies Press, 2009), 152.
107. Meier, *Law and Love*, 95.

lute right for a husband to divorce his wife.[108] CD IV, 19–V, 9 condemns polygyny and likely also remarriage after divorce. Apart from Jesus, pre-70 CE Judaism provides no extant instance of a discussion concerning the sufficient grounds for a divorce. As Meier writes:

> Therefore, despite the almost universal tendency on the part of NT exegetes to explain Jesus' prohibition of divorce against the "background" of the debate between the House of Shammai and the House of Hillel, this tendency may actually be a prime example of the anachronistic use of later texts to explain earlier ones. That is, a text written down for the first time at the beginning of the 3d century A.D. (the Mishna) is called upon to elucidate a teaching of Jesus reaching back to the early part of the 1st century A.D., with written attestation in the 50s by Paul and ca. 70 by Mark. Considering the dearth of any clear attestation of the dispute over the grounds of divorce between the Houses in the pre-70 period, we would do well, at least initially, to explain Jesus' teaching on divorce solely in light of what is truly prior to and contemporary with the Palestinian Judaism of the 1st century A.D.[109]

Meier thus pleads for an interpretation of early Christianity in the light of contemporaneous or earlier documents, especially since those documents do not offer any hint of the debate in the later mishnaic texts. Meier's plea accords with Jacob Neusner's groundbreaking body of work: What cannot be demonstrated prior to 70 CE should not simply be assumed on the basis of later rabbinic sources.

Dissimilarity (Again) and a Reconstructed "Jesus" Teaching

The Jewish Scriptures and the Second Temple witnesses provide no precedent for a strict prohibition against divorce and remarriage, with the exception of the treatment of remarriage in CD IV, 21.[110] The "historical" Jesus's strict prohibition against divorce and remarriage is largely unparalleled in the Jewish Scriptures and within Second Temple Judaism. With Elledge, however, discontinuity is a difficult criterion

---

108. Instone-Brewer ("Jewish Greek and Aramaic Marriage," 235) mistakenly describes Hillel's "new ruling" as effectively giving men the same generous divorce rights as in Greek law. There is no evidence that Jewish men ever were lacking those rights.

109. Meier, *Law and Love*, 95. Among the many exegetes who assume that Second Temple Judaism fully accepted divorce but had debated the *grounds* for divorce, as attested by the Hillel-Shammai debate, see Hays, *Moral Vision*, 350; Wolfgang Schrage, *The Ethics of the New Testament*, trans. David E. Green (Philadelphia: Fortress, 1988), 94–95; R. Collins, *Divorce*, 74–75.

110. See the discussion of this text in chapter 1, pp. 45–52.

CHAPTER 2

in view of the *multiplicity* of Second Temple Jewish views.[111] The law of Moses accepted divorce as a reality and offered only a few restrictions in discrete instances. Early Jewish sources maintain that the husband's authority to divorce was virtually unlimited until the debate recorded in the Mishnah that may or may not reflect pre-70 CE realities. Even the stricter Shammai allowed divorce. As Meier explains:

> By completely forbidding divorce, Jesus dares to forbid what the Law allows—and not in some minor, obscure halakic observance but in one of the most important legal institutions in society. He dares to say that a man who duly follows the Law in properly divorcing his wife and marrying another woman is in effect committing adultery . . . nothing short of astounding. . . . That is, precisely by conscientiously following the Torah's rules for divorce and remarriage, a Jewish man commits a serious sin against one of the commandments of the Decalogue, the commandment against adultery (Exod 20:14; Deut 5:18).[112]

Jesus therefore opposed how mainstream Judaism before, during, and after his earthly ministry viewed divorce and remarriage.

The criterion of dissimilarity confirms the strict teaching of Jesus against divorce and remarriage. To conclude more broadly on the basis of historical Jesus research, *none* of the various historical Jesus criteria argues against the authenticity of this teaching in what is "perhaps the single best-attested teaching in what we call his *halaka.*"[113] This absolute prohibition in the teaching of Jesus is of the highest probability possible in this sort of endeavor. "Jesus absolutely forbade divorce and branded divorce and remarriage as the sin of adultery."[114] Divorce followed by remarriage is adulterous in Luke 16:18 // Mark 10:11. Mark 10:9 parallels 1 Cor 7:10–11 in forbidding divorce and maintains that, if a divorce takes place, a divorcée may not marry again.

Jesus Remembered

Reconstructing a "historical" Jesus is more art than science. With flawed and imperfect criteria, certainty is not possible, only greater probability.[115] Despite

---

111. Elledge, "From the Beginning," 389, reflecting on the multiplicity of views in the Dead Sea Scrolls.
112. Meier, *Law and Love*, 113.
113. Meier, *Law and Love*, 118.
114. Meier, *Law and Love*, 126.
115. For an expression of skepticism about the historical Jesus criteria, see Rafael Rodríguez, "Authenticating Criteria: The Use and Misuse of a Critical Method," *JSHJ* 7 (2009): 152–67.

his best efforts to peel away the Jesus traditions to an earliest core, John Meier observes: "The reader will have noticed that I have not offered an opinion as to what was *the* 'original saying' or *the* 'original form' of Jesus' prohibition of divorce."[116] Meier's analysis identifies *two* divorce and remarriage formulations in Q (Matt 5:32 // Luke 16:18): the first in Luke 16:18 (with or without the clause "and marries another") and the second, tentatively, in Matt 5:32 (without the exception clause).[117] From this, Meier concludes: "This astounding and shocking teaching of Jesus called forth a great deal of debate and questioning.... Jesus probably stated his prohibition a number of times, not necessarily always in the same words."[118]

Morna Hooker goes a step further: "Perhaps, then, we shall find the 'real' Jesus, not by seeking for the 'historical,' but—as some are now arguing—in looking at the 'memory' that he left."[119] Memories are always fastened to and framed by particular times and places, and Jesus was an itinerant preacher. He was *remembered* as teaching on divorce and remarriage on multiple occasions.[120] Historical Jesus traditions may not simply be excised from narrative recollections and representations of the *remembered* Jesus.[121] Pried from those narrative contexts, the traditions may well end up mutilated and distorted. Increasingly, historical Jesus specialists have had to reckon with memory.[122]

The founder of memory studies, the French sociologist Maurice Halbwachs (1877–1945), maintained that autobiographical memory (the past to which we have direct relation) is never simply an act of recall but a complex process of reconstructing the past in light of the needs of the present and within societal frameworks.[123]

---

116. Meier, *Law and Love*, 124.

117. Meier, *Law and Love*, 124.

118. Meier, *Law and Love*, 124.

119. Morna Hooker, "Foreword: Forty Years On," in *Jesus, Criteria, and the Demise of Authenticity*, ed. Chris Keith and Anthony Le Donne (London: T&T Clark, 2012), xv.

120. Time is always structured by social groups, and places by the groups that inhabit it; see Maurice Halbwachs, *The Collective Memory* (New York: Harper & Row, 1980), 134–40, 157; Gérard Namer, *Halbwachs et la mémoire sociale* (Paris: L'Harmattan, 2000), 50–51; Edward S. Casey, *Remembering: A Phenomenological Study* (Bloomington, IN: Indiana University Press, 1987), 189.

121. Elizabeth Tonkin, *Narrating Our Pasts: The Social Construction of Oral History*, Cambridge Studies in Oral and Literate Culture 22 (Cambridge: Cambridge University Press 1992), 6.

The recent emphasis on memory studies is not necessarily exclusive of an application of the authenticating criteria of Jesus research as *one stage* in tracking the memories of Jesus's followers of what happened—thus Le Donne, *Historiographical Jesus*, 5, 13, 88–91, esp. 91.

122. E.g., the section on social memory and orality in Warren Carter, "The Things of Caesar: Mark-ing the Plural (Mk 12:13–17)," *HvTSt* 70 (2014): art. 2656.

123. Maurice Halbwachs, "The Social Frameworks of Memory," in *On Collective Memory*, trans. Lewis A. Coser (Chicago: University of Chicago Press, 1992), 43; Halbwachs, *Collective Memory*. There is also Halbwachs's notion of collective memory in which the past forms later realities.

CHAPTER 2

Memory is always a social phenomenon and not purely individual. According to Halbwachs, "It is in society that people normally acquire their memories. It is also in society that they recall, recognize, and localize their memories."[124] He further explains: "All individual remembering . . . takes place with social materials, within social contexts, and in response to social cues. Even when we do it alone, we do so as social beings with reference to our social identities."[125] A negotiation must take place between past events making their impressions and the contemporary circumstances of individuals in their social groups and circumstances.[126] Individual and collective memory are closely linked in their interactions and mutual influences.

Building on Halbwachs's work, Frederic Charles Bartlett offers a concrete illustration of social frames and cultural schemes shaping individual memory and communication of that memory.[127] In his most famous experiment, British test subjects were told an exotic, indigenous North American fairy tale, the War of the Ghosts. The subjects then had to retell the story, in some cases serially as in the telephone game (chain transmission), and in other cases repeatedly over time (repeated reproduction). As Bartlett observes, "In this process, particularly the exotic names and narrative turns, which were foreign to the local narrative conventions, disappeared, and the stories were revised to fit the sociocultural frames and linguistic and stylistic conventions of the test subjects."[128] Even more, the test subjects *did not remember* and thus did not pass on the culturally unfamiliar elements they heard as they adapted the stories to their own cultural context. Later studies have confirmed how sociocultural frames at a point in time and space operate as structural matrices for processing information while remembering.[129]

Recent work on memory from a psychological perspective has further confirmed Halbwach's social memory thesis. Human memory is not as much passive storing and recall as it is a constructive cognitive faculty that reduces the

---

124. Halbwachs, "Social Frameworks," 38.

125. Halbwachs, as explained by Jeffrey K. Olick, "Products, Processes, and Practices: A Non-Reificatory Approach to Collective Memory," *BTB* 36 (2006): 11.

126. Samuel Byrskog, "Memory and Narrative—and Time: Toward a Hermeneutics of Memory," *JSHJ* 16 (2018): 112–13.

127. F. C. Bartlett, *Remembering: A Study in Experimental and Social Psychology* (1932; repr., Cambridge: Cambridge University Press, 1995), 65, 125–29. Note the reflection and critique of these sorts of experiments in Alan Kirk, "Ehrman, Bauckham, and Bird on Memory and the Jesus Tradition," *JSHJ* 15 (2017): 91–92, 96–97.

128. Sandra Huebenthal, *Reading Mark's Gospel as a Text from Collective Memory* (Grand Rapids: Eerdmans, 2020), 101.

129. Erving Goffman, *Frame Analysis: An Essay on the Organization of Experience* (New York: Harper & Row, 1974): 11–12; Harald Welzer, *Das kommunikative Gedächtnis: Eine Theorie der Erinnerung* (Munich: Beck, 2002), 186–87.

complexity and details in what was witnessed by generalizing, abstracting, and assembling. Memories are conformed "to genre types and narrative patterns that have achieved conventional status within a culture. Besides bestowing durability and mnemonic efficiency, this encoding in conventional forms renders memories communicable, able to be externalized into the social world."[130] Memory is therefore active and constructive. It "economizes and condenses, selecting from the undifferentiated flux of experience what is most salient."[131]

Some have questioned whether the historical Jesus endeavor is even possible in view of the critique from memory studies.[132] Whereas John Dominic Crossan saw the aim of historical Jesus research as getting at what Jesus actually said or did, memory theorists point out that one can, at best, uncover an *earlier* memory of what Jesus said and did as remembered by his early followers.[133] The multiple attestation criterion only points to earlier memories. Why would a "dissimilar" Jesus who was utterly unlike his fellow Jews and first followers, ever have been remembered?[134] Gospel scholars prioritize the memories of the eyewitnesses over later Christian tradition, and yet one simply cannot pry away later "traditions," feelings, values, and literary contexts to isolate an earlier, pristine recollection of the events. As Richard Horsley warns, isolating sayings from their contexts discards the primary guide to how that saying functioned for the ancient hearers. "With

---

130. Alan Kirk, *Memory and the Jesus Tradition*, The Reception of the Jesus Tradition in the First Three Centuries 2 (London: T&T Clark, 2018), 39, 185, drawing on, especially, Bartlett, *Remembering*, 126–27; Larry R. Squire and Eric R. Kandel, *Memory: From Mind to Molecules* (New York: Scientific American Library, 1999), 46, 206. Ironically, memories are formed in a process that also involves forgetting; see Casey, *Remembering*, 284, 291.

131. Alan Kirk, "Memory," in *Jesus in Memory: Traditions in Oral and Scribal Perspectives*, ed. Werner H. Kelber and Samuel Byrskog (Waco, TX: Baylor University Press, 2009), 166.

132. E.g., Jens Schröter, "The Historical Jesus and the Sayings Tradition: Comments on Current Research," *Neot* 30 (1996): 151–68: "It is a serious question whether they [the early Christian writings] permit a reconstruction of what is called 'the historical Jesus'" (152). The wedge between "Jesus" and "Christ" "is not without problems because it presupposes that we can have a more appropriate approach to Jesus than the early Christian writings themselves had" (154). See the fuller expression of Jens Schröter's thinking in his *Erinnerung an Jesu Worte: Studien zur Rezeption der Logienüberlieferung in Markus, Q, und Thomas*, WMANT 76 (Neukirchen-Vluyn: Neukirchener, 1997).

133. John Dominic Crossan *The Historical Jesus: The Life of a Mediterranean Jewish Peasant* (New York: HarperCollins, 1991), xxxi, as critiqued by Werner Kelber, "The Works of Memory: Christian Origins as MnemoHistory—A Response," in *Memory, Tradition, and Text: Uses of the Past in Early Christianity*, ed. Alan Kirk and Tom Thatcher, SemeiaSt 52 (Atlanta: Society of Biblical Literature, 2005), 235–39.

134. Richard A. Horsley, "Prominent Patterns in the Social Memory of Jesus and Friends," in Kirk and Thatcher, *Memory, Tradition, and Text*, 66.

CHAPTER 2

no ancient guide for its meaning-context, then, interpretation is determined only, and almost completely, by the modern scholar, who constructs a new meaning-context on the basis of other such radically decontextualized sayings."[135]

The exact relationship between the individual's ability to remember and collective memory is disputed.[136] Memories will fade if they are not taken up by the groups of which an individual is part, but that collective memory is itself a construction. Some, following Halbwachs himself, are quite skeptical of the accuracy of memories of historical events (a movement called presentism). Alan Kirk explains: "Memory formations, however, do not thereby assume static, immobile forms. The activity of memory in articulating the past is dynamic, unceasing, *because it is wired into the ever-shifting* present. The remembering subject, from his or her situatedness in the present, interacts with a formative past to relate it meaningfully to contemporary exigencies and to the ongoing project of negotiating continuity and change in personal identity."[137] Social memory is *constructed*.

The gospels themselves bear witness to the need for memories to be constructed. Mark's Jesus asks that the disciples remain silent about certain events they have seen and heard in his earthly ministry until after they have also witnessed his suffering, death, and resurrection (9:9). They cannot serve as witnesses to these events in the earthly ministry until they have seen what will take place later. That later series of events will serve as the necessary context for recalling his earthly ministry. Jesus in John 2, after cleansing the temple, claims that he will rebuild the destroyed temple in three days. John nods to the reader that the disciples (collectively) *remembered* that he had said this and understood only after Jesus was risen from the dead (2:22). Again, a later context in time was necessary to understand rightly what Jesus had been saying and doing, and it was *that* understanding that was inscribed and rendered more permanent in the written gospel texts—a Jesus remembered and understood from *that* standpoint. The *Spirit* must bring to the disciples' remembrance what Jesus had taught (John 14:26). The gospels stress a necessary context for remembering properly.

Is social memory, then, *entirely* a social construction (or even fabrication) as the presentists claim? Others emphasize how the social aspect of memory enables it to *transcend* the individual and identify a stable core, what is called the *continuity* perspective.[138] Gospel scholar Chris Keith adopts this perspective in claiming

---

135. Horsley, "Prominent Patterns," 63.
136. See, e.g., Paul Ricoeur, *Memory, History, Forgetting* (Chicago: University of Chicago Press, 2004), 120–24. Individuals can place themselves in differing remembering communities.
137. Alan Kirk, "Social and Cultural Memory," in Kirk and Thatcher, *Memory, Tradition, and Text*, 10.
138. For examples of each approach, see the overview of Chris Keith, "Memory and Authenticity: Jesus Tradition and What Really Happened," *ZNW* 102 (2011): 169.

that the past *is not completely rewritable* and can set the course for its own commemoration.[139] Barry Schwartz likewise stresses a stable core in the memory of the past.[140] He faults Halbwachs for undermining established beliefs through a "pejorative" understanding of collective memory.[141] "Gospel writers inscribed... what informants led them to understand."[142] The gospel writers were *informed* by, indeed *constrained* by, the first witnesses.[143] Despite the gentile Christ-believers in the early movement, no one conveniently "remembered" Jesus as saying that circumcision was not necessary for them. True history is never a matter of indifference.[144] "Even though the past is regularly reconstructed this is done within limits, stopped by the hard edges of resistance the past provides."[145]

One should not dismiss *any* of the gospel traditions since there would have been varying perceptions among the eyewitnesses, leading to varying accounts.[146] Eyewitness memories remain stubbornly normative and constraining on later traditions. The multiple traditions attesting to Jesus's teaching on divorce and remarriage evince a stable core in the memories of the community while, at the same time, include peripheral elements that vary from text to text.[147] Again, historical research must always account for continuity in the midst of contingent expressions.[148] While Jesus's strict prohibition of divorce and remarriage is as certain as anything referenced in endeavors to reconstruct a "historical" Jesus, more importantly, his teaching made *a strong impression* in the memories of his followers. Paul's allusive appeal and unusual deference to the words of the

---

139. Keith, "Memory and Authenticity," 169.

140. Barry Schwartz, "Social Change and Collective Memory: The Democratization of George Washington," *American Sociological Review* 56 (1991): 221–36.

141. Barry Schwartz, "Christian Origins: Historical Truth and Social Memory," in Kirk and Thatcher, *Memory, Tradition, and Text*, 49.

142. Schwartz, "Christian Origins," 50.

143. Schwartz, "Christian Origins," 55.

144. Schwartz, "Christian Origins," 56. With Rafael Rodríguez: "Recalling the past, then, construes and structures historical 'facts' to make them meaningful and relevant in the present. It does so, however, within certain constraints, including the pressure exerted by previous conceptualizations of the past, both of which figure in the 'stable core' that resists restructuring at the whims of present interests." See *Structuring Early Christian Memory: Jesus in Tradition, Performance and Text*, LNTS 407 (London: T&T Clark, 2010), 62.

145. Michael Schudson, *Watergate in American Memory: How We Remember, Forget, and Reconstruct the Past* (New York: Basic, 1992), 207.

146. Keith, "Memory and Authenticity," 176.

147. Schwartz, "Social Change and Collective Memory," 221–36; Rodríguez, *Structuring Early Christian Memory*, 62.

148. Schudson, *Watergate in American Memory*, 3, 207; Rodríguez, *Structuring Early Christian Memory*, 62.

CHAPTER 2

Lord in 1 Cor 7:10–11 attest to that impression and the teaching's currency in early Christianity.[149]

Those who remember associate events with spatial settings and times since memory is always referential, temporal, and *narratival*.[150] The mind organizes events and occurrences into frames of meaning through narrative, and those frames are culturally derived and shared.[151] In other words, one cannot isolate a Jesus "behind" the gospels from the narratival recollections and settings provided by the gospel authors themselves.[152] In being integrated into a narrative, "events" become definite and meaningful.[153] Events bear meaning in connection with other events. The narrative's beginning, middle, and culmination entail reflection on the meaning of the event. Groups, such as Mark or Luke's respective communities, formed their identity through shared narratives and rituals that conveyed the significance of what their communities remembered.[154] As a recent social memory commentator on Mark has shown, a respect for social memory must respect and take seriously the narratives of those who were remembering.[155]

The Mark 10:2–12 Memory of Jesus in Narratival Context

Modern biblical scholarship has rightly stressed that the gospels were narrating the story of Jesus for specific communities and audiences. Matthew was writing for a law-observant Jewish audience that had split from their mainstream peers

---

149. Ciampa and Rosner, *First Letter to the Corinthians*, 292; following Dunn, *1 Corinthians*, 101: "He [Paul] only cites it [a word from the Lord] because he is qualifying it, whereas the allusion implies an accepted authority."

150. Byrskog, "Memory and Narrative," 118; cf. Eusebius's report of Irenaeus recalling what Polycarp looked like, his mannerisms and expressions, and where he was teaching, which served as mnemonic cues as Polycarp relayed the Jesus tradition (*Hist. eccl.* 5.20.5–7).

151. Donald E. Polkinghorne, "Narrative Psychology and Historical Consciousness: Relationships and Perspectives," in *Narration, Identity, and Historical Consciousness: The Psychological Construction of Time and History*, ed. Jürgen Straub (New York: Berghan, 2005), 5, 7.

152. Byrskog, "Memory and Narrative," 123.

153. Jürgen Straub, "Telling Stories, Making History: Toward a Narrative Psychology of the Historical Construction of Meaning," in Straub, *Narration, Identity, and Historical Consciousness*, 69–70.

154. Angela Keppler, *Tischgespräche: Über Formen kommunikativer Vergesellschaftung am Beispiel der Konversation in Familien*, 2nd ed. (Frankfurt: Suhrkamp, 1995), 28; Olick, "Products, Processes, and Practices," 6; Jerome S. Bruner, "Past and Present as Narrative Constructions," in Straub, *Narration, Identity, and Historical Consciousness*, 40.

155. Huebenthal, *Reading Mark's Gospel*. The book includes a substantive foreword by Werner H. Kelber surveying the new discipline as of 2020.

in following and worshiping the Christ. Mark's gentile audience had little need or interest to observe the cleanliness rituals of the Jewish law. The collection of the four gospels into a literary corpus would come later. The interpreter must conceptualize how these stories functioned for their first hearers. As Mark wrote for his target audience, that audience would not possess Matthew's Gospel, which in all likelihood would be penned later and in dependence on Mark.[156] The first readers of Mark would have read 10:11-12 as an absolute prohibition: "Whoever divorces his wife and marries another commits adultery against her; and if she divorces her husband and marries another, she commits adultery."[157] To marry another person after a divorce is adultery.[158] The prohibition of remarriage alongside the forbidding of divorce would have been utterly countercultural and striking to the

---

156. Matthew's changes to Mark follow discrete and understandable patterns, whereas if Mark were changing Matthew a rationale for adaptation is much harder to discern, if at all. For instance, it makes little sense that Mark, who repeatedly stresses Jesus as a great teacher (e.g., Mark 1:21-22; 4:1; 6:2; 10:1), would omit the most memorable teaching in Matthew. That Matthew was supplementing Mark's claim is more likely.

157. The second statement (v. 12) reads in the most likely original version of the text: καὶ ἐὰν αὐτὴ ἀπολύσασα τὸν ἄνδρα αὐτῆς γαμήσῃ ἄλλον μοιχᾶται "and if she divorces her husband and marries another, she commits adultery" (ℵ B C L). The latest three editions of Nestle-Aland likewise adopt this reading. The majority text (with A K N Γ) reads: καὶ ἐὰν γυνὴ ἀπολύσῃ τὸν ἄνδρα αὐτῆς καὶ γαμηθῇ ἄλλῳ μοιχᾶται "and if a woman divorces her husband and is married to another, she commits adultery." This alternative reading agrees with the first in meaning. A third reading (D f^{13} Θ) is: καὶ ἐὰν γυνὴ ἐξέλθῃ ἀπὸ τοῦ ἀνδρὸς καὶ γαμήσῃ ἄλλον μοιχᾶται "and if a woman departs from her husband and marries another, she commits adultery." This third reading appears to be a correction or softening of the first on the basis of Matt 19:9 and Luke 16:18: It was customary for Jewish men to divorce their wives but not the reverse. One possible construal of the third reading envisions the wife separating from her husband (thus the change in verb) but not a divorce since the wife could not initiate a divorce. Separation in antiquity, however, *was* a divorce, just not a documented divorce; see the discussion of this point in chapter 1, pp. 29-33; cf. Jacques Dupont, *Mariage et divorce dans l'Évangile: Matthieu 19,3-12 et parallèles* (Abbaye de Saint-André: Desclée de Brouwer, 1959), 63.

158. Andrew Cornes, *Divorce and Remarriage: Biblical Principles and Pastoral Practice* (Grand Rapids: Eerdmans, 1993), 193-94:

> It is sometimes said that because most Jews of Jesus' day clearly believed that legal divorce conferred the right to remarry, Jesus would have had to make it very clear if he meant to say that legal divorce was permissible under certain circumstances (Matt. 5:32; 19:9) but that it did not destroy the marriage bond and that therefore remarriage was out of the question. This is a valid point, but it is precisely what Jesus did do in calling remarriage 'adultery.' . . . Contemporary Jewish thinking was wrong: 'full' divorce—in the sense of destroying the marriage bond and opening the way for remarriage—is impossible.

Jesus's claim here is quite shocking.

hearer, since divorce was commonly viewed as freeing the partners to remarry.[159] Jesus did not allow for this, and the teaching in these two verses offered no exceptions for Mark's first hearers.[160] The question is how that teaching would conform to Mark's larger narrative.

Mark 10:1–12 is the first in a series of pericopes that addresses families and households: divorce and remarriage in vv. 1–12, children in vv. 13–16, property in vv. 17–22, and families, households, and farms in vv. 23–31.[161] After the change of setting in Mark 10:1, the Pharisees ask Jesus in 10:2: "Is it lawful for a man to divorce his wife?" This is a peculiar question since Jesus's contemporaries did not question the legitimacy of divorce.[162] Some interpreters have speculated that Jesus was being invited to weigh in on a controversy regarding divorce certificates that rabbinic sources trace to the first century. Interest in divorce certificates was current in Jesus's day, and Jesus responds to the Pharisees' question by turning to them.[163] The first-century teachers Hillel and Shammai had allegedly debated when those certificates would be legitimate, that is, when a man may *legitimately* divorce a wife (m. Giṭ. 9:10).

To interpret Mark 10:1–12 in light of the Hillel-Shammai debate introduces its own set of problems. First, Jacob Neusner stresses in his famous dictum: "What we cannot show, we do not know."[164] Specialists now agree that later rabbinic claims about the pre-70 CE landscape should not be taken at face value apart from corroborating evidence from the Second Temple Period itself. First-century sources do not confirm this debate. Second, and more importantly, the Pharisees posed to Jesus a very *different* question. They did not ask about *which* divorces should

---

159. Even Instone-Brewer (*Divorce and Remarriage*, 148) recognizes that this text (and its gospel parallels) "charges a person who remarries with the very specific crime of 'adultery' which a remarried person is not guilty of in any known legal system." He skirts the implications of this verse and its parallels by inserting consistently the word "invalidly" so as to read "invalidly divorces" in each instance (149–52, 169); if only Jesus had actually said that and not repeatedly conveyed an apparently absolute prohibition.

160. The strict prohibition is clear even in severe redactional investigations; see Heikki Sariola, "Streit um die Ehescheidung (10:2–12)," in *Markus und das Gesetz: Eine redaktionskritische Untersuchung*, Annales Academie Scientarum Fennicae Dissertationes Humanarum Litterarum 56 (Helsinki: Suomalainen Tidedeakatemia, 1990), 121–49.

161. John H. Elliott, "The Jesus Movement Was Not Egalitarian but Family-Oriented," *BibInt* 11.2 (2003): 199–200; John R. Donahue, *The Theology and Setting of Discipleship in the Gospel of Mark* (Milwaukee: Marquette University Press, 1983), 37–46.

162. See chapter 1, pp. 22–23; also Meier, *Law and Love*, 121.

163. See chapter 1, pp. 23–25.

164. Jacob Neusner, *Rabbinic Literature and the New Testament: What We Cannot Show We Do Not Know* (Valley Forge, PA: Trinity Press International, 1994).

be considered legitimate. They asked whether divorce *itself* was legitimate. Such a question would make sense if Jesus had taught about divorce on other occasions. Since Jesus appeared to be rejecting divorce absolutely, an unprecedented position in their day, the Pharisees wanted to ask him about this teaching.[165] Such an understanding is rendered likely, with a sideways glance, given the very different settings of Jesus's strict teaching on divorce and remarriage in the other gospels. The Pharisees therefore asked the question to test (πειράζω) him since they viewed him as teaching against the law of Moses.[166]

As Mark's Jesus tackles the topic of divorce and remarriage in the context of a controversy with the Pharisees, that controversy would call to mind several earlier incidents in the gospel. By this point in the Markan narrative, the reader has already encountered a series of controversies with the Jewish leadership, and especially the Pharisees in 2:1–3:6 (and will again in 11:27–12:37). In Mark 7:1–13 Jesus debates with the Pharisees over their human tradition of washing hands before meals. The divorce discussion was not, then, the first (or last) confrontation with the Pharisees. They were trying to entrap Jesus.

The Pharisees ask about the legality or permissibility (ἔξεστιν) of divorce (10:2), but Jesus does not answer with a simple affirmative. He responds with a question of his own: "What did Moses *command* you?" (v. 3). Was he rejecting divorce? The Pharisees respond to Jesus's apparent denial of divorce by pointing to the divorce certificates that Moses in Deut 24:1–4 had *allowed* (v. 4).[167] That passage had presupposed divorce in prohibiting a man from remarrying his divorced wife after she had married another. Jesus, however, had asked about Moses's *command*. The ad hominem censure of v. 5 is not unexpected: "Because of your hardness of heart he wrote this commandment for you." Jesus had confronted their hardened hearts before (Mark 3:5; cf. 8:17). Those familiar with the Jewish Scriptures would recognize that hardening is a stubborn refusal to hear and obey God's will, even as Pharaoh had hardened his heart against God in refusing to allow the Israelites their freedom (Exod 8:15, 32). More pertinent, however, is the reference to hardened hearts in Jer 4:4 LXX shortly after the appeal to Judah in Jer 3 to heed the warning of God's divorcing Israel. Jeremiah 3:1 opens with an allusion to Deut 24:1–4: God divorced Israel because of her unrepentant adultery (Jer 3:3, 13, 17, 20). Ironically, the God of Jeremiah reserves the right to forgive the unfaithful spouse should she repent, even though the Pharisees would in these instances

---

165. With Meier, *Law and Love*, 121.

166. Hays, *Moral Vision*, 350.

167. On the commandment/prescription versus permission dynamic, see Dupont, *Mariage*, 17, 33; Hays, *Moral Vision*, 350; Meier, *Law and Love*, 122.

CHAPTER 2

require divorce.[168] Jesus claimed that it was precisely because of the Pharisees' own hardness that Moses had issued his permission.

Moses had permitted divorce to take place because of the people's unfaithfulness, but Jesus appeals to a different commandment:

> But from the beginning of creation, "God made them male and female." For this reason a man shall leave his father and mother and be joined to his wife, and the two shall become one flesh. So they are no longer two, but one flesh. Therefore what God has joined together, let no one separate. (Mark 10:6–9)

Jesus locates God's will and command not in Deut 24:1–2 but rather in Gen 1–2. God created humans as male and female (Gen 1:27), and so the man leaves his father and mother to cleave to his wife as the two become one flesh (2:24). Sexual intercourse seals the bond of that one flesh. In Mark 10:9 Jesus rewords the Genesis verse he had just cited: "Therefore what God has joined together [συνέζευξεν], let no one separate [χωριζέτω; cf. 1 Cor 7:10–16]." Literally, what *God* joins together, a *human being* (ἄνθρωπος) is not to separate. The Greek verb "let no one separate" (χωριζέτω) is a third-person imperative with its usual imperatival force. Divorce is therefore contrary to God's will that husband and wife not be separated. Jesus takes God's original will and command in creation as the starting point for any discussion of divorce. That original intent trumps the later concession. The Pharisees in their hardness of heart were overturning God's original intention and command.

Mark notes a pattern in these controversies: Jesus says or does something that causes controversy or puzzlement, at which point he typically offers further instruction on the matter in a private setting (e.g., 4:1–9 followed by 4:10–20; 7:14–15 followed by 7:17–23; 9:14–27 followed by 9:28–29). In this particular instance, Jesus had been teaching the disciples privately in Galilee (9:30–31, 33). He then journeyed to the region beyond the Jordan (Perea) and into Judea, and in Judea the crowds are once again a factor (10:1). Jesus's debate with the Pharisees over divorce in that public setting (10:2–9) thus leads to private teaching to the disciples on the subject in 10:10–12. Here the disciples "again" (πάλιν) return to what Jesus had said to the Pharisees.[169]

---

168. Instone-Brewer, *Divorce and Remarriage*, 145–46.
169. "Again" is Markan (twenty-eight of the forty-eight instances in the Synoptic Gospels). The word appears five times in Matthew where he is dependent on Mark, and Luke has it once in a place dependent on Mark; see R. Collins, *Divorce*, 277 n. 222; Frans Neirynck and Frans van

Mark reserves what is of particular importance for private instruction away from the ears of crowds and opponents. The spatial setting of this teaching is important. As Jesus says in Mark 4:11: "To you has been given the secret of the kingdom of God, but for those outside, everything comes in parables." Then in 4:34: "He did not speak to them except in parables, but he explained everything in private to his disciples." Often this private instruction takes place in a house (7:17; 9:28, 33; 10:10). Such private settings reinforce that the teaching is for them. Jesus may teach enigmatically on the outside, but on the inside or in private with the disciples he is clear.[170] Only they will be enabled to understand and to practice what he teaches (Mark 8:22–26, see below).

Jesus's private instruction in the wake of disagreements is also in keeping with Mark's secrecy motif signaling teaching of the utmost importance for the disciples themselves and thus for Mark's community (e.g., Mark 4:10–12).[171] Although Jesus does not directly answer the Pharisees' question about the lawfulness of a man's divorcing his wife with a simple "yes" or "no," answering their question with another question, Jesus returns to that very matter in vv. 10–12 once the Pharisees are no longer on the scene. He shifts the question from the husband divorcing his wife to human beings separating what God has joined: "Whoever divorces his wife and marries another commits adultery against her; and if she divorces her husband and marries another, she commits adultery."[172] As Meier notes, "Rhetorically, the combination of the concise apodictic command in v 9 and the two-part casuistic law in vv 11–12 delivers a two-punch 'knock-out' blow."[173] According to Richard

---

Segbroeck, *New Testament Vocabulary: A Companion Volume to the Concordance*, BETL 65 (Leuven: Leuven University Press, 1984), 300. Here it functions presumptively to link the conversation in the house to the preceding events outside.

170. Heth and Wenham, *Jesus and Divorce*, 53.

171. For a concise survey of the Markan motif, see John T. Carroll, *Jesus and the Gospels: An Introduction* (Louisville: Westminster John Knox, 2016), 70–72.

172. For an alternative text-critical reconstruction, see Robert Herron Jr. "Mark's Jesus on Divorce: Mark 10:1–12 Reconsidered," *JETS* 25.3 (1982): 277–79. It does not impact the substantive issues in any major way. The woman would not be divorcing her husband with the variant reading, which is in agreement with general Jewish practice. The variant, if original, had been Hellenized by scribes into the wife's divorcing her husband. In Mark 6, then, Herodias would be at fault for having divorced her husband to marry another; so also William L. Lane, *The Gospel according to Mark*, NICNT (Grand Rapids: Eerdmans, 1974), 352 n. 5, 358. Herron ("Mark's Jesus on Divorce," 281) also notes the conspicuous setting of Jesus's discussion with the Pharisees and Herodians as he crossed over the Jordan into Perea, the territory of Herod Antipas. This is where John the Baptist had met his demise at the hands of the Herodians.

173. Meier, *Law and Love*, 123, who believes that even if the passage bears Markan features,

CHAPTER 2

Hays, "Once marriage is construed within the story told by Scripture, divorce—even if it is permissible in some narrow sense—is seen to be antithetical to God's design for male and female."[174]

Jesus's private teaching to the disciples reaches beyond the divorce to a subsequent remarriage. "The implication here is that the divorce by itself would not constitute adultery; it is the remarriage that does that."[175] In yet another surprising twist in v. 11, the husband who divorces his wife and marries another commits adultery "against her." In Jewish thought adultery was an offense against another *man* since that man's wife had been taken from him and violated.[176] As a sin of property, adultery could only be against a man since the husband was not the sexual property of his wife. Jesus "not only forbade the man to divorce his wife, but also gave her a permanent and indissoluble claim on him as her sexual property."[177] The two are so intimately united by marriage as to enjoy equal rights to the other. As Hays concludes: "Thus, Mark 10:11 is not merely a standard halakic ruling: it is a stunning reversal of convention that demands a rethinking of the character of marriage and the power of relations between husbands and wives."[178]

Usually scholars attribute the wife's divorcing of the husband in 10:12 to Mark's rephrasing for a Greco-Roman audience what in Jewish society was typically only male-initiated. On the other hand, Jesus's restatement in terms of the *wife's* initiating divorce may be intended to reinforce the sense of an equal union in marriage. Thus the man sins "against her" when the former wife remains alive.[179] Likewise, the remarrying woman sins "against him," her former husband. Husbands and wives remain responsible to their former partners despite the bill of divorce (*gēṭ*, lit. "cutting"). Divorce does not entirely sunder or "cut" the obligations to a former spouse.

Some would limit Jesus's teaching here to a situation in which a person divorced *with the intention of* remarrying, but Jesus's wording in Mark 10:11–12 does

---

an actual historical dispute between Jesus and the Pharisees lies behind the story and that Mark 10:9 need not be a creation of the later "Hellenistic" church.

174. Hays, *Moral Vision*, 351.
175. Meier, *Law and Love*, 121.
176. L. William Countryman, *Dirt, Greed and Sex: Sexual Ethics in the New Testament and Their Implications for Today* (Philadelphia: Fortress, 1988), 147–67, esp. 157–59, 175; followed by Hays, *Moral Vision*, 351.
177. Countryman, *Dirt, Greed and Sex*, 175.
178. Hays, *Moral Vision*, 351.
179. The examples of Salome and Herodias show that Mark 10:12 could be understood in the context of Palestinian society (see 1 Cor 7:11a), but this was not usual; thus Josephus, *Ant.* 15.7.10 §§259–260; 18.5.4 §136.

not mention that intent.[180] Jesus simply says in v. 11: "whoever divorce his wife *and* marries another commits adultery" (NRSV). Mark (or Jesus) could easily have rendered the intent to remarry clear by connecting the verbs with an explicit purpose clause (i.e., "in order to"). The "and" Mark uses is a regular feature in the Synoptic texts. In Semitic languages, the coordination of verbs places emphasis on the *second* verb (note the same phenomenon in Luke 16:18). Legal statements typically provide the circumstances in the first verb(s) with the decisive point coming with the final verb. Peter therefore asks Jesus in Matt 18:21—to translate the question more literally—"how often will my brother (or sister) sin against me and I forgive him (or her)?" Peter is not asking about how many times the brother or sister will sin but rather how many times he is to forgive. The sinning in the first verb is simply setting the stage for the second verb of forgiving: How many times must Peter forgive? Likewise in Mark 10:4 the Pharisees claim that Moses gave permission to give a bill of separation and to divorce. The permission pertains to the act of divorce, that is, the *second* verb. The first verb provides the condition for the second. If someone who has divorced his wife marries another, he commits adultery.[181] Thus in Mark 10:11 (and Luke 16:18, for that matter) the focus of Jesus's prohibition is on the act of remarriage after the divorce. Remarriage is an act of adultery.

At the same time, this grammatical stress on remarriage in Mark 10:11–12 is necessary to guarantee that the reader does not miss the point, despite the divorce and its certificate celebrating "freedom." What motivated this line of reasoning was the Pharisees' initial question whether *divorce* was permissible. Jesus answered that God's will in creation is for one man to be united to one woman. A divorce would violate God's will and thus be adulterous. Jesus and the Pharisees had not been talking about remarriage. In the ensuing conversation with the disciples in private, he emphasizes the sin of adulterous remarriage. As Descamps states, "if for Mark, verses 11–12 condemn remarriage, not divorce, are we not to

---

180. Hays, *Moral Vision*, 352: "The other way of reading Mark 10:11–12 is to interpret it as a restatement of verse 9: whoever divorces in order to remarry (the normal procedure) commits adultery, so divorce should be renounced altogether in the first place. This interpretation has the advantage of providing greater internal continuity in Mark 10. It is likely that Mark has taken a traditional saying of Jesus (cf. Matt 5:31–32, Luke 16:18) forbidding remarriage after divorce and radicalized its implications by placing it in conjunction with the controversy story of verses 2–9." Thus Hays interprets the prohibition of remarriage after divorce as likely being the original version of Jesus's teaching that Mark then contextualized in relation to a prohibition against divorce itself (which naturally leads to forbidden remarriage).

181. Note also Matt 9:14. See Dupont, *Mariage*, 17–18, 65–66; followed by Heth and Wenham, *Jesus and Divorce*, 48.

CHAPTER 2

extend this interpretation to verses 2–9? But how can verses 2–9 be understood to refer only to a condemnation of remarriage, if remarriage is not directly at issue there?"[182] One must conclude, then, that *both* divorce (in vv. 2–9) *and* remarriage (in vv. 11–12) are adulterous. Both are contrary to God's will for the one man and the one woman.[183]

The narratival context of Mark 10:9–11 is not just Mark 10 but includes the setting within this section of the gospel. Mark does address matters of divorce and remarriage earlier in his story, and the matter was indeed politically charged. In Mark 6:17–29 John the Baptist speaks against Herod Antipas's marriage to his brother's wife Herodias (6:18). Such a marriage would contravene Lev 18:16's command: "You shall not uncover the nakedness of your brother's wife; it is your brother's nakedness." In Lev 20:21: "If a man takes his brother's wife, it is impurity; he has uncovered his brother's nakedness; they shall be childless." John therefore speaks against the immorality in Herod's marrying his brother's wife. As a result, Herodias nurses a grudge against John and manages to receive permission to have his head served on a platter. After John the Baptist meets his demise, Jesus is then confronted with a similar, volatile question. The Leviticus texts on incest, however, are not at issue in the more general discussion of Mark 10:2–12.[184] Mark reflects the same Herodias incident that Josephus describes (*Ant.* 18.6.4 §§161–167). Of greater import is the placement of Mark 10:2–11 in this section of the gospel.

To place 10:2–12 within its larger context, Mark 8:27–10:45 is a discrete section sandwiched between the healing of two blind men. The first blind man (8:22–26)

---

182. A. L. Descamps, "The New Testament Doctrine on Marriage," in *Contemporary Perspectives on Christian Marriage: Propositions and Papers from the International Theological Commission*, ed. Richard Malone and John R. Connery (Chicago: Loyola University Press, 1984), 226.

183. Descamps, "New Testament Doctrine," 228: "[W]e discern in Jesus' saying a twofold revolution against accepted custom: first, the Jews permitted divorce, hence remarriage; second, the Jews would never think of equating remarriage by the man with adultery." The passage is deeply and directly countercultural.

184. Herron, "Mark's Jesus on Divorce," 276–77, who writes that the issue with Herodias entailed "the lawfulness of divorce and remarriage," but Mark himself signals that the issue was with marriage to the brother's wife. Herron relies on Josephus here (*Ant.* 18.5.4 §136): "Herodias took upon her to confound the laws of our country, and divorce herself from her husband, while he was alive, and was married to Herod [Antipas], her husband's brother by her father's side." Violation of the Levitical laws is most likely assumed by Josephus as well, since he does not elsewhere indicate any qualms about divorce and remarriage.

At a minimum, the Herodians would be predisposed against anyone connected with John the Baptist. Herron's reading, of course, gains greater plausibility if the textual variant is taken as original so that Herodias's divorcing of her husband to marry another was itself scandalous—thus Herron's attention to the text-critical matters.

is healed in two stages. After the first stage of the healing, the man does not yet see clearly, and Jesus completes the healing in a second stage. At the other end of the section in 10:46–52, Bartimaeus, the second blind man, praises Jesus as the "Son of David." After the healing of his blindness, Bartimaeus follows Jesus "on the way," just as the disciples had been doing. Both healings, then, bear implications for the disciples. The disciples are to follow Jesus "on the way," and Jesus must miraculously enable the disciples to see and to follow, especially since he had just criticized them in Mark 8:18 for being blind. At this point in the narrative, they only see in part. Miraculous, clear sight must await the events of Jesus's death and resurrection (cf. 8:31; 9:31; 10:33–34; 16:7).[185]

Sandwiched between these two healings are three parallel subsections that, not surprisingly, concern discipleship. In each subsection, Jesus tells his disciples that he must suffer and die (8:31; 9:31; 10:33–34), which is followed by discipleship failure (8:32–33; 9:32; 10:35–37) and, finally, by Jesus's further instruction on discipleship (8:34–9:29; 9:33–10:31; 10:38–45). The disciples and their discipleship are the focus of this section of the gospel; they must take up their crosses (8:34) to be servants of all (9:35; 10:42–45). They must be willing to make sacrifices, including giving up bodily organs (9:43–48), becoming like small children (10:15), and giving up all that they have and their families for the sake of the gospel (10:21–22, 29–30).[186] They must be ready to suffer persecution (10:30, 32–40). The inclusion of the controversy over divorce at this point of the story conveys the importance for discipleship of following God's will in marriage. Avoiding divorce and remarriage is thus included among the sacrifices that disciples must make for the sake of Christ's gospel.[187] "Those who follow Jesus are called to a higher standard of permanent faithfulness in marriage."[188] Marital fidelity entails a sacrificial service that is *central* to Christian discipleship.[189] As difficult as this sort of sacrificial discipleship is, with God, through faith, all things are possible (Mark 10:27).

---

185. As Mark 16:7 reads: "But go, tell his disciples and Peter that he is going ahead of you to Galilee; there you will *see* him, just as he told you."

186. This structure of Mark agrees with his use of *inclusio* and patterns of three; cf. the two-part parallelism of Barbara Green, "Jesus' Teaching on Divorce in the Gospel of Mark," *JSNT* 38 (1990): 68–69, 74–75. If one adopts her structure, Mark 10:1–12 would occupy the center of a chiasm and thus would be in the place of particular emphasis. Elements of emphasis appear throughout this section, quite apart from Green's proposed chiastic pattern, which is less than compelling in matching elements.

187. Hays, *Moral Vision*, 349.

188. Hays, *Moral Vision*, 350.

189. The emphasis on marital fidelity explains why Mark 10:29 does *not* include forsaking husbands or wives for the sake of Jesus and the gospel.

CHAPTER 2

Some scholars have taken the still larger canonical context of Matt 5:32 and 19:9's exception clauses as their starting point and then interpret Mark 10:11–12 and Luke 16:18 in terms of the Matthean texts. According to this approach, in the Matthean exception clauses Jesus permits divorce, if not also remarriage, in instances of the partner's sexual sin. The Matthean Jesus thus opposes all forms of *illegitimate* divorce rationalized on the basis of Deut 24:1. He does not prohibit divorce entirely. Jesus was thus forbidding in his patriarchal day the casual, unjust divorcing of wives. Mark 10:11–12 and Luke 16:18, for their parts, do not address the matter of divorce in instances of adultery; they only address the illegitimate justification for a liberal divorce policy based on Deut 24:1. This suggests that Mark and Luke were concerned with a mistaken, overly wide-ranging rationale for divorce. Scholars taking this approach believe that Mark and Luke would agree with Matthew's Jesus and that Mark and Luke would have *assumed*, although it is unstated, the propriety of divorce for sexual sin; Mark and Luke would have assumed with Matthew that remarriage would be permitted in such instances as well.[190] For these interpreters, then, Mark and Luke were concerned primarily with the wrong of divorce in instances excluding sexual sin and not the wrong of remarriage.

An interpretation of Mark that finds its inspiration in the exception clauses of Matthew is problematic and unlikely. First, the Pharisees' question in Mark 10:2 is whether divorce is *at all* lawful. Mark's Jesus does not respond by permitting divorce in instances of sexual sin but implies that divorce is against God's will and command, period. Then, when Jesus broaches the subject of remarriage in Mark 10:11 (as in Luke 16:18), these scholars assume a permission when the Markan Jesus explicitly and openly claims the exact *opposite*! One must take each gospel on its own terms and not hastily interject or overlay another gospel's context onto it. For that matter, Jesus's absolute prohibition in Mark 10:11 is of *remarriage* after the divorce. The Matthean exception clauses may pertain only to the prohibition against divorce, which would imply just as absolute a prohibition of remarriage there as well.[191]

---

190. E.g., Murray, *Divorce*, 51–52; John Job, "The Biblical View of Marriage and Divorce 4—New Testament Teaching," *Third Way* 1, Nov. 17, 1977, 13–14; C. Brown, editorial additions to H. Reisser, "πορνεύω," *NIDNTT* 1:500 (in reliance on Murray); C. Brown, "χωρίζω," *NIDNTT* 3: 540; R. T. France, *The Gospel according to Matthew*, TNTC (Grand Rapids: Eerdmans, 1985), 124; D. A. Carson, "Matthew," in *The Expositor's Bible Commentary*, ed. Frank E. Gaebelein (Grand Rapids: Zondervan, 1984), 8: 418; David E. Garland, *Reading Matthew: A Literary and Theological Commentary on the First Gospel* (New York: Crossroad, 1993), 68; Craig S. Keener, *The Gospel of Matthew: A Socio-Rhetorical Commentary* (Grand Rapids: Eerdmans, 2009), 467.

191. Cf. Heth and Wenham, *Jesus and Divorce*, 118–19, who conclude that divorce is itself adultery.

To summarize, in Mark's Gospel Jesus's teaching on divorce and remarriage is of the utmost importance. He highlights this teaching as having caused the disciples' puzzlement, a Markan emphasis. Mark includes it within a section of the gospel on the sacrificial discipleship required of Christ's own. The Pharisees may have asked about divorce, but Jesus treats the Pharisees as a foil to instruct the disciples within the private household setting against divorce and remarriage. Whereas the Pharisees stressed Moses's permission (Deut 24:1–4), Jesus countered with God's original intent and command in creation (Gen 1:27; 2:24), an intent now rendered possible by God's power at work among Jesus's own disciples (Mark 10:27). Mark's first readers would have understood Jesus's prohibition in absolute and emphatic terms in accordance with God's will in creation. Discipleship is indeed challenging, and failures do take place as Peter's story attests (Mark 14:29–31, 66–72; 16:7: "and Peter"), but God's original command remains clear. The risen Jesus will enable those who have at first failed to succeed in their discipleship (Mark 13:9–13; 14:51–52; 16:5–7). Mark's audience would have understood from Jesus's teaching that remarriage is an act of adultery.

The Luke 16:18 Memory of Jesus in Narratival Context

Like Mark's original readers and hearers, Luke's original audience encountered an absolute form of Jesus's teaching: "Anyone who divorces his wife and marries another commits adultery, and whoever marries a woman divorced from her husband commits adultery" (16:18). Once again, Jesus surprisingly teaches that men who divorce their wife to marry another woman (a commonplace event in Jewish society) are actually adulterous. Luke does not provide a parallel statement, as does Mark, for the wife divorcing her husband. Luke 16:18 *does* include, however, a statement similar to Matt 5:32: it is adulterous not only to divorce a wife and marry another but also to marry a divorced woman. The pithy formulation thus excludes any remarriage after a divorce for *either* partner.[192]

In its larger historical context, Luke's Gospel was written for gentiles grappling with their place in a sectarian form of a religion (Latin: *superstitio*) of a subjugated people, the Jews. The more immediate context for Jesus's comment on divorce and remarriage in Luke's Gospel has proved more difficult to detect. In 16:1–13 Jesus teaches about the proper use of wealth, and then in 16:14–15 confronts the Pharisees who were ridiculing him for his teaching. He then offers a statement on the permanence of even the least aspects of the law in 16:16–17. At that point,

---

192. Hays, *Moral Vision*, 357.

CHAPTER 2

Jesus makes this apparently unconnected remark about divorce and remarriage before telling a parable about wealth with the rich man and Lazarus in 16:19–31.[193] The bulk of the chapter, then, is on the proper use of possessions and the role of wealth relative to the kingdom of God. Jesus's prohibition in Luke 16:18 even seems strangely at odds with the teaching of 16:17, the verse that immediately precedes: "But it is easier for heaven and earth to pass away, than for one stroke of a letter in the law to be dropped." The law in Deut 24:1–4 envisions divorce and remarriage taking place, and yet Jesus teaches otherwise.

The immediately preceding verses, Luke 16:16–17 on the law and the prophets, appear to be preparing for the punchline of the parable of the rich man and Lazarus in vv. 29–31, which also deals with Moses and the prophets.[194] Sandwiched between the enduring claims of the law and the prophets in vv. 16–17 and vv. 19–31 (esp. vv. 29–31) is Jesus's teaching on divorce and remarriage.

Charles Talbert contends that the parable of the rich man and Lazarus develops motifs already articulated in 16:14–18 in the same order: God's looking at the heart (16:15), the inclusiveness of the kingdom (16:16), and the ongoing validity of the law and the prophets (16:17).[195] Luke 16:29–31 revisits v. 16's claim that the law and the prophets were "until John" to clarify, with v. 17, that the law and the prophets still offer guidance. The rich man thus should have known how to treat others in a proper, godly manner. The law certainly anticipates the new era arriving at the time of John the Baptist and Jesus, but Jesus is identifying moral standards that agree with the law. In other words, Jesus's teaching on divorce is an illustration of how God still expects people to live righteously in this new era.[196] The δέ in 16:17 is therefore adversative: the kingdom of God does *not* eliminate the Torah's claim as an expression of God's purposes.[197] The law points to Christ and his saving activity

---

193. E.g., Joseph A. Fitzmyer, *The Gospel according to Luke X–XXIV*, AB 28A (New York: Doubleday, 1981–1985), 1119, 1121; Richard B. Vinson, *Luke*, SHBC (Macon, GA: Smyth & Helwys, 2008), 525: "But Luke has also included three Q sayings that, to be kind, are not well integrated with the theme of the chapter; to be blunt, they look like bicycle parts left over after you've done the 'some assembly required,' which you then duct-taped to the frame in case they turned out to be necessary."

194. Robert C. Tannehill, *Luke*, ANTC (Nashville: Abingdon, 1996), 250–51.

195. Charles H. Talbert, *Reading Luke: A Literary and Theological Commentary on the Third Gospel* (New York: Crossroad, 1992), 156–58.

196. Darrell L. Bock, *Luke 9:51–24:53*, BECNT (Grand Rapids: Baker, 1996), 1344.

197. In Luke 21:33 Jesus describes the dissolution of heaven and earth while Christ's word remains. The Torah and that word are both expressions of God's will; see John T. Carroll, *Luke: A Commentary*, NTL (Louisville: Westminster John Knox, 2012), 333.

Jesus "behind" the Gospels, or Jesus Remembered

(Luke 16:19–31; 24:44–47; Acts 3:11–26). If the Pharisees truly loved the law, they would embrace Jesus and his teaching.[198]

Many commentators have concluded that the enduring teaching of the law and the prophets forms the basis for the *entirety* of Luke 16. Certainly the proper use of wealth is a central element in observing the biblical teaching.[199] This affirmation of the law is not limited to Luke 16. In Luke 10:25–28 Jesus affirms the law's command to love God and neighbor in relation to the lawyer's question about inheriting eternal life. Like the command to love God and one's neighbor, the command against adulterous remarriage in 16:18 is another key example of the law's continuing claims. That the prohibition of remarriage is a departure from the discussion about wealth in the immediate context *draws attention* to the verse and emphasizes it. It is no surprise later when the Lukan Jesus offers a partial listing of the Ten Commandments that the commandment against adultery is at the top of the list (18:20). Just before that in 18:11, the Pharisee praying at the temple singles out adultery as a particularly egregious sin while comparing himself to the tax collector. Luke highlights the forbidding of adultery as one of the most prominent commands of the law, at the top of the list for duties to one's neighbor and normative for Jesus's followers.

Luke's affirmation of an ongoing validity of the Law and his position on divorce and remarriage are in tension with Deut 24:1–4, which appears to be *sanctioning* divorce and remarriage. It is not clear, however, that the gentiles in Luke's original audience would have even noticed the discrepancy, especially since Luke does not actually cite or allude to the Deuteronomy text.[200] Even so, Luke likely viewed Jesus's teaching as an appropriate intensification of the law's teaching (cf. Matt 5:21–48).[201] Jesus continues to address the Pharisees in Luke 16:18, and this teaching would contrast sharply with their generous promotion of divorce certificates.[202] Deuteronomy 24:4 condemns as an "abomination" a man's remarrying his divorced wife after she has married another. Luke may well have viewed the logic

198. Bock, *Luke 9:51–24:53*, 1356.
199. E.g., Carroll, *Luke*, 331.
200. Carroll, *Luke*, 334.
201. Tannehill, *Luke*, 250; Carroll, *Luke*, 334, citing Joel B. Green, *The Gospel of Luke*, NICNT (Grand Rapids: Eerdmans, 1997), 603–4; Stephen G. Wilson, *Luke and the Law*, SNTSMS 50 (Cambridge: Cambridge University Press, 1983), 45–46. Perhaps like CD IV, 14–V, 1. On the other hand, John Meier (*Law and Love*, 167 n. 97) disagrees with these potential connections to the preceding context: "I must admit I have difficulty understanding how Luke took a total prohibition of divorce to be a faithful observance of the Law in the strictest way, down to 'the smallest stroke of a letter' (*keraia* in v. 17)." For Meier, Luke is simply relaying a cluster of Q material.
202. E.g., m. Giṭ. 9:10 in light of the Second Temple Jewish divorce certificates; see the discussion in chapter 1, pp. 23–25.

CHAPTER 2

of Deut 24:1–4 as extending to a second marriage with *other* women as well.[203] In that case, Luke 16:18 would be an *affirmation* of the law's teaching on marriage and divorce, even though it is actually a stricter teaching.[204]

The relationship between Luke 16:18 and the following parable is even more difficult. John Carroll suggests a connection: "A first-century audience would not overlook the relevance of the topic of marriage and divorce to a discussion of property, for that was an integral aspect of marriage."[205] Those who interpreted Deut 24:1–4 as permitting divorce were promoting a situation that placed former wives at an economic disadvantage comparable to the situation of widows, another concern of Luke's (e.g., 7:11–17; 18:1–8; 20:47; 21:1–4; cf. Acts 6:1–6). A woman's economic situation would be far more secure if her husband did not have ready access to divorce.[206]

Within its literary and historical context, then, Luke 16:18 remembers Jesus as teaching very strictly. He emphasizes the claim the Torah and the prophets make on proper conduct concerning the use of possessions, divorce, and remarriage. Luke's Jesus elsewhere stresses the commandment against adultery (18:20), and 16:18 offers yet another intensification of the Torah as an illustration of its enduring force. Luke 16:18, in its immediate context, *draws attention to itself*. Luke presents the prohibition against divorce and remarriage as *the* preeminent means by which his gentile readers may remain faithful to the law and the prophets even in the new age inaugurated by Christ and the Spirit. The teaching is therefore emphatic. For its original audience, Luke 16:18 would have made clear that there was to be no remarriage for either partner of a divorce, without exception.[207]

---

203. Which some commentators see taking place in CD IV, 14–V, 1's understanding of Deut 24:4; see Carroll, *Luke*, 334.

204. Fitzmyer, *Luke X–XXIV*, 1121, who reads this as an extension of the requirements for the priestly officeholders to Jesus's followers as a new sort of priesthood.

205. Carroll, *Luke*, 334. Sexual and monetary ethics were often conjoined in Jewish tradition, especially when criticizing the gentiles. E.g., T. Jud. 18:2: "Guard yourselves therefore, my children, against sexual promiscuity and the love of money" (Kee, *OTP*). See R. Collins, *Divorce*, 176–77; 307 n. 137.

206. Women guilty of adultery were not stoned in the Second Temple Period (cf. Lev 20:10; Deut 22:22; Jub. 30:8–9; 33:9 in relation to Num 5:11–31 and Deut 24:4). Rabbinic texts indicate that dowries were not returned after the mandatory divorce (m. Ketub. 7:4, 9; b. Qidd. 63b; b. Ketub. 45a; b. Sanh. 46a, 51a, 53a, 57a, 57b, 73a; cf. m. Soṭah 3:6; 4:2; 5:1). That a godly man must divorce an adulterous wife is mentioned in Prov 18:22 LXX. Mishnah Soṭah 2:6 assumes the possibility of such a wife being taken back despite all the other materials that seem to make this impossible.

207. The post-conversion William A. Heth believes Mark 10:11–12 and Luke 16:18 are either instances of exaggeration or generalizations that allow for exceptions. He does not recognize a

Conclusion

The authenticating criteria in historical Jesus research are imperfect and may result in a distorted picture or be vulnerable to the vicissitudes of preservation. The strongest possible results in historical Jesus reconstruction are based on several criteria employed together. The criteria of dissimilarity, embarrassment, multiple attestation, and what is common all affirm that Jesus taught against divorce and remarriage. These results do not depend on any particular solution to the literary relationship between the gospels. The researcher can be as certain as is possible in this sort of endeavor that Jesus taught strictly against remarriage as adulterous. A censure of remarriage forms the common core behind the various strands of tradition, strands that John Meier credits to Jesus's teaching on multiple occasions against remarriage.

Recent studies in social memory would stress that Jesus's disciples *remembered* his teaching against remarriage on a variety of occasions. Werner Kelber stresses how words live on when they find "an echo in people's hearts and minds."[208] Jesus's teaching on remarriage was clearly seared into his followers' memories, and they engaged with it.[209] Was this because of their easy acceptance of that teaching, or because of the challenge it posed for their lives in a world where divorce and remarriage were readily accepted?

Mark and Luke's Gospels relayed to their respective communities absolute forms of Jesus's teaching against remarriage (and divorce). Jesus's teaching, as recorded by these gospel authors, was emphasized for their audiences as having been without exception. Limited to the gospel that they had received and were hearing, these audiences would have concluded that Jesus taught strictly against remarriage. Craig Keener claims with respect to Matthew's Gospel: "*If the divorce is valid, so is the remarriage.* . . . To argue that remarriage is forbidden after a valid divorce is to argue on the basis of an inference not stated in the text."[210] In prohibiting divorce and remarriage, Mark and Luke make no mention of a distinction between valid and invalid divorces or remarriages. The prohibition is absolute. In

---

third possibility for Mark, and Luke: that this was a matter of emphasis for Jesus; see "Jesus on Divorce," 15. Heth also stresses the situations of conflict in which Jesus uttered his teaching on divorce and remarriage but overlooks how the Markan Jesus is teaching *in the house*. One would therefore need good reason to *depart* from Jesus's teaching.

208. Werner Kelber, *The Oral and the Written Gospel: The Hermeneutics of Speaking and Writing in the Synoptic Tradition, Mark, Paul, and Q* (Philadelphia: Fortress, 1983), esp. 15, 23–24, quote from 24.

209. Schröter, "Historical Jesus," 158.

210. Craig S. Keener, *And Marries Another*, 44.

a world where divorce and remarriage were widely accepted, Jesus's teaching in both Mark and Luke would have been taken as shocking, countercultural, and absolute. These authors would have needed to provide their readers indication that divorce would be acceptable in certain instances. After the absolute statements, the readers could not be expected to assume it.

Matthew's Gospel, however, conveys a Jesus who offered an *exception* to this teaching. Was Matthew embarrassed by the absolute form of Jesus's teaching on the subject and wished to soften it? Or was Jesus's teaching simply remembered differently by Matthew? Historical Jesus specialists have been too quick to peel away the exception clauses as a Matthean innovation. They deserve exploration in their own right, but the emphatic witness of Mark and Luke of Jesus's prohibition of remarriage must not be forgotten.

3

The Meaning of Words in the Matthean Exceptions

Matthew remembers Jesus's teaching on divorce and remarriage differently than the other gospel writers. Whereas Mark and Luke present a Jesus who offered no exceptions to his teaching, Matthew departs from that tradition—twice. Matthew 5:31–32 reads: "It was also said, 'Whoever divorces his wife, let him give her a certificate of divorce.' But I say to you that anyone who divorces his wife, *except on the ground of unchastity*, causes her to commit adultery; and whoever marries a divorced woman commits adultery." Then in Matt 19:9: "And I say to you, whoever divorces his wife, *except for unchastity*, and marries another commits adultery." Matthew seems to be doubly emphasizing that Jesus had indeed made an exception. If Jesus taught on divorce and remarriage on multiple occasions, as appears to be the case, he may very well have at some point qualified his teaching, just as Matthew recalls.

Both Matt 5:32 and 19:9, however, bear their fair share of exegetical puzzles, and the varying solutions to these puzzles radically shift the verses' meaning and application. One of the most challenging problems is the meaning of three key words: two verbs mutually translated as "to commit adultery" (μοιχεύω and μοιχάω) and the noun πορνεία, which the NRSV translates as "unchastity." While the first two words may be treated more briefly, πορνεία will require more extensive discussion given the array of interpretive options. Resolution of the many issues with these three words will lay a foundation for a more systematic treatment of Matt 5:31–32 and 19:3–12 in the following chapter.

CHAPTER 3

The Meaning of the Passive Forms of the Verbs μοιχεύω and μοιχάω

The meanings of μοιχεύω and μοιχάω in their passive forms are indicative of how even a single word can dramatically change the claim of a verse. In 2017 a new English translation came on the market, the Evangelical Heritage Version (EHV). Whereas almost all other English translations have "commit adultery" or its equivalent for both verbs, the EHV uniquely translates Matt 5:32: "But I tell you that whoever divorces his wife, except for sexual immorality, causes her to be *regarded as* an adulteress [μοιχευθῆναι, from μοιχεύω]. And whoever marries the divorced woman is *regarded as* an adulterer [μοιχᾶται, from μοιχάω]." The EHV translation denies the consensus among translators that a divorced wife who marries another and her new husband are adulterers. They are merely *regarded as* such.

This novel translation is the product of a group of conservative Lutheran pastors pooling their resources. Biblical interpretation in their circles has been heavily influenced by the early twentieth-century Lutheran commentator R. C. H. Lenski, who translates the verse: "But I say to you that every man releasing his wife without cause of fornication brings about that she is stigmatized as adulterous [ποιεῖ αὐτὴν μοιχευθῆναι]; and he who shall marry her that has been released is stigmatized as adulterous [μοιχᾶται]."[1] In other words, the divorced wife is the innocent victim of her former husband's action, as is her new husband. This stress on the innocent parties in a divorce may be traced to Martin Luther, who, following Erasmus, claimed that the innocent party in divorce was not adulterating in remarrying. Lenski emphasizes that the two (different) Greek verbs in Matt 5:32 possess a different meaning in the passive voice than they do in the active voice.[2] The husband, in divorcing his wife, has created the stigma or appearance of adultery for her when she marries another man. Such women are the *victims* of adultery. Jesus is therefore criticizing the lax approach to divorce in his day by censuring the original husband rather than the wrongly stigmatized former wife. Remarriage for the innocent parties in these circumstances is not adulterous but *permissible*.

Lenski and the pastors who followed him in their translation err by not recognizing that the second of these two verbs (μοιχᾶται) in Matt 5:32b is *deponent* in biblical literature and Hellenistic-era Greek (rightly BDAG), in which case the passive form of the verb always bears an active meaning. A quick scan confirms that the passive form of μοιχάω in antiquity maintained an active sense. For example, in Jer 5:7–8 LXX: "Thy sons have forsaken me, and sworn by them that are no gods: and I fed them to the full, and they committed adultery [ἐμοιχῶντο], and lodged in

---

1. R. C. H. Lenski, *The Interpretation of St. Matthew's Gospel* (Minneapolis: Augsburg, 1943), 230, with discussion on 232–35; see also 732–33 on Matt 19:9.
2. The verb μοιχεύω, at least, is not deponent.

harlots' houses. They became as wanton horses: they neighed each one after his neighbour's wife."[3] The imperfect passive form of μοιχάω is used here to describe the active adultery of the sons of Jerusalem. The Old Greek text of Jeremiah always has the passive of μοιχάω referring to active adultery.[4] Likewise, Ezekiel 16:32 LXX reads: "An adulteress [ἡ γυνὴ ἡ μοιχωμένη] resembles thee [like a harlot; ὡς πόρνη; 16:31], taking rewards of her husband." Ezekiel is criticizing Jerusalem for behaving like a guilty adulteress or prostitute. This verb is used for women's actively committing adultery in Ezek 23:37 LXX (ἐμοιχῶντο). After lamenting the incestuous relations conducted by the people of Jerusalem, Pss. Sol. 8:10–11 decries a son's relations with his mother and a father's relations with his daughter, such that, "Everyone committed adultery [ἐμοιχῶντο] with his neighbor's wife" (Wright, *OTP*).[5] Again, the passive of μοιχάω is used with an active sense for men actively adulterating with other men's wives. Second Clement 4.3 from the Apostolic Fathers reads: "We should acknowledge him by what we do, by loving one another, by not committing adultery [ἐν τῷ μὴ μοιχᾶσθαι]" (Ehrman, LCL). Here the passive infinitive is used to proscribe adultery in general. In the Shepherd of Hermas: "'If someone is married to a woman who believes in the Lord, but he discovers that she is having an adulterous relationship [ἐν μοιχείᾳ], does the man then sin if he continues to live with her?' . . . 'What then should the husband do, Lord,' I said, 'if the wife continues in her passion?' 'He should divorce her,' he replied, 'and live alone. But if he marries someone else after the divorce, he also commits adultery [μοιχᾶται].' . . . 'The same applies to both wife and husband. Not only is it adultery,' he continued, 'if a person defiles his flesh; but also, whoever behaves like the outsiders commits adultery [μοιχεία ἐστίν]'" (Herm. Mand. 4.1.4, 6, 8–9 [Ehrman, LCL]). The man commits adultery (passive form of the verb) if he marries someone else after the divorce, and the same applies to the wife. Even in an earlier era of Greek, the passive voice of this verb conveyed an active sense of committing adultery. Although the New International Version (NIV) treats the *first* Greek verb in Matt 5:32a (μοιχευθῆναι) with a (different) passive sense, it properly translates μοιχᾶται in 5:32b: "anyone who marries a divorced woman *commits adultery*."[6]

---

3. LXX translation, unless otherwise noted, from Lancelot C. L. Bretton, *The Septuagint Version of the Old Testament* (London: Bagster & Sons, 1844).

4. Jer 7:9 LXX uses μοιχᾶσθε for the commandment in the Decalogue; Jer 9:2 LXX uses μοιχῶνται to describe the people committing adultery; Jer 23:14 LXX depicts the prophet witnessing horrible things as the people commit adultery (μοιχωμένους); Jer 36:23 LXX states Israel's lawlessness includes their committing adultery (ἐμοιχῶντο).

5. Robert B. Wright, *Psalms of Solomon: A Critical Edition of the Greek Text*, Jewish and Christian Texts in Contexts and Related Studies 1 (London: T&T Clark, 2007), 114.

6. John Nolland overlooks that this verb is deponent in biblical and Koine Greek. He, nevertheless, recognizes: "[T]he related verb μοιχαν/μοιχασθαι appears to have been used both in the

CHAPTER 3

The man who marries a divorced woman in Matt 5:32b, according to Lenski and the EHV, is only stigmatized or regarded as an adulterer in marrying the wrongly divorced woman (who herself already bears the stigma of adultery). This translation of the second verb in 5:32b entails problems even beyond the grammatical error. Up to this point in the Sermon on the Mount, Jesus has been demonstrating that the man who thinks he is innocent is actually guilty, whether of anger or lust (5:21–30). Were the EHV and Lenski correct, Matt 5:32b would represent an unexpected break in that pattern with a husband thought to be guilty who is actually *innocent*.[7] Also, Lenski identifies the woman in Matt 5:32b as the *same* as the one wrongly divorced by her husband in 5:32a. The lack of the article in 5:32b *does not identify* the woman from the first part of the verse, whether innocent or guilty.[8] William Luck takes the participle "divorced" (ἀπολελυμένην) in 5:32b as a perfect middle and not, as Lenski does, as a perfect passive. If the participle is read in the middle voice, then the woman of v. 5:32b—distinct from and *unlike* the innocent woman of 5:32a—is *implicated* in the divorce process and therefore guilty. She would be the guilty woman encompassed in the exception clause of 5:32a. Again, in response, the verb employed for the man (μοιχᾶται) in 5:32b is deponent and therefore *must* have an active sense. The man in 5:32b is not stigmatized as an adulterer but is *actively* adulterating, given the verb. As Luck observes: "This makes Lenski's interpretation impossible. If the second husband is the agent of the verb, then the only way stigmatization can still be argued would be for the husband to stigmatize an already guilty woman! It seems useless to even consider stigma as a secondary concept."[9] The NIV, favoring a passive translation of the first verb in 5:32a, rightly translates the second verb in 5:32b as "commits adultery."

The first verb (μοιχευθῆναι) in 5:32a is also translated by Lenski and the EHV as "stigmatized/regarded as an adulteress." That not all is well with this translation was clear already to John Murray in the middle of the twentieth century: "the passive cannot be forced into this kind of service. The idea of merely subjective judgment on the part of others is not inherent in the passive."[10] He adds:

> First, there is nothing in the context, or in the Hebrew that lies back of the Greek, to suggest any such passive force. Secondly, the woman in this case is treated with the same degree of severity as the man. She bears the penalty of

---

active and the passive to speak without distinction of a man or a woman committing adultery"; see "The Gospel Prohibition of Divorce: Tradition History and Meaning," *JSNT* 58 (1995): 30 n. 17.

7. Luck, *Divorce and Re-Marriage*, 131.
8. Luck, *Divorce and Re-Marriage*, 131–32.
9. Luck, *Divorce and Re-Marriage*, 132–33.
10. Murray, *Divorce*, 24 n. 2.

death as the man does. If she were regarded as less guilty we might expect some kind of amelioration in the penalty executed. And if she were the helpless victim of the adulterer's lust, we may be sure that more merciful provisions would have been enacted, as in the case of Deuteronomy 22:25–27.[11]

As William Luck counters, this does not mean that the passive voice of μοιχεύω should not be translated in a fitting fashion, even if "stigmatized" or "regarded" as an adulteress is not possible.[12]

Another possible approach respecting the passive form of μοιχεύω suggested by John Nolland and, more boldly, by William Luck and R. T. France is that the woman is a *victim* of adultery.[13] She has been *adulterated*. Unlike most English translations, which use "commit adultery" as their translation of μοιχευθῆναι, the NIV reflects the passive voice in translating Matt 5:32a as: "But I tell you that anyone who divorces his wife, except for sexual immorality, *makes her the victim* of adultery, and anyone who marries a divorced woman commits adultery."[14] Luck stresses the fact that whereas μοιχᾶται in Matt 5:32b is deponent (NIV: "commits adultery"), μοιχευθῆναι in Matt 5:32a is *not deponent*. The passive voice of the verb μοιχευθῆναι should therefore be translated as such unless there are good reasons otherwise.[15] Luck claims that there are very few cases where the passive form of the verb bears an active meaning.[16] (He did not offer evidence for this claim.) The

---

11. Murray, *Divorce*, 22 n. 2.

12. Luck, *Divorce and Re-Marriage*, 115–26.

13. Nolland does not offer any primary source evidence for what "might be" the case here, and other commentators do not mention the possibility; see Nolland, *Gospel of Matthew*, 244; also Nolland, "Gospel Prohibition," 30. Nolland appears unaware of Lenski's earlier work.

R. T. France likewise suggests: "To thus brand her unjustly as an adulteress *may* also be part of what is meant by to 'make her the victim of adultery'"; see *The Gospel of Matthew*, NICNT (Grand Rapids: Eerdmans, 2007), 211 (emphasis mine), see also 192–93 n. 48. The wife is "victimized," "branded," or "stigmatized" as an adulteress in this approach to the passive verb forms.

14. Craig L. Blomberg, a member of the NIV translation oversight committee, justifies the NIV translation decision in his blog and draws on it in order to make a case for an innocent party in Matt 5:31–32. See Blomberg, "Victims of Adultery," *New Testament Musings* (blog), July 7, 2011, https://newtestamentmusings.wordpress.com/2011/07/07/victims-of-adultery/; Blomberg, "Marriage, Divorce, Remarriage, and Celibacy"; cf. Naselli, "What the New Testament Teaches," 19–20, who relays Blomberg's reasoning. Blomberg and France do not offer more than Luck, *Divorce and Re-Marriage*, who has articulated this argument in its most detailed form.

15. Luck, *Divorce and Re-Marriage*, 122. This places a burden of proof on those who take a passive form of the verb as something other than passive (e.g., to suffer adultery); cf. *Divorce and Re-Marriage*, 119, 133–24: Deut 22:14–19—for Luck, the woman is unjustly stigmatized as an adulteress.

16. Luck, *Divorce and Re-Marriage*, 119–26.

CHAPTER 3

innocent wife was made a victim of adultery in the first husband's unjust action. She was not adulterating to remarry. The passive voice of the verb does not make any claim that the victim is committing adultery to marry another.[17]

Both the EHV and Lenski on the one hand and the NIV, Nolland, Luck, and France on the other have unfortunately not consulted how μοιχεύω is used in ancient literature. Were they correct in their claims, one would expect the passive form of μοιχεύω to bear *of itself* the sense of "stigmatized as an adulteress" or "was made the victim of adultery" elsewhere in Greek literature, at least once! John 8:4 offers an initial test case: "Teacher, this woman was caught in the very act of *committing adultery* [μοιχευομένη]." The woman is accused of being an active adulteress, one who had been caught in the act (γυναῖκα ἐπὶ μοιχείᾳ κατειλημμένην; 8:3), such that the men were about to stone her. "Stigmatized as an adulteress" is not a viable translation in this instance; the middle-passive participle bears the sense of actively committing adultery. Luck responds that one should not be surprised by a *middle* form of this verb with an active sense. Passive verb forms should be taken differently.[18] Leviticus 20:10 LXX employs another middle/passive form (μοιχεύσηται) that could be a passive with an active sense reflecting active adulterating but, again, Luck would dismiss the example as irrelevant if the verb is actually in the middle voice.

What Luck and others who stress the passive voice of μοιχεύω do not recognize is that the passive form of this verb follows a clear pattern of use. They are correct that the verb is not deponent. The passive form of μοιχεύω is used in a consistent, twofold pattern. Justifying the non-deponent classification of the verb, some instances do indeed express that the woman is a victim of adultery by a man. However, *in each case* where the woman is victimized by adultery, the active agency of the man is made explicit *by an accompanying prepositional phrase*. Apollodorus describes a woman debauched *by* a man (*Ep.* 2.11: μοιχευθείσα ὑπ' αὐτοῦ). Athenaeus uses the same preposition to describe a woman seduced *by* Antenor (*Deipn.* 13.578–79: ὑπὸ δ' Ἀντήνορος μοιχευομένην). Diodorus Siculus relays "the debauching of Lucretia *by* Sextus" (*Bib. hist.* 10.21.1: τῆς Λουκρητίας μοιχευθείσης παρὰ Σέστου). Lucian mentions a woman who had been adulterated *by* someone (*Dial. mar.* 12.1: ὑπὸ τινος μεμοιχεῦσθαι). Pausanias describes the husband of a wife who has been debauched *by* a herdsman (*Descr.* 4.20.9: ὑπὸ τοῦ βουκόλον μοιχουομένης ὁ ἀνήρ). Plutarch offers two instances of the pattern: Aphrodite debauched *by* Ares (*Adol. poet. aud.* 4 [*Mor.* 19f]: μοιχευομένην ὑπ' Ἄρεος), and a wife debauched

---

17. Craig S. Keener tentatively suggests Luck's claim as a possibility; see *And Marries Another*, 36.
18. Luck, *Divorce and Re-Marriage*, 116.

by someone (*Virt. vit.* 37 [*Mor.* 315b]: μοιχευθεῖσα ὑπό τινος).[19] These are the *only* instances where the passive voice bears a passive meaning and, again, *in each case* the accompanying prepositional phrase specifies the male as the active agent.[20] The *necessity* of the accompanying prepositional phrase to create a passive sense will be clear from the other uses of the passive form of μοιχεύω.

Apart from this particular construction with the accompanying prepositional phrase (rarely with παρά, mostly with ὑπό), *all other instances* of the passive voice *bear an active meaning*: a woman's actively "committing adultery." This result is not surprising. Almost always, the ancients used the active voice for a *man's* committing adultery, and the passive voice for a *woman's* active adulterating. Thus the usual distinction in voice is simply a convention for identifying male or female active agency. Again, apart from an accompanying prepositional phrase specifying a different active agent, the passive voice *always* bears an active sense. In fact, the regular use of passive forms for active adultery renders it likely that middle/passive forms are also being used in the passive voice for active adultery (e.g., John 8:4 above, contra Luck).

Demonstrating this pattern is Sir 23:23, which employs the passive form of μοιχεύω: "She has trespassed against her own husband; and thirdly, she hath *played the whore in adultery* [ἐν πορνείᾳ ἐμοιχεύθη], and brought children by another man." The woman is blamed for trespassing against the rights of her husband by actively (and not merely apparently) engaging in adultery. As Murray puts it:

> [A]ctive wrongdoing on the part of the woman is contemplated in the use of the aorist passive. She is not simply a woman who has been wronged by the aggressive assault of a man; far less is she a woman who has been simply "stigmatized as adulterous". She is the woman "who leaves her husband", "who is disobedient to the law of the Most High" and "trespasses against her own husband". Without question, ἐμοιχεύθη here denotes the most notorious kind of adulterous behaviour on the part of the woman.[21]

The passive form of the verb here, in relation to the actions of a woman, bears an active sense.

---

19. For the same construction in reference to animals, see Aristotle, *Hist. an.* 619a10.

20. Nolland ("Gospel Prohibition," 30) advocates for a passive sense to μοιχεύω as having adultery committed against him or her, but then he tellingly admits: "[T]his usage is not documented." He had not done a search. The examples here provide the data Nolland himself had not collected, and they refute his claim.

21. Murray, *Divorce*, 23. In this context, Luck's preferred translation "made to suffer adultery" does not work for the verb. See *Divorce and Re-Marriage*, 117.

CHAPTER 3

As for non-biblical Jewish literature, the early first-century CE author Philo writes about those committing adultery: "We cannot even say that it is only the body of the [active] adulteress [τῆς μοιχευομένης γυναικός] which is corrupted, but the real truth is that her soul rather than her body is habituated to estrangement from the husband, taught as it is to feel complete aversion and hatred for him" (*Decal.* 24 [Colson, LCL]). Philo describes the effects in the adulterous woman's soul and the hatred she feels for her husband. Elsewhere he describes a woman suspected by her husband of committing adultery (*Cher.* 5: μεμοιχεῦσθαι). In *Spec.* 3.10 the adulteress (τὴν μεμοιχευομένην) is compared to the wild beasts that copulate without discrimination, unlike the innocent wife, and her act of adultery (τὸ μεμοιχεῦσθαι) is revealed by the priestly test. Likewise, the late first-century CE author Josephus writes in his history of the Jewish people of a man who suspects his wife to have committed adultery (μεμοιχεῦσθαι) and requires her to swear to her innocence before the priest (*Ant.* 3.11.6 §270). Later Josephus writes of King David and Bathsheba: "He was captivated by the beauty of the woman and, as he was unable to restrain his desire, he sent for her and lay with her. And when she became pregnant and sent to the king, asking him to contrive some way of concealing her (lit. the) sin—for, according to the laws of the fathers, she was deserving of death as an adulteress [μεμοιχευμένην]—he summoned the woman's husband, whose name was Uriah" (*Ant.* 7.7.1 §131 [Marcus, LCL]). The pregnant Bathsheba was considered deserving of death because of her apparent act of active adultery.

Those who have sought a passive translation of the passive voice of μοιχεύω are unaware that this form, when referring to women, reflects an ancient circumlocution. As Kyle Harper explains, the word μοιχός is used for a man who violates a woman. Since there was no feminine equivalent to the noun, Greek authors would use a circumlocution for the woman implicated in adultery, typically the passive form of μοιχεύω.[22] In the play *Pax*, Aristophanes recognizes female agency in instances of adultery when women are looking for men to ensnare, again with the passive form of μοιχεύω: "Do not do as the women who adulterate do" (979–980: μὴ ποίει γ᾽ ἅπερ αἱ μοιχευόμεναι δρῶσι γυναῖκες).[23] Aristotle mentions a Sicilian woman committing adultery (μοιχευθεῖσα) with an Ethiopian man (*Hist. an.* 586a3). Achilles Tatius depicts a similar situation. After Thersander ac-

22. Μοιχεία is best translated *not* as "adultery" but as "violation of a woman's honor," and not the husband's marital bond. The word means violation even in Jewish and Christian usage; see Kyle Harper, "*Porneia*: The Making of a Christian Sexual Norm," *JBL* 131 (2011): 367; contra LSJ.

23. My translation; compare with "Act you not as the wantons do" (Rogers, LCL) or "Act not like the harlot train," in C. A. Wheelwright, *The Comedies of Aristophanes* (Oxford: Talboys, 1837), 44.

cuses his wife Melitte (*Leuc. Clit.* 5.23) of adultery, she explains herself to him: "If my story is false in any respect, I admit myself convicted of unfaithfulness [μεμοίχευμαι]" (*Leuc. Clit.* 6.9.7 [Gaselee, LCL]). If the crime were true, Melitte would freely admit her *active* role in unfaithfulness. The novelist Chariton describes a scoundrel hoodwinking Chaereas concerning his wife's infidelity: "So I have to tell you that your wife is unfaithful [μοιχευομένην] and, to convince you, am ready to show you the adulterer in the act" (*Chaer.* 1.4.6 [Goold, LCL]). Chaereas then rushes to go punish his wife for her adulterating.[24] Apollodorus describes the wives of Greek husbands committing adultery (*Ep.* 6.9: μοιχευθῆναι). Wanton women, according to Aristophanes, actively adulterate (*Pax* 558: μοιχευόμεναι δρῶσι γυναῖκες). Demosthenes describes an immoral daughter who was faulted for committing adultery (*Neaer.* 110: μοιχευομένην). Athenaeus describes how a bird spots a married woman committing adultery (*Deipn.* 9.388c: μοιχευομένης) and contrasts a man's committing adultery (μοιχεύειν) with a woman's doing so (12.521b: μοιχευθησομένην). Diodorus Siculus expresses a concern regarding a woman committing adultery (*Bib. hist.* 12.21.1: εἰ μὴ μοιχευομένην). Lucian states that a man who lets his wife go wherever and do whatever she wants is inducing her to commit adultery (*Tim.* 16: μοιχευθησομένην). He also notes that Aphrodite was unfaithful (*Sacr.* 7: μοιχεύεται).

Although translations such as "stigmatized as an adulteress," "considered an adulteress," or "be adulterated" neatly suit an understanding of Matt 5:32 that recognizes an innocent party, the passive forms of both μοιχεύω and μοιχάω are not used that way for women in antiquity but rather refer to their active committing of adultery, as English translations and commentators almost universally recognize. As BDAG attests, the passive form of μοιχεύω with a woman as the subject has an active meaning: by wrongful divorce the husband "*causes her [the wife] to commit adultery* (if she contracts a subsequent marriage)"; the word should be translated

---

24. Lutheran commentator Jeffrey A. Gibbs, *Matthew 1:1–11:1*, Concordia Commentary (St. Louis: Concordia, 2006), 291, translates the passive verb form in Matt 5:32 as "he adulterated her" and "makes her to be adulterated," but then concedes that in the other instances he could locate from antiquity (Sirach and Josephus's *Antiquities*) "there is no doubt that the woman fully participated in the sexual sin." Gibbs then reveals how essential his translation is to his interpretation when he employs it to claim the *exact opposite* of what Matt 5:32 says: "The Lord's words 'everyone who divorces his wife ... makes her to have adultery committed [against her]' (Mt 5:32) can hardly be understood as saying that the *innocent party* in a cruel divorce must not remarry, lest she be guilty of permanent adultery with her second husband." Such an understanding of the passive verb forms serves as the *basis* for an innocent party interpretation, and thus the translation recommendations of Lenski, Gibbs, France, and Nolland while interpreting Matt 5:32. A better approach begins with how the passive verb forms are used elsewhere in Greek literature. The extant pattern is uniform and conveys active adultery.

CHAPTER 3

in Matt 5:32: "she commits adultery."[25] Likewise, BDAG identifies the meaning of μοιχάω, a variant reading in Matt 5:32, as "be caused *to commit adultery.*"[26] Surely it should be cause for pause that the Greek-speaking authors in the early centuries of the Christian movement never interpret the passive verb forms of μοιχεύω and μοιχάω with anything other than an active sense.[27]

Narrower Understandings of Πορνεία

The most difficult term to translate in Matt 5:32 is the Greek word πορνεία. Four interpretations take πορνεία in a *narrower* sense in which the word stands in the way of recognizing the marriage as legitimate. An invalid or illicit marriage may thus be annulled, although it is unclear whether one or both of the parties may

---

25. See BDAG, s.v. μοιχεύω, bβ. It is difficult to understand how Gibbs (*Matthew 1:1–11:1*, 291) squares this citation of BDAG with his translation of Matt 5:32: "he adulterated her" or "makes her to be adulterated."

26. So also LSJ on the active use of the passive forms of these verbs.

Evald Lövestam postulates that the background for the passive form of the verbs should be located in later rabbinic texts, which point the Decalogue's divorce commandment, a *qal* verb form in the MT, as a *hiphil* instead: "You shall not *cause* adultery to be committed" (e.g., b. Šeb. 47b). See "Divorce and Remarriage in the New Testament," *JLA* 4 (1981): 53. As John P. Meier pointed out in response, the talmudic instance forbids a *panderer* from procuring prostitutes for an adulterous man; see *Law and Love*, 169 n. 105. This is rather different than a man's forcing his wife into an adulterous second marriage in Matthew's Gospel.

One of the editors of the EHV translation, John F. Brug, "An Exegetical Brief," *Wisconsin Lutheran Quarterly* 90 (1993): 143, contends—like the EHV translation—that the passive form of μοιχεύω in Matt 5:32 should be translated "causes her to be looked upon as an adulteress and whoever marries her is looked upon as an adulterer." He does not consult any other uses of the passive form of the Greek verb in antiquity and overlooks its active meaning. Against those who object to his position that "this is not the normal force of the passive of the verb," Brug strangely responds by appealing to what the *hutqattel* of "be unclean" (*ṭāmēʾ*) in Deut. 24:4 *might* mean—one of only four *hutqattel* forms in the Old Testament, based on John H. Walton, "The Place of the 'HUTQAṬṬĒL' within the D-Stem Group and Its Implications in Deuteronomy 24:4," *HS* 32 (1991): 7–17. Why not simply consult how the passive form of the verb is used elsewhere *in Greek*, even *biblical* literature in Greek?

27. See chapter 6, pp. 234–72.

Sadly, the church body whose pastors created the EHV drew on the erroneous understanding of the verb forms to justify, in part, its official policies regarding the remarriage of innocent parties; see Wisconsin Evangelical Lutheran Synod Conference of Presidents, "A Study of Marriage, Divorce, Malicious Desertion, and Remarriage in the Light of God's Word," 1989 (revised in 2015), 17, https://synodadmin.welsrc.net/download-synodadmin/documents-from-the-wels-conference-of-presidents/?wpdmdl=3438&ind=1518035141222.

then marry another. Had the marriage been *valid*, then the dissolution of the marriage would not be an option. If any of these four approaches is correct, then Jesus would not be providing for divorce or remarriage for those legitimately married, only for those who were not ultimately married after all. Matthew would be just as absolute about there being no exception to Jesus's teaching as Mark and Luke. Besides these four narrower interpretations of πορνεία, still others have proposed potentially *wider* meanings of πορνεία. A review of that debate will require a fresh look at the use of the word throughout antiquity and how its meaning evolved. Between the narrower and broader meanings proposed for πορνεία, the plot has clearly thickened.

Spiritual Idolatry

Acts 15:20, 29, and 21:25 each include πορνεία among four items that are to be avoided by the gentile Christ-believers. Some have identified a common thread in all four prohibited items: an association with idolatry. Ben Witherington, for instance, takes his lead from the first of the four items, ἀλίσγημα, which refers to meat sacrificed in the presence of idols. The second and third items in these lists, "blood" and "strangled items," both refer, for Witherington, to pagan priests' consuming blood.[28] Witherington concludes that πορνεία, the fourth item, must be sacral prostitution at pagan temples.

In his treatment of the Matthean divorce clauses, Aidan Mahoney has extended the idolatrous associations from the temple prostitute to marriage with a non-Christ-believer as *spiritually idolatrous* πορνεία. As witnessed in the Greek version of the prophet Hosea, πορνεία could bear the metaphorical connotation of idolatry. Hosea indicted Israel for violating its marriage covenant with God by idolatry.[29] According to this interpretation, the Matthean divorce clauses state that a believer may therefore let the nonbeliever initiate a divorce—and this does

---

28. Ben Witherington III, *The Acts of the Apostles: A Socio-Rhetorical Commentary* (Grand Rapids: Eerdmans, 1998), 462–63. Walter J. Houston thinks the prohibition may originally have related to sacrifice. See "Foods," *Dictionary of the Old Testament: Pentateuch*, ed. T. Desmond Alexander and David W. Baker (Downers Grove, IL: InterVarsity, 2003), 330–31. E. P. Sanders, however, points out that pagan sacrifices would bleed the animal victim to death and drain the blood before sacrificing the animal; see *Jewish Law from Jesus to the Mishnah: Five Studies* (Philadelphia: Trinity Press International, 1990), 278; see also Hans-Josef Klauck, *The Religious Context of Early Christianity: A Guide to Graeco-Roman Religions*, SNTW (Edinburgh: T &T Clark, 2000), 16–17.

29. E.g., Hos 6:10; see also Jer 3:6–9; Rev 17:2; 18:3; 19:2. See Aidan Mahoney, "A New Look at the Divorce Clauses in Mt 5.32 and 19,9," *CBQ* 30 (1968): 31.

not contradict the stricture against divorce in 1 Cor 7:10–11—since the marriage was not legitimate in the first place but spiritually idolatrous. For Mahoney, Paul reserves genuine marriage for what takes place between two Christians.[30] The covenant union of grace in Christ takes precedence over the covenant union of marriage with unbelievers, allowing divorce in the context of mixed marriages. Legitimate, sacramental marriage, on the other hand, remains entirely indissoluble.

Mahoney's spiritual idolatry approach to πορνεία is unlikely. Cultic prostitution, the inspiration for Mahoney's spiritual idolatry metaphor, is now widely recognized as not being prominent in the ancient Near East.[31] Further, as Witherington notes, "when πορνεία is used in that sense [idolatry] in the LXX and NT it is usually in the context of Israel's corporate sin, not the sin of individuals (cf. Hos 6:10, Jer 3:2, 9, Rev 19:1)."[32] In 1 Cor 7:12–16 Paul instructs the Christ-believer to remain married to the nonbeliever. This plea is comprehensible only if a genuine marriage is at stake. If the "marriage" was spiritually idolatrous, Paul would surely not enjoin the Christ-believer to strive to remain within it. Paul uses language typical for an ordinary marital union (e.g., "if a brother has a wife," εἴ τις ἀδελφὸς γυναῖκα ἔχει), with no indication that the situation is otherwise. Matthew likewise does not provide a context to suggest something other than the ordinary sexual sin involved in πορνεία, nor does Matthew indicate that one of the partners is nonbelieving. If πορνεία refers metaphorically to spiritual idolatry, then some contextual signal would be necessary that something other than ordinary πορνεία is in view in Matt 5:32 or 19:9. The *symbolic* context of Rev 17:2, 18:3, and 19:2 signals this meaning. The Matthean context does not (e.g., 15:19).[33]

A Prohibited Marriage Due to Consanguinity or Affinity

Leviticus 18:6–18 identifies illegitimate marriages based on a degree of consanguinity and affinity (kinship), and some contend that πορνεία refers to these sorts of illegitimate marriages, unlike the broader μοιχεία used for adultery.[34] Matthew 15:19 distinguishes πορνεία from μοιχεία (adultery), and such a distinc-

---

30. Mahoney, "New Look," 35–36.

31. E.g., Karin Adams, "Metaphor and Dissonance: A Reinterpretation of Hosea 4:13–14," *JBL* 127.2 (2008): 291–305, esp. 293–94, who helpfully catalogues the various factors in that widespread dissent.

32. Ben Witherington III, "Matthew 5.32 and 19.9—Exception or Exceptional Situation," *NTS* 31 (1985): 572.

33. Robert Banks, *Jesus and the Law in the Synoptic Tradition*, SNTSMS 28 (Cambridge: Cambridge University Press, 1975), 155 n. 3.

34. On the biblical laws against consanguinity and affinity, see E. Neufeld, *Ancient Hebrew*

tion may be the case elsewhere in Matthew (and also in Mark 7:22; 1 Cor 6:9; Heb 13:4).[35] Paul's condemnation of πορνεία in the case of the man sleeping with his stepmother in 1 Cor 5:1 may be grounded in the Leviticus passage. Some have thought this restricted meaning of πορνεία may also be behind the Acts decree for the gentiles (15:20, 29; 21:25). If πορνεία bears this more restricted meaning in the New Testament (via Lev 18), then Matthew's Jesus would be permitting divorce in these instances, since such marriages were never really marriages in the first place. They were invalid unions proscribed by Lev 18:6–18 and thus exceptions to Jesus's prohibition against divorce.[36]

As support for this thesis, proponents have noted how three of the four prohibitions listed in Acts 15:20, 29, and 21:25 appear related to Lev 17's dietary restrictions, which apply also to the strangers in Israel's midst: avoiding meat sacrificed to idols (Lev 17:8–9), avoiding the consumption of blood (17:10–12), and avoiding meat that has been strangled (i.e., improperly butchered, 17:15; also Exod 22:31). If these first three items listed in Acts 15:20, 29, and 21:15 are all related to Leviti-

---

Marriage Laws: With Special Reference to General Semitic Laws and Customs (London: Longmans, Green, 1944), 191–212. See also Lev 20:11–12, 14, 17, 19–21; Deut 22:30; 27:20, 22–23.

35. Πορνεία had to be used for incest since no other technical term existed for the sin prior to the Byzantine era. On the prohibition of incest, see also T. Reu. 1:6; T. Jud. 13:3.

36. This position enjoyed some popularity in the latter half of the twentieth century; for example Joseph Bonsirven, *Le divorce dans le Nouveau Testament* (Paris: Desclée, 1948), although he takes the terminology more broadly than just the forbidden unions of Lev 18:6–18, including *any* unlawful Jewish marriage ("concubinage"; see 46–60). See also Heinrich Baltensweiler, "Die Ehebruchsklauseln bei Matthäus: Zu Matth. 5,32; 19,9," *TZ* 15 (1959): 340–56; Baltensweiler, *Die Ehe im Neuen Testament*, ATANT 52 (Zurich: Zwingli, 1967), 88–102; W. K. Lowther Clark, "The Excepting Clause in St Matthew," *Theol* 15 (1927): 161–62; F. Gavin, "A Further Note on *PORNEIA*," *Theol* 16 (1928): 102–5; F. F. Bruce, *The Acts of the Apostles: The Greek Text with Introduction and Commentary*, 3rd ed. (Grand Rapids: Eerdmans, 1990), 342–43; Bruce, *New Testament History* (London: Nelson and Sons, 1969), 270–72; John Dominic Crossan, "Divorce and Remarriage in the New Testament," in *The Bond of Marriage*, ed. W. W. Bassett (Notre Dame: Notre Dame University Press, 1968), 18–26; Jospeh A. Fitzmyer, "The Matthean Divorce Texts and Some New Palestinian Evidence," *TS* 37 (1976): 197–226, esp. 210; Tord Fornberg, *Jewish-Christian Dialogue and Biblical Exegesis* (Uppsala: Studia Missionalia Upsaliensia, 1988), 17–18; J. Carl Laney, *The Divorce Myth* (Minneapolis: Bethany House, 1981), 62–81; Ralph P. Martin, "St. Matthew's Gospel in Recent Study," *ExpTim* 80 (1969): 136; John P. Meier, *Law and History in Matthew's Gospel: A Redactional Study of Mt. 5:17–48*, AnBib 71 (Rome: Biblical Institute Press, 1976), 140–50; James R. Mueller, "The Temple Scroll and the Gospel Divorce Texts," *RevQ* 10 (1980): 247–56; Augustine Stock, "Matthean Divorce Texts," *BTB* 8 (1978): 24–33. For earlier, European advocates of this approach, see the listing in Dupont, *Mariage*, 106–7 n. 3. One author even goes so far as to deny remarriage after these invalid (!) marriages were dissolved; see Francis J. Moloney, "Matthew 19,3–12 and Celibacy: A Redactional and Form-Critical Study," *JSNT* 2 (1979): 42–60, esp. 44–46, 56–57 n. 14; Witherington, "Matthew 5.32 and 19.9," 571–76.

CHAPTER 3

cus—and they occur in the very same order in all three Acts passages as they do in Lev 17—then the fourth and final item on the list, πορνεία, may be related to the prohibition of sexual relations with close family members in Lev 18:6–18 (cf. Lev 20:11–21; Deut 27:20; Ezek 22:10).[37] It is unlikely that Acts 15:29 would be proscribing sexual sin in general when the πορνεία involved here prevents the gentiles from fellowship with Jewish Christians.[38] Something more specific seems to be at issue. The divorce clauses in Matthew would thus be explaining how the apostolic decree reported in Acts 15 should be applied among his audience.

As witnessed earlier, such a concern also emerges in Matt 14:3–4 (also Mark 6:17–18) when John the Baptist declares Herod Antipas's marriage to the former wife of his brother Philip to be unlawful and adulterous.[39] In the narratives of Matthew and Mark, the Pharisees' questioning of Jesus on the subject of divorce may have been motivated by John the Baptist's earlier condemnation of Herod Antipas.[40] Roman law also opposed marriage among those related by blood, but Roman law was more tolerant in instances of affinity. A woman could marry her former husband's brother and a man his former wife's sister *if both sets of parents were different*. In other words, stepbrothers and stepsisters could marry one another under Roman law, unlike in Lev 18:8, 16, 18. According to the *Institutes of Gaius*: "I may not marry a woman who was previously my mother-in-law or daughter-in-law or step-daughter or step-mother."[41] This would explain why Paul comments that a man sleeping with his stepmother in 1 Cor 5:1 is an instance of immorality (πορνεία) that does not even occur among the gentiles. John the Baptist was reminding Herod Antipas that his marriage, although permitted under Roman law, was contrary to the law of Moses.

Maintaining that Matthew's community entertained the possibility of gentiles joining the early Christ-believing movement, proponents of this view think that violations of Lev 18:6–18 due to marriage among close family members would have been a lively concern.[42] Situations could have existed where gentile couples

---

37. Fitzmyer, "Matthean Divorce Texts," 209; Laney, *Divorce Myth*, 73.

38. Garland, *Reading Matthew*, 70.

39. Noted by Tertullian, *Marc.* 4.34; Laney, *Divorce Myth*, 75–76. It would not be a levirate marriage since she had birthed a child by her former husband, who was still alive (Deut 25:5–10).

40. Mahoney, "New Look," 33.

41. Gaius, *Institutes of Gaius*, trans. W. M. Gordon and O. F. Robinson (Ithaca: Cornell University Press, 1988), 49–55 (1.18–23 §§58–67; here 1.18 §63).

42. E.g., Donald Senior, *Matthew*, ANTC (Nashville: Abingdon, 1998), 78–79 presents a viable interpretation. Putting aside Roman law, see the acceptability or tolerance of marriage among close family relations in Greece and the Egyptian lands as documented by Baltensweiler, *Ehe*, 96–97.

entering the community were in an incestuous union (cf. Paul's violent reaction in 1 Cor 5:1). This πορνεία would be an invalid union that would require a divorce to take place. God would not have joined two people who were forbidden to be together. As Garland explains, "Therefore, Matthew's church, in a mission setting quite different from that of Jesus, adapted Jesus' repudiation of divorce to make clear that this did not apply to a situation that they believed required divorce."[43] Heth and Wenham comment, "Nor does it take more than a few cases of such 'marriages' to cause church leaders, whether at the Jerusalem council or among Matthew's readers, to stand up and take notice of it. This seems evident from the amount of space Paul devotes in 1 Corinthians to the proper course of action to be taken with the brother who was having relations with his step-mother (1 Cor. 5:1–13)."[44] The New Jerusalem Bible (NJB) translation of Matt 5:32 and 19:9 adopts this approach: "except for the case of an illicit marriage." According to Garland, "Jesus' prohibition of divorce applies only to valid marriages, and the exception clause applies only to quite exceptional cases—marriage within forbidden degrees of kinship—and does not provide an escape hatch for husbands whose wives have committed adultery."[45] Remarriage would simply be forbidden.

Several scholars have affirmed this position over the years, and it entails a very strict position against divorce and remarriage consonant with Mark and Luke's absolute prohibitions. That Matthew's πορνεία exceptions refer to the illegitimate marriages of Lev 18:6–18 is not immediately obvious. The word *zənût* is used in the Hebrew Bible for sexual sin and prostitution (e.g., Jer 3:2, 9 [cf. Old Greek: πορνεία]; Ezek 23:27) and for idolatrous unfaithfulness (Num 14:33). While Lev 18:6–18 does not actually use the term *zənût*, the Damascus Document uses the term in its prohibition of marriages within degrees of kinship or incestuous marriages (CD IV, 12–V, 14a), a development that would eventually lead to rabbinic discussions of Lev 18:13.[46] Those advocating for this proposal believe that the meaning of πορνεία would be likewise affected and narrowed.

This approach, while popular for a time, suffers from several intractable problems. The church fathers do not interpret the Matthean exception clauses as referring to the sort of unlawful marriage described in Lev 18:6–18. They also never translate πορνεία in terms of incest. Incest was widely enough rejected in the Greco-Roman world for it not to be a factor in the interpretation of Matt 5:32 or

---

43. Garland, *Reading Matthew*, 70.
44. Heth and Wenham, *Jesus and Divorce*, 160.
45. Garland, *Reading Matthew*, 70. Garland allows this as the second of two viable interpretive options, the first being an exception from the divorce prohibition in cases of sexual sin.
46. Thus Fitzmyer, "Matthean Divorce Texts," 220–21.

CHAPTER 3

19:9 among the church fathers. Matthew's Jewish Christ-believer audience would have been aware of Lev 18, and violations of Lev 18:6–18 would have been too rare among them to justify Matthew's exception clauses.[47] Matthew would not likely have included an ethical teaching here of little relevance for his Jewish-Christian audience, especially in view of Jesus's reference to "what was said" among the Jews of his day about the issuing of divorce certificates.[48] This approach must then assume a *different* situation in the Matthean community, that is, that gentiles are also present in the community. Critiquing this reconstruction of the Matthean community, Barton writes, "the hypothesis makes the meaning of text dependent on the prior acceptance of an elaborate hypothetical reconstruction of a possible historical context, independent of evidence for which is fairly meagre."[49] Moreover, such a concern does not make sense in the context of Matthew's narration of a pre-70 CE discussion between Jesus and the Pharisees.[50]

Since the Old Greek of Lev 18:6–18 does not use the word πορνεία for the sins it describes, it is unlikely that Matthew's use of the word refers or alludes to Lev 17–18. Matthew 5:32's λόγος πορνείας, "the ground of unchastity," more likely refers to Moses's teaching on divorce in Deut 24:1, especially considering that the Pharisees remind Jesus of this text again in Matt 19:3.[51] Contextual cues limiting the meaning

---

47. Abel Isaksson, *Marriage and Ministry in the New Temple: A Study with Special Reference to Mt. 19.3–12 and 1 Cor. 11.3–16*, trans. N. Tomkinson with J. Gray, ASNU 24 (Lund: Gleerup, 1965), 131; Craig S. Keener, who documents the primary and secondary source evidence, concludes that "the incest taboo is almost universal, although the range of forbidden degrees of kinship outside the direct parental line varies considerably from one culture to the next"; see *Gospel of Matthew*, 468. The instances are too infrequent to be a factor in Matthean interpretation.

48. Donald A. Hagner, *Matthew 1–13*, WBC 33A (Dallas: Word, 1993), 125: "What evidence, in fact, do we have that Matthew's community was specifically concerned with the lives of gentile converts to Christianity?"

49. Stephen C. Barton, *Discipleship and Family Ties in Mark and Matthew*, SNTSMS 80 (Cambridge: Cambridge University Press, 1984), 196–97. He writes, with respect to the presence of gentiles in the Matthean community, "Now you see them, now you don't."

50. Barton, *Discipleship*, 197.

51. E.g., Davies and Allison, *Matthew*, 1:530. The connection to Deut 24:1 is even stronger in the minds of many scholars because of the later report of the Hillel-Shammai debate in Jesus's day. Matthew 5:32's λόγος πορνείας may reflect the school of Shammai's reversal of the order of the words in Deut 24:1 (*'erwat dābār* changed to *dəbar 'erwāh*, the Hebrew *dābār* in the LXX is most frequently translated by the Greek λόγος), as reported in the late second or early third-century m. Giṭ. 9:10. See John Meier's critique of this position as anachronistic in chapter 2, pp. 79–81, as well as the discussions of Hillel and Shammai in chapter 4, pp. 151–53.

Were Jesus siding with Shammai, πορνεία would bear the Shammaite meaning of immodest and impure acts, which for a woman includes going out on the street with her hair unfastened, bathing where men bathe, and spinning cloth in the streets with one's armpits uncovered, but

of πορνεία in the Matthean divorce texts to a technical term referring back to the sins of Lev 17–18 are simply absent (as well as in Acts 15).[52] It is the *context* of the Damascus Document that identifies incest as its central issue (nine lines later after the use of the term), as does the *context* of 1 Cor 5:1 (and even in 1 Cor 5:1 πορνεία may be translated more generally as "sexual sin").[53] However, the Hebrew word *zənût* and the Greek word πορνεία were not viewed as technical terms for the violations of Lev 17–18 in Jesus's day.[54]

Acts scholars dispute whether the apostolic decree in 15:20, 29, and 21:25 refers to the prohibitions of Lev 17–18 since the precise meaning of πορνεία in Acts is unclear. Although Acts 15 uses the word (as do Matt 5:32 and 19:9), Luke does not explicitly mention incestuous marriages. Acts 15:28 labels the four prohibitions of the decree "essentials" (τῶν ἐπάναγκες) to be observed everywhere and not just by those under

---

none of this is encompassed by the Greek word πορνεία. The Shammaite emphasis on "shameful" could be translated as "nakedness," as in b. Ber. 24b, in which case a man could not say the Shema. Nakedness might refer to her bare legs, her hair, or even her voice. In m. Yebam. 1:2 a woman is forbidden to a man because of the laws of consanguinity. What is clear is that the Hillelites understood the justification for a divorce more broadly than the Shammaites; see David Janzen, "The Meaning of *Porneia* in Matthew 5.32 and 19.9: An Approach from the Study of Ancient Near Eastern Culture," *JSNT* 80 (2000): 73–74.

Given Matthew's use of πειράζω "to test," in 19:3–12, where is the evil intent to trap Jesus in asking him to choose between Hillel and Shammai? If Matthew is indeed an early witness to what is reported much later in the Mishnah, then the Pharisees' lodging of the question in Matt 19 may have been motivated by Jesus's wording in Matt 5:32 because of their sensitivity to the interpretation of Deut 24:1. For scholars making this connection, see I. Abrahams, *Studies in Pharisaism and the Gospels* (Cambridge: Cambridge University Press, 1917), 71; George Foot Moore, *Judaism in the First Centuries of the Christian Era: The Age of the Tannaim* (Cambridge: Harvard University Press, 1927–1930), 2:124 n. 4; Dupont, *Mariage*, 87, 111–12; Jacob J. Rabinowitz, "The Sermon on the Mount and the School of Shammai," *HTR* 49.1 (1956): 79: Shammai also would have agreed with Matt 5:22, 28 that an evil intention is the equivalent of an evil act (m. B. Meṣ. 3:12); see Heth and Wenham, *Jesus and Divorce*, 183–84, 236 n. 47. To see the motivation for the Matt 19:3 query in Matt 5:32, however, is to render unnecessary an appeal to the Hillel-Shammai debate. Jesus had already taken an apparently radical position permitting divorce for only one reason.

52. With Hays, *Moral Vision*, 355. Vawter flags how this approach to πορνεία in the exception creates an "irrelevancy" to the context of Matt 19:9 with the Pharisees' concern about divorce and is unfitting in Matt 5:32, which is about the "perfecting of the Mosaic Law, not perpetuating its refinements." See "Divorce Clauses," 163.

53. Heth and Wenham, *Jesus and Divorce*, 167; Robert A. Guelich finds problematic that 1 Cor 5:1 does not allude to Lev 18:6–18 and that Paul should spend extended space on meat sacrificed to idols in 1 Cor 8 and yet not these incestuous marriages; see *The Sermon on the Mount: A Foundation for Understanding* (Waco, TX: Word, 1982), 205.

54. A point emphasized by Lövestam, "Divorce," 56.

CHAPTER 3

the Jewish law. Furthermore, Lev 17–18 applies only to gentiles who are living in the land of Israel and not those outside of it (see Lev 17:8–9, 10–13).[55] It would certainly not apply to the recipients of the apostolic decree of Acts 15. Acts 15 does not indicate that these requirements would be necessary for shared meals (cf. Gal 2:11–13).[56] The apostolic decree only corresponds to Lev 17–18 in the requirement to avoid blood (Lev 17:10–13) and, perhaps, also in avoiding sexual sin (Lev 18:6–26, although the Old Greek translators did not use πορνεία). Leviticus 17–18 does not mention anything about strangled items.[57] Idolatry and sexual immorality are regularly linked in the Scriptures and in Second Temple Jewish texts, quite apart from Leviticus (e.g., Exod 32:6–8; 34:15–16; Hos 4:11–14). Others think the apostolic decree refers to Noahic laws, and still others to avoiding idolatrous temple activities.[58] If either alternative is correct, then the sorts of illicit unions described by Lev 18 are not in view.

Moreover, if the Greek word πορνεία provides a link to Leviticus, the word would function as a summarizing term for *all* the sexual offenses mentioned in Lev 18–20.[59] Leviticus 18 also prohibits intercourse during menstruation, adultery, homosexuality, and bestiality (see vv. 19–23), all of which are identified as sins elsewhere.[60] Thus even if Jesus were referring to Lev 17–18 in Matt 5:32 and 19:9, which appears unlikely, his use of πορνεία should be interpreted more broadly, and divorce for more than just incestuous unions would be justified.[61]

If the marriages Jesus describes in Matt 5:32 and 19:9 were indeed illicit, then the marriages themselves would not have been genuine and would not have re-

55. Beverly Roberts Gaventa, *Acts*, ANTC (Nashville: Abingdon, 2003), 222.
56. Gaventa, *Acts*, 222.
57. See the critique of Witherington, *Acts of the Apostles*, 464–65.
58. A problem raised already by Gordon D. Fee, "Εἰδωλόθυτα Once Again: An Interpretation of 1 Corinthians 8–10," *Bib* 61 (1980): 172–97, esp. 186: "Every mention of εἰδωλόθυτα in the NT is also accompanied by πορνεία; Acts 15,29; Rev 2,14.20; and here [1 Cor 10:7–8]. It is highly probable, therefore, that in each case these two sins really belong together, as they did in the OT and pagan precedents. And εἰδωλόθυτα and πορνεία go together at the temples."
59. Hays, *Moral Vision*, 355. Carl R. Holladay thinks Lev 17–18 is among the texts that offer instructions for the gentiles living among the Israelites, but he too considers the list of sexual sins in Lev 18 more broadly focused; see *Acts: A Commentary*, NTL (Louisville: Westminster John Knox, 2016), 302–3.
60. Boaz Cohen, "On the Theme of Betrothal in Jewish and Roman Law," *PAAJR* 18 (1948–1949): 127 n. 336; Isaksson, *Marriage*, 130. On incest, see 1 Cor 5:1–5; on adultery, see Rom 13:9; on idolatry, see 1 Cor 10:7; on homosexuality, see Rom 1:27 and 1 Cor 6:9. That homosexuality should be included in the list has been debated; see, e.g., Martin, *Sex and the Single Savior*, 37–64; Robert A. J. Gagnon, *The Bible and Homosexual Practice: Texts and Hermeneutics* (Nashville: Abingdon, 2001), Hays, *Moral Vision*, 379–406. Regardless of the resolution of that debate, Leviticus itself casts the net of sexual sin more widely.
61. Hays, *Moral Vision*, 355.

quired a divorce.[62] Why would one require a divorce for an illicit marriage (which was not really a marriage) and yet not for adultery, which was punished by the death penalty in the Jewish Scriptures?[63] Paul in 1 Cor 7:12–15 does not require believers to divorce unbelievers, and in 1 Cor 5 he does not address the issue of a man's sexual relations with his stepmother in terms of Leviticus—and there was no *marriage* involved.[64] If the term πορνεία was used more broadly in ancient Greek—a matter that requires further exploration—then a narrow reference to Lev 18 is implausible.

Again, the Pharisees challenge Jesus on the basis of Deut 24:1 in Matt 19:3, 7, and Mark 10:4.[65] In these passages, Jesus responds to their appeal to Moses by appealing instead to God's will in creation. It would be very strange indeed if Matthew's Jesus then allowed for an exception to this creation-oriented teaching on the basis of Moses's instructions in Lev 17–18.[66] This once-popular approach may be dismissed.

Intermarriage between Jews and Gentiles

A third approach takes πορνεία as referring to marriages between Jews and gentiles that are prohibited in Deut 7:1–5, a danger also warned against in Exod 34:16. Jubilees 30:7, 10–11 labels an Israelite woman's marriage to a gentile as the equivalent of fornication (perhaps also Tob 4:12). The Old Greek of Num 25:1 describes Israel's relationship with the daughters of Moab with the related Greek verb ἐκπορνεύω. The Temple Scroll from Qumran (second half of the second century BCE) forbids the king to marry a foreigner, and this particular prohibition was extended to the people as well.[67] Along these lines, Acts 15:20, 29, and 21:25 would also be proscribing marriages of Jewish Christians to gentile Christians at this early stage in the growth of the church as contrary to Moses's law. Although the gentile Christians were free from such legal prohibitions (1 Cor 10:23–33; Rom 14), they

---

62. Phillip Sigal, *The Halakah of Jesus of Nazareth according to the Gospel of Matthew* (Lanham, MD: University Press of America, 1986), 100–101; Charles H. Talbert, *Matthew*, Paideia Commentaries on the New Testament (Grand Rapids: Baker, 2010), 233.

63. Guelich, *Sermon on the Mount*, 205; Hays, *Moral Vision*, 255.

64. Barton, *Discipleship*, 197.

65. Deuteronomy 24:1 is a question of a defect *after* marriage whereas Acts 15 concerns reasons *not* to marry (i.e., forbidden unions); see Descamps, "New Testament Doctrine on Marriage," 244.

66. Lövestam, "Divorce," 55.

67. Jacob Milgrom, "The Temple Scroll," *BA* 41 (1978): 115; David Daube, *The New Testament and Rabbinic Judaism* (Peabody, MA: Hendrickson, 1956), 86.

CHAPTER 3

were asked not to indulge for the sake of the Jewish Christians in the regions of Syria and Cilicia (Acts 15:23, 30), the very regions to which Matthew may have been addressed.

This third approach is also unlikely. The prohibition in the Torah of Jews marrying gentiles (Deut 7:3) was for the people of Israel because mixing with the gentiles would lead to idolatry (Judg 3:1–6; 1 Kgs 11:1–6; 16:31–33; Ezra 9–10). Idolatry would not have been an issue among the gentile Christ-believers. Acts 10–11 and Paul's Letter to the Galatians both stress that the barrier between Jews and gentiles had been torn down in Christ. Perhaps the concern was for Jewish Christians to maintain a good witness with their fellow Jews. Would a divorce from a gentile be permitted under these circumstances (to avoid the "faithlessness" of Ezra 9:2, 14, and 10:3, or the perception of it)? Were mixed marriages between Christians not real marriages and thus had to be dissolved? Such an approach to πορνεία is not obvious in Acts 15 and would need to be explained, especially after the apostles spoke positively of the gentile Christ-believers in their deliberations. Likewise, Matthew nowhere makes clear that Jews are forbidden from marrying gentiles, and gentiles are absent from the immediate contexts of Matt 5:32 and 19:9. Although Paul censures incest in 1 Cor 5:1, he requires Christ-believers to remain with unbelievers in 1 Cor 7:12–16. For fellow Christ-believers, divorce is categorically not an option according to 1 Cor 7:10–11.

Betrothal Infidelity

A fourth and final narrower approach takes πορνεία in the Matthean exception clauses as referring to the infidelity of a fiancé during the betrothal period. Abel Isaksson explains that first-century betrothals differed from modern engagements.[68] The modern engaged couple is not married until after the wedding ceremony, whereas the betrothed couple in antiquity was already considered husband and wife even though they had not yet consummated their marriage (Deut 22:23–29; 2 Sam 3:14; Matt 1:18–25; cf. John 8:41). As was the case in ancient Assyria and Babylonia, a betrothal would often consist in the presentation of gifts and the payment of a purchase price.[69] The betrothed woman was called a "wife" and the man a "husband." Separation after that point would require a bill of

---

68. Isaksson, *Marriage*, esp. 135–42. For earlier advocates of this approach, see the listing in Dupont, *Mariage*, 106–7 n. 3. For a robust recent defense of this view, see David W. Jones, "The Betrothal View of Divorce and Remarriage," *BSac* 165 (2008): 68–85, who expresses concern at the lack of serious engagement with this position by scholars.

69. Neufeld, *Ancient Hebrew Marriage Laws*, 142–43; Cohen, "On the Theme of Betrothal," 67–135; Anthony Phillips, "Another Look at Adultery," *JSOT* 20 (1981): 11; on the rabbis and be-

The Meaning of Words in the Matthean Exceptions

divorce. According to the Mishnah, the marriage ceremonies and consummation took place twelve months after the proposal (m. Ketub. 5:2).[70] In Matt 19:5 Jesus quotes Gen 2:24 that the two become one flesh in the sexual union. The legal betrothal contract could therefore be annulled prior to consummation. Matthew's exception clause would make sense for his Jewish audience, assuring them that a divorce during the betrothal period prior to consummation remained permissible. This would be the lone exception to his otherwise strict teaching against divorce and remarriage.

In making his case Isaksson contends that the Greek word πορνεία was never used for a wife's adultery. That was always indicated by the word μοιχεία.[71] Thus Matt 5:32 and 19:9 do not address adultery *after* the consummation. The clue to Matt 5:32 and 19:9, from this point of view, would be Joseph's intent to divorce his betrothed in Matt 1:18–25. Deuteronomy 22:13–24 appears to require divorce of the unfaithful, betrothed wife in these situations, since the death penalty was no longer being carried out in the first century, or so reasoned the later rabbis (m. Soṭah 1:2; 5:1; 6:1–3; m. Yebam. 2:8). Deuteronomy 22 in the Septuagint employs the verb ἐκπορνεύω (a πορνεία cognate) for situations of prebetrothal and betrothal sexual sin where the wife had put the man into a situation where he had no choice but to divorce her for unfaithfulness.[72] The wedding of a virgin, according to the rabbis, was celebrated on the fourth day of the week since the courts were open on the fifth day in case the husband wanted to lodge a complaint about the wife's lack of virginity (m. Ketub. 1:1).

To apply this to Joseph's situation, he had not yet "taken" Mary to his father's house to consummate the marriage (Matt 1:20: παραλαβεῖν; cf. λάμβανω in Deut. 20:7 LXX). The charge of adultery had to be made public, unlike the private agreement to divorce by mutual consent.[73] Joseph was planning to administer the divorce privately. Mary's pregnancy could have been a result of seduction (cf. Deut 22:23–24), in which case both parties were to be punished, or violation

---

trothal, see M. Mielziner, *The Jewish Law of Marriage and Divorce in Ancient and Modern Times and Its Relation to the Law of the State* (Cincinnati, OH: Bloch, 1884), 75–77, 81.

70. The date could be sooner for a soldier. See Deut 20:7; cf. Gen 24:54–55.

71. Isaksson, *Marriage*, 132–35. While the verbal forms of the πορν- and μοιχ- stems are used together in Jer 3:6–9, Isaksson takes this as metaphorical language applied to a situation that includes orgiastic rites with the worship of other gods (i.e., πορνεία, temple prostitution). In Hos 2:4 LXX the wife had been guilty of πορνεία *prior* to the marriage. Isaksson concedes the potential evidence of T. Jos. 3:8. Sirach 23:23, like Tob 8:7, refers to the sexual desire (πορνεία) that leads to adultery (μοιχεία).

72. Lövestam, "Divorce," 59; see the later discussions of this point in b. Ned. 90b–91a.

73. m. Soṭah 1:3–4; 9:9 (cf. Num 5); Abrahams, *Studies*, 70–75, esp. 72–73; Moore, *Judaism*, 2:125.

(22:25–27), in which case only the one party was punished.[74] The Jews placed great emphasis on the virginity of the bride.[75] Matthew's Joseph appears to reflect these concerns. Like the priests of Lev 21:7, Jesus's followers in the eschatological new temple were to marry only virgins.[76]

Isaksson's betrothal divorce hypothesis has its problems as well. First, Matthew does not label Mary's perceived sin as πορνεία. Had Matthew used that word in 1:18–25, a connection to the divorce texts in 5:32 and 19:9 would be secure. Second, Matt 19:3–9 is motivated by an interpretation of Deut 24:1–4 with its bill of divorce from a marriage and not Deut 22:21 on premarital unchastity or Deut 22:23 on betrothal infidelity. The latter two are not even mentioned.[77] Marriage—more generally—and divorce are at issue both in Deut 24 and in Matt 5 and 19. This may include betrothal infidelity but may not be limited to it. Third, it is unclear why only Lev 21:7 and its regulation regarding the priests marrying only virgins should apply to Christ's followers as opposed to any of the other ceremonial provisions for the priests mentioned in 21:1–9, which have no New Testament counterparts.[78] Fourth, the issue as posed to Jesus in Matt 19:3 regards divorce in general. Again, no indication is given that the question regards infidelity in the betrothal period or even premarital sex. Is Jesus more concerned about sexual infidelity *prior* to the consummation of the marriage than after it?[79] Fifth, the word πορνεία could refer to a wider range of sexual sins than betrothal infidelity, as will be clear shortly.[80] Betrothal infidelity would be a specialized use of the term, and Matt 5:32 and 19:9 do not offer contextual cues for such a meaning of the word. In fact, Heth and Wenham concede their inability to find an unequivocal instance of πορνεία describing unchastity during the betrothal period, a rather serious problem for this position.[81] Several times in the Septuagint, words from the Greek πορν- group, translating the Hebrew root *z-n-h*, appear side by side with words from the μοιχ- group, which translate the Hebrew root *n-ʾ-p*. In such cases, both words refer to the same sin: adultery.[82] In other words, there are contexts where the πορν- and μοιχ-

---

74. Angelo Tosato, "Joseph, Being a Just Man (Matt 1:19)," *CBQ* 41 (1979): 548.

75. Thus m. Ketub. 1:1 places marriages with virgins on Wednesdays and with widows on Thursday since the courts were in session Mondays and Thursdays, thus allowing husbands of women who were not virgins to go to court the next day.

76. Isaksson, *Marriage*, 145–47.

77. Witherington, "Matthew 5.32 and 19.9," 572.

78. Blomberg, "Marriage," 176.

79. Thomas R. Edgar, "Divorce and Remarriage for Adultery or Desertion," in *Divorce and Remarriage: Four Christian Views*, ed. H. Wayne House (Downers Grove, IL: InterVarsity, 1990), 173.

80. See the discussion of this point in the section that follows.

81. Heth and Wenham, *Jesus and Divorce*, 276.

82. E.g., LXX of Jer 3:1–9; Ezek 16:38–41; 23:35–37, 43–45; compare T. Jos. 3:8's use of πορνεία

word groups are used side by side for the same sin. Richard Hays voices the struggles of many to understand how Matthew's Jesus would allow divorce for betrothal infidelity but not for sexual sin after the consummation of the marriage.[83]

The Meaning of Πορνεία in Antiquity Revisited

The Matthean exception clauses are not really exceptions for those in consummated, legitimate marriages in the four narrower understandings of πορνεία, but these readings have not proven viable and a broader understanding of the term is warranted. The *Journal of Biblical Literature* has witnessed a recent flurry of scholarship on πορνεία authored by Kyle Harper (2011), Jennifer Glancy (2015), and David Wheeler-Reed, Jennifer Knust, and Dale Martin (2018). These three articles come to overlapping but also differing conclusions regarding the broader use of πορνεία. Kyle Harper argues that πορνεία evolved in meaning over time and came to include for Second Temple Jews and early Christians sexual activity outside of the marital relationship. Jennifer Glancy largely agrees with Harper's conclusions but qualifies that the primary sources never condemned the sexual use of slaves. A married man's sexual use of his own female slaves remained permissible even in early Christianity. David Wheeler-Reed, Jennifer Knust, and Dale Martin take a still broader approach to πορνεία: *any* sexual desire is illicit, even within marriage, which is intended for procreation only. The consensus among these interpreters is that Jewish literature departed from the original meaning of the term in the classical period, and the first Christians inherited that Jewish legacy. In tracing the meaning of πορνεία, one must therefore track the contexts in which the word occurs, especially with respect to changes in use, household slaves, and the extent that desire is a factor.

---

with 4:6 and 5:1's use of μοιχεύω to describe the attempted action of Potiphar's wife. For the Greek text, see R. H. Charles, *The Greek Versions of the Testaments of the Twelve Patriarchs* (Oxford: Oxford University Press, 1908), 186, 188–89. See Lövestam, "Divorce," 56–58. who demonstrates how the Hebrew verbs *zānâ* and *nā'ap* are treated as synonyms in later rabbinic literature (e.g., Num. Rab. 9:2, 25a). In the LXX, πορνεία and μοιχεία really do appear as synonyms, and not just πορνεία as a mere desire that *leads* to adultery or as anything other than adultery in this context; see rightly Sigal, *Halakah*, 96. He adds: "Though aware that *porneiai* need not mean adultery, in that particular context [Matt. 5:31–32; 19:9] it appeared better to the author to use synonyms than to be redundant by using *moikheia* twice" (97).

83. Hays, *Moral Vision*, 354; Guelich, *Sermon on the Mount*, 204: "To suggest that the 'except-clause' permits divorce in the case of discovering one's wife's premarital fornication, but does not include extramarital adultery appears arbitrary, to say the least." For Isaksson (*Marriage*, 126–27, 145), in view of Jesus's appeal to Gen 2:24, the consummation cements the marital bond fully and permanently, even in the face of a bill of divorce.

CHAPTER 3

The Classical Period

Nonbiblical Greek authors from antiquity into the first centuries CE consistently use the πορν- word group for prostitution.[84] The noun πορνεία, the substantive of the verb πορνεύω, in its four occurrences in classical authors means "prostitution of oneself," selling access to one's body (Demosthenes, *Fals. leg.* 200; cf. Dionysius of Halicarnassus, *Ant. rom.* 4.24.4; Aeschines, *Fals. leg.* 144; cf. Theopompus, *Frag.* 253).[85] The verb πορνεύω always refers to prostitution, whether literally or metaphorically.[86] Demosthenes uses the verb metaphorically to insult a man's sexual availability to other men (*Fals. leg.* 233). The feminine πόρνη occurs more frequently and always in reference to prostitutes (e.g., *BGU* 4.1024).[87] Πόρνος was the male equivalent (e.g., Xenophon, *Mem.* 1.6.13; Polybius, *Hist.* 12.15.2). Dionysius of Halicarnassus describes slaves—even males—selling themselves sexually to earn the money to buy their freedom (*Ant. rom.* 4.24.4). The late first-century BCE *Oneirocritica* of Artemidorus refers to a brothel as τὸ πορνεῖον (*Onir.* 1.78). The pimp who paid the brothel tax was the πορνοβοσκός (e.g., *PSI* 9.1055b; *SB* 20.14517).[88] Thus, the πορν- word group was *not* used in classical Greek for illicit sexual activities in general. This limitation is reflected by the translation of πορνεία using an older Latin word in a new way. Prostitutes would often stand under the "archway" (*fornix*) when attracting customers. A form of *fornix* began to refer to prostitutes and prostitution, with the noun *fornicatio* in particular describing the visiting of a prostitute.[89]

For ancient Greek and Roman authors, the status of the woman determined whether the sexual intercourse was legitimate.[90] They distinguished between

---

84. David Wheeler-Reed, Jennifer W. Knust, and Dale B. Martin helpfully review the context of *each* instance of the πορν- word group in classical Greek literature; see "Can a Man Commit πορνεία with His Wife?," *JBL* 137.2 (2018): 383–98.

85. The Ionic form of the noun (πορνείη) is used in the Hippocratic text *Epidemics* for "lechery" (7.122 [Smith, LCL]).

86. E.g., Herodotus, *Hist.* 1.93; Aeschines, *Tim.* 52 (more of an insult than a literal claim); cf. the noun in Aeschines, *Fals. leg.* 144.

87. E.g., Bernard P. Grenfell and Arthur S. Hunt, *The Oxyrhynchus Papyri*, Part III (London: Egypt Exploration Fund, 1903), 3.3.528.

88. Wheeler-Reed et al., "Can a Man," 385; Roger S. Bagnall, "A Trick a Day to Keep the Tax Man at Bay?," *BASP* 28.1–2 (1991): 5–12; C. A. Nelson, "Receipt for Tax on Prostitutes," *BASP* 32.1–2 (1995): 23–33.

89. Wheeler-Reed et al., "Can a Man," 387. On prostitution in the classical era, see now Konstantinos Kapparis, *Prostitution in the Ancient Greek World* (Berlin: de Gruyter, 2018).

90. Kyle Harper, *From Shame to Sin: The Christian Transformation of Sexual Morality in Late Antiquity*, Revealing Antiquity 20 (Cambridge: Harvard University Press, 2013). 12.

marriageable and unmarriageable women.⁹¹ Respectable women (ἐλεύθεραι, lit. "free women") maintained virginity until marriage and then chastity within marriage.⁹² They were wives, daughters, and widows whose sexual honor was a concern to a male citizen, her κύριος.⁹³ Unmarriageable women (not ἐλεύθεραι) included prostitutes, courtesans, and slaves.⁹⁴ Tradition had Solon opening a public brothel in Athens.⁹⁵ At the end of antiquity, Salvian of Marseilles summarized Roman sexual policy: "They thus forbade adultery, but set up brothels" (Salvian, *Gub.* 7.22).⁹⁶

In classical Greek literature, μοιχεία is better translated not as "adultery" but as "violation of a woman's honor," since it was the violation of a respectable, "free" woman.⁹⁷ A man would not be a μοιχός if he had sex with a woman in a brothel or out selling herself (Demosthenes, *Neaer.* 67). The woman's consent was a secondary matter since μοιχεία, while a violation of the woman, was a crime against another man.⁹⁸ The μοιχός could be a seducer or rapist. In his first oration Lysias writes, "Eratosthenes had an intrigue with [ἐμοίχευεν, lit. "adulterated"] my wife, and not only corrupted her but inflicted disgrace upon my children and an outrage on myself by entering my house" (*Or.* 1.4 [Lamb, LCL]). Referring to the violator

---

91. Rosanna Omitowoju, *Rape and the Politics of Consent in Classical Athens*, Cambridge Classical Studies (Cambridge: Cambridge University Press, 2002), 222–23; Daniel Ogden, *Greek Bastardy in the Classical and Hellenistic Periods*, Oxford Classical Monographs (Oxford: Oxford University Press, 1996), 100–6; cf. James N. Davidson, *Courtesans and Fishcakes: The Consuming Passions of Classical Athens* (New York: HarperCollins, 1997), 74.

92. Omitowoju, *Rape*, 88, 101, 120–21; Harper, *From Shame to Sin*, 19–20.

93. For Roman parallels, see Thomas A. J. McGinn, *Prostitution, Sexuality, and the Law* (Oxford: Oxford University Press, 1998), 194–202.

94. Edward E. Cohen, "Free and Unfree Sexual Work: An Economic Analysis of Athenian Prostitution," in *Prostitutes and Courtesans in the Ancient World*, ed. Christopher A. Faraone and Laura K. McClure (Madison: University of Wisconsin Press, 2006), 95–124; Harper, *From Shame to Sin*, 19–20.

95. E.g., Philemon, *Adelphoi*, frag. 3 (569e–f); Athenaeus, *Deipn.* 13.569d; cf. *Deipn.* 13.568c; 569–70; Augustine, *Ord.* 2.4.12, which speaks against brothels, pimps, and prostitutes in general. See Laura K. McClure, *Courtesans at Table: Gender and Literary Culture in Athenaeus* (New York: Routledge, 2003), 113, who also provides the text of Philemon by means of Athenaeus. See the fuller discussion of Solon's brothels in Kapparis, *Prostitution*, 34–46: Solon was not innovating, and it is a mistake to dismiss the testimony of the primary sources on Solon's actions.

96. Translation from Jeremiah F. O'Sullivan, *The Writings of Salvian, The Presbyter*, FC 3 (Washington, DC: Catholic University of America Press, 1947), 219.

97. Thus Aristotle, *Mag. mor.* 1.8; Harper, "*Porneia*," 367; Harper, *From Shame to Sin*, 39; Omitowoju, *Rape*, 73–78, contra David J. Cohen, *Law, Sexuality and Society: The Enforcement of Morals in Classical Athens* (Cambridge: Cambridge University Press, 1991), 98–170.

98. Omitowoju, *Rape*, 25, 69.

of a respectable woman, the word μοιχός did not have a feminine equivalent. Greek authors used a passive form of μοιχεύω as a circumlocution for the woman implicated in adultery.[99]

Unmarriageable women were therefore considered sexually available, especially slaves, although the Greek word πορνεία was reserved for prostitution and not for a man's sexual use of his own slave. Slaves were a common sexual outlet for men (e.g., Homer, *Od.* 1.430). They were subject to the master's power and sexual advances (e.g., Petronius, *Sat.* 75.11; Horace, *Sat.* 1.2.116–129).[100] In fact, demand for commodified sexual availability drove the slave trade in antiquity (Herodotus, *Hist.* 2.134–135).[101] This Greek and Roman perspective led Jennifer Glancy to theorize that the New Testament authors, in identifying blameworthy extramarital sex as μοιχεία or πορνεία, left the door open for "a male slaveholder's sexual use of domestic slaves."[102] The early Christians, she claims, would have assumed the moral legitimacy of the practice.

The Jewish Scriptures

The Old Greek translators chose πορνεία to translate the Hebrew root *z-n-h* and maintained the classical and Koine use of words from the πορν- word group for prostitution wherever that was the sense of the Hebrew. For example:

> *zānâ* (verb): Gen 34:31; 38:15; Judg 16:1; Jer 2:20; Mic 1:7
> *zənût* (noun): prostitution, or unfaithfulness *like* prostitution; Num 14:33; Jer 3:2; Hos 4:11)
> *zənûnîm* (noun): prostitution, or metaphorically for promiscuity more generally; Hos 1:2; Nah 3:4
> *taznût* (noun): prostitution or lust; Ezek 16:15; 23:7, 11.

Some instances refer to idolatry as a metaphorical prostitution (e.g., Jer 2:20; Ezek 23). For Wheeler-Reed, Knust, and Martin, the classical use of πορνεία for prostitution is thus paralleled by the Hebrew root *z-n-h*.[103]

---

99. See the discussion and documentation of this point earlier in this chapter.

100. Moses I. Finley, *Ancient Slavery and Modern Ideology* (New York: Viking, 1980), 95–96; Harper, *From Shame to Sin*, 19–20, 42, 45–46.

101. Leslie Kurke, *Coins, Bodies, Games, and Gold: The Politics of Meaning in Ancient Greece* (Princeton: Princeton University Press, 1999), 220–27. On the ancient Greek sex industry, see Davidson, *Courtesans and Fishcakes*, 77.

102. Jennifer A. Glancy, "The Sexual Use of Slaves: A Response to Kyle Harper on Jewish and Christian *Porneia*," *JBL* 134.1 (2015): 217 n. 10.

103. Wheeler-Reed et al., "Can a Man," 387.

The Meaning of Words in the Matthean Exceptions

Phyllis Bird offers a very different conclusion regarding the Hebrew root *z-n-h*.[104] Bird stresses that one should not take as determinative the Hebrew *qal* feminine participle *zônâ*, which is used for prostitutes, and then assume that meaning for the Hebrew root.[105] She criticizes translations that render the Hebrew verb in relation to the professional prostitute. With masculine subjects the verb refers to pursuing other gods (Judg 2:17; 8:33) and participating in illicit cultic activity (Lev 17:7; 20:5; Judg 8:27). Numbers 25:1 is a particularly difficult usage as the Israelites interacted with the daughters of Moab. The primary meaning of the root, as rightly noted by BDB and *TDOT*, is to "commit fornication," that is, "to engage in sexual relations outside of or apart from marriage."[106] In fact, the *pual* and *hiphil* uses for *zānâ* are *all* for "fornication," whether sexual or religious. Thus the root *znh* pertains to sexual intercourse apart from marriage, including premarital sex by a daughter who has thereby offended against her father or family (Lev 21:9; Deut 22:13–21; cf. Gen 34:31), or sex by a levirate-obliged widow (Gen 38:6–11, 24–26). The prostitute represents *another* instance of promiscuous sexual behavior, the second meaning identified for the Hebrew root. A different Hebrew word is used for offenses against a husband's sexual rights (*nā'ap* "adultery").

Bird also objects to the notion that the prostitute assumed by many for the Hebrew root must be a *cultic* prostitute. Hebrew and other ancient Semitic languages do not rely on the root *z-n-h* alone to express cultic prostitution but always combine it with an additional word that means "sacred or consecrated woman."[107] Neither the verb nor the noun forms of the root *znh* bear any cultic connotations in and of themselves.

Bird notes that the two classes of activity described by the Hebrew root are both present in the story of Judah and Tamar in Gen 38.[108] Judah initially thinks Tamar is a prostitute in v. 15 (note the participial form, *zônâ*, used exclusively for prostitutes). He thus condemns her in v. 24 for "playing the harlot." In v. 24, how-

---

104. A conclusion followed by Harper (*"Porneia,"* 369–71), whom Wheeler-Reed et al., "Can a Man" are critiquing. Wheeler-Reed et al. do not directly interact with Phyllis Bird, "'To Play the Harlot': An Inquiry into an Old Testament Metaphor," in *Gender and Difference in Ancient Israel*, ed. Peggy L. Day (Minneapolis: Fortress, 1989), 75–94, since they relied on Greco-Roman and Second Temple Jewish sources.

105. Bird, "To Play the Harlot," 78. So also Mary Joan Winn Leith, "Verse and Reverse: The Transformation of the Woman, Israel, in Hosea 1–3," in Day, *Gender and Difference*, 97.

106. S. Erlandsson, "*zānāh*," *TDOT* 4: 100. Bird's and Erlandsson's conclusion has been endorsed by more recent researchers; see the listing in Adams, "Metaphor and Dissonance," 301.

107. In support of Bird's point see, more recently, the widespread dissent against temple prostitutes as an institution in the ancient Near East catalogued by Adams, "Metaphor and Dissonance," 293–94.

108. Wheeler-Reed et al. "Can a Man," do not track the differing uses in this story.

CHAPTER 3

ever, she is defined by a differing sociolegal status: *"your* daughter-in-law," which determines the crime.[109] The noun alone refers to a prostitute, but in apposition to "woman" it means "the promiscuous or unchaste woman," who is defined by activity in relation to men with whom she is not married. As Bird explains:

> Virtually all discussions of the root reverse the order of influence, pointing to prostitution as the determining content of the verbal usage and thereby perpetuating the fixation on the professional model exhibited in the common English translations "play the harlot" and "go awhoring." . . . Nevertheless, the basic meaning of the verb as describing fornication or illicit marital relations should be the starting point for interpreting any given use.[110]

More importantly, Bird notes the birth of a new metaphorical use of the Hebrew root *znh* in the book of Hosea when the prophet is directed to marry and have children with a woman. "The woman is not described as a *zônâ*, although most commentators speak inaccurately of Hosea's marriage to a harlot."[111] She is simply a woman of loose sexual morals, a fornicator. The abstract plural noun emphasizes not a profession but rather habitual behavior and inclination (Hos 4:12; 5:4). Her children are thus "of promiscuity" with the author suggesting the same nature for the children as for their mother. The point is that the land is fornicating in the same manner as its children. "In the primary texts of Hosea the root *znh* has the same basic meaning exhibited elsewhere in historical-legal usage, namely 'to engage in illicit/extramarital sexual activity, to fornicate'; and as a professional noun (*zônâ*), a 'prostitute.' The subject is always female and the activity has, in itself, no cultic connotations."[112] Again, cultic connotations, when present, are expressed by other words and cues in the context. Hosea thus metaphorically *in-*

---

109. Phyllis A. Bird, "Prostitution in the Social World and Religious Rhetoric of Ancient Israel," in *Prostitutes and Courtesans in the Ancient World*, ed. Christopher A. Faraone and Laura K. McClure (Madison: University of Wisconsin Press, 2006), 43. Tamar had been promised to her brother's brother and thus had a married or betrothed status.

110. Bird, "To Play the Harlot," 78. See Gen 34:2, 31 (treat our sister like a harlot); Deut 22:21–22; Hos 2:4; cf. 2:2, 5. In other words, Judah and Samson are not censured for sex with prostitutes (Gen 38:15–26; Judg 16:1).

111. Bird, "To Play the Harlot," 80.

112. Bird, "To Play the Harlot," 88. Gerlinde Baumann agrees with Bird and others, but she also traces a trajectory in the use of the verb *zānâ* and the *qal* participle: "The *qal* participle of the verb, זנה, designates any woman who lives her sexuality outside of marriage; she may do so in order to earn her livelihood. However, זונות are not only professional prostitutes, but all women who have sexual relations with men to whom they are not betrothed or married"; see *Love and Violence: Marriage as Metaphor for the Relationship between YHWH and Israel in the Prophetic Books* (Collegeville, MN: Liturgical, 2003), 43–46.

cludes men as guilty of the illicit female pursuit of lovers. As Bird writes, "It is easy for patriarchal society to see the guilt of a 'fallen woman'; Hosea says, 'You (male Israel) are that woman!'"[113] The prophet Hosea thus exhibits a new development in the metaphorical extension of the Hebrew root to include men acting like the fallen woman in their religious infidelity and idolatry (Hos 4:18; cf. Hos 1:2; 4:12–13; Num 25:1; Jer 13:27; Ezek 43:7–9).[114] The covenantal relationship was likened to a marital relationship that had been defiled by men.

The Jewish Scriptures would thus exert a pressure in a different direction for πορνεία than in common Greek usage. The Jewish root *z-n-h* refers to extramarital intercourse more generally, and Hosea included men too as having acted like the fallen woman. In the Greek translation of the Jewish Scriptures, πορνεία would sometimes mean illicit sexual activity by women *and* men, including the married (e.g., LXX Jer 2:20; 3:2, 9; Ezek 16:15; Hos 2:4, 6; Amos 7:17).

Second Temple Judaism

In a departure from non-biblical Greek usage and reflecting the use of *z-n-h* in the Hebrew Bible, πορνεία in the Old Greek translation of the Jewish Scriptures could refer to a woman's illicit sexual behavior in general and not just prostitution. The word was also sometimes associated with idolatry and expanded to include men as subjects. Kyle Harper explains that Second Temple texts, under the influence of the Hebrew Scriptures, would expand the use of *z-n-h* and πορνεία even further to include illicit acts by men within a moral system in which legitimate sex was limited to marriage.[115] In terms of group sexual identity, the Jews began to characterize outsiders as guilty of *znh*, which reinforced the importance for insiders (fellow Jews) to limit themselves to licit sexual acts.[116] Πορνεία came to be an illegitimate form of sexual practice for both the male customer and the female professional.[117] Jennifer Glancy qualifies Harper's thesis: although πορνεία is used more widely in an expanded sense in the Old Greek translation of the Scriptures and in Second Temple Judaism, rarely is πορνεία used for sexual activity with slaves who were not prostitutes.[118] The Jews appear to have tolerated sexual activity with one's slaves, as did their Greco-Roman peers.

---

113. Bird, "To Play the Harlot," 89.
114. Harper, "*Porneia*," 370; Harper, *From Shame to Sin*, 89.
115. Harper, "*Porneia*," 371–74.
116. Jennifer Wright Knust, *Abandoned to Lust: Sexual Slander and Ancient Christianity*, Gender, Theory, and Religion (New York: Columbia University Press, 2006), 51–53, although Knust is concerned with the first Christians and not the Hebrew term.
117. Harper, "*Porneia*," 371.
118. Glancy, "Sexual Use," 218; Catherine Hezser, *Jewish Slavery in Antiquity* (Oxford: Oxford

CHAPTER 3

In Sir 23:16–18 three sorts of sinful men are described. The first two are ἄνθρωπος πόρνος. One sins "in the body of his own flesh," and in the other instance, "all bread tastes sweet." In contrast to classical usage, the meaning of πόρνος here includes male sexual transgression and not just male (or female) prostitution. The word refers more generally to the "sexually sinning man." The third sinful man disgraces the marriage bed.[119] Sirach 23:22–23 then turns to the adulterous *wife*: "Through her fornication she has committed adultery [ἐν πορνείᾳ ἐμοιχεύθη] and brought forth children by another man." Μοιχεία, used for *men's* transgression against women of honorable status, requires a passive verbal form when used in the case of the woman's agency.[120] The added ἐν πορνείᾳ emphasizes her choice of dishonorable behavior.[121] In Sir 41:17 the male hearer is to "be ashamed of sexual immorality [περὶ πορνείας] before your father or mother." In 41:20–22 one is not to be "looking at a prostitute" (γυναικὸς ἑταίρας) or "gazing at another man's wife" or "meddling with (that man's) servant girl." Sirach elsewhere warns against prostitution on practical grounds (9:8; 19:2). Harper contends that these passages illustrate the emerging belief in a conjugal sexual morality, ruling out sex with prostitutes or the slaves of other men.[122] Glancy faults Harper for not recognizing the significance that the slaves were those of *another* male slaveholder's household (7:29; 33:25–32); the text remains silent about sexual relations with one's *own* female slaves.[123] Glancy therefore rephrases the conclusion: "Discouraging men from violating other men's households, the passage promotes a domestic sexual morality without endorsing an exclusively conjugal sexual morality."[124]

University Press, 2005), 191–94 and the quote on 386: "Slaves were sexually exploited in both Jewish and Graeco-Roman society. The phenomenon that masters would sleep with and produce children with their slaves is taken for granted by both Jewish and Roman writers. The Hebrew Bible already knows of the slave concubine, the girl sold by her father to be the mistress of another man." On the Torah's regulation of sex with slaves, see Exod 21:7–11; Lev 19:20–22; and Deut. 21:10–14; discussed in Hezser, *Jewish Slavery*, 192–93; David P. Wright, "She Shall Not Go Free as Male Slaves Do: Developing Views About Slavery and Gender in the Laws of the Hebrew Bible," in *Beyond Slavery: Overcoming Its Religious and Sexual Legacies*, ed. Bernadette J. Brooten (New York: Macmillan, 2010), esp. 131–32, 138, 141 n. 23.

119. Harper, "*Porneia*," 372.
120. Harper, "*Porneia*," 371. Wheeler-Reed et al. ("Can a Man," 387) emphasizes that ἐν πορνείᾳ in 23:23, 27 refers to the spouse's adultery metaphorically as "playing the whore" with πορνεία and πόρνος clearly used in an expanded sense for spousal infidelity.
121. Harper, "*Porneia*," 371.
122. Harper, "*Porneia*," 371–72.
123. Glancy, "Sexual Use," 218–19. Harper, in private correspondence, has conceded the point.
124. Glancy, "Sexual Use," 219.

The Meaning of Words in the Matthean Exceptions

To prohibit a man from enjoying sexual relations with prostitutes or with slaves in *other* households nevertheless *is*—contra Glancy—a decisive move toward conjugal sexual morality when compared with the larger Greco-Roman world where such sexual activity was freely permitted. If a man is not to have sex with a prostitute, then the distinction between marriageable and unmarriageable women is no longer the criterion for legitimate sexual relations. Male sexual behavior is severely limited.

Ben Sira, the eponymous author of Sirach, describes as shameful any "trifling with a servant girl of yours, and of violating her bed" (Sir 41:22 MS M, as restored from the Greek translation).[125] Glancy concedes: "So far as I know, this is the clearest statement by a Jewish writer of the Second Temple period discouraging a slaveholder from sexual contact with his own slave."[126] Despite the original author's strict stance, Ben Sira's grandson, who translated his work from Hebrew into Greek, adjusted the wording of the passage to apply to the enslaved women of *other* men's households in order to justify sex with one's own slave.[127] Glancy takes the grandson's "studied silence on the sexual use of household slaves" as agreeing not only with the wider Hellenistic world but *also* with Second Temple Judaism. Thus "Ben Sira himself is an isolated voice daring to criticize a man who took sexual advantage of his slave, not unlike Musonius Rufus [frag. 12], whose criticism of the sexual use of slaves was not adopted by fellow moralists."[128] Ben Sira, however, is not the only Second Temple voice advocating conjugal sexual morality.

The Testaments of the Twelve Patriarchs witnesses the enlarging of πορνεία to refer to a broad range of illicit female and *male* sexual activity, including incest (T. Reu. 1:6: Reuben with his father's concubine), prostitution (T. Jud. 13:3; 14:2, 3), exogamy (T. Levi 9:9; cf. Jub. 7:21; 25:8; cf. 20:3, 6; 23:15), Sodomite sexuality (T. Benj. 9:1; T. Sim. 5:3; cf. Jub. 16:4), and πορνεία in general (T. Reu. 4:7), especially with respect to the young (T. Jud. 14:2; T. Reu. 4:6).[129] In his testament Joseph re-

---

125. Patrick W. Skehan and Alexander A. Di Lella, *The Wisdom of Ben Sira*, AB 39 (New York: Doubleday, 1987), 476, 479, 481; cf. Pancratius C. Beentjes, *The Book of Ben Sira in Hebrew*, VTSup 68 (Leiden: Brill, 1997), 169.

126. Glancy, "Sexual Use," 219 n. 16.

127. Carolyn Osiek, "Female Slaves, *Porneia*, and the Limits of Obedience," in *Early Christian Families in Context: An Interdisciplinary Dialogue*, ed. David L. Balch and Carolyn Osiek (Grand Rapids: Eerdmans, 2003), 265–66.

128. Glancy, "Sexual Use," 219.

129. Harper, "*Porneia*," 372. Testament of Levi 9:9's condemnation of πορνεία as exogamy (and miscegeny)—sexual relations outside the rightful people or kin—also figures in Tobit's socially charged admonition to his son Tobias to avoid πορνεία by marrying a woman from his own people (i.e., a good Jewish girl) and not one of the loose, foreign women (4:12; 8:7); see Harper, "*Porneia*," 373; Amy-Jill Levine, "Diaspora as Metaphor: Bodies and Boundaries in the

CHAPTER 3

calls how Potiphar's wife tried and failed to lead him into πορνεία (T. Jos. 3:8). In an instance that seems to limit sex to conjugal relations, T. Iss. 7:1–2 reads: "I am a hundred and twenty-two years old, and I am not aware of having committed a sin unto death. I have not had intercourse with any woman other than my wife, nor was I promiscuous [πορνεία] by lustful look" (Kee, *OTP*).[130] Glancy notes that Jacob was not criticized for sex with the slaves Bilhah and Zilpah (T. Jud. 4:13; T. Naph. 8:1).[131] Nevertheless, T. Iss. 7:1–2 celebrates not having known or looked upon *any* other woman except for one's wife.[132]

David Wheeler-Reed, Jennifer Knust, and Dale Martin agree with Kyle Harper that sexual relations are indeed to be within the confines of marriage, but they interpret Second Temple authors at times as even *more* restrictive. They point to Second Temple texts condemning lust and sexual desire even for the married. For Philo, legitimate sexuality was exclusively marital, and even there temperance is to be observed lest pleasure overcome the rational soul (*Spec.* 3.2). While Philo never explicitly critiques sexual relations by owners with their own slaves, Philo views the Jews as distinct from the other nations: "Before the lawful union we know no mating with other women, but we come as virgin men to virgin maidens." (*Ios.* 43 [Colson, LCL]). Both admonitions—to purity in entering marriage and to avoiding pleasure even within marriage—militate against sexual relations with slaves. Elsewhere, Philo depicts pleasure and virtue as two dueling forces in the soul personified by two women: the one a πόρνη and the other an ἐλευθέρα (*Sacr.* 20–33). The former is outwardly beautiful and promises sensual delight, but the latter is modest and promises righteousness.

Other Second Temple authors take the same approach as Philo. Pseudo-Phocylides condemns any sexual activity outside procreative sex with one's lawful

---

Book of Tobit," in *Diaspora Jews and Judaism: Essays in Honor of, and in Dialogue with, A. Thomas Kraabel*, ed. J. Andrew Overman and Robert S. MacLennan (Atlanta: Scholars, 1992), 105–17; so also Wheeler-Reed et al., "Can a Man," 388. When the angelic "Watchers" have mixed sexual relations with human women in 1 En. 10:9–10 (cf. Gen 6:1–4), the Enochic text condemns πορνεία as producing bastard children because of "intercourse to forbidden decrees"; see George W. Nickelsburg, *1 Enoch 1*, Hermeneia (Minneapolis: Fortress, 2001), 223. Πορνεία is used for intercourse in forbidden degrees and more broadly.

130. Harper, "*Porneia*," 372–73. Wheeler-Reed et al., "Can a Man," 389: "By this time, many Jews have taken a word that classically meant prostitution and used it to refer to any kind of sexual behavior they condemned."

131. Glancy, "Sexual Use," 220. As Glancy observes, in his Testament Reuben recounts having intercourse with a female sexually subject to another man (θηλείας ὑπάνδρου), not a married woman (γυναικὸς ὑπάνδρου). It would be difficult to condemn men who confined extramarital sexual activity to female slaves within their own household.

132. This text is therefore problematic for Glancy's position.

wife or husband (Ps.-Phoc. 175–176). Husbands are not to "outrage" their wives with shameful ways of intercourse (189) and sexual relations during pregnancy (186).[133] In 4QD^e 7 I, 12–13 we read, "Whoever approaches to have illegal sex [*liznôt*] with his wife, not in accordance with the regulation, shall leave and never return." Here the Hebrew infinitive likely even refers to sexual intercourse within marriage and, apparently, for pleasure.[134] In Tob 8:17 Tobias instructs his bride on their marriage night to get out of bed to pray rather than to consummate the marriage by sex so that he can say that he is "taking" his "kinswoman" not on account of lust (διὰ πορνείαν) but with sincerity (ἐπ' ἀληθείας). The text "obviously assumes that even sex with one's wife can count as πορνεία if indulged for the wrong reason."[135] Josephus states that faithful Jews engage in marriage and sexual relations "only for the procreation of children" (*Ag. Ap.* 2.24 §199 [Thackeray, LCL]).[136] In the same context, a Jewish man will not have sex with his wife if she is pregnant, implying that there is to be no sex where pregnancy is not possible. Thus for some Second Temple authors, the avoidance of sexual desire and pleasure would require sexual relations strictly within a conjugal context. Anything outside of that would be sinful.

New Testament Evidence

The Greek root πορν- is used fifty-six times in the New Testament, and πορνεία figures prominently in early Christian sexual ideology. The largest number of πορν- instances is in 1 Corinthians. Outside 1 Corinthians, a third of the remaining are in Rev 17–18 with its personification of the Roman Empire as a prostitute. Πόρνη refers to the professional prostitute in Luke 15:30, Heb 11:31, and Jas 2:25. Πορνεία is used seven times in vice lists.[137] Πόρνος is used three times for a male engaging in illicit sex (1 Cor 6:9; Eph 5:5; 1 Tim 1:10). Πόρνος is used once for Esau (probably for exogamy) in Heb 12:16. The Matthean exception clauses and the apostolic decree of Acts 15 also use the word group.

The New Testament often *distinguishes* πορνεία from μοιχεία (Matt 15:19; Mark 7:21; 1 Cor 6:9; Heb 13:4). Matthew regularly uses μοιχεία and its cognate verbal forms (e.g., Matt 5:32; 19:9!) and yet chooses πορνεία for the exception clauses. Some have appealed to a series of prophetic texts for an identification of the

---

133. Wheeler-Reed et al., "Can a Man," 391.
134. Wheeler-Reed et al., "Can a Man," 389–90, with Hannah K. Harrington, *The Purity Texts*, Companion to the Qumran Scrolls 5 (London: T&T Clark, 2004), 47.
135. Wheeler-Reed et al., "Can a Man," 389.
136. Wheeler-Reed et al., "Can a Man," 390.
137. See Matt 15:19; Mark 7:21; 2 Cor 12:21; Gal 5:19; Eph 5:3; Col 3:5; Rev 9:21.

CHAPTER 3

two terms, most notably the Greek versions of Jer 3:8, Ezek 16, and Hos 2:2. Francis I. Andersen and David Noel Freedman, however, demonstrate that in Hos 1–2 and Ezek 16 sexual immorality and adultery are not synonymous.[138] Those who identify πορνεία with adultery rely especially on Sir 23:23: "Through her fornication [ἐν πορνείᾳ], she has committed adultery [ἐμοιχεύθη] and brought forth children by another man." Jensen translates the verse: "She has wantonly committed adultery."[139] The verse appears to be referring to the *sexual desire* that leads to adultery.[140] The same may well be the case in Tob 8:7, which reads: "I now am taking this kinswoman of mine, not because of lust [οὐ διὰ πορνείαν], but with sincerity." Rather than equate πορνεία and μοιχεία, Wheeler-Reed, Knust, and Martin contend that these passages could be referring to the sexual desire that *leads to* adultery: Even sexual relations within marriage can be instances of πορνεία when inordinate sexual desire or pleasure is present. In 1 Thess 4:3–6 Paul contrasts the sexual possession of one's vessel—that is, one's wife—with the *passion of desire* characteristic of gentiles who do not know God.[141] They observe that, "If we were to ask Paul, then, if a man can commit πορνεία with his wife, he would say, 'Yes!' especially if he has sex with her out of lustful desire. In our opinion, Matthew likely thinks the same thing."[142] Wheeler-Reed, Knust, and Martin even see sinful desire as the meaning of πορνεία in the Matthean exception clauses.

The Revised Standard Version (RSV) translates the key clause in 1 Thess 4:4 as, "that each one of you know how to take a wife for himself." The verb "take" (κτάομαι) is used for taking a wife in LXX Ruth 4:5, 10, and "vessel" (σκεῦος) can indeed be used for a wife (cf. 1 Pet 3:7). Out of concern over sexual sin (πορνεία), Paul in 1 Cor 7:2 states that each man should "have his own" wife. Gordon Fee considers an identification of 1 Thess 4:3–6's "vessel" with a wife so "riddled" with difficulties that it remains the minority position.[143] How would one acquire his

---

138. Francis I. Andersen and David Noel Freedman, *Hosea*, AB 24 (Garden City, NY: Doubleday, 1980), 157–63.
139. Joseph Jensen, "Does *Porneia* Mean Fornication? A Critique of Bruce Malina," *NovT* 20 (1978): 172–73.
140. Isaksson, *Marriage*, 133–34.
141. Wheeler-Reed et al., "Can a Man," 394.
142. Wheeler-Reed et al., "Can a Man," 395; reiterated on 398.
143. Gordon D. Fee, *The First and Second Letters to the Thessalonians*, NICNT (Grand Rapids: Eerdmans, 2009), 147–48. Fee lists a series of problems: (1) Paul does not use "wife"; (2) "each of you" would require all the men to get married; (3) "your own" would be more fitting if a warning against other men's wives, but this context is too general; (4) the man is also a "vessel" in the 1 Peter parallel; (5) "acquiring a wife in passionate lust" is anachronistic since in the first century wives were "acquired" for household management and procreation; (6) how does one

own wife?[144] Fee, for his part, follows the majority in taking Paul's contrast as between those who know God with their self-control versus gentiles with their passionate desires. The reference in 1 Sam 21:5 to David's men having avoided sexual relations, leaving their "vessels" consecrated, strengthens a connection to the male sexual organ.[145] The gentiles express those desires in ways that are contrary to those who know God. Paul is more likely faulting the passionate, lustful gentiles for their sexual relations apart from the marital union. One should know how to gain control over one's own vessel.[146] The NRSV thus revised the RSV to read: "that each one of you know how to control your own body." Wheeler-Reed, Knust, and Martin's interpretation of this verse is less likely.

Taking πορνεία as lustful passion and desire in the Matthean exception clauses is likewise problematic. Such an identification would allow the husband to divorce his wife for *enjoying* sexual relations or for indulging in nonprocreative *conjugal* sex. Matthew does not offer any indication to support such an interpretation. The Pharisees in Matt 19:7 invoke Deut 24:1 as a basis for divorce. In Deut 24:1 LXX the man may divorce his wife for any "unseemly deed" (ἄσχημον πρᾶγμα). This is the language of shame and prostitution, since ἄσχημον and πορνεία were closely associated (e.g., Sir 26:8–9).[147] The dispute, then, is not about inordinate desire. A wife who has fallen into sexual shame may be divorced, and not one who simply enjoys conjugal sex.[148] Moreover, Matthew opts for πορνεία and not μοιχεία since the latter meant in the larger Graeco-Roman world a *man's* violation of a married woman. The *woman's* shameful transgression required the use of πορνεία.[149] The New Testament does not offer any clear indication that sexual desire should be classified as πορνεία.[150]

First Corinthians offers the most abundant use of πορν- language. First Corinthians 5:1 uses πορνεία for incest prohibited by Lev 18:8 (a man sleeping with his father's wife). This passage parallels the Second Temple expansion of πορνεία

---

avoid defrauding a brother by acquiring his own wife, and not in passionate lust. Thus Fee favors taking "one's own vessel" as "one's own *body*."

144. Jay E. Smith, "1 Thessalonians 4:4: Breaking the Impasse," *BBR* 11.1 (2001): 76–80.

145. Fee, *First and Second Letters to the Thessalonians*, 149.

146. An ingressive sense of the verb is possible in this understanding; see Nijay K. Gupta, *1 & 2 Thessalonians*, Zondervan Critical Introductions to the New Testament 13 (Grand Rapids: Zondervan, 2019), 127; cf. Smith, "1 Thessalonians 4:4," 84–85.

147. Harper, "*Porneia*," 375.

148. Harper, private correspondence.

149. Harper, "*Porneia*," 375–76.

150. This poses a problem for those who would expand the Matthean exception clauses to refer to lust or even pornography. While those actions are sinful, even adulterous (Matt 5:27–28), the exception clauses are referring to sexual relations apart from one's spouse.

CHAPTER 3

to refer to illicit sexual activity, and in this instance refers to illicit sexual activity not even tolerated by the pagans.[151] The πόρνος of 1 Cor 5:9–11 refers not to male prostitutes in the Corinthian world, as one would expect from classical and secular Greek usage, but rather to illicit sexual activity that would otherwise be acceptable. Certainly prostitution would be included among illicit sexual activities (1 Cor 6:12–20). While the Corinthians may have approved of prostitution in agreement with their larger culture, the Jewish Paul did not. Paul is expressing a very different understanding of licit sexual activity than the Greeks and Romans. Both πόρνοι and μοιχοί are listed among the unrighteous individuals Paul condemns in 1 Cor 6:9. Harper distinguishes male violators of honorable female sexuality (μοιχοί) from a broader category (πόρνοι) that refers to *men* "with a lascivious lack of self-control."[152]

In 1 Cor 6:12–20 Paul refers to a female prostitute in v. 16, with the articular τῇ πόρνῃ identifying sexual activity with a prostitute.[153] Although Greco-Roman society would accept sexual relations with this category of dishonored women, Paul does not. Jennifer Glancy stresses that Paul censures only sex with prostitutes but not the exploitation of a man's own property, the female slave.[154] Glancy does not appear to have accounted for how the Romans considered a *wife's* sexual activity with a slave adulterous.[155] Further, Paul has already expanded illicit πορνεία to include sexual activity permitted in the larger society (i.e., prostitution). He has also expanded the term to include a man's sleeping with his father's wife (1 Cor 5:1). Paul is clearly working with a broader understanding of the term. The apostle comments that many things may be permissible or lawful and yet not be beneficial or even licit (1 Cor 6:12). Prostitution may be "lawful" in the Greco-Roman world, but it must still be avoided as sinful (as πορνεία; 6:18).[156] Paul invokes the two becoming one flesh in the creation account as an argument against sex with a prostitute (6:16). How would it honor that appeal to the exclusive relationship in Genesis of a man and his wife for a man to be united to his female slave? When

---

151. Fee, *First Epistle to the Corinthians*, 219.

152. Harper, "*Porneia*," 377–78.

153. Joseph A. Fitzmyer, *First Corinthians*, AB 32 (New Haven: Yale University Press, 2008), 265; followed by Harper, "*Porneia*," 378.

154. Glancy, "Sexual Use," 227: "However, there is no evidence that Paul, Philo, or any other first-century Greek-speaking Jew used the term πορνεία to refer to a man's exploitation of a woman who was his property."

155. E.g., Livy, *Ab urbe cond.* 1.58.4; Tacitus, *Ann.* 6.40; 14.60; Justinian, *Dig.* 48.5.25. See Craig A. Williams, *Roman Homosexuality*, 2nd ed. (Oxford: Oxford University Press, 2010), 33, 55–56 on this double standard.

156. Harper, private correspondence.

confronted with those who would avoid sexual activity entirely, Paul posits in response the permissibility of sexual relations *within marriage* (7:2–3, 5). For Paul, the marital union is where licit sexual activity takes place.[157] Not surprisingly, then, what leads Glancy from an initial position of agnosticism regarding Paul's stance on the sexual use of slaves is *not* evidence from Paul himself but rather the larger Greco-Roman social context.[158]

In short, the apostle never countenances as licit the relations between a male owner and his female slave. Paul does not just confine sexual activity to a household—as per Glancy—but to a man and his wife. The husband's body *belongs to his wife* and *not* to the husband's female slave (1 Cor 7:4)! The wife maintains authority over her husband's body, a rather countercultural idea. He cannot do whatever he wants sexually. Marriage is Paul's solution to sexual desire and potential πορνεία (7:2) as he warns against extramarital sex. Sexual desires are satisfied within a reciprocal marital relationship (7:4, 9), and in *that* context nothing would suggest that such relations are wrong.

Adultery

The Matthean exception clauses are best understood in light of widespread ancient Near Eastern customs and preoccupation with the question of when a husband could justifiably divorce his wife. If the divorce were legitimate because of the wife's sexual infidelity—her sexual intercourse with a man other than the husband—then the husband would not owe the wife her dowry or bridal gift or any additional penalties (m. ʿArak. 6:1–2; m. Yebam. 15:7; m. Soṭah 6:1; m. Ketub. 7:6 [without dowry]). Raymond Westbrook traces the distinction between justified and unjustified divorces (for the sake of the dowry return) in the ancient Near East to the Code of Hammurapi. Old Babylonian law, and neo-Babylonian marriage contracts.[159] Betrothal was the beginning of a marital relationship, and from that point on a divorce would be required to sever the relationship, and the financial

---

157. Dale B. Martin, "Paul without Passion: On Paul's Rejection of Desire in Sex and Marriage," in *Constructing Early Christian Families: Family as Social Reality and Metaphor*, ed. Halvor Moxnes (New York: Routledge, 1997), 201; republished in Dale B. Martin, *Sex and the Single Savior: Gender and Sexuality in Biblical Interpretation* (Louisville: Westminster John Knox, 2006), 66; Harper, "*Porneia*," 379: "It is revealing that, whereas authors of the Roman period saw sex with prostitutes or slaves as the solution to adultery, Paul saw marriage as the solution to the temptations of easy sex with dishonored women (see, e.g., Horace, *Sat*. 1.2.31–35)."

158. Glancy, "Sexual Use," 227–28.

159. Westbrook, *Old Babylonian Marriage Laws*, 71–79, esp. 141; Janzen, "Meaning of *Porneia*," 75–78.

CHAPTER 3

recompense to the wife would depend on the circumstances surrounding the divorce.[160] Translations using the archaic "unchastity" and "fornication" obscure the ancient Near Eastern cultural context. Matthew's exception clause, for his Jewish audience, would signal a divorce for a *justifiable* cause.[161] The use of the term πορνεία thus casts the net more widely than just adultery after the consummation of the marriage. David Janzen maintains that the word πορνεία allows Jesus in Matthew's Gospel to target *also* sexual infidelity during the betrothal period.[162] In this cultural context, the Pharisaic question about divorce for "every" cause (Matt 19:3) bears profound, practical implications. Jesus limited divorce to illicit sexual relations in a marriage, including also the betrothal period, as the example of "just" Joseph shows in Matt 1:18–25. Matthew's use of πορνεία thus should be interpreted within its cultural context.

Conclusion

The proper definition and understanding of Greek words is pivotal. Μοιχάω is a deponent verb that has been wrongly interpreted with a passive sense by some conservative Lutherans in their zeal to justify the concept of an innocent party. Whereas a significant scholarly minority has stressed the passive voice of μοιχεύω, thus permitting remarriage of the innocent party, ancient usage of the passive voice of the verb (without an accompanying ὑπό or παρά prepositional phrase) was consistently active: "to commit adultery." The verb was normally used for men violating other men's property, and the passive voice became a means of referring to women's active adulterating. The passive voice of the verb thus does not substantiate the concept of an innocent party but rather undermines it.

Others have sought to minimize any exceptions to Jesus's prohibition of divorce and remarriage by means of narrow uses of the word πορνεία, whether for

---

160. Mielziner, *Jewish Law of Marriage*, 76–83.

161. Janzen, "Meaning of *Porneia*," 66–67. Janzen thinks that Jesus must be stricter than Shammai, who had advocated for divorce in situations of adultery (68), but Janzen overlooks how the Shammaites appear to have taken a looser approach to what is shameful than just adultery itself.

162. Janzen ("Meaning of *Porneia*," 70) faults Kampen for interpreting πορνεία in terms of purity issues as disloyalty to a Jewish sect: "[The argument] places a lot of weight on a very hypothetical double entendre. While *z'nût* can refer to disloyalty to the sect, at least at Qumran, we once again encounter the difficulty that only once, and only at Qumran, does it refer to incestuous marriages." Contra John Kampen, "The Matthean Divorce Texts Reexamined," in *New Qumran Texts and Studies: Proceedings of the First Meeting of the International Organization for Qumran Studies, Paris 1992*, ed. G. J. Brooke, STDJ 15 (Leiden: Brill, 1994), 149–67.

The Meaning of Words in the Matthean Exceptions

spiritual idolatry, a prohibited marriage due to consanguinity or affinity (Lev 18), intermarriage between Jews and gentiles, or betrothal infidelity (but not marital infidelity; cf. David Janzen's thesis). The failure of these suggestions indicates that Matthew's exception clauses to Jesus's teaching represent genuine exceptions.

As for the New Testament authors' understanding of πορνεία, these authors remained indebted to the Jewish Scriptures and to their Second Temple Jewish heritage and likewise adopted a broader understanding of πορνεία beyond simply prostitution. Neither the gospel writers nor the apostle Paul ever explicitly mentions or legitimates male slaveholders' sexual activity with their female slaves. The New Testament authors do not identify passion within the marital relationship as sinful or problematic. Jesus in the gospels appeals, instead, to the creation account of one man cleaving to one woman (Matt 19:4–6). The New Testament's use of πορνεία thus appears to be a broad term referring to sexual relations outside that marital context.

The term πορνεία more frequently refers to *women's* violation of the marital relationship since "adultery" (μοιχεία) was used primarily in reference to men's activity. This distinction is even more common with πόρνη and μοιχός (e.g., Isa 57:3 LXX).[163] This does not mean that μοιχεία could not be used as a term inclusive of both men's and women's adultery (e.g., Matt 15:19; Mark 7:22).[164] The distinction is not hard and fast. Occasionally, μοιχεία was used for a woman's adulterous action (e.g., John 8:4).[165] Nevertheless, the use of a term that points especially toward the inclusion of women's activity (πορνεία) is conspicuous in Matt 5:32. Both the passive form of μοιχεύω and the use of the broader term πορνεία converge in placing the focus in this verse on the *wife*. Illicit sexual activity forms a genuine exception to the prohibition against divorce.[166]

Matthew's exception clauses in 5:32 and 19:9 are understandable in view of the requirement for divorce in situations of spousal sexual infidelity among many first-century Jews (Prov 18:22 LXX; m. Soṭah 5:1; b. Giṭ. 90b; T. Reu. 3:15).[167] Precisely

---

163. Johannes B. Bauer, "Bemerkungen zu den matthäischen Unzuchtsklauseln (Mt 5,32; 19,9)" in *Begegnung mit dem Wort*, ed. Josef Zmijewski and Ernst Nellessen (Bonn: Hanstein, 1980), 26–27; Harper, "*Porneia*," 364, 366–67, 371, 375–76; France, *Matthew*, 209 n. 107.

164. The word groups are used synonymously in Jer 3:8–9 LXX.

165. The use of πορνεία also avoids semantic confusion with μοιχεύω later in Matt 19:9; see Blomberg, "Marriage," 178.

166. Bruce Malina, "Does *Porneia* Mean Fornication?," *NovT* 14 (1972): 10–17, and Jensen "*Porneia*," both agree that πορνεία may be translated as "adultery," while Jensen corrects Malina by pointing out that πορνεία may also refer to premarital sex.

167. Markus Bockmuehl, "Matthew 5.32; 19.9 in the Light of Pre-Rabbinic Halakah," *NTS* 35 (1989): 291–95, esp. 293–94, citing 1QapGen XX, 15.

CHAPTER 3

that sort of situation arises in Matt 1:19–25 when Joseph is faced with Mary's apparent marital infidelity. Joseph was "just" in his desire to divorce Mary quietly (1:19). As Dale Allison explains, had Matthew not relayed an exception clause in Jesus's prohibition of divorce, Joseph would not have been "righteous" to divorce her.[168] His actions would have been contrary to Jesus's teaching against divorce later in the gospel. Ultimately, these conclusions reinforce the sense that a careful rereading of the Matthean divorce texts is in order.

---

168. Dale C. Allison Jr., "Divorce, Celibacy and Joseph (Matthew 1.18–25 and 19.1–12)," *JSNT* 49 (1993): 3–5.

4

The Matthean Divorce-Remarriage Texts in Context

In both Matt 5:32 and 19:9 Jesus identifies an exception to his prohibition of divorce, but is Matthew's Jesus also permitting remarriage in these instances? Critical clues are now in place.[1] First, the passive verbal forms for both μοιχεύω and μοιχάω bear active senses throughout Greek literature: "to commit adultery." Second, the Greek word πορνεία does not appear to be used in a narrower sense for a particular type of illicit marriage, whether because of sexual sin during the betrothal period, marriage to a gentile or one's kin, or spiritual idolatry. The word is used for sexual sins in general. The πορνεία in Matt 5:32 and 19:9 refers to sexual sin in the context of the marital relationship. Even so, questions yet abound, especially what light the immediate contexts of these verses shed on their interpretation.

Matthew 5:31–32 is the first of the two texts and provides a testing ground for the value of the divorce certificates of the day. Is it true that with divorce certificate in hand a permission to remarry may simply be assumed, as some have claimed? Before turning to the interpretation of Matt 19:9, a few preliminary matters must be addressed. Some ancient manuscripts of Matt 19:9 read very differently and prohibit remarriages. Once the original text has been established, some scholars claim that the Greek should be translated with the *opposite* sense of an exception clause: *including* even sexual sin. There is to be no divorce or remarriage even when a spouse has sinned sexually. Or perhaps the clause is expressing not an exception but rather a matter *irrelevant* to the discussion, that is, sexual sins are of no consequence for this teaching. In reviewing Matt 19:1–9, especially Jesus's climactic statement in v. 9, most scholars take the exception clause as modifying

---

1. See chapter 3.

CHAPTER 4

both "divorce" and "(re)marry," but some maintain that the exception clause modifies only "divorce." In Matt 19:10–12 Jesus mentions eunuchs, and a dispute rages over the exact relationship of these verses to the prior paragraph. It is not clear if the eunuch comment is independent of or further commentary on how to understand Jesus's teaching on divorce and remarriage. Matthew's divorce-remarriage texts bear their fair share of questions.

Matthew 5:31–32 in Context and the First Exception Clause

The Sermon on the Mount (Matt 5–7) is the first of five extended discourses in Matthew's Gospel (also chs. 10, 13, 18, and 23–25). Matthew signals the departure from narration and the beginning of the discourse with: "Then he began to speak, and taught them, saying" (5:2). The sermon closes in 7:28 with, "Now when Jesus had finished saying these things." Following an introduction and the Beatitudes in 5:1–16 is a programmatic set of four statements in 5:17–20 that stress the importance of teaching and obeying the entirety of the law. Jesus has come not to abolish but to fulfill the law and the prophets (5:17). Righteousness must "exceed that of the scribes and Pharisees," or the individual "will never enter the kingdom of heaven" (5:20). The emphasis on obeying and fulfilling the law and the prophets brackets the entire sermon (5:17; 7:12).

Immediately following Matt 5:17–20 are six antitheses that will help the teacher avoid becoming the least in the kingdom of heaven—matters that are to be emphasized in the instruction of Jesus's followers. Each antithesis begins with "You have heard that it was said" or an equivalent (vv. 21, 27, 31, 33, 38, and 43), followed by Jesus's reply, "But I say to you." This section concludes in v. 48 with Jesus's command to, "Be perfect, therefore; as your heavenly Father is perfect," a statement that parallels 5:20 and creates the sense that 5:17–48 is a discrete unit of thought. The setting of Jesus's teaching about the law is on a mountaintop, reminiscent of God's revelation to Moses at Mount Sinai (Exod 19:3, 12; 24:15, 18; 34:1–2, 4). Jesus's repeated "*I* say to you" statements contrast God's original commands only in the sense of *intensifying* the requirement of complete, radical obedience, including even the intentions and dispositions that lead to action.[2]

In the first antithesis Jesus interprets "You shall not murder" to include also anger against a brother or sister. Reconciliation is to take place in situations of enmity (Matt 5:21–26). Next, in 5:27–30 Jesus intensifies the command "You shall not commit adultery" to include also the lust that leads to adulterous sexual re-

---

2. E.g., Senior, *Matthew*, 76.

lations.³ Losing an eye or a hand would be better than for the whole body to be cast into hell (5:30). The third of the six antitheses in vv. 31–32 begins not with an actual quotation from the Torah or Decalogue but rather with an *inference* from Deut 24:1–4's mention of a divorce certificate: "Whoever divorces his wife, let him give her a certificate of divorce."⁴

The second-century CE mishnaic tractate Giṭṭin identifies the formula this widely attested bill of divorce is to take: "Lo, you are free to marry any man" (m. Giṭ. 9:3).⁵ The bill of divorce was understood as ratifying the dissolution of the marital bond, thus permitting the partners to marry others. The Jews understood remarriage after an *invalid* divorce as adultery.⁶ Neither a woman given a divorce certificate who subsequently remarried nor her new husband would be adulterating, since the certificate rendered the divorce valid.

Jesus challenges that custom: "But I say to you that anyone who divorces his wife, except on the ground of unchastity, causes her to commit adultery; and whoever marries a divorced woman commits adultery" (Matt 5:32).⁷ Jesus's teaching *contradicts* the bill of divorce and charges the divorced wife who remarries and her second husband with adultery. As Hagner puts it, "Jesus introduces the new and shocking idea that even properly divorced people who marry a second time may be thought of as committing adultery."⁸ Even more shocking, a man's unwarranted act of divorce is placed parallel to and equivalent to the other sins warned against

---

3. Jesus in Matt 5:21–26 expands the command against murder to what was not technically murder: anger. He does the same with the command against adultery, extending it to lusting after a woman. Jewish literature frequently censures lustful thoughts in general (e.g., Prov 6:25; T. Iss. 4:4; Ps. Sol. 4:4; T. Isaac 4:53; cf. Herm. Vis. 1.1.2—1.2.4). "Woman" in Matt 5:28 should therefore not be limited to a married woman. Jesus does not identify the woman as "your neighbor's wife" (τοῦ πλησίον [σου]); see Hagner, *Matthew 1–13*, 120. R. Alan Culpepper stresses how the law typically identifies the woman's marital status: "The implication [from the omission here] is that Jesus extends the protection from man's lust to every woman"; see *Matthew: A Commentary*, NTL (Louisville: Westminster John Knox, 2021), 110. Likewise, Jesus is not just targeting married men; see Eduard Schweizer, *The Good News according to Matthew*, trans. David E. Green (Atlanta: John Knox, 1975), 121–22.

4. France, *Gospel of Matthew*, 206. Cf. a similar paraphrase of Deut 24:1 in Josephus, *Ant.* 4.8.23 §253. A divorce must be certified in writing.

5. See chapter 1, pp. 23–25, for Second Temple examples of bills of divorce that regularly included an expression of freedom from the marital bond, if not also explicit permission to remarry.

6. Instone-Brewer, *Divorce and Remarriage*, 125–32.

7. Ἀπολύω for divorce; see also Matt 1:19; Josephus, *Ant.* 15.7.10 §259. The culpability of the divorcing husband is clear even if, with the rabbis, one points, reads, and translates the Hebrew of Exod 20:14 with a *hiphil* form of the verb *nā'af*: "You shall not *cause* adultery to be committed"; see Lövestam, "Divorce," 53.

8. Hagner, *Matthew 1–13*, 125.

CHAPTER 4

in Matt 5:21–48.[9] Initiating a wrongful divorce is therefore adulterous just as lust is adulterous in 5:29–30, and the punishment would, again, be hellfire.[10] The only way to avoid adultery is to avoid divorce. For Jesus, Deut 24:1–4's divorce certificate is unnecessary and ultimately irrelevant since there is to be no divorce for the man and no marrying of a divorced woman. These strictures against divorce itself and against remarriage—whether the divorced woman or a man's marrying a divorced woman—are unique in this period.[11] Whereas Jesus posits in the other five antitheses an intensification in terms of prohibiting sinful *thoughts* and *intents*, his teaching on divorce and remarriage is no doubt equivalent to the others with respect to its difficulty, even though its intensification is in terms of *actions*.[12]

R. T. France disputes whether Jesus considered the divorce itself adulterous for the husband since "it is not at all obvious how the term 'adulterous' could be applied to the dissolution of a marriage if it does not result in subsequent sexual activity—who would be committing adultery with whom?"[13] Jesus does not explicitly label a man's divorce of his wife as adultery, but he does make clear that the divorcing husband is equally guilty when he causes her to remarry.[14] Again, one should not overlook that the action of the divorcing husband in Matt 5:30–32 stands parallel to murderous anger and adulterous lust, both of which lead to hellfire. Jesus will, of course, return to these matters later in Matt 19:3–9 and remind his hearers that God's intent is for the one man to be married to the one woman. Anything contrary to that is a violation of God's will and therefore sin. Although not appealing to Matt 19, Georg Strecker observes: "In Jesus' understanding every divorce is illegal because it contradicts the divine creative will of God; hence,

---

9. John J. Kilgallen, "To What Are the Matthean Exception-Texts (5,32 and 19,9) an Exception?," *Bib* 61 (1980): 102–3; Fitzmyer, "Matthean Divorce Texts," 203; followed by Heth and Wenham, *Jesus and Divorce*, 69–70, 223–24.

10. Keener, *Gospel of Matthew*, 189.

11. Hagner, *Matthew 1–13*, 123. The focus on the man, however, is to be expected since Jewish law was phrased in terms of the *husband's* right to divorce (Josephus, *Ant.* 15.7.10 §259).

12. Hagner, *Matthew 1–13*, 123.

13. France, *Matthew*, 212 n.117.

14. Not all divorced wives would remarry, even if most needed to for survival. Some might return to their fathers' homes. Craig L. Blomberg therefore stresses the possibility of adultery as something other than literal sexual intercourse. He points to the prophets' use of "adultery" for spiritual idolatry and suggests that Matt 5:32 parallels v. 28 in structure and thus should be interpreted similarly: "divorce itself, except when it is for sexual sin, is metaphorical adultery-faithlessness to the person to whom one promised permanent loyalty"; see "Marriage, Divorce, Remarriage, and Celibacy," 174–75. Perhaps more precisely, the adultery involves violation of God's will in creation that one man is to be united to one woman in marriage (Matt 19:4–6). The divorce *itself* is adulterous, as also would be a subsequent remarriage, should it take place.

there can be no talk of a dismissal that would be in harmony with the original divine law."[15]

Erasmus and the Reformers popularized the concept of an innocent party in a divorce. Jesus himself censured condemning the innocent (Matt 12:7) and stressed instead the principle of mercy (23:23). Matthew 5:32 identifies a situation in which, in most instances, a wife is being divorced against her will by her husband. She had not initiated the divorce proceedings and, apart from any sexual sin, is the innocent party.[16] In 1 Cor 7:15 unbelieving spouses may force divorce on their believing partners even when the believing partner is striving to preserve the marriage. Craig Keener exemplifies that longstanding consensus in explaining that such passages "exonerate those who genuinely wished to save their marriage but were unable to do so because their spouse's unrepentant adultery, abandonment, or abuse de facto destroyed the marriage bonds."[17]

Jesus's teaching bears profound implications for the concept of an innocent party in divorce. The problem for the innocent wife in Matt 5:32 is that the divorce places her in an incredibly difficult situation. Even as an innocent party, people would assume that her divorce was not without reason.[18] Further, as Luz writes, "This prohibition [of remarriage] could be devastating for the divorced woman."[19] Out of necessity, the innocent wife is made (i.e., caused to become) an adulteress by marrying another man. In other words, God's will for the original marital union renders any subsequent union adulterous, despite the legality of the divorce, the declared freedom to remarry in the divorce certificate, and the divorced wife's innocence.[20] Any man who marries the innocent former wife, even with her divorce certificate in hand, would also be guilty of adultery. Apart from sexual sin, Jesus explains in Matt 5:32 that the innocent divorced wife who marries another and the one who marries her are adulterating.[21] The implications of Jesus's teaching

---

15. Georg Strecker, *The Sermon on the Mount: An Exegetical Commentary*, trans. O. C. Dean Jr. (Nashville: Abingdon, 1988), 204 n. 34. The exception would be divorce due to a wife's adultery.

16. *All* the exceptions to the New Testament's divorce teaching are in contexts where one spouse seeks or would seek to maintain the marriage.

17. Keener, *Matthew*, 192.

18. David Werner Amram, *The Jewish Law of Divorce according to the Bible and Talmud* (New York: Hermon, 1968), 104–5.

19. Ulrich Luz, *Matthew 1–7: A Commentary*, trans. Wilhelm C. Linss, CC (Minneapolis: Augsburg, 1985), 302.

20. Dupont, *Mariage*, 57, 131.

21. Craig S. Keener inserts an assumed conclusion into the text: "In any case, this passage clearly permits the innocent party to remarry"; see *And Marries Another*, 33. One looks in vain within Keener's pages for a *rationale* to overturn the ostensive claim of Matt 5:32.

CHAPTER 4

for the key concepts justifying divorce and remarriage (divorce certificates and innocent parties) should not be underestimated.

Since the passive verb forms of μοιχεύω and μοιχάω bear an active sense elsewhere in Greek literature, the husband's action leads to a situation in which the wife *commits adultery*.[22] In fact, he is guilty of *causing* her (ποιεῖ αὐτήν) to adulterate. Most single women in Jesus's day could not survive apart from the support of a father or another man without turning to begging, prostitution, or slavery.[23] The Jewish Scriptures attest to the economic difficulties of single women (e.g., Ruth 1:3–5, 20–21; Ps 94:6; Isa 1:23; 10:2; 54:4). Matthew 5:32 thus in the very next clause naturally envisages (not coincidentally) a subsequent marriage after the divorce of the woman.[24] The man marrying her, however, must be cognizant that such a marriage would constitute adultery. Matthew's Jesus does not even specify that the remarriage is prohibited to allow for repentance and reconciliation.[25] Remarriage is simply adulterous.

The logic of Jesus's reasoning indicates that, somehow, divorce does not completely dissolve a marriage, although Jesus does not explicitly claim that the bonds of the first marriage are not severed by the divorce. Why then is it adulterous for the innocent wife to remarry? Most likely, Matt 5:32 anticipates Jesus's teaching in Matt 19:5–6: "The two shall become one flesh. Therefore, what God has joined together, let no one separate." God's *intention* is that one man and one

22. On the active use of the passive verb forms, see chapter 3, pp. 106–14.

23. Hagner, *Matthew 1–13*, 125. Raymond F. Collins (*Divorce*, 304 n. 100) imagines that the husband could be forcing the wife to become a prostitute for her economic survival, if not a second marriage. One would expect in that case the verb πορνεύω for what the husband causes rather than μοιχεύω; see Meier, *Law and Love*, 169 n. 105. The mention of the subsequent husband in the second half of the verse clarifies that the first husband has *caused* the wife to remarry. At several points, the rabbis would require steps be taken to verify that the original husband had in fact died. Testimony was necessary to that effect. The verification of the death of the widow's husband indicates that the first husband, if alive and had a divorce taken place, would need to facilitate his former wife's remarriage (see t. Yebam. 14.5, 7–8, 10; y. Yebam. 2:11, 4b; 16:5, 15d; b. Yebam. 25b, 115a, 116b, 122a; cf. m. Yebam. 15:1–2; 16:6–7); Tal Ilan, *Jewish Women in Greco-Roman Palestine* (Peabody, MA: Hendrickson, 1995), 151. Both R. Collins (*Divorce*, 167) and Ilan (*Jewish Women*, 151) note the economic and social pressures forcing widows to remarry.

Dowries were to be returned unless the wife was guilty of adultery. Marriage contracts are mentioned in Tob 7:13. A wife would return to her father's house but, with the high mortality rate in antiquity and paltry dowries in a generally impoverished society, many divorced women would find themselves in a dire situation.

24. It is not an alien notion being introduced into the text to recognize the woman's social situation after divorce, since the latter part of 5:32 assumes that the divorced woman will be remarrying and renders that remarriage explicit.

25. Stressed by Luz, *Matthew 1–7*, 306 n. 45.

woman should be joined together as one flesh not to be separated. The human act of divorce does not cancel the will and command of God that the two remain united. A subsequent marriage would be contrary to God's will and intent and is thus adulterous.

Thankfully, Matthew's Jesus includes an exception to this unprecedented and strict teaching: for reasons of unchastity. The wording of the exception is unusual (παρεκτὸς λόγου πορνείας) and reminiscent of Deut 24:1's *'erwat dābār* "the shame of a thing."[26] Deuteronomy 24:1 was the focus of a debate reported by the later rabbis between Jesus's contemporaries Hillel and Shammai. Good reasons indicate that the Hillel-Shammai debate mentioned by the later rabbis may well be a *retrojection* and not contemporaneous with Jesus, as became clear in the historical Jesus reconstruction conducted.[27] Second Temple Jewish texts did not debate where divorce was legitimate or the proper grounds for divorce. Permission for divorce was simply assumed. One cannot assume rabbinic claims about the pre-70 CE setting such as the Hillel-Shammai debate without corroborating evidence from that period. Perhaps one might introduce that leverage by means of the questions lodged to Jesus in Matt 19:3 and Mark 10:2 about the causes for divorce (any for Matthew, or at all, for Mark). Although Matthew was writing after 70 CE (and Mark not long before), his gospel is making the claim that such a question was current in the pre-70 CE period. In that case, it would be unwise to ignore the frequent concern among commentators about how Jesus's comments agree or disagree with Hillel and Shammai.

Shammai presumably allowed divorce only for sexual matters, whereas Hillel allowed divorce for any offense at all, including spilling food or talking too loudly. At the heart of their differences was the interpretation of Deut 24:1's "the shame of a thing."[28] Hillel stressed the word "thing" (*dābār*) in the phrase *'erwat dābār*: *any* "thing" or reason would suffice to justify a divorce. Shammai stressed the word "shame" (*'erwat*): the cause for divorce must involve shame and thus sexual infidelity.[29] The phrase in Matt 5:32 (λόγος πορνείας) is the opposite of what would be expected on the basis of Deut 24:1, leading some interpreters to suggest an emphasis on the Shammaite approach.[30]

---

26. Nolland, *Gospel of Matthew*, 244–45.
27. See also the discussion of the Hillel-Shammai debate in chapter 2, pp. 79–81.
28. Nolland, *Matthew*, 244–45.
29. Senior, *Matthew*, 78.
30. E.g., Instone-Brewer, *Divorce and Remarriage*, 158–59. The Septuagint translates the Hebrew with ἄσχημον πρᾶγμα. This phrase is also used in Sus 63 (in the Theodotion revision): "Therefore Chelkias and his wife expressed praise concerning their daughter together with her husband Ioakim and all the relatives, because no shameful deed [ἄσχημον πρᾶγμα] was found

CHAPTER 4

Hillel's liberal permission to divorce represents the standard view among Second Temple Jews. Josephus was displeased with his wife over a matter and decided to divorce her (*Life* 76 §§426–27; *Ant.* 4.8.23 §253; cf. Sir 25:26). Were Shammai's position current in Jesus's day, it would have been a minority position and largely forgotten after 70 CE when Matthew was writing his gospel. A limitation of divorce to sexual sin would have been radical in Jesus's Second Temple environment. If Jesus agreed with that position, his view would have been understood as radical as well.[31] Jesus would be effectively agreeing with the much stricter, minority position of Shammai over against Hillel. Jesus would not be contradicting "what was said" in 5:31 (about providing divorce certificates in a divorce) but, again, would be agreeing with the much stricter approach to the law.[32] At the same time, it must be stressed that Jesus would be stricter *even than Shammai* if he allowed divorce but no subsequent remarriage in instances of sexual infidelity.

John Meier, who considers the Hillel-Shammai debate a later retrojection into the Second Temple period, further objects that the Septuagint does not translate Deut 24:1's *'erwat dābār* with Matt 5:32's λόγος πορνείας but rather with ἄσχημον πρᾶγμα. Comparisons of Jesus's teaching with Shammai's overlook the fact that Amoraic period rabbis claimed that Shammai also allowed a man to divorce his wife for going outside with her hair unfastened, for spinning cloth in the streets with her armpits uncovered, and for bathing with men, all of which were, in effect, other areas of shameful impurity or immodesty (b. Giṭ. 90a–b; cf. m. Ketub. 7:6; m. Giṭ. 9:10).[33] Jesus's exception would not include those instances of shamefulness. Jesus's teaching would in that case definitely be stricter than Shammai's teaching. Other scholars, however, endorse the notion that Shammai had limited divorce to *sexual* sin, but these scholars (e.g., Sonne, Abrahams, Moore, Neufeld, and Zakovitch) appear to overlook the evidence provided by the Talmud (b. Giṭ. 90a–b).[34]

---

against her" (NETS). The author of Susanna is alluding to and interpreting the Deut 24 phrase. The charge here is *adultery*. Modern interpreters do not usually follow in this conclusion since Deut 22:22 identifies death as the penalty for adultery; see the discussion in Scacewater, "Divorce and Remarriage," 67–70. Perhaps the Shammaites would have agreed with the author of Susanna on the meaning of the phrase.

31. France, *Matthew*, 209.

32. Hagner, *Matthew 1–13*, 124. Shammai's position would have declined with Hillel's ascendency at the time of the composition of Matthew's Gospel, in which case Jesus would be presenting a stricter teaching for Matthew's day; see Davies and Allison, *Matthew*, 1:530.

33. Meier, *Law and History*, 143–44 and 143 n. 44.

34. Contra Isaiah Sonne, "The Schools of Shammai and Hillel Seen from Within," *Louis Ginzberg: Jubilee Volume*, ed. Saul Lieberman et al. (New York: American Academy for Jewish Research, 1945), 287–89; David W. Amram, "Divorce," in *Jewish Encyclopedia*, ed. Isidore Singer and Cyrus Adler (New York: Ktav, 1901–1925), 4:624–25; I. Abrahams, *Studies in Pharisaism and*

In short, Jesus may have been as strict as Shammai or even stricter, and it is more likely the latter was the case.

Putting aside the Hillel-Shammai debate, which really does not advance in any way the interpretation of Matt 5:32, the exception clause raises its own set of difficulties. Jesus's logic is that if the woman was divorced because of πορνεία, then she would already be an adulteress (and no one should marry an adulteress). If she was divorced for some other reason, the divorce was *unlawful* (since πορνεία is the only legitimate reason), and the woman is not free to marry another.[35]

Both Jewish and Roman law (e.g., the *Lex Iulia de adulteriis coercendis* 18–16 BCE) *required* divorce in cases of adultery.[36] Under the Julian law of Rome, a man who did not divorce a wife caught in adultery was guilty of condoning it.[37] Whereas a wife's adultery was in Roman law generally a private family matter to be dealt with by the husband, Jewish law held that the wife's adultery was a sin not just against the husband but also against God (Exod 20:14; Prov 2:16–17) that was punishable by death (Lev 20:10; Deut 22:22 [also a man adulterating with another man's wife]).[38] The Jewish community stopped administering capital punishment for the adulterer no later than the early first century CE, since Rome reserved the

---

the Gospels (Cambridge: Cambridge University Press, 1917), 71; Moore, *Judaism*, 2:123–24; Neufeld, *Ancient Hebrew Marriage Laws*, 178, but citing only m. Giṭ. 9:10 and no other texts; Zakovitch, "Biblical Law of Divorce," 33–34, also citing only m. Giṭ. 9:10 and no other texts. William Heth and Gordon Wenham (*Jesus and Divorce*, 128) dismiss as anachronistic the later talmudic understanding of Shammai's position, and yet do not recognize the irony that they themselves may be anachronistically reading the mishnaic version of Shammai's position into the pre-70 CE period.

35. Davies and Allison, *Matthew*, 1:532.

36. Julius Paulus, *Opinions*, 2.26.1–17 (on *Lex Iulia* see chapter 1, pp. 30–32), esp. 2.26.6 and 8: "After having killed the adulterer, the husband should at once dismiss his wife ... It has been decided that a husband who does not at once dismiss his wife whom he has taken in adultery can be prosecuted as a pimp"; as cited in Lefkowitz and Fant, *Women's Life*, 104; Gardner, *Women*, 85–86, 89. The husband did not need to pay the *kətûbâ*; S. Safrai, "Home and Family," in *The Jewish People in the First Century: Historical Geography, Political History, Social, Cultural, and Religious Life and Institutions*, ed. S. Safrai and M. Stern, CRINT 2 (Philadelphia: Fortress, 1974, 1976), 2:790; Z. W. Falk, "Jewish Private Law," in Safrai and Stern, *Jewish People in the First Century*, 1:518; m. Ketub. 7:6; Justinian, *Dig.* 48.5; Gardner, *Women*, 131–32; Amy Richlin, "Approaches to Adultery at Rome," *Women's Studies* 8 (1981): 227; Susan Treggiari, "Marriage and Family in Roman Society," in *Marriage and Family in the Biblical World*, ed. Ken. M. Campbell (Downers Grove, IL: InterVarsity, 2003), 165–69; Treggiari, *Roman Marriage: Iusti Coniuges from the Time of Cicero to the Time of Ulpian* (Oxford: Oxford University Press, 1991), 264–75.

37. Corbett, *Roman Law*, 133–46, esp. 142.

38. On Roman law, see F. Hauck, "μοιχεύω," *TDNT* 4:733; F. W. Hall, "Adultery (Roman)," in *Encyclopedia of Religion and Ethics*, ed. James Hastings (New York: Scribner's Sons, 1928), 1:134–35.

CHAPTER 4

right to that form of punishment.[39] It was expected that the husband *not* pardon the wife.[40] In fact, David Hill claims that the husband would be *compelled* to divorce the wife when her sexual sin had become public (e.g., Matt 1:18–19; m. Soṭah 5:1; cf. 3:6; 4:2).[41] Certainly the Jews did not allow sexual relations with an adulterous wife. In 2 Sam 20:3 David did not sleep with his concubines after Absalom raped them (2 Sam 16:22). In T. Reu. 3:10–15 Jacob is never said to have had sexual relations with Bilhah after Reuben slept with her. The tannaitic rabbis prohibited sexual relations between a couple after a wife adulterated (m. Yebam. 2:8; m. Soṭah 5:1; m. Ketub. 3:5; b. Giṭ. 90b).[42] The wife was often thought of as having become unclean (Jub. 33:7–9; 41:20; T. Reu. 3:15).

It is not entirely clear that adultery *required* divorce in first-century Jewish society, as Hill and Loader assert, but, clearly, many frowned on a continuation of the marriage. Loader explains that exceptions to divorce for adultery would take place in instances of duress.[43] Matthew 1:18–19 has Joseph contemplating just such an action. He could either expose his betrothed's apparent adultery or handle the matter privately without public revelation and trial. Deuteronomy 22:22 required adulterers be executed. John 8:3–6 shows that the original penalty was still being discussed, although the extant texts indicate that divorce was viewed as the equivalent since adultery had already ruined the one-flesh marriage relationship. It would have been improper to retain the unfaithful wife who had defiled herself with another man. Rabbinic sources describe various situations that required a husband to divorce his wife. He was to divorce her if she appeared in public with torn clothing or bathed with men (a Roman custom; see t. Ketub. 7.6;

On Jewish legal customs, see Boaz Cohen, "Concerning Divorce in Jewish and Roman Law," *PAAJR* 21 (1952): 31–32; Phillips, "Another Look at Adultery," 3–25.

On the widespread assumption that an adulterer is to die, see Prov 2:16–19; 7:25–27; Sir 9:9; Sus 22; Philo, *Spec.* 3.2; *Hypoth.* 7.1; Josephus, *Ant.* 3.12.1 §§274–275; 7.7.1 §§130–132; *Ag. Ap.* 2.30 §215.

39. b. Sanh. 15a–b, 41a–b; Sir 23:21, 24 in the second century BCE already envisions a public scourging, and Prov 6:33–35 mentions compensation; cf. Jer 13:22–26; Ezek 16:37, 39; 23:26, 29.

40. 1QapGen XX, 15; m. Yebam. 2:8; Abrahams, *Studies in Pharisaism*, 72–75; Lövestam, "Divorce," 61.

41. David Hill, *The Gospel of Matthew*, NCB (Grand Rapids: Eerdmans, 1972), 125, 281; Tosato, "Joseph," 547–51; so also Abrahams, *Studies in Pharisaism*, 74; more recently William R. G. Loader, "Did Adultery Mandate Divorce? A Reassessment of Jesus' Divorce Logia," *NTS* 61 (2015): 68; also 2 En. 71:7 (J).

42. Luz, *Matthew 1–7*, 306.

43. E.g., captivity; Josephus, *Ant.* 6.14.6 §§357, 364–365; 6.13.1 §309; 7.1.4 §§25–26; 16.3.3 §85; *J.W.* 1.22.1 §432. See Ze'ev Safrai, "Halakhic Observance in the Judaean Desert Documents," *Law in the Documents of the Judaean Desert*, ed. Ranon Katzoff and David Schaps, JSJSup 96 (Leiden: Brill, 2005), 217.

m. Ketub. 7:6; b. Giṭ. 90a–b; y. Giṭ. 44b, 2:3). A man must divorce his wife if she had been prevented from going to the bathhouse at a reasonable time and was to pay her the sum agreed on in the marriage contract (y. Ketub. 31b, 7:4).[44] The Shepherd of Hermas in the Apostolic Fathers says that a husband may stay with a guilty wife if he does not know about the sin. If he becomes aware of it and she does not repent, he must divorce her (Herm. Mand. 4.1.4–10; so also Justin, *2 Apol.* 2; Tertullian, *Marc.* 4.34.7).[45]

As Matthew writes for a Jewish audience sensitive to the pressures (or, for many, requirement) to divorce the sexually unfaithful, an absolute prohibition of divorce would have been a stumbling block. Matthew's Jesus clarifies that the prohibition did not keep husbands from divorcing adulterous wives, as expected in their legal traditions. Divorce would be permissible in these circumstances.[46] The exception clauses in Matthew would be a concession to the Jewish pressures for a mandatory divorce in the wake of adultery and may or may not bear any implications for the permissibility of remarriage.[47] Such a man cannot cause his wife to become an adulteress by the divorce since she *already is* one.

Some have emphasized the Jewish tradition that sexual misconduct was so serious a violation that it *destroyed the marital bond*. A reconciliation was *not possible*.[48] Note, however, the precise logic of Matt 5:32's exception clause: A man may not divorce a faithful wife lest he implicate himself in causing her to commit adultery. A man *may* divorce an adulterous wife without sinning himself. Whereas many first-century Jews *required* divorce in these situations, Jesus *did not*.[49] Is there an allusion to Hosea's image of God's faithfulness in the face of Israel's infidelity, an infidelity likened to sexual sin in the context of a marriage relationship? Matthew uniquely stresses Jesus's appropriation of Hosea's statement, "I desire mercy, not sacrifice" (Hos 6:6; Matt 9:13; 12:7), a mercy that may be granted the adulterous spouse. Just as God has remained faithful where the people did not, the husband may retain the adulterous wife. Jesus's wording allows for that option

---

44. Safrai, "Home and Family," 762; Bockmuehl, "Pre-Rabbinic Halakah," 291–95.

45. Afterward, according to the Shepherd of Hermas, the husband is to remain single or be ready to take her back if she should repent.

46. Keener (*And Marries Another*, 34) inexplicably claims that the exception clause has no function if it does not permit remarriage, but Jesus had prohibited *divorce* in 5:32. Jesus says nothing about a permission to remarry. In fact, he labels the marrying of a divorced woman adulterous.

47. Contra Murray, *Divorce*, 51–52.

48. E.g., Talbert, *Matthew*, 84.

49. A fact recognized by Murray, *Divorce*, 21, who adds: "Preoccupation with the one exception should never be permitted to obscure the force of the negation of all others."

CHAPTER 4

even as it allows a divorce to take place without the husband's sinning. Not to *require* divorce by the aggrieved husband is, again, shockingly countercultural.[50]

As for Mark's and Luke's absolute proscriptions against divorce, many scholars have opined that they were *assuming* what would be obvious (at least to scholars), that with πορνεία an intact marital relationship would no longer exist. Divorce would be impermissible in any *other* instance since the marital relationship remains in those cases intact. R. T. France in his commentary spells out the logic:

> It can be argued that when in Mark and Luke Jesus forbids divorce *tout simple* this is understood to mean the voluntary breaking of a marriage which is hitherto intact, it being assumed that in the case of πορνεία (*porneia*) by the wife the marriage was already destroyed and could not be allowed to continue. On that view, Matthew is merely making explicit what was assumed by Mark and Luke to be already obvious to their readers.[51]

What such commentary overlooks is the very question of whether Matthew makes such an assumption explicit.

Jesus does not explicitly claim that the wife's sexual infidelity (in the exception clause) has irrevocably broken the marital bond. Likely that is why assuming such a claim in Jesus's teaching leads to difficulties. Whereas it is adulterous for an innocent wife to marry another man, since the bond is *not* broken in that instance, the exception clause would remove that impediment if the sexual infidelity had already irretrievably broken the bond. If the marital bond is already broken by the sexual sin, the guilty woman would be free to marry another man whereas the innocent woman is not. The guilty, divorced wife would enjoy a prerogative that the innocent, divorced wife does not have. If, on the other hand, the guilty divorced wife cannot remarry but the aggrieved, innocent, former husband *may* remarry, since the bonds of marriage are broken, then why cannot the guilty divorced wife *also* remarry? Or is she *not* actually severed from bonds of the prior marriage but only separated from the husband? The husband would be polygamous, then, in marrying another woman.[52] These are the conundrums that the notion of sexual

---

50. Loader overlooks this nuance in Jesus's teaching in Matthew; "Did Adultery Mandate Divorce?," 74–78; following Instone-Brewer, *Divorce and Remarriage*, 153, 184. Although Jews in Jesus's day viewed divorce after adultery as mandatory, Matthew's Jesus—with the exception clauses—permits it but never requires it. Loader recognizes that his argument is an argument from silence: since other Jews considered divorce mandatory in *situations of adultery*, Jesus in Matthew must have as well even if he did not say so (74).

51. France, *Matthew*, 211.

52. Dupont, *Mariage*, 131; followed by Heth and Wenham, *Jesus and Divorce*, 50.

sin as a complete dissolution of a marital bond creates within this passage. These conundrums equally plague the notion that the innocent spouse of an *illegitimate* divorce may *not* remarry, while the guilty spouse of a *legitimate* divorce would be free to do so.[53]

The matter of remarriage in Matt 5:31–32 remains to be addressed. Does Jesus's teaching render remarriage adulterous? The question is ultimately whether the exception clause of Matt 5:32 permits only divorce or whether the exception clause permits both divorce and subsequent remarriage. Does Matt 5:32 indicate that remarriage is *always* adulterous or only when the wife's πορνεία is not the cause? The near consensus of scholarship is that the wife's sexual sin permits both divorce *and* remarriage for the aggrieved husband should he divorce his wife. In allowing divorce under these circumstances, it is striking, nevertheless, that Matthew *does not say that the aggrieved husband could remarry*. The absolute form of Jesus's teaching in Mark and Luke warns against simply assuming that the divorced husband enjoys that freedom. What of the innocent wife divorced against her will? The lack of an article before "a divorced woman" in 5:32 indicates that the referent is broader than the particular woman mentioned in the first part of the verse: marrying *any* divorced woman entails adultery for the man.[54] Nothing in Matt 5:32 sanctions remarriage; the verse only warns against adultery.[55]

Most scholars resist this conclusion and argue that a divorce already entailed in that culture the freedom to remarry, just as the divorce certificates of the day

---

53. Stressing legitimate versus illegitimate divorces is Murray, *Divorce*, 25–26, 98–101, who also struggles with the notion that the divorced adulterous wife may herself remarry. He writes: "[I]t is difficult to discover any biblical ground on the basis of which to conclude that remarriage of the guilty divorcee is to be considered in itself an act of adultery and as constituting an adulterous relation" (100). Then: "[W]e are not able to find biblical warrant for affirming that the person who has been divorced for adultery commits another act of adultery when he or she remarries" (101). The situation would be otherwise if remarriage itself is adulterous while the former spouse still lives.

Against Murray, Matt 5:31–32 never expresses any permission for remarriage for *any* situation. Note that, from Murray's perspective, divorce certificates issued for illegitimate divorces were ineffectual. Freedom to remarry could not be assumed from the issuance of the certificate, no matter how acceptable and assumed it would be in the larger world. Arguments from the freedom expressed in divorce certificates are therefore problematic and may not be employed without serious qualification.

54. Dupont, *Mariage*, 131–32; so also Joseph MacRory, *The New Testament and Divorce* (Dublin: Burns, Oates, and Washbourne, 1934), 25, who adds: "And, indeed, it would surely be strange if an innocent wife that had been put away were forbidden remarriage under pain of adultery, while one who was already an adulteress were permitted to remarry with perfect impunity."

55. Dupont, *Mariage*, 132.

said (e.g., m. Giṭ. 9:3).⁵⁶ Remarriage would be implicitly sanctioned when the divorce itself was legitimate. A permission for divorce would assume permission to remarry for the aggrieved party. Persuaded by the reasoning of David Instone-Brewer on this matter, R. T. France declares, "The Jewish world knew nothing of a legal separation that did not allow remarriage."⁵⁷

If only Jesus's teaching here were so easily tamed. The marriage certificates were precisely what set the stage for that teaching. The whole point of the divorce document was to declare the wife free to remarry without any charge of adultery (m. Giṭ. 9:3). Jesus declares that men are *not* free to divorce their wives at will, certificate notwithstanding. A man's action in divorcing, where sexual sin is not a factor, is parallel to other sins deserving of hellfire. God's will for that original union is not so easily dispensed. Then, the innocent, wrongly divorced wife *herself* becomes an adulteress when she marries another, certificate notwithstanding. She would be consigned either to a life of sinless singleness or a life of sin in seeking the social safety and patriarchal protection of a subsequent marriage. The only permission for divorce is sexual sin. As shockingly countercultural as this passage is with respect to the divorce certificates, should one *assume* a freedom to remarry? If divorce certificates have indeed been rendered null and void by Jesus's teaching, apart from instances of sexual sin interpreters are entirely missing the point of the passage in continuing to appeal to them for a freedom to remarry, as if *that* were the one claim from the certificates that Jesus would endorse.⁵⁸ Even with the exception clause, Hays candidly observes, "A divorced woman . . . could never remarry under the terms of this teaching without committing adultery."⁵⁹ If

---

56. See the instances at pp. 23–29 in chapter 1 helpfully located and catalogued by David Instone-Brewer. Or with Keener, *And Marries Another*, 34: "The husband's right to remarry was assumed. . . . [Jesus] allows for a valid remarriage for the innocent party." If so, why then is the *innocent wife* after a divorce guilty of adultery to marry another? Again, Jesus is teaching counterculturally here.

57. France, *Matthew*, 212, drawing on Instone-Brewer, *Divorce and Remarriage*, 117–25. Even before Instone-Brewer's documentation of divorce certificates, many were coming to this conclusion; e.g., Descamps, "New Testament Doctrine on Marriage," 257: "a legitimate divorce brought the right of the husband to remarry."

58. Note the contradictions that advocates of remarriage then face. Remarriage, Keener explains (*Matthew*, 469), is adulterous because the original union *remains* in God's sight in cases of illegitimate divorce, but then Keener appeals to the divorce certificates as permitting a freedom after divorce, which he believes would have been assumed! How can one simply assume what is stated on divorce certificates if they are wrong in cases of illegitimate divorce?

59. The passage does not address whether remarriage is possible for the man who divorced an unfaithful wife, provided he marries a woman who has not been married; Hays, *Moral Vision*, 356–57. The passage focuses on the implications for the wife.

The Matthean Divorce-Remarriage Texts in Context

the innocent woman may not remarry, how much more the adulterous woman? Divorced women are simply granted no provision for remarriage.

Matthew allows divorce when a husband has been aggrieved by his wife's sexual sin. May the innocent husband do what the innocent wife could not? Would the divorce certificate avail for him where it did not for her in providing freedom to remarry? Davies and Allison conclude: "In our judgment, the issue cannot, unfortunately, be resolved on exegetical grounds: Matthew's words are simply too cryptic to admit of a definitive interpretation."[60] Davies and Allison direct their readers instead to Matt 19:1–10. If the innocent wife is divorced and may not remarry, would not the same apply to an innocent husband after divorce?

Matthew 5:32 remains focused entirely on men wrongly divorcing their wives, and the situation for the wife after that illicit divorce. Technically, the verse does not address the innocent husband's rights after divorce from an unfaithful wife.[61] Perhaps the innocent *wife* may not remarry because she resides in a patriarchal society. Perhaps the aggrieved, innocent husband enjoys a privilege the innocent wife does not. It is an *assumption* that the marital bond has been entirely dissolved by the wife's sexual infidelity. Certainly a divorce is permissible, but remarriage may not be. After all, any man who marries a divorced woman also commits adultery, her possession of a certificate and innocence notwithstanding. Even in the face of human sin, God's original intent may remain that one man be united to one woman. These are the very issues that Matthew turns to later in the gospel. Does *that* passage substantiate the assumption that remarriage after a legitimate divorce is permissible, at least for the husband?

Craig Keener qualifies Jesus's teaching in the Sermon on the Mount, including the teaching against remarriage in 5:31–32, as "rhetorical overstatement."[62] Jesus's teaching is indeed exceedingly difficult. Keener affirms that Jesus is teaching against remarriage, and yet he comments in general on the Sermon on the Mount, ironically:

> The earliest Christians, whose interpretations appear in New Testament epistles and documents like the Didache and the writings of church fathers, demand obedience to Jesus' teaching recorded in this sermon. . . . Jesus himself apparently expected full compliance with his teaching, not in the legalistic or

---

60. Davies and Allison, *Matthew*, 1:529.
61. Hays, *Moral Vision*, 356–57. Or with Garland, *Reading Matthew*, 69: "[The exception] seems to say that the bond is permanent only until *the wife* does something to break that permanence, and it allows divorce on demand for the husband (only) as long as the wife has committed some sexual sin."
62. Keener, *Matthew*, 190.

CHAPTER 4

ascetic ways he himself condemns, "but as signs of God's Kingdom"..., expressions of submission to God's reign over the lives of his followers.[63]

In other words, Keener's quick and easy label of "rhetorical overstatement" should not be used to set aside Jesus's teaching, at least according to Keener himself elsewhere.[64] That teaching bears a declaratory legal form that is reminiscent of the casuistic law of the Old Testament.[65] In other words, Jesus is not promoting a "hyperbolic" "ideal" but rather a *standard* for his followers.[66] Only perilously should the modern interpreter dismiss Jesus's teaching as "hyperbolic" or idealized and not normative. Craig Keener, in tortured logic, appeals to Jesus's teaching of mercy in Matt 9:13 and 12:7 as allowing "the remarriage of the innocent party."[67] What Jesus says is that there is forgiveness for sin, in this case adultery, but not permission to adulterate (through remarriage) or to commit murder or any other sin. Forgiveness is not sanction for sin. To divorce an innocent wife is adulterous. To marry a divorced woman, whether innocent or guilty, is adulterous.

Matthew 19:9's Exception Clause: Preliminary Questions and Context

Matthew 19:9 narrates a second occasion when Jesus addresses divorce and remarriage, also with an exception clause. The exception clause presents several potential issues. If the original Greek text of Matt 19:9 reads in a fashion that parallels Matt 5:32, then Matt 19:9 would be interpreted similarly. Assuming the traditional

---

63. Keener, *Matthew*, 161, following Martin Dibelius, *Jesus* (Philadelphia: Westminster, 1949), 122–23, and drawing on Robert M. Grant, "The Sermon on the Mount in Earliest Christianity," *Semeia* 12 (1978): 215–31, esp. 216–19. According to Grant, the author of James would have taken the Sermon literally as what the disciple is to do, and Paul would not have neglected Jesus's moral teaching, nor the Didache and 1 Clement. He writes, "The authors we have thus far considered [cf. the Gnostics] have taken the Sermon or Sermon-like materials literally as commands to be obeyed" (219).

64. H. G. Coiner documents at length the historic Lutheran position that the innocent party may remarry. As for the Matthean texts, he candidly concedes: "The words merely say that in the case of *porneia* the husband is not responsible for committing adultery. Jesus does not say... that there can be remarriage without adultery"; see "Those 'Divorce and Remarriage' Passages (Matt. 5:32; 19:9; 1 Cor. 7:10–16) with Brief Reference to the Mark and Luke Passages," *CTM* 39 (1968): 379.

65. Fitzmyer, *Luke X–XXIV*, 1120.

66. Rightly the "pre-conversion" opinion of Heth, "Divorce and Remarriage," 70; contra Keener, *And Marries Another*, 24.

67. Keener, *And Marries Another*, 35.

The Matthean Divorce-Remarriage Texts in Context

reconstruction of the text of 19:9, on the other hand, some have concluded that the verse does not actually include an exception and the verse agrees with the absolute teaching against divorce and remarriage in Mark 10:11 and Luke 16:18—and with Matt 5:32's forbidding a wrongly divorced wife from marrying another or for a man to marry her. A genuine exception in Matt 19:9 is a necessary precondition for a reading that permits remarriage. These two questions must be addressed before interpreting Matt 19:9 in its immediate context.

The Original Greek Text of Matthew 19:9

Whereas Matt 5:32 is more stably attested in the ancient Greek manuscripts, significant variant readings are present for Matt 19:9. Critical editions of the Greek text favor the Sinaiticus's reading:

> ὃς ἂν ἀπολύσῃ τὴν γυναῖκα αὐτοῦ μὴ ἐπὶ πορνείᾳ καὶ γαμήσῃ ἄλλην μοιχᾶται.
>
> Whoever divorces his wife, except for unchastity, and marries another commits adultery.

Sinaiticus's reading "except for unchastity" identifies an exception to the prohibition. One could divorce and perhaps also remarry under these circumstances.

One key variant is present in the valuable and prominent Vaticanus manuscript.[68]

> ὃς ἂν ἀπολύσῃ τὴν γυναῖκα αὐτοῦ παρεκτὸς λόγου πορνείας ποιεῖ αὐτὴν μοιχευθῆναι καὶ ὁ ἀπολελυμένην γαμήσας μοιχᾶται, (cf. the parallel wording in Matt 5:32)
>
> Whoever divorces his wife, except on the ground of unchastity, causes her to commit adultery; and he who marries a divorced woman commits adultery.

The Vaticanus reading parallels Matt 5:32 and identifies as adulterous any remarriage by the divorced wife or any marriage to her by a subsequent husband. In other words, this textual version of Matt 19:9—like Matt 5:32, Mark 10:11, and Luke 16:18—does not sanction remarriage but identifies it as adulterous in these instances.

A few ante-Nicene thinkers appear to have drawn upon the same reading of Matt 19:9 as Vaticanus. Clement of Alexandria (150–215 CE) appears to quote this

---

68. This variant also appears in p[25], the sixth-century uncial C, family 1, the Bohairic tradition, and an eighth-century Latin manuscript.

CHAPTER 4

version of Matt 19:9 from memory: "Therefore he who divorces his wife except for fornication makes her an adulteress" (*Strom.* 3.6 [Oulton and Chadwick, LCC]). Origen also quotes the relevant portion of Matt 19:9 in his discussion of that chapter: "Whoever divorces his wife, except for the reason of sexual immorality, makes her commit adultery" (*Comm. Matt.* 14.24). The reading in Vaticanus and p[25] is universally attested in the Greek church fathers until the middle of the fifth century CE and in the Latin church fathers until the middle of the fourth century CE, with authors referencing the Sinaiticus reading thereafter.

Despite the strong external attestation for the Vaticanus reading in the first centuries of Christianity, modern critical editions of the Greek text favor the Sinaiticus reading. According to text-critical principles, the most difficult reading is to be preferred, and the Sinaiticus includes an exception clause that may permit remarriage where the other gospel divorce and remarriage texts clearly prohibit it. While the Sinaiticus reading may be the easier one for churchly practice, it is the more difficult reading in the sense that it does not match the parallel passages' explicit prohibition of remarriage.

Another principle in modern textual criticism is that the more original reading is the one that can explain the origin of the others. Were Sinaiticus original, the Vaticanus reading is easily explained as a later harmonization with the language of Matt 5:32. Were Vaticanus the original reading, on the other hand, the origin of Sinaiticus would be difficult to understand (convoluted, in fact). While the last four words of Sinaiticus could be derived from Mark 10:11, the unique language of the exception clause is unparalleled. The Sinaiticus exception clause of Matt 19:9 must be accounted for in any interpretation. It is unlikely the Sinaiticus scribe would borrow from Mark 10:11 and invent a unique exception clause rather than what is already in Matt 5:32. The Vaticanus's rendering might well have been motivated by the first Christians' perspective that remarriage was impermissible.[69] Vaticanus offers a reading that agrees with Jesus's otherwise absolute teaching against remarriage in Mark 10:11–12 and Luke 16:18. The Sinaiticus reading is therefore most likely the original.

On the other hand, the Vaticanus's exception (παρεκτὸς λόγου πορνείας) may have been original if a scribe had switched out the Semitic expression for a form that better reflected Greek style. The Sinaiticus reading would in that case be *later*.[70] The external witnesses for the Vaticanus are strong, and the attestation of early Christian authors is sobering. Also, later instances of Matthean doublets

---

69. For more on this, see chapter 6.
70. Robert H. Gundry, *Matthew: A Commentary on His Literary and Theological Art* (Grand Rapids: Eerdmans, 1982), 381.

typically restate the first.[71] If Vaticanus preserves the original reading of Matt 19:9, then the gospels would be universally proscribing remarriage. The text-critical conclusion here in favor of Sinaiticus (μὴ ἐπὶ πορνείᾳ) must remain tentative in view of the challenge posed by the Vaticanus reading.[72] Jesus in Matt 19:9, as with all the other gospel texts, would have explicitly forbidden remarriage.

Ante-Nicene authors, had they been aware of the Sinaiticus reading, were it original, may not have commented on the exception clause because they interpreted it as not permitting remarriage, only divorce. MacRory objects:

> But is it not strange that all of them should set forth Christ's teaching as so clear and unequivocal, without any reference to a text that certainly creates at least a very apparent difficulty? . . . The argument from silence is admittedly precarious, but certainly a silence like this in regard to a text that presented so obvious an objection to their view is remarkable.[73]

At a minimum, the Vaticanus reading attests to how the earliest Christians understood Jesus to be teaching against the possibility of remarriage.

To summarize: Were the Sinaiticus variant the original reading of Matt 19:9 and known to the earliest interpreters, then the interpretation of Christian authors up to 325 CE that remarriage is not permitted would be all the more stunning since it would represent their understanding of the Matthean exception clauses. On the other hand, the absence of early Christian witnesses to the Sinaiticus reading of Matt 19:9 is a powerful argument that it was unknown prior to the Council of Nicaea.

The Inclusive and Preteritive Views That Deny Any Exception to Jesus's Teaching

The words μὴ ἐπὶ πορνείᾳ, "except for unchastity," in Matt 19:9 may not actually be an exception clause. These words are translated by some as "*not even* in the case of unchastity"—what is called the "inclusive" understanding of the exception clause. In other words, a man is *not* to divorce his wife and marry another *even* in cases of

---

71. G. D. Kilpatrick, *The Origins of the Gospel according to St. Matthew* (Oxford: Oxford University Press, 1946), 84–100.

72. On the text-critical reconstruction, see Jean Duplacy, "Note sur les variantes et le texte original de Matthieu 19,9," in *Études de critique textuelle de Nouveau Testament*, BETL 78 (Leuven: Leuven University Press, 1987), 387–412; Corrado, *Parole di Gesù*, 250–311; Ulrich Luz, *Matthew 8–20*, Hermeneia (Minneapolis: Fortress, 2001), 486.

73. MacRory, *Divorce and Remarriage*, 54–55.

sexual unchastity.[74] This translation has not gained many adherents since there are no other instances in Greek literature where the two words μὴ ἐπὶ are used with the sense of "not even."[75] Were there an inclusive sense in Matt 19:9—"*not even* for adultery"—one would expect μηδέ and not μή.

If the inclusive approach to Matt 19:9 were correct, one would expect the parallel exception clause in Matt 5:32 to be inclusive as well, even though the wording is different (παρεκτὸς λόγου πορνείας, "except on the ground of unchastity"). Normally an adverb, the word παρεκτὸς when with a genitive noun functions as an improper preposition and means "apart from" (an *exclusive* sense). In Acts 26:29 the preposition means to become as Paul "except for" or "apart from" (παρεκτός) the chains that are on Paul. The exclusive sense is also clear in 2 Cor 11:28: "apart from" or "besides" (παρεκτός) the other things, Paul is under daily pressure because of his anxiety for all the churches (see also Did. 6.1; T. Zeb. 1:4).[76] Similarly in Matt 5:32 the word signals an exception to the absolute prohibition. The exclusive use of the exception clause in Matt 5:32 renders further unlikely an inclusive sense for μὴ ἐπὶ πορνείᾳ in the Matthean doublet of 19:9.

In what is called the preteritive view (as opposed to the inclusive view), Bruce Vawter takes Matt 19:9's exception as expressing a parenthetical sort of "no comment" on the matter of unchastity.[77] The μή functions as a negative particle nullifying ἐπί, where the preposition signifies a circumstance or state. In this reading, the exception of Matt 19:9 (μὴ ἐπὶ πορνείᾳ) would modify *the entire sentence* and not just the verb for divorce (ἀπολύω).[78] The word "unchastity," or better "uncleanness" (πορνεία) would then serve as an allusion to Deut 24:1. As Banks writes, "Here, in the climactic saying of the narrative, it is perfectly in accord with Matthew's redactional method that he should round the encounter with a reference to the

---

74. E.g., Michael Brunec, "Tertio de clausulis divortii Mt 5,32 et 19,9," *Verbum Domini* 27 (1949): 3–16; U. Holzmeister, "Die Streitfrage über die Ehescheidungstexte bei Matthäus 5,32, 19,9," *Bib* 26 (1945): 133–46; Karl Staab, "Die Unauflösigkeit der Ehe und die sog. 'Ehebruchsklauseln' bei Mt 5,32 und 19,9," in *Festschrift Eduard Eichmann zum 70. Geburtstag*, ed. Martin Grabmann and Karl Hofmann (Paderborn: Schöningh, 1940), 435–52; for a list of older adherents, see Dupont, *Mariage*, 98 n. 1. A survey of the Perseus database for μὴ ἐπὶ confirms Dupont's conclusion.

The inclusive approach is only viable in Matt 19:9. Allen R. Guenther helpfully reviews the use of παρεκτός throughout ancient Greek literature and its parallels to παρέκ to confirm that Matt 5:32 includes a genuine exception clause; see "The Exception Phrases: Except πορνεία or Excluding πορνεία? (Matthew 5:32; 19:9)," *TynBul* 53.1 (2002): 86–92.

75. Vawter, "Divorce Clauses," 155–67.

76. See the fuller case in Guenther, "Exception Phrases," 86–92.

77. Others took this position before Vawter gave it its preeminent expression. For a list, see Dupont, *Mariage*, 96–97.

78. Vawter, "Divorce Clauses," 163–65.

provision around which the controversy revolved."[79] Likewise, the supposed exception clause in Matt 5:32 (παρεκτός) is not actually an exception of the absolute prohibition of divorce but rather *to the very question of divorce itself*.[80] Vawter translates Matt 19:9 from this perspective: "I say to you, whoever dismisses his wife—Dt 24, notwithstanding—and marries another, commits adultery," or "I say to you, however, that if anyone dismisses his wife—*porneia* is not involved—and marries another, he commits adultery; and whoever marries one who has been dismissed, commits adultery."[81] A similar grammatical use of μὴ, Vawter claims, is in Matt 26:5 with "not during the festival" (μὴ ἐν τῇ ἑορτῇ) modifying the entirety of the prior verse about the attempt to arrest Jesus.[82] As Vawter understands Matt 19:9 in context, the Pharisees confronted Jesus with the debate between Hillel and Shammai about the grounds for divorce in Deut 24:1 (i.e., πορνεία). Jesus did not give them a direct answer. He simply placed the matter of πορνεία and Deut 24 *to the side*. Vawter then harmonizes Matt 19:9 with Mark 10:11: Jesus's full answer to the question would come in private, as narrated by Mark, and there Jesus would rule out divorce even in those cases. For that moment in public with the Pharisees described in Matt 19:9, Jesus did not offer a judgment on the matter. He labeled divorce adulterous without commenting on those instances involving infidelity. Jesus's prohibition of divorce was therefore absolute.

In an analysis paralleling Vawter's in Matt 19:9, Allen Guenther reviews the ancient Greek usage of μὴ ἐπί and identifies three categories. First are constructions that would be translated "not" followed by a preposition (for ἐπί; e.g., "not for," "not in," or simply "not"). In this case, μὴ ἐπί does not introduce an exception. The second and third categories are εἰ μὴ ἐπί and ἐὰν μὴ ἐπί, in which εἰ and ἐὰν function as subordinating constructions with the phrase meaning "except" (with εἰ) or "unless" (with ἐάν). Guenther could find *no instance* of μὴ ἐπί by itself or in constructions with other words meaning "except" or "unless." Matthew 19:9 should be translated, then, "Whoever divorces his wife *apart from / excluding / not introducing the factor of* πορνεία and marries another commits adultery." In other words, whoever divorces his wife, apart from instances of sexual sin, and marries another commits adultery. The translation "except for sexual sin" would not be viable, argues Guenther.[83]

---

79. Robert Banks, *Jesus and the Law in the Synoptic Tradition*, SNTSMS 28 (London: Cambridge University Press, 1975), 157. Cf. 15:20.

80. Banks (*Jesus and the Law*, 156) stresses that παρεκτός means "apart from" rather than "except" in the other New Testament instances.

81. Vawter, "Divorce Clauses," 164, 166; Banks, *Jesus and the Law*, 156.

82. Banks, *Jesus and the Law*, 156 n. 2.

83. Guenther, "Exception Phrases," 92–95.

CHAPTER 4

The preteritive approach is not likely. Grammatically, the preteritive appeal to Matt 26:5 for μή as simply a negative particle nullifying ἐπί ("not for πορνείᾳ," i.e., πορνείᾳ is not involved) is problematic. The μή in Matt 26:5 is *not* a simple negative particle but is functioning within a conditional relative clause (ὅσοι ἄν = ἐάν τις,"whoever"), which renders the negative μή here the equivalent of (ἐάν) μή (unless, except).[84] Thus BDAG places μή in Matt 26:5 in a different grammatical category than Matt 19:9's use of μή.[85] Matthew 19:9's μὴ ἐπὶ πορνείᾳ functions as an ellipsis for a longer conditional clause (with an understood εἰ "if"): "Whoever puts away his wife, *if he does not put her away for unchastity*, and marries another, commits adultery."[86] The grammar of the verse therefore rules out the preteritive approach. The chief advocate for this view, Vawter, tellingly abandoned this position in his later work.[87] Jewish authors often understood divorce as *required* in instances of sexual sin and, as Jesus addressed a Jewish audience, he allowed an exception to his no-divorce teaching in these instances. Finally, in Matt 19:10 the disciples' shocked reaction to Jesus's claims is difficult to imagine had he not rendered a position on the matter of the permissibility of divorce.[88] Whether the inclusive approach or the preteritive view, the question lodged by the Pharisees was whether divorce is permissible for any reason, which leads the reader to recognize a potentially good reason for divorce in the exception clause.[89]

Matthew 19:9 in Context

Prior to Matthew 19, Jesus had foretold his suffering in Jerusalem (Matt 16:21; cf. 17:22), and in 19:1 steps foot on Judean soil nearing the fulfillment of his prediction. Teaching the large crowds following him about the self-denial required of disciples (19:27–30; cf. 16:24), he also revisits teachings first shared in the Sermon on the Mount: the lowly worldly status of those in the kingdom (19:14; cf. 5:3–10), Moses's commands (19:18–19; cf. 5:17–48), the command to be per-

---

84. Maximilian Zerwick, *Biblical Greek Illustrated by Examples*, Scripta Pontificii Instituti Biblici 114 (Rome: Pontifical Biblical Institute, 1963), 148–49 §442: μή by itself does not mean "except"—thus an understood ἐάν; Dupont, *Mariage*, 102–3; followed by Heth and Wenham, *Jesus and Divorce*, 188.

85. Matt 19:9 has a negative particle and negative clause, within a conditional clause.

86. Dupont, *Mariage*, 102.

87. Bruce Vawter, "Divorce in the New Testament," *CBQ* 39 (1977): 534–35.

88. MacRory, *New Testament and Divorce*, 47.

89. Descamps, "New Testament Doctrine," 243, who adds concerning the preteritive and inclusive approaches: "They are suspect, first from the fact that they are somewhat subtle, second because they eliminate as if by magic a difficulty that has been prominent for a long time. This leads us to think that they have been invented just in order to escape this difficulty" (242–43).

fect (19:21; cf. 5:48), treasure in heaven (19:21; cf. 6:19–21), the danger of money (19:22; cf. 6:24), obstacles to entering the kingdom of heaven (19:23; cf. 7:13–14), and the promise of reward (19:27–20:16; cf. 5:3–10).[90] Matthew 19:3–9 on divorce and remarriage thus parallels 5:31–32. Whereas Jesus's instructions on divorce and remarriage take place in private in Mark 10:10–12 in the house, Jesus's corresponding teaching in Matt 19:9 is in public in the presence of his detractors. Here the saying about eunuchs (19:10–12) is directed to the disciples but not the teaching on divorce and remarriage. The paragraphs narrating what transpired after Jesus arrives in Judea in 19:1 will continue to oscillate between instruction applicable to all (19:13–15, 23–26; 20:1–16) and instruction for only the disciples (19:16–22, 27–30).[91]

The departure from Galilee for the region of Judea after Jesus had finished speaking (19:1) signals that this is, geographically, the beginning of the events leading to Jesus's crucifixion. The conflict with the religious leaders will reach a boiling point, and it is just such a conflict that takes place immediately with the change of location. The region "beyond the Jordan" is reminiscent of John the Baptist's ministry (3:5–6) and the "brood of vipers" he encountered there (3:7).[92] Even as John the Baptist had come to a dire end because of his criticism of an illicit marriage (14:3–4), now the debate over marriage and divorce is posed to Jesus as the Pharisees "test him" (19:3; cf. Satan in 4:1–11, but also the Pharisees in 16:1; 22:15, 18). The previous encounters with the Pharisees were hardly pleasant (15:12–14; 16:1–4, 6, 11–12). Whereas the Pharisees in Mark 10:2 ask if divorce *itself* was lawful, in Matt 19:3 the question is whether divorce is permissible "for any cause," literally—and more precisely—"for every reason *whatsoever*."[93] What are the legitimate grounds for divorce? For every imaginable cause a husband might have?[94] This is the question they have for Jesus when he leaves Galilee for Judea.

90. Garland, *Reading Matthew*, 197.
91. Garland, *Reading Matthew*, 197–98.
92. Jesus had come to the region of Judea beyond the Jordan (perhaps Perea near the fortress of Machaerus; cf. 4:25), the very location where John the Baptist had met his demise. This connection is not certain since Perea—although "across the Jordan"—was *not* part of Judea. Matthew may simply be alluding to John the Baptist's area of ministry. One would need to cross the Jordan in order to avoid Samaria on the way to Jerusalem.
93. Dupont, *Mariage*, 29, 85, 150; Boris Repschinski, *The Controversy Stories in the Gospel of Matthew: Their Redaction, Form, and Relevance for the Relationship between the Matthean Community and Formative Judaism*, FRLANT 189 (Göttingen: Vandenhoeck & Ruprecht, 2000), 173.
94. He is not answering a question about separation, a distinction absent in the first-century world. See chapters 1 and 2, pp. 29–30, 33, 64–66. To separate is to divorce; see Dupont, *Mariage*, 141–44. He is also not answering the Markan question of whether divorce is permissible *at all*. Again, note Josephus's affirmation of divorce for *any* cause in *Ant.* 4.8.23 §253.

CHAPTER 4

In response Jesus reminds them of Gen 1:27 and 2:24 on humanity's being made as male and female and a man's leaving his father and mother to become one with his wife. "Therefore, what God has joined together, let no one separate." Human beings are not to separate what God has brought together. Jesus's comments in vv. 3–8 appear to be prohibiting divorce absolutely.[95]

The Pharisees rightfully recognize that, rather than providing the proper grounds for a divorce, Jesus was denying any permission for divorce at all. Even the conservative Shammai had not gone that far. Whereas Jesus questions the Pharisees in Mark 10:3, in Matt 19:7 they understandably ask *him* about Moses's commanding both divorce certificates and divorce itself (Deut 24:1): "Why then did Moses command us to give a certificate of dismissal and to divorce her?" In effect, did not Moses permit divorce, Jesus?

Starting points matter. If one starts with Deut 24:1, as did the Pharisees, one would assume divorce and then seek to regulate it. If one starts with Genesis, with Jesus, then divorce is evil, a violation of what God had done in bringing a man and a woman together into one flesh.[96] For the Pharisees, starting from Deut 24:1–4, Moses "commanded" divorce. Actually, Moses did not command divorce in Deut 24:1–4 but *presupposed* that a divorce (and a divorce certificate) had already taken place. Jesus therefore corrects the Pharisees by saying that Moses had *permitted* divorce but not commanded it (v. 8), and Moses permitted it as a concession to hardened hearts (like Pharaoh in Exod 7:13—not good company). Jesus adds that "from the beginning it was not so." God's will in creation trumps Moses's later concession. Jesus therefore reaffirms his apparently absolute position in v. 6.

In v. 9 Jesus shifts from the third person to a first-person utterance, highlighting the authoritative nature of what he is saying as he explains that any husband who divorces his wife—except for sexual infidelity—and marries another is committing adultery.[97] Whereas in Matt 5:32 the divorcing husband sins against his wife (ἐπ' αὐτήν), the omission of "against her" in 19:9 "achieves a more general character.... Consequently, in 19:9 any remarriage is considered adulterous."[98] Whereas

---

95. Stressed by Heth and Wenham, *Jesus and Divorce*, 128, but also, in a very different approach, by Martin, *Sex and the Single Savior*, 135.

96. France, *Matthew*, 714.

97. R. Collins, *Divorce*, 114, 141: "I say to *you*"; cf. 5:32. Several cues in the text indicate that 19:9 is a continuation of Jesus's response "to them," the Pharisees, as in 19:8; cf. 19:3. The "you" in 19:9 remains the same as in 19:8. The juxtaposition of Moses or what was "said" in the law with what Jesus himself says in 19:8–9 must be understood as connected, even as was the case when Jesus qualified what was said by Moses with what he himself says in Matt 5:21–48. The conversation in response to the disciples does not begin until 19:10.

98. Repschinski, *Controversy Stories*, 176.

5:32 focuses on the situation of the woman, in 19:9 the point of view is the man's own divorcing and remarrying. Jesus's permission of divorce (and remarriage?) in instances of sexual sin—with the exception clause—ultimately agrees with the traditionally reconstructed Shammaite position (m. Giṭ. 9:10).[99] The stunned disciples react in v. 10 saying that it would be better not to marry. The strong reaction indicates that Jesus had articulated a very difficult and strict position. Certainly that would be the case if he had been denying divorce entirely and permitting only annulments for illegitimate or invalid marriages, as some interpreters have concluded (contrary to the position of Shammai).[100] This, however, is unlikely.[101] Were Jesus permitting divorce but not remarriage, that too would be stricter than other Jews of the day (again contrary to the presumed position of Shammai). Perhaps the disciples were just shocked at the striking and unusual limitation of divorce to instances of sexual sin in a world of easy divorce, where men's divorcing their wives was virtually unlimited, Shammai notwithstanding.[102]

Matthew 19:9's Exception Cause As Modifying Only the First Verb

Divorce may be understood from a human legal standpoint and from a divine standpoint, and Jesus has just taught in Matt 19:4–6 that human beings are not to divide what God has joined together. God's will in marriage remains for one man and one woman. Thus *remarriage* may not be permissible or legitimate even after a divorce because of sexual sin. Ultimately, one must appeal to Matt 19:9. The grammatical structure of Matt 19:9, however, is difficult: ὃς ἂν ἀπολύσῃ τὴν γυναῖκα αὐτοῦ μὴ ἐπὶ πορνείᾳ καὶ γαμήσῃ ἄλλην. The exception for adultery (μὴ ἐπὶ πορνείᾳ) is sandwiched between two verbs—"divorces" (ἀπολύσῃ) and "marries" (γαμήσῃ)—linked by καί "and," with a negated prepositional phrase just before the coordinating καί. Protases of conditional relative clauses rarely have two verbs. Occasionally there are protases with a single verb followed by an exceptive clause. Two verbs and an exception is uncharted territory in the gospels. As Murray puts it, "The question then is: does this exception, by way of right or liberty, extend to

---

99. Again, Hillel permitted divorce for any cause, as did other Second Temple Jews (Sir 25:26; Philo, *Spec.* 3.5; Josephus, *Ant.* 4.8.23 §253), but Shammai did not; see David R. Catchpole, "The Synoptic Divorce Material as a Traditio-Historical Problem," *BJRL* 57 (1974): 94–98, 120. See the discussion of this debate in relation to Matt 5:32 and in chapter 2, pp. 79–81, above.

100. E.g., Alfred Plummer, *An Exegetical Commentary on the Gospel according to S. Matthew*, ICC (Grand Rapids: Eerdmans, 1956), 260.

101. See the discussion in chapter 3, pp. 151–53.

102. Hill, *Matthew*, 281.

the remarriage of the divorcing husband as well as to the putting away? Obviously, if the right extends to the remarriage the husband in such a case is not implicated in the sin of adultery in the event of his remarriage."[103]

Most interpreters over the years have taken the exception clause of Matt 19:9 as modifying *both* divorce and remarriage, thus allowing remarriage after a justified divorce for sexual sin. Except in cases of sexual sin, divorce and remarriage is adulterous. A significant minority of scholars has contended, on the other hand, that the exception clause permits a husband to divorce under these circumstances but *not* to remarry.[104] These interpreters have advocated for two claims embedded in Matt 19:9: (1) Divorce, except for sexual sin, is adultery. Even if the divorcing spouse remains single after an unjustified divorce, that spouse has sinned by separating what God intended to remain together as one flesh.[105] (2) Remarriage (after divorce) is *always* adulterous. Davies and Allison consider the grammatical evidence indecisive.[106] Donald Hagner, on the other hand, finds it "more convincing" that the exception clause only modifies the verb for divorce.[107]

Davies and Allison's agnosticism notwithstanding, what *is* the available evidence, and to which conclusion does it point regarding what the exception clause modifies? The verse is not addressing the question of when it is permissible to remarry but rather the fundamental sin of divorce and remarriage. An overemphasis on the exception clause reverses the thrust of the sentence.[108] For that matter, the exception clause more likely modifies only the first verb (divorce)—the minority position—for a number of reasons (most of which remain unaddressed in the scholarly literature).

(1) Commentators regularly claim on the basis of ancient divorce certificates' statements of the freedom to remarry that that freedom would have been assumed

---

103. Murray, *Divorce*, 35.

104. Thus, e.g., Talbert, *Matthew*, 233; Warren Carter, *Matthew and the Margins: A Sociopolitical and Religious Reading* (Maryknoll, NY: Orbis, 2000); Gundry, *Matthew*, 377: "True, Matthew's exceptive phrase allows formalization—according to Jewish requirement—of the break between husband and wife that has already occurred through the wife's immorality. But Matthew does not let the husband remarry." Walter Grundmann, *Das Evangelium nach Matthäus*, THKNT 1 (Berlin: Evangelische Verlaganstalt, 1968), 428 (on 19:9): "Wiederverheiratung nach Trennung von der Frau auf Grund erfolgten Ehebruchs ist Ehebruch."

105. This point escapes Wayne Grudem, *What the Bible Says about Divorce and Remarriage* (Wheaton: Crossway, 2021), 29.

106. Davies and Allison, *Matthew*, 3:17

107. Donald A. Hagner, *Matthew 14–28*, WBC 33B (Dallas: Word, 1995), 549.

108. Andrew Cornes, *Divorce and Remarriage: Biblical Principles and Pastoral Practice* (Grand Rapids: Eerdmans, 1993), 219–20.

The Matthean Divorce-Remarriage Texts in Context

by Jesus's hearers.[109] Jesus's hearers would naturally have taken the exception clause as modifying *both* the divorce and the remarriage. Earlier in the gospel, however, Matt 5:32 took a surprising view when Jesus said that a divorced woman, even with a divorce certificate in hand, is *not* actually free to marry another man, nor a man her. By the time one reaches Matt 19, the reader would take the divorce certificates with a grain of salt. The reliance in the pro-remarriage position on the very divorce certificates Jesus was challenging is ironic.

One must not assume a freedom to remarry in Matt 19:9. Were the exception clause modifying *both* verbs—apart from the wife's sexual infidelity—the man who divorces *and* marries another has committed adultery, *divorce certificates notwithstanding*.[110] Jesus declares those certificates with their expressions of "freedom" null and void in the eyes of God apart from the one exception. The partners are *not* thereby free to remarry before God. Cases in favor of remarriage must therefore rest on what *Jesus* is saying rather than on the divorce certificates.

God's will remains for the union of man and wife in one flesh to endure, and anything else is adulterous. *The entire conversation to this point in Matt 19 has been about divorce.* Jesus has said nothing about remarriage. He never sets aside what he had just explained in vv. 4–8 that God's will from the creation is for one man to cleave to one woman for the lifetime of the partners. Divorce certificates do not change that.

Intractable problems therefore plague those maintaining that a divorce completely dissolves a marriage from the standpoint of God's will. For instance, divorce supposedly includes a right to remarry if the other spouse is guilty of πορνεία, but a divorce *apart from* πορνεία does not include that same right for the innocent party (see 5:31–32). The inconsistency in the rights of the innocent party is resolved if remarriage is simply not an option. Another conundrum: if the guilty party of a divorce may not remarry, the marriage does not seem to be dissolved by the divorce. Again, these problems are resolved if Jesus was permitting divorce *without* the right to remarry.

(2) Matthew 19:9 forms a doublet with 5:32. Doublets are a common feature across the Matthean landscape (e.g., 3:2 // 4:17; 3:10 // 7:19; 13:12 // 25:29; and 5:29–30 // 18:8–9), and the second instance of a doublet usually parallels but sometimes abridges the first in content. The second instance is rightfully interpreted

---

109. E.g., Keener, *Matthew*, 469, who claims that a *valid* divorce would allow for remarriage and that that would be assumed; Instone-Brewer, *Divorce and Remarriage*, 118–25.

110. Dupont, *Mariage*, 144–46; contra Instone-Brewer, who stakes his position on divorce and remarriage on this premise.

CHAPTER 4

in view of the first.[111] Matthew 19:9, with its exception clause and use of πορνεία, should be taken in a parallel fashion to Matt. 5:32 with its exception clause and use of πορνεία.[112]

> Matt 5:32: "Anyone who divorces his wife, except on the ground of unchastity, causes her to commit adultery; and whoever marries a divorced woman commits adultery" (πᾶς ὁ ἀπολύων τὴν γυναῖκα αὐτοῦ παρεκτὸς λόγου πορνείας ποιεῖ αὐτὴν μοιχευθῆναι, καὶ ὃς ἐὰν ἀπολελυμένην γαμήσῃ, μοιχᾶται).
> Matt 19:9: "Whoever divorces his wife, except for unchastity, and marries another commits adultery" (ὃς ἂν ἀπολύσῃ τὴν γυναῖκα μὴ ἐπὶ πορνείᾳ καὶ γαμήσῃ ἄλλην μοιχᾶται).

Matthew 5:31–32 makes a *twofold* claim: divorcing a woman (except for sexual infidelity) is sinful, and marrying a divorced woman is adulterous. The twofold assertion of 5:31–32 supports a twofold assertion again in 19:9. First, divorce, except for unchastity, is adultery. Second, remarriage (after divorce) is adulterous.[113] In Matthew's other instances where the protasis of a conditional has two verbs (5:19 twice; 7:24; 10:14), the apodosis refers to *both* situations.[114] In Matt 19:9 both the di-

---

111. Dupont, *Mariage*, 149–50 and 149 n. 3.
112. Dupont, *Mariage*, 100–2; Wenham, "Matthew and Divorce," 103; Heth and Wenham, *Jesus and Divorce*, 49. For a source-critical discussion of the Matthean doublets, see Kilpatrick, *Origins*, 84–100. From the perspective of Matthean priority, see B. C. Butler, *The Originality of St. Matthew: A Critique of the Two-Document Hypothesis* (Cambridge: Cambridge University Press, 1951), 138–46. Other Matthean doublets include 4:23 // 9:35; 7:16–18, 20 // 12:33–35; 9:13 // 12:7; 9:27–31 // 20:29–34; 9:32–34 // 12:22–24; 10:15 //11:22; 10:38 // 16:24; 10:39 // 16:25; 11:15 // 13:9, 43; 12:38–39 // 16:1–2; 16:19 // 18:18; 17:20 // 21:21; 19:30 // 20:16; 20:26–27 // 23:11; 24:42 // 25:13.
113. The association of the exception clause for sexual sin with divorce in the twofold Matt 5:32 places pressure, then, for the exception clause in Matt 19:9 to modify the divorce prohibition. Contra Martin, *Sex and the Single Savior*, 135–36, who takes the exception clause as modifying not divorce but remarriage. For Martin, one may not divorce *even for sexual sin*, but an innocent husband who has suffered divorce may remarry in instances of sexual sin (i.e., where that sin was committed by a wife also initiating divorce since the innocent husband may not take that initiative). Martin stresses Bernadette Brooten's case that women could divorce their husbands, even if this was rare. Martin thereby resolves the tension between Jesus's apparently absolute comments against divorce in 19:3–8 and the exception clause in 19:9. Several of the following points (e.g., modifiers typically coming after what they modify) would also militate against Martin's contrarian position. A husband is not committing a *second* sin to remarry if the divorce was due to sexual sin. Martin may rather be taking the exception clause as not *permitting* remarriage but claiming that it is not a *second* sin for the innocent spouse in a divorce.
114. Carter, *Matthew and the Margins*, 381.

The Matthean Divorce-Remarriage Texts in Context

vorce and the remarriage would be adulterous. The exception clause in Matt 5:31–32 addresses only when a man may legitimately divorce a wife.[115]

Since Matt 5:32 permits husbands to divorce unfaithful wives without any permission expressed for remarriage—the exception clause is associated only with divorce in 5:32—the same would be the case in Matt 19:9.[116] When Matt 5:32 says that to marry a divorced woman is adulterous, no exception is mentioned. Remarriage is simply sin. One would expect the same conclusion in Matt 19:9, rendering likely that 19:9's exception clause only modifies the first verb and statement.[117] According to Luz, "The prohibition of remarriage for a divorced man in 19:9 corresponds to the prohibition in 5:32 against marrying a divorced woman."[118]

John Murray expresses the view of many in emphasizing coordination between the two verbs such that divorce alone is not sinful. What is sinful is divorce followed by remarriage, "and this coordination must not be disturbed in any way."[119] In other words, a divorce itself would not be adulterous. Adultery would take place in the remarriage. This approach, however, assumes its own conclusion. Murray must distinguish Matt 19:9's logic from 5:32's twofold expression, thus ignoring Matthew's parallelism.[120] Consider what Jesus has just said in 19:6: "Therefore what God has joined together, let no one separate." Separation would be against God's will and therefore sinful. Or in 19:8: "Moses allowed you to divorce your wives, but from the beginning it was not so." Jesus treats divorce itself as adulter-

---

115. It is unclear why Murray (*Divorce*, 40) calls the claim "nonsense" and "untruth" that the first part of 19:9 might read: "Anyone who divorces his wife except for fornication commits adultery." The "anyone who" in the second half of the sentence would simply have been elided and understood: "Anyone who marries another woman commits adultery." See Murray's full case against the approach to 19:9 adopted here in *Divorce*, 39–43.

116. Dupont, *Mariage*, 148–50; George Hayward Joyce, *Christian Marriage: An Historical and Doctrinal Study*, 2nd ed., Heythrop Series 1 (London: Sheed and Ward, 1948), 284: One would expect the exception clause to function similarly in both instances.

117. Dupont, *Mariage*, 148; Heth and Wenham, *Jesus and Divorce*, 128. Luz, *Matthew 8–20*, 493: "From the prohibition expressed there [5:32] against marrying a divorced woman one could arrive indirectly, by expanding the prohibition to divorced men, at the impossibility of a second marriage following divorce." The intervening exception clause thus breaks the coordination between the two verbs.

118. Luz, *Matthew 8–20*, 493. In other words, Murray's construction of 19:9 without the parallelism (*Divorce*, 40–41) is not the only one possible. The parallelism in 5:32 supports the same understanding in 19:9. Murray nevertheless *claims*: "But in Matthew 19:9 the case is entirely different" (41).

119. Murray, *Divorce*, 41.

120. Murray, *Divorce*, 41.

ous and not just remarriage. The only permission for divorce, just as in Matt 5:32, is when the partner has already committed sexual sin. The parallelism remains intact. Whoever divorces his wife, except for sexual sin, commits adultery, and whoever marries another commits adultery.

(3) The placement of the exception clause relative to the verbs indicates that it only modifies the first verb. The exception clause could be in one of three places. The first position would be after the conditional statement's introduction (i.e., after "whoever") and *prior* to the first verb "divorces": "Whoever does not because of unchastity divorce his wife and marry another commits adultery" (ὃς ἂν μὴ ἐπὶ πορνείᾳ ἀπολύσῃ τὴν γυναῖκα καὶ γαμήσῃ ἄλλην μοιχᾶται). This placement of the exception would require divorce and remarriage in instances of a wife's sexual infidelity.[121] Were the man to continue to live with his adulterous wife, *he* would be guilty of adultery.[122] The difficulty here is the outlandish claim that the divorcing spouse must remarry in order to avoid adultery. By avoiding this first position for the exception clause, Matthew's Jesus is not *requiring* that the man divorce his unfaithful wife and remarry.

A second position would be to place the exception clause after the second verb, "and marries another": "Whoever divorces his wife and marries another, if it is not for sexual infidelity that he divorces her and marries another, commits adultery" (ὃς ἂν ἀπολύσῃ τὴν γυναῖκα καὶ γαμήσῃ ἄλλην μὴ ἐπὶ πορνείᾳ μοιχᾶται). The placement of the exception clause after the second verb would clearly and explicitly permit both divorce *and remarriage* in instances of a wife's infidelity. Strangely, Matthew's Jesus does not place the exception clause where one would expect it were he permitting both divorce and a subsequent remarriage.

This leaves a third position: *between* the two verbs. This is the only place one could position the exception clause in order to modify only the first verb.[123] The placement of the exception clause therefore renders more likely that Jesus is permitting an exception only to divorce but not to remarriage.[124]

---

121. Dupont, *Mariage*, 149.

122. J. P. Arendzen, "Another Note on Matthew xix,3–12," *Clergy Review* 21 (1941): 26; Heth and Wenham, *Jesus and Divorce*, 115. First-century Jews did, however, expect a *divorce* in instances of a wife's infidelity.

123. Heth and Wenham, *Jesus and Divorce*, 115–16.

124. Mattthew 19:9 is the only gospel text that may allow for remarriage, in view of the exception clause. If the grammar does not clearly indicate that permission, then an ambiguous Matt 19:9 should be interpreted in a manner that agrees with the other gospel divorce-remarriage texts. Blomberg ("Marriage," 180) thinks that if Jesus wanted to forbid all remarriage, he would have said so more clearly. Jesus said precisely that in Mark 10:12, Luke 16:18, and the second half of Matt 5:32.

The Matthean Divorce-Remarriage Texts in Context

(4) Of the over 250 prepositional phrases in the first seven chapters of Matthew's Gospel, the phrase comes *right after* what it modifies by a 4:1 ratio. As for when a prepositional phrase *precedes* what it modifies, the prepositional phrase is either emphatic, part of a Septuagintal quotation, or marking the beginning of a new section of the gospel.[125] One would incline, then, toward seeing 19:9's exception clause as modifying the verb it follows.

(5) Prepositional phrases negated by an immediately preceding μή (excluding postpositives) always modify the *preceding* verb in the roughly forty New Testament instances apart from instances of special emphasis.[126]

(6) The μή in Matt 19:9 forms part of an exception clause. What leverage do Matthew's other exception clauses offer? The most frequent form is εἰ μή to introduce exceptions, qualify matters, or refine a verbal statement. Matthew's εἰ μή constructions, with one exception, always modify what precedes.[127] That exception is Matt 24:22, which is an unreal second-class condition where εἰ μή introduces an actual conditional clause.[128]

(7) Luke 16:18 eliminates remarriage as a possibility. Mark 10:9 offers no provision for remarriage. Matthew 5:32 likewise does not offer the wronged husband the option of marrying another woman after divorcing the unfaithful wife. The weight of the gospel evidence therefore favors taking the exception clause as allowing divorce in instances of sexual infidelity but not remarriage. Were the exception clause modifying only divorce, Matt 19:9 would dovetail with the emphasis on not remarrying in the other gospel texts.

(8) Early Christian writers interpreted the exception clause as applying only to the first verb and not to the second. Similarly, early Christian scribes sometimes replaced Matt 19:9's μὴ ἐπὶ πορνείᾳ, "except for unchastity," with 5:32's παρεκτὸς λόγου πορνείας "except on the ground of unchastity." The scribal change takes Matt 19:9 as an exception to the prohibition against divorce, as had been the case in 5:32.[129]

(9) The syntax of Matt 19:9 consists of a double conditional clause. The introductory ὃς ἂν is the equivalent of ἐάν and, together with the following μή, means "if

---

125. Heth and Wenham, *Jesus and Divorce*, 117–18.
126. In instances of special emphasis, the prepositional phrase *precedes* the verb it qualifies; Heth and Wenham, *Jesus and Divorce*, 117. This applies to instances where no other grammatical or lexical category is operative (e.g., Matt 11:23 // Luke 10:15; 11:11; John 7:35, 41, 52; Gal 2:2; 5:15). This does not exhaust the LXX, papyri, literary Koine, or classical Greek, nor does it examine οὐ plus the indicative (233 n. 15).
127. Matt 5:13; 11:27; 12:4, 24, 39; 13:57; 14:17; 15:24; 16:4; 17:8; 21:19; 24:22, 26.
128. Heth and Wenham, *Jesus and Divorce*, 116.
129. Bonsirven, *Divorce*, 61–62. See the discussion in chapter 6.

CHAPTER 4

not," "unless," or "except."[130] The elliptical phrase "except for sexual infidelity" does not include a verb, which must be supplied from the context. The hearer would take that understood verb as the very one that immediately preceded the exception and was fresh in the ears: "to divorce." Matthew 19:9 is therefore a shortened form of the fuller: "If a man divorces his wife—if it is not for sexual infidelity that he divorces her—and marries another, he commits adultery" (ὃς ἂν ἀπολύσῃ τὴν γυναῖκα μὴ ἐπὶ πορνείᾳ καὶ γαμήσῃ ἄλλην μοιχᾶται).

In Matthew's four other doubled relative conditional constructions, the focus is especially on one of the two actions.[131] Matthew 5:19a reads, "whoever breaks one of the least of these commandments, and teaches others to do the same will be called least in the kingdom of heaven." Then in 5:19b: "Whoever does them and teaches them will be called great in the kingdom of heaven." In both cases, it is the first of the two conditionals where the stress lies. Jesus emphasizes *doing* the commandments (e.g., 5:48; 7:21–27; 25:35–36; 28:20). In Matthew's third double conditional construction: "Everyone then who hears these words of mine and acts on them will be like a wise man" (7:24). Again, Matthew is stressing living consistently with the commands. The final instance of the pattern is in Matt 10:14: "If anyone will not welcome you or listen to your words, shake off the dust from your feet."[132] In view of this pattern, the exception clause more likely goes with the stressed verb (divorce).

Although Matthew does not provide an instance of "if" (εἰ) with two conditionals in the protasis, Matthew offers five instances of a double protasis with ἐάν, and in three of them one of the verbs could be omitted without ruining the sense of the sentence: Matt 4:9 (fall down and worship); Matt 18:3 (turn and become like children); 21:21 (have faith and do not doubt). In view of the stress on one or the other conditional clause where two are present, it is reasonable to understand the divorce itself as adulterous.[133] The exception clause modifies the first verb as the stressed verb, and not the second. Thus a man may not divorce his wife *unless* she is guilty of adultery. If she is not, then he is guilty of adultery. The second statement is not qualified: whoever marries another after divorcing his wife commits adultery. A similar construction is in Matt 7:21: "*Not everyone* who says to me, 'Lord, Lord,' will enter the kingdom of heaven, but only the one who does the will of my Father in heaven." "Not everyone who says to me" parallels how not everyone who

---

130. Zerwick, *Biblical Greek*, §442; BDF §380; BDAG, s.v. μή ΑΙ1.
131. Dupont, *Mariage*, 102–3.
132. Wenham, "Syntax of Matthew 19.9," 20–21.
133. Wenham, "Syntax of Matthew 19.9," 21.

divorces commits adultery, but everyone who remarries does (paralleling everyone who does the Father's will).[134]

(10) Had Matt 5:31–32 included the added words "and marries another" (καὶ γαμήσῃ ἄλλην) before the exception clause (cf. Luke 16:18), the verse would clearly allow for remarriage: "Anyone who divorces his wife *and marries another*, except on the ground of unchastity, causes her to commit adultery." As Robert Gundry puts it: "Had Matthew been concerned to establish the right of the husband to remarry under the exception, he would hardly have omitted remarriage here in 5:32 and then put the exception only after the matter of divorce in 19:9."[135]

The case that the exception clause modifies only the first verb must remain tentative since the two relative conditional clauses within a single protasis is unparalleled elsewhere in Matthew. Nevertheless, scholars advocating that the exception clause modifies both divorce and remarriage rarely make the attempt to address the specific lines of evidence (at least ten here) favoring that it modifies only divorce. When they do, they may mention an isolated argument but not the cumulative case.[136]

Again, in Matthew's Jewish milieu husbands were often required to divorce adulterous wives in lieu of the biblical penalty of capital punishment (cf. John 8:3–11). Jesus had been firmly teaching against divorce and remarriage in response to a query regarding the grounds for divorce (Matt 19:3–8). The addition of the exception clause in this milieu would allow for the divorce in this one particular situation—as expected of husbands by fellow Jews. The Jews were not also requiring remarriage. Matthew's Jesus offers no contextual cue that the exception should be applied more broadly to include also remarriage.

The disciples respond in v. 10 that if Jesus's teaching were to be accepted, it would be better not to marry. Were one able to divorce and remarry in instances of sexual sin, why would it be better to remain single if a second marriage was an

---

134. Wenham, "Syntax of Matthew 19.9," 21–22. The difference in the construction between 7:21 and 19:9 is that Jesus is contrasting saying "Lord, Lord" with doing the will of God, whereas in Matt 19:9 divorce is normally adultery as also is remarriage.

135. Gundry, *Matthew*, 90–91.

136. David Janzen, for instance, does not account for how Jesus had singled out remarriage to a divorced woman as fundamentally adulterous in Matt 5:32b; see "Meaning of *Porneia*," 71. In other words, an argument from the exception clause, as Janzen makes, is valid for its own conditional. He concludes that remarriage would be permitted for the husband of a justifiably divorced wife. Matthew 5:32b, however, does not provide that option to the innocently divorced wife, who is highlighted in this verse as the victim of an unjust divorce. The shocking prohibition of the remarriage of the innocent party of Matt 5:32 supports a prohibition of remarriage in Matt 19:9 as a rather "compelling" reason, contra Janzen.

CHAPTER 4

option?[137] The divorce rate in Judea has been estimated at 4 percent.[138] A more stringent statement in 19:9 is more likely the lesser the divorce rate. The shock of the disciples in v. 10 makes far better sense if Jesus had limited divorce to instances of sexual sin and prohibited remarriage entirely.[139]

The Relationship of Matthew 19:10–12 to 19:2–9

In Mark 10:2–9 Jesus is guarded in his comments to the Pharisees, but in Mark 10:10–12 privately in the house he speaks freely to the disciples on divorce and remarriage. In Matt 19:2–9, the pattern is reversed; Jesus is rather blunt in the presence of the Pharisees about divorce and remarriage, but his private teaching of the disciples in 19:10–12 is more enigmatic. Jesus prohibits divorce and remarriage in Matt 19:9. Then in vv. 10–12: "His disciples said to him, 'If such is the case of a man with his wife, it is better not to marry.' But he said to them, 'Not everyone can accept this teaching, but only those to whom it is given. For there are eunuchs who have been so from birth, and there are eunuchs who have been made eunuchs by others, and there are eunuchs who have made themselves eunuchs for the sake of the kingdom of heaven. Let anyone accept this who can.'" Interpreters debate whether there is a relationship between vv. 10–12 and vv. 3–9 and, if so, what the implications for Jesus's teaching on divorce and remarriage are.[140]

---

137. Martin (*Sex and the Single Savior*, 145) comments in response to Instone-Brewer's ability to find justification for divorce and remarriage throughout the New Testament:

> If one applied Instone-Brewer's method at all consistently, one would end up with no teaching of Jesus or Paul that would have sounded radical to Jews of their day. In fact, one of the best pieces of evidence against Instone-Brewer's claim that a literal forbidding of divorce and remarriage must not have been what Jesus meant, since that would have been unthinkable to his audience, is that his audience *did* (again, according to the narrative presented by the Gospel writers) find the teaching so radical as to be scarcely comprehensible.

138. Joachim Jeremias, *Jerusalem in the Time of Jesus: An Investigation into Economic and Social Conditions during the New Testament Period* (Philadelphia: Fortress, 1969), 371.

139. This argument is all the more compelling for Galilean fishermen than for the upper crust, who left behind literature and oral teachings justifying liberal divorce and remarriage. The divorce rate in those circles would likely have been higher because of wealth and means.

140. Martin (*Sex and the Single Savior*, 136) qualifies the eunuch saying since eunuchs in antiquity *could* indulge in sexual relations (with no fear of impregnating); see also Mathew Kuefler, *The Manly Eunuch: Masculinity, Gender Ambiguity, and Christian Ideology in Late Antiquity* (Chicago: University of Chicago Press, 2001), 32–35, 96–102. The Matthean context more clearly leans toward an ascetic application since Jesus has just identified sexual relations as belonging, properly, to marriage (Matt 19:4–6). One is not even to lust after another man's wife (Matt 5:27–28). A eunuch, in this context, avoids marriage and sexual relations entirely.

The Matthean Divorce-Remarriage Texts in Context

The Mishnah relays a similar discussion as Matt 19:12: there are eunuchs born without the ability to have children, and there are eunuchs who could be married or may have been married but are not (m. Yebam. 8:4–6). The Jews took a dim view of those who had been made eunuchs. Eunuchs were not permitted in the assembly of Israel (Deut 23:1). They could not perform priestly functions (Lev 21:18–20). Even the testicles of animal sacrifices were to be intact (Lev 22:24; Josephus, *Ant.* 4.8.40 §§290–291). Jesus's saying is therefore quite striking, especially with respect to the second and third groups of eunuchs, those made so by others or those who have made themselves eunuchs. These are people whom the Jews would have viewed with disgust. Again, how the eunuch saying of Matt 19:12 relates to its immediate context is unclear.

Verse 10 is the disciples' raw reaction to Jesus's strict teaching on divorce and remarriage. Jesus responds in v. 11 that not everyone can accept this teaching, "this word" (τὸν λόγον τοῦτον). He appears to be softening some teaching, but *which* teaching? Most scholars have viewed Matt 19:12 on the various types of eunuchs as an independent logion that Matthew connected to vv. 10–11.[141] The eunuch saying encouraging celibacy for the sake of the kingdom in v. 12 would thus represent an independent trajectory of thought *unrelated* to Jesus's comments about divorce and remarriage.

One way of understanding the relationship between these verses, then, is that Matt 19:11's "not everyone can accept this teaching" is anticipating what Jesus is *about* to say in v. 12 about three types of eunuchs: not everyone can be a eunuch. Voluntary celibacy is not for everyone. In other words, vv. 10–12, apart from the disciples' initial reaction, are largely independent of what preceded—an independent logion. Thus:

An Initial Understanding of the Relationship between Verses 9–12
Verse 9—Prohibition of Divorce and Remarriage
Verse 10—Disciples' Comment Motivated by Verse 9 on Divorce-Remarriage
Verse 11—Not Everyone Can Accept This Teaching (Regarding Eunuchs in v. 12)
Verse 12—Eunuch Logion Not Related to Verses 2–9 on Divorce-Remarriage

---

141. E.g., Isaksson, *Marriage*, 119. Some have even supposed that the saying is so independent that it really belongs elsewhere. Matthew 19:12 is without Markan parallel, and so is hypothesized as having come after Jesus's instructions for the disciples to deny themselves in Luke 9:59–62 // Matt 8:21–22; Luke 14:26 // Matt 10:37; Luke 18:29 // Matt 19:29; so Alan Hugh McNeile, *The Gospel according to St. Matthew* (London: Macmillan, 1952), 275; T. W. Manson, *The Sayings of Jesus* (Grand Rapids: Eerdmans, 1957), 214–16. Matthew would not likely have separated a conclusion uttered by Jesus from the comments that led to that conclusion, and γάρ "for," at the beginning of v. 12 relates the verse to what immediately precedes. The best interpretation would seek to understand the role that v. 12 plays in that context; with Dupont, *Mariage*, 165.

CHAPTER 4

Verse 10 would conclude the divorce-remarriage discussion with v. 11 as a fresh start anticipating v. 12.[142]

That v. 11 anticipates v. 12, however, is unlikely. According to France, "Such forward reference is usually marked by a following resumptive relative or participle, and here there is no such resumption."[143] One would expect ὅτι, "that," to begin v. 12 and not γάρ, "for," an explanatory *addition*. The ὅτι, had it been present, would thus explain what "this statement" (τοῦτον) in v. 11 is: "this statement *that*."[144]

When connected to λόγος, "teaching," in Matthew, οὗτος, "this," always refers to what preceded; this feature provides further support for taking v. 11 with what *precedes* rather than with the eunuch saying that follows in v. 12. The most proximal instance of this is Matt 19:1 when Jesus concludes his teaching from the prior chapter. Matthew 7:28 and 26:1 also refer to prior teaching that has been concluded. Each of the other instances is in relation to *Jesus's* teaching and not comments by the disciples. In other words, λόγος preceded by οὗτος in Matthew's Gospel always refers back to Jesus's prior teaching. Jesus's comment in v. 11 would thus be referring back to his comment in v. 9 (in view of vv. 3–8, as in the third approach below).[145]

A second approach to the relationship between the verses is the majority view that v. 11's comment, "not everyone can accept this teaching," is responding to the *disciples'* comment in v. 10 that it is better not to marry. Jesus would be conceding that, while it would be better not to marry, not everyone will be capable of that (cf. Paul's comments in 1 Cor 7:7). Verses 11–12 would reflect an independent logion of Jesus's teaching motivated by the disciples' comment in v. 10. Thus:

A Second Understanding of the Relationship between the Verses: The Majority View
Verse 9—Prohibition of Divorce and Remarriage
Verse 10—Disciples' Stunned Reaction to Verse 9: Better Not to Marry
Verse 11—Not Everyone Can Accept This Teaching (of Verse 10 on Not Marrying as Better)
Verse 12—Eunuch Logion Motivated by the Disciples' Comment in Verse 10

That Jesus would affirm the disciples' comment is possible. Matthew presents the disciples in a better light than does Mark.[146] Often the disciples ask foolish questions in Mark's Gospel that Matthew omits (e.g., Matt 24:1–2 // Mark 13:1–2).

142. Eph 4:17 and Justin, *1 Apol.* 15.4 are likely instances of *forward*-looking τοῦτον ("this" in "this teaching").
143. France, *Matthew*, 722 n. 32.
144. Dupont, *Mariage*, 163.
145. Carter, *Matthew and the Margins*, 382.
146. Keener, *Matthew*, 470 n. 32.

The Matthean Divorce-Remarriage Texts in Context

One can therefore imagine the disciples making a sound comment that Jesus would build on.[147] At various points in Matthew, Jesus at least partially affirms the disciples' comments (13:51–52; 17:10–11, 24–27; 18:21–22).

Davies and Allison list several supporting points for the majority view that Jesus is commending the disciples' comment, but their reasoning is problematic.[148] First, they point out, some find support for severing vv. 10–12 from vv. 1–9 because Jesus permitted remarriage for the innocent spouses in instances of adultery. Jesus would not have been encouraging celibacy for them since they could remarry. The eunuch teaching must be unrelated. A permission of remarriage in v. 9, however, is unlikely in view of the evidence that the exception clause modifies only the first verb. Second, Christian interpreters such as Clement of Alexandria understood vv. 10–12 as a freestanding teaching promoting celibacy. Nevertheless, that later Christian interpreters understood vv. 10–12 in terms of celibacy and not marriage may reflect an ascetic tendency. Even the apostle Paul argued at length in 1 Cor 7 for the superiority of the single life over the married, and this influenced the early Christian authors in their interpretation. The eunuch statement in Matt 19:11–12 could be employed alongside Paul's comments about "staying where you are" in 1 Cor 7 to promote staying single but—and this is the crucial point—Matthew's Jesus heartily affirms marriage in 19:2–9 and elsewhere in the gospel.[149] Third, v. 12 is an isolated logion, they claim, but that assumes the very point that must be argued. Fourth, celibacy is for some and not all, but the prohibition against divorce is for everyone. In response, Jesus's divorce teaching is indeed for all, but that does not mean that all are empowered in the midst of a sinful world to obey it. Some are, but not all. The question becomes who the empowered are. Fifth and finally, Davies and Allison note that vv. 11–12 do not mention a *command* not to remarry but only a recommendation. However, that command is already in v. 9, and v. 12 illustrates the consequences in that some have been made eunuchs by others (in divorce).

Further problems plague this second approach to the logic of the verses, not least of which is that Jesus would be *affirming* the disciples' conclusion that it is better not to marry (v. 10). Throughout Matthew's Gospel the disciples ask questions of Jesus, misunderstand him, or object to him. Despite the disciples' more positive reputation in Matthew than in Mark, they never express an ideal that Jesus would wholeheartedly or without qualification affirm. Jesus regularly refutes their conclusions or restates them to be more precise or restates them in stronger

---

147. Keener, *Matthew*, 470 n. 32. Keener reads Matt 16:15–17, with its more positive view of the disciples, as a Matthean insertion.

148. Davies and Allison, *Matthew*, 3:20.

149. See the discussion below. Matthew leaves wives out of his lists for what to renounce in this world (e.g., just a little later in 19:29).

terms.[150] Jesus in v. 11 does not affirm the teaching only in part; he is affirming that teaching without qualification. As Luz writes, "nowhere else is a statement of the disciples given that importance."[151]

The disciples claim that it is better *not* to marry right after Jesus had just recited and affirmed in vv. 4–6 God's institution of marriage in Genesis![152] Even *if* Jesus had agreed with them, it is doubtful that he would agree with men literally being *made* eunuchs by others or with making *oneself* a eunuch by self-mutilation.[153] He would be affirming the single life by drawing *metaphorically* on the various eunuch categories.

One might respond that the disciples did indeed make a statement that was approved and praised by Jesus back in Matt 16:15–17, but one should not overstate this point. First, this is the *only* such occasion in Matthew. Second, Peter in 16:15–17 is not dispensing with Jesus's teaching there as the disciples are in 19:10; Jesus had just affirmed marriage on the basis of Genesis only for the disciples to say that it is better not to marry. Further, the disciples in v. 10 are *expressing qualms* about Jesus's teaching on divorce and remarriage. It is unlikely, then, that Jesus's comment that "not everyone can accept this teaching" would be affirming the disciples' comment about not marrying.

The disciples in v. 10 react with shock to Jesus's teaching on divorce and remarriage in v. 9.[154] Those receiving Matthew's Gospel would likewise have been shocked by such strict teaching about divorce and remarriage. Even as the disciples' focus is on that teaching, so also would be the case for the recipients of the gospel. One would need some *cue* that Jesus's reference to this word or teaching was in reference to the disciples' own comment. Jesus more likely refers by v. 11's "this teaching" (τὸν λόγον τοῦτον) to what he had just said in v. 9, but now expressed in the even starker terms of eunuchs.[155]

A freestanding v. 12 logion (or roughly vv. 10–12 as a unit) would appear to *endorse* the various eunuch categories, including the making of eunuchs through self-mutilation for the sake of the kingdom or those *made eunuchs by others*. How is a Christ-believer made a eunuch by others? Jesus nowhere else elaborates on

---

150. E.g., 8:19–20, 21–22; 14:26–27, 30–31; 15:12–13; 19:13–14, 22–26. See Quentin Quesnell, "'Made Themselves Eunuchs for the Kingdom of Heaven (Mt 19:12),'" *CBQ* 30 (1968): 343–44.

151. Luz, *Matthew 8–20*, 500.

152. Dupont, *Mariage*, 168–69.

153. Dupont, *Mariage*, 169.

154. Keener (*Matthew*, 470) believes that those who relate "this precept" in v. 11 to v. 9 ignore the intervening comment by the disciples in v. 10. On the contrary, it is the disciples' riveted focus on *Jesus's* teaching in v. 9 that keeps the reader focused there as well. An answer is therefore readily at hand for why Jesus would "jump back two verses."

155. Quesnell, "Made Themselves Eunuchs," 357–58.

or affirms such a teaching. The apostle Paul, for his part, appears *unaware* of any freestanding eunuch saying by Jesus. His comments on the celibate lifestyle in 1 Cor 7:8 are based on *his own* teaching and not the Lord's.[156] These difficulties are resolved if v. 12 is not freestanding but integrally related to what precedes with its affirmation of marriage in vv. 3–9. One may have adopted a single life for the sake of the Lord from the beginning, or one may be required to remain single (i.e., be made a eunuch) after someone else's action in a divorce.[157] In other words, Jesus is not affirming that people be literally *made* eunuchs for the sake of the kingdom. They are made eunuchs when they are divorced and not permitted to marry again. *Like* those who were made eunuchs, they are to remain celibate.[158]

A third understanding of the relationship between the verses, then, is that the "this" (οὗτος) does indeed refer backward to Jesus's own teaching. When Jesus says in v. 11 that not everyone can accept what was said, he is referring back and appearing to soften his divorce and remarriage teaching in v. 9. He would be conceding that a strict avoidance of adultery and remarriage may not be possible for everyone, only for those given to it.[159] If that is the case, the eunuch saying in v. 12 would be in relation to the disciples' comment in v. 10 that it is better *not to marry*. Thus:

A Third Set of Relations of the Relationship between Verses 9–12
Verse 9—Prohibition of Divorce and Remarriage
Verse 10—Disciples' Stunned Reaction to Verse 9: Better Not to Marry
Verse 11—Not Everyone Can Accept This Teaching (of Verse 9 on Divorce and Remarriage)
Verse 12—Eunuch Logion Motivated by the Disciples' Comment (Not to Marry) in Verse 10[160]

---

156. Dupont, *Mariage*, 189.

157. Some stress the decision to remain single for the sake of the kingdom *irrespective* of divorce as if this obviated the connection to the situation of divorce in 19:9; Jerome Kodell, "The Celibacy Logion in Matthew 19:12," *BTB* 8 (1978): 19–23; followed by Instone-Brewer, *Divorce and Remarriage*, 168 n. 68. What such interpreters overlook is that these verses need not necessarily be stated as an either-or but *may* apply to both situations and were occasioned by the discussion of divorce and remarriage in 19:9.

158. Geoffrey W. Bromiley, *God and Marriage* (Grand Rapids; Eerdmans, 1980), 40: "Jesus describes [in Matt 19:3–9] remarriage after divorce as adultery.... Even ordinary people, including those whose marriages break down but who recognize that marriage is not everything, can become celibate for the sake of God's kingdom."

159. W. D. Davies, *The Setting of the Sermon on the Mount*, BJS 186 (Atlanta; Scholars Press, 1989), 393–94.

160. Nolland (*Matthew*, 776) objects that this approach would leave v. 12 unconnected to what came before, but he is assuming an independent eunuch logion. Jesus may have introduced this saying in *support* of 19:9 in response to the disciples' comment.

CHAPTER 4

According to this approach, Jesus would be granting that his teaching in v. 9 may be too strict for his followers and may need to be softened. Even in this third approach, v. 12 *could* function as an independent logion only loosely related to the disciples' response in v. 10.

This third option, however, can be understood—and *should* be understood— rather differently. Jesus was not likely mitigating his teaching about divorce and remarriage after all. He was granting that *outside* his own disciples, this teaching about divorce and remarriage may be too difficult. Those outside may not accept it.[161] When Jesus says in v. 11, "Not everyone can accept this teaching, but only those to whom it is given [οἷς δέδοται]," this is not a contrast between *some* believers and *other* believers, as if some are capable of a life of celibacy while others are not. Whenever Matthew contrasts in his gospel those who receive Jesus's teaching with those who do not, the contrast is with those *outside* the Jesus movement. Matthew is similar to Mark in this regard. Mark 4:11 says: "To you has been given the secret of the kingdom of God, but for those outside, everything comes in parables." Thus in Matt 13:11: "To you it has been given [ὑμῖν δέδοται γνῶναι] to know the secrets of the kingdom of heaven, but to them it has not been given [ἐκείνοις δὲ οὐ δέδοται]." Those who follow Jesus's teaching stand contrasted as insiders with those outside.[162]

Some conclude that, since people outside the Jesus movement may not be *able* to "accept" this teaching, Jesus must not be referring to a divine standard for all people (vv. 6, 9); he must be referring rather to the celibacy comment of the disciples in v. 10.[163] A closer look at v. 11 is in order. Jesus simply says that not everyone will accept it. He does not say that they are not required to do so.[164] He does not even say that they are categorically unable to do so, despite the NRSV's translation, "not everybody can accept this teaching."[165] Some in the world may do so. What Jesus says is that *empowerment* "is given" to some (i.e., his own).[166] In other words, Jesus's comments in v. 11 are not disconsonant with the teaching in vv. 6 and 9 on "this matter."[167] In a world of rampant sexual sin and infidelity, such concerns are un-

---

161. See, e.g., Theodor Zahn, *Das Evangelium des Matthäus*, 4th ed. (Leipzig: Deichertsche, 1922), 592–95.

162. Gundry, *Matthew*, 254–55, 381–83; Willoughby C. Allen, *A Critical and Exegetical Commentary on the Gospel according to S. Matthew*, 3rd ed., ICC (Edinburgh: T&T Clark, 1985), 205–6.

163. E.g., Descamps, "New Testament Doctrine," 252. On this matter, D. A. Carson, "Matthew," in *The Expositor's Bible Commentary*, ed. Frank E. Gaebelein (Grand Rapids: Zondervan, 1984), 8:419 rightly stresses the grounding of these requirements in creation, intended for *all* people, even if his ultimate conclusion is problematic.

164. Contra France, *Matthew*, 722 n. 31.

165. A point missed by Blomberg, "Marriage," 183.

166. Again, contra France, *Matthew*, 723.

167. Λόγος may refer not to a verbal utterance but a "matter" or "concern."

The Matthean Divorce-Remarriage Texts in Context

avoidable, and God's command for there to be one man and one woman in marriage may seem impossible. So in v. 12 let the one who has been *empowered* accept it.

When Jesus in Matt 19:11 points to his followers as those empowered to obey his teaching, this is consonant with Matthew's repeated stress on the disciples' comprehension of Jesus's teaching (e.g., Matt 13:51; 16:17; 17:13; cf. Mark 4:13; 8:29; 9:9–10). The disciples are the ones who bear fruit (Matt 13:3–9, 18–23). Matthew stresses the disciples' comprehension even in places where Mark does not. The disciples recognize Jesus's identity after he approached them walking on the water in Matt 14:32–33. They worship him whereas Mark comments on their failure to understand and does not narrate the worship (6:51–52). In the story of the leaven of the Pharisees (Matt 16:5–12; cf. Mark 8:14–21), Matthew notes the disciples' comprehension after Jesus snaps them out of their confusion (16:12). Peter enjoys God's revelation in Matt 16:17 in a way that Mark 8 does not narrate. Similarly in the story of Elijah's return on the mountain (Matt 17:10–13; cf. Mark 9:11–13), Matthew again stresses the disciples' comprehension (17:13).[168] Jesus praises God in Matt 11:25 for revealing heavenly truths to infants and not to the wise and intelligent. His teaching is not optional for his followers (e.g., Matt 11:15; 13:9, 43, with their ears to hear).[169] Bearing fruit is not optional (e.g., Matt 3:8, 10; 7:16–20; 12:33; 13:23, 26, 30, 43; 21:43; 25:34–40), but the followers of Jesus are empowered to do God's will.

Matthew 13 and 19 in many ways parallel each other and may be usefully set alongside each other. Matthew 13:11 says that certain people—those outside the Jesus movement—have not been granted understanding of God's revelation.[170] Then in Matt 19:11 it is "given" to some and not others. Matthew 19:11 and 12 use the verb "accept, understand" (χωρέω) while 13:11 employs "know" (γινώσκω), but the difference is not significant since Matthew employs a number of words to convey the disciples' understanding. Although Jesus is demanding something very difficult, Jesus's "accept" in 19:11–12 goes beyond understanding to *acting* on that teaching.[171] Jesus is "giving" or *enabling* an obedience that is quite difficult (but possible) for those who are not his followers. Matthew 5:48 offers a helpful parallel: the law requires a radical, perfect obedience for all people. Such radical, seemingly impossible obedience must therefore be enabled, and that enablement is found only among Jesus's followers.

---

168. Matthew 17:23 omits the mention made in Mark 9:32 about the disciples' not understanding.

169. With Dupont, *Mariage*, 173–74, 178–88.

170. Hays (*Moral Vision*, 377 n. 17) stresses this verse as proof that "this word" in Matt 19:11 refers to Jesus's teaching on divorce and remarriage, and that teaching was intended for the disciples. The teaching on divorce and remarriage is to be obeyed as part of Jesus's commands and teaching for the disciples in 28:16–20.

171. P. Schmidt, "χωρέω," *NIDNTT* 1:742; followed by Heth and Wenham, *Jesus and Divorce*, 66.

CHAPTER 4

As Craig Keener helpfully explains, the disciples are concerned in v. 10 with the danger of marrying without an escape clause. "To marry without the possibility of divorce in a painful marriage seemed worse than not marrying at all! Responding to this objection, Jesus replied that some would indeed be better off not marrying."[172] The strong divorce-remarriage statement in v. 9 casts its shadow over the verses that follow, as Keener at *that* point recognized.

Matthew was never interested in the eunuch saying for its own sake. Explaining the rationale for juxtaposing a eunuch saying, if purely for the purpose of encouraging celibacy, to a passage encouraging faithfulness in marriage—all within a section that bears Matthew's editorial hand—would be quite difficult.[173] The "for" (γάρ) signals an integral connection to what came before, and Matthew heartily affirms the relationship between husbands and wives. Whereas Luke's Jesus includes *wives* among the people that the disciple must be willing to leave behind for the sake of the kingdom (18:29), the parallel statements in Matt 19:29 and Mark 10:29 do not mention leaving wives behind. Jesus in Luke 14:26 says: "Whoever comes to me and does not hate father and mother, *wife* and children, brothers and sisters, yes, and even life itself, cannot be my disciples." The parallel in Matt 10:37 reads: "Whoever loves father or mother more than me is not worthy of me; and whoever loves son or daughter more than me is not worthy of me." Matthew's Jesus does not require the disciple to abandon his wife.[174] Similarly, in the parable of the big dinner in Luke 14:16–24 the invited guests give excuses for not coming, and one mentions having recently married (14:20). In the parable of the wedding feast in Matt 22:2–14, Jesus does not make the point in the same way since no one offers an excuse about being too busy marrying a wife.

Whereas Matt 22:22–33 has Jesus's contrasting marriage in this age with no marriage in the age to come (cf. Mark 12:24–27), in Luke 20:27–40's version of that incident, the wording is rather different in vv. 34–35: "Those who belong to this age marry and are given in marriage; but those who are considered worthy of a place in that age and in the resurrection from the dead neither marry nor are given in marriage." Luke's Jesus divides the world into those who belong to this age *as opposed to* those worthy of the age to come and the resurrection, and the *latter* do not marry. While Matthew affirms that there is no marriage in the *resurrection*, he does not divide those on this side of the resurrection into those who marry and those who do not. In fact, Matthew has the dead man leave behind children

---

172. Keener, *Matthew*, 471.
173. R. Collins, *Divorce*, 121.
174. Blomberg ("Marriage," 184) tries to blunt the force of this point, but Luke still relativizes the marriage relationship for the sake of the kingdom in a way that Matthew is consistently avoiding.

in 22:24, whereas the Lukan parallel has the brother leaving behind *a wife* (20:28; as also Mark 12:19).[175] Matthew is very supportive of the marital relationship, and the eunuch saying should be interpreted in view of that context.

Matthew 19:10–12 is therefore best taken as continuing the topic of 19:2–9.[176] Had Jesus allowed remarriage after divorce for sexual sin, Jesus's teaching would not have been overly difficult—certainly not to the point that the disciples would have objected in v. 10 that it is better not to marry. When the disciples object to Jesus's teaching (v. 10), he responds by dividing the world into those *empowered* to accept the teaching and those who are not (v. 11). The eunuch saying in v. 12 conforms well to Jesus's teaching about divorce and remarriage. Some eunuchs are born that way, but some are made so by others. Then there will be those who have made themselves eunuchs for the sake of the kingdom. To express the parallel, some will forgo sexual relations by not ever marrying for the sake of the kingdom. Matthew's Jesus assumes that his followers *can* live in a celibate fashion in 5:29–30: "If your right eye causes you to sin, tear it out and throw it away; it is better for you to lose one of your members than for your whole body to be thrown into hell. And if your right hand causes you to sin, cut it off and throw it away; it is better for you to lose one of your members than for your whole body to go into hell." It is not at all coincidental that the eunuch saying in 19:11–12 bears such striking similarities to 5:29–30, since both are in the context of *not remarrying* (cf. 5:32). For those divorced by others, they have been *made* eunuchs for the sake of the kingdom.[177] As difficult as a life of such discipleship may be, as the disciples' objection in 19:10 recognizes, Jesus insists that the celibate lifestyle remains possible thanks to the help of God. The disciples do what Pharisees and unbelievers cannot readily do because "for God all things are possible" (Matt 19:26, shortly after Jesus's divorce and remarriage teaching).[178]

---

175. Quesnell, "Made Themselves Eunuchs," 344–46.

176. So Hays, *Moral Vision*, 377 n. 17: "In the Matthean context it [Jesus's teaching about eunuchs] must be understood as a response to the disciples' complaint about the difficulty of Jesus' teaching against divorce" and not because Jesus is calling for celibacy."

177. So also Gundry, *Matthew*, 377, 382–83; Barton, *Discipleship*, 191–204, esp. 194–99, here 198: "[R]emarriage subsequent to divorcing one's wife is prohibited. The saying about 'eunuchs for the sake of the kingdom of heaven' (19.12c), whatever its meaning(s) at an earlier stage in the history of the tradition, is joined by Matthew to this stringent teaching in order to support those among his audience in this position." They are to remain single and celibate for the sake of the kingdom. Barton stresses that the eunuch saying is *not* about celibacy *per se*. Rather he states: "[I]t is a word for those who have accepted the discipline of Jesus' rigorous teaching prohibiting the disciple who has divorced his unchaste wife from remarrying. . . . [T]he call to remain single once a divorce has taken place is a necessary corollary of what it means to be a member of that one family" (199).

178. Dupont, *Mariage*, 173–74.

CHAPTER 4

This connection between God making all things possible in 19:26 and the disciples' eunuch-like celibacy after divorce in vv. 10–12 is rendered more plausible by the connections between the two sections.[179] Matthew 19:1–12 bears structural similarities to vv. 16–30 with its story of the rich man who approached Jesus.[180] First, both stories begin with a question posed to Jesus (19:3, 16). Second, Jesus responds to and challenges the question (19:4–6, 17). Third, Jesus's dialogue partners raise a counterquestion on the basis of the Scriptures (19:7, 18–20). Fourth, Jesus dismisses the objections (19:8 [hardened hearts], 21 [sell what you own]). Fifth, both stories conclude with very difficult teaching—in v. 9 regarding divorce and remarriage and in v. 24 with, "It is easier for a camel to go through the eye of a needle than for someone who is rich to enter the kingdom of God." Sixth, the disciples in both instances respond with astonished, stunned reactions—in v. 10 it is better not to marry and in v. 25 with, "Then who can be saved?"[181] Seventh and finally, Jesus answers in both v. 11 and v. 26 by affirming the teaching: "For mortals this is impossible, but for God all things are possible."[182] In view of the parallels, even as v. 26 reinforces Jesus's original teaching in v. 24, Jesus's comments in vv. 11–12 would reinforce his original teaching in v. 9 about divorce and remarriage—further evidence that vv. 11–12 are narratively related to v. 9. Perhaps the resemblance between 19:1–12 and 19:16–30 cannot be pressed too far since the harsh words of v. 26 respond to the question in v. 25, and Jesus normally answers the disciples' questions (e.g., 13:10–11, 36–37; 24:3–4). A seven-part pattern, nonetheless, is hardly coincidental.

Several additional factors indicate that the requirement for celibacy (Matt 19:12) should be interpreted in view of the divorce/remarriage saying (v. 9). R. Jarrett Van Tine notes the lack of lexical support for translating v. 10's ἡ αἰτία as "case," "situation," or "relationship."[183] The Greek word is normally used in legal contexts, meaning "charge," "accusation," "guilt," "crime," "blame," or "pretext/ground," and just such a legal context is present with Jesus's pronouncement in 19:9. The disciples' reaction in v. 10 should thus be translated: "If the man who has (illegitimately)

---

179. Moloney, "Matthew 19:3–12 and Celibacy," 46–47.

180. Hays (*Moral Vision*, 377 n. 17) points to the parallels to Matt 19:23–26 as convincing that God will enable the disciples to obey the difficult teaching about divorce and remarriage; see also R. Collins, *Divorce*, 122–24.

181. Blomberg ("Marriage," 184) ignores this series of parallels since the disciples' reaction is in one instance a statement but is a question in the other. The parallels, however, speak for themselves.

182. Adapted from Wenham, *Jesus, Divorce, and Remarriage*, 75.

183. R. Jarrett Van Tine, "Castration for the Kingdom and Avoiding the αἰτία of Adultery (Matthew 19:10–12)," *JBL* 137.2 (2018): 402–4. The *one* parallel BDAG identifies for a Latinism (P.Ryl. 63) is best explained differently. The lexicons offer no other parallel.

divorced his wife is *charged* with adultery by marrying another, it would be better for such a one not to marry another" (lit. "the charge against the man with his wife").[184] The "charge" against the man in v. 10 would parallel the "charge" (αἰτία) against the wife in 19:3 that provides the potential basis for a divorce. The charge against the wife, justifying divorce, has now ironically become a charge against the husband after the divorce (in marrying another).[185] The disciples are not claiming that it is better not to marry at all. Their comments are a response to what Jesus has said about divorce and *remarriage*. With Van Tine:

> In this reading the disciples [*sic*] statement is logically sound and entirely appropriate to the context; it really is "better" for such a man who has illicitly divorced his wife "not to marry [another]" if, in so doing, he incurs the charge/guilt of adultery. That is to say, the context drives the reader to fill in the gap of 19:10b in light of 19:9 and 19:10a: εἰ οὕτως ἐστιν ἡ αἰτία τοῦ ἀνθρώπου μετὰ τῆς γυναικός, οὐ συμφέρει [τῷ ἀνθρώπῳ ἑτέραν] γαμῆσαι.[186]

"*The* man" remains the one in v. 9 related to a new wife after a divorce now "charged" with adultery. The remarriage would be adulterous.

The notion of castration in 19:12 is most naturally understood in view of the parallel in Matt 5:27–30 where one is to cut off one's members in order to *avoid adultery*.[187] Both Matt 5:27–30 and 19:10–12 are in the immediate contexts of Jesus's teaching on divorce, remarriage, and the avoidance of adultery. The eunuch saying is not independent of that context. Second Temple authors therefore suggest dismemberment as a means to avoid the sin of adultery. Philo writes:

> And so, to my thinking, those who are not utterly ignorant would *choose to be blinded* rather than see unfitting things, and *to be deprived of hearing* rather than listen to harmful words, and *to have their tongues cut out* to save them from uttering anything that should not be divulged. . . . *It is better to be made a eunuch than to be mad after illicit unions* [ἐξευνουχισθῆναί γε μὴν ἄμεινον ἢ πρὸς συνουσίας ἐκνόμους λυττᾶν]. All these things [i.e., sinful illicit unions], seeing that they plunge the soul in disasters for which there is no remedy, would prop-

---

184. Van Tine, "Castration," 406. See 406–7 for examples of the common usage of the phrase as "charge *against* someone."

185. Note the several parallels in vocabulary between vv. 3 and 10; Van Tine, "Castration," 408–9.

186. Van Tine, "Castration," 410–12.

187. Van Tine, "Castration," 414–15.

CHAPTER 4

erly *incur the most extreme vengeance and punishment* (*Det.* 48; cf. 47 [Colson and Whitaker, LCL; emphasis mine]).[188]

Likewise, Justin Martyr in his *First Apology* interprets Matt 5:29 and 19:11–12 on dismemberment in relation to the avoidance of adultery, in the case of 19:11–12, by "*second* marriages."

> Concerning chastity [Jesus] said this: "Whosoever looks upon a woman to lust after her has already committed adultery with her in his heart before God." [5:28] And: "If your right eye offends you, cut it out; for it is better for you to enter into the Kingdom of Heaven with one eye, than with two eyes to be cast into eternal fire." [5:29] And: "Whosoever shall marry her that is divorced from another husband, commits adultery." [5:32b/19:9b] And: "There are some who have been made eunuchs by men, and some who were born eunuchs, and some who have made themselves eunuchs for the Kingdom of Heaven's sake; but not all can receive this saying." [19:12, 11] So that all who according to human law make second marriages are sinners in the sight of our Master, as are those who look on a woman to lust after her. For not only the man who in act commits adultery is condemned by Him, but also the man who desires to commit adultery; since not only our deeds but also our thoughts are open before God (*1 Apol.* 1.15).[189]

Richard Hays has perceptively recognized that the eunuch saying serves as commentary on the discussion about marriage in Matt 19:2–9.[190] The disciples respond with incredulity at Jesus's teaching that it would be better not to marry. Such a response is far more likely had Jesus eliminated remarriage as adulterous.[191] Provision for divorce *and remarriage* is a far more comfortable teaching than to allow for divorce but not a subsequent remarriage. The eunuch saying about celibacy is comprehensible in a context in which the divorced may not remarry.

Stephen Barton rightly stresses that the eunuch saying was prompted by Jesus's demanding marital ethic, one that distinguished the followers of Jesus from other Jews of the day and became a source of identity for the first Christians, adding: "In the exceptional case where a man's wife is guilty of sexual immorality (πορνεία), divorce

---

188. A passage emphasized by Van Tine, "Castration," 415, as also the following Justin Martyr text.
189. Justin Martyr, *The First and Second Apologies*, trans. Leslie William Barnard, ACW 56 (New York: Paulist, 1997), 32–33.
190. Hays, *Moral Vision*, 377 n. 17.
191. Rightly Luz, *Matthew 8–20*, 493.

is permitted the offended husband: however, remarriage after divorce is prohibited on the grounds that 'they are no longer two but one flesh' (v. 6a)."[192] Barton continues, "Matthew's rhetorical intention [in the teaching about eunuchs] is to surprise and shock the disciple who has divorced his unchaste wife into imagining the possibility of a new mode of existence: remaining single and celibate, and thereby transcending family ties, for the kingdom's sake."[193] The eunuch saying in 19:12 bears implications for the *innocent* party as well. Even as the wrongly divorcing husband must remain celibate (he is one who has made himself a eunuch through divorce), so also there are those "who have been made eunuchs by others" (by being divorced). The eunuch saying reinforces that remarriage is not an option after divorce.

Conclusion

Matthew recalls Jesus giving an exception to his teaching against divorce. In Matt 5:32, even as a person is not to lust or be angry, a man may not divorce his wife. He sins by placing his wife in a vulnerable position such that, in most instances, he is causing her as the innocent party to commit adultery herself by remarrying. Any man who marries her, even though she is innocent, would be adulterating. This situation contradicts the notion that innocent parties may remarry. One must therefore modulate the pro-remarriage reasoning to the innocent parties in a *legitimate* divorce. A wife who has already committed sexual sin, on the other hand, has already adulterated. Her husband's divorcing her would be legitimate.[194] As for the husband who has legitimately divorced his wife for the cause of adultery, Jesus returns to whether that man may marry again in Matt 19:9. Although focused on the actions of men, Matt 5:32 indicates that no divorced wife may marry again.

The original text of Matt 19:9 requires reconstruction. Two readings compete for authenticity. The first, most notably attested in Vaticanus, is parallel to Matt 5:32 with identical implications. The other, most notably attested in Sinaiticus, includes an exception clause that may also modify remarriage. In other words, Matt 19:9 represents the *one* place in the gospels that *may* speak to the possibility of legitimate remarriage, assuming the Sinaiticus reading. Vaticanus enjoys stron-

---

192. Barton, *Discipleship*, 202–4, here 202.
193. Barton, *Discipleship*, 201.
194. If an innocent husband in a legitimate divorce can remarry but an innocent wife in an illegitimate divorce cannot, then divorce is not severing the marital bond in instances of illegitimate divorce. The divorce and its divorce certificate would simply be irrelevant. Then the question is whether there is such a concept as a legitimate remarriage.

CHAPTER 4

ger external attestation, but the internal evidence favors Sinaiticus. Thus most scholars deem the reading of Sinaiticus as original, but the notion that Vaticanus may be original may not be casually dismissed, in which case Matt 19:9 would definitely be prohibiting remarriage.

Assuming the Sinaiticus reading, as reflected in English translations, the question is whether the exception clause in Matt 19:9 modifies the first verb (divorce) or also the second (divorce and remarry). If it modifies both, in instances of sexual sin (the exception) one may both divorce and marry again. Both actions would be legitimate for the innocent partner. The guilty party would already be an adulterer. Several lines of reasoning favor the exception clause modifying the first verb and not the second, in which case the usual Matthean parallelism is maintained. Matthew would be making two distinct but interrelated claims: a man who divorces his wife commits adultery, unless she is already adulterous. A man who marries again after divorce commits adultery. Since the exception clause modifies the first verb and not the second, Jesus makes no provision for the husband who has validly or legitimately divorced his wife for adultery to marry another. God's will in creation remains for one man and one woman to be joined together in a lifelong union whenever a marriage takes place.

Further supporting this reading is Matt 19:12 with Jesus's eunuch saying. The disqualification of each alternative construal leaves a connection between 19:12 and 19:9 the most viable understanding. Furthermore, understanding Matt 19:12 in relation to 19:9 neatly parallels Jesus's comments on dismemberment to avoid adultery in 5:27–32. In other words, in the wake of divorce some have either made themselves eunuchs by divorcing a spouse or been made eunuchs for the sake of the kingdom by others who have divorced them. Jesus's eunuch saying thus reinforces that the parties of divorce are to remain single and not remarry.

In short, the balance of the evidence favors a prohibition of remarriage without exception—even in Matthew. Where Matthew departs from the historical Jesus and the Gospels of Mark and Luke is in his provision for divorce in instances of sexual sin. As the sole passage in the gospels that may allow for remarriage, Matt 19:9 cannot bear the burden that has been placed on it. Matthew 19:9 does not have to bear this burden alone; many see the same permission for remarriage in the apostle Paul. As for Jesus in the gospels, God's will in creation remains for there to be one man and one woman in marriage.

5

"Not Bound" and "Free" in the Apostle Paul?

The earliest witness to Jesus's teaching on divorce and remarriage is from the early 50s, only twenty years after his earthly ministry and fifteen years before the first written gospel. The apostle Paul reports in 1 Cor 7:10–11: "To the married I give this command—not I but the Lord—that the wife should not separate from her husband (but if she does separate, let her remain unmarried or else be reconciled to her husband), and that the husband should not divorce his wife." What is debated is the extent to which Paul may be softening or amending Jesus's teaching throughout 1 Cor 7. Immediately after relating the Lord's strict command, Paul already identifies an exception.

To recap the chapter: In 1 Cor 7:1 Paul turns for the first time to a prior letter the Corinthians had sent him and a matter they had raised: "Now concerning the matters about which you wrote." He answers their question about whether a husband is to refrain from sexual relations with his wife. Paul admonishes husband and wife not to deprive each other in vv. 1–7. He leaves the married behind in 1 Cor 7:8–9 to turn to "the unmarried and the widows," urging them to "remain" as they are, if at all possible. He allows them to marry if they are aflame with passion. After relaying the Lord's command on divorce and remarriage in vv. 10–11, in 1 Cor 7:12–16 Paul turns to mixed marriages with a believer and a non-Christ-believer. Again, his instructions are to stay as they are, if at all possible. He allows the Christ-believer to consent to divorce if the non-Christ-believer insists. In the next paragraph, 1 Cor 7:17–24, Paul instructs the circumcised not to seek uncircumcision nor the uncircumcised circumcision. They should stay as they are. Paul also states that slaves should not be concerned about their status and should stay as they are, but they are permitted to enjoy their freedom if it is offered. Echoing Paul's introduction of the content of the Corinthians' letter in 7:1, in v. 25 he writes:

CHAPTER 5

"Now concerning virgins." Apparently, this is another concern the Corinthians had raised in their letter to him: Should a man bound to a wife seek to be free? Paul urges the man to stay as he is, and the one free from a wife should not seek one. They both should stay as they are since, in v. 31, "the present form of this world is passing away." Because the time is short, serving the Lord is far more imperative. In vv. 32–35 the unmarried are told to stay as they are in order to devote themselves more fully to the Lord's service. If someone is not behaving properly toward a fiancée, Paul allows that person to marry. The widow in vv. 39–40 should remain as she is but has Paul's permission to remarry if she feels compelled to do so.

The chapter thus exhibits a regular pattern. Each believer should stay in his or her initial state or calling. Being anxious about the affairs of the Lord is much better than having to be concerned about the needs of a person with whom one finds oneself in relationship.[1] Whenever a possibility to change status is a viable option, Paul makes that clear. In other words, one expects an express declaration of the freedom to change one's status or condition when Paul deems it possible. In 1 Cor 7:10–11 Paul reports Jesus's prohibition of divorce and Jesus's command for the divorced wife not to marry another man. She is to stay as she is after the divorce. Paul conspicuously does *not* add to the Lord's teaching that she is free to remarry. That freedom should not be assumed in view of Paul's pattern in the chapter: stay as you are except when he provides an alternative. The absence here is conspicuous after his frequent exceptions elsewhere. One would therefore need good reason to think the divorced may remarry in view of Paul's leaving Jesus's teaching unqualified.

The dominical command in 1 Cor 7:10–11, in prohibiting both divorce and the divorced from marrying another, anticipates that a divorce may nevertheless take place. The command here agrees with Jesus's teaching on the subject as reported by the gospels.[2] Although Paul is paraphrasing Jesus's command (e.g., ἀφίημι; χωρίζω; cf. the Synoptic use of ἀπολύω), he maintains the two-part structure: the prohibition of divorce followed by the prohibition of the divorced person's remarrying. While Paul's vocabulary for divorce is different from the Jesus tradition, he is not making a distinction by the verb χωρίζω, "separate," between a divorce and a separation. The language is synonymous.[3] Paul's choice of vocabulary is attested in the divorce certificates of the day. The passive verb form for the woman's being

---

1. On Stoic parallels to this line of thought, see David L. Balch, "1 Cor 7:32–35 and Stoic Debates about Marriage, Anxiety, and Distraction," *JBL* 102.3 (1983): 429–39.
2. See the review of 1 Cor 7:10–11 and the remainder of the Jesus tradition in chapter 2, pp. 60–67.
3. To "separate" is to divorce. Divorce in the Greco-Roman world took place by separation. Formal documentation was optional; cf. the ancient Near Eastern divorce certificates common in Jewish circles. See Instone-Brewer, *Divorce and Remarriage*, 190–91.

separated or divorced is also attested in the papyri for "separating themselves" with a reflexive sense: "separate from each other" (e.g., *BGU* 4.1101 [GM-13]). The passive form is therefore used in 1 Cor 7:15 for the unbelieving partner *initiating* divorce. Paul's paraphrase of the command may reflect a specific situation at Corinth since he addresses the wife first in v. 11 as a "casuistic aside."[4]

First Corinthians 7:11 is not what the Lord "says," as in vv. 6, 8, and 12, but rather what the Lord *"commands"* (cf. 11:17; 14:37; 1 Thess 4:15). Ultimately, 1 Cor 7:10–11 conveys an emphatic imperative from the Lord against divorce that prohibits a divorced wife from marrying another man—and the husband is simply not permitted to divorce his wife.[5] The Lord's twofold command thus represents a rhetorically highlighted starting point by which Paul's other comments are to be judged. The question is whether and to what extent he modifies Jesus's original command. Cornes writes that "Christ, as reported by Paul, *does not say*: 'If she divorces, she must remain unmarried *in order to be* reconciled' with the implication, perhaps, that if she cannot be reconciled (because her partner remarries) then she no longer remains unmarried herself."[6] There are only two options: be reconciled, thus resuming the marriage, or remain single.

Some interpreters would limit the Lord's command to an *illegitimate* divorce (i.e., on non-biblical grounds) and would assert that remarriage is perfectly acceptable for the wife if her divorce had been on biblical grounds and legitimate.[7] William F. Luck claims that reconciliation is only required of a guilty party; thus the sinner is reconciled *to God*. Since the wife is told to remain single or be reconciled, she must be the guilty party of the divorce and there are no implications with respect to remarriage for the innocent party.[8] She, as the *guilty* party, should initiate her reconciliation to God (and to her husband). Luck's position on the permission to remarry in 1 Cor 7:10–16 relies on the veracity of this claim, but he does not substantiate it. In Pauline literature God is always the *initiator* of recon-

---

4. Murphy-O'Connor, "Divorced Woman," 602–4; Raymond F. Collins, *First Corinthians*, SP 7 (Collegeville, MN: Liturgical, 1999), 263; Ciampa and Rosner, *First Letter to the Corinthians*, 292–93; Garland, *1 Corinthians*, 281. For additional reasons that a specific situation may be in view, see R. Collins, 23–29. The four gospel divorce sayings begin with the husband. The admonition to remain married is countercultural. A funerary inscription (ca. 18–2 BCE) remarks on how uncommon it is for a marriage to last to the forty-first year without estrangement; see Horsley, *New Documents*, 3:33–36.

5. That the divorced wife is to remain single or be reconciled to her husband parallels Matt 5:32 and Luke 16:18 in the double tradition. A divorced woman's remarriage to another man is adulterous.

6. Cornes, *Divorce and Remarriage*, 233–34.

7. E.g., Naselli, "What the New Testament Teaches," 30.

8. Luck, *Divorce and Re-Marriage*, 187, 193.

ciliation and *never the object* of the verb (ἀπο)καταλλάσσω, contradicting Luck's appeal to the guilty human to be reconciled to God. In Jewish and Greco-Roman literature, a reconciliation takes place between two warring parties. Second Maccabees is the only ancient Jewish or Christian text, apart from Pauline literature, that uses reconciliation language in the context of the relationship with God (1:5; 5:20; 7:33; 8:29). The author of 2 Macc 1:5 asks God to respond to the pleas of the Jewish people by overlooking their sins and to be reconciled *to them* (καταλλαγείη ὑμῖν). In 2 Macc 5:20, after a period of divine anger as Antiochus was permitted to pillage the temple, a reconciliation with God became possible (cf. 8:29) and the merciful Lord was reconciled to his servants. In 2 Macc 7:32–33 God vents disciplinary anger, but the suffering of the seven brothers moves God to forgive and to be reconciled *to* the Jewish people (καταλλαγήσεται τοῖς ἑαυτοῦ δούλοις). In these instances, God *as the innocent party is being reconciled to the guilty party*.[9] Luck's claim, then, is not justifiable, and his argument that 1 Cor 7:10–11 does not proscribe remarriage for the innocent party proves unworkable. Paul is requiring the divorced parties to be reconciled to each other and does not mention God as a party. The divorced wife is to remain single or be reconciled *to her husband* (τῷ ἀνδρὶ καταλλαγήτω). The two verses relay yet another dominical command to remain unmarried.

Unfortunately, Paul does not include any language to allow for an exception to marry another in cases of legitimately grounded divorces, and one should not assume so in view of the emphatic instructions. Although the Lord's command is phrased in terms of wives (perhaps reflecting the Corinthian situation), Paul places that instruction within an immediate context maintaining a mutuality of requirements for both the man and the woman, which indicates that the Lord's command is binding on the husband as well.[10] Paul's discussion of divorce and

---

9. For reconciliation in the Scriptures, see A. Andrew Das, "Reconcile, Reconciliation," *NIDB*, 4:745–48.

10. William F. Orr and James Arthur Walther, *1 Corinthians*, AB 32 (Garden City, NY: Doubleday, 1976), 213.

As for the focus on wives in 1 Cor 7:10–11, note also the instructions on male and female obligations in 1 Cor 11:2–16 and 14:33–36. Margaret Y. MacDonald stresses a concern for both men and women, and yet a special concern for female members remaining unmarried (1 Cor 7:34); see "Women Holy in Body and Spirit: The Social Setting of 1 Corinthians 7," *NTS* 36 (1990): 161–81, esp. 164: "Were women especially drawn to the strongly ascetic teaching? ... Having separated from their husbands, had some entered into questionable liaisons with other males, as is perhaps suggested by 1 Cor 7. 10–11?" Had some taken an element of "no male and female" in Paul's teaching (Gal 3:28) too far? See also Judith M. Gundry-Volf, "Male and Female in Creation and New Creation: Interpretation of Galatians 3:28C in 1 Corinthians 7," in *To Tell the Mystery: Essays on New Testament Eschatology in Honor of Robert H. Gundry*, ed. Thomas E. Schmidt and Moisés

remarriage, except for brief comments in Rom 7:1–6, is clustered in the single chapter of 1 Cor 7, and the Lord's command prohibiting divorce and remarriage casts its shadow over all Paul has to say.

Five Places Where Paul Might Be Qualifying the Lord's Command

Interpreters point to five pressure points in 1 Cor 7 where Paul may be qualifying or even overturning the command against divorce and remarriage that he relayed from the Lord. The first is 1 Cor 7:1–7. In these verses Paul describes sexual relations in marriage as a safe haven from temptation. "Because of the cases of sexual immorality, each man should have his own wife and each woman her own husband" (v. 2). The spouses should not deprive each other of sexual relations and, if so, only temporarily for prayer lest Satan tempt them when they lack self-control (v. 5). Not all enjoy the same gift as Paul (vv. 6–7). Paul would surely affirm that the divorced who do not share his gift for celibacy need a safe haven from sexual sin as well.

A second pressure point emerges in vv. 8–9 when Paul explicitly mentions remarriage. The motivation for the permission is the same as in vv. 1–7. "But if they are not practicing self-control, they should marry. For it is better to marry than to be aflame with passion" (v. 9). As several commentators rightly recognize, Paul does not have in mind at this point the fires of hell mentioned in 1 Cor 3:15 (cf. 6:9).[11] Loveday Alexander helpfully catalogues a wide array of references in Greco-Roman novels and erotic poetry to sexual desire as "burning," and the flames are "quenched" through sexual activity. For example, in his novel Achilles Tatius writes: "However angry you make me, I still burn with love for you. . . . Make a truce with me at least for now; pity me. . . . A single consummation will be enough. It is a small remedy I ask for so great an illness. Quench a little of my fire" (*Leuc. Clit.* 5.26.2).[12] Other Greco-Roman and Jewish authors similarly describe "burning," erotic passion.[13]

Silva, JSNTSup 100 (Sheffield: Sheffield Academic, 1994), 95–121; Gundry-Volf, "Controlling the Bodies, A Theological Principle of the Corinthian Sexual Ascetics (1 Cor 7)," in *The Corinthian Correspondence*, ed. R. Bieringer, BETL 125 (Leuven: Leuven University Press, 1996), 519–41.

11. As suggested by F. F. Bruce, *1 and 2 Corinthians*, NCB (Grand Rapids: Eerdmans, 1971), 68; Graydon F. Snyder, *First Corinthians: A Faith Community Commentary* (Atlanta: Mercer University Press, 1992), 97.

12. Translation of Achilles Tatius from John J. Winkler, "Leucippe and Clitophon," in *Collected Ancient Greek Novels*, ed. B. P. Reardon (Berkeley: University of California Press, 1989), 247–48.

13. E.g., Epictetus, *Diatr.* 3.22.76; 4.1.147; Soranus, *Gyn.* 1.7.31; Prov 6:27–29; Sir 9:8; T. Jos. 2:2; Philo, *Decal.* 24; *Spec.* 3.36. See Loveday Alexander, "'Better to Marry than to Burn': St. Paul and the Greek Novel," in *Ancient Fiction and Early Christian Narrative*, ed. Ronald F. Hock, J. Bradley Chance, and Judith Perkins, SBLSymS 6 (Atlanta: Scholars Press, 1998), 252–53.

CHAPTER 5

After Paul's comments about marital desire requiring sexual expression in 7:1–7, a reference to the fire of passion is clear in vv. 8–9. Those fiery desires, for Paul, must be satisfied in the context of marriage and not through sexual relations outside of it.[14] This advice in vv. 8–9 is to "the unmarried and the widows." If the "unmarried" is a broad category inclusive also of those who were *once* married, then Paul would be including the divorced among those who may burn with passion and who should get married. He would be advising them to marry again.[15]

Still a third pressure point is in vv. 12–15 as Paul turns from the Lord's command to a situation not anticipated in that teaching: a mixed marriage between a believer and an unbeliever. Although Christian spouses are not to divorce a spouse, an unbelieving spouse may insist on it even when the Christian rightly seeks to continue in the marriage. Paul states in v. 15: "But if the unbelieving partner separates, let it be so; in such a case the brother or sister is not bound. It is to peace that God has called you." As Paul words it, when the unbelieving spouse insists on a divorce, the believing spouse is "not bound." He or she may permit the divorce to take place. In the divorce certificates of the ancient world, a divorce entailed a corresponding "freedom" to remarry.[16] Verses 12–16 therefore appear to offer a qualification to the strict teaching of vv. 10–11: In some situations, a believing spouse is no longer "bound" and therefore free to remarry.[17]

A fourth pressure point is in 1 Cor 7:27–28 where Paul appears to address the situation of divorce and remarriage yet again: "Are you bound to a wife? Do not seek to be free. Are you free from a wife? Do not seek a wife. But if you marry, you do not sin, and if a virgin marries, she does not sin." The verses appear to be contemplating both the never-married "virgin" and the formerly married who have been "loosed" from those marital bonds (by divorce). Neither sins by marrying or remarrying.[18]

---

14. Garland, *1 Corinthians*, 274–75; Martin, "Paul without Passion," 201.

15. Craig S. Keener, *And Marries Another: Divorce and Remarriage in the Teaching of the New Testament* (Peabody, MA: Hendrickson, 1991), 81.

16. Instone-Brewer's case from the divorce certificates is the primary evidence many interpreters rely on for taking these verses as permitting remarriage; e.g., Garland, *1 Corinthians*, 291, 296; Ciampa and Rosner, *First Letter to the Corinthians*, 302.

17. On this approach, see David Instone-Brewer, "Jewish Greek and Aramaic Marriage," 239–42.

18. Craig Keener is so impressed by the value of these two Pauline verses that he even refers to them as support for remarriage (!) in *Matthew*, 191 n. 95. Colin Brown makes much of vv. 27–28 as evidence that the divorced could remarry without any concern of sin, along with the fact that divorced people need the release of sexual relations with marriage as well; see "Separate, Divide," *NIDNTT* 3:536–38. Elsewhere, Keener writes:

> Paul does not say "free," but "freed." The person who is "freed" can therefore only be a person who was previously bound, and in the context this can only mean that the person was pre-

At the heart of this discussion is the meaning of the Greek word for "unmarried" (οἱ ἄγαμοι)—a word that occurs only in this New Testament chapter (vv. 8, 11, 32, and 34). In 7:11 Paul emphasizes the Lord's command that the divorced "unmarried" may not remarry. In a fifth pressure point in 1 Cor 7:32 and 34, Paul appears to be offering a qualification of the Lord's teaching against remarriage yet again. In 7:34 Paul distinguishes the "unmarried" woman from the never-married "virgin." In other words, it seems, the "unmarried" woman in this verse is *not* a virgin but someone who has been married previously. Paul will not turn to the widow until vv. 39–40, which confirms for many interpreters that he is imagining a divorced woman in 7:34. Correspondingly, Paul posits in v. 32 an "unmarried" man who does not need to strive to please a wife. Perhaps this man has never been married, but it is more likely that his situation parallels the corresponding woman in v. 34. The "unmarried" men envisioned in v. 32 would include those who have been divorced, since they stand alongside "unmarried" divorced women. Paul hopes to discourage them from considering (re)marriage, but that option is apparently *not forbidden* in these verses. Paul appears to be softening the Lord's command.

The structure of the passage is also a factor in how the five pressure points are resolved. Roy Ciampa and Brian Rosner outline the chapter as having an A-B-A′-B′ structure:

A—Married people (7:1–7)
B—Unmarried people in general and widows (7:8–9)
A′—Married people (7:10–16)
B′—Unmarried people in general (7:25–38) and widows (7:39–40)

This structuring of the chapter reinforces the conclusion that later in the chapter Paul is still treating a broad category of the unmarried that is inclusive of the divorced.[19]

1 Corinthians 7:1–6—The Married Couple

Paul posits marriage between *one* man and *one* woman as the solution to sexual desire. Spouses are not to deprive each other of sexual relations, since the apostle grants

---

viously married. Given the fact that "freed" in the first line refers to divorce, we must take it as referring to divorce in the second line as well" (*And Marries Another*, 63).

The context, however, may actually indicate something *other* than a prior marriage—an option Keener overlooks, to anticipate a later discussion.

19. Ciampa and Rosner, *First Letter to the Corinthians*, 287.

CHAPTER 5

that not all have the same gift as he (vv. 6–7).[20] Each man is to have his own wife, and each woman her own husband (v. 2). Paul envisions one man and one woman together in a marital relationship, and in this context sexual desire may be satisfied.[21] Since Paul is addressing in these verses the relations between a husband and a wife, it is not yet clear how he would apply his thinking to the divorced or to other categories of relationships, such as widowers, widows, and the never married. He had just mentioned in the prior paragraph (6:16) the travesty of sexual relations with a prostitute, which defiles how "the two shall become one flesh." The one-flesh relationship of the one man and one woman in marriage is the rightful place for sexual relations and not with a prostitute. Paul does not claim, at least in 7:1–7, that a *second* man or woman may enter into a one-flesh relationship with the original husband or wife through remarriage.[22] Again, in vv. 1–7 he freely grants that believers often experience sexual desire, but he offers only *one* man with *one* woman in marriage as the solution.

1 Corinthians 7:8–9—Unmarried and Widows

In 1 Cor 7:8–9 Paul turns to a group that includes widows: "To the unmarried and the widows, I say that it is well for them to remain unmarried as I am. But if they

---

20. A point stressed, representatively, by Stanley B. Marrow in an argument for the freedom to remarry; "Marriage and Divorce in the New Testament," *AThR* 70.1 (1988): 3–6.

21. For the married to abstain from sexual relations was not unheard of among the Jews. In T. Naph. 8:8: "There is a time for having intercourse with one's wife, and a time to abstain for the purpose of prayer" (Kee, *OTP*). Egyptian deity cults have left their remains in Corinth, with one of the five temples dating to the first century CE at Cenchreae; cf. Apuleius, *Metam.* 10.35; 11.4, 6, 12, 17. The Egyptian cults encouraged celibacy, especially among Isis's devotees; see Juvenal, *Sat.* 6.535–537; Plutarch, *Is. Os.* 2 [*Mor.* 351f–352a]; Propertius, *Eleg.* 2.28a.60–62; 3.33.1–4; 4.5.28–34; Tibullus, *Eleg.* 1.3.23–26; Richard E. Oster Jr., "Use, Misuse and Neglect of Archaeological Evidence in Some Modern Works on 1 Corinthians (1 Cor 7,1–5; 8,10; 11,2–16; 12,14–26)," *ZNW* 83 (1992): 59–64. The Corinthian Christian interest in celibacy is culturally explicable. David L. Balch points to Q sayings that could be interpreted as supportive of abstinence; see "Backgrounds of 1 Cor. VII: Sayings of the Lord in Q; Moses as an Ascetic ΘΕΙΟΣ ΑΝΗΡ in II Cor. III," *NTS* 18 (1972): 352–58. Philo praised Moses for abstaining from sexual relations (*Mos.* 2.13–14); see the discussion in Balch, "Backgrounds," 358–60. On the drive toward sexual relations in marriage and marital obligations, see Alexander, "Better to Marry," 235–56. Judith M. Gundry-Volf even proposes that Paul is countering an interest in divorce in order to be celibate; see "Controlling the Bodies," 527–28; similarly, Gundry-Volf, "Male and Female," 118. If responding to a Corinthian interest in divorce for the sake of celibacy, Paul would be focused in these verses on the propriety of divorce, and remarriage would simply not be in view.

22. Were divorce to take place, Paul would presumably direct them back to their original spouses, just as the Lord "commands" in 1 Cor 7:11.

are not practicing self-control, they should marry. For it is better to marry than to be aflame with passion." The practical implications of these verses depend on whether the "unmarried" include the divorced. If Paul's "unmarried" is a general term inclusive of the divorced, then he has urged these people to marry if they are not able to practice self-control.[23] One can imagine many divorced "unmarried" people who burn with passion, and Paul appears to be encouraging them to get married.[24] Nevertheless, Norbert Baumert recognizes that the pairing with "widows" severely limits who should be included among the "unmarried."[25] Four hurdles stand in the way of taking "unmarried" in vv. 8–9 more generally and inclusive of the divorced.

First, despite the use of "unmarried" in 1 Cor 7:10–11 for those remaining single after divorce, one searches Greek literature elsewhere in vain for a clear use of this

---

23. The term is used *strictly* for divorcées in vv. 10–11. Some would argue that the word refers to divorcées, or is inclusive of them, in each of the four instances in 1 Cor 7, the only place where the word occurs in the New Testament.

24. Ben Witherington III questions whether "not married" is an inclusive category for widowers, the single and separated, or divorced, but (καί) *especially* widows; see *Women in the Earliest Churches*, SNTSMS 59 (Cambridge: Cambridge University Press, 1988), 30. For a wide array of commentators favoring an inclusive term, see Anthony C. Thiselton, *The First Epistle to the Corinthians*, NIGTC (Grand Rapids: Eerdmans, 2000), 515. Similarly C. K. Barrett, *A Commentary on the First Epistle to the Corinthians*, HNTC (New York: Harper & Row, 1968), 160–61; Jean Héring, *The First Epistle of Saint Paul to the Corinthians* (London: Epworth, 1962), 51; P. E. B. Allo, *Première épître aux Corinthiens*, 2nd ed., EBib (Paris: Gabalda, 1956), 162; Archibald Robertson and Alfred Plummer, *A Critical and Exegetical Commentary on the First Epistle of Paul to the Corinthians*, 2nd ed., ICC (New York: Scribner's Sons, 1911), 138; Johannes Weiss, *Der erste Korintherbrief*, 9th ed. (Göttingen: Vandenhoeck & Ruprecht, 1910), 176–77; Bruce, *1 and 2 Corinthians*, 68; Heinrich August Wilhelm Meyer, *Critical and Exegetical Handbook to the Epistles to the Corinthians* (New York: Funk & Wagnalls, 1884), 155; Simon J. Kistemaker, *New Testament Commentary: Exposition of the First Epistle to the Corinthians* (Grand Rapids: Baker, 1993), 217–18; Friedrich Lang, *Die Briefe an die Korinther*, NTD 7 (Göttingen: Vandenhoeck & Ruprecht, 1994), 91; Christophe Senft, *La première épître de Saint-Paul aux Corinthiens*, Commentaire du Noveau Testament 7 (Paris: Delachaux & Niestlé, 1979), 91; Philipp Bachmann, *Der erste Brief des Paulus an die Korinther*, Kommentar zum Neuen Testament (Leipzig: Deichert, 1905), 271. Widows are singled out because of their frequent need for help, but see Garland, *First Corinthians*, 276: "Although this view has much to commend it, the word ἄγαμος has a broad semantic range, as its application in this chapter to both males and females attests. It does not seem warranted to restrict its meaning here to 'widowers,' since it was also used to refer to 'bachelors' (LSJ 5)." Although Witherington (*Women in the Earliest Churches*, 30, 234 n. 29) entertains the possibility that the word could refer to a wide array of the unmarried, including the divorced, he settles on the word here meaning "widower" for a number of reasons.

25. Norbert Baumert, *Woman and Man in Paul: Overcoming a Misunderstanding* (Collegeville, MN: Liturgical, 1996), 48: They are most likely older, never-married men and widowed men.

word (ἄγαμος) in reference to the "divorced." Caution is therefore in order before assuming reference to the divorced in the word's other occurrences in 1 Cor 7. The LSJ lexicon lists "widowers" as one of the ways ἄγαμος is used in ancient Greek literature for men, alongside bachelors. The male equivalent of χήρα "widow," was χῆρος, but this Greek word is rare *and unattested in the Koine period* of the New Testament.[26] Consequently, the masculine form χῆρος does not occur in the Septuagint or the New Testament, and the only word in this period that referred to a "widower" was ἄγαμος, the very word used in 1 Cor 7:8. As Raymond Collins states, "Paired with 'widows,' the 'unmarried' of v. 8 are most likely widowers."[27] Thus ἄγαμοι in v. 8 is *not* referring to unmarried people in general, inclusive of divorcées.[28] Many well-regarded Pauline specialists, such as Richard Hays and Gordon Fee, have come to this conclusion.[29]

Roy E. Ciampa and Brian S. Rosner fault Fee and Hays among others since: "[T]here is no evidence that it [ἄγαμος] ever means 'widower.'" Ciampa and Rosner further fault these interpreters' "failure to distinguish between denotation and reference" before providing their readers a list of introductory linguistic textbooks.[30] Hays, for his part, never claims that the word *denotes* or *means* widowers. He says that Paul is *referring* to them. That the term may refer to widowers is manifest from ancient Greek usage. Nevertheless, it would not be a misunderstanding to insist on "widower" as the *meaning* of the word in this particular instance. A word has a semantic range, and its meaning depends on that word's syntagmatic relationship to other words in the context. To refine the argument, alongside χήρα in the specific construction ἄγαμοι καὶ χῆραι, the word ἄγαμος would mean "widower."[31] Whether or not the word ultimately *means* "widowers," as is arguable, it is certainly *referring* to them in this verse.

---

26. Fee, *First Epistle to the Corinthians*, 319, and thus nowhere in the LXX or the NT, a matter (conveniently) overlooked by Luck, *Divorce and Re-Marriage*, 204.

27. R. Collins, *Divorce*, 236 n. 33.

28. If in use here, this would be "widowers and widows" rather than a general category of unmarried; so also William F. Orr, "Paul's Treatment of Marriage in 1 Corinthians 7," *Pittsburgh Perspective* 8 (1967): 12–14; Jeremy Moiser, "A Reassessment of Paul's View of Marriage with Reference to 1 Cor. 7," *JSNT* 18 (1983): 108; G. J. Laughery, "Paul: Anti-Marriage? Anti-Sex? Ascetic? A Dialogue with 1 Corinthians 7:1–40," *EvQ* 69 (1997): 121 n. 50; R. Collins, *First Corinthians*, 268–69; Orr and Walther, *1 Corinthians*, 210; Barrett, *First Epistle to the Corinthians*, 160–61.

29. Richard B. Hays, *First Corinthians*, IBC (Louisville: John Knox, 1997), 118: "The word 'unmarried' (*agamoi*) is used here to refer specifically to widowers, not in a generic fashion to include all those who are not married"; so also Fee, *First Epistle to the Corinthians*, 319; William Loader, *Sexuality and the Jesus Tradition* (Grand Rapids: Eerdmans, 2005), 164; Wolfgang Schrage, *Der erste Brief an die Korinther*, EKKNT 7.1–4 (Neukirchen-Vluyn: Neukirchener, 1995), 2:94–95.

30. Ciampa and Rosner, *First Letter to the Corinthians*, 287 n. 82.

31. Contra Ciampa and Rosner, *First Letter to the Corinthians*, 286 n. 79.

Second, Paul repeatedly treats men and women in parallel mutual relations throughout vv. 1–16 (eight times [!] with further instances later in the chapter).[32] To review the pattern in the first sixteen verses: In v. 2 a man should have his own wife and a wife her husband. In v. 3 the husband should allow his wife conjugal relations and the wife her husband. In v. 4 the husband has rights over his wife's body even as she has rights over her husband's. Skipping the parallel relations in vv. 8–9, the next pairing is in the Lord's command in vv. 10–11 where the wife is not to separate from her husband nor the husband his wife. Paul's own instructions resume in vv. 12–13 that a believing husband should not divorce his unbelieving wife, nor the believing wife an unbelieving husband. In 7:14–15 the unbelieving husband is made holy by a believing wife as is the unbelieving wife by the believing husband. In v. 16 the wife might save the husband and the husband might save the wife. The pattern of parallel circumstances in vv. 1–16 is therefore repeated, conspicuous, and consistent. This pattern offers strong evidence that the "unmarried" in vv. 8–9 are widowers, thus matching the "widows."

After discussing circumcision and uncircumcision and slaves and freedpersons in vv. 17–24, the new section in vv. 25–40 returns to the paired sets, but the repeated, staccato effect of vv. 1–16 is no longer present. In 7:28 if the man marries it is not a sin, just as if a virgin marries she has not sinned. In vv. 32–34 the unmarried man is concerned about matters of the Lord and the married man his wife, just as the unmarried woman is concerned about the things of the Lord and the married woman her husband. The pattern is not as pronounced as in vv. 1–16, but instances are frequent later in the chapter.

Ciampa and Rosner observe that Paul does not *always* present men and women in parallel in the chapter, even if he does so rather frequently.[33] They point to vv. 36–38, which address the engaged man who is unsure whether to marry his fiancée but do not tackle the same problem from *her* standpoint. The lack of parallelism here, on the other hand, is understandable since unmarried women did not enjoy the same social ability to initiate marriage as men. In vv. 39–40 Paul mentions the situation of the widow but not the widower but again, as Ciampa and Rosner concede, the social situations of widower and widow are not parallel since widows faced severe economic threats that widowers typically did not.[34] In other words, the two breaks in the pattern of male-female balancing

---

32. Wayne A. Meeks, "The Image of the Androgyne: Some Uses of a Symbol in Earliest Christianity," *HR* 13.3 (1974): 199: "monotonously parallel statements made about the obligations, respectively, of men and women." See also Robin Scroggs, "Paul and the Eschatological Woman," *JAAR* 40.3 (1972): 294–95; Schrage, *Erste Brief an die Korinther*, 2:94.

33. Ciampa and Rosner, *First Letter to the Corinthians*, 287.

34. Schrage, *Erste Brief an die Korinther*, 2:94; Garland, *1 Corinthians*, 272, Ciampa and Rosner,

CHAPTER 5

that Ciampa and Rosner seize on are both explicable. Furthermore, Ciampa and Rosner overlook in their critique the consistent, repeated, staccato-like pattern in vv. 1–16. Again, that consistent pattern in vv. 1–16 provides strong evidence that Paul is discussing unmarried *widowers* and widows in 7:8–9.[35]

Third, Roman society placed tremendous pressure on *both* widowers and widows to remarry throughout the empire. In Roman society widows were expected to remarry within a year, especially in view of the need for a woman to bear at least three children during her lifetime and her low life-expectancy (including the five to ten percent death rate for mothers in childbirth).[36] Male mortality rates during this time were high as well, especially because of participation in the military. Augustus's marital legislation in 18 and 17 BCE and 9 CE restricted the right of inheritance for men who had not married and reproduced (Dio Cassius, *Hist. rom.* 54.16.1–2).[37] Widowers could remarry right away with no restriction.[38] Augustus's caducary laws required "the widower" to "remarry at once to escape their provisions."[39] As Csillag writes, "It followed from the *obligation of the Augustan laws* binding on both men and women to live in a state of matrimony *within the specified age limits* that if the marriage of the parties came to an end for some reason or another, e.g., divorce, death, etc., the party so affected *had to contract a new marriage*."[40] For men, this requirement was for those ages twenty-five through sixty. According to Thiselton, "These factors mean that the issue of 'whether to marry' or 'whether to have physical intimacy' was a much larger and more widespread issue for widowers and widows than we can easily comprehend today if we merely project our modern situation back into the Graeco-Roman world."[41] Augustus and Tiberius were especially worried about the decline in upper-class Roman birth rates.[42] The rationale for Roman widowers to remarry reflects peren-

---

First Letter to the Corinthians, 287. Thus widows are regularly singled out (e.g., Exod 22:22; Isa 1:17; Jer 22:3; Zech 7:10; Sir 4:10; Acts 6:1; Jas 1:27).

35. Ciampa and Rosner think that vv. 8–9 may be referring to widows *and their suitors* since vv. 25–38 are about virgins and their suitors; see *First Letter to the Corinthians*, 287. They provide no evidence that the suitors of vv. 8–9 are *not* primarily widowers *or* that the suitors may indeed include also the divorced.

36. Aline Rousselle, "Body Politics in Ancient Rome," in *From Ancient Goddess to Christian Saints*, vol. 1 of *A History of Women in the West*, ed. Pauline Schmitt Pantel (Cambridge: Harvard University Press, 1992), 297–99 (noting high infant mortality rates as well), 316, 319; Gardner, *Women*, 51.

37. Rouselle, "Body Politics," 313–14, 316.
38. Corbett, *Roman Law*, 249.
39. Corbett, *Roman Law*, 150.
40. Csillag, *Augustan Laws*, 87.
41. Thiselton, *First Corinthians*, 516.
42. See chapter 1, pp. 30–33, on Augustus's marital legislation.

nial concerns in antiquity. Plato would *require* the childless widower to remarry (*Leg.* 930b). The apostle is therefore reflecting this acute social pressure for *both* widowers and widows to remarry in vv. 8–9, although the motivation for Paul is to avoid sexual temptation and not procreation.

Fourth, if 1 Cor 7:8–9 is offering advice for unmarried people in general—whether the divorced or those never married—it creates at least three contradictions and replications with the rest of the chapter.

(1) Paul will address men acting improperly toward their betrothed in 7:36 and urge marriage. This would needlessly repeat what Paul had already said in v. 9 if the same people are in view or included.

(2) If Paul is including divorcées among the "unmarried" of vv. 8–9, then he is counseling them preferably to stay single but to get married if they feel they are aflame with passion. In 1 Cor 7:10–11, however, there is no option for marriage to a different spouse after a divorce. The divorced are only allowed to return to the former spouse. Paul says nothing about the flames of passion after divorce. For Paul to counsel remarriage in these situations would be contrary to the Lord's command in vv. 10–11.

(3) When Paul explicitly discusses remarriage for someone previously married, it is for the widow in 7:39. He does not mention the divorced among those who may remarry. To put that point differently, Paul's two clear statements on the subject of remarriage are in vv. 10–11 and in v. 39: the divorced woman is to remain unmarried, but the widow may remarry.

If the "unmarried" of vv. 8–9 does *not* include the divorced, then there is consistency to the instructions throughout the chapter.

Some believe that 1 Cor 7:1–7 provides the general principles that the remainder of the chapter then unpacks. The first seven verses do offer the general principle that the married may enjoy sexual relations, especially in v. 2. Fee responds: "But that founders on the sections that follow, which are structurally tied to this one, but which do not deal with *getting* married at all."[43] Hays rightly explains that Paul's instructions are not given to the divorced until v. 11 and to the never-married until vv. 25–38.[44]

Paul turns to widowers and widows because their situation may be the same as his own as one likely once married.[45] Later rabbinic sources stress the need for the law-observant male to marry (e.g., m. Yebam. 6:6). In the Babylonian Talmud

---

43. Fee, *First Epistle to the Corinthians*, 319.
44. Hays, *First Corinthians*, 118.
45. R. Collins, *First Corinthians*, 263. Alternatively, Christian Wolff judges the evidence for Paul as a widower less than certain and maintains that Paul is presenting himself as an older unmarried (never-married) man (Paul does not address divorce until vv. 10–11); see *Der erste Brief des Paulus an die Korinther*, THKNT 7 (Berlin: Evangelische Verlagsanstalt, 1996), 139. That Paul

CHAPTER 5

(b. Yebam. 62b–64a, esp. 63a): Only when male and female were united were they called "Adam." The Babylonian Talmud faults the twenty-year-old unmarried male for spending his days in sin (b. Qidd. 29b). Paul stresses his observance of the law and adherence to the customs of the fathers (Acts 22:3; Gal 1:14; Phil 3:4–6). This student of the law likely fulfilled the biblical command to be fruitful and multiply (Gen 1:28; 9:9), at least in getting married. As Garland observes, "It would have been exceptional, though not impossible, for Paul to have been as successful in Pharisaic Judaism, as he claims to have been . . . , without having been married."[46] The comparison to Paul himself in 7:8–9, on the other hand, may be in relation to the gift of being able to remain single, mentioned in 7:7, and thus no indication of Paul's former marital status.[47] Regardless, the widower and widow should ideally not marry again, but "Paul is a realist," and it is better to marry than to burn.[48] He does not, however, offer that option for the divorcée, who should return to the former spouse, as is clear in the immediately following verses (vv. 10–11).[49]

1 Corinthians 7:12–16—Marriage to Nonbelievers

Paul writes in 1 Cor 7:15: "But if the unbelieving partner separates, let it be so; in such a case the brother or sister is not bound. It is to peace that God has called you." Many interpreters find in this verse the permission for remarriage that was absent in 1 Cor 7:10–11, pointing to Paul's claim in 7:15 that the brother or sister is "not bound" (οὐ δεδούλωται). The divorce certificates of the Jewish and Greco-Roman worlds certified that a divorced partner was "free" (ἐλευθέρα) to remarry. The "not bound" of 1 Cor 7:15, it is argued, would be the *equivalent* of being "free," the very claim Paul makes for the widow who may remarry in 1 Cor 7:39 and Rom 7:3.[50]

This line of reasoning suffers from several shortcomings, the first of which is that the passage is not addressing remarriage. Paul is arguing against the believer

---

had formerly been married is an ancient perspective, already held by Clement of Alexandria at the end of the second century (*Strom.* 7.11).

46. Garland, *First Corinthians*, 276; Snyder, *First Corinthians*, 96. See also Joachim Jeremias, "War Paulus Witwer?," *ZNW* 26 (1926): 310–12; Jeremias, "Nochmals: War Paulus Witwer?," *ZNW* 28 (1929): 321–23 on rabbis needing to be married. At the same time, the case for Paul as a widower himself is somewhat speculative.

47. Schrage, *Erste Brief an die Korinther*, 2:94–95.

48. R. Collins, *First Corinthians*, 263.

49. Paul's discussion thus places the onus on the divorced to find their desires satisfied in a return to the former marriage; contra Martin, *Sex and the Single Savior*, 138–39.

50. E.g., Instone-Brewer, "Jewish Greek and Aramaic Marriage," 241, followed by Ciampa and Rosner, *First Letter to the Corinthians*, 302, who stress the "freedom" language of the divorce certificates.

dissolving a marriage to a nonbeliever. When he does address the matter of remarriage in vv. 10–11, he follows the Lord in prohibiting it.[51]

Second, 1 Cor 7:15 is not at all parallel to 1 Cor 7:39 and Rom 7:3:

> Rom 7:3: Woman "bound" to husband as long as he lives—husband dies—widow "free" to "marry"
>
> 1 Cor 7:39: Woman "bound" to husband as long as he lives—husband dies—widow "free" to "marry"
>
> 1 Cor 7:15: Spouse "not bound" (?)

First Corinthians 7:15 and these two other Pauline verses differ from each other in at least three ways. (1) In 1 Cor 7:39 and Rom 7:3, "freedom" (ἐλευθέρα) is explicitly mentioned, but Paul does not use "freedom" language in 1 Cor 7:15.[52]

(2) Romans 7:3 and 1 Cor 7:39 both explicitly permit remarriage; 1 Cor 7:15 does not. Further, the woman who may remarry in both Rom 7:3 and 1 Cor 7:39 is identified as a widow.

(3) The widow in 1 Cor 7:39 and Rom 7:3 is "bound" (δέδεται) to her husband until he dies (cf. 7:27). In 1 Cor 7:15 one might translate οὐ δεδούλωται more literally as "not *enslaved*."[53] In other words, Paul does not employ the "not bound" language one would expect if he intended a parallel to the remarrying widows of 1 Cor 7:39 and Rom 7:3. Paul does not use 1 Cor 7:15's δουλόω, "enslave, subject," anywhere else when speaking of the marital bond. Paul never says that the wife is "enslaved" to her husband in the marriage relationship. One must therefore question taking "enslave" and "bind" as synonyms in 1 Cor 7.[54]

Third, the ancient divorce certificates do not use the terminology of being no longer "bound" but rather "free" to remarry.[55] Expressions of the divorced's being

---

51. It would be odd that remarriage is forbidden where adultery has taken place, even for the innocent, but permissible in the case of mixed marriages when the unbeliever departs.

52. Contra e.g., Atkinson, *To Have and to Hold*, 124.

53. David Instone-Brewer frequently translates οὐ δεδούλωται as "not bound," no doubt to give the impression that it is the same language as in 1 Cor 7:39 when it is not; e.g., "Graeco-Roman Marriage," 111; Instone-Brewer, "Jewish Greek and Aramaic Marriage," 237.

54. Contra e.g., Instone-Brewer, "Jewish Greek and Aramaic Marriage," 238–40; followed by Naselli, "What the New Testament Teaches," 32–33. Pat Edwin Harrell even claims that the two verbs share "a common root"; see *Divorce and Remarriage in the Early Church: A History of Divorce and Remarriage in the Ante-Nicene Church* (Austin, TX: Sweet, 1967), 129. "Binding" is a different verb and does not mean "enslaved."

55. Keener (*Matthew*, 191) amazingly (and falsely) claims: "Paul's words ['not bound'] recall the *exact* language for freedom to remarry in ancient divorce contracts, and his ancient readers, unable to be confused by modern writers' debates on the subject, would have understood his words thus."

CHAPTER 5

"free" or "permitted" to remarry are characteristic of and virtually ubiquitous in the certificates. Instone-Brewer notes: "All Jewish divorce certificates and most Graeco-Roman ones contained the words 'You are free to marry any man you wish,' or something similar. These words were so important that they were the only words that were essential in a Jewish divorce certificate."[56] It is rhetorically conspicuous, then, that the apostle *limits* the divorce certificates' language of "freedom" to the *widow* (1 Cor 7:39; Rom 7:3). Paul could very easily have used the language of the certificates in 1 Cor 7:15 but, again, conspicuously avoids it. One should not therefore *assume* a freedom to remarry in 1 Cor 7:15 when Paul appears to be *deliberately avoiding* that language.

Fourth, the assertions in 1 Cor 7:39 and Rom 7:3 that a woman is bound to her husband as long as he lives agrees with the Lord's command in 1 Cor 7:10–11. To place the passages alongside each other:

> 1 Cor 7:10–11: The wife should not separate from [divorce] her husband (but if she does separate, let her remain unmarried or else be reconciled to her husband)
> 1 Cor 7:39: A wife is bound [δέδεται] as long as her husband lives. But if the husband dies, she is free [ἐλευθέρα] to marry anyone she wishes, only in the Lord.
> Rom 7:2–3: Thus a married woman is bound [δέδεται] by the law to her husband as long as he lives; but if her husband dies, she is discharged from the law concerning the husband. Accordingly, she will be called an adulteress if she lives with another man while her husband is alive. But if her husband dies, she is free [ἐλευθέρα] from that law, and if she marries another man, she is not an adulteress.

In other words, in relation to 1 Cor 7:10–11, a divorce may be forced upon the woman—and 1 Cor 7:12–15 sketches just such a situation with an unbelieving spouse—but the divorced wife is not free to marry someone else. First Corinthians 7:10–11 dovetails with the teaching of 1 Cor 7:39 and Rom 7:3. Remarriage is only an option for the woman whose spouse has died.

Instone-Brewer makes the strong claim that if Paul had meant anything other than to express a freedom for the divorced to remarry in v. 15, "he would have had to state this very clearly."[57] This entirely misses Paul's rhetoric in 1 Cor 7 as should by now be clear. Again, Paul *conspicuously avoids* the standard "freedom" language of

---

56. Instone-Brewer, *Divorce and Remarriage*, 202.
57. Instone-Brewer, "Jewish Greek and Aramaic Marriage," 240–41, a repeated claim. Craig S. Keener makes the same claim; see *And Marries Another*, 61, also relying on the "freedom" expressed in the divorce certificates of the day.

208

the divorce certificates. He does not use the word "bound" (δέω). He then uses *that very language* in v. 39 for the *widow*, who is "not bound" but "free" to marry again. In short, Paul's choice of vocabulary in v. 15 appears deliberately designed to *avoid the very conclusion* Instone-Brewer is making![58] When the New Testament regularly conveys *prohibitions* of divorce and remarriage, one would need a clear text indicating an exception.[59] Instone-Brewer's point could be also be reversed: In view of many Corinthians' resistance of marriage and sexual relations (e.g., 1 Cor 7:1), Paul would have needed to render explicit for this audience the possibility of remarriage.

Fifth, the language of being "enslaved" (δουλόω) is not part of the wording of the divorce certificates of Paul's day. Paul uses "enslaved" differently in his writings, usually with respect to the obligations required by Moses's law or the nefarious powers of this present evil age (e.g., Rom 7:25; Gal 4:8, 24–25; 5:1). "Not enslaved" in 1 Cor 7:15 would be in natural relation to a command, here the Lord's rule not to separate from a spouse. He states throughout 1 Cor 7:10–15:

> To the *married* I give this command—not I but the Lord—that the wife should *not separate from* [divorce] her husband (but if she does separate, let her remain unmarried or else be *reconciled* to her husband), and that the husband should *not divorce* his wife. To the rest I say—I and not the Lord—that if any believer has a wife who is an unbeliever, and she consents to live with him, he should *not divorce* her. And if any woman has a husband who is an unbeliever, and he consents to live with her, she should *not divorce* him. For the unbelieving husband is made holy through his wife, and the unbelieving wife is made holy through her husband. . . . But if the unbelieving partner *separates, let it be so*; in such a case the brother or sister is *not bound*. It is to peace that God has called you.

The "command" of the Lord requires that there be no divorce (vv. 10–11), and Paul himself issues repeated imperatives against divorce (vv. 12–13), and yet he adds

---

58. Keener (*And Marries Another*, 62–63) claims that anyone forbidding remarriage has simply read their own thinking into Paul's words. Really? Keener overlooks how 1 Cor 7:12–16 *avoids* the very language of the divorce certificates that he invoked.

59. Despite Instone-Brewer's regular insertion of "freedom" in his discussion; see *Divorce and Remarriage*, 201–2. He adds elsewhere: "If Paul had meant something else, he would have had to state this very clearly, in order to avoid being misunderstood by everyone who read his epistle"; see "Jewish Greek and Aramaic Marriage," 241. How much clearer can Paul be? He restates the Lord's command for the divorced woman to remain single or be reconciled to the former husband. He conspicuously *avoids* the use of the language he uses elsewhere for freedom to remarry (for the widow).

that the individual is "not enslaved" to that command.[60] The subsequent imperative to let the spouse depart bears a permissive force that responds directly to those prohibitions of divorce in the prior verses.[61] Not only does Paul forbid divorce four times in these verses, he also repeatedly stresses the advantages of continuing the marriage.[62] Nevertheless, the believing spouse need not continue to struggle against the divorce when the unbelieving spouse remains determined.[63] This is the peace to which God calls the believing spouse when he or she has not been able to save the marriage. The conscience of the believer is not to be troubled in this situation. Thus Paul allows for a divorce to be insisted on by the unbelieving spouse, but he never says that the believer is permitted to remarry.[64]

In fact, *the concern for the original spouse continues even after the divorce* (!) in v. 16 with the hope yet to save the original spouse, still a "husband" or "wife." Even as vv. 10–11 call for the divorced, believing wife to remain single or be reconciled to her former husband, in v. 16 the divorced spouse still acts in a way that might yet save the unbelieving spouse who has "separated" (the same verb in vv. 10–11 and 15,

---

60. Rightly Barrett, *First Epistle to the Corinthians*, 166.

61. Rightly Murray, *Divorce*, 68–69, who does not recognize the implications of the focus on the command against divorce. Remarriage is simply not in view in 1 Cor 7:15. Murray claims on 71 that there is no injunction in these verses to remain unmarried but misses the one already norming the following discussion in 7:10–11. He assumes on 72 that dissolution of the marital bond through divorce allows the innocent party to remarry, even as he recognizes that divorce in 1 Cor 7:15 may also be understood *without* a permission for subsequent remarriage (see 76 n. 13).

62. One might contend that "not enslaved" does *not* refer to the admonition to stay married, since Paul would assume they have already left. If the partner has left, on the other hand, there would be nothing remaining to which one might be enslaved. Two problems hinder such reasoning. First, Paul admonishes the nondeparting spouse to "let" the separating one go. Second, the use of the verb χωρίζεται in the papyri involves *mutual* agreements to divorce; see Moulton and Milligan, *Vocabulary*, 696; Fee, *First Epistle to the Corinthians*, 334 n. 153.

63. H. G. Coiner documents at length the historic Lutheran position that the innocent party may remarry, and yet he candidly concedes with respect to 1 Cor 7:15 that Paul has in mind just "Christ's prohibition of divorce as to be afraid to depart when the heathen partner insists on separation"; see "'Divorce and Remarriage' Passages," 382 n. 54. He adds: "Some commentators, Luther and Calvin among them, maintain that when St. Paul says that in circumstances such as these the Christian husband is 'not bound,' he means that they are at liberty to marry again. This right is not explicitly stated by St. Paul" (383). He concludes: "Does St. Paul make allowance here for the remarriage of the deserted spouse? An allowance for remarriage is not specifically stated, and this freedom cannot be substantiated by valid exegesis. To conclude that remarriage is allowable is to go beyond the clearly stated words of the text" (383). Such candor is commendable since it is against the grain of this interpreter's own tradition.

64. Myrna and Robert Kysar, *The Asundered: Biblical Teachings on Divorce and Remarriage* (Atlanta: Knox, 1978) print the admonitions against divorce in 1 Cor 7:10–16 in bold (65) and then conclude: "If divorce does occur, in spite of the injunction against it, let there be no remarriage" (70).

another connection). Paul does not want his readers to relinquish that continuing hope both for the original marriage and for that former spouse's salvation.

That v. 16 maintains hope for the original marriage is confirmed by the structure of the paragraph:

> Paul's mandate: Do not divorce a pagan spouse (vv. 12–13)
> The reason ("for," γάρ): They are sanctified in you (v. 14)
> The exception ("but," δέ): If they choose to leave, let it be so (v. 15ab)
> The reason (for the ideal, instead of the exception): "But/rather" (δέ) God has called us to peace "for" (γάρ) perhaps you will yet save your spouse (vv. 15c–16)[65]

The exception in v. 15ab is to the command not to divorce in vv. 12–13. If the unbeliever demands it, the believer is no longer enslaved by the prohibition and is therefore exempt from blame over the divorce. This reading connects v. 15ab naturally to its context (vv. 12–13) and adheres to the Lord's strict command in vv. 10–11 to remain single after a divorce or be reconciled.

Verses 15c–16 are introduced as a *contrast* (adversative δέ). The δέ of v. 15c does not introduce causal support for letting the partner leave in v. 15ab. Paul is not saying "let the nonbeliever go *because* God has called us to peace." In that case, he would have written γάρ rather than δέ. The call to peace functions as a contrast to v. 15ab by stressing the importance of preserving the marriage (with vv. 12–14). Verses 15c–16's contrast to v. 15ab thereby links to the reasoning of vv. 12–14. The call to peace is a call to remain in the marital relationship or, at least in the wake of separation, to maintain hope for that spouse. Verse 16 then explains *why* God has called believers to peace within marriage and even in the face of divorce: to *save* that spouse. Verse 16 thus grounds all of vv. 12–15 with an ever-present hope for the unbelieving, divorcing spouse.[66]

The Mishnah describes various instances of Jews striving to act "in the interest of peace" toward non-Jews (Giṭ. 5:8–9). Paul too admonishes living peaceably to-

---

65. Adapted from Fee, *First Epistle to the Corinthians*, 336.

66. At the same time, Andrew Cornes stresses that v. 15c's δέ may still be translated as "and" if v. 15b had *already* given a reason for allowing the divorce (the believer is not enslaved); see *Divorce and Remarriage*, 252–53. Verse 15c would thus provide an *additional* reason for allowing the divorce: God's call to live in peace.

On the optimism of seeing the non-Christian partner come to faith, see the pioneering case of Joachim Jeremias, "Die missionarische Aufgabe in der Mischehe (1 Cor 7 16)," in *Neutestamentliche Studien für Rudolf Bultmann zu seinem siebzigsten Geburtstag*, ed. Walther Eltester, BZNW 21 (Berlin: Töpelmann, 1954), 255–60, esp. 258–60. For an evaluation of the varying approaches, see esp. R. Collins, *Divorce*, 60–63.

CHAPTER 5

ward all people (Rom 12:18). Such peaceable relations provide opportunities for the sake of the gospel and salvation, as does the believing spouse's peaceable behavior toward the divorcing spouse.[67] David Instone-Brewer documents how "for the sake of peace" is used in early rabbinic writings for a pragmatic solution that "did not necessarily conform with the legalistically correct procedure."[68] In this context, that legally correct procedure is the Lord's command in 1 Cor 7:10–11 against divorce.[69]

Some modern translations do not capture the force of v. 16's hope for the original marriage, especially when they relate v. 16 to v. 15. The NASB in its translation of v. 16 renders the chance of the spouse's conversion to be remote: "For [δέ] how do you know, O wife, whether you will save your husband? Or how do you know, O husband, whether you will save your wife?" Nevertheless, many translations recognize the proper relationship between v. 16 and what precedes it. The NRSV and CSB both read: "Wife, for all you know, you might save your husband. Husband, for all you know, you might save your wife." The NEB is similar: "Think of it: as a wife you may be your husband's salvation; as a husband, you may be your wife's salvation." These translations properly express the continuing hope for conversion of the divorcing, unbelieving spouse.

One further clue confirms that Paul is not permitting or even envisioning remarriage in 7:15. The Stoics and Cynics in Paul's day used "slavery" language in relation to marriage even though Paul himself does not.[70] Philo reports Essene philosophers claimed that one who marries becomes a slave rather than a freeperson (*Hypoth.* 11.17). Musonius Rufus describes a married woman who wanted to study philosophy as *already* enslaved (*Disc.* 3).[71] The parallels for marriage as

---

67. Fee, *First Epistle to the Corinthians*, 337. See also David Daube, "Pauline Contributions to a Pluralistic Culture: Re-Creation and Beyond," in *Jesus and Man's Hope*, ed. Donald G. Miller and Dikran Y. Hadidian (Pittsburgh: Pittsburgh Theological Seminary, 1971), 2:233–35, who notes how the rabbis often used this language to extend Jewish privileges and peaceable relations even to gentiles, citing b. Giṭ. 61a; m. Giṭ. 5:9; Rom 12:18.

68. Instone-Brewer, *Divorce and Remarriage*, 203.

69. Instone-Brewer, of course, believes that permission for a (valid) divorce would have entailed freedom to remarry, but that conclusion is derived on the basis of *other* grounds and not what is stated in 1 Cor 7:12–16; see *Divorce and Remarriage*, 204. Instone-Brewer is simply *assuming* and *reading his own perspective into the text* when he writes: "Paul's general principle is therefore that a man or woman who has been divorced against his or her will should be free to remarry" (204). John P. Meier lodges a similar complaint: "As so often with Instone-Brewer's presentation, pivotal claims are simply asserted rather than proven"; see *Law and Love*, 168 n. 101.

70. Will Deming, *Paul on Marriage and Celibacy: The Hellenistic Background of 1 Corinthians 7*, 2nd ed. (Grand Rapids: Eerdmans, 2004), 147–50.

71. Translation from Cora E. Lutz, "Musonius Rufus: 'The Roman Socrates,'" *Yale Classical Studies* 10 (1947): 42 line 8.

"slavery" suggest that a believing husband or wife did not need to be "enslaved" *to the marital relationship* when the unbelieving spouse initiated divorce. To say that the believing spouse was "not enslaved" meant the exact *opposite* of entering into a *new* marriage (enslaved state) in Paul's social milieu.[72] He does not envision or advocate for remarriage in 7:15.[73]

Known for his work on both the apostle Paul and the historical Jesus, E. P. Sanders begins his analysis of 1 Cor 7:10–16 with vv. 10–11 as Paul relays the Lord's command that a wife is not to divorce her husband but if she does she is to remain single or be reconciled. The husband is not to divorce his wife. Sanders then relates the Lord's command in vv. 10–11 to Paul's own advice in vv. 12–16 and notes a remarkable consistency. Just as the Lord had contemplated that a divorce might take place, so does Paul in vv. 12–16 in instances of mixed marriages—"a live possibility for the Christians in Corinth." Sanders continues, "In the form of the saying divorce is not entirely forbidden, but remarriage to another person apparently is. This is the point on which Paul in fact fixes."[74] For that matter, as long as the believing spouse is not responsible for the divorce, the Pauline "permission" is not really a permission per se but "a mere concession to a factual situation" when unbelieving spouses abandon their believing partners.[75] Typically, there was little, if anything, a deserted spouse could do.[76] The abandoned spouse may be at peace about the situation, but Jesus's instructions (vv. 10–11) remain in effect. It may also be that Paul is envisioning more than desertion on the part of the nonbeliever that may cause the divorce.[77]

---

72. A point stressed by Thiselton, *First Epistle to the Corinthans*, 535, following Deming.

73. As F. Neirynck stresses: "Paul has no other instruction on second marriages than his final word of ch. 7 on marriage that is for life: a wife is accorded freedom to marry again after the death of her husband (7,39–40, cf. vv. 8–9; Rom 7,2). Remarriage is not mentioned in v. 15." See "The Sayings of Jesus in 1 Corinthians," in *The Corinthian Correspondence*, ed. R. Bieringer, BETL 125 (Leuven: University Press, 1996), 173–74.

74. Sanders and Davies, *Studying*, 324 (from one of the chapters authored by Sanders). Similarly, in response to Craig Keener's advocacy of remarriage on the basis of 1 Cor 7:12–16, Dale Martin finds "much more likely ... simply that Paul was saying that the Christian was not *bound* to insist on continuing the marriage, not that the Christian was then free to remarry (about which Paul says nothing in that immediate context)." See *Sex and the Single Savior*, 143.

75. Fitzmyer, "Matthean Divorce Texts," 200.

76. David Instone-Brewer, "Graeco-Roman Marriage," 109.

77. Wayne Grudem surveys other instances of the Greek phrase "in such instances as these" in v. 15 (ἐν τοῖς τοιούτοις) and concludes that desertion is not the only action by the nonbeliever necessitating a divorce; see *What the Bible Says*, 39–53. Grudem adds sexual sin, as Jesus did in the gospels, and abuse of a spouse or children, threat of murder or serious harm, addiction to pornography, and drug and alcohol addiction. Although Paul is not permitting remarriage, he may be allowing for *divorce* "in such instances as these." It is important to note, however,

CHAPTER 5

1 Corinthians 7:27–28—Release from a Fiancée

Paul turns to respond to another matter the Corinthians raised in their letter in v. 25: "Now concerning virgins [παρθένοι]." Three possible understandings have been proposed for who these "virgins" are, determined in part by how one understands vv. 36–38. The first approach has been advocated for by the very first interpreters of 1 Corinthians: Paul is addressing fathers who would be giving their "virgin" daughters away in marriage.[78] Paul shifts from the Greek verb γαμέω, "marry," to γαμίζω in v. 38, the latter of which in the gospels means "to give in marriage." The phrase "his own virgin" suggests a jurisdictional relationship rather than one with a fiancée. This approach, despite its antiquity, has not proven persuasive since Paul does not explicitly address fathers, guardians, and daughters in this passage, and nothing in vv. 25–35 would suggest it.[79] The ancients also did not describe the daughter in relation to her father as "his virgin." The words for "behaving improperly" in v. 36 (ἀσχημονεῖν) and "strong passions" (ὑπέρακμος) often bear sexual connotations that would not be suitable for a father (Rom 1:27; 1 Cor 12:23).[80] A father would neither be out of control with respect to his own daughter nor under necessity to give her away in marriage (v. 37).[81] If a father is at issue, then no suitor appears in the context.[82] Also, women in first-century Corinth enjoyed

---

that Paul *limits himself* in this context to desertion by an unbeliever, and it is unclear whether or how Paul would expand the permission since he does not make such a view explicit. Paul is equally clear that the believer is not to initiate divorce against the unbeliever when the unbeliever wishes to continue the marriage. This study is more limited in its focus and will not resolve the matter, although Martin (*Sex and the Single Savior*, 145) critiques such expansions of exceptions, and in relation to Instone-Brewer's comments: "It is therefore rather bizarre that his basic argument is not so much based on what the texts actually say but on what an *ancient Jewish reader must have assumed* the texts meant even if they did not say it." These additional instances "must have been" exceptions Paul would sanction, or so the reasoning goes. Paul struggles mightily throughout 7:12–16 to allow for the believer to let the nonbeliever go in view of Jesus's strict command. One would need more explicit justification to expand the list of exceptions but, again, such questions go beyond the purview of this study.

78. J. B. Lightfoot, *Notes on Epistles of St. Paul: 1–II Thessalonians, 1 Corinthians 1–7, Romans 1–7, Ephesians 1:1–14* (Grand Rapids: Baker, 1980), 231.

79. Fee, *First Epistle to the Corinthians*, 360; Ciampa and Rosner, *First Letter to the Corinthians*, 331; James F. Bound, "Who Are the 'Virgins' Discussed in 1 Corinthians 7:25–38?," *EvJ* 2 (1984): 8.

80. Bound, "Who Are the 'Virgins'," 8–9.

81. Witherington, *Women in the Earliest Churches*, 37–38.

82. J. K. Elliott, "Paul's Teaching on Marriage in 1 Corinthians: Some Problems Considered," *NTS* 19 (1972–1973): 219; Witherington, *Women in the Earliest Churches*, 37: "On this view, Paul suddenly introduces a third party into the discussion (the daughter's husband-to-be), without any prior reference to him."

greater choice in matters of marriage.[83] The most recently mentioned man in the passage was the unmarried man in vv. 32–34. The shift from the Greek verb γαμέω to γαμίζω in v. 38 may have been for the sake of variety, since the distinction between -εω and -ιζω Greek verbs was breaking down during Paul's era.[84] Finally, one would expect in v. 36 "let *her* marry" if the father were giving away his daughter in marriage and not "let *them* marry."[85]

A second view takes "virgins" as referring to men and woman in "spiritual marriages" in which spouses live as if they were not married.[86] According to *Acts of Thecla* 5, men who have wives are to live as if they did not have them. Such relationships, on the other hand, are not attested in the first or early second century, and 1 Cor 7:2–6 makes clear that Paul would oppose such spiritual marriages: Married couples are not to deprive each other of sexual relations except for an agreed upon time for prayer. There would be no reason to address the matter again here.[87] In v. 36 one party *wishes* to marry, and so this group does not refer to the already married as the spiritual marriages position maintains.[88] The feminine definite articles in vv. 28, 34, 36, and 38 indicate that women are in view rather than the unmarried of both sexes, even as Paul addresses a man in vv. 27–28 and 36–38 in relation to that woman. The word "virgins" (παρθένοι) is typically used for females, that is, for unmarried women who have not had sexual relations with men.[89] At this point early in the life of the Corinthian church, many of the men had already experienced sexual relations prior to coming to faith.[90] "Let them marry" in 7:36 would not be the solution appropriate for situations of people already married, albeit choosing to be in a spiritual marriage relationship.

The distinction in 7:34 between the "unmarried woman" and the "virgin" suggests that "virgin" refers to a specific class of unmarried women and not to all

---

83. Witherington, *Women in the Earliest Churches*, 38

84. Fee contends that Paul uses γαμίζω transitively with objects of the verb and γαμέω intransitively, but that this distinction had weakened in Koine Greek; see *First Epistle to the Corinthians*, 391; Elliott, "Paul's Teaching," 220, prefers to take the two verb forms as synonymous.

85. Bound, "Who Are the 'Virgins,'" 9. Note the textual variant with the third-person singular in the Western textual family and the Vulgate.

86. H. Achelis, *Virgines Subintroductae: Ein Beitrag zum VII. Kapitel des I. Korintherbriefs* (Leipzig: Hinrichs, 1902); see the historical overview in Greg Peters, "Spiritual Marriage in Early Christianity: 1 Cor 7:25–38 in Modern Exegesis and the Earliest Church," *TJ* 23 (2002): 211–24.

87. Ciampa and Rosner, *First Letter to the Corinthians*, 331.

88. Witherington, *Women in the Earliest Churches*, 37.

89. E.g., Matt 1:18, 23; 25:1, 7, 11; Luke 1:27; Acts 21:9; 2 Cor 11:2, with the one exception being the men in Rev 14:4 who have not had relations with women.

90. Ciampa and Rosner, *First Letter to the Corinthians*, 331–32.

CHAPTER 5

marriageable unmarried women.[91] Another clue is v. 36's reference to a man potentially behaving improperly toward "his" (αὐτοῦ) virgin. Most commentators have therefore maintained a third position: that Paul has in mind *betrothed women* in this section.[92] All major English translations have adopted this approach except for the Jerusalem Bible.[93] As Richard Hays explains, "Paul first begins to address those who have not yet been married only in verse 25" (and not in v. 8).[94] Paul is tackling in this section misgivings about going through with the marriages. Such an understanding of the word has the advantage of remaining consistent throughout 7:25–38.[95] The same man would be addressed in vv. 27–28 and vv. 36–38.[96]

Some object to the possibility that Paul has betrothed women in view in these verses since a betrothal "was tantamount to marriage.... The vows to become one flesh were stated at the time of the engagement." [97] The problem with this reasoning is that it assumes a Jewish understanding of betrothal as the equivalent of marriage. In the Greco-Roman world, a betrothal functioned differently. By the time of Paul, ancient approaches to giving a daughter away in marriage had ceased or become uncommon and were replaced by a precursor to the modern form of marriage in which a betrothal preceded the marriage itself, and the betrothal "carried no legal obligations."[98] Pliny therefore complains about betrothals as among the trifles littering the everyday landscape (*Ep.* 1.9). Augustus's 18 BCE legislation

---

91. Elliott, "Paul's Teaching," 221; Garland, *First Corinthians*, 320.

J. Massingberd Ford thinks that Paul has in mind the impending levirate marriage to a brother-in-law of a young widow; see "Levirate Marriage in St Paul (I Cor. VII)," *NTS* 10 (1963–1964): 361–65. As Fee (*First Epistle to the Corinthians*, 360 n. 254) responds, this approach is difficult to reconcile with Paul's description of the women as virgins (παρθένοι) and the notion that the Corinthian congregation would be *that* concerned with Jewish legal issues. Paul offers no cues in that direction.

92. The commentary consensus finds its origin in Werner Georg Kümmel, "Verlobung und Heirat bei Paulus (I. Cor 7.36–38)," in *Neutestamentliche Studien für Rudolf Bultmann zu seinem siebzigsten Geburtstag*, ed. Walther Eltester, BZNW 21 (Berlin: Töpelmann, 1954), 290–95; Matt 1:18, 23; Luke 1:27; cf. 2 Cor 11:2.

93. The JB reads in 7:25: "About remaining celibate"; the NJB changed this to: "About people remaining virgin."

94. Hays, *First Corinthians*, 126; so also Moiser, "Reassessment," 112; Fee, *First Epistle to the Corinthians*, 356–62; Vincent L. Wimbush, *Paul the Worldly Ascetic: Response to the World and Self-Understanding according to 1 Corinthians 7* (Macon, GA: Mercer University Press, 1987), 14; Richard A. Horsley, *1 Corinthians*, ANTC (Nashville: Abingdon, 1998), 104–6.

95. Garland, *First Corinthians*, 320.

96. Fee, *First Epistle to the Corinthians*, 336.

97. Luck, *Divorce and Re-Marriage*, 202.

98. Jérôme Carcopino, *Daily Life in Ancient Rome* (New Haven: Yale University Press, 1968), 80; Justinian, *Dig.* 23.1.1–2, 9, 14; 24.1.32.27; 24.2.2.2; Philip Lyndon Reynolds, *Marriage in the*

(*Lex Iulia de ordinibus maritandis*) singled out betrothed men. Carcopino writes, "He [Augustus] forbade the breach of a betrothal because he had observed that hard-boiled bachelors took advantage of a series of engagements, capriciously cancelling one after the other, to postpone the wedding indefinitely."[99] The Greco-Roman custom of pre-wedding betrothal is in view at Corinth as opposed to the Jewish custom. Paul's instructions regarding whether or not to follow through with the marriage make sense against that background. Thus in 1 Cor 7:36 the man in this situation should "marry . . . his virgin" (παρθένον αὐτοῦ).[100]

Paul makes a few statements in vv. 25–38 that have been understood as sanctioning remarriage, the first of which is in vv. 27–28: "Are you bound [δέδεσαι] to a wife? Do not seek to be free [λύσιν]. Are you free [λέλυσαι] from a wife? Do not seek a wife. But if you marry, you do not sin, and if a virgin marries, she does not sin." The man who is "free" or "loosed from a wife" may marry again, and it is not a sin. Those "loosed" from their marital bonds may remarry, it seems.[101] Colin Brown, in fact, emphasizes the point by stating multiple times on the basis of 1 Cor 7:27–28 that "Remarriage is not a sin."[102] Unfortunately, a number of problems beset this approach, quite apart from the fact that Paul is not identifying women in general but rather the betrothed.

(1) A rather serious problem is that taking vv. 27–28 as commenting on remarriage after divorce interrupts what Paul announced he would be talking about (v. 25). According to Oster, "Even though Paul explicitly states that he is dealing with virgins from 7:25, many translations and interpreters have Paul abandon his stated topic and begin to discuss the issue of divorce and remarriage."[103]

Western Church: The Christianization of Marriage during the Patristic and Early Medieval Periods, Supplements to Vigiliae Christianae 24 (Leiden: Brill, 1994), 3–6.

99. Carcopino, *Daily Life*, 97. See Dio Cassius, *Hist. rom.* 54.16; Suetonius, *Aug.* 34.

100. "*His* virgin" offers the very sort of syntagmatic cue that *engaged* virgins are in view; contra Roland H. A. Seboldt, "Spiritual Marriage in the Early Church: A Suggested Interpretation of 1 Cor 7:36–38," *CTM* 30.2–3 (1959): 113. As for why Paul does not use a Greek word for "betrothed," his stress in this passage is on the superiority of the virgin-unmarried condition since that affords greater opportunity to serve the Lord—thus the repeated "virgin" (παρθένος); contra Bound, "Who Are the 'Virgins'," 10. It is better to *remain* a virgin.

101. Again, Keener, *Matthew*, 191 n. 95. James F. Bound stresses what he believes is decisive evidence that these verses refer to those once married: the use of the perfect tense; see "Who Are the 'Virgins'," 5. Bound overlooks that the perfect tense would make equally good sense for those having once been engaged. The "you" of v. 28 may therefore be single males, after all.

102. Brown, "Separate, Divide," 536–38. Brown even leverages these verses against the absolute statements of Mark and Luke (540).

103. Richard E. Oster Jr., *1 Corinthians*, The College Press NIV Commentary (Joplin, MO: College Press, 1995), 178.

(2) To be "free" or "loosed" with respect to a wife does not necessarily mean that one has been freed *from* a wife as in a divorce. The BDAG Greek lexicon entry for λύω stresses in relation to 1 Cor 7:27: "a previous state of being 'bound' need not be assumed." The lexicon cites Simplicius (as relayed by Epictetus): "One who does not found a family is free." In other words, "loosed" may simply mean "unmarried" with no implication that a divorce has taken place.[104] The original NIV therefore translated v. 27: "Are you married? Do not seek a divorce. Are you unmarried? Do not look for a wife." The apostle would not be assuming a prior marriage or advocating for remarriage.

(3) Paul clarifies that he is writing about a matter for which he does *not* have a command of the Lord (v. 25), but he *did* have a command of the Lord about divorce and remarriage (vv. 10–11). Whereas the Lord in vv. 10–11 *commands* the divorced wife not to marry another, here remarriage would not be a sin, and Paul merely *advises* that the divorced remain single.[105] If the situations are the same, Paul's advice in v. 28 would contradict the Lord's command earlier in vv. 10–11 at several points.[106]

(4) Verse 28's qualification of v. 27 that the *virgin* is not sinning to marry would make little sense if v. 27 had been concerned with those who had *divorced*.

(5) Verses 27–28 would not be a balanced pair, as the pattern is elsewhere in 1 Cor 7, since the man would be divorced but the woman would remain a virgin.

(6) Paul uses "bound" for the marital relationship in 1 Cor 7:39 and Rom 7:3. The language of being "bound," however, is not how the ancients typically described

---

104. A point J. Carl Laney also stresses; see "No Divorce, No Remarriage," in *Divorce and Remarriage: Four Christian Views*, ed. H. Wayne House (Downers Grove, IL: InterVarsity, 1990), 47; so also Fee, *First Epistle to the Corinthians*, 366.

105. Schrage, *Erste Brief an die Korinther*, 158; but F. W. Grosheide, *Commentary on the First Epistle to the Corinthians*, NICNT (Grand Rapids: Eerdmans, 1953), 176. Verse 27 is closely connected to vv. 10–11 and therefore consists of "very definite precepts," unlike in v. 28. For Grosheide, "loosed" would not mean to be divorced but simply unmarried.

106. Wolff, *Erste Brief des Paulus an die Korinther*, 156: "Eine Hinwendung zu verheirateten und geschieden Männern wäre jetzt unerwartet, zumal Paulus bereits in V.10f. zu ihnen gesprochen und dort ein Wort des Herrn, nicht aber seine eigene Meinung (V.25) angeführt hatte." Loader (*Sexuality*, 175 n. 124) writes in favor of "bound" as betrothal or engagement: "It is not about divorce which would need to be more careful than this in the light of 7:11."

One possibility Luck raises (*Divorce and Re-Marriage*, 206) is that vv. 27–28 concern the innocent parties of divorce whereas vv. 10–11 refer only to unjust divorcing. The problem is that vv. 10–11 simply state as a rule that one is not to marry another, whether unjust or not. Likewise, vv. 27–28 do not offer any indication that Paul's instructions at this point are limited to an "innocent" party. Luck appears to be reading his own conclusions into the texts.

"Not Bound" and "Free" in the Apostle Paul?

the relationship of a man to his wife.[107] Being "bound," perhaps more frequently, would describe a man's relationship to his betrothed, as in 1 Cor 7:27.[108] Susan Treggiari remarks on how much of the vocabulary for marriage is used within the betrothal agreement.[109]

(7) Neither the noun "loosening" (λύσις) nor the verb "to loose" (λύω) is attested in antiquity for divorce.[110] Such words represent well-attested *contractual* language used to describe discharge from a bond, debt, or contract.[111] Indeed, Aulus Gellius (*Noct. att.* 4.4) describes betrothal as a contract. According to Jews such as Philo, to seduce or rape a betrothed woman before her marriage is adultery, since the betrothal contract was taken as equivalent to marriage (*Spec.* 3.12; cf. Deut 22:23–27).[112] On breaking off the betrothal to a virgin, one need only consider Joseph pondering breaking off (ἀπολύω) his betrothal to Mary in Matt 1:19–20, 24 (not the ἀφίημι of 1 Cor 7:11–13's divorcing).[113] Many have therefore concluded that much of vv. 25–38 is in reference to betrothed women and their fiancés.[114]

By using contractual language here, Paul is saying: "Are you bound/under contractual obligations [δέδεσαι] to a woman? Do not seek to be free of those obligations [λύσιν]. Are you free of such obligations [λέλυσαι] from a woman? Do not seek a wife. But if you marry, you do not sin, and if a virgin marries, she does not sin." Paul is primarily concerned here with those who are contracted or betrothed to be married.[115] This approach neatly maintains the balance and parallelism of

---

107. Deming, *Paul on Marriage and Celibacy*, 171.

108. On δέω being used for betrothal, see Wolff, *Erste Brief des Paulus an die Korinther*, 156; also Baumert, *Woman and Man in Paul*, 86–89.

109. Susan Treggiari, *Roman Marriage: Iusti Coniuges from the Time of Cicero to the Time of Ulpian* (Oxford: Clarendon, 1991), 155–59; seconded by Ciampa and Rosner, *First Letter to the Corinthians*, 339, as support for this section of the letter as addressing the betrothed.

110. Instone-Brewer (*Divorce and Remarriage*, 207), despite his blanket claim that this is marital contract language, struggles to find a parallel. He does not find any examples in Paul's era or before. He does identify the 201 CE P.Oxy. 1473 that uses the language of a "discharged contract" (συγγραφὴ ἐλύθη). In other words, this Greek verb goes unattested in marital contexts for almost 150 more years from the time of Paul's writing. Additionally, contra Instone-Brewer, it is doubtful how useful P.Oxy 1473 is here, since it uses this language for *the discharge of a bank debt contract* for a dowry, not a marriage.

111. Moulton and Milligan, *Vocabulary*, 382, 384.

112. So also Schrage, *Erste Brief an die Korinther*, 158.

113. Elliott, "Paul's Teaching," 221–22, here 222.

114. E.g., Baumert, *Woman and Man in Paul*, 82–84, 86–93, 120–26. He even concludes that 7:39 was not about a typical widow but rather a betrothed woman whose fiancé had died (126–29). She therefore *remains* so (unmarried).

115. Johann Christian Konrad von Hofmann, *Die heilige Schrift Neuen Testaments: Zusammen-*

a man and a woman in the same situation. Both have never been married. Also, by using the term "woman" (γυνή) at various points in theses verses rather than "virgin" or "betrothed" (παρθένος), Paul is able to state the matter with the broader implication of not seeking a *wife*. Paul is at this point including *all* single people with the betrothed.[116] Verses 27–28 are Paul's advice for the betrothed that should also be taken as applicable more generally.[117] One should not seek an engagement or a wife *in general*. Nevertheless, the man potentially seeking a wife in v. 27 would be *unbetrothed* since Paul has in mind the situations of men and women relative to engagement as those who have never married.

Despite the fact that "loosed" most likely means to be freed of betrothal obligations (λύσιν), some have pressed further that the word γυνή should be translated as "wife" rather than "betrothed." For these interpreters, Paul would not primarily have in mind the betrothed in these verses after all. Thiselton responds by noting how frequently γυνή is used without reference to marital status.[118] BDAG includes "bride" among the meanings of γυνή. Since Thiselton does not see 1 Cor 7:15 as offering any evidence or permission for remarriage, he concludes that "continuity of topic and argument" requires betrothal, not marriage, to be in view in vv. 25–28.[119]

To review: Paul is addressing *unbetrothed* men in v. 28 who are considering marriage to virgin women, and unbetrothed virgin women who are considering getting married. Throughout, Paul advocates the single life as less encumbered with worldly concerns. Verses 36–38 will turn to men *already* betrothed to virgins. Verses 27–28 do not provide any counsel for the divorced. Paul had already offered that earlier in the chapter.

If one insists that v. 27 *does* in fact have the married in view and not the betrothed—avoiding conflict with vv. 10–11—one may simply take γυνή "woman," and παρθένος "virgin," *in opposition*. Verse 28 would thus have in view marrying someone *not previously married* (with BDAG). "When bound to a wife, do not seek separation; when separated from a wife, do not seek a wife. And, also, if you are getting married, you do not sin; and if the girl is getting married, she does not sin."[120] The first half of the verse would be teaching against divorce and remar-

---

hängend untersucht (Nördlingen: Beck, 1862–1878), 2.2:164; Weiss, *Erste Korintherbrief*, 194–95 ("spiritual engagement"); Elliott, "Paul's Teaching," 220–23; Baumert, *Woman and Man in Paul*, 420–25. J. Carl Laney stresses also the discussion in the immediate context of virgins and not the married; see "Paul and the Permanence of Marriage in 1 Corinthians 7," *JETS* 25.3 (1982): 290–91.

116. With Fee, *First Epistle to the Corinthians*, 366–67.

117. Fee, *First Epistle to the Corinthians*, 366–67.

118. E.g., Matt 9:20, 22; 15:22, 28; Mark 14:3; see 1 Cor 7:34 for the *unmarried* woman. See Thiselton, *First Epistle to the Corinthian*, 576–77.

119. Thiselton, *First Epistle to the Corinthians*, 577.

120. Piet Farla, "'The Two Shall Become One Flesh': Gen. 1.27 and 2.24 in the New Testament

riage in a manner consistent with earlier in the chapter. The second half of the verse would be addressing those who had never been married, "virgins" and their suitors. For them, it is no sin to get married. The verse is not, in that case, offering remarriage as an option.

1 Corinthians 7:32–34—The Unmarried as Noninclusive of Divorcées

Another instance in which Paul could be offering teaching on remarriage is 1 Cor 7:32 and 34, if the term "unmarried" is inclusive of the divorced. The "unmarried" woman in v. 34 appears to be a separate category from the never-married "virgin" woman, mentioned separately, in which case Paul is giving marital instructions to an "unmarried" group inclusive of the divorced, especially since the instructions for widows does not occur for a few more verses. Paul contrasts the situation of this unmarried woman (divorced) with the married woman in v. 34 as if to discourage the unmarried from considering (re)marriage—although it is permissible. At least so goes the reasoning.

Verse 34 rests on a shaky textual foundation with several variant readings attested in the ancient manuscripts. The reading of v. 34 in the twenty-eighth edition of Nestle-Aland remains preferable, since it could account for the other variants. The Nestle-Aland also more likely represents the original, since it is the most difficult reading as other readings tend to resolve grammatical incongruities.[121] Whereas Paul employs the active voice for the verb μερίζω in Rom 12:3, 1 Cor 7:17, and 2 Cor 10:13, the passive voice and perfect tense of 1 Cor 7:34's use of the verb match 1 Cor 1:13's "Is Christ divided?" The married man of 1 Cor 7:32–34 is therefore a "divided" man.[122] The "and" (καί) that appears before the verb "is divided" in v. 34

Marriage Texts," in *Intertexuality in Biblical Writings: Essays in Honour of Bas van Iersel*, ed. Sipke Draisma (Kampen: Kok, 1989), 81 n. 12.

121. With p[15], B, P, 6, 104, 365, 1175, 1505, *pc*, t, vg, co, Eusebius. A comprehensive discussion of the text-critical issues in vv. 33–34 is in Jeffrey John Kloha, "A Textual Commentary on Paul's First Epistle to the Corinthians" (PhD diss., The University of Leeds, 2006), 1:160–87; https://etheses.whiterose.ac.uk/296/.

122. Tertullian, the Peshitta, Methodius, and Chrysostom understand the verb as "there is a difference between." To express a distinction or difference between two things, Paul elsewhere uses διαστολή with coordinated genitives (Rom 10:12) or a plural dative (1 Cor 14:7). The standard lexicons do not offer any examples of "to distinguish between two separate objects." Their examples all imply the division of single object into two. The ancient lexicographers also show this understanding. Harpocration, Apion, Apollonius, Ps.-Zonoras, Hesychius, and the Suda all use μερίζω to gloss δαίω "to divide," or δαίομαι "to divide among themselves." Therefore, the most likely meaning of the verb μεμέρισται at 1 Cor 7:34 is "he is divided (in loyalty)." See Kloha, "Textual Commentary," 173–74.

CHAPTER 5

is the result of Semitic influence, since it indicates a conclusion (like οὖν) as if an apodosis of a conditional sentence. "The one who marries" in v. 33 is functioning as a sort of conditional participle—again, a Semitic grammatical construction.[123] The variants resolve these difficulties.

Of greater significance, however, is the use of the singular verb "is anxious about" (μεριμνᾷ) with *two* subjects: the unmarried woman and the virgin (ἡ ἄγαμος καὶ ἡ παρθένος). This is yet another matter resolved by the variants. One possible understanding of the two subjects takes the "and" as a disjunctive "or": "the unmarried woman or the virgin." A disjunctive approach to the two subjects would thereby match the singular verb. Paul would be *distinguishing* the unmarried woman *from* the virgin or never married.

Commentators still understand this as effectively *both* the unmarried woman and the virgin, who are not anxious about the affairs of a husband.[124] This grammatical option, however, requires an unnatural use of the conjunction καί. As Guenther points out, καί means "or" only when linking successive numbers ("two or three" in 2 Cor 13:1) or successive events (e.g., in the middle of night" or "near dawn" in Luke 12:38).[125] Were the "unmarried" woman defined broadly and inclusively of the divorced, then v. 34 would be at odds with v. 11's prohibition of the divorced remarrying.

On the other hand, even if one were to adopt this first approach to the grammar, the verse would not necessarily provide support for remarriage. The feminine article prior to "virgin" leads commentators to identify this woman as the "betrothed." Since most commentators are of the opinion that the "virgin" (παρθένος) in question in vv. 25–38 is the *betrothed* woman, then the "unmarried" woman would be the *non-betrothed*, never-married woman. Both women would number among the never married, one unbetrothed and the other betrothed. Thus Paul is not envisioning by "virgin" *any* unmarried woman, or even any never-married woman.[126] The "betrothed" woman—like other "unmarried women"—would still be anxious about the affairs of the Lord, but that would change when she became a "married woman."[127] In other words, these verses offer little support, if any, for remarriage. There are, however, other viable grammatical options to be explored.

A second possibility is to take both ἡ ἄγαμος and ἡ παρθένος as adjectival modifiers of "woman" (ἡ γυνή), that is, "the unmarried chaste woman."[128] Support for this position is as follows:

123. Kloha, "Textual Commentary," 174–75.
124. Thus a long line of commentators translating καί as a normal conjunction "and," in spite of the singular verb; see e.g., Thiselton, *First Epistle to the Corinthians*, 590.
125. Allen R. Guenther, "One Woman or Two? 1 Corinthians 7:34," *BBR* 12 (2002): 43.
126. Fee, *First Epistle to the Corinthians*, 381.
127. Contra Guenther, "One Woman," 39.
128. Thus Guenther, "One Woman," 33–45.

1. A singular subject would match the singular verb.
2. The word "virgin" often functions adjectivally in Greek literature (e.g., Isa 37:22).[129] "Unmarried" is also used adjectivally in Greek literature (e.g., Demosthenes, *Leoch.* 44.32; Dionysius of Halicarnassus, *Ant. rom.* 9.22.2; Euripides, *Hel.* 689, *Iph. taur.* 220).
3. Verses 32–34 would retain the balance that is characteristic of 1 Cor 7, in this case between the unmarried man and the married man in vv. 32–33 and the "chaste unmarried woman" and the married woman of v. 34.[130]
4. This approach also avoids the conflict with the Lord's command in v. 11 for the divorced to remain unmarried.
5. Verses 32–34 would conform better to a paragraph in which Paul turns from the married discussed in vv. 1–16 to the unmarried "virgins."
6. Ἄγαμος and παρθένος frequently occur together in Greek literature to stress both singleness and celibacy (e.g., Malalas, *Chron.* 71.19).[131] Plutarch (*Rom.* 3.3.2–3) describes Amulius's fear that a brother's daughter would end up unwedded and a virgin (ἄγαμον καὶ παρθένον). The two words thus function together in Greek literature as adjectives.[132]
7. Many divorced and widowed women are *not* free of constraints to serve the Lord as are unmarried women, since many divorced and widowed women have parental obligations.[133]

The weakness of this approach, critics have noted, is that "virgin" is used substantivally elsewhere in the New Testament.[134] Nevertheless, the "adjectival use of παρθένος in Greek literature" is "common," and this approach avoids the problems of two distinct categories of women in the verse and neatly resolves the use of singular verbs (μεριμνᾷ and ᾖ).[135] Of course, in this case the divorced would simply not be in view.

A final possibility that has circulated since the time of Jerome is to take ἡ παρθένος as epexegetical and further describing ἡ ἄγαμος: "the unmarried woman,

129. For further examples, see Guenther, "One Woman," 37.
130. Guenther, "One Woman," 40.
131. *Ioannis Malalae Chronographia*, ed. Ioannes Thurn, Corpus Fontium Historiae Byzantinae 35 (Berlin: de Gruyter, 2000), 50. For the English, see Elizabeth Jeffreys, Michael Jeffreys, and Roger Scott, trans., *The Chronicles of John Malalas*, Byzantina Australiensia 4 (Leiden: Brill, 2017), 34 (Book 4.6).
132. Of almost fifty instances of ἄγαμος in antiquity, over half refer to the never married, often specified as such by means of the word "virgin" (παρθένος), which is frequently adjectival.
133. Guenther, "One Woman," 44.
134. So Ciampa and Rosner, *First Letter to the Corinthians*, 353.
135. Garland, *1 Corinthians*, 334.

that is, the virgin."¹³⁶ This third possibility is viable as well. Paul uses two adjectives to modify a single noun elsewhere (τέκνον ἀγαπητὸν καὶ πιστόν, 1 Cor 4:17; ἀδελφοί μου ἀγαπητοὶ καὶ ἐπιπόθητοι, Phil 4:1).¹³⁷ If the second or third possibility is adopted, Paul would be discussing *one* category of women in v. 34 and not two. These approaches maintain the consistency of Paul's instructions throughout the chapter. With the Lord's command in vv. 10–11, the divorced are to remain single or be reconciled. As Guenther writes, "The implication is that reconciliation would express itself in remarriage to the former spouse if both were still unmarried. If reconciliation is not possible, for whatever reason, the 'default' condition is singleness."¹³⁸ The weakness of this third approach is that there would be *other* unmarried women also devoted to the Lord who would be excluded from the affirmation.

Whichever of the grammatical options one adopts for v. 34, these verses explain the superiority of the unmarried state, since the unmarried are free to serve the Lord more fully. Verses 32–34 contrast the situation before the Lord of the unmarried and married. Even if one grants that Paul is including the divorced among the "unmarried," which is a possibility (albeit an unlikely one), it is important to recognize what Paul is saying and what he is not saying. Nowhere does he advocate for a change in these verses. He does not advocate that the unmarried should be married. He does not say that the divorced now enjoy a freedom that 1 Cor 7:10–11 denied. One should not assume what Paul does not say in these general remarks on the various situations in which people find themselves. As for the permission to marry, Paul will explicitly turn to that possibility in vv. 36–38, but there he envisions the potential marriage of a man and his "virgin."

1 Corinthians 7:39—Instructions to the Widows Revisited

"A wife is bound as long as her husband lives. But if the husband dies, she is free to marry anyone she wishes, only in the Lord" (1 Cor 7:39).¹³⁹ The parallels between this verse and Jewish divorce bills are hard to miss: "Lo, thou art free to marry any man. . . . Lo, thou art a freedwoman: lo, thou belongest to thyself" (m. Giṭ. 9:3). The

---

136. E.g., R. Collins, *First Corinthians*, 296.
137. Kloha, "Textual Commentary," 175 n. 137.
138. Guenther, "One Woman," 45.
139. NA²⁸ does not take "by the Law" (νόμῳ) as original, despite good external witnesses. Were the word present, the verse would parallel Rom 7:2–3 more closely and thus may reflect the influence of the Romans parallel. The inclusion or noninclusion of the word does not change the implications of this verse regarding remarriage.

"Not Bound" and "Free" in the Apostle Paul?

divorce certificates render explicitly the *freedom* to marry another. Paul's "anyone she wishes" likewise parallels the Jewish divorce certificates.[140] *Here* is the divorce certificate language that was missing earlier in 1 Cor 7:15. In view of the freedom for the widow to marry again, Paul offers a qualification that the second spouse is to be "in the Lord." With Tomson, "Meanwhile his [Paul's] one glaring omission is the other legal means of terminating the marriage bond: divorce.... [H]e supports the tradition of Jesus that marriage is life-long and is terminated only by the death of a partner."[141] As common as divorce was, Paul does not mention it. Fee comments on this fact: "The first statement, 'A woman is bound to her husband as long as he lives,' runs so counter to Jewish understanding and practice at this point in history that it almost certainly reflects Paul's understanding of Jesus' own instructions (see on v. 10). As such it is a final word against divorce and remarriage."[142] The apostle does, however, offer yet another instance of instruction on divorce and remarriage in his letters, and the question is whether that passage takes the same position at 1 Corinthians 7. Perhaps Paul softens his teaching in *another* context.

Romans 7:2–3—A Woman Bound to Her Husband As Long As He Lives

Paul explains in Rom 7:1 that the Mosaic law rules over a person as long as that person lives. Verses 2–3 illustrate his point:

> Thus a married woman is bound by the law to her husband as long as he lives; but if her husband dies, she is discharged from the law concerning the husband. Accordingly, she will be called an adulteress if she lives with another man [ἐὰν γένεται ἀνδρὶ ἑτέρῳ] while her husband is alive. But if her husband dies, she is free from that law, and if she marries another man [γενομένην ἀνδρὶ ἑτέρῳ], she is not an adulteress.

---

140. See chapter 1, pp. 23–25, for earlier examples of the certificates and also those in Peter J. Tomson, "What Did Paul Mean by 'Those Who Know the Law'?" (Rom 7.1)," *NTS* 49 (2003): 579.

141. Tomson, *Paul and the Jewish Law*, 120. In fact, Tomson notes later: "The exactness of the halakhic formulations in 1 Cor 7:39 give the impression that it is a direct quotation" (124).

In fact, Paul betrays the widespread *acceptability* of the remarriage of widows when he rhetorically appeals to his possession of God's Spirit in v. 40 for the possibility of remaining single in widowhood; see Stanley N. Olson, "Epistolary Uses of Expressions of Self-Confidence," *JBL* 103.4 (1984): 593, 596. *Widows* enjoy that permission.

142. Fee, *First Epistle to the Corinthians*, 391.

CHAPTER 5

Paul concludes that a death must take place to free a person from the law. In the illustration the woman bound to a husband is called an adulteress if she "becomes another man's" by marriage.[143] The only means for a woman to enjoy a second marriage without being called an adulteress is for the first husband to die. Paul assumes that death is necessary to release a person from the marital bond in vv. 2–3 and that his audience would take this for granted. He argues *from* these comments to the need for a death to take place to free a person from the Mosaic law as well.[144] The fact that elsewhere in 1 Cor 7:39 Paul mentions as normative the wife's being bound to her husband until he dies demonstrates that "*the metaphorical use* [in Rom 7:2–3] *does not cancel out the literal meaning of this law.*"[145] Again, Paul assumes the normativity of this legal principle in order to apply it metaphorically: A death must take place for the wife to enjoy freedom from her husband.

What is shocking about this illustration is that Paul writes this to the *Romans*. Roman divorce law allowed either partner to divorce the other (cf. Mark 10:11–12). An ordinary reader in a Roman context would have found Paul's premise problematic: a woman is *not* bound to her husband as long as he lives, such that marrying another man would be adulterous. Divorces took place regularly. According to Hellenistic law, for instance, a woman could simply "leave" her husband. As Wolff explains, "Both spouses could dissolve the marriage at will and without formality, by mutual agreement, or by expelling or deserting the other partner."[146] Although a wife could freely instigate divorce, if the divorcing woman should later decide to marry another, a second husband would want to be cautious not to violate the rights of a former husband. A former husband's divorce certificate (annulment) would be prudent. A Greco-Roman parallel to Rom 7:2–3 highlights the differences:

> If on the other hand he [the husband] were dead, she would be free of the charge [of adultery], for no one exists to suffer the injury of the adultery, and when a marriage lacks a man, it cannot be insulted. But *if* on the other hand the marriage has not been *annulled*, because the husband is still alive, then a

---

143. James D. G. Dunn, *Romans 1–8*, WBC 38A (Dallas: Word, 1988), 361; Robert Jewett, *Romans: A Commentary*, Hermeneia (Minneapolis: Fortress, 2007), 432 points to the ostrakon *O.Wilck.* 1530 for "it belongs to me" (τὸ γινόμενόν μοι).

144. Stressed also by Witherington, *Women in Earliest Churches*, 62–64. Only a death dissolves the marital bond.

145. Tomson, "What Did Paul Mean," 577.

146. H. J. Wolff, "Hellenistic Private Law," in Safrai and Stern, *Jewish People in the First Century*, 1:540; H. J. Wolff, *Written and Unwritten Marriages*. Either partner could dissolve the marriage freely.

stranger corrupting the wife has poached on another man's property. (Achilles Tatius, *Leuc. Clit.* 8.10.11–12)[147]

What rendered the woman an adulteress after she had married another man while her first husband was still alive was that her original marriage had not been annulled. Without a divorce certificate, a wife was not necessarily entirely free of the first husband. Another husband could be stealing the first husband's property. Precisely that possibility of annulment or a divorce certificate is what is lacking in Rom 7:2–3.[148] Paul's illustration *omits* precisely what the average Roman hearer *would have expected.* The point would have been clear.

Even the Jews posed two options: *either* the death of the husband *or* the divorce bill would allow a woman to enjoy her freedom. "She acquires her freedom by a bill of divorce or by the death of her husband" (m. Qidd. 1:1; cf. Josephus, *Ant.* 15.7.10 §259). It is no coincidence that Paul's language in Rom 7:2–3 is *identical* to Deut 24:2's in an immediate context of the issuing of *divorce certificates*: ([ἐὰν] ἀπελθοῦσα γένηται ἀνδρί ἑτέρῳ)![149] In other words, *both* Jewish and Greco-Roman sources regularly identify both the death of the husband *and divorce* as means by which a wife enjoys the freedom to marry another. The wife could apply pressure for her husband to divorce her if she had not initiated it herself. Divorce certificates therefore abounded in this world with their "freedom" for the wife.[150] The apostle conspicuously does not allow divorce as an option here, only the death of the husband—and he *assumes* this in order to argue another point.

Paul addresses the Roman gentiles as those who know the law in Rom 7:1, but this is also an aspect of the law that he had apparently *been engaged in teaching*, if 1 Cor 7:10–11, 39–40 is any indication. He had been instructing his gentile converts into a very different approach to marriage as a lifelong union.[151] Peter Tomson concludes that an "apostolic marriage law" was widely disseminated in

---

147. Translated by Winkler, *Collected Ancient Greek Novels*, 279, a text that drew the attention of Jewett, *Romans*, 433.

148. Commentators have regularly noted that Paul does not mention divorce; e.g., Douglas J. Moo, *The Letter to the Romans*, 2nd ed., NICNT (Grand Rapids: Eerdmans, 2018), 438 n. 649; followed by Thomas R. Schreiner, *Romans*, BECNT (Grand Rapids: Baker, 1998), 355. These commentators do not recognize how countercultural and striking that omission is; see e.g., Brendan Byrne, *Romans*, SP 6 (Collegeville, MN: Liturgical, 1996), 213. Joseph A. Fitzmyer is closer here: "The freedom of the wife to have relations with another comes with her husband's death; it has nothing to do here with divorce"; see *Romans*, AB 33 (New York: Doubleday, 1993), 458.

149. In view of 1 Cor 7:10–11, the source must be the teaching of Jesus.

150. See chapter 1, pp. 23–29, for further examples.

151. On the gentile audience of Romans, see A. Andrew Das, *Solving the Romans Debate* (Minneapolis: Fortress, 2007), and on these verses in particular, 85–87. With Peter J. Tomson:

CHAPTER 5

early Christianity.[152] Commentators advocating for remarriage claim that Paul does not mention here the possibility of divorce since it simply was not in view. These interpreters overlook that Paul *does* explicitly envision a woman married to *another man* after the first. He then states that it is *not possible* for her to avoid the charge of adultery in that second marriage as long as the first husband remains alive. The Roman Christ-believing audience would have immediately recognized divorce as an exception to lifelong marital relationships in their larger world—*unless there had been prior teaching to the contrary*. Paul does not go further to mention divorce simply because, for the apostle, a divorce would not eliminate the adultery in marrying another man or change the situation. As Peter Tomson rightly concludes, Rom 7:3 "is an explicative corollary which *excludes divorce* as a means of terminating the marriage by stating that, as long as the husband lives, the woman cannot 'become another man's.'"[153]

Conclusion

To review: Roy Ciampa and Brian Rosner outline the structure of 1 Cor 7:

    A—Married people (vv. 1–7)
    B—Unmarried people in general and widows (vv. 8–9)
    A'—Married people (vv. 10–16)
    B'—Unmarried people in general (vv. 25–38) and widows (vv. 39–40)[154]

For Ciampa and Rosner, this structure reinforces the conclusion that Paul is addressing a broad category of the unmarried, inclusive of the divorced, both in vv. 8–9 and later in the chapter. Such an outline depends on how one interprets the individual subsections of the chapter, especially vv. 8–9 and 25–38. With that investigation complete, the time has come to revisit their outline.

In 1 Cor 7:1–7 Paul encourages couples to enjoy the outlet that marriage provides for one man and one woman to satisfy sexual desire. A man has "his own wife" and a woman "her own husband" (7:2). They belong to each other. Paul does not indicate or suggest that they might subsequently belong to someone else.

"What is more, the fact that Paul cites this rule in letters to two different churches suggests that this halakha was part and parcel of his basic paranesis" (*Paul and the Jewish Law*, 120).

152. Tomson, "What Did Paul Mean," 580; followed in this judgment by Arland J. Hultgren, *Paul's Letter to the Romans: A Commentary* (Grand Rapids: Eerdmans, 2011), 269.

153. Tomson, "What Did Paul Mean," 576.

154. Ciampa and Rosner, *First Letter to the Corinthians*, 271–72.

Strong indications mark vv. 8–9 as a turn from the married in vv. 1–7 to widowers and widows. The LSJ lexicon includes "widowers" among the referents of this word since the related masculine form for "widower" (χῆρος) is rare and unattested in this period. The syntagmatic key is the contextual linkage to "and widows." Verses 1–16 faithfully and repeatedly match men and women in the *same* situations, evidence that the "unmarried" linked with the female "widows" in vv. 8–9 must be male "widowers." Roman society placed intense pressure on widowers to remarry as well, especially if they did not yet have three children. This approach also avoids a contradiction with vv. 10–11, which immediately follow and which require a single life for the divorced.

Paul relays the emphatic command of the Lord in vv. 10–11 that divorce is not an option for believers but, if a woman nevertheless divorces, that divorcing woman must remain single. Verses 12–16 then raise the matter of innocent believing spouses whose non-Christ-believing partners insist on divorce. These people, in view of vv. 10–11, would be required to remain single. Many interpreters, however, seize on Paul's "not bound" language. The word is better translated as "not enslaved." The term appears to be a deliberate departure from the "free" language of the divorce certificates and from the "bound" language that Paul applies only to widows in 1 Cor 7:39 and Rom 7:2–3. In other words, when offered a chance to declare "freedom" for the innocent, divorced spouse, Paul conspicuously passes on the opportunity. The concept of an innocent partner in divorce being justified in remarriage is absent in Paul. "Not enslaved" is language Paul uses in relation to the law of Moses and divorce. "Enslaved" is also language used by the philosophers of Paul's day for those in a marital relationship: Not to be enslaved for the philosophers was to *not be in a marriage*, whether a first or a subsequent one. A first-century hearer would not, then, envision remarriage. After the apostle has repeatedly and emphatically insisted that believing partners are not to divorce their spouses, he grants the believing partner "peace" when the non-Christ-believer insists on it. Even then, the hope is ever for the restoration of the original marital bond (v. 16).

Verses 25–38 take up the topic of the "unmarried." Some have identified a permission to remarry in vv. 27–28, but Paul employs *contractual* language and not the language of marriage itself. These are "virgins" who have been contractually *betrothed*. The betrothed are not "bound" and are free to be "loosed" from or to break off those agreements, and it is likewise no sin to follow through on the betrothal with marriage. Ultimately, the single life in devotion to the Lord is to be preferred, if possible.

Paul mentions the "unmarried" again in vv. 32 and 34 in comments explaining why the unmarried are in a better position to serve the Lord more fully. When

CHAPTER 5

Paul discusses those who are free to marry, he explicitly identifies the betrothed elsewhere in this section (e.g., vv. 25–28, 36–38). Grammatically, good indications suggest that he is referring to the never married in vv. 32–34 as well.

Pulling together these observations, a different structure for the chapter is preferable to the one offered by Ciampa and Rosner above. Paul discusses the merits of sexual relations or abstinence among the married in vv. 1–7. He proceeds to the situation of those no longer married (but not the divorced) in vv. 8–9. He admonishes against divorce in v. 10 and against remarriage in the wake of divorce in v. 11. In vv. 12–16 he turns to the special case of those married to nonbelievers, permitting the believer to allow the nonbeliever to divorce. Verses 25–38 takes up the new topic (from their letter, v. 25) of those who have not been married and are betrothed. Finally, Paul tackles the situation of the widow in vv. 39–40. Widows enjoy permission to remarry, if they are not able to remain single. Much of the chapter maintains the same gender parity as first exhibited in 7:2–4.[155] Ultimately, each section of the chapter is addressing a discrete situation.[156]

The married (vv. 1–7)
Widowers and widows (vv. 8–9)
Divorce in the context of believers, the Lord's command (vv. 10–11)
Divorce in the context of mixed marriages (vv. 12–16)
Circumcision and uncircumcision, slave and free (vv. 17–24)
The betrothed and the preference for being single over the married state (vv. 25–38)
Widows (vv. 39–40)

In 1 Cor 7:1 Paul begins to answer the question the Corinthians posed to him in their letter: "It is well for a man not to touch a woman." The Corinthians were asking about the propriety of avoiding sexual relations entirely, even with one's spouse. The concern that has prompted Paul's discussion in vv. 1–16 is the possibility that the Corinthians would abandon their marriages by divorce or by abstaining from sexual relations. Paul *is not addressing remarriage*. The matter of remarriage is only explicitly mentioned in vv. 11 and 39 when Paul denies it as an option apart from the death of a spouse. The rest of the chapter, even 7:15, simply does not mention it. Paul actively promotes marriage for those who have never been married who need a release from their sexual desires, but he never promotes remarriage.

155. R. Collins, *First Corinthians*, 262.
156. Rightly Fee, *First Epistle to the Corinthians*, 297–300; Collins, *First Corinthians*, 262, 288; Hays, *First Corinthians*, 118: "Paul's advice to other classes of non-married persons—the divorced and the not-yet-married—is given separately in vv. 11 and 25–38."

"Not Bound" and "Free" in the Apostle Paul?

Throughout the chapter Paul urges people to *stay as they are* in whatever situation they find themselves.[157] They are not to divorce. Ideally, they are to remain single. Paul qualifies and allows for the single to be married, and for the divorced believer in a mixed marriage to become single again. He never allows for remarriage with the exception of the widow in 7:39. Even there, it would be better for the widow to remain single. One must therefore hunt for *indirect* clues in 1 Cor. 7 that Paul envisions remarriage as a possibility, but the possible clues do not bear the weight placed on them. What remains at the end of the day is the firm, unqualified command of the Lord in 1 Cor 7:11 that the divorced are not to marry another.

In 1 Cor 7:39 Paul states: "A wife is bound [δέω] as long as her husband lives. But if the husband dies, she is free [ἐλευθέρα] to marry anyone she wishes, only in the Lord." So also Rom 7:2–3 reads: "Thus a married woman is bound [δέω] by the law to her husband as long as he lives; but if her husband dies, she is discharged [ἐλευθέρα] from the law concerning the husband. Accordingly, she will be called an adulteress if she lives with another man while her husband is alive. But if her husband dies, she is free from that law, and if she marries another man, she is not an adulteress." In making his point about being freed from the law, he takes for granted that only a prior spouse's death can prevent a subsequent marriage from being adulterous, and the premise assumes his prior teaching on marriage.

One element has been passed over in this discussion: how the earliest Christian thinkers interpreted 1 Cor 7. The Christian witnesses in the first several centuries, many of whom were native Greek speakers, did not understand 1 Cor 7:15's language of "not bound" and "free"—or anything else in 1 Cor 7—as permitting remarriage. They too connected 7:16 to hopes for the original marriage in vv. 12–13. That witness is a telling confirmation of the interpretation of 1 Cor 7 supported by this chapter, but it requires further discussion in itself, especially concerning those early Christian thinkers closest to the pages of the New Testament who were writing prior to the Council of Nicaea in 325 CE.

---

157. Many scholars have commented on Paul's philosophy of "staying" where one is, e.g., David W. Kuck, "The Freedom of Being in the Word 'As If Not' (1 Cor 7:29–21)," *CurTM* 28 (2001): 585–93, but with provision for marriage.

6

The Witness of the Early Church

The post-apostolic era through the Council of Nicaea (325 CE) offers a testing ground for how the New Testament witness was received. Did early Christians oppose remarriage? Were there differences in viewpoint and practice? How did these authors interpret individual biblical texts? As with historical Jesus research, an abundance of riches greets the interpreter: Several authors and councils address the subject. The Council of Nicaea represents a natural *terminus* for this inquiry, since the emperor Constantine's conversion, the Edict of Milan legalizing Christianity, and Constantine's involvement at Nicaea would lead to the masses flocking to the church and the increasing influence of the larger, more permissive society. Social pressures would eventually and inevitably exert a strong countervailing influence.

Despite the winds of change in the air, most *post*-Nicene thinkers would censure remarriage after divorce as adulterous. Augustine throughout his writings, for instance, championed the sacramental indissolubility of the marital bond. In his 410 CE *Faith and Works*, he defends how one is saved by faith alone, inspiring Luther's later emphasis, and yet he still writes of divorced and remarried persons wishing to receive baptism: "But these persons are not admitted, because the Lord Christ declares without any doubt that such marriages are not marriages but adulteries" (1 §2).[1] Remarriage is not an option while the former partner remains

---

1. Augustine, *On Faith and Works*, trans. and ed. Gregory J. Lombardo, ACW 48 (New York: Newman, 1988), 8, 15. He adds in 7 §10 with respect to remarriage: "Let us not feel that in correcting such evils we are destroying the bond of matrimony." For Augustine, the remarriages are not genuine marriages. This position is a function of Augustine's teaching a sacramental bond in marriage that cannot be done away with through divorce.

alive. Later in the same work, Augustine holds that even his opponents recognize that remarriage is adulterous (7 §10).

John Chrysostom in the East writes at length on divorce and remarriage as well. If a couple divorce, the wife must remain single, be reconciled to her husband, or wait for him to die (*Virginit.* 40–41).[2] Chrysostom makes no provision for remarriage, even for the innocent party. If a divorcing man does not marry another, he is still an adulterer by forcing his wife to remarry since she continues to be his wife even after the divorce (*Hom. Matt.* 17.4). When a wife adulterates, one must divorce her to avoid sharing in the sin but, again, Chrysostom makes no mention of remarriage for the innocent partner (*Hom. 1 Cor.* 19 [on 1 Cor 7:12]). Chrysostom often uses the phrase "second marriage," *but only in relation to widows* and, even then, he prefers a single marriage in view of Gen. 2:24's one man and one woman (*Iter. conj.* [*Against Remarriage*]; *Hom. 1 Cor.* 19 [on 1 Cor 7:28, 36]).

Although most Christian authors in the fourth and fifth centuries agreed with Augustine and Chrysostom (including Basil of Caesarea, Ambrose, and Jerome), dissent began to grow (e.g., Ambrosiaster). The post-Nicene story is complex and not easily addressed in a relatively short discussion.[3] The question here is a more limited and manageable one: whether the *ante*-Nicene Christian writers and councils endorsed remarriage after divorce in certain situations.[4]

One cannot address the question of remarriage in early Christianity without exploring a related matter. Modern readers—especially scholars concerned about consistency—often forget that ancient discourse was regularly marked by paradox.[5] Contemporary Protestantism generally finds in Paul's letters a celebration of marital sexual relations, and the earliest mainstream Christians did indeed defend sexual relations within a marital context against more extreme positions.[6]

---

2. John Chrysostom, *On Virginity; Against Remarriage*, trans. Sally Rieger Shore, Studies in Women and Religion 9 (New York: Mellen, 1983), 60–61.

3. See the entirety of Henri Crouzel's famous monograph on the topic, *L'église face au divorce: du premier au cinquième siècle*, ThH 13 (Paris: Beauchesne, 1971).

4. Some of the relevant texts have been collated in David G. Hunter's *Marriage and Sexuality in Early Christianity*, Ad Fontes: Early Christian Sources (Minneapolis: Fortress, 2018), including the ante-Nicene Hermas, Tertullian, Clement of Alexandria, Lactantius, and the Canons of the Council of Elvira, which is ante-Nicene in part.

5. Jennifer A. Glancy, *Corporal Knowledge: Early Christian Bodies* (Oxford: Oxford University Press, 2010), 119–20.

6. E.g., Ed and Gaye Wheat, *Intended for Pleasure: Sex Technique and Sexual Fulfillment in Christian Marriage*, 3rd ed. (Grand Rapids: Revell, 1997), 17, 24–25.

William A. Heth comments: "'Celibacy' is a word that makes modern Protestants uncomfortable. Ever since the Reformation when Martin Luther boldly broke from the Catholic Church,

Nonetheless, early Christian authors frequently celebrate the single life. Many modern interpreters, especially in the Protestant tradition, dismiss early Christian thinking on divorce and remarriage as a reflection of the wrongheaded asceticism of their age.

Elizabeth Clark's *Reading Renunciation* provides a comprehensive survey of ascetic patterns of thought in early Christianity. Her most pronounced evidence for a stringent asceticism comes from *after* 325 CE, but not exclusively.[7] Inspiring these varying perspectives among ancient Christian authors are certain biblical texts exerting their influence, especially 1 Corinthians 7. Early Christian appropriation of the biblical witness exhibits the paradox characteristic of ancient thought: both a defense of sexual relations within marriage and an advocacy for the single life in service to the Lord. If ancient Christian authors found their inspiration in biblical texts, even on matters ascetic, then the modern Protestant who values the biblical witness may not find that witness as easy to dismiss.

The Shepherd of Hermas

The Shepherd of Hermas, written in the first half of the second century (ca. 140–150 CE), enjoyed considerable popularity.[8] Several early Christian authors cite it, including Irenaeus, Clement of Alexandria, Tertullian, Origen, Jerome, and Augustine. Origen concluded that it was written by one of Paul's companions in view of the Hermas mentioned in Rom 16:14. Some early Christian communities even esteemed the Shepherd of Hermas as Scripture, as did Clement of Alexandria. The Codex Sinaiticus included the work just after the New Testament. The older of the two Latin manuscripts of the Shepherd is from 200 CE, and the work was translated into Sahidic and Ethiopic. Tertullian, in his later, rigorist Montanist phase, spoke vehemently against it, no doubt due to the work's popularity. The Shepherd is also the earliest extant witness to post-apostolic teaching on divorce and remarriage.

---

denounced compulsory clerical celibacy as the work of the devil, and abandoned monastic vows for married life, Evangelicals in Reformed traditions have associated celibacy with unscriptural excess." See "Unmarried 'For the Sake of the Kingdom' (Matthew 19:12) in the Early Church," *Grace Theological Journal* 8.1 (1987): 56–57. Consequently, Heth adds (58), Protestants have never explained how Jesus's "eunuch" saying in Matt 19:10–12 or Paul's counseling celibacy in 1 Cor 7 are to be applied among believers.

7. Elizabeth Clark, *Reading Renunciation: Asceticism and Scripture in Early Christianity* (Princeton: Princeton University Press, 1999), 259–329, apart from the gnostics and Encratites.

8. Translation of Hermas from Ehrman, LCL.

The work begins with an angel coming to Hermas dressed as a shepherd to deliver revelation from the Lord. The second section of the work is divided into twelve commandments or mandates. In mandate 4 Hermas receives the Lord's instruction about avoiding sexual sin. Hermas describes a believing wife, faithful "in the Lord" (Herm. Mand, 4.1.4), that is, in Christ (1 Cor 4:17; 7:39).[9] Those following Christ may choose to marry rather than live an ascetic or celibate lifestyle. In a marital relationship the man is to keep his thoughts focused on his wife in order to avoid sexual immorality, which would be "a great sin." To act on lust toward another woman would bring upon oneself death (Herm. Mand. 4.1.1–2). As Lyn Osiek comments, "The injunction to remember one's own wife (when tempted toward another) is straightforward and appealingly relational rather than legalistic."[10]

Hermas then asks the Lord what is to be done with an adulterous wife. Should the husband sin by continuing to live with her (Herm. Mand. 4.1.4)? The angel responds that if the husband is ignorant of the wife's sin, he does not himself sin. If he *does* know about the wife's sin, and she has not repented, then he shares in her immorality and guilt (4.1.5). Hermas naturally asks what the husband should do once aware of a wife's adultery. The angel responds that the husband is to divorce the unrepentant wife and live alone. "But if he marries someone else after the divorce, he also commits adultery" (4.1.6). Remarriage after divorce for this (innocent!) spouse, whether the husband or the wife, is categorically adulterous.[11] Notions of innocent parties or valid divorces are nonfactors in the reasoning.

The Shepherd of Hermas offers an early witness to how the New Testament texts on divorce and remarriage were interpreted and understood (Matt 5:32; 19:9; Mark 10:11; Luke 16:18; 1 Cor 7:10–11).[12] Augustus's *Lex Iulia de adulteriis coercendis* (18–16 BCE) required the divorce of adulterous wives.[13] Hermas expands that requirement to include a wife's response to an adulterous husband (Herm. Mand. 4.1.8–10).[14] The requirement to divorce an adulterous partner may be grounded in Paul's forbidding sexual relations with a prostitute as contrary to the

---

9. Carolyn Osiek, *The Shepherd of Hermas*, Hermeneia (Minneapolis: Fortress, 1999), 110–11 n. 7; cf. Norbert Brox, *Der Hirt des Hermas*, Kommentar zu den Apostolischen Vätern 7 (Göttingen: Vandenhoeck & Ruprecht, 1991), 205.

10. Osiek, *Shepherd*, 110.

11. J. P. Arendzen, "Ante-Nicene Interpretations of the Sayings on Divorce," *JTS* 20 (1919): 231.

12. Crouzel, *L'église*, 51; Anton Ott, *Die Auslegung der neutestamentlichen Texte über die Ehescheidung*, NTAbh 3 (Münster: Aschendorffschen, 1911), 10.

13. Crouzel, *L'église*, 47; Osiek, *Shepherd*, 111.

14. Brox (*Der Hirt des Hermas*, 206) notes the difference that the Julian law was only for the husband, but the mandate here is for both the innocent husband *and* the innocent wife in such cases.

CHAPTER 6

union with Christ (1 Cor 6:15–17). Paul uses the πορν- word group in 1 Cor 6:15–17 after explaining that Christ-believers are not to associate with the immoral in their midst (1 Cor 5:9–11).[15] Whereas the Roman *Lex Iulia* penalized those who did *not* remarry, the Shepherd of Hermas counterculturally forbids it.[16] One would need good reason, then, to conclude that the Shepherd permitted exceptions to this prohibition. Only one exception is mentioned in what immediately follows, and it is to restore the original marital union. The work offers no provision for the divorced to marry anyone else. They are to remain single, thereby avoiding adultery. Importantly, the Shepherd does not qualify that singleness is *only* when repentance remains a possibility (i.e., the guilty spouse has not yet remarried). The Shepherd countenances only a life of singleness in the wake of divorce apart from restoration to a former spouse (cf. 1 Cor 7:10–11).

The Shepherd of Hermas's next follow-up question envisions *another* situation: a wife's repenting after the divorce, in which the case the former husband is to receive her back. Again, this is countercultural and contrary to the *Lex Iulia*. If the husband does not receive her back, he himself sins (Herm. Mand. 4.1.8). "Because of repentance, therefore, the husband ought not to marry. The same applies to both wife and husband" (4.1.8). There is "but one repentance. . . . This is why you have been ordered to remain by yourselves, whether a husband or wife; for repentance is possible in such cases" (4.1.10). The angelic figure stresses *twice* in response that the single life after divorce is for the sake of the adulterous spouse's repentance and the restoration of the original union (4.1.8, 10).

---

15. Kirsopp Lake theorizes that the Roman Christians were resolving a tension between 1 Cor 5:11 about not associating with the immoral people and Jesus's prohibitions of divorce. See "The Earliest Christian Teaching on Divorce," *The Expositor* 7 (1910): 425; so also Heth and Wenham, *Jesus and Divorce*, 25. According to Lake, the solution was to stay single after the divorce and then take back the repentant spouse. "That is to say it [Hermas] enjoins on the husband of an unfaithful wife the duty of separating from her, but does not set him free to marry again" (426). If Hermas was aware of and commenting on Matthew, then Hermas would be confirming that the Matthean exception clauses were intended to permit a divorce for an unfaithful spouse but without the provision for remarriage.

Crouzel, *L'église*, 50, 68: Jerome, Basil, and Ambrose all cite 1 Cor 6:16 on why separation is required after adultery in an extension of Paul's prostitute comments to marital infidelity; so also Heth and Wenham, *Jesus and Divorce*, 25 (i.e., not based on the *Lex Iulia* but 1 Cor 6:15–17). Paul quotes Gen 2:24 on the one-flesh of marriage (cf. Matt 5:32; 19:9)—apparently making divorce an obligation. The one-fleshness of the adultery would render the original marriage adulterous (Crouzel, *L'église*, 53).

16. C. W. Emmet, "The Teaching of Hermas and the First Gospel on Divorce," *The Expositor* 8 (1911): 69 stresses against Lake that people *assumed* the permission to remarry in that culture, but that is precisely what makes Hermas's teaching so *countercultural* and inexplicable unless it is based on the similarly countercultural teaching of Jesus and the first Christians.

The Witness of the Early Church

Some therefore propose that the Shepherd of Hermas envisions remarriage as a possibility in cases where the spouse was *repeatedly* sinful and there was *no* opportunity for repentance or restoration, perhaps because the adulterous spouse had married another. Leaving the door open for repentance would thus, for these scholars, be the only reason one is to remain single after divorce.[17] Otherwise, they conclude, one may remarry.

Certainly repentance is a major motif, if not the theme, of the Shepherd of Hermas.[18] In this passage, the wife's unrepentant adultery places the knowing husband in the position of being required to divorce her. He must remain single, and the given rationale for this is the possibility of her repentance and restoration. Even more, the discussion of marital matters in 4.1 is separated from its natural continuation in 4.4 by a section that seems out of place—at first (4.2–3). The intervening material is about repentance/conversion (μετανοέω/μετάνοια).[19] In this context, an adulterous wife's repentance is analogous to a conversion, or reconversion. The Shepherd of Hermas has already explained the death-dealing consequences of adultery (4.1.3).

The stress in this section on repentance raises another possible interpretation. Since the author is repeatedly emphasizing repentance *throughout* the work, one should not assume that the mandate to remain single after divorce is *only* for the purpose of repentance and restoration. That is simply the rationale the author stresses for his *own* purposes in keeping with his theme. One would need more explicit evidence that remarriage after divorce is possible. The angel conveys no permission to marry anyone else in 4.1, nor does the angel even raise that as a possibility. One is left, then, with the stern, lingering warning that to marry someone else would be adulterous, even for the innocent husband (4.1.6).

The Shepherd *will* eventually allow for remarriage later in Herm. Mand. 4.4, but only after the death of a spouse, and Hermas is so hesitant to admit even *that* as a possibility that he requires revelatory verification by means of a follow-up question. He expresses his concern that remarriage *even in the event of the death of a spouse would be adulterous*: "If a wife or, again, a husband, should die and the survivor marry, does the one who marries commit a sin?" (4.4.1). The response is that it is not a sin or adultery to marry another in these instances. Ideally, one would remain single (cf. 1 Cor 7:39; Rom 7:2–3). Hermas's concern attests to a growing

---

17. Osiek, *Shepherd*, 111 is representative, but tentatively so: "The implication almost seems to be that if it were not for that contingency, it would be permitted to marry another." Strangely, Osiek (111) then endorses Kirsopp Lake's reading of Hermas as not permitting remarriage after divorce over Emmet.

18. Osiek, *Shepherd*, 28–30.

19. Osiek, *Shepherd*, 109–10.

CHAPTER 6

opposition of "second marriages" (after a spouse's death) in favor of celibacy.[20] If Hermas envisions potential adultery for a widow or widower to marry again, a potential scandal that requires the Lord's revelation, how much more would it be adulterous for a divorced individual to marry another (contrary to Herm. Mand. 4.1.6)? The single life after divorce is to continue. To remarry someone other than one's former spouse would be adulterous unless that spouse had died.

William Luck, an advocate of remarriage, was forced to admit that the Shepherd of Hermas is a unique witness to remarriage as adulterous.[21] David Instone-Brewer concludes from the Shepherd: "[I]t is more likely that remarriage was completely forbidden unless the spouse died (which is allowed in *Command* 4.4), and that the apparently superfluous reason [the adulterous spouse may repent] was given to bolster the argument."[22] Instone-Brewer apparently did not realize the implications of his reasoning for his claim that anyone in this era would recognize that divorce *assumed* the right to remarry. If the Shepherd rejected such a right, the New Testament authors could have as well. Far more likely, the New Testament authors' censure of remarriage influenced Hermas to take this unusual, countercultural position.

Justin Martyr

Chapters 15–17 of Justin Martyr's 150 CE *First Apology* offers catechesis on entry into the new life at baptism, renouncing heathen idolatry and vices, worshipping God, submitting to God and the elders in social virtues, and in watching and praying.[23] Chapter 15 discusses the matter of chastity, beginning with a quotation from memory of Matt 5:28–29: "'Whosoever looketh upon a woman to lust after her, hath committed adultery with her already in his heart before God.' And, 'If thy right eye offend thee, cut it out; for it is better for thee to enter into the kingdom of heaven with one eye than, having two eyes, to be cast into everlasting fire.'"[24] Justin then continues with another quote, from Matt 5:32: "And, 'whosoever shall marry her that is divorced from another husband committeth adultery.'"[25] Justin

20. Osiek, *Shepherd*, 116; see 1 Tim. 3:2; Tertullian, *Mon.* 16.3; *Exh. cast.* 1.
21. Luck, *Divorce and Re-Marriage*, 290.
22. Instone-Brewer, *Divorce and Remarriage*, 240–41.
23. A. J. Bellinzoni, *The Sayings of Jesus in the Writings of Justin Martyr*, NovTSup 17 (Leiden: Brill, 1967), 54–55. He reconstructs which gospel texts stand behind Justin's discussion of divorce and remarriage on 70–71 and 96–97.
24. Translation of Justin Martyr from *ANF* 1.
25. Crouzel (*L'église*, 54) comments that we do not know why he does not also quote the first

summarizes Matt 5:32's teaching by citing just the second half of the verse, leading Arendzen to comment: "Now it seems unreasonable to suppose that someone who summed up the Christian marriage law in that one sentence was not really certain whether remarriage after divorce was allowable or not."[26] At that point, Justin quotes Matt 19:12, which follows Matthew's *second* divorce/remarriage passage in 19:1–9: "And 'there are some who have been made eunuchs of men, and some who were born eunuchs for the kingdom of heaven's sake; but all cannot receive this saying.'" Justin therefore interprets the eunuch saying in Matt 19:12 as a further elaboration on Jesus's teaching regarding divorce and remarriage (via Matt 5:32). Justin concludes from the Matt 19:12 citation: "So that all who, by human law are *twice married* (διγαμίας ποιούμενοι), are in the eye of our Master sinners, and those who look upon a woman to lust after her. For not only he who in act commits adultery is rejected by Him, but also he who desires to commit adultery: since not only our works, but also our thoughts are open before God" (emphasis mine).

The question is what Justin means by "twice married" or "doubly married." One possibility is bigamy: to have a second wife while a lawful first wife is still alive and present. A second possibility is marriage to a second wife after divorcing the first. The third is a second wife after the death of the first. The decisive interpretive key in this context is that Justin has just cited Matt 5:32, which forbids a man from marrying a woman divorced from her husband. This favors the second possibility for "twice married." Justin does not mention the exception clauses of Matthew (cf. Luke 16:18): The woman may be an innocent victim of a divorce, but for a man to marry her would be adulterous sin.[27] Justin's Jesus is proclaiming that his followers

---

part of the verse, but the rationale for the omission of Matt 5:32a is likely twofold: (1) Justin is quoting the passage from memory; and (2) Justin is concerned with *second* marriages that would take place *after* the dissolution of the original marriage. Matthew 5:32a would be irrelevant.

26. Arendzen, "Ante-Nicene Interpretations," 232.

27. Luck (*Divorce and Re-Marriage*, 291) offers a convoluted attempt to circumvent this by positing that Justin has in view *only* the man who had been lusting after a married woman. For *him* to marry an innocently divorced woman—after he had lusted after her in her married state—would be adultery. Otherwise, she would be free to remarry. Also, Luck holds that the innocent *divorcing* spouse may remarry. While such a reading conforms to Luck's understanding of the divorce/remarriage biblical texts, it falters on Justin's stress on "*all*" who, by human law are twice married." "All" who are "twice married" are charged with adultery. Justin does not offer any clarification in his teaching that only *some* "twice-married" situations are problematic and not all such situations. Justin never actually *says* that his further comments have in view *only* the lusting man at the beginning of the chapter. Luck does not take "human law" as referring to the general custom in Roman society of permitting remarriages. For Luck, it must refer to "twice married" *in the specific situation where a man had been lusting after a married woman*. If only

CHAPTER 6

are to be "once-married" people.[28] Justin offers no provision for the divorced to remarry after a former spouse has married another. He does not offer any provisions for the innocent parties of a divorce. He simply replicates Jesus's general censure of marrying a divorced woman, regardless of whether she is innocent.

Chastity entails avoiding adulterous sin, whether it be "twice marriage" or lust after a woman. Justin follows Matthew in articulating this in terms of the man. He continues in *First Apology* 15:

> And many, both men and women, who have been Christ's disciples from childhood, remain pure at the age of sixty or seventy years; and I boast that I could produce such from every race of men. For what shall I say, too, of the countless multitude of those who have reformed intemperate habits, and learned these things? For Christ called not the just nor the chaste to repentance, but the ungodly, and the licentious, and the unjust.

For Justin, Christ's followers live in a chaste and pure manner that distinguishes them from the outside world.[29] Justin is an early witness to handbooks or rubrics for the proper behavior of a follower of Christ, which includes being "once married." An ascetic or celibate lifestyle is not required so long as one avoids adulterous lust and a double-married state. If Justin's teaching against the double-married state also includes widows and widowers, he would be proscribing any remarriage at all. For Instone-Brewer, Justin Martyr is contrasting "human law" with Jesus's teaching, which allows for no remarriage. The church's position would be clear.[30]

Justin addresses divorce again in his *Second Apology* (2.1–7). He describes a woman who had, like her spouse, enjoyed extramarital pleasures, but then she

---

Justin had said as much. Against Luck, Justin signals that he is providing what Jesus had to teach about chastity *more generally* by not limiting himself to statements regarding a man who lusts.

28. Victor J. Pospishil *ignores* Justin's emphasis on the once-married state to claim, without the text's saying so, that the innocent husband in a divorce for adultery may himself remarry; see *Divorce and Remarriage: Toward a New Catholic Teaching* (New York: Herder and Herder, 1967), 141.

29. Justin then quotes Matt 9:13, but he does so by means of Luke 5:32—shifting back and forth from memory between the two gospels: "I have come not to call the righteous, but sinners to repentance."

30. Strangely, Reynolds limits himself to the Shepherd of Hermas and quickly moves on to Tertullian, thereby overlooking Justin Martyr's agreement with the Shepherd. See Philip Lyndon Reynolds, *Marriage in the Western Church: The Christianization of Marriage during the Patristic and Early Medieval Periods*, VCSup 24 (Leiden: Brill, 1994), 187–200. See also the witness of Athenagoras.

came to the knowledge of Christ's teaching and resolved to be faithful to her husband. The husband, meanwhile, remained unconverted and intemperate. Even when she warned him of punishment in the eternal fires, he remained dissolute. At some point, despite her desire to help him amend his life, his behavior became even worse. Her friends urged her to divorce him. The wife's hope for her husband's conversion reflects the influence of 1 Cor 7:12–16. That hope could not endure forever. Lest she "become a partaker also in his wickedness and impieties," she offered him a bill of divorce and separated. The husband did not take that well and charged her with being a Christian. Justin's account attests to the pressure on believers to divorce spouses guilty of sexual sin (cf. Herm. Mand. 4.1.4–6). Remarriage is not at issue in this passage and is not presented as an option. Instone-Brewer concludes from the *Second Apology* account: "[W]e are not told whether the Church would have allowed such a remarriage" (i.e., for the wife of the divorced, adulterous husband).[31] With respect to the *First Apology* passage, and despite his own inclinations otherwise, Instone-Brewer is more definite: "[Justin Martyr] quoted a series of sayings by Jesus and concluded that it is sinful to remarry."[32]

Athenagoras

In his 177 CE *Plea for the Christians* (*Legatio pro Christianis*), Athenagoras publicly appeals to the Emperors Marcus Aurelius Antoninus and Lucius Aurelius Commodus. In chapter 33 he describes for them Christian chastity:

> Therefore, having the hope of eternal life, we despise the things of this life, even the pleasures of the soul, each of us reckoning her his wife whom he has married according to the laws laid down by us, and that only for the purpose of having children. For as the husbandman throwing the seed into the ground awaits the harvest, not sowing more upon it, so to us the procreation of children is the measure of our indulgence in appetite.[33]

A Christian man and woman are therefore free to marry and even to "indulge in appetite," but the indulgence should be for sake of children. The believer need not remain celibate for life or engage in an ascetic lifestyle. Marital pleasure for the sake of children is permissible. Athenagoras continues:

31. Instone-Brewer, *Divorce and Remarriage*, 242.
32. Instone-Brewer, *Divorce and Remarriage*, 241.
33. Translation from *ANF* 2.

CHAPTER 6

> Nay, you would find many among us, both men and women growing old unmarried, in hope of living in closer communion with God. But if the remaining in the state of an eunuch brings nearer to God, while the indulgence of carnal thought and desire leads away from Him, in more do we reject the deeds. For we bestow the exhibition and teaching of actions,—that a person should either remain as he was born, or be content with one marriage; for a second marriage is only a specious adultery.

Athenagoras relays the advice of Paul in 1 Cor 7 to remain in the state one finds oneself unless one should choose to be married, and here to "be content with one marriage; for a second marriage is specious adultery." Is Athenagoras condemning second marriage after divorce or *any* second marriage, even after the former spouse has died? While Justin Martyr was unclear whether the censure of the "twice-married" also included remarriage after a spousal death, Athenagoras provides clues in this regard:

> "For whosoever puts away his wife," says He, "and marries another, commits adultery;" not permitting a man to send her away whose virginity he has brought to an end, nor to marry again. For he who deprives himself of his first wife, even though she be dead, is a cloaked adulterer, resisting the hand of God, because in the beginning God made one man and one woman, and dissolving the strictest union of flesh with flesh, formed for the intercourse of the race.

After admonishing that one be satisfied with a single marriage, Athanagoras cites Mark 10:11 (without ἐπ' αὐτήν; "against her") and Matt 19:9 (without the exception clause).[34] These verses admonish the husband not to divorce his wife and marry another. The rationale for a single marriage is Jesus's teaching in Mark 10:6–9 and Matt 19:4–6 that in creation God intended for one man to be united to one woman.[35] Athenagoras apparently takes the exception clause of Matt 19:9 as *irrelevant* to the question of remarriage and therefore omits it. As Arendzen states:

---

34. Theodore Mackin stresses that Athenagoras should not be taken as an advocate of "anti-sexual rigorism" as was the case for some of the Fathers, most notably Athenagoras's contemporary Tatian; see his *Divorce and Remarriage*, Marriage in the Catholic Church 2 (New York: Paulist, 1984), 125. Had Athenagoras been "an Encratite rigorist," he would not have endorsed a single marriage. Mackin concludes that Athengoras had taken his cues from Gen 1–2 and "the proto-typical monogamy of the first marriage" (125). One might add that Jesus too had started there.

35. Arendzen, "Ante-Nicene Interpretations," 232; Heth and Wenham, *Jesus and Divorce*, 29–30.

The Witness of the Early Church

"The exceptional clause introduced in St Matthew could be omitted by the writer, because, according to him, whatever its meaning, it applied only to the first part of the legislation about the dismissal of the wife, not to the second regarding remarriage."[36] "A quasi-everlasting relation was set up between the two partners, alive or dead."[37] Athenagoras may reflect a growing asceticism in the early church, but he grounds his approach in Christ's teaching. To remarry after divorce would be contrary to God's will in creation.

Athenagoras extends the prohibition of a second marriage to include even those who have experienced the death of a spouse: "For he who deprives himself of his first wife, *even though she be dead*, is a cloaked adulterer" (emphasis mine). For that matter, Athenagoras clarifies by this comment that marrying again, or second marriage, is *only conceived of as a possibility* by his peers in the wake of the death of a spouse. Only a second marriage after a spouse's death *needed* to be addressed. Apparently, no one was countenancing a second marriage after divorce. Athenagoras's explicit prohibition of a second marriage after spousal death is unique in this era.[38] How much more, then, is a second marriage prohibited in instances where a spouse is contemplating it after divorce? "It is plain that a union with another partner during the lifetime of the first is a crime against nature."[39] Athenagoras's stress on the one marriage goes against Paul's teaching that permits a second marriage after a spouse's death (1 Cor 7:39; Rom 7:2–3). Other early Christian authors will not go as far as Athenagoras to contradict Paul and deny a second marriage for those whose spouses have died. Instone-Brewer concludes that "a concept of an unbreakable 'one flesh' marriage" may be in view.[40] As was the case with the Shepherd of Hermas, Instone-Brewer does not recognize the challenge such a conclusion would pose for his own position that a divorce in antiquity, even in Christian circles, would always include the right to remarry.

---

36. Arendzen, "Ante-Nicene Interpretations," 232.

37. Arendzen, "Ante-Nicene Interpretations," 233.

38. Crouzel, *L'église*, 57–60: All the Christian writers of this period, however, were concerned with chastity and purity. Crouzel ultimately defends the position that the Christian authors of this age only prohibited remarriage after divorce, Athenagoras notwithstanding. Pospishil casually dismisses Athenagoras's testimony as "exaggerated" and "preposterous." See *Divorce and Remarriage*, 142.

39. Arendzen, "Ante-Nicene Interpretations," 233. Luck (*Divorce and Remarriage*, 228) tries to insert the notion of an "unjustified" divorce as being at issue, even if the evidence is not decisive. In other words, an innocent party would be free to remarry. The problem is that Athenagoras never introduces the concept of an innocent party. Luck must assume his conclusion in the face of an admitted absence of evidence.

40. Instone-Brewer, *Divorce and Remarriage*, 243.

CHAPTER 6

Theophilus of Antioch

Theophilus served as bishop of Antioch in Syria in 171–183 CE and died shortly thereafter (ca. 185). His 181 or 182 CE letter to Autolycus (*Ad Autolycum*) includes a section on chastity (3.13). The first half of the discussion warns against even thinking lustfully about another man's wife. Theophilus concludes the admonition with Matt 5:28: "Whosoever looketh on a woman who is not his own wife to lust after her, hath committed adultery with her already in his heart."[41] He adds that the object of the lust in this instance is a married woman. Theophilus shifts from Matt 5:28 to a quotation of Matt 5:32 (cf. Luke 16:18):

> "And he that marrieth," says [the gospel], "her that is divorced from her husband, committeth adultery; and whosoever putteth away his wife, saving for the cause of fornication, causeth her to commit adultery." Because Solomon says: "Can a man take fire in his bosom, and his clothes not be burned? Or can one walk upon hot coals, and his feet not be burned? So he that goeth in to a married woman shall not be innocent" [Prov 6:27–29].[42]

The warning from Proverbs against being burned explains why one may not marry a woman divorced from her husband. It would be like playing with fire. Theophilus's conclusion is in relation to the prohibition of marrying a divorced woman. He labels the divorced woman "a *married* woman." Even after the divorce, she remains married.

Theophilus *inverts* the order of Matt 5:32 // Luke 16:18, quoting the prohibition of marrying a divorced woman *first* (Matt 5:32b // Luke 16:18b) before admonishing against divorcing a spouse (Matt 5:32a // Luke 16:18a). Justin Martyr only cites the latter prohibition, Matt 5:32b // Luke 16:18b, omitting the first part of the verses. For both Justin Martyr and Theophilus, then, the prohibition against marrying a divorced woman is a matter of *emphasis*. "It looks as though Theophilus interprets Jesus' conditional saying about divorce (Matt 5:32a) in the light of the unconditional and absolute saying about marriage to a divorcée (Matt 5:32b/Luke 16:18b)."[43] Thus it is adultery to divorce one's wife, and it is adultery to marry

---

41. Translation of Theophilus from *ANF* 3.
42. See the discussion in Crouzel, *L'église*, 61.
43. Heth and Wenham, *Jesus and Divorce*, 31. Following Joseph Bonsirven (*Divorce*, 64–65), Heth and Wenham go further to contend that the original marriage may not be dissolved by divorce. Bonsirven emphasizes a perpetual conjugal bond in marriage, which is indissoluble. Jesus, however, urges human beings not to rend asunder what God has joined, which assumes that human beings can, in fact, dissolve the marital union.

As with his reading of Justin Martyr, Luck (*Divorce and Remarriage*, 227–28) concludes that

a divorced woman. Theophilus does not qualify whether this divorced woman is innocent or not. As in Matt 5:32, the prohibition appears absolute. Consequently, Theophilus does not quote Matt 19:9, which also pertains to the matter of divorce and remarriage. He does not offer any permission for the innocent husband to remarry.

Irenaeus

In his *Against Heresies* (4.15.2), Irenaeus attributes the permission for divorce to Moses's softening God's original law against divorce.[44] Elsewhere in the work, Irenaeus combats the (inconsistently) ascetic approach of the gnostic teachers Basilides and Saturninus, who labeled marriage and procreation "from Satan" (*Haer.* 1.24.2).[45] Irenaeus cites the Samaritan woman as an example of someone "who did not remain with one husband, but committed fornication by [contracting] many marriages" (*Haer.* 3.17.2; cf. John 4:17–18).[46] Irenaeus thus labels marriage to more than one partner fornication. A Christian remains limited to a single spouse.

Tertullian

Tertullian wrote at length over the years on divorce, marriage, and remarriage. During his later life, however, Tertullian joined the Montanist sect and adopted their more stringent ethical perspective. His attitude toward the Shepherd of Hermas serves as a bellwether: he approved of the Shepherd of Hermas early in his

---

Theophilus must have in mind a *connection* between the prohibition of a man's lusting and the prohibition of remarriage, thereby *limiting* the prohibition against remarriage to the man who had lusted after the woman prior to her divorce. This assumes a great deal that remains unstated in the Matthean text. The prohibition against lust in 5:27–30 appears to be a self-contained admonition parallel to murder and oath-taking as self-contained admonitions. Matthew 5:27–30 neither mentions marital status nor provides additional wording to limit lust to the married in 5:31–32. Luck appears to be "over-reading," a common complaint he has for those whom he critiques.

44. The line of approach here parallels Ptolemy's *Letter to Flora* (4) in which the gnostic teacher ascribes the proscription of divorce to the law of God but the permission for divorce to Moses (with Matt 19:1–9). Although human beings are not to put asunder what God has joined together, Ptolemy does not identify a position on remarriage; see Crouzel, *L'église*, 65–66.

45. Crouzel, *L'église*, 64–65.

46. Translation of Irenaeus from *ANF* 1.

career, but disapproved of it in his more rigorous, Montanist phase. One must therefore track his thinking at different points over time.

Elizabeth Clark maintains that Tertullian ultimately adopted a negative stance regarding even a first marriage. Clark's Tertullian is a prime representative of asceticism in early Christianity. Tertullian does defend marriage as God's ordinance against Marcion and other heretics of an extremely ascetic bent (*Marc.* 4.34; *Praescr.* 33; *Mon.* 15).[47] Marriage is necessary in order to avoid temptation and for the sake of procreation, but the avoidance of marriage would be better (1 Cor 7:8, 36).[48] Clark's view that Tertullian ultimately views marriage as a concession to human weakness has been challenged by other readers, especially since Tertullian appraises marriage positively in other places in his writings, and not just in response to heretics.[49]

Tertullian condemns remarriage already in his pre-Montanist years.[50] His *Of Patience* (*De patientia*), which may have been written as late at 202 CE, is likely his earliest reference to marriage. In 12.5 he compares the personified discipline of patience to:

> a disjunction of wedlock (for that cause, I mean, which makes it lawful, whether for husband or wife, to persist in the perpetual observance of widowhood), she waits for, she yearns for, she persuades by her entreaties, repentance in all who are one day to enter salvation.... The one she prevents from becoming an adulterer; the other she amends [*Alterum non adulterum facit, alterum emendat*].[51]

Those legitimately divorced because of a partner's infidelity (the cause that renders a disjunction of wedlock lawful) are to stay unmarried until the partner reconciles, even as a widow remains unmarried. The innocent partner is thereby

---

47. Elizabeth A. Clark, "Status Feminae: Tertullian and the Uses of Paul," in *Tertullian and Paul*, ed. Todd D. Still and David E. Wilhite, Pauline and Patristic Scholars in Debate 1 (New York: Bloomsbury, 2013), 140.

48. Clark, "Status Feminae," 140–43. See also Margaret Y. MacDonald, "A Response to Elizabeth A. Clark's Essay, 'Status Feminae: Tertullian and the Uses of Paul,'" in Still and Wilhite, *Tertullian and Paul*, 156–64.

49. For a helpful corrective and for Tertullian's positive comments about a single marriage "in the Lord," see Coleman Ford, "'Tantum in Domino': Tertullian's Interpretation of 1 Corinthians 7 in His *Ad Uxorem*," *TynBul* 69 (2018): 241–58.

50. Christine Trevett, *Montanism: Gender, Authority and the New Prophecy* (Cambridge: Cambridge University Press, 1996), 112–14.

51. Translation from *ANF* 3. Other manuscripts read *ex ea tamen causa qual licet seu viro seu feminae ad viduitatis perseverantiam susineri*, but the manuscript evidence is weak; see Crouzel, *L'église*, 95.

prevented from becoming an adulterer, even as the guilty party is to repent. In Tertullian's example, it is the wife waiting for her husband to be restored from sin, whereas Matthew has the husband causing the wife to become an adulteress. Tertullian does not explicitly address in this text whether remarriage is permissible, only that it is not when a partner sins and reconciliation remains possible. The comparison with the *widow*, however, strongly suggests that one is to remain unmarried after a divorce even in cases where the partner does not reconcile.[52]

The next reference to divorce and remarriage is in Tertullian's *To His Wife* (*Ad uxorem*) from his pre-Montanist phase, which was written sometime between 203 and 207 CE.[53] In *Ux.* 1.1 Tertullian writes: "I am even at this early period instilling into you the counsel of (perpetual) widowhood." He exhorts his wife not to marry again after his death. In 1.2 he offers as an example the marriage of Adam and Eve: Only one man is to be united to a single woman, despite the biblical patriarchs lawfully marrying multiple wives. Matters are to be different in the church. Marriage is a "lesser good," but the Scriptures nowhere support an abolishing of marriage (1.3): "In fact, in that it is written, 'To marry is better than to burn.'" Marriage is permitted, even if it is not the best option since the married are not able to serve the Lord wholeheartedly. Tertullian is not an extreme ascetic but tempered by the biblical witness. In 1.5 he writes: "For of our own salvation we are secure enough, so that we have leisure for children!" In *Ux.* 1.7 Tertullian explains to his wife that it is better to remain a widow than to marry again.[54] If the passions are a problem and require another marriage, then it is not a sin (following Paul in 1 Cor 7:27; cf. 1 Cor 7:8–9).[55] Paul in 1 Cor 7 commends virginity and widowhood as affording

---

52. Crouzel, *L'église*, 94–95. Instone-Brewer (*Divorce and Remarriage*, 245–46) overlooks this passage in his discussion.

53. Translation of *Ad uxorem* from *ANF* 4. Johannes Quasten dates *Ad uxorem* to the early third century, *De exhortatione castitatis* to a few years later, and *De monogamia* to the Montanist phase; see *The Ante-Nicene Literature after Irenaeus*, vol. 2 of *Patrology* (Westminster, MD: Christian Classics, 1950), 302, 305–6. Clark (*Reading Renunciation*, 268 n. 34) responds to this approach to dating the documents: "It could be argued that the dating of Tertullian's treatises as 'late' on the basis of their increased rigor is a dubious methodological procedure." The dating of Tertullian's various treatises must therefore be viewed as tentative.

54. David G. Hunter, in his comments on patristic interpretation of 1 Tim 3:2, 3:12, and Titus 1:6, misses how Tertullian embeds his discussion of church leaders and "second marriages" or "twice married" in an immediate context declaring the necessity of the death of a husband for a marriage to cease (*Ux.* 1.7). See "'A Man of One Wife': Patristic Interpretations of 1 Timothy 3:2, 3:12, and Titus 1:6 and the Making of Christian Priesthood," *Annali di Storia dell'Esegesi* 32.2 (2015): 338. Tertullian is not envisioning a second marriage as having taken place after divorce for *any* Christian and not just the clergy.

55. Crouzel, *L'église*, 95.

CHAPTER 6

opportunities for a closer dependence on God (*Ux.* 1.8). If one ultimately opts for marriage, "one rib" for Adam means "one woman" (1.2).[56]

The second book of *Ad uxorem* turns to the marriage of a Christian with a pagan. Tertullian again tackles what a wife is to do after the death of a spouse or a divorce, which is to remain continent (2.1), but Book 2 deals with marriage to pagans.[57] Divorce is not an option in these situations, except where there is fornication (*Ux.* 2.2). In *Ux.* 2.8 Tertullian commends at length the original marriage if that marriage had been "in the Lord." The *Christian* married couple pray in the Lord together and enjoy a union blessed by God and attended by angels.[58] Even better is to remain unmarried in the first place, and certainly one should not enter into a union with a nonbeliever.[59] Tertullian thus does not address remarriage more generally or with respect to the divorced.[60] However, when he does identify remarriage as permissible, again, it is in the context of a widow in the first book of *Ad uxorem* and not the divorced (following 1 Cor 7:39). As Carly Daniel-Hughes

---

56. Reynolds, *Marriage*, 189, does not account for Tertullian's "one rib" principle. Tertullian begins *Ux.* 2.1 by condemning those who have not only remarried but have done so with new partners who are not even believers! These are "fallen" marriages. They have acted contrary to the rules that govern those "in the Lord." As for marriages that are "in the Lord," Tertullian cites 1 Cor 7:8–9 that it is better to remain single, but that there is permission to marry. Pierre Nautin changes Tertullian's condemnation of divorcées remarrying to an acceptance of it by claiming that Tertullian views the unmarried in 1 Cor 7:8 as including the divorced; see "Divorce et remariage dans la tradition de l'église latine," *RSR* 62 (1974): 10–11. Whereas Tertullian's condemnation singles out those who were divorced before remarrying, his admonition on the basis of 1 Cor 7:8 never includes the divorced in Paul's permitted remarriage.

57. Tertullian complains in *Ux.* 2.1 that Christian women failed in their chance to remain continent after the death of, or divorce by, their pagan husbands. They rejected remaining celibate and, further, in their remarrying did not even marry Christians. Mackin contends: "Nowhere does he [Tertullian] scold those among these women because they have remarried after divorce." He concludes that the passage "apparently permitted remarriage after divorce." See Mackin, *Divorce and Remarriage*, 135. Mackin's logic is difficult to follow here, since Tertullian is clearly censuring these women for remarrying after the divorce or death of their spouses and, for that matter, not even seeking to marry believers. One cannot help but sense in these women's marrying of pagans after already having been married to pagans a further *criticism* of their behavior, not an approval of their actions. Mackin *reverses* Tertullian's logic! In fact, what immediately follows in *Ux.* 2.1 is a discussion of marrying "in the Lord" *in relation to widows* and not the divorced. Even Pospishil (*Divorce and Remarriage*, 143) recognizes, against the grain, that in *Ad uxorem* Tertullian is "disapproving of remarriage in general."

58. See Carly Daniel-Hughes, "'Only in the Lord'? Debates over Paul's View of Remarriage in Early Christianity," *ScEs* 66 (2014): 275–80 for Tertullian's argumentation against Christians choosing to enter afresh into mixed marriages in view of 1 Cor 7:12–16.

59. Crouzel, *L'église*, 95–97.

60. Heth and Wenham, *Jesus and Divorce*, 36.

explains, Tertullian is heavily dependent on 1 Cor 7 (and 1 Tim 3:2: one marriage only): "In this letter [*Ux.* 1], Tertullian walks a precarious balance between condoning marriage—for he admits that the apostle allows it and Christ preaches against divorce—and giving ground to his opponents who seek a second marriage after the death of their spouse."[61]

In his semi-Montanist period in 208–211 CE, Tertullian wrote *Against Marcion* (*Adversus Marcionem*). He reports that Marcion did not permit marriage at all, but Tertullian disagrees, quoting 1 Cor 7:10–11 that the wife is not to depart from the husband or else remain unmarried or be reconciled (*Marc.* 5.7). Although Christ "plainly forbids" divorce, should it nevertheless take place, one must hope for the marriage "to be resumed by reconciliation."[62] Tertullian does not allow here for any possibility of remarriage to someone else. Arendzen comments: "[Tertullian] does not discuss the question of the remarriage of the innocent party because, whatever happens, the parties are husband and wife. Asking whether the innocent party might remarry was to him whether the innocent party might have two wives or husbands."[63]

In *Marc.* 4.34 Tertullian writes at length against Marcion on the question of when divorce is legitimate and when it is not. Marcion had denied divorce in Christ's teaching altogether. Tertullian does not treat the topic of remarriage in this section except tangentially.[64] From the perspective of the man, Tertullian explains why it is adulterous to marry a woman wrongly divorced from her husband. The marital union remains "permanent" unless it has been "rightly dissolved." Tertullian does not express the obvious: that one is not to marry a woman *rightly* dissolved from her husband since that woman would *already* be an adulteress. What of the innocent husband in this situation? While commenting on Matt 5:32 and Luke 16:18, Tertullian *never says* that the innocent husband of an adulterous wife may subsequently marry another. He only allows for the innocent husband to divorce the adulterous wife. In fact, the section repeatedly proscribes divorce and yet permits it when the other spouse is adulterous. In equally repetitious manner, Tertullian refuses to say that a remarriage for the innocent is possible. The absence is conspicuous. One must not, then, *assume* that, for Tertullian, the inno-

---

61. Daniel-Hughes, "Only in the Lord," 275.
62. Translation from *ANF* 3.
63. Arendzen, "Ante-Nicene Interpretations," 233.
64. Mackin (*Divorce and Remarriage*, 136–37) cites *Marc.* 4.34 on when divorce may be permitted and when the marriage bond continues after a wrongful divorce. Mackin concludes that remarriage is permissible after a rightful divorce by the innocent husband even though Tertullian never actually claims that.

cent husband could marry someone else.[65] Tertullian censures Herod for marrying Herodias as a widow. Many interpreters have therefore concluded that Tertullian here is also forbidding remarriage.[66] If so, Tertullian's discussion here would agree with and be consistent with his comments against remarriage in his later works from his Montanist period. Even early in his writings, Tertullian grapples mightily with a permission to remarry in cases of the death of a spouse and never appeals to a permission to remarry after a valid divorce, a telling absence.[67]

In his *Exhortation to Chastity* (*De exhortatione castitatis*), which *could* have been composed as early as 206 CE but was more likely written during his Montanist years, Tertullian explicates "the law of once marrying" (*Exh. cast.* 5). In Genesis the two become one flesh. One rib from Adam means that there is to be only one wife and "one marriage, sanctioned for mankind" (*Exh. cast.* 5).[68] Lamech was the first to sin by polygamy. In *Exh. cast.* 9 Tertullian claims that "second marriage" is "no other than a species of fornication." Here Tertullian's attitude shifts from viewing the second marriage of a widow as a "lesser good" to seeing it as a lesser evil in view of Paul's dark description of a widow's "burning" in 1 Cor 7:9.[69] Sinful desire

---

65. Contra e.g., Pat Edwin Harrell, *Divorce and Remarriage in the Early Church: A History of Divorce and Remarriage in the Ante-Nicene Church* (Austin, TX: Sweet, 1967), 179, who makes Tertullian say what he does not: "The entire tenor of this passage is to suggest that divorce and remarriage are possible under proper conditions." So also Nautin ("Divorce et remariage," 11–14). Alex R. G. Deasley faults such an argument as one that "overlooks the ad hominem element in Tertullian's argument, not to mention his lawyer's style of stating a position in unqualified form first, addressing the qualifications later." See *Divorce and Remarriage in the Bible and the Church* (Kansas City, MO: Beacon Hill, 2000), 197. Tertullian thus goes on to stress how Christ returned to the Creator's original intent and prohibited divorce. Tertullian *repeatedly* qualifies the teaching against divorce to *allow* it in one particular situation, adultery.

66. Crouzel, *L'église*, 97–108; Bonsirven, *Divorce*, 66–67. Cf. Reynolds (*Marriage*, 189–90), who claims that Tertullian "seems to assume both that remarriage after divorce on the ground of fornication is not strictly forbidden and that it is contrary to the spirit of the Gospel." Later on 193–95 Reynolds struggles mightily to have Tertullian in this particular document—but not in his later work—allow for remarriage after a valid and permitted divorce, even though, as he himself admits, "Tertullian did not say that a man who divorced his wife on the ground of fornication could marry again." Tertullian in this passage repeatedly allows for a divorce and goes no further.

67. Anthony J. Bevilacqua, "The History of the Indissolubility of Marriage," *Proceedings of the Annual Convention of the Catholic Theological Society of America* 22 (1967): 256.

68. Translation of *Exhortation to Chastity* from *ANF* 4.

69. Andrew M. Bain, "Tertullian: Paul as Teacher of the Gentile Churches," in *Paul and the Second Century*, ed. Michael F. Bird and Joseph R. Dodson, LNTS 412 (London: T&T Clark, 2011), 221. Interpreters such as Nautin, not surprisingly, ignore "the law of once marrying" lest one be guilty of fornication in this passage. Tertullian here allows an exception to the prohibition against remarrying for the widow, but not for the divorced.

leads to these "second marriages." "Be thankful if God has once for all granted you indulgence to marry." A failure of continence is resolved by a first marriage and no more. Even the lack of children from a first marriage does not justify a second (*Exh. cast.* 12). Children are a burden that distracts from serving the Lord. As for Paul's comment in 1 Cor 7:28 that the one who (re)marries has not sinned, Tertullian minimizes that as Paul's *own* opinion rather than the Lord's through the Holy Spirit (*Exh. cast.* 4; see also *Mon.* 11). For those whose spouses have died, Tertullian takes Paul's teaching in 1 Cor 7:39 and Rom 7:2–3 as teaching *in the Spirit* that it is better to remain *unmarried* and simply belong to Christ (*Exh. cast.* 4; see also *Mon.* 13) again linking the discussion of remarriage only to those whose spouses have died.[70] If abstinence even for the married is advantageous in 1 Cor 7:5, how much more advantageous is it to avoid remarriage (*Exh. cast.* 10). As soldiers of Christ in 2 Tim 2:3–4, believers should avoid the worldly entanglements of marriage (*Exh. cast.* 12). In this advice Tertullian is following Paul's teaching in 1 Cor 7:39–40.[71] Tertullian grants that for Paul remarriage was lawful or licensed, but Tertullian makes a case that it should not be permitted of widows (*Exh. cast.* 8). Paul's appeal to the Spirit in 1 Cor 7:40, in the end, requires remaining single (*Exh. cast.* 4; 11). As for instances of divorce, *Exh. cast.* 16.17–18 states that there is to be "perseverance in widowhood, or else a reconciliation of peace." Whereas virginity is to be preferred over the married state, widowhood is *required* after divorce. Tertullian does not envision a second marriage as permissible for the divorcée. The possibility does not usually cross his mind.

Tertullian's work *On Monogamy* (*De monogamia*) from his Montanist period (217 CE) represents a perspective from within the movement. As Christine Trevett writes, "If the original New Prophecy had outlawed remarriage then it came as music to Tertullian's ears and probably bolstered a distaste for remarriage which he had harboured for some time."[72] Nevertheless, as Trevett concedes, "Is all this just Tertullianism or does it represent the teachings of the earliest Asia Minor New Prophecy on remarriage? We cannot be certain and Tertullian cited no oracle in support."[73] According to Tertullian, even unclean birds did not enter the

---

70. Characteristically, Hunter discusses remarriage without specifying whether it is in the context of the death of a spouse or divorce; "Man of One Wife," 338–39.

71. Contrary to Bain ("Tertullian," 221), Tertullian is *not* making a case "against the evidence" but rather for the option Paul himself deems more preferable.

72. Trevett, *Montanism*, 112.

73. Trevett, *Montanism*, 113. Trevett holds that it is more probable that the New Prophecy must have outlawed digamy. She concludes: "While not condoning the extremes of asceticism, and while allowing marriage, they were more closely aligned with those Christians in Asia who looked to celibacy as the superior option. Hence remarriage [of widows] would not be

CHAPTER 6

ark with two females (*Mon.* 4). Tertullian teaches against divorce since "from the beginning" the two become one flesh. Jesus set the pattern by taking only one spouse: the church (*Mon.* 5). A person "loosed" from a husband or wife may not marry someone else unless it is by death and not divorce. He adds later, "As to the *divorced*, he [the Lord] would grant no permission to marry" (*Mon.* 11).[74] The widow may be permitted a "second" marriage, but not the divorced. Tertullian's inconsistency about the *widow* remarrying appears elsewhere in *On Monogamy*: "Therefore, if those whom God has conjoined man shall not separate by divorce, it is equally congruous that those whom God has separated by death man is not to conjoin by marriage; the joining of the separation will be just as contrary to God's will, as would have been the separation of the conjunction. . . . God wills not a divorced woman to be joined to another man 'while her husband liveth,' as if He will do it 'when he is dead'" (*Mon.* 9). In the back-and-forth on the remarriage of widows, again, remarriage of the divorced is categorically rejected.

On Monogamy 9 may be a new development in denying remarriage even after a spouse's death.[75] What motivates this teaching is a shift in focus away from those Pauline texts allowing the widow to marry again to a stress on Jesus's teaching that in creation the one man is to be united to the one woman—and no more. Since the time is short for the world in its current form (1 Cor 7:29)—and how much more so in Tertullian's Montanist phase—the laity must assume the role of priests and remain satisfied with a single spouse (*Mon.* 11). Tertullian never permits the divorced to marry again and vacillates in *On Monogamy* on the permissibility of the "second marriage" of the widow. Although 1 Tim 3:2 and Titus 1:6 allow for more than one wife, Tertullian notes that in Rev 1:6 all Christians are "priests" (*Mon.* 12; cf. *Ux.* 1.7). That means, for Tertullian, the "husband of one wife" is married only once. He writes, "The New Prophecy (abrogates) second marriage, (which is) no less a divorce of the former (marriage)" (*Mon.* 14). Tertullian "considers remarriage to be forbidden and invalid in any circumstance."[76] This would apply to widows, but in *Mon.* 11 he interprets 1 Cor 7:39's apparent permission for the widow to remarry "in the Lord." He seizes on the qualification and interprets it as a *first* marriage "in the Lord" for those widows who had previously been married as unbelievers. Paul's tension between permitting remarriage for the widow and yet urging against it in 1 Cor 7:39 and Rom 7:2–3 leads to a similar tension in

---

condoned. Paul had felt much the same (1 Cor. 7:40) and what was his personal opinion had now metamorphosed. It was a ruling of the Paraclete" (114).

74. Translation of *De monogamia* from *ANF* 4.
75. Crouzel, *L'église*, 104–8.
76. Reynolds, *Marriage*, 190.

the ante-Nicene writings. Tertullian's vacillations with respect to Paul's apparent permission for widows to marry again leads him to allow second marriage in some instances but advise against it in others, ultimately denying it altogether.[77] Nowhere does Tertullian permit remarriage after divorce, even for an innocent party. In view of his struggles with respect to the second marriage of widows, one would expect even *more* discussion of the possibility of remarriage for the divorced, had Tertullian deemed it conceivable.

Clement of Alexandria

Clement of Alexandria traveled widely for the sake of his own education, eventually receiving instruction in 180 CE from a man named Pantaenus, the head of the Alexandrian Christian school.[78] Clement succeeded him and strove mightily in his lecturing and writing to win a hearing for the Christian faith among the Alexandrian educated. The second and third volumes of his *Stromateis* address marriage and may be dated to 199–201 CE. The gnostic Christian teachers of his day were divided between ascetic and licentious camps (*Strom.* 3.5.40). Clement inclined sympathetically toward the ascetics. He does grant that the apostles took their wives with them in their ministries, since Paul says as much in 1 Cor 9, with couples living with each other as brothers and sisters. The wives would preach in the women's quarters (3.6.53).[79] Marriage is best, he maintains, when it is without sexual relations. Whereas the pagan ascetic still feels desire but does not give in to it, thanks to God's grace the Christian is not to feel desire at all (3.7.57–58).[80]

Despite Clement's advocacy of "spiritual" marriages, he opposed the ascetic gnostic teachers of his day. Since Clement's sympathies were with asceticism, his comments on this matter are "against the grain" and likely reflect mainstream early Christian thought. In *Strom.* 3.12.89 Clement condemns those who call marriage fornication as guilty themselves of blasphemy. Marriage is necessary for the sake of having children (3.7.58). Even the married state is to be received as a gift of God, and not just the unmarried state (3.12.79). In *Strom.* 3.6.45, 49 those who entirely reject marriage and the procreation of children manifest the spirit of

---

77. Clark, "Status Feminae," 147–49.

78. John Ernest Leonard Oulton and Henry Chadwick, *Alexandrian Christianity: Selected Translations of Clement and Origen with Introductions and Notes*, LCC 2 (Philadelphia: Westminster, 1954), 16. Unless otherwise noted, all translations of Clement of Alexandria in this chapter are from Oulton and Chadwick.

79. Cf. *Did. apost.* 16 for deaconesses ministering to women.

80. Oulton and Chadwick, *Alexandrian Christianity*, 34.

CHAPTER 6

the antichrist. Clement here recognizes the seed of Christian sexual relations as holy (3.6.46).[81] In *Strom.* 3.12.81 Clement claims wise married couples will know when it is time to be continent and when to have sexual relations for the sake of children. Against false teachers who reject marriage, Clement cites Paul's positive comments about the institution in 1 Cor 7 (3.6.51). Here Clement notes that several of the apostles were therefore married (3.6.52–53). The Apostle Paul had also been married, like the other apostles, but did not take his wife with him in his travels since it would have been an inconvenience (3.6.53). Clement views this position as threading the proper line between the two Gnostic ethical extremes (3.5.40). Earlier in the *Stromateis* after reviewing ancient Greek thought on marriage, Clement offers his own opinion: humans are to practice intercourse not as animals do (2.23). To be subjected to extreme passion is slavery. Marriage is for the procreation of children. Some people may not need to marry and will be able to serve the Lord more fully, but others will not possess that same ability.[82] Only *some* Christians are capable of abstinence (3.1.4).

In *Strom.* 2.23 Clement states that marriage must be kept pure. On the basis of Matt 5:32 and 19:9, Clement advises that the husband is not to divorce his wife except for fornication, "and it [the law] regards as fornication, the marriage of those separated while the other is alive."[83] With these words, Clement renders explicit that the Matthean texts implicitly teach that a spouse must first die before a remarriage is possible. He makes no allowance for innocent partners of a divorce to remarry.[84] Second unions while an original partner remains alive are simply fornication. The one who marries a divorced person commits adultery.[85] Clement then observes how the law had commanded that the adulteress be put to death, whether by flames (for cases within priestly families) or by stoning. The law thus agrees with the gospel, says Clement. The harlot must repent of the fornication

---

81. Crouzel, *L'église*, 72–73.

82. Willy Rordorf is representative of those who dismiss Clement of Alexandria's comments on marriage and remarriage since he was inclined toward asceticism and thus preferred celibacy to marriage; see "Marriage in the Early New Testament and in the Early Church," *JEH* 20 (1969): 203 n. 1. Rordorf would have done well to reread Paul's preference for the celibate lifestyle in 1 Cor 7. Such a lifestyle allows believers to serve the Lord more single-mindedly. Clement is merely echoing Paul's original comments.

83. Translation here from *ANF* 4.

84. Crouzel, *L'église*, 72.

85. Contra Harrell, *Divorce and Remarriage*, 177, Clement does not offer any indication that this is only for those who have divorced their wives for causes *other* than adultery (i.e., *illegal* divorces) and that the innocent husband could remarry. The blanket censuring of remarriage in the ante-Nicene writers never admits exceptions for innocent parties. That must be read *into* these authors.

and enjoy the "regeneration of repentance." Clement's third book of *Stromateis* returns to the matter of divorce and remarriage. In *Strom.* 3.6.47 a husband is not to render a wife an adulteress through divorce, except in instances where the wife is already guilty of fornication. In 3.12.80 Clement quotes both Rom 7:2 and 1 Cor 7:39–40, stating that the death of the husband allows the woman the freedom to marry again.

David Instone-Brewer, strangely, limits his discussion of Clement of Alexandria to *Strom.* 2.23, concluding: "One may assume that he [Clement] would have been against all remarriage, but this is not stated."[86] Instone-Brewer appears unaware of Clement's advocacy of the "single marriage" against gnostic asceticism in *Strom.* 3.12.89: "As idolatry is an abandonment of the one God to embrace many gods, so fornication is apostasy from single marriage to several."[87] Clement promotes the "single marriage" since "several" (i.e., remarriage) is immoral fornication. The presbyter, deacon, or layman is to be the husband of *one* wife according to the Apostle Paul (1 Tim 3:2, 12; Titus 1:6) (3.12.90). Even as Scripture constrained Clement to defend marriage, he draws on Scripture as his rationale for a man to enjoy only one wife in a "single marriage." Clement offers no exception to his teaching and no provision for remarriage while the former spouse lives.[88]

Clement comments on the eunuch saying in Matt 19:11–12 and explains that this is in direct relation to Jesus's teaching on divorce (*Strom.* 3.6.50): "What the questioners wanted to know was whether, when a man's wife has been condemned for fornication, it is allowable for him to marry another. It is said, however, that several athletes abstained from sexual intercourse, exercising continence to keep their bodies in training, as Astylos of Croton and Crison of Himera. Even the cithara-player, Amoebeus, though newly married, kept away from his bride. And Aristotle of Cyrene was the only man to disdain the love of Lais when she fell for him." Clement here draws on Matt 19:11–12 to explain that the man whose wife was divorced for adultery must abstain from sexual relations. Clement's Jesus offers no provision for the innocent husband to remarry.[89] "For Clement celibacy

---

86. Instone-Brewer, *Divorce and Remarriage*, 244.

87. Cf. the "single marriage" of *Strom.* 2.12. See also Clark, *Reading Renunciation*, 326, who claims Clement cites these verses to oppose remarriage.

88. Crouzel, *L'église*, 72.

89. Crouzel, *L'église*, 73; Heth and Wenham, *Jesus and Divorce*, 33. God will provide the divorced what they need to remain celibate. Early Christian authors appropriated Jesus's eunuch comments with ambivalence because of their opposition to paganism and cultic eunuchs; see Mathew Kuefler, *The Manly Eunuch: Masculinity, Gender Ambiguity, and Christian Ideology in Late Antiquity*, Chicago Series on Sexuality, History, and Society (Chicago: University of Chicago Press, 2001), 245–82, 378–90.

is, according to Christ in Matt 19:3–12, the condition of the husband who has had to leave his adulterous wife."[90]

One passage in Clement's *Stromateis* may, at first, seem at odds with his prohibition of remarriage. After recognizing that not all people are capable of sexual abstinence, Clement writes: "We admire monogamy and the high standing of single marriage, holding that we ought to share suffering with another and 'bear one another's burdens,' lest anyone who thinks he stands securely should himself fall. It is of second marriage that the apostle says, If you burn, marry" (3.1.4). When this passage is placed alongside the passages later in *Strom.* 3 that condemn the second marriage as adultery, it becomes clear, as Crouzel explains, that the "second marriage" is for those whose spouses have died.[91] Later Clement returns to the admonition to marry if one burns in 1 Cor 7:9 and explains that "second marriage" in these cases is not sin, adding: "But he gains heavenly glory for himself if he remains as he is, and keeps undefiled the marriage yoke broken by death" (3.12.82). Clement interprets 1 Cor 7:9 as applicable to widows and widowers for whom the marriage yoke had been "broken by death."[92] Clement would prefer widows and widowers remain single, but if they lack self-control—with 1 Cor 7:8–9, 32–35, 39–40 (which Clement cites)—they may marry again. Clement of Alexandria therefore helpfully defines "second marriage" in the ante-Nicene context as the marriage of widows and widowers.[93] Apart from the remarriage of widows or widowers, to depart from a single marriage to several is to engage in wicked fornication.

Origen

Eusebius, the third-century church historian, describes Origen as a colorful figure. He writes that the young Origen, already a teacher in the church of Alexandria, was hoping to study divine things with women as well as men without scandal

---

90. Henri Crouzel, "Remarriage after Divorce in the Primitive Church: A Propos of a Recent Book," *ITQ* 38 (1971): 29. Heth ("Unmarried," 82–87) surveys each of Clement's Matt 19:12 references and concludes that Jesus is also applying it to those "made eunuchs" by others through divorce. They are enabled by God, like a eunuch, to forgo remarriage.

91. Crouzel, *L'église*, 74.

92. Crouzel, *L'église*, 74.

93. R. Alan Culpepper claims Clement of Alexandria (*Strom.* 3.1) as a witness to the early church permitting second marriages, but Culpepper does not seem aware of the fact that this was only for widowers and widows; see *Matthew: A Commentary*, NTL (Louisville: Westminster John Knox, 2021), 359. His claim is therefore misleading and erroneous.

(*Hist. eccl.* 6.8.1–2). For the sake of those labors, he took literally Jesus's instructions on those who have made themselves eunuchs for the sake of the kingdom of heaven (Matt 19:12).[94]

Origen writes at length on divorce and remarriage in his commentary on Matthew.[95] He begins his discussion by emphasizing the necessity of divorcing a wife guilty of adultery (*Comm. Matt.* 13.25). He quotes Matt 5:29–30 that, when it comes to lust, it is better to lose a body part than one's soul, adding: "And so also one is saved with one eye, who has cut out the eye of his own house, his wife, if she commit fornication, lest having two eyes he may go away into the hell of fire . . . let us not spare them."[96]

In his *Commentary on Matthew* (14.16), Origen exposits Matt 19:1–9. He begins with the Pharisees' question in v. 3 whether a divorce may occur for any reason. Jesus rejects their position, emphasizing that God joined the two together into one flesh that is not to be separated: "And because God joins together, there is a gift in the relationship between those joined together by God. Paul understood this to be equal to the gift of the pure unmarried state, and speaks of marriage according to the word of God as a gift when he says, 'I wish all people were as myself.'"[97] The marital union is thus a gift of God's grace just as much as Paul's own celibacy in 1 Cor 7:7. Origen concludes *Comm. Matt.* 14.16 by recognizing that humans may indeed break apart what God has joined together.

In *Comm. Matt.* 14.17 Origen expands on humans wrongfully severing what God has joined together. A husband may not divorce his wife unless she has committed adultery and thereby cut herself off from him. The Lord left the Father to join with his own wife, the church (Origen cites Phil 2:6 and John 1:14). Adultery is therefore the only ground for divorce.[98] Origen does not say at this point whether a new

---

94. Crouzel, *L'église*, 81.

95. Several translations are available, including the longstanding one by John Patrick in the *ANF*. More recent is the translation of the Greek manuscript of Origen's commentary (the thirteenth-century Codex Monacensis 191) in the first volume of Ronald E. Heine, *The Commentary of Origen on the Gospel of St Matthew*, 2 vols., Oxford Early Christian Texts (Oxford: Oxford University Press, 2018). The second volume of Heine's work translates the Latin manuscript of the work (the *Vetus Interpretatio*). See also the translation of selections by Judith L. Kovacs, with some modifications, in *1 Corinthians: Interpreted by Early Christian Commentators*, ed. Robert L. Wilken, The Church's Bible Series (Grand Rapids: Eerdmans, 2005), 107–9.

96. Crouzel, *L'église*, 74–75. Translation of Origen here from *ANF* 9.

97. Translation from Heine, *Commentary*. Unless otherwise noted, all translation of Origen's *Commentary on Matthew* are from Heine.

98. Crouzel, *L'église*, 78.

marriage is possible for the innocent partner of divorce (cf. 14.19).[99] Origen never grants that a second marriage is possible whenever he invokes the Matthean exception clause.[100] That absence is conspicuous.

Next, Origen compares Christ's relationship to the synagogue with a marriage to a wife who has been adulterous (14.17). In fact, she plotted against her husband and killed him.[101] Since Christ's new spouse is the church, Origen appears to be justifying remarriage for the innocent party of a divorce (despite the killing of the innocent husband). Luck describes this as "a clear case of disciplinary divorce followed by remarriage" in a section not taken "seriously" by those who deny remarriage in Origen.[102] Origen continues this topic in 14.18–20.[103] Here Origen contrasts what Paul had said with what Moses had said as Origen strives to "investigate [the law's] spiritual meaning":

> The person who wants to interpret these things figuratively will compare Paul's confident assertion based on the divine grace he had, that 'a wife is bound for as long as her husband lives, but if the husband die, she is free to be married to whom she wishes, but only in the Lord. She is more blessed, however, if she remains as she is, in my opinion, and I think that I too have the Spirit of God'. . . . In the same way, Moses too, because he had been granted the authority to give laws permitting certain things, including the divorcing of wives because of the hardness of heart of the people, could have thought that the legislation came from the Spirit of God even in the case of the laws based on his own opinion. (*Comm. Matt.* 14.18)

One must therefore investigate Moses's spiritual meaning. In *Comm. Matt.* 14.19 Origen states that the mother of the (Jewish) people removed herself from Christ without a bill of divorce. Christ later wrote that bill of divorce when a shameful deed was discovered in her withdrawal: "Therefore, he gave up all claim to her and married another, if I may speak this way, after he gave the bill of divorce 'into the hands' of his former wife." This bill of divorce became clear in Jerusalem's destruction. Origen continues: "Now Christ can have taken the synagogue as wife and lived with her in marriage first but later not have been pleased by her. The ground

---

99. Contra Luck, *Divorce and Remarriage*, 295, who simply assumes that remarriage of the innocent party will take place.
100. Crouzel, *L'église*, 82.
101. Heine, *Commentary*, 1:179.
102. Luck, *Divorce and Remarriage*, 295.
103. *Comm. Matt.* 14.20 is missing in the *Vetus Interpretatio* Latin text. 14.18–20 are present in their entirety in the Greek text.

of her not pleasing him was that a shameful deed was found in her." She preferred Barabbas and had Jesus crucified. Consequently, he wrote a bill of divorce for her and sent her away from his house. The former wife departed and became the wife of another man, Barabbas.

Origen explains in 14.20 that the divorced wife cannot go back to her former husband. He recognizes that this "will seem inconsistent with the saying" that all Israel will be saved (Rom 11:25–26). The divorce thus appears to be *temporary* and *remedial*, with the divorced wife taken back, "a characteristic Origenist understanding of divine chastisement. God's 'divorce' of the Israelites . . . cannot be taken as a sanction for human divorce."[104] In other words, Origen himself recognizes that the spiritual meaning cannot be pressed too literally. Origen describes in 14.21 the adulterous wife kicked out by her original spouse for marrying a second husband, getting kicked out from his house for "a shameful deed," and yet she is not to return to the former husband since she has been defiled. The line of reasoning echoes Deut 24:1–4, thereby demonstrating that Origen is still thinking in terms of the law.

To return to 14.18, Origen explains that Paul went beyond the literal meaning of the Law to interpret it spiritually (or figuratively) in Christ. Here Origen quotes 1 Cor 7:39–40 on how the wife is bound to her husband as long as he lives. After he dies, she does better to remain single but may remarry. In other words, the spiritual interpretation takes the bond as lifelong, but what of Christ's marriage to the church after his original marriage to the synagogue? Henri Crouzel cautions that one cannot press the details of allegorical exegesis too far.[105] Origen is tackling the subject of the synagogue on *its own terms* as the Pharisees confront Jesus with the grounds for divorce (and remarriage). Origen's exegesis may even at this point be ad hominem in view of the freedom among the Jews to divorce and remarry. How ironic, then, that God effectively did the same to Israel. The question, Crouzel insists, is whether divorce and remarriage are possible *now* in the era of the church. Again, one cannot press the allegorical exegesis in *Comm. Matt.* 14.17–20 too hard or there are contradictions.[106] As Crouzel points out, Origen speaks of Christ's love for the church as having existed before creation and thus as preexistent even though it is also after the marriage to the synagogue.[107] Christ's union with the *church* is therefore inseparable and would *predate* the union with the synagogue.[108] Instone-Brewer comments: "When Christ marries the Church,

---

104. Clark, *Reading Renunciation*, 238.
105. Crouzel, *L'église*, 78.
106. Crouzel, *L'église*, 81.
107. Crouzel, *L'église*, 79,
108. Crouzel, *L'église*, 80; Crouzel ("Remarriage after Divorce," 35) stresses caution before applying literally the allegorical genre. To take the passage literally ends up in terrible contra-

CHAPTER 6

this would presumably be a remarriage after a divorce. However, Origen did not conclude that humans can remarry because he regarded Christ as being above the Law."[109] Origen also was not content to leave matters with the analogy with Christ's marriage to the synagogue and continues the topic in a nonfigurative fashion. Origen will also leave the realm of the law behind. In the ensuing comments, Origen's condemnation of remarriage is clear.

In *Comm. Matt.* 14.22 Origen quotes 1 Tim 3:2 that the bishop is the husband of one wife. Origen concludes: "Paul wants no one in the church who has accepted any authority over the masses, such as in the sacramental rites, to have been married a second time." Church leaders are allowed only one marriage.[110] Origen then quotes at length from the section on widows in 1 Tim 5. In 1 Tim 5:9–10 no widow is to enjoy the church's support unless she is at least sixty years old and has been married only once. She is to be a virtuous woman in how she cared for children and raised them. As for the younger widows, they are to marry again (1 Tim 5:14). Origen marvels from these restrictions that the bishop or the supported widow has been married only once:

> We raise the question at this point of why Paul does not permit twice-married people to be appointed to ecclesiastical offices, since we perceive it to be possible that some who have been married twice are much better than those married only once. Such an issue seems to me worth investigating. It is possible that someone who failed in two marriages was still a young man when he divorced the second wife and that he passed the rest of his life into his elderly years in a chaste and pure manner.

Paul restricts church office to a person married only once even though there are people who have divorced two times, only to live subsequently in a chaste and pure manner.

In 14.23 Origen ascribes the second marriage to hardened hearts.[111] He quotes Jesus's words that Moses allowed divorce for hardened hearts and juxtaposes

---

dictions since Christ is married to the church since creation, and to be married also to the synagogue would be bigamy (36). Christ remains faithful to his original bride. Even the synagogue, according to Rom 11:25–26, will be restored to Christ.

109. Instone-Brewer, *Divorce and Remarriage*, 247. Pospishil (*Divorce and Remarriage*, 145) is also among those who seize on Christ's synagogue divorce and remarriage: "From this comparison it is apparent that Origen regarded divorce and remarriage as permissible."

110. Crouzel, *L'église*, 81.

111. Crouzel, *L'église*, 82.

those words with Rom 7:2–3 that the woman is bound to her husband as long as he lives and is only free from him after his death. Origen concludes:

> Now already some leaders of the church have permitted things beyond what has been written so that a woman is married 'while her husband is living', acting contrary to the written word which says, 'A wife has been bound for as long as her husband lives', and the further word, 'Therefore, the woman who marries another man while her husband is living will be called an adulteress'. The latter is not at all unreasonable for it is likely that this accommodation was permitted in contrast to worse things contrary to laws which had been ordained and recorded from the beginning.[112]

Origen here recognizes that there were in his day some church officials who were permitting spouses to remarry.[113] As Joyce writes, Origen's "words do not suggest that the laxity of practice was common: they are more easily understood of a few exceptional instances which had aroused comment among the faithful."[114] Origen emphasizes *three times* that what they were doing in their official acts was contrary to the Scriptures, and that biblical teaching takes precedence.[115] He cites Rom 7:3 and 1 Cor 7:39 as clear teaching, especially when combined with Gen 2:24, Matt 19:5, and Mark 10:7–8. As long as the former husband still lives, any new marriage by the former wife would be adulterous.

---

112. The Latin translation (Heine, *Commentary*, 2:440) reads:

For I know that some who preside over churches have gone beyond Scripture and permitted a woman to take a husband while her previous one is living—and some have acted contrary to the Scripture (which says, "A wife has been bound as long as her husband lives," likewise: "While her husband is living she will be called an adulteress if she is with another man"); they have not, however, permitted this without any reason at all. Perhaps they permitted it because of this kind of weakness in incontinent people in comparison to things which are evil, as opposed to those things which were written "from the beginning": "But I say to you that whoever shall divorce his wife, except because of fornication, and marry another commits adultery, and he who marries a divorced woman commits adultery."

113. Victor J. Pospishil even prioritizes this text as preferable to other ante-Nicene statements on the subject, since Origen offers a glimpse into actual practice whereas the surviving statements are, effectively, ivory-tower pronouncements; see "Divorce and Remarriage in the Early Church," *ITQ* 38.4 (1971): 344.

114. George Hayward Joyce, *Christian Marriage: An Historical and Doctrinal Study*, 2nd ed., Heythrop Series 1 (London: Sheed and Ward, 1948), 309.

115. Crouzel, *L'église*, 83. Crouzel, "Remarriage after Divorce," 36: "As those who have any acquaintance with him will know, no condemnation could be stronger or more explicit in Origen, for whom Scripture is the supreme norm."

CHAPTER 6

After criticizing those of his peers who were officiating over marriages after divorce, Origen offers an extensive discussion of the topic in 14.24, this time opposing a Jewish man who would allow for remarriage.[116] The Jewish man might reason that since Jesus provided for divorce in instances of a wife's adultery, then *any* unseemly thing in a woman could be reckoned as adulterous and justify divorcing the wife. Origen responds that the Old Testament penalty for a wife's adultery was that she should be stoned. The severity of the punishment proves that the sin was no ordinary "shameful deed/thing" by which she had lost her husband's favor. Origen reminds his readers that Jesus allowed divorce only for adultery and not for other reasons, even if utterly heinous: "For to put up with such great sins, which are likely worse than adultery and sexual immorality, will appear to be irrational. But on the other hand, everyone would agree that it is impious to act contrary to the intention of the Saviour's teaching."[117] Origen stresses that one must follow the Scripture's literal teaching.

Origen at that point offers one of his most pointed discussions of remarriage, and the passage is best cited at length (here from the Greek text):

> For there is no question that *the husband who divorces a wife who is not committing sexual immorality makes her commit adultery* so far as lies in his power to do so. For if it is true that a woman 'will be called an adulteress if she marries another man while her husband is living' and *the husband, by divorcing his wife, gives her the occasion for a second marriage, he obviously, by this action, makes her commit adultery.*...
>
> Furthermore, *the husband who abstains from his wife often makes her commit adultery because he does not fulfil her desires*, even if he does it under the illusion of practicing greater holiness and self-control. And perhaps the husband who, so far as lies in his power, makes his wife commit adultery because he does not fulfil her desires is more deserving of blame than the one who divorces his wife on grounds other than sexual immorality, *such as witchcraft or murder or any of the most serious sins*. And just as *a woman is an adulteress even though she appears to be married to another man while her former husband is still living, so too a man, although he appears to marry a woman who has been divorced, does not so much marry as commits adultery with her according to the words of our Saviour* [key comments italicized].[118]

---

116. Crouzel, *L'église*, 85–86, who also cites it in its entirety.

117. The Latin text reads: "For to put up with such sins of a woman which are worse than acts of adultery and fornication will seem to be irrational; in the same way, everyone will admit it is impious to act contrary to the intention of the Saviour's teaching" (Heine, *Commentary*, 2:441).

118. The Latin text (Heine, *Commentary*, 2:441–42) follows the Greek very closely.

The Witness of the Early Church

This section is a stumbling block to those who claim that Origen permits a second marriage after divorce, even for the innocent party of a divorce due to adultery.[119] Origen never grants that an innocent partner may subsequently remarry. The last sentence in the section asserts that while the former spouse lives, a subsequent marriage is adulterous. All Origen allows, then—with Christ's teaching—is for a divorce to take place after adultery.[120] Origen hews closely to the Matthean text in never speaking of an innocent spouse's marrying again.[121] Also, reflecting the influence of 1 Cor 7:3–4 and opposing the extreme ascetic approaches of his day, husband and wife enjoy equal conjugal rights. If the husband does not satisfy the wife's desires, he is more culpable than a man who puts his wife away for some reason other than fornication (e.g., poisoning or murder).

In 14.25 Origen takes stock of all the possible risks and difficulties that can take place in a marriage in view of its permanency. Origen imagines potentially great hardships for a husband. Celibacy may be the easier path. Origen quotes the disciples in Matt 19:10 on it being better not to marry, but Origen stresses that Christ explained in that passage that the ability must be "given" them: "Let the person who wants it ask, trusting and believing in the one who says, 'Ask and it will be given to you', and he will receive if he has no doubt regarding the saying, 'Everyone who asks receives.'"

In commenting on Matt 19:12 in *Comm. Matt.* 15.1, Origen distinguishes three types of eunuchs: those born that way who are naturally impotent; those made that way by others (e.g., those influenced by worldly philosophers); and those who have made themselves eunuchs. The latter are praiseworthy: "This happens when, for the sake of the kingdom of heaven, they have cut off the desire for physical things by means of the very sharp Word." In 15.4 Origen heaps further praise on those who have made themselves eunuchs for the sake of the kingdom. He nevertheless warns, even in the face of that praise: "Others, however, impelled by human words practise abstinence from sexual pleasures and all intemperance connected with the topic. It was truly not the word of God which produced in them such purpose, discipline and, if I may call it this, achievement, but human words, either from Greek philosophers or heretics 'who forbid marriage and com-

---

119. E.g., Bonsirven, *Divorce*, 72.

120. Crouzel, *L'église*, 83. He explains later that Origen is commenting on the grounds for divorce since Origen viewed the prohibition of remarriage while a spouse lived as a *settled matter* going back to the Shepherd of Hermas and his predecessor, Clement of Alexandria (87).

121. Crouzel, *L'église*, 88. Even as Matt 5:32 never speaks of an innocent spouse's marrying again, Origen does not either, and the wife—whether innocent or guilty of sexual sin—is denied that by both Matthew and Origen. Even as Matthew did not address a wife divorcing an adulterous husband, neither does Origen because he is adhering in his comments to the Matthean text that he is expositing.

mand abstinence from foods.'" Origen censures those who are eunuchs for an ungodly, human reason, including those who would "forbid marriage." The heretics' prohibition of marriage is thus not from God. Origen vehemently opposes those whose asceticism goes beyond the bounds of Scripture as he strikes the same balance as in Matt 19:9–12.

Bevilacqua comments in conclusion: "Origen does not indicate if the husband who dismisses his wife for adultery can remarry. . . . No positive argument, however, can be drawn from this silence."[122] At the same time, Origen does not authorize it. He never offers permission for an innocent husband to remarry after divorcing an adulterous wife despite ample opportunities to do so.[123] Instead, throughout his discussion, Origen repeatedly cites Rom 7:3 and 1 Cor 7:39–40 that remarriage is adulterous unless the spouse is deceased. He asserts that to marry a divorced woman is adulterous without any comment on whether she is innocent. Origen permits divorce for adultery, but that is as far as he goes. As Instone-Brewer comments: "Origen remained committed to the teaching that divorce was only on the ground of adultery and remarriage was not permitted before the death of a spouse."[124] Curiously, Instone-Brewer once again does not reconcile these comments with his own position that a divorce in the ancient world would have entailed a corresponding and assumed freedom to remarry. Origen, for his own part, is constrained by his explication of the Scriptures, even if it is countercultural.

Pseudo-Clementine Homilies

The early third-century Pseudo-Clementine Homilies (3.54) preserves a fictional conversation between Peter and the magician Simon (cf. Acts 8) in which Peter juxtaposes the woman with seven husbands whom the Sadducees presented to Jesus (Matt 22:22–33) with Jesus's own recognition that Moses had conceded di-

---

122. Bevilacqua, "Indissolubility," 273.

123. For example, note Origen's Fragments on 1 Corinthians §§28, 33–36; see Crouzel, *L'église*, 92–93. Original text available in Claude Jenkins, "Documents: Origen on I Corinthians. II," *JTS* 9.35 (1908): 353–72; Jenkins, "Documents: Origen on I Corinthians. III," *JTS* 9.36 (1908): 500–14. For instance, Origen interprets 1 Cor 7:8–9 as applying to widows and widowers, but these remarried couples cannot say "bone of my bones," since theirs was not the original marriage. See Fragments on 1 Corinthians §35 (Jenkins, "Documents III," 503–4). So also Methodius of Olympus, who apparently concludes that Paul himself was a widower (*Symp.* 3.12). Origen says *nothing* about how "bone of my bones" might apply to those married after divorce—he does not even consider it as a possibility worthy of discussion.

124. Instone-Brewer, *Divorce and Remarriage*, 248–49.

vorce because of hardened hearts (Matt 19:8).[125] Jesus appeals to creation over against the Mosaic permission for divorce. One man is to be joined to one woman in marriage. By juxtaposing the two passages, this section of the Homilies interprets Jesus's comments on the basis of creation as censuring the remarriages of the woman with seven husbands.[126]

Novatian

Novation represents an early to mid-third-century CE witness. He died around 257 CE. In his *On the Discipline and Advantage of Chastity* (*De bono pudicitia*), he says that "a separation without return should not afford any occasion to a stranger" as the two have been made one (5).[127] He adds in his next section that there should be no separation, and adultery is the sole cause for divorce (6). Novatian does not offer any permission for remarriage for either of the divorced parties.[128] As will be clear from the Council of Nicaea, Novatian's followers denied remarriage. "Not affording any occasion to a stranger" therefore censures remarriage in the wake of divorce.

Minucius Felix

Minucius Felix died around 250 CE in Rome. He authored one of the earliest Latin defenses of the Christian faith. In his *Octavius* he writes: "It is our pleasure to abide by the bond of a single marriage; in our desires for begetting children, we know one woman or none at all. . . . Very many of us preserve (rather than take pride in) the perpetual virginity of our undefiled bodies; and indeed, desires of incest are so far removed from our minds that even modest intercourse causes not a few of us to blush" (31.5).[129] His affirmation of "a single marriage" and to "know one woman or none at all" should not be taken as opposing polygamy since Rome did not permit multiple wives at the same time. Minucius Felix is celebrating the early Christian practice of a single marriage, if not perpetual virginity.

---

125. English text is in *ANF* 8. For the Greek text, see Bernhard Rehm, *Die Pseudoklementinen I: Homilien*, 3rd ed., GCS (Berlin: Akademie Verlag, 1992), 76.
126. Crouzel, *L'église*, 67–68.
127. The document was wrongly attributed to Cyprian. Translation from *ANF* 5.
128. Crouzel, *L'église*, 110.
129. Translated by G. W. Clarke, *The Octavius of Marcus Minucius Felix*, ACW 39 (New York: Newman, 1974). Crouzel comments on some difficult phrases in the passage in *L'église*, 110–11.

CHAPTER 6

Minucius Felix is a further witness with Tertullian to the older Republican ideal of the *univira* having made its way into early Christianity: Married people, especially wives, would choose to remain single after the death of a spouse.[130] Early Christians in their inscriptions praise the *univira*. One such inscription reads: *mihi uno marito*, "I have one husband" (*ILCV* 4318 A.5). Another inscription, possibly from Carthage, celebrates a *protogamia* (*ILCV* 1003). Even non-Christians in this era would occasionally express disapproval of second marriages.[131] The influence of the older Roman ideals on early Christianity would explain the hesitancy in permitting widows to remarry in the second century (e.g., Herm. Mand. 4.1, 4; Clement of Alexandria, *Strom.* 3.1.4, 3.12.82).

The *Didascalia Apostolorum*

The *Didascalia Apostolorum* is a third-century Christian document describing church customs and practices. *Didascalia Apostolorum* 14 discusses the situation of those who hold the church office of widow.[132] Such widows are not to be less than fifty years old and no longer likely to have "a second husband." A younger woman would bring shame on the office of widowhood if she became a wife to another man. She would, in that case, have had "two husbands" when she had "promised to be a widow unto God."[133] For a younger widow to become the wife of *more* than a second man "is to be accounted a harlot." A "second husband" is therefore granted to the younger widow. The document nowhere allows a second husband to the divorced woman.

This chapter of the *Didascalia* is not entirely focused on widows. At one point it addresses the younger woman "who has been for a short time with her husband and her husband dies, or for some other cause there be a separation, and she remains by herself alone, being in honor of widowhood—she shall be blessed by God. For she resembles the widow of Sarepta of Sidon. . . . Or again, she shall be like Annah, who praised the coming of Christ." The chapter here envisions a woman divorced from her husband. Like the widow, she "remains by herself alone." The provision for a second marriage granted to the younger widow is conspicuously not extended to the divorcée. Younger women separated from

---

130. See the discussion of the *univira* in chapter 1, pp. 33–43.
131. E.g., Plutarch, *Queaset. Rom.* 105 (*Mor.* 289a–f).
132. Crouzel, *L'église*, 115–16.
133. Translation from Arthur Vööbus, *The Didascalia Apostolorum in Syriac: Chapters XI–XXVI*, CSCO 408 (Leuven: Peeters, 1979).

their husbands are to remain single like the widow of Sarepta or the prophetess Anna.[134] The *Didascalia* is therefore another witness to the language of "second husband" or "two husbands" being restricted in early Christianity to widows and not the divorced.

Lactantius

Lactantius died at roughly the time of the Council of Nicaea after serving as an advisor to the emperor Constantine. His *Divine Institutes* may date to 305 or 310 CE. In *Divine Institutes* 6.23 he writes:

> For such is not the case, as is the interpretation of public law, that she alone is the adulteress who has another man, while the male is free from the charge of adultery, though he may have many mistresses. The divine law so joins two with equal right into a marriage, which is two in one flesh, that whoever breaks apart the joining of the body is regarded as an adulterer ...
>
> These are the things which are prescribed by God for continency. But, however, lest anyone think that he is able to circumscribe the divine precepts, there are added these points, that all calumny and chance for fraud be removed; he is an adulterer who takes a wife who has been sent away by her husband; and so is he who has, aside from the crime of adultery, put a wife away that he may take another. God did not intend for that 'one flesh' to be separated and torn apart.[135]

Interpreters often tend to fill in the gaps and silences in the ante-Nicene witness. Matthew 5:31–32 and 19:9 explain that it is adulterous to divorce one's wife unless that wife is guilty of sexual sin. Lactantius follows the Matthean text and does not mention the possibility that an innocent party of a legitimate divorce may marry again.[136] That silence does not prevent Reynolds from claiming that Lactantius "probably" held that husbands who had divorced their wives for adultery may remarry.[137] The problem is that this silence is *never filled in* that way in any of the

---

134. The Syriac and Greek texts of the *Didascalia Apostolorum* are not the same in this section. Some manuscripts go further to label the younger widow's second marriage as *also* a sin.

135. Translation from Mary Francis McDonald, *The Divine Institutes Books I–VII*, FC 49 (Washington, DC: Catholic University of America, 1964), 460–61.

136. Crouzel, *L'église*, 111–12.

137. Reynolds, *Marriage*, 182; so also Nautin, "Divorce et remariage," 15–17, who believes that Lactantius is following Roman law. Predictably, Pospishil, *Divorce and Remarriage*, 148: "Although

other ante-Nicene fathers and thus should not be assumed. When writers are following the Matthean text, that text never states whether the innocent party may marry again. One searches in vain for an ante-Nicene author to render such a permissive logic explicit and thereby set a precedent. Instead, one encounters the repeated struggle to justify remarriage for widows in spite of Paul's explicit permission (cf. 1 Cor 7:39–40; Rom 7:2–3). The struggle for a widow's right to remarry should leave one hesitant to assume a right to remarry for the divorcée, even if innocent and the divorce legitimate.

Church Councils Culminating in Nicaea

Council of Elvira (306 CE)

The canons of the Council of Elvira from Spain were composed at varying times. Some are likely earlier and ante-Nicene, even as the council itself is dated to roughly 306 CE.[138] Among the more likely original, Canon 8 reads: "Women who without acceptable cause leave their husbands and join another man may not receive communion even when death approaches."[139] Remarriage in that instance requires permanent excommunication. The canon does not address the possibility of whether a woman could receive communion if she had left her husband for an *acceptable* cause and remarried. To forestall that very conclusion, the Council of Elvira immediately adds in Canon 9: "A baptized woman who leaves an adulterous husband who has been baptized, for another man, may not marry him. If she does, she may not receive communion until her former husband dies, unless she is seriously ill." The wife may leave an adulterous Christian husband but is not to remarry. If she does, she is to be excommunicated. She must wait until the first husband dies before she may marry again.[140] When there is no cause for the divorce, Canon 8 is severe in its judgment, but Canon 9 is less severe since it reflects the Matthean exception clauses allowing divorce for a proper cause. Unlike the Matthean exception clauses, however, Canon 9 is worded in terms of the woman's

---

he does not say so explicitly, he permitted thereby the husband to contract a new marriage" since he must have been following the secular customs of the day.

138. See the discussions in Maurice Meigne, "Concile ou collection d'Elvire?" *RHE* 70 (1975): 361–87; Josep Vilella, "The Pseudo-Iliberritan Canon Texts," *ZAC* 18 (2014): 21–59.

139. English translations are readily available online. See, e.g., http://legalhistorysources.com/Canon%20Law/ElviraCanons.htm.

140. Bonsirven, *Divorce*, 75; Ott, *Auslegung*, 47.

response to the *man's* adultery.[141] The woman who divorces for a proper cause and remarries must remain excommunicated until the former husband dies.[142]

Philip Lyndon Reynolds notes the council's focus on women: "The Council of Elvira did not prohibit the remarriage of men who had divorced their wives for adultery, but in due course the rejection of the double standard became another crux."[143] The council's reasoning may therefore seem misogynous. Reynolds's reasoning does not account for how the Council of Elvira was responding in these decisions to a recent law enacted by Emperor Diocletian in 293 that women could dissolve their marriages by writing a bill of divorce. They did not have to wait to serve the bill to their husbands or to make it known to them.[144] The council was therefore focused on the wife's situation in view of the new law and simply did not address the situation of the husband in a similar situation.[145] In fact, Canon 10 *continues* to focus on the wife: "If an unbaptized woman marries another man after being deserted by her husband who was a catechumen, she may still be baptized [*si ea quam catechumenus relinquit duxerit maritum, potest ad fontem lavcari admitti*]. This is also true for female catechumens [*hoc et circa feminas catechumenas erit observandum*]. If a Christian woman marries a man in the knowledge that he deserted his former wife without cause, she may receive communion only at the time of her death."[146]

---

141. The two canons do not address marriages to nonbelievers. They address situations within the churches, in contrast to the secular world; cf. the 293 law of Diocletian.

142. Harrell (*Divorce and Remarriage*, 181) dismisses the council's prohibition of the innocent wife's remarrying as reflecting the "rigorism growing with the church," but he produced no example of an ante-Nicene writer explicitly permitting innocent parties in legitimate divorces to remarry. All one finds in these authors is the prohibition of remarriage while a former spouse lives.

143. Reynolds, *Marriage*, 145, 181, who recognizes that Jesus's teaching suggests that remarriage after divorce is adulterous, with remarriage "perhaps" being permitted for the husband who divorced his wife for adultery (145).

144. MacRory, *New Testament and Divorce*, 79; Belivacqua, "Indissolubility," 288–89.

145. Contra e.g., Nautin, "Divorce et remariage," 18–20; Pospishil, *Divorce and Remarriage*, 183.

146. Crouzel, *L'église*, 117–20, who questions the translation of Canon 10 since the subject of *potest* is unclear. Grammatically, it would be the *ea* and *not* the catechized, but in that case the next clause becomes difficult. A wife who abandoned her husband cannot be the catechumen. Canon 10 therefore supports two affirmations: (1) A catechumenate divorces his wife and she remarries; he can be admitted to baptism. (2) The same practice applies to women who divorce their husbands if the man remarried. In this case, even if she left her spouse with proper reason, he does not have the excuse of the Matthean exception clause, as it is not possible to require the catechumen that he or she be restored to the partner since that partner has remarried. If the text is read in this way, there is reference to 1 Cor 7:12–16. The separation is during a catechetical period or in unbelief and not after he had become a Christian.

CHAPTER 6

Council of Arles (314 CE)

Canon 11 from the Council of Arles states "concerning those who apprehend their wives in adultery" that "they be counseled not to take other wives while their own wives are still living, even if the latter are adulterous."[147] As Reynolds comments: "The decree does not so much permit as tolerate or concede remarriage."[148] MacRory explains that this toleration is a function of Roman law permitting divorced men to marry again.[149] The innocent husband may *not* marry again, but the council opens the door to a pastoral attitude in these cases.[150] In other words, the Gaul church's position remains that a man may not remarry even after divorcing an adulterous wife.[151] The council is cognizant that the position is countercultural and difficult in practice. G. H. Joyce comments:

> Roman public opinion in 314 A.D., it must be remembered, was still governed by pagan standards. In the circumstances indicated, remarriage would have seemed to most men the only natural course. The Christian law requiring the injured husband to live a single life would have appeared very unreasonable. What wonder if not a few young Christians, faced with such a difficulty, dropped the practice of their religion, and followed the custom of society.[152]

Despite the pressures and difficulty of upholding the requirement to remain single after divorce, even after a divorce for just cause, the council continued to censure a man's remarriage.

Council of Neocaesarea (315 CE)

The Council of Neocaesarea declares in Canon 8: "If the wife of a layman has committed adultery and been clearly convicted, such [a husband] cannot enter the ministry; and if she commit adultery after his ordination, he must put her away; but if he retain her, he can have no part in the ministry committed to him."[153]

---

147. Translation available at https://www.fourthcentury.com/arles-314-canons/.
148. Reynolds, *Marriage*, 182; Crouzel, *L'église*, 122. Toleration is one thing, permission another.
149. MacRory, *Divorce and Remarriage*, 80.
150. Crouzel, *L'église*, 125.
151. Bonsirven, *Divorce*, 75. Even Harrell recognizes: "Remarriage was not possible even on the grounds of adultery" (*Divorce and Remarriage*, 182).
152. Joyce, *Christian Marriage*, 307.
153. Translation from *NPNF*² 14.

The *innocent* husband of an adulterous wife is not permitted to enter the ministry. If she adulterates *after* his ordination, he is required to divorce her or else resign from the ministry.[154] Canon 3 reads: "Concerning those who fall into many marriages, the appointed time of penance is well known; but their manner of living and faith shortens the time."

Thus, those who have contracted more than one marriage must go through a time of penance for the sin. Likewise Canon 7 of Neocaesarea reads: "A presbyter shall not be a guest at the nuptials of persons contracting a second marriage; for, since the digamist is worthy of penance, what kind of presbyter shall he be, who, by being present at the feast, sanctioned the marriage?" Those in multiple marriages are to repent, and church officials are not even to be present at such weddings. Such is the severity of remarriage as a sin.

Council of Nicaea (325 CE)

In Canon 8 of the Council of Nicaea is the requirement "that they [the Novatians, called Cathari (καθαροί)] will communicate with persons who have been twice married; and with those who having lapsed in persecution have had a period [of penance] laid upon them, and a time [of restoration] fixed."[155] In the middle of the third century, Novatian and his followers broke away from the Roman church because its bishop was willing to restore after a period of penance those who had apostasized during the Decian persecution. The breakaway church under Novatian was more rigorous in its practice, including its approach to the "second married." The Council of Nicaea responded to the continuing existence of Novatianists by requiring their clergy to be willing to commune with the "twice married" and the "lapsed" after a period of penance.

Some have taken "twice married" as including divorcées who had remarried, especially Giovanni Cereti in his interpretation of Canon 8 of Nicaea.[156] So also Reynolds, who concludes: "The canon regards the second marriage as adultery, since this is what Jesus taught, but it does not consider the marriage to be invalid."[157] Cereti

---

154. This parallels the requirement to put away an adulterous wife in Canons 65 and 70 of the Council of Elvira.

155. Translation from *NPNF*² 14.

156. Giovanni Cereti, *Divorzio, nuove nozze e penitenza nella Chiesa primitiva*, Collana Studi e Ricerche 26 (Bologna: Edizioni Dehoniane Bologne, 1977): 270–354; Cereti, "The Reconciliation of Remarried Divorcees according to Canon 8 of the Council of Nicaea," in *Ius Sequitur Vitam: Law Follows Life, Studies in Canon Law Presented to P. J. M. Huizing*, ed. James H. Provost and Knut Walf, Annua Nuntia Lovaniensia 32 (Leuven: Peeters, 1991), 193–207.

157. Reynolds, *Marriage*, 148–49, here 149.

CHAPTER 6

argues that the church did not require the dissolution of remarriages after *illicit* divorces but merely the recognition of the sin involved and a period of penance. Such remarried divorcées could eventually be received back into communion. Cereti even argues that this was the position of the church fathers even before Nicaea.

Cereti's position has since been dismissed by early Christian specialists.[158] In his interpretation of Canon 8 he does not account for the Novatianist practice the council was pronouncing against. Epiphanius (*Pan.* 59.4.1–3) explains that the Novatians had required of the laity what 1 Tim 3:2, 8 limited to bishops and deacons: *All* married people were to have only a single spouse and remain single in widowhood. Wallraff in his review of the literature notes how Cereti stands alone in this opinion among early Christian specialists.[159] Eastern Novatianists, for instance in Phrygia, were excluding "twice married" from communion, whereas the Novatians in Constantinople were undecided.[160] Crouzel explains that "twice married" in early Christianity refers to those who had married after being widowed.[161] The Council of Nicaea had taken a position on those who had remarried after the death of a spouse, with the "twice married" serving as a technical term. The council was *not* requiring the Novatianists, or anyone for that matter, to commune with those who had married again after divorce for adultery.

Ascetical Elements in the Ante-Nicene Witness

Many biblical interpreters claim that the witness of the ante-Nicene authors and councils on divorce and remarriage should be taken with a grain of salt since

---

158. Andreas Weckwerth, "The Twenty Canons of the Council of Nicaea," in *The Cambridge Companion to the Council of Nicaea*, ed. Young Richard Kim (Cambridge: Cambridge University Press, 2021), 170–71 and 170 n. 73; cf. Bernhard Kötting, "Digamus," in *RAC* 3:1022–23. More convincing was the case of Henri Crouzel, "Les *digamoi* visés par le Concile de Nicée dans son canon 8," *Aug* 18 (1978): 533–46, in response to Cereti.

159. Martin Wallraff, "Geschichte des Novatianismus seit dem vierten Jahrhundert im Osten," *ZAC* 1.2 (1997): 259 n. 28, who also offers a helpful review regarding this matter of the primary and secondary source documentation on the Novatians, agreeing with Kötting and Crouzel.

160. For example, see Socrates, *Historia ecclesiastica* 5.22.60: "The Novatians in Phrygia do not admit such as have twice married; but those of Constantinople neither admit nor reject them openly, while in the Western parts they are openly received." Translation of Socrates Scholasticus from *NPNF*[2] 2.

161. Crouzel, *L'église*, 124. Crouzel, "*Digamoi*," 534–35: Origen in his Homily 17 describes Anna in Luke 2:36–38 who had not become δίγαμος in her widowhood. Origen's Fragment 35 on 1 Corinthians also uses this term for those marrying a second time after being widowed; see Jenkins, "Documents III," 502–3. Other references to *digamoi* never mention a situation after divorce, a deafening silence.

272

ascetic interests were skewing their conclusions. Craig Keener is representative: the "church fathers often read their own culture's growing asceticism into these texts."[162] He later adds: "I believe that second- and third-century Christian writers ... reflect the rise of marital asceticism in the dominant culture and especially the church ... not the historical situation of the first century," and their position "against remarriage was burdened by a less than enthusiastic view of marriage."[163] David Instone-Brewer correctly summarizes the witness of the first centuries "that remarriage before the death of a former spouse involves sin," but he immediately dismisses that witness: "Ascetic beliefs, which characterize almost all the Fathers, minimized the problems with this 'plain' meaning of the texts. Many of the fathers regarded singleness or celibacy as preferable to the married state, though they acknowledged that marriage did not involve sin."[164] William Heth even attributes his change of mind on remarriage, in part, to a reevaluation of the early Christian witness; they were overly influenced by a non-biblical asceticism.[165] For these interpreters, the ascetic interests of early Christian authors render suspect their conclusions regarding remarriage. Perhaps their interpretation is too laden with cultural baggage to be of value.

Elizabeth Clark narrates a problem for this line of reasoning: The Society of Biblical Literature's Group on Ascetic Behavior in Greco-Roman Antiquity, "despite prolonged meetings throughout the 1980s, never reached consensus on a definition of asceticism."[166] Group members debated what weight to give to elements such as deprivation, pain, and the "shrinking of self." [167] Others emphasized renouncing and resisting desire.[168] Steven Fraade defines asceticism as having two components: "(1) The exercise of disciplined effort toward the goal of spiritual perfection (however understood), which requires (2) abstention (whether total or partial, permanent or temporary, individualistic or communalistic) from the sat-

---

162. Keener, *And Marries Another*, 44.

163. Keener, *Gospel of Matthew*, 469 n. 29. Craig L. Blomberg likewise flags the "general tendencies toward asceticism"; see "Marriage, Divorce, Remarriage, and Celibacy," 181.

164. Instone-Brewer, *Divorce and Remarriage*, 257.

165. William A. Heth, "A Response to Gordon J. Wenham," in *Remarriage after Divorce in Today's Church: Three Views*, ed. Mark L. Strauss, Counterpoints (Grand Rapids: Zondervan, 2006), 45.

166. Clark, *Reading Renunciation*, 14.

167. Clark, *Reading Renunciation*, 14. The group defined ascetic *behavior* as varying responses to social, political, and physical worlds that are perceived as oppressive, unfriendly, or stumbling blocks to the pursuit of heroic personal or communal goals, lifestyles, and commitments; see Vincent L. Wimbush, "Introduction," in *Ascetic Behavior in Greco-Roman Antiquity: A Sourcebook*, ed. Vincent L. Wimbush, Studies in Antiquity and Christianity (Minneapolis: Fortress, 1990), 2.

168. Geoffrey Galt Harpham, *The Ascetic Imperative in Culture and Criticism* (Chicago: University of Chicago Press, 1987), 61; Clark, *Reading Renunciation*, 15–16.

CHAPTER 6

isfaction of otherwise permitted earthly, creaturely desires."[169] William Deal contends that in a cross-cultural, universal definition of asceticism there are always controls, restrictions, and limitation on what people can do with their bodies. This raises the question of *when* self-discipline or self-denial becomes ascetic.[170] *Which* acts are construed by those within a culture as "ascetic"?[171] Thus Richard Valantasis describes differing definitions: "The theorists understand asceticism as a large and pervasive cultural system; while the historians views asceticism as specific religious practices relating to social withdrawal, restriction of food, regulation of sexuality, and the formation of religious community."[172]

Kallistos Ware stresses a distinguishing feature of *early Christian* asceticism through the fourth century. The ascetic flight for the Christian is not to escape this creation or to destroy it. "Voluntary abstinence for ascetic reasons is entirely legitimate; but to abstain out of loathing for the material creation is heretical."[173] He cites the 355 CE Council of Gangra from Asia Minor that anathematizes those

---

169. Steven D. Fraade, "Ascetical Aspects of Ancient Judaism," in *Jewish Spirituality: From the Bible through the Middle Ages*, ed. Arthur Green (New York: Crossroad, 1986), 257. Fraade's "otherwise permitted" betrays the social construction of asceticism (by whom?). Jews are commanded to abstain from pleasures that the gentiles could enjoy (e.g., pork). Fraade nevertheless does not consider Judaism itself as ascetic but rather elements *within* Judaism (e.g., the Pharisees' practice of priestly purity in their homes; see 270, 277).

170. William E. Deal, "Toward a Politics of Asceticism: Response to the Three Preceding Papers," in *Asceticism*, ed. Vincent L. Wimbush and Richard Valantasis (Oxford: Oxford University Press, 1995), 426.

171. The possibility of a universal definition is made difficult by the varying cultures of non-participant observers; Deal, "Toward a Politics of Asceticism," 426–27.

172. Richard Valantasis, "A Theory of the Social Function of Asceticism," in *Asceticism*, ed. Vincent L. Wimbush and Richard Valantasis (Oxford: Oxford University Press, 1995), 544. For a helpful historical sketch of the study of asceticism and the various problems identified at the International Conference on Asceticism, see Vincent L. Wimbush and Richard Valantasis, "Introduction," in Wimbush and Valantasis, *Asceticism*, xix–xxxiii.

Valantasis himself builds on the work of Max Weber, Michel Foucault, and Geoffrey Harpham in explaining that asceticism is "self-forming activity . . . to become an ethical subject" (with Foucault); see "Theory," 546. As Valantasis states later, "Self-denial . . . [is] necessary for a person to live within a culture so that the resistance to appetites and desires is at the heart of cultural integration and functioning" (546–47). For Valantasis, at the heart of asceticism is a self who, through behavioral changes, is seeking to become a new self, a different person, in new relationships, thereby helping form a new culture (547). Valantasis is followed by Neil Elliott, "Asceticism among the 'Weak' and the 'Strong' in Romans 14–15," in *Asceticism and the New Testament*, ed. Leif E. Vaage and Vincent L. Wimbush (New York: Routledge, 1999), 242. Ascetic activity functions as signifiers in a semiotic situation to represent specific values within a culture, as noted in Valantasis, "Theory," 548.

173. Kallistos Ware, "The Way of the Ascetics: Negative or Affirmative?" in Wimbush and Valantasis, *Asceticism*, 10.

The Witness of the Early Church

who consider marriage or eating meat as sinful. Ware concludes: "We fast, not out of hatred for God's creation, but as to control the body; also fasting enables us to help the poor, for the food that we ourselves refrain from eating can be given to others who are in need."[174] Unlike a creation-denying "unnatural asceticism," "natural asceticism" is not against the body but for it. "To refrain from marriage and sexual activity is natural asceticism; to castrate oneself is unnatural."[175] "We are not to disfigure the gifts that God confers on us."[176] Ware's distinction is a helpful corrective to those who see in early Christian asceticism something unnatural and creation-negating. As representative of this pattern, Athanasius's *Life of Antony* envisions, yes, a withdrawal from the world, but also a subsequent reengagement as a transformed person capable of self-control and the repression of sensual and selfish impulses for the sake of others and out of love for God.

Rather than trace the ascetic trajectories of early Christian thought, a project Peter Brown and Elizabeth Clark have already engaged, a better starting point is the ascetic element in the teachings of Jesus and Paul. If Jesus and Paul already manifested such tendencies, how is one to fault early Christian authors who were merely following in their footsteps, albeit under greater social and cultural pressures toward asceticism. The earliest days of Christianity were not somehow free of ascetic currents, and any presupposition otherwise "needs considerable tempering."[177] To put it differently, later Greek philosophy did not introduce ascetic notions into an "otherwise world-affirming primitive Christianity."[178] The Roman world of the New Testament authors and first Christians already manifested the "ideal of temperance and bodily discipline in matters of sex, diet, and exercise" across a range of authors and texts.[179] One may point to the ascetic interests articulated in the Dead Sea Scrolls, the writings of Philo of Alexandria, or the Testaments of the Twelve Patriarchs.[180] As Clark writes, "Scholars of early Christian asceticism now deem it misguided to try to locate some particular moment after the late second century when Christianity took an ascetic turn."[181] Ascetic elements were present from the beginning.

Jesus condemned a man's lusting after a woman as adultery (Matt 5:28). He encouraged men to "hate" their wives (Luke 14:26) and leave them for the sake of ministry (Luke 18:29). He praised those who became eunuchs for the sake of the kingdom, even if this praise was tempered somewhat by his application of this to those who

---

174. Ware, "Way of the Ascetics," 10.
175. Ware, "Way of the Ascetics," 9.
176. Ware, "Way of the Ascetics," 10.
177. Clark, *Reading Renunciation*, 20.
178. Clark, *Reading Renunciation*, 20.
179. Clark, *Reading Renunciation*, 20.
180. Clark, *Reading Renunciation*, 1.
181. Clark, *Reading Renunciation*, 22.

CHAPTER 6

are not to marry again after divorce (Matt 19:10–12). The ideal is to serve wholeheartedly the kingdom of God. Paul writes similarly, as most believe that 1 Cor 7 is Paul's response to a quotation from the Corinthian men in 7:1 that it is good not to touch a woman (i.e., to avoid sexual relations). Paul disagrees and qualifies that judgment. He recognizes a time when married couples will abstain from sexual relations for the sake of prayer, but then they are to resume sexual relations to avoid the temptation of extramarital sex (1 Cor 7:5). He urges unmarried widowers and widows to remain as he is, but if they do not have self-control and are burning, they may marry (7:8–9). He recognizes that his own ability to maintain a celibate lifestyle is a gift from God, and not all will have that same gift (7:6–7). In view of the present distress, he urges those who have never married to remain as they are, although it is not a sin to marry (7:26–28), but those who marry must recognize that they will experience trouble in this life (7:28). The married should live as though they are not, since the current form of the world is passing away (7:29–31). Those who remain unmarried may serve the Lord without distraction instead of having to please a spouse (7:32–35). In short, to marry is acceptable, but not to marry is even better (7:38). Even the widow is better off to remain unmarried rather than to remarry (7:39–40). Vincent Wimbush points to these verses to demonstrate that Paul, if not already Jesus, may be firmly classified in the ascetic camp.[182] To remain celibate in view of the times is superior to marriage even if marriage is acceptable (7:7, 9, 17, 37).[183]

Dale Martin offers a thoroughgoing reading of 1 Cor 7 and Paul's asceticism through the lens of the ancient physicians and Stoic philosophers. Stoic self-sufficiency would require the elimination of sexual desire *even within marriage*, and Martin contends that Paul shares that perspective.[184] J. Edward Ellis critiques that approach through an alternative lens, that of the popular, ancient Greek romance novels. He observes that Paul does not require all Christians to be celibate in 1 Cor 7 and affirms marriage and sexual relations in the marital context. Marriage is preferable to immorality (1 Cor 7:2) and burning (7:8–9). Further, Paul does not mention procreation in 1 Cor 7:2–5 as he urges husbands and wives not to deny each other sexually lest they be tempted. Ellis reviews how Greek novels celebrate passionate sexual desires finding their proper expression in marriage and not outside of it (cf. 1 Cor 7:9).[185] The moral of the story of *Daphnis and Chloe*, for instance, is "If you are love sick, get married."[186]

---

182. Wimbush, *Paul the Worldly Ascetic*.
183. For a helpful overview of these texts in 1 Cor 7 on the value of celibacy, see esp. Heth, "Unmarried," 61–68.
184. Martin, "Paul without Passion."
185. J. Edward Ellis, *Paul and Ancient Views of Sexual Desire: Paul's Sexual Ethics in 1 Thessalonians 4, 1 Corinthians 7 and Romans 1*, LNTS 354 (London: T&T Clark, 2007), 153–59.
186. Ellis, *Paul and Ancient Views*, 158.

In the thought world of the novels, then, erotic desire is a powerful, dangerous force. It is a painful wound, a sickness, a madness that can overcome anyone; it drives people to irrational thoughts and actions. This force is properly channeled and rendered safe in marriage. All of this, say the novels, is wonderful. First-century auditors influenced by the thought world the novels reflect would be unlikely to see in 'It is better to marry than to burn,' a disdain for marriage, sex, or sexual desire.[187]

Ellis concludes that Paul's qualified celebration of the celibate lifestyle for the ancient auditor would not be viewed as a condemnation of marriage, sex, or sexual desire as expressed within marriage. Paul in 1 Cor 7 commends the celibate or single lifestyle but also recognizes the value of marriage if one is not able to continue in that single lifestyle and wholehearted devotion to the Lord. Jesus in Matt 19:12 commends those who choose a celibate lifestyle for the sake of the kingdom. Is it really so shocking, as for Instone-Brewer, that "[s]ome, like Athenagoras and Tertullian, even used Jesus' teaching on remarriage to encourage celibacy"?[188]

The extreme ascetic impulse in the larger cultural milieu of early Christianity devalued *any* fleshly relations, including those within a marital context. Early Christian authors, on the other hand, defend sexual relations as proper and fitting within marriage, especially for the sake of children, and they appeal to the Scriptures as the raw material justifying their position. Irenaeus censures Tatian for equating marriage with fornication (*Haer.* 1.28.1).[189] Abstention from marriage was a voluntary matter and not because marriage was prohibited (Clement of Alexandria, *Strom.* 3.7.58; 3.9.66). Such abstinence is in the service of God and never a devaluation of the creation.[190] Perpetual virginity is not to be forced on people (Irenaeus, *Haer.* 4.15.2). Of course, while marriage is good, maintaining virginity for the sake of the kingdom is superior to the distractions of married life (Athanasius, *Ep. virg.* [*Copt.*] 26–27).[191] Clement of Alexandria considers continence possible even *while*

---

187. Ellis, *Paul and Ancient Views*, 159.

188. Instone-Brewer, *Divorce and Remarriage*, 357.

189. So also e.g., Tertullian, *Mon.* 14 (approving first marriages); *Marc.* 1.29; 4.11; Clement of Alexandria, *Strom.* 3.12.81; Hippolytus, *Haer.* 8.13.

190. Jenkins, "Documents III," 502–3; Clement of Alexandria, *Strom.* 3.6.52; 3.12.85; Origen, Fragments on 1 Corinthians 34 (on 7:5).

191. Athanasius, *Ep. virg.* (*Copt.*) 19. Translation from David Brakke, *Athanasius and the Politics of Asceticism*, Oxford Early Christian Studies (Oxford: Oxford University Press, 1995), 279. Other examples given for abstinence from sex include those from Origen, Fragments on 1 Corinthians 34 (on 7:5) in Jenkins, "Documents III," 502–3 (the Israelites abstaining before entering the presence of the holy); Tertullian, *Exh. cast.* 10.3–4 (abstaining for the sake of prayer); Origen, Fragments on 1 Corinthians 34 (on 7:5) in Jenkins, "Documents III," 502 (abstaining prior to receiving the Eucharist). One does not withdraw from sexual activity altogether.

having sexual relations (*Strom.* 3.12.79). The virgin remains free of worldly troubles (1 Cor 7:28).[192] Nevertheless, for Origen marriage remains a "gift,"[193] Methodius of Olympus grants that not all are capable of remaining unmarried and a eunuch for the sake of the kingdom (*Symp.* 3.13; cf. Matt 19:12). Censuring ante-Nicene authors for an extreme sort of asceticism not only evinces a failure to define the term and the standards but would also implicate the Apostle Paul. Such evaluations serve only to highlight the cultural differences between modern Christianity and ante-Nicene and biblical Christianity. As the "pre-conversion" William Heth put it: "'Celibacy' is a word that makes modern Protestants uncomfortable."[194] He adds, "Protestants have neglected to define how Jesus' saying about 'eunuchs' for the kingdom's sake and Paul's counsel to singleness in 1 Corinthians 7 apply to the believer today."[195]

David G. Hunter summarizes the ante-Nicene landscape prior to 300 CE on this point: "By the end of the third century, it appears that a kind of détente emerged between those Christians who favored sexual renunciation and those who advocated marriage. Within the mainstream of the Christian tradition, a moderate attitude toward marriage seems to have prevailed: the superiority of celibacy was asserted, but the permissibility of marriage was also upheld."[196]

Conclusion

David Instone-Brewer writes of the ante-Nicene witness: "The general consensus is that marriage is indissoluble except by death."[197] More precisely, marriage may be dissolved by divorce for instances of adultery, but that dissolution does not allow for remarriage. God's will in creation, even in the face of divorce, remains that one man be married to one woman. Several patterns are clear in ante-Nicene witness. First, biblical texts set the tone for the discussions. For instance, in 1 Tim 3:1–7 are

---

192. Origen, Fragments on 1 Corinthians 39 (on 7:28) in Jenkins, "Documents III," 509–10.
193. Fragments on 1 Corinthians 34 (on 7:7) in Jenkins, "Documents III," 502–3.
194. Heth, "Unmarried," 56–57.
195. Heth, "Unmarried," 58. Heth helpfully reviews early Christian teaching on celibacy with an eye toward contemporary evangelical application.

W. M. Calder has identified an early Christian epitaph from *prior* to 350 CE that stresses how a man, Akakios, had been married only once and remained a widower for thirty years; see "Early Christian Epitaphs from Phrygia," *AnSt* 5 (1955): 31–33, esp. 32. Such practice was therefore worthy of note.

196. Hunter, *Marriage and Sexuality*, 21. He cites as representative of that attitude Methodius of Olympus and Lactantius. His volume includes a translation of the comments on marriage in both authors (91–100 and 101–7, respectively).

197. Instone-Brewer, *Divorce and Remarriage*, 258.

the qualifications for the office of bishop: "Now a bishop must be above reproach, married only once.... He must manage his own household well, keeping his children submissive and respectful in every way—for if someone does not know how to manage his own household, how can he take care of God's church?" (vv. 2, 4–5). The bishop must be "married only once" (μιᾶς γυναικὸς ἄνδρα, lit. "the husband of one wife"). Then in 1 Tim 5:9–16 the qualifications are given for a widow to "be put on the list." She must be "not less than sixty years old and has been married only once" (v. 9: ἑνὸς ἀνδρὸς γυνή, lit. "the wife of one husband"). Does this limit bishops or enrolled widows to those who have not remarried after divorce, or those who have remarried in general, even after the death of a spouse? The first centuries of the Christian movement witnessed these passages being interpreted in terms of a second spouse after the death of a former one for bishops and enrolled widows. After the original spouse's death, those in these offices would not have taken another. Rather crucially, "second marriages" are discussed frequently and explicitly in the context of widows but *never* in the context of divorce. That absence is conspicuous and telling.

The ante-Nicene thinkers regularly cite Paul in 1 Cor 7 and Jesus in the gospel texts on God's intent in creation despite the provision of Moses for hardened hearts. Jesus responds to the Pharisees' insistence on divorce in Matt 19:5–6 and Mark 10:7–8: "For this reason a man shall leave his father and mother and be joined to his wife, and the two shall become one flesh." One man and one woman become "one flesh." In apparent tension with the one man/one woman teaching of Jesus, Paul provided for widows to be released from "the law concerning the husband" to marry again after his death. In *that* situation, she will not be labeled an adulteress (Rom 7:2–3; 1 Cor 7:39). Here is provision for the "second marriage" that Jesus's teaching does not seem to envision. The earliest Christian authors would stress one or the other passage with varying results. They felt compelled to *justify* remarriage for the widow when God's will in creation had been, according to Jesus, one man united to one woman, and despite the Pauline witness in its favor (1 Cor 7:39–40; Rom 7:2–3). Several authors *discourage* the second marriages of widows, preferring a single marriage as best, if marriage was to be entered at all. Minucius Felix (*Oct.* 31.5), however, allows for one marriage only. Clement of Alexandria (*Strom.* 2) limits the term "marriage" to the first lawful union. Conspicuously, in defending the second marriage of a widow, a similar defense of a right to innocent divorced people is entirely absent. Despite the Pauline texts explicitly allowing it, if the remarriage of widows required extensive discussion and justification, how much more would remarriages after divorce had that been viewed as an option?

One searches in vain for an ante-Nicene source that cites the Matthean exception clauses as justifying remarriage after divorce for *anyone*. Significantly, the

CHAPTER 6

ante-Nicene authors do not use the language of the divorce certificates of their day that a spouse after divorce is "free" to marry again. The ante-Nicene authors never even raise the possibility that the innocent parties in a legitimate divorce are allowed to remarry. The gospel texts claim that one must remain single after a divorce. They frequently label a wife's remarriage as adulterous irrespective of her status as innocent or guilty.

Several students of early Christianity have drawn attention to the frequent lack of explicit condemnation of the remarriage of an innocent husband who has divorced his wife for adultery. Such men, these modern authors contend, *could* marry again after divorce, even if innocent wives could not—a double standard understandable within a patriarchal society.[198] To cite V. Pospishil: "Whenever we encounter a prohibition of remarriage after divorce, it *first* is directed to wives, while there is no mention of husbands and their legal situation; or *second*, divorce is disapproved for specific causes other than adultery."[199] Atkinson therefore concludes: "What these passages really offer is a strong argument from silence: it is the absence of any explicit prohibition of divorce and remarriage that is striking."[200] It is a strange logic to conclude from the fact that all divorced women are denied remarriage that innocent divorced men of adulterous wives may remarry since most texts do not *explicitly* forbid them. Thus remarriage is *generally* permissible. Crouzel responds to the logic: "How is it conceivable that if, according to the Fathers, Matt 19:9 accepted the remarriage of a husband whose wife was unfaithful, they should never have said so?"[201]

The ante-Nicene fathers, upon examination, do not support the conclusions of Nautin, Pospishil, Atkinson, Reynolds, and others. The Shepherd of Hermas forbids divorced spouses from remarrying despite the cultural assumption that divorce included such a right—even for the husband who has divorced his wife for adultery. Former spouses are to remain single or be reconciled. When the Shepherd of Hermas *does* allow for remarriage, it is for the widow and only after expressing great concern over the possibility and requiring an angelic statement

---

198. Nautin, "Divorce et remariage," 7–54: The Latin fathers allowed the remarriage of the innocent husband of a wife who had committed adultery from the second to the fourth centuries CE. A significant number have concurred with this conclusion, including Reynolds, *Marriage*, 145, 174–83; and Atkinson, *To Have and to Hold*, 36–37).

199. Pospishil, *Divorce and Remarriage*, 49–54, here 50; followed by Atkinson, *To Have and to Hold*, 38–39.

200. Atkinson, *To Have and to Hold*, 38. Atkinson concedes that Pospishil's work was heavily criticized by Henri Crouzel. Atkinson makes no attempt to lay out the details of this debate but simply endorses Pospishil.

201. Crouzel, "Remarriage after Divorce," 29.

of permission. Justin Martyr quotes Matt 5:32b that it is adulterous to marry a divorced wife and cites Jesus's eunuch saying about remaining single. Justin labels those who are "twice married" adulterers with no qualification whether a party is innocent. Athenagoras condemns anything more than a single marriage as adultery. Tertullian urges the innocent party to wait for the guilty party of a divorce to repent and in the meanwhile to observe a single life analogous to a widow. He espouses a one-rib, one-woman approach to marriage that does not allow for multiple partners. At one point, Tertullian repeatedly forbids divorce but allows it for adultery, all the while never permitting remarriage. He calls "second marriage" fornication. Clement of Alexandria also advocates for a "single marriage," calling anything more an embrace of fornication. He too applies Jesus's eunuch saying in Matt 19:10–12 to the situation after divorce. He allows for those whose marriages were "broken *by death*" and who are still "burning" a possibility of remarriage. Origen satirizes the freedom to divorce and remarry in the synagogues under the law and emphatically condemns those church leaders who were permitting remarriage while a spouse remained alive as acting contrary to Scripture. To marry a woman after divorce is to commit adultery. The ante-Nicene authors simply never countenance *any* party of divorce—whether innocent or not, whether the divorce was legitimate or not—marrying again unless the former spouse has died.

Conclusion

The world in which the Christ-faith was born took divorce and remarriage for granted. Whether among the Jews or among the Greeks and Romans, divorce certificates regularly proclaimed the wife's "freedom" to marry another man, but more frequently that freedom was simply assumed as partners chose to part ways. Many have contended that the first Christians likewise assumed that divorce brought with it a corresponding freedom to marry again, but there were countercurrents. The older, conservative Roman ideal was for a woman to remain faithful to a single husband throughout her life and even after his death. Inscriptions praised the *univira*. Although less frequent, inscriptions also praised men who had been similarly faithful to their wives. Ancient authors, even of the likes of Vergil, would wax poetic about the *univira*. The ideal remained despite the common practice to the contrary.

The Scriptures acknowledged and regulated divorce among the Jewish people. Some in the time of Jesus claimed generous rationales for putting away their wives to marry others. Jewish women might divorce their husbands, but this was usually the husband's prerogative. Despite that widespread acceptance, even among the Jews was the conservative Dead Sea community. While they accepted divorce, some in their midst refused to recognize a corresponding right to marry again. The Christ-faith was born amid these currents and lesser countercurrents.

Scholars strive to reconstruct the Jesus who stands behind the gospels as documents of faith and where he stood on matters of divorce and remarriage. The endeavor and its criteria are imperfect and incomplete. Whatever approach to reconstruction one chooses, among the few apparent certainties in this endeavor is that the Jesus behind the gospels taught, surprisingly, that both divorce and remarriage were contrary to God's will in creation. A key shortcoming of the historical Jesus venture is its failure to grapple with how the memory of Jesus would have been socially constructed from the start. In that case, the question becomes how Jesus was *remembered*. To modulate to this more recent method of inquiry, Jesus's teaching on divorce and remarriage had a tremendous impact in the memories of his followers in view of the traditions recounted by Paul, Mark, Luke, and Matthew. For Mark, Jesus's difficult teaching against divorce and remarriage was at the center of what it means to be a disciple. Mark's Jesus assures the disciples in the face of his difficult teaching that they are uniquely enabled to live accordingly. Luke has Jesus's teaching against divorce and remarriage as the ultimate example of how he had not set aside the law and the prophets. Luke rhetorically draws attention to that teaching within his narrative.

Matthew recalls Jesus twice making an exception to his teaching: "except for πορνεία." The exception clauses modify Jesus's warning. There is disagreement whether a wife has *committed* adultery or has been *victimized* or *stigmatized by* it through her husband's divorce. One church body has even based its practice and understanding on the view that people may not actually be adulterating in remarrying, since they are only stigmatized as such or are the innocent victims of divorce. The pastors in this church body have even created their own Bible translation that reflects their approach to the divorce and remarriage texts. Clearly, much is at stake in the resolution of this debate. Despite the desire to justify a church doctrine, the meaning of the two Greek verbs for "committing adultery" (μοιχεύω and μοιχάω) in their passive voice forms may be checked against their usage in the rest of the New Testament, the Septuagint, and especially the larger ancient world. The one Greek verb (μοιχάω) is a *deponent* that always carries the active sense of "to commit adultery," as the BDAG Greek lexicon and other modern translations have already noted. The other Greek verb (μοιχεύω) bears a passive sense *only when a prepositional phrase is present that identifies the active party*. Otherwise, the verb *always bears the active sense* "to commit adultery," as the lexicons and other modern translations recognize. The active voice is used for male adulteration, and the passive voice is used for female adulteration. The ingenious attempt to ground the concept of an innocent party in the divorce and remarriage texts falters because of the grammatical error.

Even as the translation of the passive voice of verb forms might allow a more permissive approach to remarriage, the translation of πορνεία in the exception clauses may require a more restrictive approach. The exception may only be for a specialized case, and Jesus's teaching in Matthew may therefore ultimately agree with the absolute form of his teaching in Mark and Luke. One possibility is that a marriage may not be legitimate in the first place because it involved spiritual idolatry and thus may be dissolved with remarriage (i.e., a *legitimate* marriage) as an option. The exception clause should be limited to this specific situation. A second possibility is that the marriage is invalid because of a violation of the laws against consanguinity or affinity in Lev 18. A third possibility is that the marriage is invalid because a Jew has married a gentile. A fourth and final possibility is that the exception to the stricture against divorce and remarriage is only for instances of *betrothal* infidelity. Each of these four approaches would render the Matthean Jesus's teaching against divorce and remarriage arguably as absolute as the Markan or Lukan Jesus. While each approach to πορνεία has enjoyed popularity in some quarters in the past, all four have been largely rejected in recent decades and for good reasons. The word πορνεία, in view of ancient usage, refers to sexual sin. That sexual sin is taking place within a *marital* context in Jesus's teaching and is the equivalent of adultery. For that matter, adultery was a hot topic in the ancient Mediterranean context, since the divorce of a wife for a cause other than adultery would be unjustifiable and would require the release to the divorced wife of her dowry. The Matthean exception clauses thus express a genuine exception to Jesus's absolute teaching against divorce and remarriage.

The question becomes whether the Matthean exception clauses (in 5:31–32 and 19:9) permit both divorce and remarriage or only divorce. Matthew 5:32 has proven a difficult passage for those advocating that an innocent party in divorce may remarry. Jesus rules that out for the divorced wife, whether she is innocent or guilty, divorce certificate in hand or not—a result at odds with modern celebrations of a divorced spouse's freedom in these cases. A man marrying even an innocent, divorced wife is adulterating. Matthew 5:32 merely allows a husband an exception to divorce a wife guilty of adultery. Culturally, Jewish men faced pressure to divorce adulterous wives lest they be implicated in the impropriety. Jesus himself does not require the divorce but permits it with the exception clause in view of this particular instance for a Jewish audience.

Matthew 19:9 is the only gospel text that may actually *permit* remarriage. In this case, the "except for sexual sin" would modify both the verbs "divorce" and "(re)-marry," granting an exception to both. Another possibility is that the exception clause may modify only the first verb. Scholars recognize both options as grammatically admissible. Several lines of evidence, however, favor the conclusion that the exception clause modifies only the divorce verb, in which case Matt 19:9 does not offer any permission for remarriage. That cumulative case deserves greater engagement. Also in favor of this conclusion is the disciples' reaction in 19:10, which leads to Jesus's teaching on eunuchs. Of the various interpretive options, the teaching on eunuchs in vv. 11–12 is best understood as an extension of Jesus's teaching on marriage and divorce in vv. 1–9. Some are made eunuchs by others in divorce, but Jesus's own have a God-given ability to remain celibate in those circumstances that others do not have.

Conclusion

The Apostle Paul's comments in 1 Cor 7 and the first few verses of Rom 7 have also ignited controversy. Those advocating a biblical sanction for remarriage have located five areas within 1 Cor 7 where Paul appears to refer to the divorced person's marrying again. First, in 1 Cor 7:1–7 Paul recognizes that not all people have the same gift that he possesses to avoid sexual relations. He posits marriage as the solution to those desires. On the other hand, he gives no indication in these verses whether there is provision for anything more than a single marriage to satisfy those needs. Second, in 1 Cor 7:8–9 he tells the "unmarried" and widows that if they lack self-control and are burning that they should marry. Perhaps "unmarried" should be taken in a broad sense inclusive of the divorced. More likely, however, is that Paul is addressing *widowers* alongside widows. Several lines of evidence converge to support this conclusion. Third, in 1 Cor 7:15 a believing spouse is "not bound" if an unbelieving partner demands divorce. "Not bound" is thought to be equivalent to the "freedom" expressed in divorce certificates. The problem with this argument is that Paul openly proclaims "freedom" to remarry later in 1 Cor 7:39, but it is for the widow. He does the same in Rom 7:2–3. Conspicuously, Paul avoids the language of freedom at the point where it would have clearly permitted remarriage for those other than widows. Also, Paul does not use the word "not bound" but rather "not enslaved," and he uses such language in relation to legal stipulations. In this context, the believer is "not enslaved" to Jesus's and Paul's requirement not to divorce the spouse, a requirement repeatedly stated in the preceding verses. Fourth, 1 Cor 7:27–28 appears to allow those "released" from a wife to marry again, even if it is not advisable. The problem here is that Paul is discussing the situation of betrothed couples. Even if not, v. 27 would still require the divorced not to marry again, and v. 28 allows *virgins* and their suitors to marry. Finally, Paul appears to be *discouraging* remarriage in vv. 32 and 34 but does not rule it out. On the other hand, one should not *assume* a permission for something Paul has already ruled out in vv. 10–11. He never advocates for the divorced to marry. One encounters a clear and explicit permission to remarry, but only for the widow in 1 Cor 7:39–40 and again in Rom 7:2–3. One searches 1 Cor 7 in vain for any further permission to remarry.

As for the ante-Nicene thinkers and councils, biblical passages set the tone for their discussions. Ultimately inspiring the ante-Nicene pronouncements was Jesus's teaching in Matt 19:5–6 and Mark 10:7–8 that God's will in creation for marriage is for one man to be united to one woman, even to the point of challenging Paul's provision for widows to remarry in 1 Cor 7:39 and Rom 7:2–3. Other authors would *defend* marriages after the death of a spouse. "Second marriages" are therefore discussed frequently and explicitly in the context of widows, but *never* in the context of divorce. That absence is conspicuous and telling, especially in the face of the repeated praise for the "single marriage." Frequently, these authors convey a prohibition to marry again after divorce, but some specialists have seized on these prohibitions being expressed most clearly for women. Women are clearly denied divorce and remarriage under any circumstances, but what of the innocent husbands who have had to divorce their wives for adultery? These specialists would like to read into the admitted silence a permission for these men. The problem is that several ante-Nicene authors are categorical that "second marriage" is fornication and that marriage is broken only "by death." The explicit statements do not confirm these specialists' hypothesis.

If the thesis proves correct that early Christianity was characterized by a greater consistency in opposing remarriage, a crucial question remains: how is the biblical witness to be appropriated? Modern interpreters and Christian believers have adopted a variety of responses to the biblical text. While some seek to norm their practice by biblical teaching, others supplement biblical teaching with the church's historic witness, with reason, or with their own personal experience. If, on the other hand, one falls into a camp that seeks to draw upon the biblical witness as the sole or primary norm for personal or churchly practice, then such a consistency in the early Christian witness on remarriage would prove to be countercultural and difficult.

As Dale Martin observes: "One gets the feeling that the vast majority of Christians, Roman Catholic as well as Protestant, though agreeing that divorce is regrettable and to be avoided if possible, has come to accept for the most part the reality of divorce and remarriage in contemporary society, religious as well as secular."[1] John Piper, an evangelical scholar and prolific author, founded and pastored a large church in the Minneapolis–St. Paul area. He authored and defended his church's original position prohibiting remarriage. Over time, and despite Piper's continuing to maintain and teach that the biblical witness denies remarriage, others in his church's leadership changed the congregation's practice to allow for it. Whether Roman Catholic facilitation of annulments or Protestant expansions of the exception clauses, modern church bodies have largely accepted the practice of remarriage. Were an ancient Christ-believer to travel through time to visit, he or she would likely find modern practice to be foreign and facilitating adultery. The stakes with respect to this issue are obviously high.

A few have come to the conclusion that remarriage is indeed adulterous in early Christianity and have sought to live and practice accordingly. That raises the question of those who have remarried. Should they be required to dissolve their unions and return to their original spouses? Some have advocated just that.[2] Even those

---

1. Martin, *Sex and the Single Savior*, 125.
2. E.g., Joseph A. Webb, *Till Death Do Us Part?* (Longwood, FL: Webb Ministries, 1992).

opposing the remarriage-as-adultery position have suggested that the dissolution of subsequent marriages is a necessary corollary. Craig Keener writes: "If the first marriage was never dissolved in God's sight, and if adultery cannot dissolve the marriage bonds, then any subsequent sexual activity is by definition adulterous. The only solution to such an adulterous union is to dissolve it, which would mean that all second marriages can be dealt with only by repentance and separation."[3] Keener is of the opinion that a "no remarriage" position would imply that any action of sexual intercourse would be an act of adultery against the original marriage.[4] He then dismisses the no-remarriage position by appeal to the only instance of an invalid union in Matthew's Gospel. In Matt 14:3–4 John the Baptist is reported to have criticized an illicit union between Herod and his brother's wife. Keener concludes: "A union conceived in adultery, a union conceived in reckless disregard for a standing, valid marriage, can only be rectified through dissolving the new union."[5]

Keener's conclusion that all invalid remarriages must be dissolved in favor of the original union is not clear in the biblical text. John the Baptist is criticizing an unrepentant Herod: "It is not lawful for you to have her." The NRSV translation is literal but misleading. If it is not lawful "to have" her, as the English translation puts it, then Herod is to no longer have her. He should therefore divorce her, thus Keener's logic. The problem is that the Greek verb is idiomatic in this instance, meaning simply "to be married to someone."[6] The marriage was illegitimate. What to do about that situation is another matter and is simply not addressed in the text beyond the obvious need for repentance, which Herod continued to resist.

Although Matt 14:3–4 does not offer any clear direction for what to do after recognizing a remarriage as sinful, those advocating that remarriages be dissolved in favor of the original unions have provided other arguments for the position. First, according to the Scriptures, marital covenants are permanent and may not be dissolved.[7] Second, those who have committed adultery in remarriage are *continuing* to adulterate as long as they remain in that subsequent marriage. The present tense verb "to commit adultery" in the New Testament divorce and remarriage passages should be taken as continuative, indicating a continuous condition or state.[8] As long as the remarried remain so, they remain in adultery.

---

3. Keener, *And Marries Another*, 48.

4. Craig S. Keener, "Remarriage for Adultery, Desertion or Abuse," in *Remarriage after Divorce in Today's Church: Three Views*, ed. Mark L. Strauss, Counterpoints (Grand Rapids: Zondervan, 2006), 104–5.

5. Keener, *And Marries Another*, 48–49.

6. See BDAG, s.v. ἔχω, 2a.

7. Webb, *Till Death*, 33–46, 111–14.

8. Webb, *Till Death*, 184.

CONCLUSION

To address the first contention, a case has been made that the marital covenant must be permanent since there is no evidence from the Hebrew Bible that a covenant with God as a partner has ever been dissolved. God remains faithful even when the covenantal partner is unfaithful.[9] A number of problems prevent this contention from being persuasive. Hebrew Bible specialists do not view all covenantal agreements as inviolable and permanent.[10] Even if those covenants that involve God as a partner are not dissolved, is not marriage a covenant between a man and a woman? A human party may dissolve a covenant agreement or contract with another human party.[11] Ultimately, the New Testament passages on marriage never mention the covenantal aspect of the union. At the same time, while Jesus stresses God's will that marriage be between one man and one woman, he also warns against humans breaking and dissolving what God has joined together (Mark 10:9; Matt 19:6). Jesus's admonition assumes that people may indeed separate or break apart by divorce what God has joined. Thus it is a genuine admonition. Similarly, in Matt 5:32 Jesus describes men who *marry* divorced women. Certainly, it was adulterous to enter that union, but Jesus does not describe it as "trying to marry" or "presumably marrying."[12] Jesus warns against the sin of adultery, but he does not use the nouns "adulterer" or "adulteress" (μοιχός, μοιχαλίς) as if the sin were unforgiveable.[13]

---

9. David W. Jones and John K. Tarwater, "Are Biblical Covenants Dissoluble? Toward a Theology of Marriage," *Reformed Perspectives Magazine* 7.38 (September 18–24, 2005): 1–13.

10. Covenant breaking would invoke the severe curses and sanctions. Gordon P. Hugenberger summarizes the discussion in that regard in *Marriage as a Covenant: Biblical Law and Ethics as Developed from Malachi*, VTSup 52 (Leiden: Brill, 1994), 3. Tarwater and Jones contend in response that each instance of a covenant established by God has remained permanent. Jones and Tarwater ultimately appeal to *New Testament* evidence: "Perhaps the greatest proof of the unending nature of such agreements comes from the apostle Paul, who in an argument from the lesser to the greater, wrote that even a covenant between men—as opposed to a divinely initiated covenant—if confirmed, 'cannot be annulled' (Gal 3:15)" ("Are Biblical Covenants Dissoluble?," 6). The fatal flaw in this argument is that Paul is writing *not* about a covenant instrument but a *last will and testament*; see the detailed argumentation of this point in A. Andrew Das, *Galatians*, Concordia Commentary (St. Louis: Concordia, 2014), 345–49; Das, "Rethinking the Covenantal Paul," in *Paul and the Stories of Israel* (Minneapolis: Fortress, 2016), 65–92, esp. 76–81.

11. Jones and Tarwater conclude their study by frankly conceding: "[T]here is certainly more work to be done, such as proving the covenantal nature of marriage (cf. Gen. 2:24; Prov. 2:16–17; Mal. 2:10–16), [and] proving that God is a part of the nuptials (Gen. 2:23–24; Matt. 19:6)"; see "Are Biblical Covenants Dissoluble?," 12.

12. A point stressed by John Piper, "Divorce, Remarriage, and Honoring God," *Desiring God*, Aug. 16, 2016, https://www.desiringgod.org/interviews/divorce-remarriage-and-honoring-god.

13. Blomberg, "Marriage, Divorce, Remarriage, and Celibacy," 174, although the point cannot be pressed too hard in view of the use of μοιχαλίς in Rom 7:3.

Conclusion

The present tense of the verb "to commit adultery" (μοιχᾶται) does not demonstrate continuous adultery is being committed as partners remain in a remarriage. Present tense indicative verb forms may not necessarily express continuing action. They are often gnomic or timeless, and Jesus's pronouncement bears an almost proverbial or maxim-like quality.[14] Context is decisive and not the tense or indicative mood of the verb. Carroll Osburn points out that of the seven hundred present indicative verbs in Matthew's Gospel, the vast majority are "descriptive" with no sense of continuing action. For instance, in Matt 8:25 "we perish" does not have a sense of continuing action. Jesus's passing by in Matt 20:30 does not have a continuous sense. Matthew 13:44's buying or selling a field is not continuous. Continuous action in the present indicative verb form is present only in a minority of instances (e.g., Matt 15:23). Context is therefore determinative. As for the context of Matt 19:9, the question the Pharisees raised was whether it is lawful to divorce for any cause (19:3). The question is *when* a divorce is adulterous and when it is justified. Osburn labels Matt 19:9's verb form a "gnomic present" since it is stating a general truth and not continuous action (e.g., 3:10; 6:2; 7:17; 23:3).

The New Testament treats a remarriage as an actual marriage, whether or not it was appropriate or adulterous. In John 4:17–18 Jesus affirms that the Samaritan woman at the well has indeed had *five* husbands even though the man she is currently living with is not her husband. The word "husband" could also be translated as simply "man," but in that case she has had five men and the man she now has is not her man—a nonsensical understanding. To translate the word as "man" is therefore problematic. Jesus is referring to her five "husbands."

The subsequent marriage remains deeply scarred by adulterous sin, but with repentance and forgiveness may be consecrated to God. Deuteronomy 24:1–4 forbids a woman married to another man to return to her original spouse. It would be a pollution of the land before God. The Torah therefore emphasizes the severity of the sin involved in such an instance. The prophet Jeremiah returned to these verses in Jer. 3:1: "If a man divorces his wife and she goes from him and becomes another man's wife, will he return to her? Would not such a land be greatly polluted? You have prostituted yourself with many lovers, and would you return to me? says the Lord." Most modern translations have a rhetorical question here since an imperative would be "out of harmony with the whole tenor of the passage. The question at issue is whether Israel, who has sinned so deeply, may lightly decide to return to Yahweh as though nothing had happened."[15] Two factors

---

14. Carroll D. Osburn, "The Present Indicative Matthew 19:9," *Restoration Quarterly* 24.4 (1981): 193–203.

15. J. A. Thompson, *The Book of Jeremiah*, NICOT (Grand Rapids: Eerdmans, 1980), 192; Nelly

prevent the wife from returning to her original husband. First, the reference to Deut 24:1–4 reinforces the legal impossibility of a return. If the law prohibits a wife to return to her first husband after a subsequent marriage, how much more abominable is it for Israel (or Judah, in some reconstructions) to think it can return to God after affairs with several lovers—as if nothing had happened?[16] Second, the immediately following verses reinforce that the people have not repented (*šûb*). Jeremiah describes their faithlessness in vv. 6–11, and v. 8 describes the divorce of the northern kingdom because of unrepentant harlotry. Verses 12–18 look forward to a *future* (postexilic) restoration. Whether this involves Yahweh's setting aside Deut 24:1–4 is a matter of debate. It is also questionable whether the prophet envisions the people repenting.[17] David Instone-Brewer believes that Jer 3:12–22 imagines a *new* nation constituted of the children of *both* Judah and Israel: "In this way the law of Deuteronomy 24 is not broken because God does not marry exactly the same former wife, and yet the prophecy of Hosea is fulfilled because the future Israel will be reconciled when she becomes a new wife in unification with Judah."[18] If so, Jer 3 does not set aside Deut 24:1–4. Others believe that Yahweh's actions in these verses transcend or take precedence over the stipulations of the legal code.[19] Earl C. Muller comments on the prophetic "divorce" texts: "The prophetic form itself implies an ongoing relationship, not one that has been terminated" and the divorce imagery is more likely "an aggrieved spouse's poetic exaggeration."[20] Whatever interpretive path one takes, Jer 3:1–5 relies on the force of Deut 24:1–4 to stress the legal impossibility of returning to the original spouse, regardless of how Yahweh navigates the situation in the ensuing verses.[21]

Stienstra, *YHWH Is the Husband of His People: Analysis of a Biblical Metaphor with Special Reference to Translation* (Kampen: Kok Pharos, 1993), 224.

16. William L. Holladay, *Jeremiah 1*, Hermeneia (Philadelphia: Fortress, 1986), 113. On Israel versus Judah as the referent, see also e.g., C. L. Crouch, "Playing Favourites: Israel and Judah in the Marriage Metaphor of Jeremiah 3," *JSOT* 44 (2020): 594–609; Richard M. Davidson, "Divorce and Remarriage in the Old Testament," in *Marriage: Biblical and Theological Aspects*, ed. Ekkehardt Mueller and Elias Brasil de Souza, Biblical Research Institute Studies in Biblical Ethics 1 (Silver Spring, MD: Review and Herald, 2015), 191–93, esp. 191.

17. Louis Stulman, *Jeremiah*, Abingdon Old Testament Commentaries (Nashville: Abingdon, 2005), 57–58; John M. Bracke, *Jeremiah 1–29*, Westminster Bible Companion (Louisville, KY: Westminster John Knox, 2000), 42.

18. Instone-Brewer, *Divorce and Remarriage*, 42–43.

19. E.g., Peter C. Craigie, Page H. Kelley, and Joel F. Drinkard Jr., *Jeremiah 1–25*, WBC 26 (Dallas: Word, 1991), 51; Terence E. Fretheim, *Jeremiah*, SHBC (Macon, GA: Smyth & Helwys, 2002), 75.

20. Earl C. Muller, review of *Divorce and Remarriage in the Bible*, by David Instone-Brewer, *CBQ* 65 (2003): 471.

21. E.g., James D. Martin, "The Forensic Background to Jeremiah III 1," *VT* 19 (1969): 92: "All

Conclusion

The Deuteronomy text may have been influential in the minds of the first Christians. Given the acceptance and frequency of divorce and remarriage in the Jewish and Greco-Roman worlds, tellingly, Paul never requires the remarried who had joined his churches to divorce their current spouses and return to their original partners. John the Baptist and Jesus never instruct remarried people to dissolve their marriages for the sake of their former ones. Likewise, the first centuries of the early Christian movement would have seen remarried converts frequently joining their ranks even though the churches were not sanctioning remarriage among believers. The same silence greets the interpreter in the witness of the ante-Nicene authors and councils. While the act of remarriage is itself adultery and the Christian churches did not permit it or perform it, these authors and councils offer no evidence or advice to dissolve remarriages. On this point, Harrell is correct: "There is nothing to indicate in the literature of the period that a divorced and remarried catechumen was required to make any change in his marital status before being accepted for baptism."[22] Again, the silence on this point is deafening in view of the significant volume of people in their world who had remarried. What Paul *did* say is that the divorced among Christians are to remain single or be reconciled to their former partners (1 Cor 7:11). The remarried partners should repent of the adultery and then remain "where they are," to draw on Paul's language in 1 Cor 7, although he does not address this particular situation. Keener's view that to adopt a no-remarriage position requires the dissolution of subsequent marriages—a reductio ad absurdum in his mind—is not the case.

Dale B. Martin remarks on a noticeable trend in the last several decades. Whereas a century before divorce and remarriage were largely frowned upon in ecclesiastical circles, scholars and church officials in recent decades appear to be widely accepting of both.[23] He draws attention to the work of Craig Keener and David Instone-Brewer. Both are representative of the attempt to expand the exceptions to Jesus's prohibition of divorce and remarriage far beyond sexual sin or desertion by an unbeliever. Martin wryly observes how these two scholars' books were reviewed rather positively, no doubt because of their justifying a more liberal approach to divorce and remarriage on the basis of Scripture. "Keener

---

that the phrase in V. 1 'will he return to her?' is saying is 'Is it legally possible for Yahweh to take Judah back again?' The answer, on the legal analogy, is 'No!', the more so since Judah's case is much worse than that envisaged in the divorce law." See also T. R. Hobbs, "Jer 3 1–5 and Deut 24 1–4," *ZAW* 86 (1974): 27: "When the analogy is made with the behaviour of the nation the message becomes clear. Judah can no more be united with her god, whom she has forsaken for others, than can a divorced woman be united with her former husband. The nation is rejected."

22. Harrell, *Divorce and Remarriage*, 226.
23. Martin, *Sex and the Single Savior*, 125–26.

repeatedly pushes the interpretation of each passage toward leniency."[24] Thus, Martin observes: "Reviews by evangelical or conservative scholars have generally been positive about Keener's book, even if they are occasionally a bit wary of his more-lenient conclusions."[25] Martin relays from Instone-Brewer that "the proper way to understand the 'biblical teachings' on divorce, therefore, is to see them as allowing divorce and remarriage certainly in the case of adultery, but also in a case of neglect or abuse or failure to keep the marriage 'vows,' which may include 'emotional' abuse or even the withholding of love."[26] Martin comments: "It is difficult to avoid the impression that Instone-Brewer's study has been well-received among certain circles because he provides a biblical foundationalist argument for more leniency on divorce and remarriage."[27] Martin's point is that moderns frequently do not appear to be self-aware of how they are interpreting ancient texts from their own cultural vantage point. Any study that is countercultural is not likely to be well received.

Jesus, Paul, and the first Christians were opposed to remarriage. The modern will inevitably respond by seeking ways to mitigate such an unwelcome and impractical position. For Martin, the scholar should be self-aware when he or she is constructing a point of view that varies or disagrees with the ancients' viewpoint—and there is no shame in that. Nevertheless, for those who wish to base a position on the early Christian witness—if this study is a defensible reconstruction—the discrepancy between modern and ancient views will inevitably lead to cognitive dissonance that individuals and church bodies will seek to resolve in their own ways. Despite the likely bad press, this volume will hopefully encourage a renewed scholarly discussion of remarriage in early Christianity. The consistency of that witness is worth considering. The New Testament's fierce, repeated claim that apart from the death of a spouse remarriage is adulterous certainly raises the stakes.

---

24. Martin, *Sex and the Single Savior*, 143.
25. Martin, *Sex and the Single Savior*, 234 n. 52.
26. Martin, *Sex and the Single Savior*, 144.
27. Martin, *Sex and the Single Savior*, 234 n. 54.

Bibliography

Abrahams, I. *Studies in Pharisaism and the Gospels*. Cambridge: Cambridge University Press, 1917.

Achelis, H. *Virgines Subintroductae: Ein Beitrag zum VII. Kapitel des I. Korintherbriefs*. Leipzig: Hinrichs, 1902.

Achilles Tatius. Translated by S. Gaselee. LCL. New York: Putnam's Sons, 1917.

Adams, Karin. "Metaphor and Dissonance: A Reinterpretation of Hosea 4:13–14." *JBL* 127.2 (2008): 291–305.

Alexander, Loveday. "'Better to Marry than to Burn': St. Paul and the Greek Novel." Pages 235–56 in *Ancient Fiction and Early Christian Narrative*. Edited by Ronald F. Hock, J. Bradley Chance, and Judith Perkins. SBLSymS 6. Atlanta: Scholars Press, 2009.

Allen, Willoughby C. *A Critical and Exegetical Commentary on the Gospel according to S. Matthew*. 3rd ed. ICC. Edinburgh: T&T Clark, 1985.

Allison, Dale C., Jr. "Divorce, Celibacy and Joseph (Matthew 1.18–25 and 19.1–12)." *JSNT* 49 (1993): 3–10.

———. *The Historical Christ and the Theological Jesus*. Grand Rapids: Eerdmans, 2009.

———. *Jesus of Nazareth: Millenarian Prophet*. Minneapolis: Fortress, 1998.

Allo, P. E. B. *Première épître aux Corinthiens*. 2nd ed. EBib. Paris: Gabalda, 1956.

Amram, David W. "Divorce." Pages 4:624–28 in *Jewish Encyclopedia*. Edited by Isidore Singer and Cyrus Adler. New York: Ktav, 1901, 1925.

———. *The Jewish Law of Divorce according to the Bible and Talmud*. New York: Hermon, 1968.

Andersen, Francis I., and David Noel Freedman. *Hosea*. AB 24. Garden City, NY: Doubleday, 1980.

Archer, Léone J. *Her Price Is beyond Rubies: The Jewish Woman in Graeco-Roman Palestine*. JSOTSup 60. Sheffield: Sheffield Academic, 1990.

Arendzen, J. P. "Another Note on Matthew xix, 3–12." *Clergy Review* 21 (1941): 23–26.

———. "Ante-Nicene Interpretations of the Sayings on Divorce." *JTS* 20 (1919): 230–41.

Aristophanes. Translated by Benjamin Bickley Rogerts. 3 vols. LCL. New York: Putnam's Sons, 1924.

Aristophanes. *The Comedies of Aristophanes*. Translated by C. A. Wheelwright. 2 vols. Oxford: Talboys, 1837.

Arnal, William. "Major Episodes in the Biography of Jesus: An Assessment of the Historicity of the Narrative Tradition." *TJT* 13 (1997): 201–26.

Atkinson, David. *To Have and to Hold: The Marriage Covenant and the Discipline of Divorce*. London: Collins, 1979.

———. "A Response." *The Churchman* 95 (1981): 162–63.

Augustine. *On Faith and Works*. Translated and edited by Gregory J. Lombardo. ACW 48. New York: Newman, 1988.

Bachmann, Philipp. *Der erste Brief des Paulus an die Korinther*. Kommentar zum Neuen Testament. Leipzig: Deichert, 1905.

Bagnall, Roger S. "A Trick a Day to Keep the Tax Man at Bay?" *BASP* 28. 1–2 (1991): 5–12.

Bain, Andrew M. "Tertullian: Paul as Teacher of the Gentile Churches." Pages 207–23 in *Paul and the Second Century*. Edited by Michael F. Bird and Joseph R. Dodson. LNTS 412. London: T&T Clark, 2011.

Balch, David L. "1 Cor 7:32–35 and Stoic Debates about Marriage, Anxiety, and Distraction." *JBL* 102.3 (1983): 429–39.

———. "Backgrounds of 1 Cor. VII: Sayings of the Lord in Q; Moses as an Ascetic ΘΕΙΟΣ ΑΝΗΡ in II Cor. III." *NTS* 18 (1972): 351–64.

Baltensweiler, Heinrich. "Die Ehebruchsklauseln bei Matthäus: Zu Matth. 5,32; 19,9." *TZ* 15 (1959): 340–56.

———. *Die Ehe im Neuen Testament*. ATANT 52. Zurich: Zwingli Verlag, 1967.

Banks, Robert. *Jesus and the Law in the Synoptic Tradition*. SNTSMS 28. London: Cambridge University Press, 1975.

The Barna Group. "New Marriage and Divorce Statistics Released." March 31, 2008. https://www.barna.com/research/new-marriage-and-divorce-statistics-released/.

Barrett, C. K. *A Commentary on the First Epistle to the Corinthians*. HNTC. New York: Harper & Row, 1968.

Bartlett, F. C. *Remembering: A Study in Experimental and Social Psychology*. Cambridge: Cambridge University Press, 1995.

Barton, Stephen C. *Discipleship and Family Ties in Mark and Matthew*. SNTSMS 80. Cambridge: Cambridge University Press, 1984.

Bauer, Johannes B. "Bemerkungen zu den matthäischen Unzuchtsklauseln (Mt 5,32; 19,9)." Pages 23–33 in *Begegnung mit dem Wort*. Edited by Josef Zmijewski and Ernst Nellessen. Bonn: Hanstein, 1980.

Baumann, Gerlinde. *Love and Violence: Marriage as Metaphor for the Relationship between YHWH and Israel in the Prophetic Books.* Collegeville, MN: Liturgical, 2003.

Baumert, Norbert. *Woman and Man in Paul: Overcoming a Misunderstanding.* Collegeville, MN: Liturgical, 1996.

Baumgarten, Joseph M. *Qumran Cave 4.XIII: The Damascus Document (4Q266–273).* DJD 18. Oxford: Oxford University Press, 1996.

Beentjes, Pancratius C. *The Book of Ben Sira in Hebrew.* VTSup 68. Leiden: Brill, 1997.

Bellinzoni, A. J. *The Sayings of Jesus in the Writings of Justin Martyr.* NTSup 17. Leiden: Brill, 1967.

Benoit, P., J. T. Milik, and R. de Vaux. *Les grottes de Murabba'ât.* DJD 2. Oxford: Oxford University Press, 1961.

Bevilacqua, Anthony J. "The History of the Indissolubility of Marriage." *Proceedings of the Annual Convention of the Catholic Theological Society of America* 22 (1967): 253–308.

Bird, Phyllis A. "'To Play the Harlot': An Inquiry into an Old Testament Metaphor." Pages 75–94 in *Gender and Difference in Ancient Israel.* Edited by Peggy L. Day. Minneapolis: Fortress, 1989.

———. "Prostitution in the Social World and Religious Rhetoric of Ancient Israel." Pages 40–58 in *Prostitutes and Courtesans in the Ancient World.* Edited by Christopher A. Faraone and Laura K. McClure. Madison: University of Wisconsin Press, 2006.

Blomberg, Craig L. *The Historical Reliability of the Gospels.* 2nd ed. Downers Grove, IL: InterVarsity, 2007.

———. "Marriage, Divorce, Remarriage, and Celibacy: An Exegesis of Matthew 19:3–12." *TJ* 11 (1990): 161–96.

———. "Victims of Adultery." *New Testament Musings* (blog), July 7, 2011. https://newtestamentmusings.wordpress.com/2011/07/07/victims-of-adultery/.

Bockmuehl, Markus. "Matthew 5.32; 19.9 in the Light of Pre-Rabbinic Halakah." *NTS* 35 (1989): 291–95.

Bonsirven, Joseph. *Le divorce dans le Nouveau Testament.* Paris: Desclée, 1948.

Boring, Eugene M. "How May We Identify Oracles of Christian Prophets in the Synoptic Traditions? Mark 3:28–29 as a Test Case." *JBL* 91.4 (1972): 501–21.

Bound, James F. "Who Are the 'Virgins' Discussed in 1 Corinthians 7:25–38?" *EvJ* 2 (1984): 3–15.

Bracke, John M. *Jeremiah 1–29.* Westminster Bible Companion. Louisville: Westminster John Knox, 2000.

Bradley, Keith R. "Ideals of Marriage in Suetonius' *Caesares.*" *Rivista storica dell'antichità* 15 (1985): 77–95.

———. "Remarriage and the Structure of the Upper-Class Roman Family." Pages 79–98 in *Marriage, Divorce, and Children in Ancient Rome*. Edited by Beryl Rawson. Oxford: Oxford University Press, 1991.

Brakke, David, trans. *Athanasius and the Politics of Asceticism*. Oxford Early Christian Studies. Oxford: Oxford University Press, 1995.

Brenton, Sir Lancelot C. L. *The Septuagint Version: Greek and English*. Grand Rapids: Zondervan, 1851.

Brin, Gershon. "Divorce at Qumran." Pages 231–44 in *Legal Texts and Legal Issues: Proceedings of the Second Meeting of the International Organization for Qumran Studies Cambridge 1995: Published in Honour of Joseph M. Baumgarten*. Edited by Moshe Bernstein, Florentino García Martínez, and John Kampen. STDJ 23. Leiden: Brill, 1997.

Bromiley, Geoffrey W. *God and Marriage*. Grand Rapids; Eerdmans, 1980.

Brooten, Bernadette J. "Early Christian Women and Their Cultural Contexts: Issues of Method in Historical Reconstruction." Pages 65–91 in *Feminist Perspectives on Biblical Scholarship*. Edited by Adela Yarbro Collins. Chico, CA: Scholars Press, 1985.

———. "Jewish Women's History in the Roman Period: A Task for Christian Theology." *HTR* 79.1 (1986): 22–30.

———. "Könnten Frauen im alten Judentum die Scheidung betreiben?" *EvT* 42.1 (1982): 65–80.

———. "Zur Debatte über das Scheidungsrecht der jüdischen Frau." *EvT* 43.5 (1983): 466–78.

Brown, Colin. "Divorce, Separation and Remarriage." Pages 3:535–42 in *The New International Dictionary of New Testament Theology*. Edited by Colin Brown. Grand Rapids: Zondervan, 1975–78.

———. "Separate, Divide." Pages 3:534–43 in *NIDNTT*. Edited by Colin Brown. Grand Rapids: Zondervan, 1975–78.

Brox, Norbert. *Der Hirt des Hermas*. Kommentar zu den Apostolischen Vätern 7. Göttingen: Vandenhoeck & Ruprecht, 1991.

Bruce, F. F. *1 and 2 Corinthians*. NCB. Grand Rapids: Eerdmans, 1971.

———. *The Acts of the Apostles: The Greek Text with Introduction and Commentary*. 3rd ed. Grand Rapids: Eerdmans, 1990.

———. *New Testament History*. London: Nelson and Sons, 1969.

Brug, John F. "An Exegetical Brief." *Wisconsin Lutheran Quarterly* 90 (1993): 143.

Brunec, Michael. "Tertio de clausulis divortii Mt 5, 32 et 19, 9." *Verbum Domini* 27 (1949): 3–16.

Bruner, Jerome S. "Past and Present as Narrative Constructions." Pages 23–43 in *Narration, Identity, and Historical Consciousness: The Psychological Construction of Time and History*. Edited by Jürgen Straub. New York: Berghan, 2005.

Buckley, Timothy J. *What Binds Marriage? Roman Catholic Theology in Practice*. Rev. ed. London: Continuum, 2002.

Butler, B. C. *The Originality of St. Matthew: A Critique of the Two-Document Hypothesis*. Cambridge: Cambridge University Press, 1951.

Byrne, Brendan. *Romans*. SP 6. Collegeville, MN: Liturgical, 1996.

Byrskog, Samuel. "Memory and Narrative—and Time: Toward a Hermeneutics of Memory." *JSHJ* 16 (2018): 108–35.

Calvert, D. G. A. "An Examination of the Criteria for Distinguishing the Authentic Words of Jesus." *NTS* 18.2 (1971–72): 209–19.

Carcopino, Jérôme. *Daily Life in Ancient Rome*. New Haven: Yale University Press, 1968.

Carmody, Denise Lardner. "Marriage in Roman Catholicism." *JES* 22.1 (1985): 28–40.

Carroll, John T. *Jesus and the Gospels: An Introduction*. Louisville: Westminster John Knox, 2016.

———. *Luke: A Commentary*. NTL. Louisville: Westminster John Knox, 2012.

Carson, D. A. "Matthew." Pages 8:3–599 in *The Expositor's Bible Commentary*. Edited by Frank E. Gaebelein. 12 vols. Grand Rapids: Zondervan, 1984.

Carter, Warren. *Matthew and the Margins: A Sociopolitical and Religious Reading*. Maryknoll, NY: Orbis, 2000.

———. "The Things of Caesar: Mark-ing the Plural (Mk 12:13–17)." *HvTSt* 70 (2014): Art. 2656; https://journals.sagepub.com/doi/10.1177/1476993X17742292.

Casey, Edward S. *Remembering: A Phenomenological Study*. Bloomington: Indiana University Press, 1987.

Catchpole, David R. "The Synoptic Divorce Material as a Traditio-Historical Problem." *BJRL* 57 (1974): 92–127.

Catullus. Translated by Francis Cornish Warre. In *Catullus, Tibullus, Pervigilium Veneris*. Revised by G. P. Goold. 2nd ed. LCL. Cambridge: Harvard University Press, 1988.

Cereti, Giovanni. *Divorzio, nuove nozze e penitenza nella Chiesa primitiva*. Collana Studi e Ricerche 26. Bologna: Edizioni Dehoniane Bologne, 1977.

———. "The Reconciliation of Remarried Divorcees according to Canon 8 of the Council of Nicaea." Pages 193–207 in *Ius Sequitur Vitam: Law Follows Life, Studies in Canon Law Presented to P. J. M. Huizing*. Edited by James H. Provost and Knut Walf. Annua Nuntia Lovaniensia 32. Leuven: Leuven University Press, 1991.

Chariton. *Callirhoe*. Translated by G. P. Goold. LCL. Cambridge: Harvard University Press, 1995.

Charles, R. H. *The Greek Versions of the Testaments of the Twelve Patriarchs*. Oxford: Oxford University Press, 1908.

Charlesworth, James H. *The Historical Jesus*. An Essential Guide. Nashville: Abingdon, 2008.

Cherlin, Andrew J. "The Deinstitutionalization of American Marriage." *Journal of Marriage and Family* 66.4 (2004): 848–61.

Ciampa, Roy E., and Brian S. Rosner. *The First Letter to the Corinthians*. PNTC. Grand Rapids: Eerdmans, 2010.
Clark, Elizabeth A. *Reading Renunciation: Asceticism and Scripture in Early Christianity*. Princeton: Princeton University Press, 1999.
———. "Status Feminae: Tertullian and the Uses of Paul." Pages 127–55 in *Tertullian and Paul*. Edited by Todd D. Still and David E. Wilhite. Pauline and Patristic Scholars in Debate 1. New York: Bloomsbury, 2013.
Clark, W. K. Lowther. "The Excepting Clause in St Matthew." *Theology* 15 (1927): 161–62.
Cohen, Boaz. "Concerning Divorce in Jewish and Roman Law." *PAAJR* 21 (1952): 3–34.
———. "On the Theme of Betrothal in Jewish and Roman Law." *PAAJR* 18 (1948–49): 67–135.
Cohen, David J. *Law, Sexuality and Society: The Enforcement of Morals in Classical Athens*. Cambridge: Cambridge University Press, 1991.
Cohen, Edward E. "Free and Unfree Sexual Work: An Economic Analysis of Athenian Prostitution." Pages 95–124 in *Prostitutes and Courtesans in the Ancient World*. Edited by Christopher A. Faraone and Laura K. McClure. Madison: University of Wisconsin Press, 2006.
Coiner, H. G. "Those 'Divorce and Remarriage' Passages (Matt. 5:32; 19:9; 1 Cor. 7:10–16) with Brief Reference to the Mark and Luke Passages." *CTM* 39 (1968): 367–84.
Coleman, Gerald D. *Divorce and Remarriage in the Catholic Church*. New York: Paulist, 1988.
Collins, C. John. "The (Intelligible) Masoretic Text of Malachi 2:16, or, How Does God Feel About Divorce." *Presb* 20.1 (1994): 36–40.
Collins, John J. "Marriage, Divorce, and Family in Second Temple Judaism." Pages 104–62 in *Families in Ancient Israel*. Edited by Leo G. Perdue, Joseph Blenkinsopp, John J. Collins, and Carol Meyers. Louisville: Westminster John Knox, 1997.
Collins, Raymond F. *Divorce in the New Testament*. GNS 38. Collegeville, MN: Liturgical, 1992.
———. *First Corinthians*. SP 7. Collegeville, MN: Liturgical, 1999.
Constantelos, Demetris J. "Marriage in the Greek Orthodox Church." *JES* 22.1 (1985): 21–27.
Coontz, Stephanie. "The World Historical Transformation of Marriage." *Journal of Marriage and Family* 66.4 (2004): 974–79.
Corbett, Percy Elwood. *The Roman Law of Marriage*. Oxford: Clarendon, 1930.
Cornes, Andrew. *Divorce and Remarriage: Biblical Principles and Pastoral Practice*. Grand Rapids: Eerdmans, 1993.
Countryman, L. William. *Dirt, Greed and Sex: Sexual Ethics in the New Testament and Their Implications for Today*. Philadelphia: Fortress, 1988.

Cowley, A. E. *Aramaic Papyri of the Fifth Century BC*. Oxford: Oxford University Press, 1923.
Craigie, Peter C., Page H. Kelley, and Joel F. Drinkard Jr. *Jeremiah 1–25*. WBC 26. Dallas: Word, 1991.
Crossan, John Dominic. "Divorce and Remarriage in the New Testament." Pages 18–26 in *The Bond of Marriage*. Edited by W. W. Bassett. Notre Dame: Notre Dame University Press, 1968.
———. *The Historical Jesus: The Life of a Mediterranean Jewish Peasant*. New York: HarperCollins, 1991.
Crouch, C. L. "Playing Favourites: Israel and Judah in the Marriage Metaphor of Jeremiah 3." *JSOT* 44 (2020): 594–609.
Crouzel, Henri. *L'église face au divorce: du premier au cinquième siècle*. ThH 13. Paris: Beauchesne, 1971.
———. "Les *digamoi* visés par le Concile de Nicée dans son canon 8." *Aug* 18 (1978): 533–46.
———. "Remarriage after Divorce in the Primitive Church: A Propos of a Recent Book." *ITQ* 38 (1971): 21–41.
Csillag, Pál. *The Augustan Laws on Family Relations*. Budapest: Akadémiai Kiadó, 1976.
Culpepper, R. Alan. *Matthew: A Commentary*. NTL. Louisville: Westminster John Knox, 2021.
Curran, John. "'To Be or to Be Thought to Be': The *Testimonium Flavianum* Again." *NovT* 59.1 (2017): 71–94.
Danby, Herbert, trans. *The Mishnah*. Oxford: Oxford University Press, 1987.
D'Angelo, Mary Rose. "Remarriage and the Divorce Sayings Attributed to Jesus." Pages 78–106 in *Divorce and Remarriage: Religious and Psychological Perspectives*. Edited by William P. Roberts. Kansas City, MO: Sheed and Ward, 1990.
Daniel-Hughes, Carly. "'Only in the Lord'? Debates over Paul's View of Remarriage in Early Christianity." *ScEs* 66 (2014): 269–83.
Das, A. Andrew. Add as first entry for Das:
Das, A. Andrew. *Galatians*. Concordia Commentary. St. Louis: Concordia, 2014.
———. "Reconcile, Reconciliation." Pages 4:745–48 in *New Interpreters Dictionary of the Bible*. Edited by Katharine Doob Sakenfeld. Nashville: Abingdon, 2009.
———. "Rethinking the Covenantal Paul." Pages 65–92 in *Paul and the Stories of Israel: Grand Thematic Narratives in Galatians*. Minneapolis: Fortress, 2016.
———. *Solving the Romans Debate*. Minneapolis: Fortress, 2007.
Daube, David. *The New Testament and Rabbinic Judaism*. Peabody, MA: Hendrickson, 1956.
———. "Pauline Contributions to a Pluralistic Culture: Re-Creation and Beyond." Pages

BIBLIOGRAPHY

223–45 in *Jesus and Man's Hope*. Edited by Donald G. Miller and Dikran Y. Haddian. Pittsburgh: Pittsburgh Theological Seminary, 1971.

Davidson, James N. *Courtesans and Fishcakes: The Consuming Passions of Classical Athens*. New York: HarperCollins, 1997.

Davidson, Richard M. "Divorce and Remarriage in the Old Testament." Pages 179–202 in *Marriage: Biblical and Theological Aspects*. Edited by Ekkehardt Mueller and Elias Brasil de Souza. Biblical Research Institute Studies in Biblical Ethics 1. Silver Spring, MD: Review and Herald, 2015.

Davies, Philip R. *Behind the Essenes: History and Ideology in the Dead Sea Scrolls*. BJS 94. Atlanta: Scholars Press, 1987.

Davies, W. D., and Dale C. Allison Jr. *A Critical and Exegetical Commentary on the Gospel According to Matthew*. 3 vols. ICC. Edinburgh: T&T Clark, 1988–1997.

Deal, William E. "Toward a Politics of Asceticism: Response to the Three Preceding Papers." Pages 424–42 in *Asceticism*. Edited by Vincent L. Wimbush and Richard Valantasis. Oxford: Oxford University Press, 1995.

Dean, David Andrew. "Covenant, Conditionality, and Consequence: New Terminology and a Case Study in the Abrahamic Covenant." *JETS* 57.2 (2014): 281–308.

Deasley, Alex R. G. *Divorce and Remarriage in the Bible and the Church*. Kansas City, MO: Beacon Hill, 2000.

Deming, Will. *Paul on Marriage and Celibacy: The Hellenistic Background of 1 Corinthians 7*. 2nd ed. Grand Rapids: Eerdmans, 2004.

Derrett, J. Duncan M. *Law in the New Testament*. London: Dartman, Longman, and Todd, 1970.

Descamps, A. L. "The New Testament Doctrine on Marriage." Pages 217–73 in *Contemporary Perspectives on Christian Marriage: Propositions and Papers from the International Theological Commission*. Edited by Richard Malone and John R. Connery. Chicago: Loyola University Press, 1984.

Dibelius, Martin. *Jesus*. Philadelphia: Westminster, 1949.

Dio Cassius. *Roman History*. Translated by Earnest Cary. 9 vols. LCL. Cambridge: Harvard University Press, 1914–1927.

DivorceScience. "World Divorce Statistics—Comparisons among Countries." N.d. https://divorcescience.org/for-students/world-divorce-statistics-comparisons-among-countries/.

Dixon, Suzanne. *The Roman Family*. Baltimore: Johns Hopkins University Press, 1992.

Donahue, John R. *The Theology and Setting of Discipleship in the Gospel of Mark*. Milwaukee: Marquette University Press, 1983.

Dunn, James D. G. *1 Corinthians*. New Testament Guides. Sheffield: Sheffield Academic Press, 1995.

———. *Jesus Remembered*. Vol. 1 of *Christianity in the Making*. Grand Rapids: Eerdmans, 2003.

———. "Q¹ as Oral Tradition." Pages 45–69 in *The Written Gospel*. Edited by Markus Bockmuehl and Donald A. Hagner. Cambridge: Cambridge University Press, 2005.

———. *Romans 1–8*. WBC 38A. Dallas: Word, 1988.

Duplacy, Jean. "Note sur les variants et le texte original de Matthieu 19,9." Pages 387–412 in *Études de critique textuelle de Nouveau Testament*. Edited by J. Delobel. BETL 78. Leuven: Leuven University Press, 1987.

Dupont, Jacques. *Mariage et divorce dans l'Évangile: Matthieu 19,3–12 et parallèles*. Abbaye de Saint-André: Desclée de Brouwer, 1959.

Dupont-Sommer, A. *The Essene Writings from Qumran*. Translated by G. Vermes. Cleveland, OH: World Publishing, 1961.

Edgar, Thomas R. "Divorce and Remarriage for Adultery or Desertion." Pages 151–96 in *Divorce and Remarriage: Four Christian Views*. Edited by H. Wayne House. Downers Grove, IL: InterVarsity, 1990.

Ehrman, Bart D. *The Apostolic Fathers*. 2 vols. LCL. Cambridge: Harvard University Press, 2003.

Elledge, C. D. "'From the Beginning It Was Not So . . .': Jesus, Divorce, and Remarriage in Light of the Dead Sea Scrolls." *PRSt* 37 (2010): 371–89.

———. *The Statutes of the King: The Temple Scroll's Legislation on Kingship, 11Q19 LVI 12–LIX 21*. Cahiers de la Revue biblique 56. Paris: Gabalda, 2004.

Elliott, John H. "The Jesus Movement Was Not Egalitarian but Family-Oriented." *BibInt* 11.2 (2003): 173–210.

Elliott, J. K. "Paul's Teaching on Marriage in 1 Corinthians: Some Problems Considered." *NTS* 19 (1972/73): 219–25.

Elliott, Neil. "Asceticism among the 'Weak' and the 'Strong' in Romans 14–15." Pages 231–51 in *Asceticism and the New Testament*. Edited by Leif E. Vaage and Vincent L. Wimbush. New York: Routledge, 1999.

Ellis, J. Edward. *Paul and Ancient Views of Sexual Desire: Paul's Sexual Ethics in 1 Thessalonians 4, 1 Corinthians 7 and Romans 1*. LNTS 354. London: T&T Clark, 2007.

Emmet, C. W. "The Teaching of Hermas and the First Gospel on Divorce." *The Expositor* 8 (1911): 68–74.

Erickson, John H. "Eastern Orthodox Perspectives on Divorce and Remarriage." Pages 15–26 in *Divorce and Remarriage: Religious and Psychological Perspectives*. Edited by William P. Roberts, 15–26. Kansas City, MO: Sheed and Ward, 1990.

Erlandsson, S. "zānāh." *TDOT* 4:99–103.

Euripides. *Works*. 4 vols. Translated by Arthur S. Way. New York: Putnam's Sons, 1929–1935.

Evans, Craig A. "Authenticity Criteria in Life of Jesus Research." *Christian Scholar's Review* 19.1 (1989): 6–31.

———. *Matthew*. New Cambridge Bible Commentary. Cambridge: Cambridge University Press, 2012.

Eve, Eric. "Meier, Miracle, and Multiple Attestation." *JSHJ* 3.1 (2005): 23–45.

Falk, Z. W. "Jewish Private Law." Pages 1:504–34 in *The Jewish People in the First Century: Historical Geography, Political History, Social, Cultural, and Religious Life and Institutions*. Edited by S. Safrai and M. Stern with D. Flusser and W. C. van Unnik. CRINT 1. Assen: Van Gorcum, 1974.

Farla, Piet. "'The Two Shall Become One Flesh': Gen. 1.27 and 2.24 in the New Testament Marriage Texts." Pages 67–82 in *Intertexuality in Biblical Writings: Essays in Honour of Bas van Iersel*. Edited by Sipke Draisma. Kampen: Kok, 1989.

Fee, Gordon D. "Εἰδωλόθυτα Once Again: An Interpretation of 1 Corinthians 8–10." *Bib* 61 (1980): 172–97.

———. *The First and Second Letters to the Thessalonians*. NICNT. Grand Rapids: Eerdmans, 2009.

———. *The First Epistle to the Corinthians*. Rev. ed. NICNT. Grand Rapids: Eerdmans, 2014.

Field, David. "Talking Points: The Divorce Debate—Where Are We Now?" *Themelios* 8.3 (1983): 26–31.

Finley, Moses I. *Ancient Slavery and Modern Ideology*. New York: Viking, 1980.

Fitzmyer, Joseph A. "Divorce among First-Century Palestinian Jews." *Eretz-Israel* 14 (1978): 103–10.

———. *First Corinthians*. AB 32. New Haven: Yale University Press, 2008.

———. *The Gospel according to Luke*. 2 vols. AB 28–28A. New York: Doubleday, 1981–1985.

———. "Marriage and Divorce." Pages 1:511–15 in *Encyclopedia of the Dead Sea Scrolls*. Edited by Lawrence H. Schiffman and James C. VanderKam. Oxford: Oxford University Press, 2000.

———. "The Matthean Divorce Texts and Some New Palestinian Evidence." *TS* 37 (1976): 197–226.

———. *Romans*. AB 33. New York: Doubleday, 1993.

———. *To Advance the Gospel: New Testament Studies*. 2nd ed. Biblical Resource Series. Grand Rapids: Eerdmans, 1981.

Ford, Coleman. "'Tantum in Domino': Tertullian's Interpretation of 1 Corinthians 7 in His *Ad Uxorem*." *TynBul* 69 (2018): 241–58.

Ford, J. Massingberd. "Levirate Marriage in St Paul (I Cor. VII)." *NTS* 10 (1963–1964): 361–65.

Fornberg, Tord. *Jewish-Christian Dialogue and Biblical Exegesis*. Uppsala: Studia Missionalia Upsaliensia, 1988.

Fraade, Steven D. "Ascetical Aspects of Ancient Judaism." Pages 253–88 in *Jewish Spirituality: From the Bible through the Middle Ages*. Edited by Arthur Green. New York: Crossroad, 1986.

France, R. T. *The Gospel according to Matthew*. TNTC. Grand Rapids: Eerdmans, 1985.

———. *The Gospel of Matthew*. NICNT. Grand Rapids: Eerdmans, 2007.
Fredriksen, Paula. *From Jesus to Christ: The Origins of New Testament Images of Jesus*. New Haven: Yale University Press, 1988.
Fretheim, Terence E. *Jeremiah*. SHBC. Macon, GA: Smyth & Helwys, 2002.
Frey, Jean Baptiste. *Corpus of Jewish Inscriptions: Jewish Inscriptions from the Third Century B.C. to the Seventh Century A.D.* Library of Biblical Studies. Sussidi allo Studio delle Antichità Cristiane 1. New York: Ktav, 1975.
———. "La signification des termes ΜΟΝΑΝΔΡΟΣ et Univira." *RSR* 20 (1930): 48–60.
Fuller, Russell. "Text-Critical Problems in Malachi 2:10–16." *JBL* 100.1 (1991): 47–57.
Funke, Hermann. "Univira: Ein Beispiel heidnischer Geschichtsapologetik." *JAC* 8/9 (1965–1966): 183–88.
Gadd, C. J. "Tablets from Kirkuk." *Revue d'Assyriologie et d'Archéologie Orientale* 23 (1926): 49–161.
Gagnon, Robert A. J. *The Bible and Homosexual Practice: Texts and Hermeneutics*. Nashville: Abingdon, 2001.
Gaius. *Institutes of Gaius*. Texts in Roman Law. Translated by W. M. Gordon and O. F. Robinson. Ithaca: Cornell University Press, 1988.
García Martínez, Florentino. *The Dead Sea Scrolls Translated: The Qumran Texts in English*. Grand Rapids: Eerdmans, 1992.
Gardner, Jane F. *Women in Roman Law and Society*. Bloomington: Indiana University Press, 1986.
Garland, David E. *1 Corinthians*. BECNT. Grand Rapids: Baker, 2003.
———. *Reading Matthew: A Literary and Theological Commentary on the First Gospel*. New York: Crossroad, 1993.
Gaventa, Beverly Roberts. *Acts*. ANTC. Nashville: Abingdon, 2003.
Gavin, F. "A Further Note on *PORNEIA*." *Theology* 16 (1928): 102–5.
Gentry, Kenneth L., Jr. *The Charismatic Gift of Prophecy: A Reformed Response to Wayne Grudem*. Memphis: Footstool, 1989.
Gibbs, Jeffrey A. *Matthew 1:1–11:1*. Concordia Commentary. St. Louis: Concordia, 2006.
Ginzburg, Louis. *An Unknown Jewish Sect*. Moreshet Series 1. New York: Jewish Theological Seminary of America, 1970.
Glancy, Jennifer A. *Corporal Knowledge: Early Christian Bodies*. Oxford: Oxford University Press, 2010.
———. "The Sexual Use of Slaves: A Response to Kyle Harper on Jewish and Christian *Porneia*." *JBL* 134.1 (2015): 215–29.
Goffman, Erving. *Frame Analysis: An Essay on the Organization of Experience*. New York: Harper & Row, 1974.
Goldberg, Gary J. "Josephus's Paraphrase Style and the *Testimonium Flavianum*." *JSHJ* 20.1 (2021): 1–32.

Goodacre, Mark. *The Case against Q: Studies in Markan Priority and the Synoptic Problem*. Harrisburg, PA: Trinity Press International, 2002.

———. "Criticizing the Criterion of Multiple Attestation: The Historical Jesus and the Question of Sources." Pages 152–69 in *Jesus, Criteria, and the Demise of Authenticity*. Edited by Chris Keith and Anthony Le Donne. New York: T&T Clark, 2012.

Goodacre, Mark, and Nicholas Perrin, eds. *Questioning Q: A Multidimensional Critique*. Downers Grove, IL: InterVarsity, 2004.

Grant, Robert M. "The Sermon on the Mount in Earliest Christianity." *Semeia* 12 (1978): 215–31.

The Greek Anthology. Translated by W. R. Paton. 5 vols. Cambridge: Harvard University Press, 1917–1918.

Green, Barbara. "Jesus' Teaching on Divorce in the Gospel of Mark." *JSNT* 38 (1990): 67–75.

Green, Joel B. *The Gospel of Luke*. NICNT. Grand Rapids: Eerdmans, 1997.

Grosheide, F. W. *Commentary on the First Epistle to the Corinthians*. NICNT. Grand Rapids: Eerdmans, 1953.

Grudem, Wayne. *What the Bible Says about Divorce and Remarriage*. Wheaton: Crossway, 2021.

Grundmann, Walter. *Das Evangelium nach Matthäus*. THKNT 1. Berlin: Evangelische Verlaganstalt, 1968.

Guelich, Robert A. *The Sermon on the Mount: A Foundation for Understanding*. Waco, TX: Word, 1982.

Guenther, Allen R. "The Exception Phrases: Except πορνεία or Excluding πορνεία? (Matthew 5:32; 19:9)." *TynBul* 53.1 (2002): 83–96.

———. "One Woman or Two? 1 Corinthians 7:34." *BBR* 12 (2002): 33–45.

Gundry, Robert H. *Mark: A Commentary on His Apology for the Cross*. Grand Rapids: Eerdmans, 1993.

———. *Matthew: A Commentary on His Literary and Theological Art*. Grand Rapids: Eerdmans, 1982.

Gundry-Volf, Judith M. "Controlling the Bodies, A Theological Principle of the Corinthian Sexual Ascetics (1 Cor 7)." Pages 519–41 in *The Corinthian Correspondence*. Edited by R. Bieringer. BETL 125. Leuven: Leuven University Press, 1996.

———. "Male and Female in Creation and New Creation: Interpretation of Galatians 3:28C in 1 Corinthians 7." Pages 95–121 in *To Tell the Mystery: Essays on New Testament Eschatology in Honor of Robert H. Gundry*. Edited by Thomas E. Schmidt and Moisés Silva. JSNTSup 100. Sheffield: Sheffield Academic Press, 1994.

Gupta, Nijay K. *1 & 2 Thessalonians*. Zondervan Critical Introductions to the New Testament 13. Grand Rapids: Zondervan, 2019.

Hagner, Donald A. *Matthew 1–13*. WBC 33A. Dallas: Word, 1993.

———. *Matthew 14–28*. WBC 33B. Dallas: Word, 1995.
Halbwachs, Maurice. *The Collective Memory*. New York: Harper & Row, 1980.
———. "The Social Frameworks of Memory." Pages 37–189 in *On Collective Memory*. Translated by Lewis A. Coser. Chicago: University of Chicago Press, 1992.
Hall, F. W. "Adultery (Roman)." *ERE* 1:134–35.
Harper, Kyle. *From Shame to Sin: The Christian Transformation of Sexual Morality in Late Antiquity*. Revealing Antiquity 20. Cambridge: Harvard University Press, 2013.
———. "*Porneia*: The Making of a Christian Sexual Norm." *JBL* 131 (2011): 363–83.
Harpham, Geoffrey Galt. *The Ascetic Imperative in Culture and Criticism*. Chicago: University of Chicago Press, 1987.
Harrell, Pat Edwin. *Divorce and Remarriage in the Early Church: A History of Divorce and Remarriage in the Ante-Nicene Church*. Austin, TX: Sweet, 1967.
Harrington, Hannah K. *The Purity Texts*. Companion to the Qumran Scrolls 5. London: T&T Clark, 2004.
Hauck, F. "μοιχεύω." *TDNT* 4:733.
Hays, Richard B. *First Corinthians*. Interpretation. Louisville: John Knox, 1997.
———. *The Moral Vision of the New Testament: Community, Cross, New Creation: A Contemporary Introduction to New Testament Ethics*. New York: HarperCollins, 1996.
Hegy, Pierre, and Joseph Martos, eds. *Catholic Divorce: The Deception of Annulments*. New York: Continuum, 2000.
Heine, Ronald E. *The Commentary of Origen on the Gospel of St Matthew*. 2 vols. Oxford Early Christian Texts. Oxford: Oxford University Press, 2018.
Héring, Jean. *The First Epistle of Saint Paul to the Corinthians*. London: Epworth, 1962.
Herodotus. Translated by A. D. Godley. 4 vols. New York: Putnam's Sons, 1921–1926.
Herron, Robert, Jr. "Mark's Jesus on Divorce: Mark 10:1–12 Reconsidered." *JETS* 25.3 (1982): 273–81.
Heth, William A. "The Changing Basis for Permitting Remarriage after Divorce for Adultery: The Influence of R. H. Charles." *TJ* 11 (1990): 143–59.
———. "Divorce and Remarriage." Pages 219–39 in *Applying the Scriptures: Papers from ICBI Summit III*. Edited by Kenneth S. Kantzer. Grand Rapids: Zondervan, 1987.
———. "Divorce and Remarriage: The Search for an Evangelical Hermeneutic." *TJ* 16 (1995): 63–100.
———. "Jesus on Divorce: How My Mind Has Changed." *SBJT* 6.1 (2002): 4–29.
———. "Remarriage for Adultery or Desertion." Pages 59–83 in *Remarriage after Divorce in Today's Church: Three Views*. Edited by Mark L. Strauss. Counterpoints. Grand Rapids: Zondervan, 2006.
———. "A Response to Gordon J. Wenham." Pages 43–47 in *Remarriage after Divorce in Today's Church: Three Views*. Edited by Mark L. Strauss, 43–47. Counterpoints. Grand Rapids, MI: Zondervan, 2006.

———. "Unmarried 'For the Sake of the Kingdom' (Matthew 19:12) in the Early Church." *Grace Theological Journal* 8.1 (1987): 55–88.

Heth, William A., and Gordon J. Wenham. *Jesus and Divorce: The Problem with the Evangelical Consensus*. Nashville: Nelson, 1984.

Hezser, Catherine. *Jewish Slavery in Antiquity*. Oxford: Oxford University Press, 2005.

Hilberath, Bernd Jochen. "Die prinzipielle Unauflösigkeit der Ehe und die prinzipielle Bedeutung einer evangeliumgemäßen Barmherzigkeit." *TQ* 194 (2014): 399–401.

Hill, David. *The Gospel of Matthew*. NCB. Grand Rapids: Eerdmans, 1972.

Hippocrates. *Epidemics 2 and 4–7*. Edited and translated by Wesley D. Smith. LCL. Cambridge: Harvard University Press, 1994.

Hobbs, T. R. "Jer 3 1–5 and Deut 24 1–4." *ZAW* 86 (1974): 23–29.

Hofmann, Johann Christian Konrad von. *Die heilige Schrift Neuen Testaments: Zusammenhängend untersucht*. 8 vols. Nördlingen: Beck, 1862–1878.

Holladay, Carl R. *Acts: A Commentary*. NTL. Louisville: Westminster John Knox, 2016.

Holladay, William L. *Jeremiah 1*. Hermeneia. Philadelphia: Fortress, 1986.

Holmén, Tom. "Authenticity Criteria." Pages 43–54 in *Encyclopedia of the Historical Jesus*. Edited by Craig A. Evans. New York: Routledge, 2008.

———. "Divorce in *CD* 4:20–5:2 and 11QT 57:17–18: Some Remarks on the Pertinence of the Question." *RevQ* 18 (1998): 397–408.

———. "Doubts about Double Dissimilarity: Restructuring the Main Criterion of Jesus-of-History Research." Pages 47–80 in *Authenticating the Words of Jesus*. Edited by Bruce Chilton and Craig A. Evans. Leiden: Brill, 1999.

Holzmeister, U. "Die Streitfrage über die Ehescheidungstexte bei Matthäus 5,32, 19,9." *Bib* 26 (1945): 133–46.

Hooker, Morna D. "Christology and Methodology." *NTS* 17.4 (1971): 480–87.

———. "Foreword: Forty Years On." Pages xiii–xvii in *Jesus, Criteria, and the Demise of Authenticity*. Edited by Chris Keith and Anthony Le Donne. New York: T&T Clark, 2012.

———. "On Using the Wrong Tool." *Theology* 75 (1972): 570–81.

Horace. *Odes and Epodes*. Translated by C. E. Bennett. LCL. New York: Macmillan, 1914.

Horsley, G. H. R. *New Documents Illustrating Early Christianity: A Review of the Greek Inscriptions and Papyri Published in 1978*. Sydney: Macquarie University Press, 1983.

Horsley, Richard A. *1 Corinthians*. ANTC. Nashville: Abingdon, 1998.

———. "Prominent Patterns in the Social Memory of Jesus and Friends." Pages 57–78 in *Memory, Tradition, and Text: Uses of the Past in Early Christianity*. Edited by Alan Kirk and Tom Thatcher. SemeiaSt 52. Atlanta: Society of Biblical Literature, 2005.

Houston, Walter J. "Foods." Pages 326–36 in *Dictionary of the Old Testament: Penta-*

teuch. Edited by T. Desmond Alexander and David W. Baker. Downers Grove, IL: InterVarsity, 2003.

Huebenthal, Sandra. *Reading Mark's Gospel as a Text from Collective Memory*. Grand Rapids: Eerdmans, 2020.

Hugenberger, Gordon P. *Marriage as a Covenant: Biblical Law and Ethics as Developed from Malachi*. VTSup 52. Leiden: Brill, 1994.

Hultgren, Arland J. *Paul's Letter to the Romans: A Commentary*. Grand Rapids: Eerdmans, 2011.

Humbert, Michel. *Le remariage à Rome: Étude d'historie juridique et sociale*. Università di Roma 44. Milan: Giuffre, 1972.

Hunt, A. S., and C. C. Edgar, trans. *Select Papyri, Volume I: Private Documents*. LCL. Cambridge: Harvard University Press, 1959.

Hunter, David G. "'A Man of One Wife': Patristic Interpretations of 1 Timothy 3:2, 3:12, and Titus 1:6 and the Making of Christian Priesthood." *Annali di Storia dell'Esegesi* 32.2 (2015): 333–52.

———. *Marriage and Sexuality in Early Christianity*. Ad Fontes: Early Christian Sources. Minneapolis: Fortress, 2018.

Ilan, Tal. *Jewish Women in Greco-Roman Palestine*. Peabody, MA: Hendrickson, 1995.

———. "Notes and Observations on a Newly Published Divorce Bill from the Judaean Desert." *HTR* 89.2 (1996): 195–202.

———. "Women in Qumran and the Dead Sea Scrolls." Pages 123–47 in *The Oxford Handbook of the Dead Sea Scrolls*. Edited by Timothy H. Lim and John J. Collins. Oxford: Oxford University Press, 2010.

Instone-Brewer, David. "1 Corinthians 7 in the Light of the Graeco-Roman Marriage and Divorce Papyri." *TynBul* 51.2 (2001): 101–15.

———. "1 Corinthians 7 in the Light of the Jewish Greek and Aramaic Marriage and Divorce Papyri." *TynBul* 52.2 (2001): 225–43.

———. "Deuteronomy 24:1–4 and the Origin of the Jewish Divorce Certificate." *JJS* 49.2 (1998): 230–43.

———. *Divorce and Remarriage in the Bible: The Social and Literary Context*. Grand Rapids: Eerdmans, 2002.

———. "Marriage & Divorce Papyri of the Ancient Greek, Roman and Jewish World." 2000. http://www.tyndalearchive.com/Brewer/MarriagePapyri/Index.html.

———. "Nomological Exegesis in Qumran 'Divorce' Texts." *RevQ* 18 (1998): 561–79.

Isaksson, Abel. *Marriage and Ministry in the New Temple: A Study with Special Reference to Mt. 19.3–12 and 1 Cor. 11.3–16*. Translated by N. Tomkinson with J. Gray. Acta Seminarii Neotestamenticii Upsaliensis 24. Lund: Gleerup, 1965.

Janzen, David. "The Meaning of *Porneia* in Matthew 5.32 and 19.9: An Approach from the Study of Ancient Near Eastern Culture." *JSNT* 80 (2000): 66–80.

Jayson, Sharon. "Interest in Remarriage Is on the Wane." *Christianity Today*, Oct. 16, 2013.

———. "Remarriage Rate Declining as More Opt for Cohabitation." *USA Today*, Sept. 12, 2013. https://www.usatoday.com/story/news/nation/2013/09/12/remarriage-rates-divorce/2783187/.

Jenkins, Claude. "Documents: Origen on I Corinthians. II." *JTS* 9.35 (1908): 353–72.

———. "Documents: Origen on I Corinthians. III." *JTS* 9.36 (1908): 500–14.

Jensen, Joseph. "Does *Porneia* Mean Fornication? A Critique of Bruce Malina." *NovT* 20 (1978): 161–84.

Jeremias, Joachim. *Jerusalem in the Time of Jesus: An Investigation into Economic and Social Conditions during the New Testament Period*. Philadelphia: Fortress, 1969.

———. "Die missionarische Aufgabe in der Mischehe (1 Cor 7 16)." Pages 255–60 in *Neutestamentliche Studien für Rudolf Bultmann zu seinem siebzigsten Geburtstag*. Edited by Walther Eltester. BZNW 21. Berlin: Töpelmann, 1954.

———. "Nochmals: War Paulus Witwer?" *ZNW* 28 (1929): 321–23.

———. "War Paulus Witwer?" *ZNW* 26 (1926): 310–12.

Jewett, Robert. *Romans: A Commentary*. Hermeneia. Minneapolis: Fortress, 2007.

Job, John. "The Biblical View of Marriage and Divorce 4—New Testament Teaching." *Third Way* 1, Nov. 17, 1977.

John Chrysostom. *On Virginity; Against Remarriage*. Translated by Sally Rieger Shore. Studies in Women and Religion 9. New York: Mellen, 1983.

John Malalas. *The Chronicles of John Malalas*. Translated by Elizabeth Jeffreys, Michael Jeffreys, and Roger Scott. Byzantina Australiensia 4. Leiden: Brill, 2017.

———. *Chronographia*. Edited by Johannes Thurn. Corpus Fontium Historiae Byzantinae 35. Berlin: de Gruyter, 2000.

Jones, David Clyde. "A Note on the LXX of Malachi 2:16." *JBL* 109.4 (1990): 683–85.

Jones, David W. "The Betrothal View of Divorce and Remarriage." *BSac* 165 (2008): 68–85

Jones, David W., and John K. Tarwater. "Are Biblical Covenants Dissoluble? Toward a Theology of Marriage." *Reformed Perspectives Magazine* 7.38, Sept. 18–24, 2005.

Josephus. *Jewish Antiquities*. Translated by H. St. J. Thackeray et al. 9 vols. LCL. Cambridge: Harvard University Press, 1930–1965.

———. *The Life. Against Apion*. Translated by H. St. J. Thackeray. LCL. Cambridge: Harvard University Press, 1926.

Joyce, George Hayward. *Christian Marriage: An Historical and Doctrinal Study*. 2nd ed. Heythrop Series 1. London: Sheed and Ward, 1948.

Justinian. *The Digest of Justinian*. Edited by Theodor Mommsen and Paul Krueger. Translated by Alan Watson. 4 vols. Philadelphia: University of Pennsylvania Press, 1985.

Justin Martyr. *The First and Second Apologies*. Translated by Leslie William Barnard. ACW 56. New York: Paulist, 1997.

Kaiser, Walter C., Jr. "Divorce in Malachi 2:10–16." *CTR* 2.1 (1987): 73–84.

Kampen, John. "A Fresh Look at the Masculine Plural Suffix in CD IV, 21." *RevQ* 16.1 (1993): 91–97.

———. "The Matthean Divorce Texts Reexamined." Pages 149–67 in *New Qumran Texts and Studies: Proceedings of the First Meeting of the International Organization for Qumran Studies, Paris 1992*. Edited by G. J. Brooke. STDJ 15. Leiden: Brill, 1994.

Kapparis, Konstantinos. *Prostitution in the Ancient Greek World*. Berlin: de Gruyter, 2018.

Keener, Craig S. *And Marries Another: Divorce and Remarriage in the Teachings of the New Testament*. Peabody, MA: Hendrickson, 1991.

———. *The Gospel of Matthew: A Socio-Rhetorical Commentary*. Grand Rapids: Eerdmans, 2009.

———. *The Historical Jesus of the Gospels*. Grand Rapids: Eerdmans, 2009.

———. "Remarriage for Adultery, Desertion or Abuse." Pages 103–19 in *Remarriage after Divorce in Today's Church: Three Views*. Edited by Mark L. Strauss. Counterpoints. Grand Rapids: Zondervan, 2006.

Keith, Chris. "Memory and Authenticity: Jesus Tradition and What Really Happened." *ZNW* 102 (2011): 155–77.

Keith, Chris, and Anthony Le Donne, eds. *Jesus, Criteria, and the Demise of Authenticity*. New York: T&T Clark, 2012.

Kelber, Werner. *The Oral and the Written Gospel: The Hermeneutics of Speaking and Writing in the Synoptic Tradition, Mark, Paul, and Q*. Philadelphia: Fortress, 1983.

———. "The Works of Memory: Christian Origins as MnemoHistory—A Response." Pages 221–48 in *Memory, Tradition, and Text: Uses of the Past in Early Christianity*. Edited by Alan Kirk and Tom Thatcher. SemeiaSt 52. Atlanta: Society of Biblical Literature, 2005.

Kelly, J. N. D. *A Commentary on the Pastoral Epistles*. Grand Rapids: Baker, 1981.

Keppler, Angela. *Tischgespräche: Über Formen kommunikativer Vergesellschaftung am Beispiel der Koversation in Familien*. 2nd ed. Frankfurt: Suhrkamp, 1995.

Kilgallen, John J. "To What Are the Matthean Exception-Texts (5,32 and 19,9) an Exception?" *Bib* 61 (1980): 102–5.

Kilpatrick, G. D. *The Origins of the Gospel according to St. Matthew*. Oxford: Oxford University Press, 1946.

Kirk, Alan. "Ehrman, Bauckham, and Bird on Memory and the Jesus Tradition." *JSHJ* 15 (2017): 88–114.

———. "Memory." Pages 155–72 in *Jesus in Memory: Traditions in Oral and Scribal Perspectives*. Edited by Werner H. Kelber and Samuel Byrskog. Waco: Baylor University Press, 2009.

———. *Memory and the Jesus Tradition. The Reception of the Jesus Tradition in the First Three Centuries 2*. London: T&T Clark, 2018.

———. "Social and Cultural Memory." Pages 1–24 in *Memory, Tradition, and Text: Uses of the Past in Early Christianity*. Edited by Alan Kirk and Tom Thatcher. SemeiaSt 52. Atlanta: Society of Biblical Literature, 2005.

Kistemaker, Simon J. *New Testament Commentary: Exposition of the First Epistle to the Corinthians*. Grand Rapids: Baker, 1993.

Klauck, Hans-Josef. *The Religious Context of Early Christianity: A Guide to Graeco-Roman Religions*. Studies in the New Testament World. Edinburgh: T&T Clark, 2000.

Kloha, Jeffrey John. "A Textual Commentary on Paul's First Epistle to the Corinthians." 4 vols. PhD diss., The University of Leeds, 2006.

Knust, Jennifer Wright. *Abandoned to Lust: Sexual Slander and Ancient Christianity*. Gender, Theory, and Religion. New York: Columbia University Press, 2006.

Kodell, Jerome. "The Celibacy Logion in Matthew 19:12." *BTB* 8 (1978): 19–23.

Köstenberger, Andreas J. *Commentary on 1–2 Timothy and Titus*. Biblical Theology for Christian Proclamation. Nashville: B&H, 2017.

Kötting, Bernhard. "Digamus." Pages 3:106–23 in *Reallexikon für Antike und Christentum*.

Kovacs, Judith L. *1 Corinthians: Interpreted by Early Christian Commentators*. Edited by Robert L. Wilken. The Church's Bible Series. Grand Rapids: Eerdmans, 2005.

Kraeling, Emil G., ed. *The Brooklyn Museum Aramaic Papyri: New Documents of the Fifth Century B.C. from the Jewish Colony at Elephantine*. New Haven: Yale University Press, 1953.

Krause, Jens-Uwe. *Witwen und Waisen im Römischen Reich I: Verwitwung und Wiederverheiratung*. Heidelberger Althistorische Beiträge und Epigraphische Studien 16. Stuttgart: Steiner, 1994.

Kreider, Rose M. "Remarriage in the United States." *United States Census Bureau*, August 2006. https://www.census.gov/library/working-papers/2006/demo/kreider-02.html.

Kriegel, Albert, and Moritz Kriegel, eds. *Corpus Juris Civilis*. Leipzig: Baumgartner, 1987.

Kuck, David W. "The Freedom of Being in the Word 'As If Not' (1 Cor 7:29–21)." *CurTM* 28 (2001): 585–93.

Kuefler, Mathew. *The Manly Eunuch: Masculinity, Gender Ambiguity, and Christian Ideology in Late Antiquity*. The Chicago Series on Sexuality, History, and Society. Chicago: University of Chicago Press, 2001.

Kümmel, Werner Georg. "Verlobung und Heirat bei Paulus (I. Cor 7.36–38)." Pages 275–95 in *Neutestamentliche Studien für Rudolf Bultmann zu seinem siebzigsten Geburtstag*. Edited by Walther Eltester. BZNW 21. Berlin: Töpelmann, 1954.

Kurke, Leslie. *Coins, Bodies, Games, and Gold: The Politics of Meaning in Ancient Greece.* Princeton: Princeton University Press, 1999.

Kysar, Myrna, and Robert Kysar. *The Asundered: Biblical Teachings on Divorce and Remarriage.* Atlanta: Knox, 1978.

Lactantius. *The Divine Institutes, Books I–VII.* Translated by Mary Francis McDonald. FC 49. Washington, DC: The Catholic University of America, 1964.

Lake, Kirsopp. "The Earliest Christian Teaching on Divorce." *The Expositor* 7 (1910): 416–27.

Lane, William L. *The Gospel according to Mark.* NICNT. Grand Rapids: Eerdmans, 1974.

Laney, J. Carl. *The Divorce Myth.* Minneapolis: Bethany House, 1981.

———. "No Divorce, No Remarriage." Pages 15–54 in *Divorce and Remarriage: Four Christian Views.* Edited by H. Wayne House. Downers Grove, IL: InterVarsity, 1990.

———. "Paul and the Permanence of Marriage in 1 Corinthians 7." *JETS* 25.3 (1982): 283–94.

Lang, Friedrich. *Die Briefe an die Korinther.* Das Neue Testament Deutsch 7. Göttingen: Vandenhoeck & Ruprecht, 1994.

Lattimore, Richmond. *Themes in Greek and Latin Epitaphs.* Illinois Studies in Language and Literature 28.1–2. Urbana: University of Illinois Press, 1942.

Laughery, G. J. "Paul: Anti-Marriage? Anti-Sex? Ascetic? A Dialogue with 1 Corinthians 7:1–40." *Evangelical Quarterly* 69 (1997): 109–28.

Le Donne, Anthony. *The Historiographical Jesus: Memory, Typology, and the Son of David.* Waco: Baylor University Press, 2009.

Lawler, Michael G. *Marriage and the Catholic Church: Disputed Questions.* Collegeville, MN: Liturgical, 2002.

Lawler, Michael G., and Todd A. Salzman. "Catholic Doctrine on Divorce and Remarriage: A Practical Theological Examination." *TS* 78 (2017): 326–47.

Lefkowitz, Mary R., and Maureen B. Fant. *Women's Life in Greece and Rome: A Source Book in Translation.* 2nd ed. Baltimore: Johns Hopkins University Press, 1992.

Leith, Mary Joan Winn. "Verse and Reverse: The Transformation of the Woman, Israel, in Hosea 1–3." Pages 95–108 in *Gender and Difference in Ancient Israel.* Edited by Peggy L. Day. Minneapolis: Fortress, 1989.

Lenski, R. C. H. *The Interpretation of St. Matthew's Gospel.* Minneapolis: Augsburg, 1943.

Leon, Harry J. *The Jews of Ancient Rome.* Rev. ed. Peabody, MA: Hendrickson, 1995.

Levine, Amy-Jill. "Diaspora as Metaphor: Bodies and Boundaries in the Book of Tobit." Pages 105–17 in *Diaspora Jews and Judaism: Essays in Honor of, and in Dialogue with, A. Thomas Kraabel.* Edited by J. Andrew Overman and Robert S. MacLennan. USF Studies in the History of Judaism 41. Atlanta: Scholars Press, 1992.

Lewis, Jamie M., and Rose M. Kreider. "Remarriage in the United States: American Community Survey Reports." *American Community Survey Reports* 30, March 2015. https://www.census.gov/content/dam/Census/library/publications/2015/acs/acs-30.pdf.

Lewis, Naphtali, ed. *The Documents from the Bar Kokhba Region in the Cave of Letters: Greek Papyri.* Judean Desert Studies. Jerusalem: Israel Exploration Society, 1989.

L'Huillier, Peter. "The Indissolubility of Marriage in Orthodox Law and Practice." Pages 108–26 in *Catholic Divorce: The Deception of Annulments.* Edited by Pierre Hegy and Joseph Martos. New York: Continuum, 2000.

Lightfoot, J. B. *Notes on Epistles of St. Paul: 1–II Thessalonians, 1 Corinthians 1–7, Romans 1–7, Ephesisans 1:1–14.* Grand Rapids: Baker, 1980.

Lightman, Majorie, and William Zeisel. "Univira: An Example of Continuity and Change in Roman Society." *Church History* 46 (1977): 19–32.

Lipiński, E. "The Wife's Right to Divorce Her Husband in the Light of an Ancient Near Eastern Tradition." *JLA* 4 (1981): 9–27.

Livingston, Gretchen. "Four-in-Ten Couples Are Saying 'I Do,' Again." *Pew Research Center*, Nov. 14, 2014. http://www.pewsocialtrends.org/2014/11/14/chapter-1-trends-in-remarriage-in-the-u-s/#.

Livy. *History of Rome, Volume IV: Books 8–10.* Translated by B. O. Foster. LCL. Cambridge: Harvard University Press, 1926.

———. *History of Rome, Volume IX: Books 31–34.* Translated by Evan T. Sage. LCL. Cambridge: Harvard University Press, 1935.

Loader, William. *The Dead Sea Scrolls on Sexuality: Attitudes toward Sexuality in Sectarian and Related Literature at Qumran.* Grand Rapids: Eerdmans, 2009.

———. "Did Adultery Mandate Divorce? A Reassessment of Jesus' Divorce Logia." *NTS* 61 (2015): 67–78.

———. *Sexuality and the Jesus Tradition.* Grand Rapids: Eerdmans, 2005.

Lorusso, Lorenzo, and George Gallaro. "Divorced and Remarried in the Eastern Orthodox Churches." *Studia Canonica* 50 (2016): 485–502.

Lövestam, Evald. "Divorce and Remarriage in the New Testament." *JLA* 4 (1981): 47–65.

Luck, William F., Sr. *Divorce and Re-Marriage: Recovering the Biblical View.* 2nd ed. Richardson, TX: Biblical Studies Press, 2009.

Lüddeckens, Erich. *Ägyptische Eheverträge.* Ägyptische Abhandlugen 1. Wiesbaden: Harrassowitz, 1960.

Lutz, Cora E., ed. and trans. "Musonius Rufus: 'The Roman Socrates.'" *Yale Classical Studies* 10 (1947): 3–147.

Luz, Ulrich. *Matthew 1–7: A Commentary.* Translated by Wilhelm C. Linss. CC. Minneapolis: Augsburg, 1985.

———. *Matthew 8–20.* Hermeneia. Minneapolis: Fortress, 2001.

Lysias. Translated by W. R. M. Lamb. LCL. New York: Putnam's Sons, 1930.

MacDonald, Margaret Y. "A Response to Elizabeth A. Clark's Essay, 'Status Feminae: Tertullian and the Uses of Paul.'" Pages 156–64 in *Tertullian and Paul*. Edited by Todd D. Still and David E. Wilhite. Pauline and Patristic Scholars in Debate 1. New York: Bloomsbury, 2013.

———. "Women Holy in Body and Spirit: The Social Setting of 1 Corinthians 7." *NTS* 36 (1990): 161–81.

Mackin, Theodore. *Divorce and Remarriage*. Marriage in the Catholic Church 2. New York: Paulist, 1984.

———. "The International Theological Commission and Indissolubility." Pages 27–69 in *Divorce and Remarriage: Religious and Psychological Perspectives*. Edited by William P. Roberts. Kansas City, MO: Sheed and Ward, 1990.

MacRory, Joseph. *The New Testament and Divorce*. Dublin: Burns, Oates, and Washbourne, 1934.

Mahoney, Aidan. "A New Look at the Divorce Clauses in Mt 5.32 and 19,9." *CBQ* 30 (1968): 29–38.

Malina, Bruce J. "Criteria for Assessing the Authentic Words of Jesus: Some Specifications." Pages 27–45 in *Authenticating the Words of Jesus*. Edited by Bruce Chilton and Craig A. Evans. Leiden: Brill, 1999.

———. "Does *Porneia* Mean Fornication?" *NovT* 14 (1972): 10–17.

Manson, T. W. *The Sayings of Jesus*. Grand Rapids: Eerdmans, 1957.

Marrow, Stanley B. "Marriage and Divorce in the New Testament." *AThR* 70.1 (1988): 3–15.

Marshall, I. Howard. *A Critical and Exegetical Commentary on the Pastoral Epistles*. ICC. Edinburgh: T&T Clark, 1999.

Martial. *Epigrams*. Translated by Walter C. A. Ker. 2 vols. LCL. Cambridge: Harvard University Press, 1947–1950.

Martin, Dale B. "Paul without Passion: On Paul's Rejection of Desire in Sex and Marriage." Pages 201–15 in *Constructing Early Christian Families: Family as Social Reality and Metaphor*. Edited by Halvor Moxnes. New York: Routledge, 1997.

———. *Sex and the Single Savior: Gender and Sexuality in Biblical Interpretation*. Louisville: Westminster John Knox, 2006.

Martin, James D. "The Forensic Background to Jeremiah III 1." *VT* 19 (1969): 82–92.

Martin, Ralph P. "St. Matthew's Gospel in Recent Study." *ExpTim* 80 (1969): 132–36.

Marucci, Corrodo. *Parole di Gesù sul divorzio: Ricerche scritturistiche previe ad un ripensamento teologico, canonistico e pastorale della dottrina cattolica dell'indissolubilità del matrimonio*. Naples: Morcelliana, 1982.

McClure, Laura K. *Courtesans at Table: Gender and Literary Culture in Athenaeus*. New York: Routledge, 2003.

McGinn, Thomas A. J. *Prostitution, Sexuality, and the Law.* Oxford: Oxford University Press, 1998.

McGrew, Lydia. *The Eye of the Beholder: The Gospel of John as Historical Reportage.* Tampa, FL: DeWard, 2021.

———. *The Mirror and the Mask: Liberating the Gospels from Literary Devices.* Tampa, FL: DeWard, 2019.

McLaren, Elizabeth. "Marriages in England and Wales, 2013." *Office for National Statistics,* April 27, 2016, https://www.ons.gov.uk/peoplepopulationandcommunity/birthsdeathsandmarriages/marriagecohabitationandcivilpartnerships/bulletins/marriagesinenglandandwalesprovisional/2013.

McNeile, Alan Hugh. *The Gospel according to St. Matthew.* London: Macmillan, 1952.

Meeks, Wayne A. "The Image of the Androgyne: Some Uses of a Symbol in Earliest Christianity." *HR* 13.3 (1974): 165–209.

Meier, John P. *Companions and Competitors.* Vol. 3 of *A Marginal Jew: Rethinking the Historical Jesus.* ABRL. New York: Doubleday: 2001.

———. *Law and History in Matthew's Gospel: A Redactional Study of Mt. 5:17–48.* AnBib 71. Rome: Biblical Institute Press, 1976.

———. *Law and Love.* Vol. 4 of *A Marginal Jew: Rethinking the Historical Jesus.* ABRL. New Haven: Yale University Press, 2009.

———. *Mentor, Message, and Miracles.* Vol. 2 of *A Marginal Jew: Rethinking the Historical Jesus.* ABRL. New York: Doubleday, 1994.

———. *The Roots of the Problem and the Person.* Vol. 1 of *A Marginal Jew: Rethinking the Historical Jesus.* ABRL. New York: Doubleday, 1991.

Meigne, Maurice. "Concile ou collection d'Elvire?" *RHE* 70 (1975): 361–87.

Meissner, Bruno. *Beiträge zum altbabylonischen Privatrecht.* Leipzig: Hinrichs, 1893.

Meyer, Ben F. *The Aims of Jesus.* London: SCM Press, 1979.

Meyer, Heinrich August Wilhelm. *Critical and Exegetical Handbook to the Epistles to the Corinthians.* New York: Funk & Wagnalls, 1884.

Mielziner, M. *The Jewish Law of Marriage and Divorce in Ancient and Modern Times and Its Relation to the Law of the State.* Cincinnati, OH: Bloch, 1884.

Milgrom, Jacob. "The Temple Scroll." *BA* 41 (1978): 105–20.

Minucius Felix. *The Octavius of Marcus Minucius Felix.* Translated by G. W. Clarke. ACW 39. New York: Newman, 1974.

Mitteis, L., and U. Wilcken. *Grundzüge und Chrestomathie der Papyruskunde.* Vol. 2, *Juristischer Teil.* Part 2, *Chrestomathie.* Leipzig: Teubner, 1912.

Moiser, Jeremy. "A Reassessment of Paul's View of Marriage with Reference to 1 Cor. 7." *JSNT* 18 (1983): 103–22.

Moloney, Francis J. "Matthew 19, 3–12 and Celibacy: A Redactional and Form-Critical Study." *JSNT* 2 (1979): 42–60.

Moo, Douglas J. *The Letter to the Romans*. 2nd ed. NICNT. Grand Rapids: Eerdmans, 2018.

Moore, George Foot. *Judaism in the First Centuries of the Christian Era: The Age of the Tannaim*. 3 vols. Cambridge: Harvard University Press, 1927–1930.

Moulton, J. H., and G. Milligan. *Vocabulary of the Greek Testament*. Peabody, MA: Hendrickson, 1930.

Mueller, James R. "The Temple Scroll and the Gospel Divorce Texts." *RevQ* 10 (1980): 247–56.

Muller, Earl C. Review of *Divorce and Remarriage in the Bible: The Social and Literary Context*, by David Instone-Brewer. *CBQ* 65 (2003): 470–72.

Murphy-O'Connor, Jerome. "The Divorced Woman in 1 Cor 7:10–11." *JBL* 100.4 (1981): 601–6.

———. *Divorce in the New Testament*. GNS 38. Collegeville, MN: Liturgical, 1992.

———. "An Essene Missionary Document? CD II, 14–VI, 1." *RB* 77.2 (1970): 201–29.

———. "Remarques sur l'exposé du Professeur Y. Yadin." *RB* 79.1 (1972): 99–100.

Murray, John. *Divorce*. Philadelphia: Committee on Christian Education, 1953.

———. "Divorce." *WTJ* 9.1 (1946): 31–46.

———. "Divorce: Fifth Article." *WTJ* 11.2 (1949): 105–22.

———. "Divorce: Fourth Article." *WTJ* 10.2 (1948): 168–91.

———. "Divorce: Second Article." *WTJ* 9.2 (1947): 181–97.

———. "Divorce: Third Article." *WTJ* 10.1 (1947): 1–22.

Namer, Gérard. *Halbwachs et la mémoire sociale*. Paris: L'Harmattan, 2000.

Naselli, Andrew David. "What the New Testament Teaches about Divorce and Remarriage." *Detroit Baptist Seminary Journal* 24 (2019): 3–44.

National Center for Family & Marriage Research. "Fast Facts on American Marriages." Bowling Green State University, n.d. https://www.bgsu.edu/ncfmr/resources/data/fast-facts.html.

Nautin, Pierre. "Divorce et remariage dans la tradition de l'église latine." *RSR* 62 (1974): 7–54.

Neirynck, F. "The Sayings of Jesus in 1 Corinthians." In *The Corinthian Correspondence*. Edited by R. Bieringer, 141–76. BETL 125. Leuven: University Press, 1996.

Neirynck, Frans, and Frans Van Segbroeck. *New Testament Vocabulary: A Companion Volume to the Concordance*. BETL 65. Louvain: University Press, 1984.

Nelson, C. A. "Receipt for Tax on Prostitutes." *BASP* 32, nos. 1–2 (1995): 23–33.

Neufeld, E. *Ancient Hebrew Marriage Laws: With Special Reference to General Semitic Laws and Customs*. London: Longmans, Green, 1944.

Neusner, Jacob. *Rabbinic Literature and the New Testament: What We Cannot Show We Do Not Know*. Valley Forge, PA: Trinity Press International, 1994.

"New Marriage and Divorce Statistics Released." Mar. 31, 2008. https://www.barna.com/research/new-marriage-and-divorce-statistics-released/.

The Nicene and Post-Nicene Fathers. Series 1. Edited by Philip Schaff. 1886–1889. 14 vols. Repr. Peabody, MA: Hendrickson, 1994.

The Nicene and Post-Nicene Fathers. Series 2. Edited by Philip Schaff. 1890–1900. 14 vols. Repr. Peabody, MA: Hendrickson, 1994.

Nickelsburg, George W. E. *1 Enoch 1.* Hermeneia. Minneapolis: Fortress, 2001.

Niehaus, Jeffrey J. "God's Covenant with Abraham." *JETS* 56.2 (2013): 249–71.

Noam, Vered. "Divorce in Qumran in Light of Early Halakhah." *JJS* 56.2 (2005): 206–23.

Nolland, John. *The Gospel of Matthew.* NIGTC. Grand Rapids: Eerdmans, 2005.

———. "The Gospel Prohibition of Divorce: Tradition History and Meaning." *JSNT* 58 (1995): 19–35.

———. *Luke 9:21–18:34.* WBC 35B. Nashville: Nelson, 1993.

O'Collins, Gerald. "The Joy of Love (*Amoris Laetitia*): The Papal Exhortation in Its Context." *TS* 77 (2016): 905–21.

Ogden, Daniel. *Greek Bastardy in the Classical and Hellenistic Periods.* Oxford Classical Monographs. Oxford: Oxford University Press, 1996.

Olender, Robert G. "Paul's Source for 1 Corinthians 6:10–7:11." *Faith and Mission* 18.3 (2001): 60–73.

Olick, Jeffrey K. "Products, Processes, and Practices: A Non-Reificatory Approach to Collective Memory." *BTB* 36 (2006): 5–14.

Olson, David H., and John DeFrain. *Marriage and the Family: Diversity and Strengths.* 3rd ed. Mountain View, CA: Mayfield, 2000.

Olson, Stanley N. "Epistolary Uses of Expressions of Self-Confidence." *JBL* 103.4 (1984): 585–97.

Omitowoju, Rosanna. *Rape and the Politics of Consent in Classical Athens.* Cambridge Classical Studies. Cambridge: Cambridge University Press, 2002.

Orr, William F. "Paul's Treatment of Marriage in 1 Corinthians 7." *Pittsburgh Perspective* 8 (1967): 5–22.

Orr, William F., and James Arthur Walther. *1 Corinthians.* AB 32. Garden City, NY: Doubleday, 1976.

Osburn, Carroll D. "The Present Indicative Matthew 19:9." *Restoration Quarterly* 24.4 (1981): 193–203.

Osiek, Carolyn. "Female Slaves, *Porneia*, and the Limits of Obedience." Pages 255–74 in *Early Christian Families in Context: An Interdisciplinary Dialogue.* Edited by David L. Balch and Carolyn Osiek. Religion, Marriage, and Family. Grand Rapids: Eerdmans, 2003.

———. *The Shepherd of Hermas.* Hermeneia. Minneapolis: Fortress, 1999.

Oster, Richard E., Jr. *1 Corinthians*. The College Press NIV Commentary. Joplin, MO: College Press, 1995.

———. "Use, Misuse and Neglect of Archaeological Evidence in Some Modern Works on 1 Corinthians (1 Cor 7,1–5; 8,10; 11,2–16; 12,14–26)." *ZNW* 83 (1992): 52–73.

Ott, Anton. *Die Auslegung der neutestamentlichen Texte über die Ehescheidung*. NTAbh 3. Münster: Aschendorffschen, 1911.

Oulton, John Ernest Leonard, and Henry Chadwick. *Alexandrian Christianity: Selected Translations of Clement and Origen with Introductions and Notes*. LCC 2. Philadelphia: Westminster, 1954.

Page, Sydney. "Marital Expectations of Church Leaders in the Pastoral Epistles." *JSNT* 50 (1993): 105–20.

Pestman, P. W. *Marriage and Matrimonial Property in Ancient Egypt: A Contribution to Establishing the Legal Position of the Woman*. Papyrologica Lugduno-Batava 9. Leiden: Brill, 1961.

Peters, Greg. "Spiritual Marriage in Early Christianity: 1 Cor 7:25–38 in Modern Exegesis and the Earliest Church." *TJ* 23 (2002): 211–24.

Phillips, Anthony. "Another Look at Adultery." *JSOT* 20 (1981): 3–25.

Philo of Alexandra. *The Works of Philo*. 10 vols. Translated by F. H. Colson and G. H. Whitaker. LCL. Cambridge: Harvard University Press, 1937.

Pietersma, Albert, and Benjamin G. Wright. *A New English Translation of the Septuagint*. Oxford: Oxford University Press, 2007.

Piper, John. "Divorce, Remarriage, and Honoring God." *Desiring God*, Aug. 16, 2016. https://www.desiringgod.org/interviews/divorce-remarriage-and-honoring-god.

Plautus. Translated by Paul Nixon. 5 vols. LCL. Cambridge: Harvard University Press, 1924–1938.

Plummer, Alfred. *An Exegetical Commentary on the Gospel according to S. Matthew*. ICC. Grand Rapids: Eerdmans, 1956.

Plutarch. *Lives*. Translated by Bernadotte Perrin. 11 vols. LCL. Cambridge: Harvard University Press, 1914–1926.

———. *Moralia*. Translated by Frank Cole Babbitt et al. 16 vols. LCL. Cambridge: Harvard University Press, 1927–2004.

Polkinghorne, Donald E. "Narrative Psychology and Historical Consciousness: Relationships and Perspectives." Pages 3–22 in *Narration, Identity, and Historical Consciousness: The Psychological Construction of Time and History*. Edited by Jürgen Straub. New York: Berghan, 2005.

Polkow, Dennis. "Method and Criteria for Historical Jesus Research." Pages 336–56 in *Society of Biblical Literature 1987 Seminar Papers*. SBLSP 26. Atlanta: Scholars Press, 1987.

Pomeroy, Sarah B. *Goddesses, Whores, Wives, and Slaves: Women in Classical Antiquity.* New York: Schocken, 1975.

Porten, Bezalel, and Ada Yardeni. *Textbook of Aramaic Documents from Ancient Egypt.* 3 vols. Jerusalem: Hebrew University, 1986–96.

Porter, Stanley E. *The Criteria for Authenticity in Historical-Jesus Research: Previous Discussion and New Proposals.* JSNTSup 191. Sheffield: Sheffield Academic Press, 2000.

Pospishil, Victor J. "Divorce and Remarriage in the Early Church." *ITQ* 38.4 (1971): 338–47.

———. *Divorce and Remarriage: Toward a New Catholic Teaching.* New York: Herder and Herder, 1967.

Propertius. Translated by H. E. Butler. LCL. Cambridge: Harvard University Press, 1952.

Quasten, Johannes. *The Ante-Nicene Literature after Irenaeus.* Vol. 2 of *Patrology.* Westminster, MD: Christian Classics, 1950.

Quesnell, Quentin. "'Made Themselves Eunuchs for the Kingdom of Heaven.'" *CBQ* 30 (1968): 335–58.

Rabello, Alfredo Mordechai. "Divorce of Jews in the Roman Empire." *JLA* 4 (1981): 79–102.

Rabinowitz, Jacob J. "The 'Great Sin' in Ancient Egyptian Marriage Contracts." *JNES* 18.1 (1959): 73.

———. "The Sermon on the Mount and the School of Shammai." *HTR* 49.1 (1956): 79.

Reardon, B. P., ed. *Collected Ancient Greek Novels.* Berkeley: University of California Press, 1989.

Rehm, Bernhard. *Die Pseudoklementinen I: Homilien.* 3rd ed. Die Griechischen Christlichen Schriftsteller der Ersten Jahrhunderten. Berlin: Akademie Verlag, 1992.

Reisser, H. "πορνεύω." Pages 1:497–500 in *NIDNTT.* Edited by Colin Brown. Grand Rapids: Zondervan, 1975–78.

Repschinski, Boris. *The Controversy Stories in the Gospel of Matthew: Their Redaction, Form, and Relevance for the Relationship between the Matthean Community and Formative Judaism.* FRLANT 189. Göttingen: Vandenhoeck and Ruprecht, 2000.

Reynolds, Philip Lyndon. *Marriage in the Western Church: The Christianization of Marriage during the Patristic and Early Medieval Periods.* VCSup 24. Leiden: Brill, 1994.

Richlin, Amy. "Approaches to Adultery at Rome." *Women's Studies* 8 (1981): 225–50.

Ricoeur, Paul. *Memory, History, Forgetting.* Chicago: University of Chicago Press, 2004.

Robertson, Archibald, and Alfred Plummer. *A Critical and Exegetical Commentary on the First Epistle of Paul to the Corinthians.* 2nd ed. ICC. New York: Scribner's Sons, 1911.

Rodríguez, Rafael. "Authenticating Criteria: The Use and Misuse of a Critical Method." *JSHJ* 7 (2009): 152–67.

———. "The Embarrassing Truth about Jesus: The Criterion of Embarrassment and the Failure of Historical Authenticity." Pages 132–51 in *Jesus, Criteria, and the Demise of Authenticity*. Edited by Chris Keith and Anthony Le Donne. New York: T&T Clark, 2012.

———. *Structuring Early Christian Memory: Jesus in Tradition, Performance and Text*. LNTS 407. New York: T&T Clark, 2010.

Rordorf, Willy. "Marriage in the Early New Testament and in the Early Church." *JEH* 20 (1969): 193–210.

Rose, Martin. *5. Mose 12–25: Einführung und Gesetze*. Vol. 1 of *5. Mose*. ZBK 5.1. Zurich: Theologischer Verlag, 1994.

Roth, Martha T. *Babylonian Marriage Agreements: 7th–3rd Centuries B.C.* AOAT 222. Neukirchen-Vluyn: Neukirchener, 1989.

Rousselle, Aline. "Body Politics in Ancient Rome." Pages 296–336 in *From Ancient Goddess to Christian Saints*. Vol. 1 of *A History of Women in the West*. Edited by Pauline Schmitt Pantel. Cambridge: Harvard University Press, 1992.

Safrai, S. "Home and Family." Pages 2:728–92 in *The Jewish People in the First Century: Historical Geography, Political History, Social, Cultural, and Religious Life and Institutions*. Edited by S. Safrai and M. Stern with D. Flusser and W. C. van Unnik. CRINT 2. Philadelphia: Fortress, 1976.

Safrai, Ze'ev. "Halakhic Observance in the Judaean Desert Documents." Pages 205–36 in *Law in the Documents of the Judaean Desert*. Edited by Ranon Katzoff and David Schaps. JSJSup 96. Leiden: Brill, 2005.

Salvian. *The Writings of Salvian, The Presbyter*. FC 3. Edited and translated by Jeremiah F. O'Sullivan. Washington, DC: Catholic University of America Press, 1947.

Sanders, E. P. *The Historical Figure of Jesus*. London: Penguin, 1993.

———. *Jewish Law from Jesus to the Mishnah: Five Studies*. Philadelphia: Trinity Press International, 1990.

Sanders, E. P., and Margaret Davies. *Studying the Synoptic Gospels*. Harrisburg, PA: Trinity Press International, 1989.

Sariola, Heikki. "Streit um die Ehescheidung (10:2—12)." Pages 121–49 in *Markus und das Gesetz: Eine redaktionskritische Untersuchung*. Annales Academie Scientarum Fennicae Dissertationes Humanarum Litterarum 56. Helsinki: Suomalainen Tidedeakatemia, 1990.

Scacewater, Todd. "Divorce and Remarriage in Deuteronomy 24:1–4." *JESOT* 1.1 (2012): 63–79.

Schembri, Kevin. "The Orthodox Tradition on Divorced and Remarried Faithful: What Can the Catholic Church Learn." *Melita Theologica* 65.1 (2015): 121–41.

Schiffman, Lawrence H. "Laws Pertaining to Women in the *Temple Scroll*." Pages 210–28 in *The Dead Sea Scrolls: Forty Years of Research*. Edited by Devorah Dimant and Uriel Rappaport. STDJ 10. Leiden: Brill, 1992.

———. "Ordinances and Rules." Pages 145–75 in *The Dead Sea Scrolls: Hebrew, Aramaic, and Greek Texts with English Translations. Rule of the Community and Related Documents*. Edited by James H. Charlesworth et al. PTSDSSP 1. Tübingen: Mohr Siebeck, 1994.

———. *Reclaiming the Dead Sea Scrolls: The History of Judaism, the Background of Christianity, and the Lost Library of Qumran*. Philadelphia: Jewish Publication Society, 1994.

Schmidt, P. χωρέω. Pages 1:741–42 in *NIDNTT*. Edited by Colin Brown. Grand Rapids: Zondervan, 1986.

Schockenhoff, Eberhard. "Traditionsbruch oder notwendige Weiterbildung? Zwei Lesarten des nachsynodalen Schreibens 'Amoris Laititia'." *Stimmen der Zeit* 235 (2017): 147–58.

Schrage, Wolfgang. *Der erste Brief an die Korinther*. EKKNT. 4 vols. Neukirchen-Vluyn: Neukirchener, 1995.

———. *The Ethics of the New Testament*. Translated by David E. Green. Philadelphia: Fortress, 1988.

Schreiner, Thomas R. *Romans*. BECNT. Grand Rapids: Baker, 1998.

Schremer, Adiel. "Qumran Polemic on Marital Law: CD 4:20–5:11 and Its Social Background." Pages 147–60 in *The Damascus Document: A Centennial of Discovery. Proceedings of the Third International Symposium of the Orion Center for the Study of the Dead Sea Scrolls and Related Literature, 4–8 February, 1998*. Edited by Joseph M. Baumgarten, Esther G. Chazon, and Avital Pinnick. SJDJ 34. Leiden: Brill, 2000.

Schroeder, H. J. *Canons and Decrees of the Council of Trent*. St. Louis, MO: B. Herder, 1941.

Schröter, Jens. *Erinnerung an Jesu Worte: Studien zur Rezeption der Logienüberlieferung in Markus, Q, und Thomas*. WMANT 76. Neukirchen-Vluyn: Neukirchener, 1997.

———. "The Historical Jesus and the Sayings Tradition: Comments on Current Research." *Neot* 30 (1996): 151–68.

Schudson, Michael. *Watergate in American Memory: How We Remember, Forget, and Reconstruct the Past*. New York: Basic, 1992.

Schwartz, Barry. "Christian Origins: Historical Truth and Social Memory." Pages 43–56 in *Memory, Tradition, and Text: Uses of the Past in Early Christianity*. Edited by Alan Kirk and Tom Thatcher. SemeiaSt 52. Atlanta: Society of Biblical Literature, 2005.

———. "Social Change and Collective Memory: The Democratization of George Washington." *American Sociological Review* 56 (1991): 221–36.

Schweizer, Eduard. *The Good News according to Matthew*. Translated by David E. Green. Atlanta: Knox, 1975.

———. "Scheidungsrecht der jüdischen Frau? Weibliche Jünger Jesu?" *EvT* 42.3 (1982): 294–300.
Scott, S. P., trans. *The Civil Law Including the Twelve Tables, the Institutes of Gaius, the Rules of Ulpian, the Opinions of Paulus, the Enactments of Justinian, and the Constitutions of Leo.* 17 vols. Cincinnati: Central Trust Company, 1932.
Scroggs, Robin. "Paul and the Eschatological Woman." *Journal of the American Academy of Religion* 40.3 (1972): 283–303.
Seboldt, Roland H. A. "Spiritual Marriage in the Early Church: A Suggested Interpretation of 1 Cor 7:36–38." *Concordia Theological Monthly* 30.2–3 (1959): 103–19, 176–89.
Seltzer, Judith A. "Families Formed outside of Marriage." *Journal of Marriage and Family* 62.4 (Nov. 2000): 1247–68.
Seneca. *Moral Essays.* Translated by John W. Basore. 3 vols. LCL. Cambridge: Harvard University Press, 1928–1935.
Senft, Christophe. *La première épître de Saint-Paul aux Corinthiens.* Commentaire du Noveau Testament 7. Paris: Delachaux & Niestlé, 1979.
Senior, Donald. *Matthew.* ANTC. Nashville: Abingdon, 1998.
Sextus Pompeius Festus. *De verborum significatu quae supersunt cum Pauli Epitome.* Edited by Wallace M. Lindsey. Leipzig: Teubner, 1913.
Shelton, John C. *Greek and Latin Papyri, Ostraca, and Wooden Tablets in the Collection of the Brooklyn Museum.* Papyrologica Florentina 22. Florence: Edizioni Gonnelli, 1992.
Shemesh, Aharon. "4Q271.3: A Key to Sectarian Matrimonial Law." *JJS* 49.2 (1998): 244–63.
Shields, Martin A. "Syncretism and Divorce in Malachi 2,10–16." *ZAW* 111 (1999): 68–86.
Sigal, Phillip. *The Halakah of Jesus of Nazareth according to the Gospel of Matthew.* Lanham, MD: University Press of America, 1986.
Simó, C. "Atlas of Divorce and Post-Divorce Indicators." Paper presented at the XXVI IUSSP Conference, Marrakech, Morocco, 27 September–2 October, 2009. https://www.semanticscholar.org/paper/ATLAS-OF-DIVORCE-AND-POST-DIVORCE-INDICATORS-IN-Sim%C3%B3/4879712ab5db03ef5a5bb73efd100f52996e547d.
Skehan, Patrick W., and Alexander A. Di Lella. *The Wisdom of Ben Sira.* AB 39. New York: Doubleday, 1987.
Smith, Jay E. "1 Thessalonians 4:4: Breaking the Impasse." *BBR* 11.1 (2001): 65–105.
Snyder, Graydon F. *First Corinthians: A Faith Community Commentary.* Atlanta: Mercer University Press, 1992.
Sonne, Isaiah. "The Schools of Shammai and Hillel Seen from Within." Pages 275–91 in *Louis Ginzberg: Jubilee Volume.* New York: American Academy for Jewish Research, 1945.

Spijker, Jeroen A., and Montserrat Solsona. "Atlas of Divorce and Post-Divorce Indicators." *Papers de Demografia* 412 (2012): 1–110.
Sprinkle, Joe M. "Old Testament Perspectives on Divorce and Remarriage." *JETS* 40.4 (1997): 529–50.
Squire, Larry R., and Eric R. Kandel. *Memory: From Mind to Molecules*. New York: Scientific American Library, 1999.
Staab, Karl. "Die Unauflösigkeit der Ehe und die sog. 'Ehebruchsklauseln' bei Mt 5, 32 und 19, 9." In *Festschrift Eduard Eichmann zum 70. Geburtstag*. Edited by Martin Grabmann and Karl Hofmann, 435–52. Paderborn: Ferdinand Schöningh, 1940.
Statius. *Silvae*. Translated by D. R. Shackleton Bailey and Christopher A. Parrott. LCL. Cambridge: Harvard University Press, 2015.
Stein, Robert H. "The 'Criteria' for Authenticity." Pages 225–63 in *Studies of History and Tradition in the Four Gospels*. Vol. 1 of *Gospel Perspectives*. Edited by R. T. France and David Wenham. Sheffield: JSOT Press, 1980.
Stienstra, Nelly. *YHWH Is the Husband of His People: Analysis of a Biblical Metaphor with Special Reference to Translation*. Kampen: Kok Pharos, 1993.
Stock, Augustine. "Matthean Divorce Texts." *BTB* 8 (1978): 24–33.
Straub, Jürgen. "Telling Stories, Making History: Toward a Narrative Psychology of the Historical Construction of Meaning." Pages 44–98 in *Narration, Identity, and Historical Consciousness: The Psychological Construction of Time and History*. Edited by Jürgen Straub. New York: Berghan, 2005.
Strecker, Georg. *The Sermon on the Mount: An Exegetical* Commentary. Translated by O. C. Dean Jr. Nashville: Abingdon, 1988.
Stulman, Louis. *Jeremiah*. Abingdon Old Testament Commentaries. Nashville: Abingdon, 2005.
Suetonius. *Lives of the Caesars*. Translated by John Carew Rolfe. LCL. Cambridge: Harvard University Press, 1914.
Tacitus. *Agricola. Germania. Dialogus*. Translated by Maurice Hutton. Revised by R. M. Ogilvie, E. H. Warmington, William Peterson, and Michael Winterbottom. LCL. Cambridge: Harvard University Press, 1970.
———. *The Histories and the Annals*. Translated by Clifford H. Moore and John Jackson. 4 vols. LCL. Cambridge: Harvard University Press, 1925–1937.
Talbert, Charles H. *Matthew*. Paideia Commentaries on the New Testament. Grand Rapids: Baker, 2010.
———. *Reading Luke: A Literary and Theological Commentary on the Third Gospel*. New York: Crossroad, 1992.
Tannehill, Robert C. *Luke*. ANTC. Nashville: Abingdon, 1996.
Thiselton, Anthony C. *The First Epistle to the Corinthians*. NIGTC. Grand Rapids: Eerdmans, 2000.

Thompson, J. A. *The Book of Jeremiah*. NICOT. Grand Rapids: Eerdmans, 1980.
Tigay, Jeffrey H. *Deuteronomy: The JPS Torah Commentary*. Philadelphia: Jewish Publication Society, 1996.
———. "Examination of the Accused Bride in 4Q159 Forensic Medicine at Qumran." *JANESCU* 22 (1993): 129–34.
Tomson, Peter J. *Paul and the Jewish Law: Halakha in the Letters of the Apostle to the Gentiles*. CRINT 3.1. Minneapolis: Fortress, 1990.
———. "What Did Paul Mean by 'Those Who Know the Law'? (Rom 7.1)." *NTS* 49 (2003): 573–81.
Tonkin, Elizabeth. *Narrating Our Pasts: The Social Construction of Oral History*. Cambridge Studies in Oral and Literate Culture 22. Cambridge: Cambridge University Press 1992.
Tosato, Angelo. "Joseph, Being a Just Man (Matt 1:19)." *CBQ* 41 (1979): 547–51.
Towner, Philip H. *The Letters to Timothy and Titus*. NICNT. Grand Rapids: Eerdmans, 2006.
Treggiari, Susan. "Marriage and Family in Roman Society." Pages 132–82 in *Marriage and Family in the Biblical World*. Edited by Ken. M. Campbell. Downers Grove, IL: InterVarsity, 2003.
———. *Roman Marriage: Iusti Coniuges from the Time of Cicero to the Time of Ulpian*. Oxford: Oxford University Press, 1991.
Trevett, Christine. *Montanism: Gender, Authority and the New Prophecy*. Cambridge: Cambridge University Press, 1996.
Uecker, Jeremy E., and Charles E. Stokes. "Early Marriage in the United States." *Journal of Marriage and Family* 70.4 (2008): 835–46.
Valantasis, Richard. "A Theory of the Social Function of Asceticism." Pages 544–52 in *Asceticism*. Edited by Vincent L. Wimbush and Richard Valantasis. Oxford: Oxford University Press, 1995.
Valerius Maximus. *Memorable Doings and Sayings*. Edited by D. R. Shackleton Bailey. 2 vols. LCL. Cambridge: Harvard University Press, 2000.
Van Tine, R. Jarrett. "Castration for the Kingdom and Avoiding the αἰτία of Adultery (Matthew 19:10–12)." *JBL* 137.2 (2018): 399–418.
Vasoli, Robert H. *What God Has Joined Together: The Annulment Crisis in American Catholicism*. New York: Oxford University Press, 1998.
Vawter, Bruce. "The Divorce Clauses in Mt 5,32 and 19,9." *CBQ* 16 (1954): 155–67.
———. "Divorce in the New Testament." *CBQ* 39 (1977): 528–42.
Vergil. *The Aeneid*. Translated by Sarah Ruden. New Haven: Yale University Press, 2008.
Vermes, Geza. "Sectarian Matrimonial Halakhah in the Damascus Rule." *JJS* 25.1 (1974): 197–202.
Vilella, Josep. "The Pseudo-Iliberritan Canon Texts." *ZAC* 18 (2014): 21–59.
Vinson, Richard B. *Luke*. SHBC. Macon, GA: Smyth & Helwys, 2008.

Vööbus, Arthur, trans. *The Didascalia Apostolorum in Syriac: Chapters XI–XXVI.* CSCO 408. Leuven: Peeters, 1979.

Wacholder, Ben Zion. *The New Damascus Document: The Midrash on the Eschatological Torah of the Dead Sea Scrolls: Reconstruction, Translation, and Commentary.* STDJ 56. Leiden: Boston, 2007.

Wallraff, Martin. "Geschichte des Novatianismus seit dem vierten Jahrhundert im Osten." *ZAC* 1.2 (1997): 251–79.

Walton, John H. "The Place of the 'HUTQAṬṬĒL" within the D-Stem Group and Its Implications in Deuteronomy 24:4." *HS* 32 (1991): 7–17.

Ware, Kallistos. "The Way of the Ascetics: Negative or Affirmative?" Pages 3–15 in *Asceticism*. Edited by Vincent L. Wimbush and Richard Valantasis. Oxford: Oxford University Press, 1995.

Wassen, Cecilia. *Women in the Damascus Document.* Academia Biblica 21. Leiden: Brill, 2005.

Watson, Alan. *The Law of Persons in the Later Roman Republic.* Oxford: Oxford University Press, 1967.

Webb, Joseph A. *Till Death Do Us Part?* Longwood, FL: Webb Ministries, 1992.

Weckwerth, Andreas. "The Twenty Canons of the Council of Nicaea." Pages 158–76 in *The Cambridge Companion to the Council of Nicaea*. Edited by Young Richard Kim. Cambridge: Cambridge University Press, 2021.

Weder, Hans. "Perspektive der Frauen?" *EvT* 43.2 (1983): 175–79.

Weinfeld, Moshe. *Deuteronomy and the Deuteronomic School.* Winona Lake, IN: Eisenbrauns, 1992.

Weiss, Johannes. *Der erste Korintherbrief.* 9th ed. Göttingen: Vandenhoeck & Ruprecht, 1910.

Welles, C. Bradford, Robert O. Fink, and J. Frank Gilliam, eds. *The Excavations at Dura-Europos Conducted by Yale University and the French Academy of Inscriptions and Letters*. Final Report V Part 1. *The Parchments and Papyri*. New Haven: Yale University Press, 1959.

Welzer, Harald. *Das kommunikative Gedächtnis: Eine Theorie der Erinnerung.* Munich: Beck, 2002.

Wenham, David. "Paul's Use of the Jesus Tradition: Three Samples." Pages 7–37 in *The Jesus Tradition outside the Gospels*. Vol. 5 of *Gospel Perspectives*. Edited by David Wenham. Sheffield: JSOT Press, 1984.

Wenham, Gordon J. "Does the New Testament Approve Remarriage after Divorce?" *SBJT* 6.1 (Spring 2002): 30–45.

———. *Jesus, Divorce, and Remarriage in Their Historical Setting.* Bellingham, WA: Lexham, 2019.

———. "Matthew and Divorce: An Old Crux Revisited." *JSNT* 22 (1984): 95–107.

———. "The Syntax of Matthew 19:9." *JSNT* 28 (1986): 17–23.

Bibliography

Westbrook, Raymond. *Old Babylonian Marriage Law*. Archiv für Orientforschung 23. Horn: Berger & Söhne, 1988.

Whealey, Alice. "Josephus, Eusebius of Caesarea, and the *Testimonium Flavianum*." Pages 76–116 in *Josephus und das Neue Testament: Wechselseitige Wahrnehmungen*. Edited by Christfried Böttrich and Jens Herzer. WUNT 209. Tübingen: Mohr Siebeck, 2007.

———. *Josephus on Jesus: The Testimonium Flavianum Controversy from Late Antiquity to Modern Times*. StBibLit 36. New York: Lang, 2003.

Wheat, Ed, and Gaye Wheat. *Intended for Pleasure: Sex Technique and Sexual Fulfillment in Christian Marriage*. 3rd ed. Grand Rapids: Revell, 1997.

Wheeler-Reed, David, Jennifer W. Knust, and Dale B. Martin. "Can a Man Commit πορνεία with His Wife?" *JBL* 137.2 (2018): 383–98.

Williams, Craig A. *Roman Homosexuality*. 2nd ed. Oxford: Oxford University Press, 2010.

Williams, Gordon. "Some Aspects of Roman Marriage Ceremonies and Ideals." *Journal of Roman Studies* 48.1–2 (1958): 16–29.

Williams, Sally. "'I Do, I Do, I Do . . .' The Remarriage Game." *The Guardian*, Jan. 20, 2009. https://www.theguardian.com/lifeandstyle/2009/jan/31/remarriage-family.

Wilson, Stephen G. *Luke and the Law*. SNTSMS 50. Cambridge: Cambridge University Press, 1983.

Wimbush, Vincent L. "Introduction." Pages 1–11 in *Ascetic Behavior in Greco-Roman Antiquity: A Sourcebook*. Studies in Antiquity and Christianity. Edited by Vincent L. Wimbush. Minneapolis: Fortress, 1990.

———. *Paul the Worldly Ascetic: Response to the World and Self-Understanding according to 1 Corinthians 7*. Macon, GA: Mercer University Press, 1987.

Wimbush, Vincent L., and Richard Valantasis. "Introduction." Pages xix–xxxiii in *Asceticism*. Edited by Vincent L. Wimbush and Richard Valantasis. Oxford: Oxford University Press, 1995.

Winter, Paul. "Ṣadokite Fragments IV, 20, 21 and the Exegesis of Genesis 1, 27 in Late Judaism." *ZAW* 68 (1956): 71–84.

Wisconsin Evangelical Lutheran Synod Conference of Presidents. "A Study of Marriage, Divorce, Malicious Desertion, and Remarriage in the Light of God's Word." 2015. https://synodadmin.welsrc.net/download-synodadmin/documents-from-the-wels-conference-of-presidents/?wpdmdl=3438&ind=1518035141222.

Witherington, Ben, III. *The Acts of the Apostles: A Socio-Rhetorical Commentary*. Grand Rapids: Eerdmans, 1998.

———. "Matthew 5.32 and 19.9—Exception or Exceptional Situation." *NTS* 31 (1985): 571–76.

———. *A Socio-Rhetorical Commentary on Titus, 1–2 Timothy, and 1–3 John*. Vol. 1 of *Letters and Homilies for Hellenized Christians*. Downers Grove, IL: InterVarsity, 2006.

———. *Women in the Earliest Churches*. SNTSMS 59. Cambridge: Cambridge University Press, 1988.

Wolff, Christian. *Der erste Brief des Paulus an die Korinther*. THKNT 7. Berlin: Evangelische Verlagsanstalt, 1996.

Wolff, Hans Julius. "Hellenistic Private Law." Pages 1:534–60 in *The Jewish People in the First Century: Historical Geography, Political History, Social, Cultural, and Religious Life and Institutions*. Edited by S. Safrai and M. Stern. CRINT 1. Assen: Van Gorcum, 1974.

———. *Written and Unwritten Marriages in Hellenistic and Postclassical Roman Law*. Monograph of American Philological Association 9. Haverford, PA: American Philological Association, 1939.

Wright, David P. "She Shall Not Go Free as Male Slaves Do: Developing Views about Slavery and Gender in the Laws of the Hebrew Bible." Pages 125–42 in *Beyond Slavery: Overcoming Its Religious and Sexual Legacies*. Edited by Bernadette J. Brooten. Black Religion/Womanist Thought/Social Justice Series. New York: Macmillan, 2010.

Wright, N. T. *Jesus and the Victory of God*. Vol. 2 of *Christian Origins and the Question of God*. Minneapolis: Fortress, 1996.

Wright, Robert B. *Psalms of Solomon: A Critical Edition of the Greek Text*. Jewish and Christian Texts in Contexts and Related Studies 1. London: T&T Clark, 2007.

Yadin, Y. "Expedition D—the Cave of the Letters." *IEJ* 12.3–4 (1962): 227–57.

Yadin, Yigael, Jonas C. Greenfield, and Ada Yardeni. "Babatha's '*Ketubba*.'" *IEJ* 44.1–2 (1994): 75–101.

Yarbro Collins, Adela. *Mark*. Hermeneia. Minneapolis: Fortress, 2007.

Zahn, Theodor. *Das Evangelium des Matthäus*. 4th ed. Leipzig: Deichertsche, 1922.

Zakovitch, Yair. "The Woman's Rights in the Biblical Law of Divorce." *JLA* 4 (1981): 28–46.

Zehnder, Markus. "A Fresh Look at Malachi II 13–16." *VT* 53.2 (2003): 224–59.

Zerwick, Maximilian. *Biblical Greek Illustrated by Examples*. Scripta Pontificii Instituti Biblici 114. Rome: Pontifical Biblical Institute, 1963.

Ziegler, Joseph, ed. *Duodecim Prophetae*. SVTG 13. Göttingen: Vandenhoeck & Ruprecht, 1943.

Zilliacus, Henrik, Jaako Frösén, Paavo Hohti, Jorma Kaimio, and Maarit Kaimio. *Fifty Oxyrhynchus Papyri (P. Oxy. Hels.)*. Commentationes Humanarum Litterarum 63. Helsinki: Societas Scientiarum Fennica, 1979.

Index of Authors

Abrahams, I., 121n51, 125n73, 152, 154n41
Achelis, H., 215n86
Adams, Karin, 116n31, 131nn106–7
Alexander, Loveday, 197, 200n21
Allen, Willoughby C., 184n162
Allison, Dale C., Jr., 60n9, 68n52, 75, 76n88, 120n51, 144, 152n32, 153n35, 159, 170, 181
Allo, P. E. B., 201n24
Amram, David W., 149n18, 152n34
Andersen, Francis I., 138
Archer, Léone J., 23n26
Arendzen, J. P., 174n122, 235n11, 239, 242–43, 249
Arnal, William, 76n89, 77n90
Atkinson, David, 28n48, 65n33, 207n52, 280

Bagnall, Roger S., 128n88
Bain, Andrew M., 250n69, 251n71
Balch, David L., 135n127, 194n1, 200n21
Baltensweiler, Heinrich, 117n36, 118n42
Banks, Robert, 116n33, 164, 165nn79–82
Barrett, C. K., 201n24, 202n28, 210n60
Bartlett, F. C., 84, 85n130

Barton, Stephen C., 120, 123n64, 187n177, 190–91
Bauer, Johannes B., 143n163
Baumann, Gerlinde, 132n112
Baumert, Norbert, 201, 219n108, 219n114, 220n115
Baumgarten, Joseph M., 48n131, 51n144
Beentjes, Pancratius C., 135n125
Bellinzoni, A. J., 238n23
Benoit, P., 23n26, 65n37
Bevilacqua, Anthony J., 250n67, 264
Bird, Phyllis A., 131–33
Blomberg, Craig L., 2n5, 3n10, 59n7, 109n14, 126n78, 143n165, 148n14, 174n124, 184n165, 186n174, 188n181, 273n163, 288n13
Bonsirven, Joseph, 117n36, 175n129, 244n43, 250n66, 263n119, 268n140, 270n151
Boring, Eugene M., 60n12, 62
Bound, James F., 214nn79–80, 215n85, 217nn100–101
Bracke, John M., 290n17
Bradley, Keith R., 30n54, 41, 197n13
Brin, Gershon, 48, 49n137

327

Bromiley, Geoffrey W., 183n158
Brooten, Bernadette J., 72n73, 134n118, 172n113
Brown, Colin, 98n190, 198n18, 217
Brox, Norbert, 235n9, 235n14
Bruce, F. F., 117n36, 197n11, 201n24
Brug, John F., 114n26
Brunec, Michael, 164n74
Bruner, Jerome S., 88n154
Buckley, Timothy J., 10n39
Butler, B. C., 172n112
Byrne, Brendan, 227n148
Byrskog, Samuel, 84n126, 85n131, 88n150, 88n152

Calvert, D. G. A., 78n99, 79n100
Carcopino, Jérôme, 216n98, 217
Carmody, Denise Lardner, 10n39
Carroll, John T., 93n171, 100n197, 101nn199–201, 102
Carson, D. A., 98n190, 184n163
Carter, Warren, 83n122, 170n104, 172n114, 180n145
Casey, Edward S., 83n120, 85n130
Cereti, Giovanni, 271–72
Charlesworth, James H., 48n134, 75n84
Cherlin, Andrew J., 7n23
Ciampa, Roy E., 64n30, 67n49, 88n149, 195n4, 198n16, 199, 202–4, 206n50, 214n79, 215n87, 215n90, 219n109, 223n134, 228, 230
Clark, Elizabeth A., 234, 246, 247n53, 253n77, 255n87, 259n104, 273, 275
Clark, W. K. Lowther, 117n36
Cohen, Boaz, 122n60, 124n69, 154n38
Cohen, David J., 129n97
Cohen, Edward E., 129n94
Coiner, H. G., 160n64, 210n63
Coleman, Gerald D., 10n39

Collins, C. John, 22n18
Collins, John J., 50n140, 51
Collins, Raymond F., 25n33, 47nn125–26, 63n24, 63n27, 81n109, 92n169, 102n205, 150n23, 168n97, 186n173, 188n180, 195n4, 202, 205n45, 206n48, 211n56, 224n136, 230nn155–56
Constantelos, Demetris J., 11n40
Coontz, Stephanie, 7n27
Corbett, Percy Elwood, 32n62, 33n64, 153n37, 204nn38–39
Cornes, Andrew, 89n158, 170n108, 195, 211n66
Countryman, L. William, 94nn176–77
Craigie, Peter C., 290n19
Crossan, John Dominic, 85, 117n36
Crouch, C. L., 290n16
Crouzel, Henri, 233n3, 235nn12–13, 236n15, 238n25, 243n38, 244n42, 245nn44–45, 246n51, 247n52, 247n55, 248n59, 250n66, 252n75, 254n81, 254n84, 255nn88–89, 256, 257n94, 257n96, 257n98, 258n100, 259, 260nn110–11, 261n115, 262n116, 263nn120–21, 264n123, 265n126, 265nn128–29, 266n132, 267n136, 269n146, 270n148, 270n150, 272, 280
Csillag, Pál, 31, 34n71, 52nn153–54, 204
Culpepper, R. Alan, 147n3, 256n93
Curran, John, 58n4

D'Angelo, Mary Rose, 61–63
Daniel-Hughes, Carly, 248, 249n61
Das, A. Andrew, 5n15, 196n9, 227n151, 288n10
Daube, David, 123n67, 212n67
Davidson, James N., 129n91, 130n101
Davidson, Richard M., 290n16

Index of Authors

Davies, Margaret, 60nn10–12, 61n14, 63n25, 68n53, 74n80, 213n74
Davies, Philip R., 46n120, 47n129, 48n131, 50n141
Davies, W. D., 68n52, 120n51, 152n32, 153n35, 159, 170, 181, 183n159
Deal, William E., 274
Dean, David Andrew, 4n14
Deasley, Alex R. G., 250n65
DeFrain, John, 7n21, 7n24, 8n29
Deming, Will, 212n70, 213n72, 219n107
Derrett, J. Duncan M., 72n74
Descamps, A. L., 95, 96nn182–83, 123n65, 158n57, 166n89, 184n163
Dibelius, Martin, 160n63
Di Lella, Alexander A., 135n125
Dixon, Suzanne, 30n53, 32nn60–61, 33n63
Donahue, John R., 90n161
Drinkard, Joel F., Jr., 290n19
Dunn, James D. G., 64n30, 68, 69n54, 76nn86–87, 88n149, 226n143
Duplacy, Jean, 163n72
Dupont, Jacques, 89n157, 91n167, 95n181, 117n36, 121n51, 124n68, 149n20, 156n52, 157nn54–55, 164n74, 164n77, 166n84, 166n86, 167nn93–94, 171n110, 172nn111–12, 173nn116–17, 174n121, 176n131, 179n141, 180n144, 182nn152–53, 183n156, 185n169, 187n178
Dupont-Sommer, A., 46n120

Edgar, Thomas R., 126n79
Ehrman, Bart D., 84n127
Elledge, C. D., 44n111, 44n114, 45n119, 52, 81, 82n111
Elliott, J. K., 214n82, 215n84, 216n91, 219n113, 220n115
Elliott, John H., 90n161

Elliott, Neil, 274n172
Ellis, J. Edward, 276–77
Emmet, C. W., 236n16, 237n17
Erickson, John H., 11n40
Erlandsson, S., 131n106
Evans, Craig A., 3n10, 59, 78n98, 79n102
Eve, Eric, 73n78

Falk, Z. W., 153n36
Fant, Maureen B., 27n41, 53, 153n36
Farla, Piet, 220n120
Fee, Gordon D., 5n17, 62n21, 64, 122n58, 138–39, 140n151, 202, 205, 210n62, 211n65, 212n67, 214n79, 215n84, 216n91, 216n94, 216n96, 218n104, 220nn116–17, 222n126, 225, 230n156
Field, David, 64n33
Finley, Moses I., 130n100
Fitzmyer, Joseph A., 44, 46n120, 47, 49n136, 51nn148–49, 62n20, 65n37, 66n42, 66n46, 70n61, 100n193, 102n204, 117n36, 118n37, 119n46, 140n153, 148n9, 160n65, 213n75, 227n148
Ford, Coleman, 246n49
Ford, J. Massingberd, 216n91
Fornberg, Tord, 117n36
Fraade, Steven D., 273, 274n169
France, R. T., 33, 98n190, 109–10, 113n24, 143n163, 147n4, 148, 152n31, 156, 158, 168n96, 180, 184n164, 184n166
Fredriksen, Paula, 76nn86–87
Freedman, David Noel, 138
Fretheim, Terence E., 290n19
Frey, Jean Baptiste, 36n80, 40n96
Fuller, Russell, 22n18
Funke, Hermann, 34n74

Gadd, C. J., 24n28
Gagnon, Robert A. J., 122n60

329

INDEX OF AUTHORS

Gallaro, George, 11n40
Gardner, Jane F., 30n53, 52n154, 53, 153n36, 204n36
Garland, David E., 98n190, 118n38, 119, 159n61, 167nn90–91, 195n4, 198n14, 198n16, 201n24, 203n34, 206, 216n91, 216n95, 223n135
Gaventa, Beverly Roberts, 122nn55–56
Gavin, F., 117n36
Gentry, Kenneth L., Jr., 61n16
Gibbs, Jeffrey A., 113n24, 114n25
Ginzburg, Louis, 48
Glancy, Jennifer A., 127, 130, 133–36, 140–41, 233n5
Goffman, Erving, 84n129
Goldberg, Gary J., 58n4
Goodacre, Mark, 59n9, 64, 68n53, 73n79
Grant, Robert M., 160n63
Green, Barbara, 97n186
Green, Joel B., 101n201
Greenfield, Jonas C., 23n26
Grosheide, F. W., 218n105
Grudem, Wayne, 170n105, 213n77
Grundmann, Walter, 170n104
Guelich, Robert A., 121n53, 123n63, 127n83
Guenther, Allen R., 164n74, 164n76, 165, 222, 223nn129–30, 223n133, 224
Gundry, Robert H., 68n50, 70n62, 162n70, 170n104, 177, 184n162, 187n177
Gundry-Volf, Judith M., 196n10, 200n21
Gupta, Nijay K., 139n146

Hagner, Donald A., 120n48, 147, 148nn11–12, 150n23, 152n32, 179
Halbwachs, Maurice, 83–84, 86–87
Hall, F. W., 153n38
Harper, Kyle, 112, 127, 128n90, 129n92, 129n94, 129n97, 130n100, 131n104, 133–34, 135n129, 136, 139nn147–49, 140, 141n157, 143n163
Harpham, Geoffrey Galt, 273n168, 274n172
Harrell, Pat Edwin, 207n54, 250n65, 254n85, 269n142, 270n151, 291
Harrington, Hannah K., 137n134
Hauck, F., 153n38
Hays, Richard B., 46n122, 47n125, 66n42, 77, 81n109, 91nn166–67, 94, 95n180, 97nn187–88, 99n192, 121n52, 122nn59–61, 123n63, 127, 158, 159n61, 185n170, 187n176, 188n180, 190, 202, 205, 216, 230n156
Hegy, Pierre, 9n36, 11n40
Heine, Ronald E., 257n95, 257n97, 258n101, 261n112, 262nn117–18
Héring, Jean, 201n24
Herron, Robert, Jr., 93n172, 96n184
Heth, William A., 1–2, 4–5, 33, 54, 59n5, 93n170, 95n181, 98n191, 102n207, 119, 121n51, 121n53, 126, 148n9, 153n34, 156n52, 160n66, 166n84, 168n95, 172n112, 173n117, 174nn122–23, 175nn125–26, 175n128, 185n171, 233n6, 236n15, 242n35, 244n43, 248n60, 255n89, 256n90, 273, 276n183, 278
Hezser, Catherine, 133n118
Hilberath, Bernd Jochen, 10n37
Hill, David, 154, 169n102
Hobbs, T. R., 291n21
Hofmann, Johann Christian Konrad von, 219n115
Holladay, Carl R., 122n59
Holladay, William L., 290n16
Holmén, Tom, 45n117, 46n121, 75n85, 78n99, 79n101
Holzmeister, U., 164n74

Index of Authors

Hooker, Morna D., 78n95, 78n99, 79nn100–101, 83
Horsley, Richard A., 85, 86n135, 195n4, 216n94
Houston, Walter J., 115n28
Huebenthal, Sandra, 84n128, 88n155
Hugenberger, Gordon P., 4n14, 5n15, 288n10
Hultgren, Arland J., 228n152
Humbert, Michel, 30n54, 31n56, 34nn68–69, 35n75, 37n81, 42
Hunter David G., 233n4, 247n54, 251n70, 278

Ilan, Tal, 23n26, 49n139, 150n23
Instone-Brewer, David, 2, 3n9, 4, 23n26, 24nn27–28, 24n30, 25n32, 26, 27n39, 28, 29nn51–52, 32n59, 33, 42, 45n115, 46n123, 48, 65n35, 66, 80n104, 81n108, 90n159, 92n168, 147n6, 151n30, 156n50, 158, 171nn109–10, 178n137, 183n157, 194n3, 198nn16–17, 206n50, 207nn53–54, 208–9, 212, 213n76, 214n77, 219n110, 238, 240–41, 243, 247n52, 255, 259, 260n109, 264, 273, 277–78, 290–92
Isaksson, Abel, 120n47, 122n60, 124–26, 127n83, 138n140, 179n141

Janzen, David, 121n51, 141n159, 142–43
Jayson, Sharon, 8nn29–30
Jenkins, Claude, 264n123, 272n161, 277nn190–91, 278nn192–93
Jensen, Joseph, 138, 143n166
Jeremias, Joachim, 80n105, 178n138, 206n46, 211n66
Jewett, Robert, 226n143, 227n147
Job, John, 98n190
Jones, David Clyde, 22n18
Jones, David W., 4n14, 124n68, 288nn9–11

Joyce, George Hayward, 173n116, 261, 270
Kaiser, Walter C., Jr., 22n18
Kampen, John, 48n131, 51n148, 142n162, 221n120
Kandel, Eric R., 85n130
Kapparis, Konstantinos, 128n89, 129n95
Keener, Craig S., 2–4, 59n7, 98n190, 103, 110n17, 120n47, 148n10, 149, 155n46, 158n56, 158n58, 159–60, 171n109, 180n146, 181n147, 182n154, 186, 198n15, 198n18, 207n55, 208n57, 209n58, 213n74, 217n101, 273, 287, 291–92
Keith, Chris, 60n9, 86, 87n139, 87n146
Kelber, Werner, 85n133, 88n155, 103
Kelley, Page H., 290n19
Kelly, J. N. D., 54
Keppler, Angela, 88n154
Kilgallen, John J., 148n9
Kilpatrick, G. D., 163n71, 172n112
Kirk, Alan, 84n127, 85nn130–31, 86
Kistemaker, Simon J., 201n24
Klauck, Hans-Josef, 115n28
Kloha, Jeffrey John, 221nn121–22, 222n123, 224n137
Knust, Jennifer Wright, 127, 128n84, 130, 133n116, 136, 138–39
Kodell, Jerome, 183n157
Köstenberger, Andreas J., 53
Kötting, Bernhard, 272nn158–59
Kovacs, Judith L., 257n95
Krause, Jens-Uwe, 41n99
Kreider, Rose M., 6
Kuck, David W., 231n157
Kuefler, Mathew, 178n140, 255n89
Kümmel, Werner Georg, 216n92
Kurke, Leslie, 130n101
Kysar, Myrna, 210n64
Kysar, Robert, 210n64

Lake, Kirsopp, 236nn15–16, 237n17
Lane, William L., 93n172
Laney, J. Carl, 117n36, 118nn37–38, 218n104, 220n115
Lang, Friedrich, 201n24
Lattimore, Richmond, 36n76, 39n87, 40n97
Laughery, G. J., 202n28
Lawler, Michael G., 10nn38–39
Le Donne, Anthony, 59n9, 75n84, 83n121
Lefkowitz, Mary R., 27n41, 53, 153n36
Leith, Mary Joan Winn, 131n105
Lenski, R. C. H., 106, 108, 109n13, 110, 113n24
Leon, Harry J., 40n96
Levine, Amy-Jill, 135n129
Lewis, Jamie M., 6
L'Huillier, Peter, 11n40
Lightfoot, J. B., 214n78
Lightman, Majorie, 34n74, 36, 37nn82–84
Lipiński, E., 22n20, 25n32
Livingston, Gretchen, 6
Loader, William R. G., 52n151, 154, 156n50, 202n29, 218n106
Lorusso, Lorenzo, 11n40
Lövestam, Evald, 114n26, 121n54, 123n66, 125n72, 127n82, 147n7, 154n39
Luck, William F., Sr., 80n106, 108–11, 195–96, 202n26, 216n97, 218n106, 238, 239n27, 243n39, 244n43, 258
Lüddeckens, Erich, 28n47
Luz, Ulrich, 73, 149, 150n25, 154n42, 163n72, 173, 182, 190n191

MacDonald, Margaret Y., 196n10, 246n48
Mackin, Theodore, 10n39, 242n34, 248n57, 249n64
MacRory, Joseph, 157n54, 163, 166n88, 269n144, 270n149

Mahoney, Aidan, 115–16, 118n40
Malina, Bruce J., 75, 138n139, 143n166
Manson, T. W., 22n22, 179n141
Marrow, Stanley B., 200n20
Marshall, I. Howard, 53
Martin, Dale B., 10n39, 63n28, 122n60, 127, 128n84, 130, 136, 138–39, 141n157, 168n95, 172n113, 178n137, 178n140, 198n14, 206n49, 213n74, 214n77, 276, 286, 291–92
Martin, James D., 290n21
Martin, Ralph P., 117n36
Martos, Joseph, 9n36, 11n40
Marucci, Corrodo, 71n65
McClure, Laura K., 129nn94–95, 132n109
McGinn, Thomas A. J., 129n93
McGrew, Lydia, 59n7
McLaren, Elizabeth, 8n31
McNeile, Alan Hugh, 179n141
Meeks, Wayne A., 203n32
Meier, John P., 9, 19n8, 20, 22n21, 22n23, 23n24, 44n109, 45n115, 45n117, 46nn120–21, 46n123, 47n125, 47n128, 48nn131–32, 52n150, 58n3, 59, 62–63, 64n29, 65n34, 65n39, 68n51, 69–70, 71nn65–66, 71n69, 72, 73nn76–77, 75, 76nn86–87, 77, 80–83, 90n162, 91n165, 91n167, 93, 94n175, 101n201, 103, 114n26, 117n36, 120n51, 150n23, 152, 212n69
Meigne, Maurice, 268n138
Meissner, Bruno, 24n30
Meyer, Ben, 79n101
Meyer, Heinrich August Wilhelm, 201n24
Mielziner, M., 125n69, 142n160
Milgrom, Jacob, 123n67
Milik, J. T., 23n26, 65n37
Moiser, Jeremy, 202n28, 216n94
Moloney, Francis J., 117n36, 188n179
Moo, Douglas J., 227n148

Moore, George Foot, 121n51, 125n73, 152, 153n34
Mueller, James R., 117n36
Muller, Earl C., 290
Murphy-O'Connor, Jerome, 45n117, 46n120, 47n125, 50, 62, 66n43, 195n4
Murray, John, 3n10, 18n5, 18n7, 65n33, 98n190, 108, 109n11, 111, 155n47, 155n49, 157n53, 169, 170n103, 173, 210n61

Namer, Gérard, 83n120
Naselli, Andrew David, 5n15, 5n17, 33, 109n14, 195n7, 207n54
Nautin, Pierre, 248n56, 250n65, 250n69, 267n137, 269n145, 280
Neirynck, F., 92n169, 213n73
Nelson, C. A., 128n88
Neufeld, E., 116n34, 124n69, 152, 153n34
Neusner, Jacob, 81, 90
Nickelsburg, George W. E., 136n129
Niehaus, Jeffrey J., 4n14
Noam, Vered, 48n134, 51n145
Nolland, John, 20–21, 69–70, 71n69, 107n6, 109–10, 111n20, 113n24, 151n26, 151n28, 183n160

O'Collins, Gerald, 10n38
Ogden, Daniel, 129n91
Olender, Robert G., 63n28
Olick, Jeffrey K., 84n125, 88n154
Olson, David H., 7n21, 7n24, 8n29
Olson, Stanley N., 225n141
Omitowoju, Rosanna, 129nn91–92, 129nn97–98
Orr, William F., 196n10, 202n28
Osburn, Carroll D., 289
Osiek, Carolyn, 135n127, 235, 237nn17–19, 238n20
Oster, Richard E., Jr., 200n21, 217
Ott, Anton, 235n12, 268n140

Page, Sydney, 53–54
Perrin, Nicholas, 68n53, 73n79
Pestman, P. W., 28
Peters, Greg, 215n86
Phillips, Anthony, 124n69, 154n38
Piper, John, 5n17, 286, 288n12
Plummer, Alfred, 169n100, 201n24
Polkinghorne, Donald E., 88n151
Polkow, Dennis, 76n85, 77n94
Pomeroy, Sarah B., 43n108
Porter, Stanley E., 76n85
Pospishil, Victor J., 240n28, 243n38, 248n57, 260n109, 261n113, 267n137, 269n145, 280

Quasten, Johannes, 247n53
Quesnell, Quentin, 182n150, 182n155, 187n175

Rabello, Alfredo Mordechai, 22n20, 29n49
Rabinowitz, Jacob J., 19n7, 121n51
Rehm, Bernhard, 265n125
Reisser, H., 98n190
Repschinski, Boris, 167n93, 168n98
Reynolds, Philip Lyndon, 216n98, 240n30, 248n56, 250n66, 252n76, 267, 269–71, 280
Richlin, Amy, 153n36
Ricoeur, Paul, 86n136
Robertson, Archibald, 201n24
Rodríguez, Rafael, 60n9, 76n89, 77n91, 82n115, 87n144, 87nn147–48
Rordorf, Willy, 254n82
Rose, Martin, 17n3
Rosner, Brian S., 64n30, 67n49, 88n149, 195n4, 198n16, 199, 202–4, 206n50, 214n79, 215n87, 215n90, 219n109, 223n134, 228, 230
Roth, Martha T., 25n32
Rousselle, Aline, 204nn36–37

Safrai, S., 153n36, 155n44, 226n146
Safrai, Ze'ev, 154n43
Salzman, Todd A., 10n38
Sanders, E. P., 60–61, 63n25, 68n53, 73–74, 115n28, 213
Sariola, Heikki, 90n160
Scacewater, Todd, 18n7, 25n33, 152n30
Schembri, Kevin, 11n40
Schiffman, Lawrence H., 45n115, 46n120, 47n127, 48n134, 51
Schmidt, P., 185n171
Schockenhoff, Eberhard, 10n38
Schrage, Wolfgang, 81n109, 202n29, 203n32, 203n34, 206n47, 218n105, 219n112
Schreiner, Thomas R., 227n148
Schremer, Adiel, 48
Schröter, Jens, 85n132, 103n209
Schudson, Michael, 87n145, 87n148
Schwartz, Barry, 87
Schweizer, Eduard, 72n73, 147n3
Scroggs, Robin, 203n32
Seboldt, Roland H. A., 217n100
Seltzer, Judith A., 8n28
Senft, Christophe, 201n24
Senior, Donald, 118n42, 146n2, 151n29
Shemesh, Aharon, 51n145
Shields, Martin A., 22n18
Sigal, Phillip, 21n112, 123n62, 127n82
Simó, C., 8
Skehan, Patrick W., 135n125
Smith, Jay E., 139n144, 139n146
Snyder, Graydon F., 197n11, 206n46
Solsona, Montserrat, 8
Sonne, Isaiah, 152
Spijker, Jeroen A., 8
Sprinkle, Joe M., 17n4, 18n6
Squire, Larry R., 85n130
Staab, Karl, 164n74

Stein, Robert H., 72n72, 72n74, 78
Stienstra, Nelly, 289n15
Stock, Augustine, 117n36
Stokes, Charles E., 7n28
Straub, Jürgen, 88n153
Strecker, Georg, 148, 149n15
Stulman, Louis, 290n17

Talbert, Charles H., 100, 123n62, 155n48, 170n104
Tannehill, Robert C., 100n194, 101n201
Tarwater, John K., 4n14, 288nn9–11
Thiselton, Anthony C., 201n24, 204, 213n72, 220, 222n124
Thompson, J. A., 289n15
Tigay, Jeffrey H., 17n3, 48n134, 72n71
Tomson, Peter J., 45, 225, 226n145, 227–28
Tonkin, Elizabeth, 83n121
Tosato, Angelo, 126n74, 154n41
Towner, Philip H., 53–54
Treggiari, Susan, 34n73, 36n80, 153n36, 219
Trevett, Christine, 246n50, 251

Uecker, Jeremy E., 7n28

Valantasis, Richard, 274
Van Tine, R. Jarrett, 188–89, 190n188
Vasoli, Robert H., 9n36
Vaux, R. de, 23n26, 65n37
Vawter, Bruce, 65n33, 121n52, 164–66
Vermes, Geza, 49
Vilella, Josep, 268n138
Vinson, Richard B., 100n193

Wacholder, Ben Zion, 44n112, 45n118
Wallraff, Martin, 272
Walther, James Arthur, 196n10, 202n28
Walton, John H., 114n26
Ware, Kallistos, 274–75

Index of Authors

Wassen, Cecilia, 49
Watson, Alan, 29n50
Webb, Joseph A., 286n2, 287nn7–8
Weckwerth, Andreas, 272n158
Weder, Hans, 72n73
Weinfeld, Moshe, 19n7
Weiss, Johannes, 201n24, 220n115
Welzer, Harald, 84n129
Wenham, David, 63n29
Wenham, Gordon J., 1–2, 4, 5n15, 5n17, 59n5, 93n170, 95n181, 98n191, 119, 121n51, 121n53, 126, 148n9, 153n34, 156n52, 166n84, 168n95, 172n112, 173n117, 174nn122–23, 175nn125–26, 175n128, 176nn132–33, 177n134, 185n171, 188n182, 236n15, 242n35, 244n43, 248n60, 255n89
Westbrook, Raymond, 25n32, 141
Whealey, Alice, 58n4
Wheat, Ed, 233n6
Wheat, Gaye, 233n6
Wheeler-Reed, David, 127, 128n84, 128nn88–89, 130, 131n104, 131n108, 134n120, 136, 137nn133–36, 138–39
Williams, Craig A., 140n155

Williams, Gordon, 36n78, 39n88, 39n91, 40nn94–95, 43n108
Williams, Sally, 8n31
Wilson, Stephen G., 101n201
Wimbush, Vincent L., 216n94, 273n167, 274n172, 276
Winter, Paul, 50
Witherington, Ben, III, 43n106, 54, 115–16, 117n36, 122n57, 126n77, 201n24, 214nn81–82, 215n83, 215n88, 226n144
Wolff, Christian, 205n45, 218n106, 219n108
Wolff, Hans Julius, 29n51, 226
Wright, David P., 134n118
Wright, N. T., 78

Yadin, Yigael, 23n26, 50n141
Yarbro Collins, Adela, 21, 44n110, 51
Yardeni, Ada, 23n26, 24n31

Zahn, Theodor, 184n161
Zakovitch, Yair, 72n73, 152, 153n34
Zehnder, Markus, 22n18
Zeisel, William, 34n74, 36, 37n82, 37n84
Zerwick, Maximilian, 166n84, 176n130

Index of Subjects

adultery, 22n23, 24n28, 94–96, 98–99, 101–2, 183, 189–92, 226, 228, 275, 278, 286–89, 291–92; as betrothal infidelity, 125–27; in classical Greek literature, 129–30; in early Christian teaching, 235–39, 242, 244, 250n65, 254–57, 261n112, 262–65, 267, 269–72, 280–81; in the Greco-Roman world, 32; in Jewish and Old Testament teaching, 18n5, 19n7, 25, 80, 82, 93, 116, 119, 122–23, 130–31, 134, 138, 141–43, 152n30, 153–55, 156n50, 219; in relation to an innocent party, 3, 10n39, 11, 181, 207n51, 240n28; in relation to the Matthean exception clauses, 13, 56–57, 89–91, 145–50, 157–62, 164–66, 168–74, 176–77; in the teaching of the historical Jesus, 67–74; voice of the Greek verbs used, 105–14, 283–84

Arles, Council of, 270

ascetic/asceticism, 14, 160, 181, 196n10; in early Christian aversion to second marriages, 54; in early Christianity, 234–35, 240–41, 243, 245–47, 251n73, 253, 254n82, 255, 263–64, 273–78; in Jesus and Paul, 178n140

Augustus, 29–33, 36, 38, 52, 204, 216–17, 235

betrothal, 4, 18n5, 26, 132n112, 216–17, 218n106, 219–20, 222, 229–30, 285; betrothal infidelity, 124–27, 145, 154, 205, 284; in the Old Testament, Judaism, and ancient Near East, 132n109, 141–43

celibacy, 13, 31, 179, 181, 183–84, 186, 200n21, 223; in early Christian teaching, 233n6, 235, 241, 251n73, 254n82, 263, 273, 277–78; gift of, 64n29, 184, 187, 197, 257, 276n183; after marriage, 181, 187nn176–77, 188, 190, 197, 238, 240, 248n57, 255; in Roman Catholicism, 9

consanguinity/affinity marital prohibitions, 116–23, 143, 284

continuity (in memory studies), 86–87

covenant, 4–5, 19–20, 29n48, 48n133, 50, 115–16, 133, 287–88

desire, sexual, 112, 125n71, 141, 144, 190, 197–200, 228, 276–77, 285; as always

Index of Subjects

illicit, 127, 136–39; in early Christian teaching, 239, 241–42, 250, 253, 262–63, 265, 273–74; to marry again, 54, 206n49, 230

Dido, 39

dissimilarity, 59, 70n60, 75, 77–79, 81–82, 85, 103

divorce, (il)legitimate, 3–4, 98, 114–16, 143, 153, 157–59, 246, 283, 287; early Christian opposition to, 249, 267–68, 269n142, 280–81; in Greco-Roman world, 29, 128, 130; Jesus's opposition to, 167, 169, 173, 188; in Jewish teaching, 33, 90–91, 119, 133, 135–36, 141, 151; Paul's opposition to, 191–92, 195–96

divorce, valid, 3, 24n28, 52, 90n159, 114–15, 117, 119, 284, 287; in Greco-Roman thought, 26, 41; in Jewish teaching, 147, 169; a nonfactor in early Christian reasoning, 235, 250, 252, 271; in relation to remarriage, 103, 158n56, 171n109, 177n136, 192, 212n69

divorce certificate/bill, 1–4, 13–15, 17, 19, 105, 120, 145, 168, 194, 198, 282; ante-Nicene resistance to, 280; in Greco-Roman world, 32–33, 41, 64–66; Jesus's teaching against, 95, 101, 147–50, 152, 157–59, 170–71, 191n194, 284; in Old Testament and Second Temple Judaism, 23–29, 49, 65, 90–91; Paul's denial of their "freedom," 206–9, 225–27, 229, 285

dowry/dowries, 4, 17n2, 22, 26n38, 27, 29–30, 32, 102n206, 141, 150n23, 219n110, 284

Eastern Orthodox, 11

Elephantine, 22, 24, 49, 52n151

Elvira, Council of, 233n4, 268–69, 271n154, 233n4

embarrassment, 75–79, 103

Erasmus, Desiderius, 2, 11, 106, 149

eunuchs, 234n6, 278; in early Christian teaching, 242, 255, 256n90, 257, 263–64, 278, 281; in Jesus's teaching, 13, 146, 167, 178–92, 239, 275

flaminica dialis cult, 1, 34

Fortuna Muliebris cult, 34

Fortuna Virgo cult, 34

freedom/permission, to remarry, 3–4, 10n39, 90, 212; in early Christianity, 239n27, 241, 243n39, 255, 258–59, 261, 264, 280–81; as expressed on divorce certificates, 1–3, 15, 23–30, 33, 65, 95, 147, 149, 170–71, 282; in the Greco-Roman world, 42–43, 52; in Jesus's teaching, 13, 153, 156–59, 170–71, 284; in the Old Testament and Jewish teaching, 21, 23–30, 48; in Paul's teaching, 14, 194, 198, 200n20, 206–9, 210n63, 213nn73–74, 217–20, 223–27, 229–31, 236n15, 285

Herod Antipas, 46n124, 50, 72–73, 93n172, 94n179, 96, 118, 250, 287

Hillel, 18n5, 33, 79–82, 90, 120n51, 151–53, 165, 169n99

historical Jesus, 9, 12, 57–83, 85, 87, 103–4, 151, 213, 232

inclusive reading, of the Matthean exception clause, 163–64, 166

innocence/innocent party, 3, 9n35, 13–14, 109n14; in early Christianity, 233, 235, 237, 239–40, 243n39, 244–46, 249, 253–55, 258, 263–64, 267–68, 269n142, 270–71, 279–81; emphasized in the Reformation and by Protestants, 2–3, 11, 106, 142, 149; innocent stigmatized as

INDEX OF SUBJECTS

adulterers, 13, 106, 108, 110, 112–14, 142; in Jesus's teaching, 149–50, 156–60, 171, 172n113, 177n136, 181, 191–92; in Paul's teaching, 195–96, 207n51, 210n61, 210n63, 218n106, 229; in Roman Catholic teaching, 10n39
intermarriage (of Jews and gentiles), 123–24

Lex Iulia de adulteriis coercendis, 31, 153, 235
Lex Iulia de maritandis ordinibus, 31
Lex Iulia et Papia, 31–33
Lex Papia Poppaea nuptialis, 31
Luther, Martin, 11, 106, 210n63, 232, 233n6

Mater Matuta, 34
memory studies, 13, 82–88, 103, 282
multiple (independent) attestation, 52, 57–59, 63–64, 67–69, 73, 78

Neocaesarea, Council of, 270–71
Nicaea, Council of, 12, 14, 54, 163, 231–32, 265, 267–68, 271–72
Novatianists, 271–72

Pharisees, 80, 118, 120; in early Christianity, 257, 259, 274n169, 279; in Luke's Gospel, 99, 101; in Mark's Gospel, 57, 73, 90–95, 98–99, 123; in Matthew's Gospel, 121nn51–52, 123, 139, 146, 165–68, 178, 185, 187, 289
polygamy/polyandry/polygyny, 45–51, 53, 81, 156, 250, 265
presentism (in memory studies), 86–87
preteritive view (of the Matthean exception clause), 163–65
prostitute/prostitution, 114–16, 128–40, 143, 150, 200, 235–36; in the Greco-Roman world, 128–30; in the Old Testament and Judaism, 16, 45, 107, 119, 125n71, 130–37

Q, 57, 59, 63–64, 68–70, 73, 83, 100–101, 200n21

reconciliation, 17n4, 19, 56, 66, 70, 74, 150, 155, 290–91; in early Christianity, 233, 246–47, 249, 251, 264, 280; in Paul's teaching, 193, 195–96, 208–11, 213, 216n91, 224
regarded/considered as adulterer/adulteress, 3, 18n7, 30; in early Christianity, 267; in Jesus's teaching, 106, 108–9, 113, 148, 157n53, 168
remarriage, modern statistics, 6–8
Roman Catholicism, 2, 5n17, 9–12, 286

Sadducees, 264
second marriage/twice-/double-married, 18, 25, 42, 46, 50n140, 51–52, 54, 102, 114n26, 190, 279, 286–87; early Christian opposition to, 190, 233, 238, 239n25, 242–43, 247, 249–54, 256, 258, 260, 262–63, 266, 267n134, 271, 281; in Jesus's teaching, 70n62, 71n67, 150n23, 173n117, 177; in Paul's teaching, 213n73, 225–26, 228
self-control, 139–40, 197, 201, 256, 262, 275–76, 285
separation, 33, 39, 41, 89n157, 156, 158, 196n10, 287; against God's will in creation, 5, 93, 150–51, 168, 170, 173, 288; as divorce, 25, 56, 63–66, 74, 92, 95, 124, 167n94; as divorce in Paul, 193–95, 198, 201n24, 203, 206, 208–11, 220–21, 236n15; in early Christianity, 237, 241, 252, 254, 257, 265–67, 269n146

shameful thing, 17, 18n5, 22, 80, 121n51, 151–52, 258–59, 262
Shammai, 18n5, 33, 79–82, 90, 120n51, 142n161, 151–53, 165, 168–69
Sinaiticus, 161–63, 191–92, 234
spiritual idolatry, 115–16
spiritual marriage, 215, 253
stigmatized, as adulterer/adulteress, 13, 70, 106, 108–11, 113, 283

univira, 33–44, 52–55, 266, 282

Vaticanus, 161–63, 191–92
victimized, by adultery, 2–3, 13, 106, 109–10, 177n136, 239, 283
virgin, 125–26; in early Christianity, 242, 247, 251, 265, 277–78; in Greco-Roman world, 35, 37, 39, 129; in the Old Testament and Judaism, 16–18, 45n116, 52, 125, 136; in Paul's teaching, 194, 198–99, 203–4, 214–24, 229, 285

widow, 41n99, 53–55, 102, 126n75, 131; in early Christianity, 43, 233, 238, 240, 246–48, 250–53, 256, 260, 264, 266–68, 272, 278n195, 280; in the Greco-Roman world, 32, 34–38, 52, 129; in the Old Testament and Judaism, 6, 16, 40n96, 46, 49–52, 150n23; in Paul's teaching, 193–94, 198–209, 216n91, 219n114, 221, 223–25, 228–31, 276, 279–80, 285
widower, 54, 200–206, 229, 238, 240, 256, 264n123, 276, 278n195, 285

Index of Scripture

OLD TESTAMENT

Genesis
1–2	92
1:27	49, 92, 99, 168
2:23–24	288n11
2:24	92, 99, 125, 127n83, 168, 233, 236n15, 261, 288n11
7:9	47, 49
9:22–23	18
24:54–55	125n70
34:2	132
34:31	130–32
38	131
38:6–11	131
38:15	130–31
38:15–26	132n110
38:24	131
38:24–26	131

Exodus
7:13	168
8:15	91
8:32	91
18:20	19n7
19:3	146
19:12	146
20:14	147n7, 153
20:26	18
21:7–11	134n118
21:10–11	18, 80n104
22:22	204n34
22:31	117
24:15	146
24:18	146
32:6–8	122
34:1–2	146
34:4	146
34:15–16	122
34:16	123

Leviticus
17	117–18
17–18	120–23
17:7	131
17:8–9	117, 122
17:10–12	117
17:10–13	122
17:15	117
18	117, 123
18–20	122
18:6–18	117n36, 118–20, 121n53
18:6–26	122
18:8	118, 139
18:13	119
18:16	73, 96, 118
18:18	48n135, 51n148, 118, 139
18:19–23	122
19:20–22	134n118
20:5	131
20:10	3, 18, 69, 102n206, 110, 153
20:11–12	117n34
20:11–21	118
20:14	117n34
20:19–21	117n34
20:21	73, 96
21:1–9	126
21:7	16, 51, 126
21:9	131
21:13–14	16, 51
21:18–20	179

Index of Scripture

Numbers

5:11–31	18, 102n206
5:13	19
5:14	19
5:20	19
14:33	119, 130
25:1	123, 131, 133

Deuteronomy

7:1–5	123
7:3	124
17:17	47–48
20:7	125
21:10–14	18, 134n118
22	125
22:13–19	16
22:13–21	18, 131
22:13–24	125
22:14–19	109n15
22:21–22	132
22:22	3, 69, 102n206, 153
22:23–24	18, 125
22:23–27	3, 219
22:23–29	124
22:25–27	109, 126
22:28–29	16, 18
22:30	117n34
23:1	179
23:14	17–18
23:15	18
24	126, 165
24:1	17–18, 21, 23–24, 70n61, 80, 98, 120, 139, 151–52, 164–65, 168
24:1–2	92
24:1–4	17–18, 23, 25, 91, 99–102, 147–48, 168, 259, 289–90
24:2	227
24:4	17, 22, 69n57, 101, 102n206, 114n26
27:20	117n34, 118
27:22–23	117n34

Judges

2:17	131
3:1–6	124
8:27	131
8:33	131
16:1	130, 132n110

Ruth

1:3–5	150
1:20–21	150
4:5	138
4:10	138

1 Samuel

21:5	139

2 Samuel

3:14	124

1 Kings

11:1–6	124
16:31–33	124

Ezra

9–10	19, 124
9:2	124
9:14	124
10:3	124

Psalms

94:6	150

Proverbs

2:16–17	153, 288n11
2:16–19	154n38
6:25	147n3
6:27–29	244
6:33–35	154n39
7:25–27	154n38

Isaiah

1:17	204n34
1:23	150
10:2	150
37:22	223
50:1	19
54:4	150
57:3	143

Jeremiah

2:20	130, 133
3	91
3:1	289, 291n21
3:1–2	19
3:1–5	290
3:1–9	126n82
3:2	116, 119, 130, 133
3:3	91
3:6–9	115, 125n71
3:6–11	290
3:8	19, 138, 290
3:9	116, 119, 133
3:12–18	290
3:12–22	290
3:13	91
5:7–8	106
7:9	107n4
9:2	107n4
9:17	91
9:20	91
13:22–26	154n39

INDEX OF SCRIPTURE

13:27	133	4:8	133	19:2	134
22:3	204n34	4:11	130	23:16–18	134
23:14	107n4	4:11–14	122	23:21	154n39
36:23	107n4	4:12–13	133	23:22–23	134
		5:14–6:3	19	23:23	111, 125n71, 138

Lamentations

		6:6	155	23:24	154n39
1:8	18	6:10	115–16	25:13–26	21
		14:1–2	19	25:26	152, 169n99

Ezekiel

				26:8–9	139
16	138	**Amos**		33:25–32	134
16:15	130, 133	7:17	133	41:17	134
16:31	107			41:20–22	134
16:32	107	**Micah**		41:22	135
16:36–37	18	1:7	130		
16:37	154n39			**Susanna**	
16:38–41	126n82	**Nahum**		63	151n30
16:39	154n39	3:4	130		
22:10	118			**2 Maccabees**	
23	130	**Zechariah**		1:5	196
23:7	130	7:10	204n34	5:20	196
23:11	130			7:32–33	196
23:26	154n39	**Malachi**		7:33	196
23:27	119	2:10–16	19, 288n11	8:29	196
23:29	154n39	2:14–16	51n148		
23:35–37	126n82	2:16	20–21, 48, 49n137	**NEW TESTAMENT**	
23:37	107				
23:43–45	126n82	**DEUTEROCANONICAL**		**Matthew**	
43:7–9	133	**BOOKS**		1:18	215n89, 216n98
				1:18–19	154
Hosea		**Tobit**		1:18–25	124–26, 142
1–2	138	4:12	123, 135n129	1:19	144, 147n7
1–3	19n8	7:13	19, 150n23	1:19–20	219
1:2	130, 133	8:7	125n71, 135n129, 138	1:19–25	144
2:2	132n110, 138			1:20	125
2:4	125n71, 132n110, 133	**Sirach**		1:23	215n89, 216n98
2:5	132n110	4:10	204n34	1:24	219
2:6	133	7:29	134	3:2	11
2:14–15	19	9:8	134	3:5–6	167
3:4–5	19	9:9	154n38	3:7	167

342

Index of Scripture

3:8	185		171–72, 177, 245n43,	9:20	220n118
3:10	171, 185, 289		267, 284	9:22	220n118
3:14	76	5:32	3, 13, 56–57, 67–71,	9:27–31	172n112
3:15	76		73–74, 77, 79, 83,	9:32–34	172n112
4:1–11	167		89n158, 98–99,	9:35	172n112
4:9	176		105–9, 113–14, 116,	10	146
4:17	171		119–22, 125–26,	10:14	172
4:23	172n112		127n82, 137, 143,	10:15	172n112
4:25	167n92		145, 147, 148n14,	10:37	179, 186
5	126		149–52, 155, 157,	10:38	172n112
5–7	146		159–62, 164–65,	10:39	172n112
5:1–16	146		168, 171–75, 177,	11:15	172n112, 185
5:2	146		187, 190–91, 235,	11:22	172n112
5:3–10	166–67		236n15, 238–39,	11:23	175n126
5:13	175n127		244–45, 249, 254,	11:25	185
5:17	146		263n121, 281, 284,	11:27	175n127
5:17–20	146		288	12:4	175n127
5:17–48	146, 166	5:33	146	12:7	149, 155, 160,
5:19	172, 176	5:38	146		172n112
5:20	146	5:43	146	12:22–24	172n112
5:21	146	5:48	146, 167, 176, 185	12:24	175n127
5:21–26	146	6:19–21	167	12:33	185
5:21–30	108	6:27	289	12:33–35	172n112
5:21–48	101, 148, 168n97	7:12	146	12:38–39	172n112
5:27	146	7:13–14	167	12:39	175n127
5:27–28	139n150	7:16–18	172n112	13	146, 185
5:27–30	146, 189,	7:16–20	185	13:3–9	185
	245n43	7:17	289	13:9	172n112, 185
5:27–32	192	7:19	171	13:10–11	188
5:28	147n3, 190, 244, 275	7:20	172n112	13:11	184–85
5:28–29	238	7:21	176	13:12	171
5:29	190	7:21–27	176	13:18–23	185
5:29–30	148, 171, 187, 257	7:24	172, 176	13:23	185
5:30	147	7:28	180	13:26	185
5:30–32	148	8:19–20	182n150	13:30	185
5:31	70n61, 146	8:21–22	179, 182n150	13:36–37	188
5:31–32	13, 65n36,	8:25	289	13:43	172n112, 185
	74, 95n180, 105,	9:13	160, 172n112,	13:44	289
	109, 145, 147, 157,		240n29	13:51	185

343

13:51–52	180	18:18	172n112	19:9–12	263
13:57	175n127	18:21	95	19:10	166, 177–84,
14:3–4	118, 167, 287	18:21–22	180		186–89, 263, 284
14:17	175n127	19	57, 126, 148, 166, 185	19:10–12	146, 167, 178,
14:26–27	182n150	19:1	166, 180		180, 182–83,
14:30–31	182n150	19:1–9	145, 180, 239,		187–89, 234n6, 276,
14:32–33	185		245n44, 284		281
15:12–13	182n150	19:1–10	159	19:11	179–85, 187, 190
15:12–14	167	19:1–12	188	19:11–12	180–81, 185,
15:19	116, 137n137, 143	19:2–9	178, 181, 187, 190		188, 190, 255, 284
15:20	165n79	19:3	65n36, 120, 123,	19:12	13, 179, 181–83,
15:22	220n118		142, 151, 167,		187–92, 239, 257,
15:23	289		188–89, 257, 289		263, 277–78
15:24	175n127	19:3–8	168, 172n113, 177,	19:13	155
15:28	220n118		180	19:13–14	182n150
16:1	167	19:3–9	57, 126, 148, 167,	19:13–15	167
16:1–2	172n112		178, 183	19:14	166
16:1–4	167	19:3–12	13, 57, 74, 105, 256	19:16	188
16:4	175n127	19:4–6	143, 148n14, 169,	19:16–22	167
16:5–12	185		182, 188, 242	19:16–30	188
16:6	167	19:4–9	3	19:17	188
16:11–12	167	19:5	261	19:18–19	166
16:15–17	181n147, 182	19:5–6	150, 285	19:18–20	188
16:17	185	19:6	64n29, 168, 173,	19:21	167
16:19	172n112		184, 191, 288	19:22–26	182n150
16:21	166	19:7	65n36, 123, 139, 188	19:23	167
16:24	166, 172n112	19:8	168, 173, 265	19:23–26	167
16:25	172n112	19:9	3, 56–57, 65n36,	19:24	188
17:8	175n127		68–70, 74, 77,	19:25	188
17:10–11	180		89n158, 105, 116,	19:26	187–88
17:10–13	185		119–22, 125–26,	19:27–30	166–67
17:13	185		127n82, 137, 143,	19:27–20:14	167
17:20	172n112		145, 160–68,	19:29	179, 181, 186
17:22	166		170, 172–73, 175,	19:30	172n112
17:23	185n168		180, 182–84, 186,	20:1–16	167
17:24–27	180		188–89, 191–92,	20:16	172n112
18	146		236n15, 242, 245,	20:26–27	172n112
18:3	176		254, 257, 267, 284,	20:28	187
18:8–9	171		289	20:29–34	172n112

Index of Scripture

20:30	289	4:1–9	92	10:1	89n156, 90, 92
21:19	175n127	4:9	93	10:1–12	90, 97n186
21:21	172n112, 176	4:10–12	93	10:2	65n36, 90–91, 98,
21:43	185	4:10–20	92		151, 167
22:2–14	186	4:11	93, 184	10:2–9	92, 96, 178
22:15	167	4:11–12	93	10:2–12	3, 74, 88, 96
22:22–23	186, 264	4:13	185	10:3	91, 168
22:24	187	4:34	93	10:4	57, 65n36, 91, 95,
23–25	146	6	73n75		123
23:3	289	6:2	89n156	10:5	92
23:11	172n112	6:17–29	96	10:6–9	242
23:23	149	6:18	72, 96	10:7–8	261, 285
24:1–2	180	6:51–52	185	10:9	64n29, 69, 82, 92,
24:3–4	188	7:1–13	91		288
24:22	175n127	7:14–15	92	10:10	93
24:26	175n127	7:17	93	10:10–12	92, 178
24:42	172n112	7:17–23	92	10:11	68–70, 73, 82, 95,
25:1	215n89	7:21	137		98, 161–62, 165,
25:7	215n89	7:22	117, 143		235, 242
25:11	215n89	8:14–21	185	10:11–12	56–57, 65n36,
25:13	172n112	8:17	92		68, 71, 74, 89, 94–
25:25–26	176	8:18	97		96, 98, 102n207,
25:29	171	8:22–26	93, 96		226
25:34–40	185	8:29	185	10:12	72–73, 89n157, 94,
26:1	180	8:31	97		174n124
26:5	166	8:32–33	97	10:13–16	90
28:16–20	185n170	8:34–9:29	97	10:17–22	90
28:19	76	9:9	86	10:21–22	97
28:20	176	9:9–10	185	10:23–31	90
		9:11–13	185	10:27	97, 99
Mark		9:14–27	92	10:29	97n189, 186
1:7–8	76	9:28	93	10:29–30	97
1:21–22	89n156	9:28–29	92	10:30	97
2:1–3:6	91	9:30–31	92	10:32–40	97
3:5	92	9:31	97	10:33–34	97
3:24	68n50	9:32	97	10:35–37	97
3:25	68n50	9:33	92, 93	10:38–45	97
3:26	68n50	9:33–10:31	97	10:46–52	97
4:1	89n156	9:50	64n29	11:27–12:37	91

345

INDEX OF SCRIPTURE

12:19	187	16:17	100	15	121–22, 124
12:24–27	186	16:18	56–57, 65n36,	15:20	115, 117, 123
13:1–2	180		67–71, 73–75,	15:23	124
13:8	68n50		82–83, 95, 98–102,	15:28	121
13:9–13	99		161–62, 174n124,	15:29	115, 117, 122n58, 123
13:12	68n50		175, 177, 235, 239,	15:30	124
14:3	220n118		244, 249	21:9	215n89
14:29–31	99	16:19–31	75, 100–101	21:11	61
14:48	68n50	16:29–31	100	21:25	115, 117, 123
14:51–52	99	18:1–8	102	22:3	206
14:66–72	99	18:20	101		
16:5–7	99	18:29	179, 186, 275	**Romans**	
16:7	97n185, 99	20:27–40	186	1:27	122n60, 214
		20:34–35	186	7:1	225, 227
Luke		21:1–4	102	7:1–3	12, 14, 42
1:2	62n18	24:44–47	101	7:1–6	197
1:15	76			7:2	213n73, 255
1:27	76, 215n89, 216n98	**John**		7:2–3	224n139, 225–27,
1:30	76	1:14	257		229, 231, 237, 243,
2:36–38	272	2:13–22	62		251–52, 261, 268,
3:15–17	76	2:22	86		279, 285
5:32	240n29	4:17–18	245, 289	7:3	2, 51, 206–8, 218,
7:11–17	102	7:35	175n126		228, 261, 264
10:7	63n23	7:41	175n126	7:25	209
10:15	175n126	7:52	175n126	11:25–26	259
10:25–28	101	8:3–6	154	12:18	212
11:11	175n126	8:3–11	177	14	123
12:38	222	8:4	143		
14:16–24	186	8:41	124	**1 Corinthians**	
14:20	186	14:26	62, 86	2:16	62
14:26	179, 275	19:35	62n18	3:15	197
15:30	137			4:17	224, 235
16	101	**Acts**		5	123
16:1–13	99	1:21–22	62n18	5:1	117–19, 121, 124,
16:1–15	75	3:11–26	101		139–40
16:14–15	99	6:1	204n34	5:1–5	122n60
16:14–18	100	6:1–6	102	5:1–13	119
16:15	100	8	264	5:9–11	140, 236
16:16	100	10:39	62n18	6:9	117, 122n60, 137, 140,
16:16–17	99–100	10:41	62n18		197

6:12	140	7:10	61–62, 64n29, 66, 225	7:25–38	199, 204n35, 205, 216–17, 219–20, 222, 228–30
6:12–20	64n29, 140	7:10–11	3, 14, 56–57, 60–66, 73–74, 82, 88, 116, 124, 193–95, 198, 201, 205–9, 210n61, 211–13, 218nn105–6, 220, 224, 227, 229–30, 235–36, 249, 285		
6:15–17	236			7:25–40	203
6:16	140, 200, 236n15			7:26–28	276
6:18	140			7:27	207, 218–19, 247
7	14, 180–81, 193, 197, 202, 207, 213n73, 218, 223, 225, 228, 231, 234, 247, 249, 254n82, 276–79, 285, 291			7:27–28	198, 214–18, 220, 229, 285
				7:28	203, 215, 218n105, 220, 233, 251, 276, 278
7:1	193, 209, 230, 242, 276	7:10–15	66, 209–10	7:29	2, 252
7:1–6	199	7:10–16	12, 92, 160n64, 195, 199, 210n64	7:29–31	276
7:1–7	193, 197–200, 205, 228–30, 285	7:11	70, 195, 199, 200n22, 205, 218n106, 230–31, 291	7:31	194
				7:32	199, 221, 229, 285
7:1–16	203–4, 206, 229–30			7:32–33	223
		7:11–13	219	7:32–34	203, 215, 221, 223–24, 230
7:2	138, 141, 197, 200, 205, 228, 276	7:12	61–62, 233		
		7:12–13	66, 203, 209, 211, 231	7:32–35	194, 256
7:2–4	230			7:32–40	53
7:2–5	276	7:12–14	211	7:34	199, 215, 220n118, 221–24, 229, 285
7:3	203	7:12–15	123, 198, 208		
7:3–4	263	7:12–16	3, 63, 79, 116, 124, 193, 198, 209n58, 212n69, 213, 229–30, 241, 248n58, 269n146	7:36	205, 214–15, 217, 233, 246
7:3–5	141				
7:4	141, 203			7:36–38	203, 215–16, 224, 230
7:5	197, 251, 276, 277n191				
7:6	62			7:37	214, 276
7:6–7	197, 200, 276	7:14	211	7:38	214–15, 276
7:7	62, 180, 257, 278n193	7:14–15	203	7:39	12, 42, 51, 199, 205–8, 218, 224, 225n141, 226, 229–31, 235, 243, 248, 251–52, 261, 279, 285
		7:15	63, 64n29, 149, 195, 198, 206–13, 220, 225, 230, 285		
7:8	62, 183, 199, 202, 216, 248n56				
		7:15–16	211		
7:8–9	193, 197–201, 204–5, 213n73, 228–30, 246–47, 248n56, 256, 276, 285	7:16	211–12, 231	7:39–40	194, 199, 203, 213n73, 227, 230, 251, 255–56, 259, 264, 268, 276, 279
		7:17	221, 276		
		7:17–24	203, 230		
		7:25	61, 193, 214, 216–18		
7:8–12	62			7:40	61–62, 225n141, 251, 252n73
7:9	141, 205, 250, 256, 276	7:25–28	230		
		7:25–35	214	9	253

9:1–18	62	5:1	209	**2 Timothy**	
9:5	63n23	5:15	175n126	2:3–4	251
9:14	63	5:19	137n137		
10:7	122n60			**Titus**	
10:7–8	122n58	**Ephesians**		1:6	43, 247n54, 255
10:23–33	123	4:17	180		
11:17	62, 195	5:5	137	**Hebrews**	
11:23–25	63			11:31	137
12:23	214	**Philippians**		12:16	137
12:28	62	2:6	257	13:4	117, 137
12:28–29	60	3:4–6	206		
14:3	60	4:1	224	**James**	
14:5	60			1:27	204n34
14:16–23	61	**Colossians**		2:25	137
14:37	62, 195	3:5	137n137		
14:37–38	61			**1 Peter**	
15:3–5	63n23	**1 Thessalonians**		3:7	138
15:4	63n26	4:3–6	138	5:1	62n18
15:5	63n26	4:4	138		
15:7	63n26	4:11	62	**2 Peter**	
15:16	62n18	4:15	195	1:16	62n18
2 Corinthians		**1 Timothy**		**1 John**	
11:2	54, 215n89, 216n98	1:10	137	1:1–3	62n18
11:28	164	3	54		
12:1–4	62	3:1–7	278	**Revelation**	
12:9	60–61	3:2	43, 53, 247n54, 249, 252, 255, 260, 271, 279	1:6	252
12:21	137n137			2:14	122
13:1	222			2:20	122
		3:4–5	279	3:20	61
Galatians		3:8	271	3:22	61
1:11–2:14	62	3:12	247n54, 255	9:21	137n137
1:14	206	5	54–55, 260	14:4	215n89
2:2	175n126	5:9	43, 53–54, 279	17–18	137
2:11–13	122	5:9–16	279	17:2	115–16
3:15	288n10	5:11–12	54	18:3	115–16
4:8	209	5:14	54, 260	19:1	116
4:24–25	209			19:2	115–16

Index of Other Ancient Sources

OLD TESTAMENT PSEUDEPIGRAPHA

1 Enoch
10:9–10   136n129

Jubilees
7:21   135
16:4   135
20:3   135
20:6   135
23:15   135
25:8   135
30:8–9   69n57, 102n206
33:7–9   154
33:9   69n57, 102n206
41:20   154

Psalms of Solomon
4:4   147n3
8:10–11   107

Pseudo-Phocylides
175–176   137
186   137
189   137

Testament of Benjamin
9:1   135

Testament of Isaac
4:53   147n3

Testament of Issachar
4:4   147n3
7:1–2   136

Testament of Joseph
2:2   197n13
3:8   125n71, 126n82, 136
4:6   127n82
5:1   127n82

Testament of Judah
4:13   136
13:3   117n35, 135
14:2   135
14:3   135
18:2   102n205

Testament of Levi
9:9   135

Testament of Naphtali
8:1   136
8:8   200n21

Testament of Reuben
1:6   117n35, 135
3:10–15   154
3:15   143, 154
4:6   135
4:7   135

Testament of Simeon
5:3   135

Testament of Zebulun
1:4   164

INDEX OF OTHER ANCIENT SOURCES

Dead Sea Scrolls

Damascus Document
IV	52
IV, 9–V, 2	51
IV, 12–V, 14a	119
IV, 14–V, 1	101n201, 102n203
IV, 19–V, 3	45
IV, 19–V, 9	45, 48, 81
IV, 20–21	48n132, 49–51
IV, 21	45, 47, 51, 81
V, 1	47
V, 1b–2a	45n118
V, 2	47
XIII, 7	49
XIII, 14–18	51n148
XIII, 15–18	48
XIII, 17	47n128, 48

1QapGen (Genesis Apocryphon)
XX, 15	143n167, 154n40

4Q76 (Minor Prophets[a])
	21, 49n137
II, 4–7	21, 48

4QD[a] (4QDamascus Document[a])
III, 5	49

4QD[e] (4QDamascus Document[e])
7 I, 12–13	137

4QD[f] (4QDamascus Document[f])
3 5–10	51
3 10–15	49–52

4Q159
2–4	48
9–10	48

11QT[a] (Temple Scroll[a])
LIV, 4–5	45n116, 48, 49n137, 51n148
LVII	45, 51n148, 52
LVII, 15–19	44, 47, 51
LXVI, 8–11	44n114, 45n116, 49n137, 51n148
LXVI, 11	48

Ancient Jewish Writers

Josephus

Against Apion
2.24 §199	137
2.30 §215	154n38

Antiquities
3.11.6 §270	112
3.12.1 §§274–275	154n38
4.8.23 §253	23, 147n4, 152, 167n94
4.8.40 §§290–291	179
6.13.1 §309	154n43
6.14.6 §357	154n43
6.14.6 §364–365	154n43
7.1.4 §§25–26	154n43
7.7.1 §§130–132	154n38
7.7.1 §131	112
15.7.10 §259	65, 147n7, 148n11, 227
15.7.10 §§259–260	24, 94n179
16.3.3 §85	154n43
17.1.2 §14	46n124, 50n140
18.3.3 §§63–64	58
18.5.2 §§116–119	77n90
18.5.4 §136	94n179, 96n184
18.6.4 §§161–167	96
18.6.6 §180	38

Jewish War
1.22.1 §432	154n43
1.24.2 §477	46n124, 50n140

Life
76 §§426–427	23, 152

Philo of Alexandria

De cherubim
5	112

De decalogo
24	112, 197n13

De Iosepho
43	136

De sacrificiis Abelis et Caini
7	113
20–23	136

De specialibus legibus
3.2	136, 154n38
3.10	112
3.12	219
3.30–31	22

Index of Other Ancient Sources

3.36	197n13	Soṭah		90b	143, 154
De vita Mosis		1:2	125	Ketubbot	
2.13.14	200n21	1:3–4	125n73	45a	102n206
		2:6	102n206	Nedarim	
Hypothetica		3:6	69n57, 102n206, 154	90b–91a	125n72
7.1	154n38	4:2	69n57, 102n206, 154	Qiddušin	
11.17	212	5:1	102n206, 125, 143, 154	63b	102n206
Quod deterius potiori		6:1	141	Sanhedrin	
insidari soleat		6:1–3	125	15a–b	154n39
47	189–90	9:9	125n73	46a	102n206
48	189–90	Yebamot		51a	102n206
		1:2	23, 121n51	53a	102n206
Rabbinic Sources		2:8	125, 154n40	57a	102n206
		6:6	205	57b	102n206
Mishnah		8:4–6	179	73a	102n206
'Arakin		15:1–2	150n23	Šebi'it	
6:1–2	141	15:7	142	47b	114n26
Baba Meṣi'a		16:6–7	150n23	Yebamot	
3:12	121n51	**Tosefta**		25b	150n23
Giṭṭin		Ketubbot		62b–64a	206
1:1	227	7.6	154	63a	206
5:9	212n67	Yebamot		115a	150n23
9:3	23, 147, 158, 224	14.5	150n23	116b	150n23
9:10	79, 90, 101n202, 120n51, 152, 153n34, 169	14.7–8	150n23	122a	150n23
		14.10	150n23	**Jerusalem Talmud**	
Ketubbot		**Babylonian Talmud**		Giṭṭin	
1:1	125, 126n75	Berakot		44b, 2:3	155
1:2	51	24b	121n51	Ketubbot	
3:5	154	Giṭṭin		31b, 7:4	155
5:1	51	29b	206	Yebamot	
5:2	125	61a	212n67	2:11, 4b	150n23
7:4	102n206	90a–b	152, 155	16:5, 15d	150n23
7:6	141, 152, 153n36, 155				
7:9	102n206				

Related Literature

Numbers Rabbah
9:2	127n82
9:25a	127n82

EARLY CHRISTIAN WRITINGS

Athanasius

Epistula ad virgines
19	277n191
26–27	277

Athenagoras

Plea for the Christians (Legatio pro Christianis)
33	241–42

Augustine

De ordine
2.4.12	129n95

Faith and Works
1 §2	232
7 §10	232n1, 233

2 Clement
4.3	107

Clement of Alexandria

Stromateis
2	279
2.23	254
3	256
3.1	256n93
3.1.4	254, 256, 266
3.5.40	253–54
3.6.45	253
3.6.46	254
3.6.47	255
3.6.49	253
3.6.50	255
3.6.51	254
3.6.52	277n190
3.6.52–53	254
3.6.53	162, 254
3.7.57–58	253
3.7.58	253, 277
3.9.66	277
3.12.79	278
3.12.80	255
3.12.81	254
3.12.82	266
3.12.85	277n190
3.12.89	253, 255
4.15.2	277
7.11	206n45

Didache
6.1	164

Didascalia apostolorum
14	266
16	253n79

Epiphanius

Panarion
59.4.1–3	272

Eusebius

Historia ecclesiastica
5.20.5–7	88n150
6.8.1–2	257

Hippolytus

Refutatio omnium haeresium
8.13	277n189

Irenaeus

Adversus haereses
1.24.2	245
1.28.1	277
3.17.2	245
4.15.2	245

John Chrysostom

De non iterando conjugio
	233

De virginitate
40–41	233

Homily on 1 Corinthians
19	233

Homily on Matthew
17.4	233

Justin Martyr

Apologia I
1.15	190
15	238, 240
15–17	238
15.4	180n142

Apologia II
2	155
2.1–7	240

Dialogus cum Tryphone
134	50n140

Index of Other Ancient Sources

Lactantius

Divine Institutes
6.23   267

Methodius

Symposium
3.12   264n123
3.13   278

Minucius Felix

Octavius
31.5   265, 279

Novatian

De bono pudicitia
5   265
6   265

Origen

Commentarium in evangelium Matthaei
13.25   257
14.16   257
14.17   257, 258
14.17–20   259
14.18   258–59
14.18–20   258
14.19   258
14.20   258n103, 259
14.21   259
14.22   260
14.23   260–61
14.24   162, 262–63
14.25   263
15.1   263
15.4   263

Pseudo-Clementine Homilies
3.54   264

Ptolemy

Letter to Flora
4   245n44

Salvian

De gubernatione Dei
7.22   129

Shepherd of Hermas

Mandate(s)
4   235
4.1   237
4.1.1–2   235
4.1.3   237
4.1.4   107, 235, 266
4.1.4–6   241
4.1.4–10   155
4.1.5   235
4.1.6   107, 235, 237–38
4.1.8   236
4.1.8–9   107
4.1.8–10   235
4.1.10   236
4.2–3   237
4.4   237–38
4.4.1   237

Visions
1.1.2–1.2.4   147n3

Socrates

Historia ecclesiastica
5.11.60   272n160

Tertullian

Ad uxorem
1   249
1.1   247
1.2   247
1.5   247
1.7   247, 252
1.7–8   43n107
1.8   248
2.1   43n107, 248
2.2   248

Adversus Marcionem
4.34   246, 249
4.34.7   155
5.7   249

De exhortatione castitatis
4   251
4–7   43n107
5   250
8   251
9   250
10   251
10.3–4   277n191
11   43n107, 251
12   251
13   43n107

De monogamia
5   252
8   43n107
11   251–52
12   252
13   43n107
14   252
15   246
17   43n107

INDEX OF OTHER ANCIENT SOURCES

De patientia
12.5 — 246

De praescriptione haereticorum
33 — 246

De pudicitia
16 — 43n107

De virginibus velandis
9 — 43n107

Theophilus

Ad Autolycum
3.13 — 244

Ancient Inscriptions and Papyri

BGU
4.1024 — 128
4.1101 — 66
4.1102 — 24
4.1103 — 27
4.1104 — 27

Carm. Epigr.
455 — 36n77
548.5 — 36n77
558.4 — 35
597.3 — 36n77
643.5 — 36n78
652.7 — 36n77
693.4 — 36n78
736.3 — 36n78
968.3 — 36n78
1142.15–17 — 36n77
1306 — 35
1523.7 — 36n78
1571.3 — 40

Chr.M.
283 — 42n103
284 — 42n103
285 — 42n102
291 — 26
293 — 27
295 — 27

CIJ
1.81 — 40n96
1.158 — 40n96
1.392 — 40n96
1.541 — 40n96

CIL
2.301 — 39
2.3596 — 39
3.1537 — 36
3.1992 — 36
3.2667 — 36
3.2739 — 41n98
3.2741 — 36
3.2868 — 41n98
3.3241 — 38
3.3572 — 35
3.7553 — 41n98
3.7694 — 41n98
3.8178 — 36
3.10577 — 41n98
3.14292 — 36
3.14910 — 41n98
5.7763 — 35
6.304 — 35
6.434 — 38n86
6.1779 — 39n87
6.2308 — 35
6.2318 — 35
6.5162 — 37
6.6976 — 35
6.7243 — 38–39
6.7579 — 39
6.7732 — 36
6.9693 — 39
6.9810 — 36
6.10867 — 36
6.11082 — 38n86
6.12405 — 35
6.12652 — 39
6.12829 — 36
6.13303 — 35–36
6.13528 — 39n87
6.14404 — 39
6.14771 — 35
6.15546 — 38–39
6.15806 — 38–39
6.18817 — 39
6.19008 — 39n87
6.19253 — 36
6.19838 — 37
6.25392 — 35
6.25427 — 39
6.26268 — 35
6.30111a — 38n86
6.30115 — 39
6.30428 — 36
6.31711 — 35, 37
6.37207 — 36, 41n98
8.648 — 38n86
8.1542 — 36
8.7384 — 35
8.11294 — 35
8.16737 — 39
8.19470 — 35
8.27380 — 39
9.2272 — 36
9.5142 — 35
9.5517 — 36
10.1310 — 38
10.3058 — 35–36
10.3351 — 35

10.3720	36, 40	P.Eleph.		P.Oxy.Hels.	
10.7196	43	1.2.1–18	42n103	35	27
10.37207	36				
11.216	36	P.Fam.Tebt.		P.Ryl.	
11.800	35	13	27	2.154	28
11.4593	35				
11.6281	36	P.Fay.		PSI	
12.2244	40n97	22	26n38	8.921–31	27
12.5193	39			9.1055b	128
13.2000	36	P.Freib.		P.Tebt.	
13.2056	37	3.30	42n103	1.104	42n102
13.2189	41n98				
13.2216	36	P.Gen.		SB	
13.5383	36	1.21	42n103	20.14517	128
14.418	35				
14.839	35	P.Giss.		**Greco-Roman**	
14.963	35	2	42n103	**Literature**	
14.1641	36				
14.2841	41n98	P.Grenf.		Aeschines	
14.5210	40n97	2.76	27	*De falsa legatione*	
		P.Lips.		144	128
CPJ		27	27	*In Timarchum*	
2.144	24			52	128n86
		P.Mil.Vogl.			
IG		3.184	27	**Aeschines Milesius**	
12.8.449.12–14	39n87	3.185	27	*Anthologia Graeca*	
ILCV				7.260	41
1003	266	P.Münch.			
1581	43	3.62	42n103	**Apollodorus**	
4318 A.5	266			*Epitome*	
		P. Mur.		2.11	110
P.Brookl.		19	23	6.9	113
8	27				
		P.Oxy.		**Apuleius**	
P.Dura.		906	27	*Metamorphoses*	
31	28	1473	219n110	8.8.7	43
32	28	2770	28		

INDEX OF OTHER ANCIENT SOURCES

10.35	200n21	**Cicero**		**Epictetus**	
11.4	200n21				
11.6	200n21	*De oratore*		*Diatribai*	
11.12	200n21	1.40.183	29	3.22.76	197n13
11.17	200n21	1.56.238	29	4.1.147	197n13

Aristophanes

Pax
558   113
979–980   112

Aristotle

Historia animalium
586a3   112
619a10   111

Magna moralia
1.8   129n97

Artemidorus

Onirocritica
1.78   128

Athenaeus

Deipnosophistae
9.388c   113
12.521b   113
13.568c   129n95
13.569–70   129n95
13.569d   129n95
13.578–79   110

Chariton

De Chaerea et Callirhoe
1.4.6   113
3.6.6   39

Demosthenes

Contra Leocharem
44.32   223

De falsa legatione
200   128
233   128

In Neaeram
67   129

Dio Cassius

Historia romana
54.10.5–7   31
54.16   217n99
54.16.1–2   204
60.16.6   38n85

Diodorus Siculus

Bibliotheca historica
10.21.1   110
12.21.1   113
12.18.1–2   65

Dionysius of Halicarnassus

Antiquitates romanae
2.25.7   65
4.24.4   128
9.22.2   223

Euripides

Andromache
973   65

Helena
689   223

Iphigenia taurica
220   223

Gaius

Institutes
1.18 §63   118n41
1.18–23 §§58–67   118n41

Gellius

Noctes atticae
4.4   219

Herodotus

Historiae
1.93   128n86
2.134–135   130
5.39   65n38

Hippocrates

Epidemics
7.122   128n85

Index of Other Ancient Sources

Homer

Odyssea
1.430 — 130

Horace

Odes
3.14.5 — 38

Satirae
1.2.31–35 — 141n157
1.2.116–129 — 130

Julius Paulus

Opinions
2.26.1–17 — 153n36
2.26.6 — 153n36
2.26.8 — 153n36

Justinian

Codex Justinianus
5.4.14 — 25
5.10.1 — 25
6.46.2 — 25
8.39.2 — 26
9.18 — 53

Digesta
23.1.1–2 — 216n98
23.1.9 — 216n98
23.1.14 — 216n98
24.1.32.27 — 216n98
24.2.2 — 25
24.2.2.2 — 216n98
24.2.11 — 26
24.3.66 — 26
45.1.19 — 25
48.5 — 153n36
48.5.25 — 140n155

Juvenal

Satirae
6.535–537 — 200n21

Livy

Ab urbe condita libri
1.58.4 — 140n155
34.7.12 — 42

Lucian

Dialogi marini
12.1 — 110

Timon
16 — 113

Lysias

Orations
1.4 — 129

Malalas

Chronographia
71.19 — 223

Martial

Epigrammata
1.13 — 38n85
1.42 — 38
6.7 — 30

Musonius Rufus

Discourses
3 — 212

Ovid

Epistulae
7.123–124 — 39n89

Tristia
5.14.7 — 38
5.14.38 — 38

Pausanias

Graeciae descriptio
4.20.9 — 110

Petronius

Satyrica
75.11 — 130
111 — 40

Philemon

Adelphoi
3 — 129n95

Plato

Leges
930b — 205

Plautus

Mercator
817–829 — 30

Mostellaria
187–189 — 40
199–202 — 40
223–226 — 40

357

INDEX OF OTHER ANCIENT SOURCES

Pliny the Younger

Epistulae
6.24   38

Plutarch

Cato Minor
25.2–5   30

De amore prolis
2   31

De Iside et Osiride
2   200n21

De virtute et vitio
37   111

Quaestiones romanae et graecae
105   38, 266

Quomodo adolescens poetas audire debeat
4   110

Romulus
3.3.2–3   223

Polybius

Historiae
12.15.2   128

Propertius

Elegiae
2.6.41–42   40
2.15.29   40
2.15.36   40
2.20.17–18   40
2.28a.60–62   200n21

3.13.23   38
3.33.1–4   200n21
4.5.28–34   200n21
4.11.36   37
4.11.68   37

Seneca

De beneficiis
3.16.2   30

Soranus

Gynaeceia
1.7.31   197n13

Statius

Silvae
2.7.126–129   38
5.1.43–74   37
5.3.240   37

Suetonius

Divus Augustus
34   217n99

Tacitus

Annals
2.86   34
3.25   31
6.29   38n85
6.40   140n155
11.26   35
14.60   140n155
15.44   58
15.64   34n73
16.34   38n85

Germania
19.2   35
19.4   35

Historiae
1.2   31

Tatius

Leucippe et Clitophon
5.23   113
5.26.2   197
6.9.7   113
8.10.11–12   226–27

Theopompus

Fragments
253   128

Tibullus

Elegiae
1.3.23–26   200n21

Valerius Maximus

Factorum ac dictorum memorabilium libri IX
2.1.3   37
4.3.3   37
4.6.2   41
4.6.3   41
4.6.5   38

Vergil

Aeneid
1.343–346   39
4.18–19   39
4.27–29   39

Index of Other Ancient Sources

4.45	39	4.316	39	**Xenophon**	
4.123–128	39	4.551–552	39	*Memorabilia*	
4.165–168	39	4.575	39	1.6.13	128
4.171–172	39	6.450–475	39		
4.307	39	6.473–474	39		